FAUQUIER COUNTY
IN THE REVOLUTION

T. TRIPLETT RUSSELL
and
JOHN K. GOTT

HERITAGE BOOKS
2019

HERITAGE BOOKS
AN IMPRINT OF HERITAGE BOOKS, INC.

Books, CDs, and more—Worldwide

For our listing of thousands of titles see our website at
www.HeritageBooks.com

Published 2019 by
HERITAGE BOOKS, INC.
Publishing Division
5810 Ruatan Street
Berwyn Heights, Md. 20740

Copyright © 1977 T. Triplett Russell and John K. Gott

Originally privately printed
Warrenton Printing and Publishing Company
Warrenton, Virginia
1977

All rights reserved. No part of this book may be reproduced or transmitted in any form or by any means, electronic or mechanical, including photocopying, recording or by any information storage and retrieval system without written permission from the author, except for the inclusion of brief quotations in a review.

International Standard Book Number
Paperbound: 978-1-888265-60-6

CONTENTS

Fauquier County Board of Supervisors iv
Introduction v
Acknowledgements viii
Chapter I, The Forest Land 1
Chapter II, The Kindling Flame 28
Chapter III, The Great Bridge 60
Interlude - Norfolk to Haarlem 94
Chapter IV, The Heights of Haarlem
and the White Plains 97
Interlude - White Plains to Trenton 129
Chapter V, Trenton and Princeton 133
Interlude - Princeton to Brandywine 162
Chapter VI, Brandywine 165
Interlude - Brandywine to Germantown 207
Chapter VII, Germantown 211
Interlude - Valley Forge 243
Chapter VIII, Monmouth 245
Interlude - Monmouth to Stony Point 282
Chapter IX, Stony Point 285
Interlude - The War Moves South 321
Chapter X, Charleston 323
Interlude - Kings Mountain 354
Chapter XI, Cowpens 359
Interlude - The War Returns to Virginia 388
Chapter XII, Yorktown 393
Epilogue - The Forest Land Revisited 437
Fauquier Countians in the Revolution 445
Index 481

Fauquier County Board of Supervisors

1971

John B. Adams, Chairman
(Scott District)

William D. Doeller
(Marshall District)

James F. Austin
(Centre District)

David A. Botts
(Cedar Run District)

Samuel Butler
(Lee District)

1976

Jason Paige, Jr., Chairman
(Marshall District)

Robert Gilliam
(Centre District)

David A. Botts
(Cedar Run District)

Samuel Butler
(Lee District)

Stevenson McIlvaine
(Scott District)

Fauquier County American Revolution Bicentennial Committee

(Appointed by Board of Supervisor, 14 January 1971)

Mrs. Charles G. Turner } Co-Chairmen
Mr. William D. Doeller }

Mr. John K. Gott, Historian

Introduction

"Fauquier County in the Revolution" is an appropriate title for this book, but it requires a word of explanation. Anyone with even cursory knowledge of the story of the American war for independence is aware that Fauquier County, Virginia, had no important part in that classic struggle. No battle or even minor skirmish took place within her borders. None of her sons held key positions in either the military or political field. Her boundaries were never violated by enemy troops and, with a single exception, not even the friendly armies of neighboring states crossed her rolling countryside. One might ask, therefore, "Why Fauquier?"

It is for these very reasons (and a few others) that we have chosen to write about Fauquier. We readily concede that such a book might be written about a score of counties in Virginia, about hundreds of shires and counties throughout the thirteen original states. In a quiet county, remote from the maelstrom, the average man could view the great panorama of human conflict and decide for himself the extent of his involvement. The men who went to war from Fauquier, for the most part, did so because they believed it to be their duty. Many remained behind but contributed heavily to the cause. By accident of geography and the fortunes of war, Fauquier County was ideally situated to accomplish that purpose.

In the first place she lies near the center of the original colonies and the course of events carried her sons from the ramparts of Quebec to the pine barrens around Savannah. She lay midway between the great plantations of the lower James and the lonely outposts along the Ohio. Her sons fought at Kaskaskia, at Vincennes and at Broadway and 116th Street, just off Riverside Drive. They fought in the narrow streets of Trenton and on the open wastes of Cowpens. They fought, were beaten, got up and fought again.

Secondly, by a curious turn of fate, the records of Fauquier are, relatively speaking, intact. They escaped the depredations of hostile armies from 1861 to 1865, with some minor exceptions.

However, sad to say, years ago they did not entirely escape neglect and, sometimes, wanton vandalism. It is now, therefore, doubly important that we see that the great heritage we have left, is preserved, protected and lovingly restored.

And, thirdly, Fauquier County has not been swept up in the devastating result of urban sprawl and exploitation in the name of progress. Many of her landmarks remain, subject, it is true, to gentle decay, but at least not to ruthless spoilation by greedy speculators. Today we can still almost visualize the tired soldier returning from the war, trudging along narrow roads, through woods, along streams tumbling over ancient rocks, by rail fences and field-stone walls, until at last he reaches home.

It is through the soldier's eyes that we have tried to see the Revolution. Although we have tried to give essential biographical detail, this is not a book of genealogy. If family tradition holds that your ancestor served in the Revolution from Fauquier and his name does not appear here, it is family tradition that is probably correct. We offer no assurance that our list of Fauquier men is complete. On the contrary, we can assure you that it is not. There are many reasons for this, and it might be well to cite a few.

Although the county records are reasonably intact, the military records of the war are woefully incomplete. Very few muster rolls exist and payroll records are spotty at best. Documents of all sorts have been destroyed, discarded or lost. The first major loss of National Archives came when the British burned Washington on the 25th of August, 1814. While the most important records had been removed to Virginia, many, today considered priceless but then considered to be only of routine interest, went up in flames. Far more devastating, however, was the neglect and wanton abuse of records during the mid-nineteenth century, when they were haphazardly thrown into damp cellars where mildew, rats, insects and water did their irrevocable worst.

Records of the State of Virginia met a similar fate. The counties were encouraged, especially between 1861 and 1865, to place their records in a supposedly safe depository in Richmond. Many did so, keeping no copies at the county seats. Most of them were destroyed when the capital of the Confederacy was deliberately burned on the night of 3 April 1865.

An almost endless source of fascinating detail about the life of participants in the Revolution is in the collection of pension records in the National Archives. It is so large that, even though abstracting the applications has been going on for years, the end is still a long way off. Even these are not as extensive as they should be because Congress provided for veterans only when forced to do so and then so little as to be scarcely worth the effort.

The first pension act was not passed until 1818, 37 years after Yorktown. Most of those pensioned were then in their sixties. The mortality rate at the time was such that at least two thirds of those who survived the Revolution were dead. Furthermore, to qualify for a pension, the veteran had to demonstrate that he was totally indigent. No man with an ounce of pride and two cents to rub together would submit to the humiliating confession that not only was he totally impoverished, but that his children and grandchildren were either too poor or too indifferent to care for him.

In the pension act of 1831 the indigency test was dropped but, by that time the average veteran was nearing eighty. Comrades who could verify his service were hard to find among the living. His own memory was failing and it all seemed so long ago. This should explain why we may have overlooked your ancestor, whose military record went up in flames and who either died too soon or had too much gumption to wallow in protestations of poverty for a few measly dollars.

Finally let us say that the writers offer no apology for loving Fauquier or for taking pride in her splendid heritage. However, our own ancestors are not the subject of this book and are not mentioned in it, except in a footnote or two for the record.

T. Triplett Russell
John K. Gott

Acknowledgements

Fauquier County has been favored with Boards of Supervisors who have been interested in and made provisions for the preservation of our county's history. When called upon to commemorate a significant milepost in the history of the County, State and Nation they have given their enthusiastic approval and provided financial support.

Very few other counties in the Commonwealth of Virginia can boost so much cooperation in these efforts by the Board of Supervisors. First, in 1959 when Fauquier County celebrated the 200th anniversary of its creation by the Colony of Virginia with the publication of *Fauquier County, 1759-1959*. This was the product of many hands but would have been impossible without the able guidance of the late Dr. William Hodgkin. This was followed six years later with *Years of Anguish, Fauquier County, Virginia, 1861-1865*, by Emily G. Ramey and John K. Gott.

In the preparation of the present book in commemoration of our nation's bicentennial we owe much to many. The records of two hundred years have been difficult to ferret out of collections and would have been impossible without the aid of the following people who listened, searched, made suggestions, read and offered constructive criticism, answered innumerable letters and pointed the way: John A. C. Keith and Mrs. John C. McDonnell of Warrenton; John Melville Jennings, Director and Howson W. Cole, Curator of Manuscripts, Virginia Historical Society; John W. Dudley, Assistant Archivist, Virginia State Library; James W. Walker, Research Specialist and Ms. Dorinda Cartwright, Archives Technician, National Archives; Archie Motley, Curator of Manuscripts, Chicago Historical Society; Mrs. Harva Sheeler and Mrs. Dorothea de Wilde, Librarians, Virginia Room, Fairfax County Public Library; Mrs. Sara Collins, Virginiana Room, Arlington County Public Library and Mrs. Doris Townsend, Langley High School.

Special mention and gratitude (from all who have had occasion to use the records of Fauquier County) goes to those men who, through the years, have been the Clerk of the Fauquier County Court. We owe a debt to Humphrey Brooke who kept the first records of the Court (1759-1793) so beautifully and completely. To the late Thomas E. Bartenstein whose love and care of the records brought out seemingly insignificant records and to the present Clerk, Harvey H. Pearson, who so ably carries on the business and traditions of the office. Mr. Pearson's help and interest made research at distant points easier.

The Fauquier County Bicentennial Commission, especially the Co-Chairpersons, Mrs. Charles G. Turner and William D. Doeller, have given encouragement and aid most generously. To all of those not mentioned who have helped—we thank you.

I
The Forest Land

In 1775, the County of Fauquier in Virginia spread like a great forested blanket over the lap of the piedmont. To the west, veiled in violet haze rose the Blue Ridge, a wall separating her from the lush valley of the Shenandoah beyond. Many years before, Robert Beverley wrote of these mountains dimly seen on the horizon as mysterious, beckoning, known only to the inhabitants because they "shew themselves above the tops of the trees."

That was no longer true. Over the length and breadth of the county the smoke from the chimneys of cabins in small clearings curled upward through the forest. The population was thinly scattered. Relatively speaking, it is today. It is one of the chief charms of Fauquier County. In 1775, the people might have wished that their neighbors were a bit closer, that their holdings were not separated by broad swaths of primeval forest. The ancient trees, taller than any man-made objects, arched over their heads. The forests were still thronged with wild life. The roads through them were dark, sometimes hardly visible and always incredibly bad, especially in winter.

Though the population of Fauquier was small in 1775, possibly fewer than 14,000 souls,[1] there was not in all its 664 square miles one town or village of any importance.

1. No exact figure can be found for the population of Fauquier County in 1775, but interpolation of census records beginning in 1782 and continuing for the rest of the century indicates that there were about 13,500 people living in the county at the beginning of the Revolution. Of these about 8,700 were white and the rest (4,800) slaves and a few free blacks. The slaves were, however, owned by only about 15 per cent of the white male population, or about 650 persons. At least half of these owned between 1 and 4 slaves. The remainder of the Negroes were owned by roughly 325 families, many of whom did not live in Fauquier County. In 1782, 44 per cent of all the slaves were owned by 88 of the principal landowners, one of whom, Charles Carter of "Cleve", near Falmouth, had 188. It is doubtful if the ratio had changed greatly during the seven years preceeding.

On the site of an ancient Indian town on Hedgman's River, in the area of Elk Marsh, the forest was broken by savannahs of rich, dark soil which supported reeds that reached incredible heights. In these sunlit glades in the lower county, the settlement of Fauquier had begun some sixty years before. The settlers had been few, brave and cautious, because the Indians still used the Shenandoah Hunting Path that skirted the Bull Run Mountains and crossed Fauquier to a ford across Hedgman's River. In 1687 a block house had been built at Brent Town on Town Run to "observe" the Indians and offer some shelter for the few hardy souls who had ventured so far from civilization.

In 1722, in the Treaty of Albany, Governor Spotswood had put an end to that threat. The Indians promised to keep their "young men" west of the Blue Ridge and not to disturb the settlement of the piedmont, if the white man would not penetrate beyond the mountains.[2] The Indians kept their promise, though the white man did not, and no Indian raids are known to have taken place in Fauquier in the fifty-three years before the Revolution.

Thus, Fauquier County was not, and never had been, the frontier in the sense that we usually think of it, a land subject to intermittent attack by hostile savages. Secure behind the crenelated battlements of the Blue Ridge, the settlers cleared the forest and sowed their crops undisturbed.

We normally think of the development of America as having been carried on by people of diverse ethnic background, pursuing their native customs, until swept into the vast melting-pot of American life. To this Fauquier was an exception. The historian, scanning lists of tithables or militia rosters remaining in the county, is struck by the fact that the names reveal a common English background. They are, by and large, the same names one encounters in the lower tidewater counties of the Northern Neck, where the families that settled Fauquier gained their first foothold in Virginia.

There had been attempts to settle foreigners in the county but, somehow, none had had a lasting influence on its development. As early as 1686 the proprietors of the Brent Town tract, of which part lay in Fauquier, had tried to induce immigrant French Huguenot families to settle there. Despite alluring terms and the blan-

---

2. Journals of the House of Burgesses, 1712-26, pp. 319, 347. See also Council Journal, Nov. 1, 1722, in Va. Mag. XII, p. 340.

dishments of Nicholas Hayward in England and Giles Brent in Virginia, the Huguenots had, to a man, refused to come.[3]

In 1718 a small group of German miners from the principality of Westphalia applied to Robert Carter, agent for the vast Fairfax Proprietary, for a grant of land on Licking Run. They had been brought to Virginia by Governor Spotswood to mine the iron ore supposed to lie in what is now Culpeper County but were dissatisfied by his somewhat highhanded treatment. On Licking Run they built the tiny village of Germantown. Much has been written about this settlement, but many seem to forget how few these prople were and how quickly they dispersed. There were only twelve families comprising some forty-two persons. Germantown lasted less than twenty years. By 1745, many had moved back to Culpeper County. The remainder had secured grants elsewhere and their children had intermarried with their English neighbors. In 1775, on the site of Germantown, stood the abandoned glebe of Hamilton Parish, then owned by Jeremiah Darnell, and the old home of Tilman Weaver.[4] The other buildings, including the church, were in ruins. The only real relic of the German settlement was the continuance of a few old names like Holtzclaw, Fishback, Rector and Weaver. In those families was preserved the tradition of thrifty husbandry for which Germans have always been noted.

Possibly the nearest thing to a lasting influence from an alien ethnic group came from the Scotch-Irish. These unfortunate people had had bitter experiences that they would not easily forget. They were mostly lowland Scottish Protestants who had been planted in northern Ireland in Cromwell's time in a vain British effort to curb the wild Irish tribesmen and to convert them from the Catholic faith. Among them was a sprinkling of Scottish Highlanders and southern Irish Protestants.

They were established as tenants under absentee British landlords who cared nothing for their welfare and whose only

---

3. Both Nicholas Hayward and Giles Brent left descendants who were afterwards prominent in Fauquier. Nicholas Hayward's daughter, Hester, married Richard Foote, who emigrated to Virginia. Col. William Brent, great grandson of Giles, was a member of the Virginia Convention of 1776.

4. Harrison, Fairfax: **Landmarks of Old Prince William**;...(Richmond, 1924) Vol. I, pp. 207-221. An account of the rise and fall of the Germantown settlement. The log house of Tilman Weaver, built in 1721, stood until about 1925. Not much more remained in 1775.

interest was in wringing from them every shilling their backbreaking labor could earn. At the same time they became victims of the seemingly unrelenting hostility and disgraceful neglect of the English parliament.

Finally, in 1717 and 1718, many of their 60 year leases expired, leaving them impoverished and hopeless. The English landlords had mercilessly evicted them by the thousands from the land into which they had poured all of their strength and energy, so that they could reap the profit from sheep-raising. By the thousands they emigrated to America, most to more northern colonies, but some to Virginia. They hated the English, they hated Catholics but, most of all, they hated landlords.

By that time most of the good land in Fauquier had been taken up by Robert Carter and his friends. On these vast tracts, Carter expected to erect manors to be leased in smaller tracts to tenant farmers. He visualized great estates cultivated by a happy tenantry, prosperous but subservient to the landed proprietor. It was the one notable miscalculation in Carter's otherwise capable management of the proprietary estates of Lord Fairfax.

He reckoned without the Scotch-Irish. They would put up with quite a lot in terms of hardship, but they had seen enough of landlords. Forced to the hostile terrain and poor soil of the broken hillsides by the appropriation of prime lands, they bypassed Carter's alluring acres in search of land to be obtained in fee simple. Some settled on the rugged, rocky hills east of the Pignut Mountain and in other less desirable areas along the Bull Run Ranges, but their numbers were never great and, as the result of the poverty of their acres, their economic state was seldom flourishing before the Revolution. By that time their ethnic peculiarities, except for an inherent love of a good fight, had largely disappeared.

As a result of Carter's inability to secure tenants for his huge tracts of prime land in the center of the County and the negligence of his heirs, these immense holdings had meanwhile lain idle. In 1775, they were still largely so. On one huge Carter tract in upper Fauquier an aged retainer, who had been put there under the terms of the original grant, complained that he could not feed one cow because he could not clear enough pasture and had no hand to help him. The Carters remained unmoved by his distress. Their quit rents were long in arrears. Landon Carter owed the Proprietor

---

5. Duke University Collection. Letters, Carter to Fairfax, 13 July 1772; 28 Sept. 1773 and 12 Sept. 1774.

quit rents in the huge total of £678 16s 3d. The imperious "Councillor" Robert Carter of Nomini Hall, with "long arrearages of quit rents due," had asked forbearance in 1772.[5] Lord Fairfax, who earlier had implored them to see about settling their land, to no avail, was somewhat less than sympathetic.

Though the earliest settlement was on Elk Run, that community remained a loose assortment of farmhouses around a church and a wayside ordinary. It never coalesced into a commercial center of any promise or the hub of any development. In 1775, there were still fewer than a thousand people. The English settlers built a church some distance from the center on Elk Run, a building that was, at the time of the Revolution, by a wide margin the finest structure in the entire county.[6] However, as we will soon see, the fortunes of the established church at the beginning of the Revolution were in sad disarray and even the handsome church was then showing signs of neglect. Not far away was an ordinary, Hardin's,[7] a blacksmith's shop and a grist mill on Hedgman's River or one of its tributaries. The exact location of the last is unknown. If there was a general store, its name and location have also vanished with the passage of time. The church and ordinary appear on Fry and Jefferson's map of 1755 and on Bishop Madison's map of 1818, but on neither is there any indication of a town nearby.

Another natural clearing in the forest was found at White Plains, just west of the gap called Thoroughfare, in the Bull Run Mountains that separated Fauquier and Prince William. Here, too, was a loosely organized settlement, oriented more closely to the County of Prince William and the Parish of Dettingen than it was to the County of Fauquier and the newly created Parish of Leeds.[8]

The only formally established town in Fauquier was Maidstone, the idea of an enterprising alumnus of the old German

---

6. Completed in 1769, the life of this cruciform brick church was brief. Bishop Meade thought that the roof had collapsed by 1811 and the walls not long after. (Meade, Bishop William: **Old Churches Ministers and Families of Virginia**. Baltimore, 1966) Vol. II, Pp. 216f).

7. In 1775 Mark Hardin, who was operating the ordinary in 1759, had moved to Augusta County. His son, Martin Hardin, may have run it before selling it in 1802 to Joseph Blackwell.

8. West of The Plains an immense Carter grant tended to block westward expansion which took place only after the construction of the Manassas Gap Railroad in 1854.

settlement at Germantown named John Rector.⁹ Rectortown, as it was known later, existed mostly on paper. The merchants who, in the words of its founder in 1772, "desired to settle there" had, in 1775, not arrived. Rectortown was known especially by the polemic delivered against it by George Washington when told by his nephew, Fielding Lewis, that he had invested in a lot. After reluctantly granting him permission to cut timber on his Fauquier land to build a house, he wrote testily, "...now let me ask what your views were in purchasing a Lott in a place which, I presume, originated with and will end in two or three Gin Shops, which probably will exist no longer than they serve to ruin the proprietors and those who make most frequent application to them." Happily Rectortown failed to live up to Washington's dire prophecy. It was, and is today, a tiny village of great charm and quiet inconsequence.

The metropolis of Fauquier County at the time of the Revolution was the county seat, which then bore the uninspired name of Fauquier Courthouse. It was located at almost the exact center of the county on property that had been patented in 1718 by the powerful Lee family. It is said that Richard Henry Lee had pulled strings in the House of Burgesses to secure the location of the county seat on his property. Be that as it may, its site could hardly have been more fortunate. On an eminence near the junction of two main highways through the county, convenient as it possibly could be to all the inhabitants, it was by its very nature the hub about which the county revolved.¹⁰ It boasted a brick courthouse completed in 1769, measuring thirty-six by twenty feet, to which a sixteen foot addition had been made in 1771. The quality of the building was such that it was already looking somewhat delapidated. The initial budget had forced the contractor to take unwise shortcuts, and there was visible evidence of hard usage.

There was a gaol, barely strong enough to hold those who had no particular desire to escape. It was also much too small according to Sheriff Joseph Blackwell, who "came into Court and

---

9. Hening, **Statutes**, Vol. VIII, p. 621. The German spelling of the name is Richter and it appears so in old documents.

10. The town of Warrenton was not officially laid out until 1790 when, by direction of Richard Henry Lee, James Routt prepared a plat of 12 half-acre lots. Main Street was a part of the Dumfries-Rappahannock Road, straightened for the purpose and widened to 55 feet, 7¼ inches. A deed dated 11 August 1797 refers to it as "Fauquier Court House now called the Town of Warrenton." See Fauquier Historical Society: **Bulletin**. (Richmond, 1921), p. 74f.

protested against the prison for the insufficiency thereof." Its inadequacy was so evident that in 1779, during the war, it was replaced by the building that is now being restored. (1975). In the center of the town was a building known as the "Red Store," established as a trading post before 1764 by Alexander Cunninghame of Falmouth. This thriving general store was, in 1775, receiving stiff competition from one across Main Street run by Martin Pickett. The best known tavern in the town was run by Andrew Edwards, to whom a licence was granted 26 July 1759, although there were almost certainly others. An ordinary run by Thomas Maddux in 1790 probably was standing in 1775. There was also a tavern run by one Waters and several other "grog shops" to supply the thirsty litigants on court days, though not in continuous operation.

There was a blacksmith's shop, a saddler's shop and, probably, a cabinet shop. In addition, in the few private homes thereabouts, a certain amount of trade was carried on, as millinery, clock making and tailoring, according to notices posted on the porch of the ordinary. Somewhat remotely situated and, of course, complained of by its near neighbors, was a tannery.

In 1775 there were perhaps a dozen houses. The finest was probably "Paradise", home of Martin Pickett and his wife, Ann Blackwell. They were married in May, 1764, and built at least part of the present structure soon after. William Allason, the merchant, was building a stone house on the outskirts, now known as "North Wales." It is the only known use of stone for an entire dwelling in Fauquier antedating the Revolution, though most had stone foundations and chimneys. Joseph Blackwell also had a town house in Fauquier Courthouse which existed until 1963, when it was demolished for a parking lot. Other houses are lost or survive only as appendages to more recent structures.

The only church was on Turkey Run about two miles south of town. It was a great barn-like frame building of no architectural merit, but it held a large congregation. In 1775 it was frequently empty or nearly so. Mr. Craig, the rector, was discouraged by the lack of attendance and attributed it to the times.

The County Court usually sat on the fourth Monday in the month and might last into the second day. Coinciding with it in reasonably propitious weather in April or May and again in October or November, Muster Day was held, when the county militia went through its paces on the muster field at the edge of town. The militiamen and their fractious admirers added an element of excitement to Court Day. Spirits ran high and tempers flared, leading sometimes to lethal consequences.

It must be remembered that fighting in the eighteenth century was governed by no Marquis of Queensbury rules. To have one's eye gouged out, nose bitten off or to receive a swift knee in the groin were commonplace social hazards, scarcely worth mentioning. However, if one had an ear bitten off one would do well to make it a matter of public record. The severance of an ear was also a prescribed punishment for theft. Mayhem was acceptable, but conviction of a felony carried with it a certain social stigma. Public records of ears respectably detached are frequent in Fauquier County Minute Books.

At Fauquier Courthouse the people gathered when court was in session, settled their deals, replenished their supplies, spread their gossip and aired their views on politics, religion and the state of the world. They had come also for news, that rare and precious commodity in colonial days. Copies of one or more of the three Virginia Gazettes [11] published in Williamsburg were posted on the porches of the taverns or the courthouse. They were seldom recent and the news was often inaccurate, but they were the best that could be had. Also posted were handbills, advertisements and notices of local significance.

In the several more or less disorderly taverns the booze flowed, the stakes were high and the gentlemen vied with each other for the distinction and sometimes lucrative advantage of public office in the backwoods county. The future town of Warrenton was tame by comparison with Winchester where the gaudier aspects of frontier life could be found in violent excess, but it had its moments.

These four centers of population were linked by a system of roads too awful for modern experience to contemplate. When, in 1772 Lord Fairfax ordered a "chariot" from London, his agent William Allason, in Falmouth, wondered how under the sun he would deliver it to Greenway Court, Lord Fairfax's seat on the other side of Ashby's Bent. Apparently it came knocked down and

---

11. The Virginia Gazettes are quite confusing. In January 1775 there were two in Williamsburg, both titled "Virginia Gazette," one published by Dixon and Hunter and another "Printed by John Pinkney for the benefit of the children of Clementina Rind." Purdie, a former partner of Hunter's, was about to launch his own paper which he proposed to call "The Virginia Gazette". It first appeared 3 February 1775. In June of the previous year William Duncan and Company in Norfolk had launched a paper with the same name. In a token effort to avoid confusion, they called theirs also "The Norfolk Intelligencer". As the various Gazettes often held varying opinions, subscribers in Fauquier were indeed fortunate that they did not receive them at the same time, if at all.

Allason seriously considered shipping it in pieces. He finally decided to assemble it in Falmouth and get some "good horses" to pull it over the treacherous roads. Weeks later it arrived at Greenway Court in a somewhat battered state and there it remained, seldom used. It was simply too much trouble, considering the limited distance over which it could safely travel. Its progress through Fauquier provided a useful bit of education for small boys, most of whom had never before seen so elaborate a conveyance.

Travel in Fauquier was thus on horseback or on foot. Women stayed home or rode behind their menfolk. It was usually inconvenient for them to appear in court. Their depositions were taken at home or in the house of a neighbor when the need arose. Opportunities for shopping, that great restorative of female morale, came seldom, if at all.

Ordinaries existed at most of the major cross-roads. We have mentioned one run by the Hardins near Elk Run Church where the main road branched to now almost deserted Germantown. Another, also on the main road where it was joined by the Dumfries Road, was run by Joseph Neville. Where the main road crossed Goose Creek, just before a fork leading to Calmes Gap, was an ordinary run by Thomas Watts. On the Dumfried Road, where it crossed the old Carolina Road, George Neville ran what was possibly the most frequented ordinary in the Piedmont.[13] And, finally, in the fork in the Alexandria Road serving the northern part of the county was an ordinary run by William West, son of a family whose Potomac River estates lay close to Belvoir. In addition to these many planters had licenses to entertain paying guests in their homes for long or short periods. The ordinaries were all primitive, but a traveller no longer had to sleep in the out-of-doors as in the past, unless dirty linen, fleas and bedbugs bothered him.

Travelling was not, however, something that one did for pleasure. Except for infrequent trips to the county seat for legal matters, most farmers stayed home and tended their crops. One thing he had to do was to have his corn ground, so reasonable access to a water powered grist mill was necessary. The locations of

12. Watts' Ordinary was shown on maps after 1760, but it appears that the operation of the ordinary was, in fact, taken over by Robert Ashby, whose home, "Yew Hill," was licensed for that purpose.

13. It is, surprisingly, the only Fauquier landmark noted on the splendid "General Map of the Middle British Colonies in America," published in London by Sayer and Bennett, 15 October 1776.

these mills are useful in spotting areas of intensive cultivation. Permission for the construction of one had to be obtained from the county authorities, as they frequently involved the flooding of adjacent areas, the condemnation of property on the opposite bank of the stream, or the interruption of navigable water courses and the maintenance of access roads. Therefore their sites can usually be identified from public records.[14]

In 1775 at least twenty such mills were in operation. The earliest included Col. Thomas Harrison's mill on Cedar Run, which existed for many years prior to its first record in 1744, Jonathan Chapman's on Broad Run, probably in use in 1742, though not in the building still standing, and a mill at Germantown on Licking Run, which certainly existed soon after 1722 but is not precisely located. Mention of the last mill indicates that it was also operated as a saw mill, the first in Fauquier.

There must have been a mill to serve the Elk Marsh Settlement at an early date. It was probably on the Rappahannock or its tributaries, but which of several later mills occupied the site of the early mill is unknown.

It is not surprising that the most progressive and best equipped mills in Fauquier in 1775 were those owned and operated by the well-heeled and enterprising Westmoreland County families who showed an interest in developing their Fauquier land only in the years immediately prior to the Revolution. Of these the mills established at the mouth of Carter's Run in 1760 by the Pickett family were probably best equipped in 1775. In addition to the usual grist mill for grinding corn there was a roller mill for bleached flour and a saw mill. Another roller mill was established about 1764 on Goose Creek about a mile from Rectortown by George Lamkin of Westmoreland.

Joseph Blackwell's mill on Deep Run, built in 1765, was also a saw mill as well as a grist mill. There was a grist mill at George Neville's ordinary at Auburn in 1768, and that same year Charles Chinn had one on Cromwell's Run. Piper's Mill on Thumb Run near Orlean had been in existance for some time in 1770. It was near old Piper's Church, one of four frame chapels established after the creation of Leeds Parish in 1769.

The early seventies saw a great boom in mill construction throughout the county, of which at least ten were completed before 1775. One on Crooked Run was probably built by Captain John

14. Moffett, Lee: **Water Powered Mills of Fauquier County, Virginia.** (n.p., n.d.). A careful study locating a number of mills, traces of which are fast disappearing.

Ashby, and a mill on Ashville or Bolling Run was built by Thomas Marshall shortly after he bought "Oak Hill" in 1773. In 1770 John Churchill applied for a mill on Cedar Run and the following year bought additional land on both sides of Cedar Run from Wharton Ransdell for that purpose.

If the reader is laboring under any delusion that there were private houses dating from before the Revolution that were even reasonably comfortable or attractive, then such fancies should be promptly squelched. There is no positive record of any brick houses as were frequently found in the Tidewater counties. Field stone, which could be had in abundance, was in general used only for chimneys. Entire houses of stone were uncommon, though outbuildings subject to fire hazard, as kitchens and blacksmith's shops, were frequently stone. Because of better insulation, so also were at least the lower parts of ice houses and dairies.

There were many log houses, but Tidewater tradition and the building of saw mills on the rapid streams facilitated the use of a sort of balloon frame construction made of timbers dressed at least on one side and covered with wood siding. The homes even of the wealthy were tiny by modern standards. Usually there were two rooms below and a loft above. The rooms below, which could be heated by a fireplace, housed the adults. The loft, which was often divided but seldom sheathed, was for children, sometimes house servants and miscellaneous odd bodies like tutors and stray visitors who were neither one nor the other. The lofts were ventilated by narrow openings in the gable ends. It is said that "Yew Hill" was the first house in Fauquier to have glass windows, and dormers were far too sophisticated for general use.

Without screens and with the customary intimate association with draft animals, control of flies and fleas was next to impossible. Lice, bedbugs and ticks were inevitably at home, however resolute the war against them. Writers, Washington among them, complained bitterly but accepted them with resignation and took their sleeping bags into the woods. Most were not so particular.

Perhaps the most interesting example of the pre-Revolutionary Fauquier house is Thomas Marshall's own house, "The Hollow," near Markham. Its chief interest lies in the fact that it has survived virtually unchanged since Thomas Marshall's time, and we can deduce a great deal about their style of living from what remains. Unless something is done quickly, by the way, it will not remain long - it appears about to collapse.

Thomas Marshall leased 330 acres of the Aylett patent in 1765 from Richard Henry Lee and built the house shortly after.[15] He moved his family from the vicinity of Germantown and occupied the house until he moved to "Oak Hill" in 1773. We must assume that, in addition to the house, he built a barn, a separate kitchen, quarters for the nine Negroes he had at the time and other necessary outbuildings. Even at that, the size of the house astonishes one today.

It measures 16½ by 24½ feet, about the size of a living room in a medium priced modern house. The ground floor was originally a single room with a broad fireplace at one end. Later, presumably in desperate search for a little privacy, a bedroom was partitioned off, 11½ by 15½ feet. Above, reached by an incredibly steep box stair, is a loft divided into two narrow rooms with ceilings only 6½ feet high. John Marshall could barely stand in the rooms-had to stoop to go through the door and contort his lanky frame uncomfortably to negotiate the narrow stair.

Into this dwelling Thomas Marshall moved in 1765 with a family of eight, three boys and three girls. While he was there five more children were born. In addition, for one year, the house sheltered James Thomson, John Marshall's tutor and, intermittently, a number of visitors.

Obviously the place must have been crowded to the point of suffocation. The family must have slept in every room. Privacy was impossible and, in extreme weather conditions, living conditions must have been nearly unbearable.

At this time, it must be remembered, Thomas Marshall was a man of considerable consequence. For most of the time he was a member of the House of Burgesses. He was Sheriff in 1767, which was a lucrative and important office, and as County Surveyor his income from surveying was fairly constant. We can therefore conclude that "The Hollow" was one of the better houses in Fauquier. The reader must imagine the worst.

Somewhere in these houses there must have been a place for a few books and somehow the quiet and leisure necessary to read them must have been possible. Education was the touchstone that assured wealth and position then as, in some measure, it is today. Wills frequently provide for schooling for sons and often daughters, usually two or three years. It was enough to teach them to read,

---

15. Richard Henry Lee and his brother, Thomas Ludwell Lee, married sisters, daughters of William Aylett of Westmoreland County. In 1741 William Aylett patented what is believed to have been the 2,825 acre tract at present day Markham, previously surveyed for Col. Charles Burgess.

write and cipher, but an introduction to the classics was highly desirable. School in England was beyond the reach of the planters of Fauquier unless they were steering sons toward the Anglican ministry. In 1775 that was not a popular goal.

Those who could afford it, as Marshall, the Chiltons, Blackwells and Eustaces, hired private tutors - usually young Scotsmen with some academic qualifications. Often several families would pool their resources and set up a "field school" under the auspices of the local parson. As will be seen, the products of this rather haphazard schooling were often amazingly literate. Their letters contain quotations from Cicero, Virgil and sometimes Homer. Bishop Meade says that, under the tutelage of James Thomson, John Marshall was reading Horace and Livy in Latin, a remarkable achievement after two year's schooling. Most people had some knowledge of the Bible and were beginning to ransack it for exotic names for their numerous progeny.

For those who would dabble in the law, as those who hoped to serve as Justices or hold other public office, Blackstone's "Commentaries on the Laws of England" was a prime requisite. There was also "The Practice of Physick," in which hair-raising remedies for common ailments make one wonder how anyone survived. And, with greater frequency in 1775, we find a book bearing the ominous title "The Art of Warr," a treatise on military tactics.

However, we must concede the fact that the overwhelming majority of books that found their way into Fauquier homes were religious books of almost paralyzing dullness. One of the most widely owned, (if not read), was "The Complete Duty of Man." It would be a challenge to a modern reader to plough through its 551 mind-boggling pages. Some must have read it, though, for we find many little nuggets from it in contemporary writing.

Practical how-to-do-it books were also widely used, especially those on carpentry. In almost every really old house there is some recognizable detail that is evidence of an honest effort to copy a plate from, for instance, the "Four Books of Architecture" of Palladio, with such materials as were at hand. Nevertheless, we must conclude that the skills and materials sufficient to create any convincing replica of one of the great tidewater plantations were simply not available in Fauquier before the Revolution. When Lord Fairfax moved to Greenway Court in 1750 he dreamed of building a manor house in Leeds Manor worthy of an English nobleman of his rank and state. He was obliged to give up the idea. It was

16. By H. Venn, A.M., Vicar of Hudderfield, Yorkshire. Published 1765.

clearly impossible to do so. Wearily his nephew, Thomas Bryan Martin, who would have liked more comfortable quarters than rustic Greenway Court, wrote in 1767 that plans "remain in status quo and in quo state they are likely to remain, ...we are building castles, tho' not on earth where one is greatly wanted, but castles in the air." Lord Fairfax's brother Robert found the primitive life among "strange, brutish prople ... past all conception."

The costume of the back country was usually simple homespum, but it is nonsense to suppose, as some writers have, that men like Thomas Marshall and James Scott, delegates from Fauquier, wore such a rig on the floor of the House of Burgesses. When in Williamsburg, and on state occasions, they dressed like "men of fashion." They had the means and they certainly had the opportunity. A probable exception to current fashion was that they "wore their own hair." A powdered wig was messy, uncomfortable and a confounded nuisance in the backwoods. Wigs were not as prevalent in Virginia as is usually imagined. Our forefathers, like ourselves, were not above presenting an image to a portrait painter as more stylishly dressed than they normally were. In modern pageants, common soldiers found wandering around with wigs under their tricorns are absurd.

The fact that we have been at pains to demolish the pre-Revolutionary stately homes and deflate the elegant people of Fauquier does not mean that they were impoverished or wholly without creature comforts. In an effort to portray John Marshall in the nineteenth century tradition of having been born in a log cabin, his biographer, Beveridge, has reduced his grandfather, John Marshall "of the Forrest," to bare subsistence level. However, Thomas Marshall, his eldest son, inherited substantially more land than George Washington inherited from his father, together with several Negroes and some cash.[17]

A very high percentage of the people in Fauquier owned slaves. Few families had many, but there were usually enough to help substantially with household chores. The planter and his sons usually worked their land along with his Negroes. Except for the settlement of estates or the satisfaction of hopeless debt they were rarely bought or sold. The population growth among the slaves was about what one would expect from normal increase. This is not to

17. Westmoreland Co. D. B. 11, p. 1. John Marshall devised to his son Thomas by will dated 1 April 1752, 300 acres in addition to the 200 acre home place. Thomas Marshall sold the 300 acres immediately to the Vestry of Washington Parish for use as a glebe. This transaction has escaped the notice of biographers.

suggest that, under the law, they had a square deal.

If life in Fauquier County was rugged before the Revolution it also had many compensations. The climate was salubrious, food plentiful and the troubles of a beleaguered world seemed remote and irrelevant. If anything troubled them it was the religious question and that, in Fauquier, was both clear cut and perplexing. They were all Protestants and, as a matter of fact, belonged for the most part to one or the other of only two sects. Though Quakers from Pennsylvania had settled in the Kecocton Hills in Loudoun County, none seemed to have pushed south beyond the Pantherskin Branch of Goose Creek. The Scotch-Irish brought their Presbyterian religion with them, but somehow seemed to have mislaid it along the way. No pre-Revolutionary Presbyterian congregation seems to have been active in Fauquier. The Methodists had not yet begun to germinate in the Virginia backwoods.

There were no Catholics. In fact, one who had Catholic leanings would do well not to mention it. Not only did candidates for public office have to swear to uphold the Protestant succession, but they had also to abjure belief in the doctrine of transubstantiation, under oath.[18] To profess Catholicism was to court political and social oblivion. If any votive candles burned in Fauquier before the Revolution, they have escaped the notice of historians.

The two remaining sects were, therefore, members of the established Church of England (not yet called Anglican) and the Society of Baptists. At first the Baptists were very much the underdogs, persecuted, reviled, and sometimes imprisoned. By 1775, the balance had shifted, and it was the established church that was fighting for survival. Fauquier County offers an almost classic example of the factors that brought about this abrupt change.

Fauquier County had been created in 1759, within the Anglican Parish of Hamilton, which had been taken from Overwharton in 1730. Its first minister was the Reverend Mr. James Keith, whose daughter married Thomas Marshall. Mr. Keith was a worthy man, utterly frustrated by the immense size of his parish. In 1745, partly as a result of his urgent pleas, Hamilton Parish was split and most of Prince William County fell in the new Parish of

---

18. Known as "the Test" it read "I do declare that I do believe there is not any Transubstantiation in the Sacrament of the Lord's Supper or in the Elements of bread and wine at or after the consecration thereof by any person whatsoever." F. H. S.: **Bulletin (July 1924)**, p. 423.

Dettingen. Mr. Keith remained Rector of Hamilton and moved to a new glebe on the site of old Germantown in Fauquier County. He died in 1751 leaving behind a respectable, if not distinguished, reputation as a man of the cloth.

There were then two churches, the new brick church at Elk Run built just before the division, and Saint Mary's on Turkey Run, a large frame building near Fauquier Court House.

Keith's successor, named in 1753, was a man of entirely different sort. No more devastating calamity could have befallen the established Church in Fauquier than the appointment of the Reverend Mr. John Brunskill, Jr. as Rector of Hamilton Parish. By 1757, even the most lethargic of his parishioners were up in arms. A catalogue of his crimes includes, according to Governor Dinwiddie, almost everything but murder, and that nearly. The kindest thing the Governor could say was that "the unhappy man is almost constantly drunk." It was the disagreeable task of Joseph Blackwell, a vestryman and Burgess, to arrange his ouster, which took two years to effect. In the meantime, the Vestry had been dissolved and the church was in shambles.[19]

When a new vestry was elected, they chose as Rector the Reverend Mr. James Craig, who assumed the pulpit in 1762. Mr. Craig was probably a good man, but his influence had been permanently sapped by Mr. Brunskill's didoes. He was also a speaker of paralyzing dullness. Soon the northern part of the county was clamoring for another division. It came in 1769, with the creation of Leeds Parish, above an east-west line passing through the southern outskirts of present Warrenton, just above Turkey Run Church. As Hamilton Parish retained the only two churches, it was assessed a sum toward the building of four small frame chapels in the new parish.[20]

The new vestry included a high percentage of the men who would be the leaders of Fauquier in the Revolutionary period. They were Martin Pickett, John O'Bannon, James Scott, Henry Peyton, William Edmonds, Humphrey Brooke, Samuel Grigsby, William Pickett and Charles Chinn, who took the oath on the first day of the July Court, 1770. Three other members, Thomas Marshall, John Chilton and John Moffett, were sworn a day or two later.

The four chapels were completed before March of 1772: Taylor's Church near Bethel, Goose Creek near Salem (Marshall), Bull Run in Prince William County, just across the line, and

---

19. Fauquier Historical Society: **Bulletin** (June 1923), pp. 258-60.

20. ibid., p. 265.

Piper's Church on Thumb Run on the road between Orlean and Hume. The glebe was established on Little River, between Salem and The Plains on land purchased mostly from John Glascock.

As minister, the vestry selected a Scotsman who had come to Virginia in 1763, and was tutor to the children of Thomas Marshall at "The Hollow". His name was James Thomson. He was conscientious, persevering and daring to his support of colonial independence. Though his control of syntax was marginal, there is no question that his heart was in the right place. In 1775, he was 38 years old and had been Rector of Leeds for six years. It was a trying period for a clergyman of Anglican persuasion. Not only was support from England slipping out from under the clergy, but there was an alarming growth of dissent in the colonies. Such characters as Mr. Brunskill had been few but conspicuous. Tithes paid to such an establishment were resented, and new light on the subject of religion was sought by many.

Into this vacuum, created by the waning influence and mounting rejection of the established church, dissenting sects, as the Baptists, moved effectively. It is not surprising that their "new light" doctrine caught on, but that it all happened so completely and so fast. Before 1770, they were persecuted and scorned. By 1775, theirs seemed the new way to salvation.

The Society of Baptists had been established in Virginia as early as 1743, and even in Fauquier County a small group worshipped in a church on Barker's Branch near Broad Run in 1762. They attracted little attention until there appeared among them a young minister, David Thomas, who was learned, articulate and eloquent. Because of his lasting influence over the people of Fauquier, we should know something of his background.

He was born in Pennsylvania in 1732 of a prosperous and highly respected family. Deeply religious, he was soon attracted to the teachings of such proponents of the "Great Awakening" as George Whitefield and Samuel Davies. He received his education at Hopewell, New Jersey, a stronghold of Baptist teaching, established by a number of young ministers from the Philadelphia Baptist Association who had been associated with the New Light Presbyterians during the Great Awakening. While subscribing to the teachings of Whitefield, they deplored the ascendency of "ignorant ranters" who threatened to turn the Baptist movement into an emotional binge rather than an expression of enlightened religion.

Thomas espoused the "New Light" doctrine based on a literal interpretation of the Bible and baptism by immersion, but seems to have resisted the teachings of the more extreme members of the church, known as "Separates," who leaned heavily towards Arminianism. After having obtained a degree in theology from Hopewell, he embarked on a preaching career in Virginia that was spectacular. The organization of Broad Run Church, 3 December 1762, marked the start of a movement that soon spread through the county. Men came from elsewhere to hear him preach and were profoundly shaken.

The reaction of the established church to this new challenge was, at the beginning, indifference. Under the Toleration Act of 1689 freedom of worship had been granted to all "except Papists and such as deny the Trinity." So long as the Baptists paid tithes and their ministers obtained licenses from the government in Williamsburg to preach under the Toleration Act, they were relatively unmolested. There was some complaint about their "absenting themselves from their parish church," and at least once Elder Thomas "was pulled down from his pulpit" and a snake thrown into the midst of the congregation, "but no hurt done." Elder Thomas went right on preaching.

Several congregations took their inspiration from Broad Run, but not all followed Elder Thomas' "Regular" Baptist precepts. The Separate Baptists influenced a number of the younger converts who introduced a manner of preaching wholly alien to the teaching at Hopewell, where Thomas had his training. Elder Robert Semple, a Baptist minister himself, wrote of them:[21]

> Their manner of preaching was, if possible, much more novel than their doctrines ... (they) had acquired a very warm and pathetic address, accompanied by strong gestures and a singular tone of voice. Being often deeply affected themselves while preaching, correspondent affections were felt by their pious hearers, which were frequently expressed by tears, trembling, screams, shouts and acclamations.

More significant than the oddities of their preaching was the fact that they took the position that no one should need a license to preach the Word of God and, furthermore, paying tithes to support a church not of one's choosing was both unnecessary and probably sinful. Carried to its logical conclusion, this doctrine was bound to bring about a conflict with the law.

---

21. Semple, Robert B.: **A History of the Rise and Progress of the Baptists in Virginia.** Rev. & Extended by Rev. G. W. Beale. (Richmond, Va., 1894). p. 15, et. seq.

The first Separate Baptist Church in Fauquier was planted on Carter's Run in 1769 by John Pickett. This personable and earnest young man (he was 28) did not have Elder Thomas' educational advantages, but he had a commanding presence and eloquent, if somewhat perfervid, delivery. He was not, however, an ignorant rabble-rouser of obscure origin. His brother, Martin Pickett, was a Justice and one of the leading men in the county. He had other impressive family connections. It is important to remember that the Baptist movement was not, and had never been, a class struggle. Yet Pickett was probably the most persecuted man in Fauquier. Arrested on the 26th of February, 1770, "by a precept under the hand and seal of William Edmonds, Gent. for preaching contrary to Act of Parliament (he) was brought into Court. Having refused to give security for his Good behavior ordered that he be remanded to Gaol there to remain until he give Security for his good behavior himself in the sum of Two hundred pounds and two securities in the sum of One hundred pounds." [22] The gaol, incidently, had been built by his own brother, William Pickett, four years earlier.

While the record indicates a measure of due legal process, the account given by Elder Robert Semple, himself no sympathizer with Pickett's viewpoint, is more factual: "The mob broke into the meeting house and split to pieces the pulpit and table, while the magistrates issued their warrant and, seizing Mr. Pickett thrust him into Fauquier prison. There he continued for about three months preaching through the grates and admonishing as many as came to him to repent and turn to God. The word of God was not bound! Great numbers were awakened under his prison labours." His diet was "rye bread and water, to the great injury of his health."

If Fauquier officials and supporters of the established church had wanted to strengthen the Baptist movement, they had gone about it in exactly the right way. While unjustly imprisoning its most eloquent spokesman, they gave him opportunity to harangue the mob. Naturally his fellow workers in the vineyard were inspired to new heights of oratory and rebellion.

One of these was William Marshall, younger brother of Thomas Marshall, who was formerly a Burgess and was then Sheriff of Fauquier. William Marshall was older than Pickett, (he was nearly 40), and had been known as a young man for his "devotion to fashionable amusement." He beheld the "New Light,"

---

22. Fauquier County Minute Book, 26 Feb. 1770. Armistead Churchill presided and William Edmonds, Joseph Hudnall and John Moffett, gentlemen justices, were present.

which was so blinding that "one of the most remarkable seasons of in-gathering which Virginia has ever known resulted from his labours." For this he was seized and was saved from being thrown into gaol only by the timely intervention of his brother.

Others were similarly harassed. In 1769, Elder William Fristoe was pursued by the Sheriff, (Original Young), gun in hand and ready to kill him. Fristoe later wrote: "This same Sherief is since become a baptist; and a most humble and contrite cristian he is." [23] So much so, in fact, that we find in record of the May Court of 1775 a request for permission to "erect a meeting House on the land of Mr. Original Young."

The most imaginative effort of mob violence was reserved for the unfortunate James Ireland, who preached occasionally at Carter's Run, but more regularly in Culpeper County. There they not only threw him in gaol but, according to him, attempted to blow him up with gun powder, suffocate him by burning brimstone at the door of his cell, and even to poison him. The fact that he was exceptionally handsome and adored by the ladies possibly generated a special ire among the menfolk.

This activity resulted in the planting of a number of Baptist congregations where there had been none before. Thumb Run Church, growing out of old Piper's Church (called "the Manor Church"), was organized in 1772. Goose Creek Church on Goose Creek near Upperville was erected 4th February, 1775. By 1775 whatever official opposition there had been to the Baptists of any persuasion had collapsed. Several other churches were about to be erected or awaited approval by the court. In addition to Mr. Young's church, another, approved in the May Court of 1775, was proposed by the "Anabaptists" to be "in the lower part of this County ... on the lands of John Kelly."[24]

Although Elder David Thomas was forced to accept a measure of evangelical "enthusiasm" and some "ranting," there is concrete

23. Morgan Edwards gives this account but is mistaken in that Original Young was only a deputy sheriff. His home adjoined that of Col. Thomas Harrison near Sowego.

24. Fauquier County Minute Book, 22 May 1775. William Grant presiding. The location of this meeting house is uncertain; however, Dr. Woodford B. Hackley, Past Executive Secretary, Virginia Baptist Historical Society, believes that it was this congregation which later removed across the Rappahannock River and became the Hedgman River Baptist Church (now Jeffersonton Baptist Church).

evidence that he still hoped for an educated and inspired clergy. [25] Another graduate of Hopewell (and Princeton as well) had been James Manning, who was sent to Warren, Rhode Island, where he had started a Latin School. In 1766 the Warren Academy received a collegiate charter from the General Court of Rhode Island, with little trouble since Rhode Island was the spiritual home of the Baptists in America and the colony had no college. Its success was immediate and was soon known in the other colonies.

In 1770 this institution was moved to Providence and became the College of Rhode Island. Later it became Brown University. Thus a Warren Academy was the predecessor of the ninth and last of the great colonial colleges existing today.[26] Its importance as an institution of learning and the soundness of its theological teaching was well known in Virginia. The growing influence of the Regular Baptists in Fauquier County as exercised by Elder David Thomas is evident in the events following.

Among the Princeton graduates of 1766, (the year that Warren Academy received its collegiate charter), was a young man named Hezekiah Balch. It is not unlikely that James Manning, seeking a trained faculty for his new Academy would turn to the recent graduates of his alma mater, Princeton. While it is not certain that young Balch served on the faculty at any time during the period from 1766 to 1776, he well may have. Possibly he was there in 1770 when, at the suggestion of James Manning, the College of Rhode Island was pleased to grant an advanced degree in theology to the distinguished clergyman from Virginia, Elder David Thomas. It was Balch's burning ambition to start a Latin school of his own in which young men would be guided through the classics and the basic fundamentals of Christian learning to ornament the pulpits of those churches adhering to the true faith. But where?

What better place could there be than the beautiful foothills of the Blue Ridge where the "New Light" had flared so brightly and the Word of God was being preached somewhat indifferently to the hungry multitudes? What was needed was something like the

---

25. Thomas, David, A.M., of Kentucky: **The Observer trying the Great Reformation in This State,** ... (Lexington: Printed by John Bradford, (1802). In the year 1786 Elder David Thomas resigned the pastorate of Broad Run Baptist Church and migrated to Kentucky. It was his opinion, after much reflection, that the Great Revival was the "work of God."

26. Pomfret, John E.: "Colonial Colleges" in: **Pennsylvania Gazette**, June 1975. Dr. Pomfret was formerly President of William and Mary College.

Warren Academy. In 1775 Warren Academy was just in the talking stage but, two years later, it formally opened its doors at the edge of the village called Fauquier Courthouse, whose name would be changed to Warrenton in its honor.[27] In his enthusiasm Hezekiah Balch hoped that Warren Academy in Fauquier would meet with the same success that had crowned the achievement of James Manning. It is a pity that it did not.

Aside from periodic outbursts of mayhem on Muster Days and occasional exercise of mob violence against unoffending ministers of the gospel, public records indicate that the people of Fauquier were moral and law-abiding. The County Court Minutes for 1774 and 1775 are generally routine—runaway servants, debt, theft and rather vague allegations of disturbance of the peace in which the defendants were enjoined to "be of good behavior toward all his Majesty's liege people for twelve months and a day, and especially towards" the plaintiff, whoever he was. However, capital crimes were not unknown and, in the March Court of 1774, were the first faint rumblings of a sensational bit of news. The cause was not stated but we know that the crime was murder, and furthermore, murder in one of the county's most exalted families. The Sheriff was ordered to summon a Grand Jury of Inquest.

Not much can be found in the Fauquier County records about the Harrison murder case. William Harrison, eldest son of Colonel Thomas Harrison of Dorrell's Run, was found brutally slain in his plantation house on the Harrison estate not far from Sowego. His father had been prominent in Fauquier, Justice and Burgess for the first ten years of the county's existence. He had died in 1773 leaving a large estate.[28] When his son was killed in the early spring

27. It is generally conceded that Warrenton owes its name to the establishment there of the Warren Academy in 1777. It is commonly assumed that the Academy was named in honor of Dr. Joseph Warren, a Massachusetts patriot of unquestioned distinction, who was killed at Bunker Hill. Possibly Hezekiah Balch had some deep attachment to the memory of Dr. Warren but the latter, having died long before any Virginia troops had taken part in the Revolution, was hardly a folk hero in Virginia. It is much more probable that Balch selected a name known in Virginia and identified with an established seat of learning.

28. Fauquier County Will Book 1, pp. 231-35: Dated 26 Sept. 1773, probate 26 Jan. 1774. Col. Thomas Harrison was a grandson of Burr Harrison of Chappawamsic. He married ca. 1730 Ann Grayson, widow of John Quarles of Spottsylvania County. His youngest son Benjamin of "Glanville" (1744-1798) was the Captain Benjamin Harrison of the Third Virginia Regiment who is mentioned later in these pages.

of 1774 the immediate assumption was that he had been done in by his slaves, a possibility that sent cold chills down the spine of this slave-oriented society. But the answer was not that easy. The administration of his father's estate had not gone smoothly. He had made enemies, some within his own family. There were many rumors. He was not, it was said, a very attractive character. Nothing has been found that offers a solution to the mystery, but it was the talk of the county while it lasted.[29]

It is not surprising that records of such mishaps in the families of the rich and powerful should have vanished mysteriously over the years. The office of the County Clerk was easily accessible to those who knew their way about, and those having vested interests were not reluctant to improve upon the record or delete it entirely if the occasion demanded. Fauquier County is full of legends, but the public records make rather bland reading unless one has special knowledge. When we say, therefore, that the people were "moral and law-abiding," we must still remember that it was a violent time, that the plantation houses were far apart, and that time lay heavy on many hands. The old houses kept their secrets well; the cemeteries were even less talkative. Few of the descendants of those who lived in the county in 1775 are without at least one family skeleton, grinning impudently over their shoulders.

Looking backward over a span of two centuries into the hearts and minds of the people of Fauquier on the threshold of Revolution, one finds many curious anomalies. The elaborate historical facade we have built over the years has many carefully carved niches into which they do not fit. They were not pioneers, facing unknown danger in unexplored wilderness. Life was hard, but not heroically so.

Neither were they tidewater grandees in powdered perukes perpetually dressed as though for a court ball. They were neither rich nor poor. There were few temptations to lavish spending, and they were seldom heavily in debt as were their tidewater cousins. The stern Calvinism that was sweeping the county encouraged frugality, and the boycott of luxury goods from England introduced early in the war scarcely touched them.

29. Fauquier County Order Book, February Court, 1775. Jane Harrison, widow, was granted letters of administration of the estate of William Harrison, dec'd., and guardianship of three minor children. She was Jane Humston, daughter of Edward Humston. She married (2) Philip Mallory. The children were: 1. William, d.s.p. 1791; 2. Burr, apparently died insane after 1822 (Fauquier Co. Order Book, 1822) and 3. Lucy, married 1785, William Mallory.

Politically they were confused. They were still transplanted Englishmen struggling with a hostile environment and their roots were still deep in English culture, but almost none had visited England and fewer wanted to do so. They had no cash crop that made trade with England important. They grew little tobacco and that of poor quality. They had no ports and many had never glimpsed the sea. They might yearn for independence, but their reasons for doing so were often ambivalent.

If the ringing phrases of Rousseau and Thomas Paine had reached their ears, they were but imperfectly understood. That "all men are created equal" was an engaging concept. It meant, of course, that all white freeholders over twenty-one were created equal. They had no concept of a classless society. Secure in their English heritage and their ties by blood and marriage to the ruling families of the Northern Neck, they were well aware that some were born to rule and that others labored in the vineyard. The number of families from which all of the chosen leaders were expected to come was small indeed. Nepotism, far from being frowned upon, was a way of life. To an almost unbelievable extent the leading families were related, by blood or marriage or both. There are several interesting reasons for this fact which prevailed in degrees of consanguinity often frowned upon by modern geneticists.

In the first place the settlers often moved in family groups, taking up tracts of land in close proximity. Great tracts of land were patented and held on speculation. On the death of the original patentee, it was divided among his children, thus establishing several brothers and sisters on adjoining farms. Travel was difficult and young people were confined for relatively long periods of time within a short radius of their homes. For most young men in the back country the "girl next door" was very likely to be his first cousin. Propinquity did the rest.

Another reason not to be overlooked was snobbery, greater in the eighteenth century than today, greater in Virginia than elsewhere. No one wanted his children to "marry beneath them," and as each man's family was thought to be superior to all others except those to whom it was already related, social equality was often narrowed to the limits of kinship. An enterprising young son who chose a bride outside the colony or even the county risked family censure because no such person could possibly be "good enough."

As an illustration of the complexity of inter-twining family relationships among the men in positions of authority in Fauquier in 1775, we might take the Fauquier County Court. The Justices of this body filled most of the local offices except that of Sheriff and

County Lieutenant, so the members of the Court set a pattern that comprised most of the County's officialdom.

The presiding justice in 1775 was Armistead Churchill who, by virtue of his relationship to Judith Armistead, first wife of Robert "King" Carter and Priscilla Churchill, wife of his son Robert of "Nomini Hall," may be said to have represented the vast interests of the powerful absentee Carter heirs.[30] He and his brothers John and William had inherited "Pageland," the 10,600 acre tract on Turkey Run that had belonged to Mann Page, Carter's son-in-law.

His wife was Elizabeth Blackwell, daughter of Samuel Blackwell of "Walnut Lodge," long a Burgess from Northumberland County.[31] The Blackwell family accounts for two more members of the court. They were Elizabeth Churchill's cousin, John, married to her sister Ann, and her uncle, Joseph Blackwell. The latter's daughter had married Martin Pickett, another Justice.[32] The Sheriff, William Edmonds, though not on the Court, was married to another Elizabeth Blackwell, first cousin of the former.[33] Joseph Blackwell's daughter, Judith, was married to another Justice, Thomas Keith.[34] Keith's sister was the wife of Thomas Marshall, Burgess from Fauquier.

The tangled web did not stop there. Laetitia Blackwell, daughter of Joseph, married John Chilton. He was not only a Justice but also County Surveyor. When Armistead Churchill was not presiding in 1775 his place was taken by William Grant. It should surprise no one to learn that his daughter, Judith, was the wife of Thomas Blackwell. Grant had also been Sheriff and

30. He was a son of the Hon. Armistead and Hannah (Harrison) Churchill of "Bushy Park", Middlesex Co., Va.

31. Hardy, Stella Pickett: **Colonial Families of the Southern States of America,** ... 2nd ed., rev. (Baltimore, 1958) Also, Fauquier Historical Society **Bulletin** (July 1924), pp. 486-99.

32. The Picketts also came from Westmoreland County. William Pickett, b. Westmoreland County, ca. 1710; d. Fauquier County, 1766, married Elizabeth (Buckner) Cooke, daughter of Mordecai and Elizabeth Cooke, of Gloucester County.

33. All three sons of Capt. Samuel Blackwell had daughters named Elizabeth. The third was the wife of Capt. Charles Chilton.

34. The Reverend James and Mary Isham (Randolph) Keith had six children who survived childhood. Three sons, Isham, Thomas and Alexander D. Keith, served with distinction in the Revolution.

coroner.[35] Humphrey Brooke, the County Clerk, may seem a stranger to this family gathering, but look more closely.[36] One of his sons married a daughter of Martin Pickett, another a daughter of Thomas Marshall.

One might go on like this forever, but the point would seem to have been proved. If one had arranged to have been born in one of the chosen families and was even reasonably intelligent and circumspect, one had only to wait until public office fell like a ripe plum into one's lap. If born outside this charmed circle, however, one might as well be a Papist. Public office was an unlikely career.

Many of those mentioned above will present themselves in the pages to come. There is no merit in laboring a point, but it would be useless to deny that family connections and preferments played a large part in their military as well as civilian careers. When they emerge as outstanding it is owing to personal quality rather than the circumstance of birth or position. Considering this fact, it is remarkable that so many did so well.

Next below the "gentlemen" came the freeholders who had, by enterprise and hard work, gained title to smaller amounts of land and lesser estates. They were farmers, or "planters" as they preferred to call themselves. While the great estates lay idle they tilled their acres, bred their livestock and raised sturdy families to carry on their names. They seldom sought public office and were not ashamed to sign their names with a firm "X" when the occasion demanded. They were proud, penny-pinching and sometimes contrary, but they usually voted with the gentry because power and money were, to them, almost the same. Their sons were the rank and file in the war that was soon to come.

35. Capt. John Grant (16 -1748) of Stafford County patented with John Graham 1,175 acres on the south side of Goose Creek in 1741. He married 17 August 1727 Hester Foote, daughter of Richard Foote of Chotank, and secondly, Margaret Watts, widow of William Strother. By his first marriage he had William Grant, of Fauquier, Justice, 1772; Sheriff, 1765. By his second marriage he had Peter Grant who served as clerk to the meeting of the freeholders of Fauquier that framed the Fauquier Resolutions.

36. Humphrey Brooke (1730-1803) was a son of Humphrey and Elizabeth (Braxton) Brooke of King William County. He was a first cousin of Carter Braxton, signer of the Declaration of Independence. He, too, represented Carter interests in Fauquier, as he was a nephew of Mary (Carter) Braxton, daughter of Robert "King" Carter. His uncle, Robert Brooke, surveyed the Fairfax Proprietary along the Potomac and Shenandoah Rivers including the vast Carter tracts in Frederick County.

Below them came "the meaner sort of people," the dropouts from society, convicts and the perpetually indigent and irresponsible. They were a cause for some concern in an established community, but not much. If they caused trouble they were whipped, if too much trouble they were hanged. Those who were concerned about their welfare did not, of course, know them. They lived in the next county, over the nearest mountain or, at least, beyond the bend in the road.

At the bottom of the heap were, of course, the blacks. Too much has been written about slavery in Virginia for us to hope to add anything new. In Fauquier County their number was about the same as that of the whites. Economics and a measure of humanitarian interest determined that it was better to keep them together in family groups. Their living conditions were atrocious but usually better than those of the lower class whites. As potential warriors they were of no use. Their owners were understandably reluctant to furnish them with arms, and they had no compelling impulse to fight for abstract principles. Their role was to stay at home and take care of things while their masters fought for life, liberty and the pursuit of happiness, concepts that meant nothing to them. Generally they performed their tasks without complaint. Only Lord Dunmore imagined that they might do otherwise.

II

The Kindling Flame

In 1775 Fauquier had been a Virginia county for only sixteen years. Before the year 1759 the area had been only a piedmont backwoods of Prince William County, expected to furnish troops when the Indians in the Shenandoah Valley became restless, but otherwise to remain quiet and pay taxes. Vast tracts of land owned by tidewater families remained unsettled, and the thinly scattered population had no voice to speak for them in Williamsburg. In 1755, the year of Braddock's defeat, they petitioned the Assembly in Williamsburg for a new county with a county seat that would be reasonably accessible and a governing body that would be sensible of their immediate needs. The tidewater members of the Governor's Council, lacking any confidence in the character of the "back inhabitants" refused to act.[1]

One factor that may have influenced the Council in its reluctance to create a new county upland of Prince William was the fact that it lay wholly within the Fairfax Proprietary of the Northern Neck. The interesting story of this curious political entity is long and need not detain us here, but the inhabitants paid quitrents, not to the Colony of Virginia, but to Thomas, Lord Fairfax, Baron of Cameron, and with them were obligated under certain semi-feudal terms to an extent that had not then been fully determined.[2] Lord Fairfax was not an indolent absentee landlord content to live in idle splendor in his English castle of Leeds,

1. **Journals of the House of Burgesses of Virginia, 1752-1758,** Vol. 8, pp. 247, 249, 253, 255, 263 and **Legislative Journals of the Council of Colonial Virginia,** Vol. III, p. 1136. Also, **Journals,** pp. 430, 436, 444, 445, 448, also Vol. 9, 1758-1761, pp. 22, et seq. Hening, **Statutes,** Vol. VII, p. 311.

2. H. C. Groome, **Fauquier During the Proprietorship,** pp. 35-36. Administrative powers granted to the proprietor under the Charter of 1663 were so sweeping as to be almost feudal. No attempt was ever made by Lord Fairfax to enforce many of his prerogatives, but the Colony had no assurance that he might not try.

leaving the management of his Virginia estates to others. Quite to the contrary, he had established himself in 1750 at "Greenway Court," a rough-hewn forest mansion in Frederick County, with the obvious intention of administering his estates himself, defending them if necessary, and seeing to it that they were promptly and advantageously settled. Furthermore, to assist him, he brought over his twenty year old nephew, Thomas Bryan Martin, in 1751. Protection against Indian attack was soon a matter of concern, and it was evident by the winter of 1754 that local militia could not provide it. Reluctantly George II sent two regiments of British regulars under the command of Major General Edward Braddock, a popular and able Coldstream Guardsman, to settle the matter.[3]

Unfortunately General Braddock had little but contempt for the advice on Indian warfare proffered by the Virginians, including the youthful George Washington. For that he reaped his reward on the 9th of July, 1755, in a forest thicket near Green Meadows in western Pennsylvania. If Fauquier men were among the militia that accompanied this expedition they have not been identified, but it was Jack Ashby who brought the news to Greenway Court and carried it thence to Williamsburg with incredible speed.[4]

Captain Jack Ashby was not born in Fauquier, but he belonged to a family which, if any can be said to have done so, pioneered the early settlement of northern Fauquier.[5] After the French and Indian Wars he settled in Fauquier and his sons and nephews took active part in the Revolution, especially his nephew and namesake Captain John Ashby, son of Robert Ashby of "Yew Hill."

3. Governor Dinwiddie called for 200 militia under 21 year old Major George Washington in 1753, to be joined by Frederick and Augusta County volunteers under the young Scottish doctor, Adam Stephen. Washington's regiment was never up to strength and Lord Fairfax had little luck in raising volunteers in the valley. In May of 1754 Washington had only 159 men.

4. B. J. Peters, **Reminiscences**, pp. 9, 13-14, 32, has it that Ashby covered 210 miles in thirteen hours using thirteen horses most of which were "never of any value afterward." Another writer says the journey was 200 miles and the number of horses only six. The Pony Express never equaled either version.

5. Thomas Ashby, Captain Jack Ashby's father, probably settled near Ashby's Bent after the Treaty of the Long House in 1722 but certainly before 1730, when we have record of him there and the gap in the Blue Ridge had acquired his name. He and his six stalwart sons were expert woodsmen, tireless hunters and crack shots. Fairfax relied heavily upon them in 1736.

The news of Braddock's defeat was received in England with shock and amazement. The success of British arms in the European theatre of war had not prepared them for what a horde of savages might do to them in the American backwoods. It was a cruel lesson that the Americans had to learn again nearly two hundred years later in Viet Nam. After the dust had settled in 1755 it was only too obvious that Britain would not send another expeditionary force to protect the back country from Indian attack. They had had enough.

Without help from Britain it was obviously necessary for the colonies to defend themselves with their own resources. Those resources were slim and unreliable. Their store of arms and ammunition was meagre and what they had was jealously held in the colonial capitals under the eye of the Royal Governor. Manpower often could not be counted on. Most would defend their homes, but they were reluctant to march the distance necessary to help the next man defend his.

The only solution was a strong militia ready for immediate action, and ready to be summoned in the event of a surprise attack. The House of Burgesses, meeting in Williamsburg in March of 1756, passed an act for raising militia in the counties of Fairfax, Prince William, Culpeper and Hampshire to man a line of forts from Great-Cape Capon in Hampshire County to the south fork of the Mayo River in Halifax. The Prince William militia was commanded by Major John Frogg.[6] There were three Captains, Foushee Tebbs of "Tebbsdale" near Dumfries and William and John Baylis, whose home is now in Fauquier County. The Lieutenant of Horse, Richard Taylor, had under him forty mounted troopers among whom many Fauquier names are recognizable: John Fishback, Henry Kemper, Richard Byrne, Thomas Marshall, Peter Peirce, John Cornwell, William Peake and Robert Nevill. The Lieutenant of Foot, James Seaton, had 21 foot soldiers including Isaac Settle and Moses Coppage who were probably from Fauquier.

It was this militia who gave grudging help to those few who chose to remain and defend their homes in the Valley when the Indian raids reached their peak of terror in 1757. Lord Fairfax's threats and cajolery failed to arouse most of the Pennsylvania Germans and Quakers to take up arms in their own defense. Fairfax wrote the Governor, "if we are not in some way supported this next summer these back parts will be entirely deserted," adding, "I have never deserted...but have endeavored to encourage

---

6. Major John Frogg was on the first commission of peace for Fauquier County, 7 May 1759. His home was near Morrisville.

the people to stand by their plantations, but must confess to very little purpose."[7] His plea for help from neighboring counties brought little response.

In 1759, however, two events combined to reduce tension in the Valley. In September came the fall of Quebec. Bereft of their French allies, the Indians fell to intertribal warfare and lost interest in sporadic raids on white settlements. In May the new County of Fauquier had been created on the other side of the Blue Ridge Mountains. There, at least, concern would be felt for the peril that had all but wrecked the splendid Valley of the Shenandoah. Lord Fairfax could breathe more easily.

Circumstances had combined to convince the Governor's Council that the creation of a new county "on the head of" Prince William was indeed desirable. The first of these was the rapid development west of the Bull Run Mountains by descendants of tidewater families who had taken up vast tracts of forest land during the agency of Robert Carter in the first third of the eighteenth century. Since Carter himself lived in Lancaster County, it is not surprising that the majority of these families had their origins in the counties of Lancaster, Northumberland, Westmoreland, Richmond, King George and Stafford. However, while the validity of the Northern Neck grants remained in doubt, they had been slow to settle those lands. Even the sweeping victory of Thomas, Lord Fairfax before the Privy Council on the 11th of April, 1745, setting at rest any doubts that proprietary grants were good as gold, had not moved them to any precipitate action.[8]

In 1755 the situation was changing. The tobacco lands in the lower Northern Neck were wearing out. In any event they could not support any but the eldest sons of these families in the style they maintained, and cutting up these once-prosperous fiefs was unthinkable. Now the younger sons, born between 1720 and 1730, were coming of age. The reason for securing the Fauquier grants in the first place had been to provide for them. Increasingly the list of tithables in Prince William's "back country" began to turn up the names of old tidewater families—Churchill, Blackwell, Wright, Peyton, Chilton, Ransdell, to name only a few. Through these men the backwoods inhabitants could seek representation in Williamsburg.

---

7. Edward D. Neill, **The Fairfaxes of England and America**, p. 100. The letter was not to Dinwiddie but to John Campbell, 4th Earl of Loudoun and titular Governor of Virginia.

8. H. C. Groome, op. cit., p. 64.

Another contributing factor in the decision to establish the County of Fauquier must have been the character of Lord Fairfax himself. If the House of Burgesses was wary of an English nobleman with vested rights of uncertain limits over a vast principality within their borders, they had ample precedent for misgivings. The examples of both Virginia and Maryland had been anything but reassuring. Even when the Proprietor was himself wise and tolerant, his heirs had managed to throw the colonies into chaos. Fairfax was, however, from a different bolt of cloth.[9]

Fairfax had accepted the responsibility for the territory under his control without demanding any extraordinary powers of administration. While belonging to the county governments, as was his right, he yielded to their counsel and abided by their laws. His behavior during the French and Indian Wars had been exemplary. Not only did he refuse to desert his tenants but acted on their behalf with courage and wisdom, not only at "Greenway Court" but also in Williamsburg.[10] His nephew, Colonel Thomas Bryan Martin, though not always in the best of health, could be counted upon in an emergency to act promptly and with considerable resource. Not only had he won his spurs but had proved without question his loyalty and devotion to Lord Fairfax and to Virginia during the terrible years that followed Braddock's defeat.

When the County of Fauquier was created in 1759, Lord Fairfax was approaching seventy. His administrative abilities were unimpaired but, increasingly, he was leaving the details of the management of his estates to Bryan Martin. Most of the area of the new county had by then been granted to others, subject to annual quit-rents, but Lord Fairfax had reserved for himself and the heirs of his sister, Martin's mother, the immense Manor of Leeds, part in Fauquier and part in Frederick and Loudoun Counties. The Fauquier portion, some 122,850 acres, extended from Carter's Run along Hedgman's River (Rappahannock) to the crest of the Blue Ridge and north to Ashby's bent. The settlement of these manors, (there were others besides Leeds, not in Fauquier), was Bryan Martin's responsibility, which he handled with efficiency and tact. Between 1759 and 1775 he had negotiated more than 100 major leases in Fauquier alone.[11]

9. Stuart E. Brown, Jr., **Virginia Baron.** An excellent biography of Thomas, Sixth Lord Fairfax.

10. Ibid., pp. 60, 149.

11. Josiah Look Dickinson, **The Fairfax Proprietary,** index pp. 8-15 and accompanying map.

In 1775 Lord Fairfax was eighty-two, long past taking any part in the politics of the counties formed within his immense suzerainty. Details and, to a large extent, protection of the Fairfax interests, were left to his nephew who was almost his alter ego. He even left letter-writing to Bryan Martin and, if Bryan's letters reflect the old man's opinions, then some surprising thoughts whirled under his powdered wig—thoughts that would not have pleased His Majesty, the King.

When, on the 17th of May, 1759, sufficient pressure had been brought to push the bill for the creation of Fauquier County through the House of Burgesses, the justices first appointed included Thomas Harrison, Joseph Blackwell, John Wright, William Blackwell, John Frogg, John Bell, William Eustace, John Churchill, William Grant, (of the quorum), John Crump, Duff Green, Yelverton Peyton, Thomas Marshall, George Lambkin, Wharton Ransdell, Elias Edmonds, Thomas McClanahan and Richard Foote, Gentlemen.[12] Even a casual inspection of this list is enough for one to conclude that control of the new county rested in the hands of descendants of those who had exercised the same control in the lower part of the Northern Neck or, more recently, in Prince William County.

Colonel Thomas Harrison, presiding Justice of the first court, had succeeded his father, also Thomas Harrison, in the same position in Prince William County. However, in anticipation of the creation of a new county, he had built a new house on the west side of Dorrell's Run on part of his inherited estate and now considered himself as a resident of Fauquier. He served as Burgess from Fauquier from 1760 to May, 1769, and died in 1773.[13]

The County Clerk was Humphrey Brooke, a relative newcomer to the county who qualified, probably, because of his superior education. He was then 31, the son of Humphrey and Elizabeth (Braxton) Brooke of Dumfries. The Brooke family had first settled in old Rappahannock County (now Richmond) and his uncle, Robert Brooke, had been the surveyor for most of the Fairfax holdings in Frederick County. His first cousin, Carter Braxton, signed the Declaration of Independence. Humphrey Brooke served the County as Clerk for 34 years, retiring in 1793 in favor of his son, Francis.

12. Fauquier Historical Society, **Bulletin**, July, 1924, p. 399.

13. Ibid., p. 390. Bertram Ewell's survey of the Fauquier-Prince William boundary line shows "Col. Harrison's old house" in Prince William and "Col. Harrison's," in Fauquier, about ½ mile from it.

The Sheriff was Joseph Blackwell, aged 44, son of Samuel and Margery (Downing) Blackwell of "Walnut Lodge," Northumberland County.[14] Joseph Blackwell and his brother William had left Northumberland County before 1748 and had settled in part of Prince William that was now Fauquier. He had represented Prince William County in the House of Burgesses intermittently from October, 1748, through October, 1755. Though listed as a Justice of the new county, he did not qualify, preferring the office of Sheriff instead. It was his unpleasant duty to oust the miscreant parson John Brunskill as Rector of Hamilton Parish, as previously mentioned.

Most of the Justices and other officials who attended the first Fauquier Court on that lovely spring day in May of 1759 had passed to their reward or were no longer participating in the affairs of the county in 1775, but there was one conspicuous exception. Thomas Marshall, gentleman, in 1759 "produced a commission from under the hands and seals of the President and Masters of the College of William and Mary appointing him to be Surveyor of this County."[15] As Thomas Marshall was destined to play a major role in the history of Fauquier during the Revolution, it would be well at this point to know more about him. In many respects he was a remarkable man, a statement in which his eldest son, Chief Justice John Marshall, concurred.[16]

Thomas Marshall, son of Captain John and Elizabeth (Markham) Marshall, was born 2 April, 1730, on his father's plantation on Mattox Creek, Westmoreland County, about five miles from the Washington plantation on Bridges Creek. In fact some of the Marshall land was part of a tract once granted to ancestors of George Washington, but "by them lost for want of seating."[17] George Washington was two years younger. The two

14. Ibid., pp. 486-499. Stella Pickett Hardy, **Colonial Families of the Southern States of America**, pp. 49-70, "The Blackwell Family."

15. The right to commission county surveyors, for a substantial fee, was one of the curious colonial prerogatives of the College of William and Mary. There is no evidence that the candidates were expected to attend that college.

16. Joseph Story, **An Address by Mr. Justice Story on Chief Justice Marshall**, p. 8: "My father," would he say with kindled feelings and emphasis, "my father was a far abler man than any of his sons. To him I owe the solid foundation of all my own success in life."

17. Grants were usually given subject to "seating" (i.e. building a house of prescribed dimensions) within a limited period of time.

families were probably acquainted, but it was not until both were in their teens that Thomas Marshall was thrown into frequent contact with Washington.

For young men of good family who had, nevertheless, to make their way in the world there was no profession more useful than surveying. The long term prospects of neither Marshall nor Washington could be termed propitious. The Washington lands were extensive, but there were several older sons to inherit. The Marshall lands were more modest and, though he was the eldest son and would inherit, they were reaching the end of useful cultivation. Both Washington and Marshall were trained in surveying, but Washington had an advantage that Marshall conspicuously lacked, an important client.

The client was, in fact, none other than Lord Fairfax, the nominal owner of the mind-boggling total of five million, two hundred and eighty thousand acres of land in northern Virginia, most of which needed surveying. George Washington was connected by marriage with the Fairfax family and enjoyed Fairfax's complete confidence.[18] His Lordship stood in dire need of a number of surveyors on whose work he could rely.

When Washington was only seventeen, in 1749, Lord Fairfax proposed his name to the College of William and Mary as county surveyor of Culpeper County.[19] It was a staggering responsibility for a teenage boy, but it would not have been in character for Washington to have felt any doubt of his qualification. He named Thomas Marshall as his deputy. Their duties were not confined to Culpeper; in fact, most of their work was in the counties of Fauquier and Frederick, where Fairfax's needs were most pressing. For almost two years they had ranged the Piedmont together, amid the towering forest in the shadow of the Blue Ridge. Here they hunted, swam rivers and rested at night under the open sky. Headquarters was at "Greenway Court."

There was no grandeur at Greenway Court but there was a bountiful table, the constant attendance of the great and near-great who came to pay their respects to Lord Fairfax, and there was always something doing. There, too, one had the latest news. With everything from the latest London scandal sheets to the works of Dryden and Pope, Lord Fairfax was well supplied.

18. His elder half-brother, Lawrence, married Anne, daughter of William Fairfax of "Belvoir," a cousin of Lord Fairfax.

19. Culpeper County then included Madison and Rappahannock Counties, where little of Fairfax holdings had been surveyed.

This halcyon existence came to an end in September of 1751, when Washington was called to accompany his elder brother, Lawrence, to Bermuda in search of a cure for tuberculosis. Not long after Thomas Marshall, the fourth child but eldest son and heir, was called to the bedside of his ailing father. He laid his transit aside and returned with reluctance to Westmoreland County.

John Marshall "of the Forest" died on his Westmoreland County plantation in April or May of 1752. Thomas Marshall, as executor of his estate, sold most of his father's property. The most valuable land was 300 acres conveyed by deed dated 28 August, 1753, to the Vestry of Washington Parish for use as a glebe.[20] He settled his mother, two younger brothers and two unmarried sisters in the old Marshall homestead with 200 acres of marginally productive land. It was not expected to be a permanent arrangement.

His three older sisters were all married. The eldest, Ann, wife of Augustine Smith, was moving with her family to Fauquier County. When he returned to Fauquier in 1753, he took his youngest brother, Markham (called Abraham in his father's will), aged thirteen, with him. The other brothers followed. In 1768, his mother, his sister Sarah, widow of Robert Lovell, and her son William Lovell were given a lease for lives near Oven Top Mountain by Thomas Bryan Martin, acting for Lord Fairfax.[21] At the same time, his brother John, who had married Mary Quesenbury, took a lease that included their son Thomas, on Buck Run.

In 1754 Thomas Marshall married Mary Randolph Keith, daughter of the Reverend Mr. James Keith and his wife Mary Isham Randolph. She was a daughter of the Randolphs of "Tuckahoe," one of the most powerful families in the colony. This marriage brought to Thomas Marshall a whole coterie of useful connections. Mary (Keith) Marshall, like another Randolph daughter, the mother of Thomas Jefferson, figured but slightly in the known history of her distinguished family. Jefferson never

---

20. Westmoreland County Deed Book 11, p. 1. Westmoreland Court Orders 1752-55, folio. 123 d.

21. A "lease for lives" was a device to assure continunity in leaseholds. The lease was for the duration of three lives, sometimes more. The lessees were, for instance, a man, his wife and one child; a widow and two sons; a man, his son and grandson; or some other combination that would secure the lease for a long period.

mentioned his mother, but a son of Mary Marshall was more explicit. On her gravestone in Kentucky is the laconic inscription:[22]
> She was good, not beautiful
> Useful, not ornamental
> And she was the mother of fifteen children.

They settled in what was said to have been a log cabin near Midland. Whether this is true, or merely conforms to nineteenth century tradition that has all patriots born in log cabins, is unknown. Anyway, it was there on the 24th of September, 1755, that his eldest son, John, was born. Whatever the house was made of, Thomas Marshall had done well. Had his position not been secure he would not have been named County Surveyor when the new county was formed four years later, or Burgess in 1761.

On the agenda of the first Fauquier County Court in May of 1759 were many items such as the appointment of persons to survey the condition of roads (bad), take a list of tithables (elusive), and to obtain some law books so that the justices could talk their way out of an emergency. Two were of major importance: choosing a site for a courthouse, and organizing a county militia.

The matter of the location of the courthouse had, in reality, already been settled. The approximate center of population was, at the time, in the vicinity of Elk Marsh, and it seemed logical to locate the courthouse there, on a site near present Morrisville. There were a few powerful and highly articulate objectors to that location. They favored a tract in the geographical center of the county that happened to be owned by Richard Henry Lee of Westmoreland County, a member of the House of Burgesses.[23] The objectors were represented most forcefully by John Bell, Duff Green, Wharton Ransdell and Elias Edmonds, "four of the Gent named in the Commission of Peace of this county" who refused to qualify themselves as justices unless they had their way. It would be churlish to observe that three, at least, of these gentlemen had been prescient enough to buy land close to or adjoining the Lee property. Lee had, of course, been useful in getting the bill for the creation of the county through the House of Burgesses. One would like to think that the excellent choice of the site for the county seat was the result of some long-range planning by skillful experts among

---

22. The grave is at "The Hill," home of her son Thomas, Washington, Mason Co., Kentucky.

23. Richard Henry Lee, 1732-1794, was the fifth son of Col. Thomas and Hannah Harrison (Ludwell) Lee of "Stratford." His home was "Chantilly," Westmoreland County.

our forefathers. Alas, it was pure chance.

It was, of course, among the first duties of the new county to set up a militia that would react more promptly to the needs of the inhabitants of the back counties. Among the first acts of the court was to appoint a County Lieutenant to represent the Governor or President of the Council in matters pertaining to the militia. The choice fell upon 28 year old Henry Churchill, son of Colonel Armistead Churchill and brother of John Churchill, newly appointed Justice. He was one of the heirs of the great estate called "Pageland." [24] What talents this young aristocrat may have had for so responsible an office will forever remain unknown. He died of pleurisy on Christmas Eve, 1760, remembered chiefly for the elegance of his wardrobe.

His place was taken by Colonel Thomas Harrison, but, as Harrison was also one of the Burgesses, a delegation of authority was necessary. This fell on a much more down-to-earth individual, Captain William Edmonds, who had real military experience. He quickly put together a militia of 70 well-trained men, officially organized 29 August, 1761, for frontier defense. As 1st Lieutenant there was nineteen year old Martin Pickett. The 2nd Lieutenant was William Ransdell, and William Norris was Ensign. There were six sergeants and Stephen Bailey and John Hudnall, "Patrolers." [25]

The activities of the Fauquier Militia between 1761 and 1775 are not easily ascertained. One has the feeling that Bailey and Hudnall did most of the steady work. The rest were on call, except on Muster Days when it was their duty to "raise Cain" in Fauquier Courthouse and bedevil the local constabulary. An order in the Virginia Council dated 1 August, 1763, outlines the scope of their responsibility. It reads: [26]

> Two groups of militia, numbering each about 500 men were authorized (by the Council). One group under the command of Adam Stephen, was to be made up of men taken proportionately from the militia of the counties of Hampshire, Frederick, Culpeper, Fauquier and Loudoun

---

24. 10,610 acres on Turkey Run granted in 1724, granted by Robert Carter as agent for Lord Fairfax to his son-in-law, Mann Page, later bought by Col. Armistead, a near relative.

25. Fauquier County Bicentennial Committee, **Fauquier County, Virginia,** 1759-1959, pp. 170-171.

26. **Legislative Journals,** op. cit., August 1, 1763.

to protect the frontier from the Potomac to Lord Fairfax's southern line. (near New Market in the Shenandoah Valley.)

Another group under Colonel Andrew Lewis was to carry this line of defense to the Carolina line. "In case of emergency the one was to aid the other." It is not known that such an emergency ever arose.

There was, however, an emergency in Frederick County in 1764. Captain Edmonds received the following:[27]

On His Majesty's Service...to Capt. William Edmonds:
> Sir: By a letter I have just received from Col. Hite in Frederick, desiring assistance against the Indians, I have thought proper to call the Militia together; I therefore desire you to meet at the Courthouse on Tuesday next at 10 o'clock with your officers and men, equipped according to law. I am, Sir, your Humble Servant, John Bell.

The outcome of this order is unrecorded.

In the quiet years between 1759 and 1763 Fauquier County seems to have prospered. New settlers came to take up ungranted lands everywhere. They still came, for the most part, from the lower counties of the Northern Neck. Except for the manor lands, there was not much Fairfax land left for disposal but several of the large tracts previously granted were now broken up to settle the estates and satisfy the heirs and creditors of the original patentees. Enormous Carter tracts were in escheat and Burgess, Ball and others left no direct descendants in Fauquier.

There were problems. Occasional drought and cruel spring frosts were a constant threat. Abnormally cold summers ruined the crops. The new settlers had to accustom themselves to the fact that farming the rocky hillsides was quite different from planting tobacco in the flat sandy soil of the tidewater. Even the instruments of husbandry were changing. A man named Stephen McCormick, overseer on the land in Fauquier owned by Peter Hedgman, was working on a new sort of plow. When Hedgman died in 1765 he left 500 acres of this land to Stephen's wife, Margaret. Their son, born after the Revolution, patented a cast iron mold board plow in 1816

---

27. Fauquier County Historical Society, **Bulletin**, No. 2, 1922, p. 145. John Bell was Edmonds' brother-in-law, having married his sister, Frances.

which he made in his blacksmith shop at Auburn. He always acknowledged the pioneering attempts of his father in developing a plow that would revolutionize cultivation of soil in the Piedmont.[28]

Local affairs diverted their attention from larger events developing in the world that would, one day, affect their lives. The machinations of the English Parliament were remote and of only passing interest. There was a new King in 1760, George III who, at least spoke English. They thought that might be some help. The fact was that the new King had troubles of his own. The Seven Years' War, with which the colonists had never consciously identified themselves, although they were an integral part, had left him flat broke.

The result was the Stamp Act of 1765. Somehow the enormous National Debt created by the Seven Years' War had to be paid and it fell upon George III's Prime Minister, Lord North, to find a way to do so. He had but two choices. He could tax the nobility or he could tax the colonies. He chose to tax the colonies. The resulting uproar in the colonies left him stunned.

It is surprising though, that the Stamp Act could arouse such passionate indignation in Fauquier. The county was new, public opinion was diverse and the whole matter would seem more likely to concern those in the tidewater who depended more directly on English imports. Fauquier County was largely self-sufficient and the revenue collected there would have been paltry in comparison with taxes in the tidewater counties. Nevertheless in 1766 the farmers were angry. Philip Martin, Bryan's younger brother, happened to be visiting Greenway Court. He wrote home, 30 April 1766, "Anxiety is great" the colonists were "impatient to know their destiny, - whether they are to sink under a load they say it is impossible to support, or once more be a happy people." [29]

Some of the "anxiety" in Fauquier County was generated by the exertions of a man about whom we will have much to say later. Although Richard Henry Lee owned vast tracts of land in Fauquier, he made his home in Westmoreland County and there he formulated Virginia's most impassioned protest against the Act,

---

28. Stafford County Deed Book, Liber O, 1748-1763, pp. 188-191. Will of Peter Hedgman, dated 29 Nov. 1764; proved 12 Aug. 1765. Hedgman left the remainder of the tract called "Merry Hill" to John Knox, a Falmouth merchant. Knox sold it to Hancock Lee. Fauquier White Sulphur Springs was established on this part of the Hancock Lee land.

29. Wykeham-Martin MSS. Letter Philip Martin to Robert Fairfax, 30 April 1766. Quoted in Brown, **Virginia Baron**, p. 159.

the Leedstown Resolutions. Not all of his friends and neighbors joined in this rash statement of colonial rights, (his own brother, Philip Ludwell Lee, denounced it), but 113 did. Among them were many whose ties in Fauquier were strong and many would later take up residence there. News of the Leedstown Resolutions reached Fauquier from many quarters.[30]

Three of the signers were sons of Major Thomas Chilton of Cople Parish, Westmoreland County. A fourth son, John Chilton, had already moved to the tract of land on Baldwin's Ridge in Fauquier County and was thus not able to add his signature. Later two of the signers, William and Charles Chilton would join him there, leaving "Currioman," the Chiltons' Westmoreland estate, to the eldest son, Thomas. Wharton Ransdell, another signer, was their nephew. We find him just before the Revolution presiding over the meeting at which the men of Fauquier protested the Boston Port Bill. Reading a little further we find the names of John and Joseph Blackwell, sons of Samuel Blackwell of Northumberland County.

Others who signed at Leedstown in 1766 and later turned up in Fauquier County included Peter Grant, John Lee, Jr., Joseph Peirce, Edward Ransdell and Hancock Eustace. All were heirs of Fauquier land or had family interests there.

The Stamp Act was soon repealed but the National Debt was still enormous and new taxes soon replaced it. In 1767 came the Townshend Acts, if anything, more offensive than their predecessor. Under this new set of regulations import duties were to be collected in America by officers of the Crown and, in part, used there to make Royal officials independent of Colonial appropriations. The reaction was exactly what might have been expected, a movement towards a boycott of British manufactures. Again the indignation in Fauquier was somewhat out of proportion to the degree of real privation encountered. Few British manufactures found their way to Fauquier and luxuries were certainly not essential to their way of life, but they were angry just the same, if we can judge by the utterances of their representatives in the House of Burgesses. They were clearly aligned with a new group that was forming around that bright, particular star from another upland county, Patrick Henry.

30. The Leedstown Resolutions (often called Westmoreland Resolves incorrectly) in the handwriting of Richard Henry Lee, is in the archives of the Virginia Historical Society. It is dated 27 February 1766.

The senior delegate from Fauquier was Colonel Thomas Harrison, mentioned earlier, who was 66 in 1765, but had lost none of his fire on that account. His long experience in the House of Burgesses had made for him many friends - and enemies. The Harrisons of the Northern Neck (as opposed to the James River Harrisons) had never been part of the tidewater aristocracy that had controlled the House of Burgesses for so many years. His interests lay in the upland county and its welfare, as far as he was concerned, lay in freedom from British domination. If the British could not protect the back counties, and obviously they could not, then "by G-- they had no right to exploit them."

The junior delegate was, in 1765, Thomas Marshall. Marshall and George Washington had entered the House of Burgesses the same year, in 1761. Washington was elected from Frederick County, where he had spent much of the intervening time since 1752. Together they shared the problems of the delegates from the back counties whose influence was negligible in comparison with those represented by the tidewater grandees. Neither was a brilliant speaker but they were willing to work, especially on committees that best served their constituencies. One of these concerned the militia. In 1764 they found themselves, together with Fielding Lewis, Washington's brother-in-law, William Green and Thomas Rutherford appointed as commissioners for the counties of Hampshire, Frederick, Culpeper, Prince William, Loudoun and Fauquier to "examine, state and settle the accounts of . . . the militia." [31] In that duty they had ample opportunity to weigh for themselves the zeal with which the local inhabitants had met their obligation for military service. It had not been an encouraging experience. Frederick and Hampshire Counties had furnished most of the men and provisions. Marshall was probably embarrassed to learn that Fauquier's sole contribution was maintaining one deserter in gaol for an unspecified time.

In spite of his real desire to serve in the House of Burgesses Thomas Marshall faced a situation in 1767 that did not bother either Washington or Harrison. Both of the latter could afford the honor and privilege of sitting in an elected body where men were supposed to live on incomes derived from their landed estates. Washington had married an heiress and Harrison was wealthy. By contrast Marshall had a growing family to support. In 1767 he was

---

31. Hening's **Statutes**, Vol. 8, p. 10.

forced to quit the House to take the more lucrative job of Sheriff of Fauquier County.³²

By the spring of 1769, he had his fill of the shrievalty and was again looking toward the House of Burgesses. Much had happened in his absence. In March he learned that his old friend, Colonel George Washington was in Fauquier. Although Washington now held his seat from Fairfax County, Marshall was fairly certain that his allegiance to the back country was unchanged.

Washington was staying with his old friend Robert Ashby at "Yew Hill" near Delaplane, only about five miles from "The Hollow", Marshall's home near Markham. His business was the survey of the land he had bought from the estate of George Carter who had died in London some years before. Carter had not taken the slightest interest in the land and had probably not even visited it. Yet, it was beautiful, untouched acreage which Washington considered a wise investment. He had bought 2,768 acres astraddle the Fauquier-Loudoun line, between Upperville and Paris, neither of which villages was then in existence. He planned to survey it himself.

According to his diary, Captain Marshall spent the afternoon and evening of 12 March 1769, probably discussing the last session of the House of Burgesses. A new Governor was on the way to replace Francis Fauquier who had died 3 March 1768. Whatever Washington may have said, convinced Marshall that he was needed in the House of Burgesses.

In June, Marshall announced his candidacy and caused official notices to be read. His enormous influence as Sheriff almost assured his election, but he was taking no chances. He resorted to a strategy that might convince us that political chicanery is not a modern invention. The voting franchise at that time, was given to landowners irrespective of their place of residence. A man owning land in two counties voted in two counties. In June, Marshall resigned as Sheriff of Fauquier, because a Sheriff could not also be a Burgess. Before his resignation, he calmly set the date of the forthcoming election, the 18th of September. One of his most formidable rivals for the office was from the lower county and confidently expected the support of twenty residents of Stafford County who were qualified to vote in Fauquier.

By a strange coincidence the election in Stafford had been set on—the 18th of September! No helicopter was available to ferry the

---

32. For some reason Thomas Marshall is not listed in **Fauquier County, Virginia 1759-1959**, p. 75, among the Sheriffs of the county. William Blackwell, Jr., is listed 1767-69.

voters from Stafford Courthouse to Fauquier. As the total number of landowners likely to vote in Fauquier was about 400, this was a substantial coup. William Eustace, Marshall's successor as Sheriff, ran the election. It was for Marshall marvelously successful.[33]

After 1769, except for a brief period in 1773 when Marshall was County Clerk of newly-formed Dunmore County, he was in the House of Burgesses. It is a fair assumption that he normally voted with the back country delegates. However he was not in Williamsburg in May, 1774, when Governor Dunmore, shocked by the radical tenor of the debate, dissolved the assembly. At that time Fauquier County was represented by a single voice, that of the youthful James Scott.

In many ways James Scott was a curious choice for a seat in the House of Burgesses by the voters of Fauquier County. He was a son of the Reverend James Scott, Rector of Dettingen Parish. Young (aged 27), charming, fashionably dressed, generous he certainly was, but his past history did not promise a brilliant career. Whereas most of Fauquier County's officialdom had credentials extending back for a number of years, Scott was a relative newcomer. Although most came from old and distinguished families, they had to work hard for their places in the narrow circle of preferment. James Scott had been handed everything on a silver platter. Events would prove that he was brave and conscientious, but not temperamentally suited to withstand the rigors of the life that was to come. None of this had been evident in 1769. His personal popularity had been the deciding factor.

The Scott family fortunes originated in the shrewd business sense of the young man's uncle, the Reverend Alexander Scott, Rector of Overwharton Parish. He had come from Morayshire, Scotland shortly after he was ordained for the ministry in 1710 and along with his clerical duties, managed a number of profitable land deals that rapidly made him a man of means. Most of these were in what later became Fauquier County. The most important, in 1727, was an immense grant of 2,823 acres "on a branch of the Rappahannock River in King George County on the head of a branch of the Broad Run of Occoquan River in Stafford." This bewildering and incorrect description was, in fact, of land in Fauquier County on the west side of the Pignut and included the present town of Marshall. When the land was accurately surveyed it was found to contain, not 2,823 acres but really 3,533 acres, the

---

33. Charles S. Sydnor, **American Revolutionaries in the Making**, p. 69.

sort of "robbery by survey" of which Lord Fairfax had reason to complain.[34]

Before he died in 1738, Parson Scott added an adjoining 481 acres on which the manor house of Gordonsdale was later built. He had married Sarah Gibbons, the widow of William Brent, and another source of a substantial estate, but they had no children. About 1736 Alexander Scott invited his much younger half-brother James, recently ordained, to come to Virginia as his heir. The Reverend James Scott handled the assignment with considerable finesse. In 1744, the vast Parish of Hamilton, which had superseded Overwharton, was divided. The upper parish which included all of Fauquier County retained the name of Hamilton. The Reverend James Scott became Rector of the other called Dettingen Parish.[35]

The Reverend James Scott was a strait-laced clergyman of conservative bent and considerable learning. By the laws of primogeniture his large estate would go to his eldest son Alexander, to be doled out to the rest if he thought fit. It was fortunate therefore, that his eldest son was handsome, bright and capable. This was especially true because his second son, James, was quite a problem. He was "wild and difficult to manage", and had gambled away his share of his father's estate by the time he was sixteen. Parson Scott sent Alexander off to Aberdeen to finish his education. Lacking any idea what to do with James, who was in addition a stranger to books, he apprenticed him to a carpenter. James hated it, whether carpentry or work of any sort, is not clear.[36]

In 1758, came the dreadful news. The ship on which the eighteen year old Alexander Scott was returning to Virginia from Scotland had come to grief. Young Alexander died at sea. His father was heartbroken but, true to his principles, recognized that James was next in line. James took the news without notable anguish. "Farewell, jackplane," he said lightly, laying it down forever.

He married Elizabeth Harrison, daughter of Colonel Cuthbert and Frances Osborne (Barnes) Harrison of "Fairview", Prince

34. Josiah Look Dickinson, op. cit. This was a major issue in the Hite vs. Fairfax suit.

35. Fairfax Harrison, **Landmarks of Old Prince William**, pp. 292-294.

36. It was by no means unusual in the colonies for sons of wealthy parents to serve as apprentices. Many successful planters boasted that, in their youth, they had become proficient at bricklaying, carpentry and other skilled trades.

William County in 1760.[37] He was eighteen, she twenty. Sometime thereafter they moved to the huge Scott tract in Fauquier and built "Clermont" (of which there is no trace today). They had eight children, of whom at least six were born before 1775. During 15 years of married life, James Scott had settled down a bit, but his commitment to the cause of Virginia against the Crown was not too clear. The aging Rector of Dettingen had sent three more sons abroad to be educated. One of them was chaplain to the Royalist Governor of Maryland, Robert Eden, and was said to share his views about American independence.[38] Another was graduated from Aberdeen, entered the Middle Temple in 1771 and became a member of the English bar in 1772. Returning to practice law in Dorchester County, Maryland, he kept his ideas to himself. Though he later revealed himself as an ardent patriot, the fact was not then apparent. Of course none of this was known in Fauquier County when James Scott was elected to the House of Burgesses. Independence had not then been thought of, except by the radical few.

Nevertheless, when James Scott entered the House of Burgesses many of the portents of an ominous conflict loomed in the Virginia sky. The first was the advent of a new Governor to replace the genial Lord Botetourt. Entirely different from either of his predecessors, John Murray, Earl of Dunmore and Baron Fincastle, was a Scottish nobleman who came to Virginia reluctantly, late in 1771. He had little but contempt for the rustic inhabitants but, to Lord Fairfax's dismay, immediately identified himself with his Lordship, whom he considered the only Virginian of station as exalted as his own. That Lord Fairfax was also a Scottish Baron seemed especially fortuitous to Dunmore. It did not occur to him that the Barony of Cameron had been bought by one of Lord Fairfax's ancestors from an impecunious James I and that his Lordship had not one drop of Scottish blood.[39]

Arriving in Virginia Lord Dunmore hastened to "Greenway Court" to pay his respects, thereby giving the Fauquier inhabitants

37. Cuthbert Harrison was a brother of Col. Thomas Harrison, Burgess from Fauquier. He, too, owned land in Fauquier in addition to his Prince William holdings.

38. Sir Robert Eden secured for John Scott the living of Eversham Parish in Somerset County on the eastern shore of Maryland.

39. Cameron was a parish in Fife on the east coast of Scotland, six miles from St. Andrews. The Barony carried with it no land of value, there or elsewhere.

the rare treat of watching the "progress" of a Royal Governor, even though he was a thrifty Scotsman who did not spend much along the way. Oozing charm and deference to Lord Fairfax he struck Bryan Martin as "remarkable for his affability." It was not an impression that Bryan was to hold very long. The simple fact was that Lord Fairfax's opinions and those of his nephew, Colonel Martin were those of the colonists. This may be seen by a letter written by Bryan Martin to his brother, Denny, in England in August of 1770, nearly two years before Lord Dunmore's visit.

The Reverend Denny Martin of "Salts" near Maidstone in Kent was a quiet, plodding English clergyman with absolutely no influence and probably only marginal interest in the situation between England and her colonies.[40] It was true that he might inherit one day some preposterous amount of wasteland in this remote outpost of civilization, but the day would not come soon, if ever, and the eventuality promised to be a headache. He must have been quite bewildered to receive from his younger brother this thundering epistle; bewildered, and suspicious that Bryan had lost his mind:[41]

> Virginia is now determined to punish you for your crimes and we are come to a resolution to have only such goods as they cannot live without. Till the laws imposing taxes on us are repealed, we shall be dressed in our own clothing ... silks and finery are not permitted to be landed here. Your merchants in England will feel the weight and curse the folly of your politicians ... you force us to be frugal contrary to our nature .. you send troops to break the peace and treat us as rebels when you yourselves are the cause of our disputes.

Yet if Lord Dunmore was given no reason to suspect that Lord Fairfax and his nephew were not in sympathy with his views, it is not surprising. Though they were well established in Virginia, the Fairfax estates in England still hung on the slender thread of royal favor. One word of the dissidence in Virginia could, if it got back to London, do Lord Fairfax and his English relatives irreparable harm. Their cue was silence. Lord Dunmore displayed, as he did

---

40. Denny Martin was the eldest son of Lord Fairfax's sister, Frances. He first came to Virginia in 1784 to claim the estate. He died in England, 3 April 1800. See Groome, op. cit., pp. 223-240.

41. Wykeham-Martin MSS., quoted in Brown, op. cit., 165.

later, no awareness of colonial problems, no ability to see things from the colonists' point of view. They watched him ride off with deep misgiving.

For a while the events leading to further conflict with Britain took place on other stages with a different cast of characters. In Fauquier the chief concern was for those of their number who had gone into Kentucky and the Ohio River Valley where the Shawnee tribes were stirring up trouble. Under the leadership of Thomas Bullitt a number of young men from Fauquier had sought land grants in the area northeast of present Lexington, centering about Limestone (now Maysville) on the Ohio River.[42] On the 8th of July 1773, Dunmore left Williamsburg "on a tour of the back country" ostensibly routine but intended mainly to get a slant on the Indian situation. The journey convinced Dunmore of the need for action and he returned to Williamsburg to prepare for it.

In the meantime elsewhere "Indians" of a different sort had started quite a ruckus. The news of the "Boston Tea Party" reached Fauquier in the dead of winter and caused no particular reaction. It is probable that the rather conservative inhabitants deplored the action and thought that the unruly Bostonians should be punished. However the news of the drastic act of vengeance by the British Parliament against a whole city, which reached Williamsburg on the 19th of May, 1774, and Fauquier County a few days later, was received with rage and disbelief.

Fauquier County was having a bad time anyway. A nearly fatal May frost had almost destroyed wheat, corn and tobacco and left prospects of famine in its wake. Furthermore the news from Ohio was unrelentingly bad. Bryan Fairfax wrote to his brother:[43]

> I cannot silently pass over the many misfortunes that attend this unhappy country ... just complaints are not heard or injuries readjusted. England, once our support, seems now determined to reduce us to an implicit obedience to her arbitrary will to which we will never submit .. our trade at Boston stopped to force obedience to which she has no right to claim ... our Assembly dissolved

---

42. Thomas Bullitt (1730-1778) was a son of Benjamin and Elizabeth (Harrison) Bullitt and a brother of Cuthbert Bullitt. He was Commander at Fort Frederick in 1756 and afterwards made extensive surveys in Kentucky. During the Revolution he was Adjutant General in the Southern Department.

43. Wykeham-Martin MSS., quoted in Brown, op. cit., p. 172.

KINDLING FLAME

for supporting her sister in distress, our courts of justice shut.

With rising anger he continued:

Your merchants no longer enjoy the fruits of American labor and all (Americans are) determined to pay their debts already due England.

For, in cold fury at their reaction to the Boston Port Bill, Lord Dunmore had, on the 26th of May, dissolved the House of Burgesses. Fauquier County's sole representative, the youthful James Scott, along with most of the others, ambled over to Raleigh Tavern to continue the discussion. He was not among those selected to attend a convention to be held in Philadelphia 5 September, 1774, but there was plenty to do at home.

Fauquier County was in an uproar but it is only fair to say that so were most of the other Virginia counties. Meetings were being held in which the arbitrary act of the Parliament against Boston were castigated from Hell to breakfast. The Town of Fredericksburg led the parade on the 1st of June. Then came Prince William and the Town of Dumfries on the 6th, Frederick County on the 8th, Dunmore County (now Shenandoah) on the 16th, Westmoreland on the 22nd, Richmond on the 29th, and Prince George. James City County met on the 1st of July, followed by Culpeper on the 7th. Then it was Fauquier's turn.

The Resolutions dated 9 July, 1774, began impressively: [44]

At a General Meeting of the Freeholders of the COUNTY OF FAUQUIER in Virginia, on the 9th of July, 1774, at the Court House of the said County:
Mr. Wharton Ransdell being chosen Moderator, The following Resolutions were unanimously agreed to:
RESOLVED, That it is an undoubted right of British subjects, and without which freedom cannot exist, to be taxed only by their own free consent, either personally given, or by their Representatives legally assembled.

And so forth through eight resolutions, each more indignant than the last. The Moderator was the youthful Wharton Ransdell, son of William and Mary (Chilton) Ransdell and nephew or cousin

---

44. Fauquier Historical Society, **Bulletin**, June 1923, p. 27.

to half of the officials of Fauquier County. The document was signed by Peter Grant as Clerk.[45] Presumably that meant clerk of the meeting, as Humphrey Brooke was County Clerk.

So, according to the above, we must conclude that in Fauquier County in July of 1774 the recently voiced complaint that "taxation without representation is tyranny" had been accepted as a basis for protest. It is interesting to consider what our forefathers really had in mind. Whose rights were being trampled upon?

The Virginia House of Burgesses had, during the 150 or so years of its existence, built up a rather impressive degree of autonomy as far as the conduct of colonial affairs was concerned. If by "representation" it was meant that each of the colonies should have one or more seats in the English Parliament, it is difficult to understand how they could have expected so small a voice to have had any appreciable effect.

If by "representation" they meant some degree of universal suffrage, they were well before their time. The House of Burgesses represented the ruling class, not the people. The same was true of Parliament, and would remain so in both England and America until well into the twentieth century. Let us look at the voting record. We do not have complete statistics in Fauquier but we do have the next best thing - the record in the neighboring county of Culpeper.[46]

Culpeper had a slightly larger population than Fauquier but, proportionately, the voting pattern was, as nearly as we can judge, almost identical. In 1790 in Culpeper there were just over 22,000 people of whom about 40 per cent were black and could not vote. Of the remaining 13,800 about one half were women who, of course, could not vote. We are now down to, to be exact, 7,127 white males. However the span of life at the time was such that half of these were under sixteen. Considerably more were under twenty-one, which was the voting age. In fact tithable white males of voting age numbered only 1,786.

But we must not stop there. In order to cast a ballot a man must own at least 25 acres of land. Only 935 qualified in that respect. Of these an average of only 359 chose to exercise their franchise between 1786 and 1789. This is not an isolated figure.

45. Peter Grant (1734-1815) was a son of Capt. John Grant of Westmoreland County and his second wife, Margaret Watts. He married in Fauquier, Susannah Winn, bond dated 23 Nov. 1767. Minor Winn gave security.

46. Sydnor, op. cit., Appendix I. This valuable study of Virginia politics provided most of the statistics used in the next paragraph.

Culpeper's voting population was at its height in 1761 and, by the time of the Revolutionary War had *dwindled* - a trend that continued after the war. Membership in a dissenting sect might have been an additional reason for disenfranchisement but, in spite of the dis-establishment, the number of voters still decreased.

In 1769 Fauquier had 399 voters - more than Culpeper had that year. This might argue that Fauquier, with a smaller population, was slightly more democratic than Culpeper - about .3 of 1 per cent more. However, be that as it may, the Fauquier lads who went off to fight the British, did so to uphold the rights of less than 3 per cent of the population. There is no use in becoming unduly exercised by this curious anomaly but it does serve to demonstrate that universal suffrage was not really uppermost in the minds of the eighteenth century politicians.

Nevertheless, the people were in an uproar, however small their representation was likely to be under any circumstances known in the 18th century. So also, reflecting popular opinion, was the liberal clergy. The Reverend James Thomson, Rector of Leeds Parish, struck out, probably on his own, but possibly to some extent under the influence of Colonel Thomas Marshall. Mounting the pulpit of one of the chapels in Leeds Parish, he said: [47]

> You have all heard before now of the measures taken by the British Parliament to deprive his Majesty's subjects of these Colonies of their just and legal rights by imposing several taxes upon them destructive of their liberties as British subjects. And to enforce those acts they have for some time blocked up the harbour of the city of Boston with ships of war and overawed the inhabitants by British troops. By which illegal steps the people in general have endured great hardships by being deprived of their trade, and the poor reduced to great want. It is therefore incumbent upon every one of us, as men and Christians, cheerfully to contribute according to our ability toward their relief.
>
> And as we know not how soon their case may be our own, I would likewise recommend to you to contribute something toward supplying the country with arms and ammunition, that if we be attacked we may be in a posture

---

47. Bishop William Meade, **Old Churches, Ministers and Families of Virginia**, p. 219.

of defence. And I make no doubt that what you bestow in this manner will be employed in the use you intend it for. If you want to be better informed with respect to the Acts which have been passed with a view to impose illegal taxes upon us and deprive us of our liberties, I shall refer you to the gentlemen of the committee for this county who will satisfy you on that head.

The ink was scarcely dry on the "Fauquier Resolutions" when the good people of the county had an opportunity, if they chose to avail themselves of it, to present it to Lord Dunmore in person. On the 11th of July, 1774, he passed through Fauquier on his way to Greenway Court, behaving very much as though the events of the last two months had never happened. The House of Burgesses, before its dissolution, had asked him to take action against the Indians in the Ohio Valley, and he was about to do so. He may have attempted to annex the Fauquier militia along the way but, if so, he had little success. Few Fauquier pensioners ever claimed that they had served in "Lord Dunmore's War".[48]

After five weeks at Greenway Court, during which the Fairfax good nature was sorely tried, he departed westward, leaving behind the ailing and reluctant Colonel Bryan Martin in command of reserves in Frederick and adjoining counties. Surprisingly Dunmore was successful, thanks mostly to the gallant performance of Colonel Andrew Lewis and the men from the back counties of Augusta, Botetourt and Fincastle, who fought the Indians to a standstill at Point Pleasant near the mouth of the Great Kanawa on the 10th of October. After this bloody battle in which, of course, Lord Dunmore took no active part, he returned in triumph to Williamsburg in December.

It was his last triumph and it was short-lived. The greater problem, which he had left behind in Williamsburg, was soon to catch up with him. It would make Indian fighting on the banks of the Ohio seem comparatively peaceful. In spite of the success at Point Pleasant the atmosphere in Virginia worsened. In November Bryan Martin wrote again to his brother: [49]

48. One Fauquier County man contributed largely to the success of Lord Dunmore's War though it was unrecognized at the time. He was Simon Kenton, Dunmore's chief scout. He was then using an assumed name because he believed that he was wanted for murder in Fauquier County. He was born near Hopewell Gap, 3 April 1755.

49. Wykeham-Martin, MSS., quoted in Brown, op. cit., p. 174.

Confusion worse confounded and desolation have fixed their sable banners here. Oppression's iron rod hangs o'er our head prepared to give the fatal blow, — America is determined to defend her right, — your merchants must be ruined.

He still hoped that restrictions against the importation of British goods might succeed in arousing English merchants on behalf of the colonials, but they had little or no effect on the government. That the English merchants, as a class, would rise to demand that the government alter its colonial policy was an idea that bemused many responsible colonists. The power of the mercantile interests was strong, but it was not organized. The government was pressed for money and the tax rate in England was as high as the commons might safely be expected to bear. Bryan Martin was dreaming an impossible dream.

The last Christmas before the war was quiet in the foothills. The Indians no longer worried them. There was a ball at the Palace at Williamsburg to celebrate Lord Dunmore's return and the birth of a daughter to Lady Dunmore. In a burst of rare good feeling he named her Virginia in honor of his sometimes aggravating constituency. It was true that the Port of Boston was still closed and the city was now swarming with redcoats. However Boston was far away and news of General Gage's strenuous measures to implement the blockade of Boston, taken in November, did not reach Virginia by way of London until mid-January. Public indignation for acts already two months old is not easily aroused.

The apparent calm, however, was deceptive. The House of Burgesses had met in Dunmore's absence and after token expressions of loyalty to the mother country, had passed a dozen resolutions designed to give her a swift kick in her tenderest spot, her economy. It was Lord Dunmore's unpleasant duty on Christmas Eve to pen his report to the Secretary for the Colonies, Lord Dartmouth. 1774 had been bad enough but for 1775 he could see only further trouble. This required no great prescience. The Continental Congress meeting in Philadelphia in September had passed certain resolutions that must be ratified in Virginia. A meeting for that purpose had been set for Monday, the 20th of March, 1775.

In order that Lord Dunmore might not be forced into any intemperate action by a confrontation in the capital, the 2nd Virginia Convention decided to meet elsewhere, where they could deliberate with more freedom and without a platoon of the Governor's redcoats hanging about. Events of the past months had demonstrated that the Governor burned at the end of a rather short fuse. They chose the barnlike St. John's Church near the falls of the James River, one of the few buildings outside the capital that could hold so large a gathering.[50] About 120 delegates filled the narrow, cramped pews to capacity, leaving the spectators to line the walls and crowd about outside the open windows.

As delegates from Fauquier, James Scott was again joined by Thomas Marshall. Marshall was then forty-five, a large, slightly florid man, whose appearance is known to us only through a rather bad portrait. He appears slackjawed, with a somewhat lop-sided face and shifty eyes. It is the painter's fault - as he was both intelligent and decisive. We have no portrait of James Scott, his junior by twelve years. He was no longer the light-hearted playboy of his younger days. Lines of worry were already beginning to form that in four years would change him to the gaunt, broken man we will meet later at Lord Stirling's Headquarters in New Jersey.

The first three days of the Convention were almost routine. Thursday morning began with the reading of a petition to the King by the Jamaica Assembly in support of American rights. Upon hearing this the Virginia delegates adopted a resolution thanking their Jamaican friends and assuring them that it was "the most ardent wish of this colony ... to see a speedy return to those halcyon days when we lived a free and happy people."

This nonsense was too much for Patrick Henry, the delegate from Hanover County. For ten long years he and his colleagues from the back counties had battled in the House of Burgesses for the rights of the colonists against the Crown. Now, after three days of futile bickering, all the delegates wanted to do was to return to the good old days! To Hell with the good old days! As far as he was concerned the British government had shown nothing but contempt for colonial yearning to live as "a free and happy people." With Marshall, Scott and other back county delegates he believed that some of those from the tidewater were beginning to waver. Abruptly he rose to his feet with a proposal. It was that an independent militia be immediately established, responsible to the Convention, not to the Governor, to serve in the defense of the rights and liberties of the colonies.

The delegates gasped. Those who had the same thoughts were suddenly united. Promptly the moderates raised their protest. The English merchants, they said, were clutching their empty pockets

---

50. St. John's Church (without its present tower) is very much as it was in 1775. The village of Richmond, formerly Byrd's Warehouse, had about 1,800 inhabitants.

and calling for a settlement. Rumor had it that the King himself was almost ready "to look upon America's sufferings with an eye of pitie." Furthermore British navies rode triumphant on every sea, her army never marched but to certain victory! Was this the time to provoke the lightning?

When they had had their say, Henry rose again. While it cannot be said that anyone remembered exactly the words that followed, the power of his oratory would reverberate down the corridors of time: [51]

> "Is life so dear or peace so sweet as to be purchased at the price of chains and slavery? Forbid it, Almighty God! I know not what course others may take, but as for me, - give me liberty or give me —"

The delegate from Hanover paused, brandishing aloft a small ivory letter opener. Slowly he lowered it into the folds of his shirt front,

"DEATH."

The absurdity of the gesture would have been fatal to one without the speaker's gift for histrionics. Somehow Patrick Henry made the whole performance spell-binding. The delegates sat in stunned silence, possibly uncertain whether to laugh or cry. The men who had supported Henry were not prepared for this. Thomas Marshall later said that the speech was "one of the most bold, animated and vehement pieces of eloquence that had ever been delivered." That his immediate reaction was the same is debatable.[52]

Marshall looked about him speculatively. He had served his county of Fauquier in the House of Burgesses off and on for fourteen years. He knew how such words would fall upon the ears of the tidewater crowd, with whom he was himself connected by blood and marriage. He knew also a great deal about the feelings of the people in his county. There had been a great amount of talk in Fauquier about British "tyranny" and drastic measures proposed to withstand it, but there was some difference between talk and action. Fauquier people had never been long on action.

51. No copies of Henry's speeches exist. What we know of them today is the result of the efforts of his biographer, William Wirt, to refresh the memories of his hearers many years later.

52. Leonard Baker, **John Marshall, A Life in Law**, p. 25. This appears to be what John Marshall told William Wirt many years later, not Thomas Marshall's written comment.

Reviewing the past he had reason to suspect that the impassioned speeches in the highly charged atmosphere of St. John's Church might echo rather hollowly in the mountains of Fauquier. Most of the planters, even as late as March of 1775 were in favor of another twist of the lion's tail - but not breaking it off entirely. It would be his and Scott's duty in the months to come to kindle the fires of patriotism in the lovely peaceful foothills. But whatever the people thought, Fauquier's reaction would be determined by a small group of powerful men who owned vast tracts of land in that untamed country. However, when Henry resumed his pew, it was such a man who rose to speak.

Richard Henry Lee did not live in Fauquier County. Nevertheless he held, by inheritance, a tract of 4,200 acres in the exact center of the county, shaped like a large Virginia ham. It was the tract his father, Thomas Lee, had set aside in 1718 when he had served briefly as land agent for the Fairfax proprietary. By the judicious use of influence and a little purposeful prodding the Assembly had been pleased to locate the county seat on this land. Now he was carving neat slices from his ham to serve to the local inhabitants in the form of leases.[53] Those who attended Court in Fauquier Courthouse knew him well. Among such men Lee's endorsement of Patrick Henry's proposal would have great influence.

Tall, beaked-nosed, elegant, Richard Henry Lee was of a family that had been powerful in Virginia for generations. Logic would have placed him on the side of the moderates, opposed to Henry's resolution, but Lee was a bit of a maverick. The Leedstown Resolutions against the Stamp Act nine years before had demonstrated that. Now many of its signers lived in Fauquier County; Blackwells, Chiltons, Ransdells, Washingtons and others. He spoke in quiet, reasoned terms. With "elegance" of speech greater than Henry's, he used "rules of persuasion" to accomplish everything which such rules could effect. Yet, "under the impulse of the tempest which Henry had created" he "trampled upon rules and yet triumphed at this time perhaps beyond his expectations."[54] Jefferson and Thomas Nelson, Jr., followed Lee to the podium. Neither spoke with eloquence but both with deep sincerity. Both favored the resolution.

One of Fauquier County's greatest landowners remained silent. Miserably uncomfortable, Colonel George Washington had

---

53. Casenove Gardner Lee, Jr., **Lee Chronicle**, p. 128.

54. William Wirt, **Patrick Henry**, pp. 123-125.

jack-knifed his huge frame into one of the narrow, hard pews. He was resplendent in the uniform of the Fairfax Militia, the only delegate in uniform and one of the few who truly understood to what end the road they were taking might lead. Yet he said nothing. Thomas Marshall did not expect him to do so. In the long years he had known George Washington he had seldom seen him rise to his feet in a public gathering. The uniform voiced his opinion. He was ready to fight. No more need be said.

As Marshall looked around him he saw others becoming enthusiastic on whose support he would not have counted. Robert Carter Nicholas, originally conservative, now wanted to enlarge the whole enterprise and, instead of arming a militia, proposed that the colony raise ten thousand regulars for war.[55] His proposal was not accepted, probably because many delegates, like Marshall, realized that the cold light of dawn might reveal that the counties they represented had no appetite for battle. Oratory was a powerful force but, like some wines, does not travel well.

Marshall was not naive enough to think for a moment that England would give up without a fight. Against the British regulars he knew how limited was the experience and skill of the Fauquier militia and, quite probably, the militia of the other Virginia counties. Privately he suspected that the other colonies were in the same boat. On occasion the backwoods militia had fought effectively in the forests. Against fixed positions manned by trained European troops they were helpless. The training of an American army had a long, rough road ahead, and Marshall knew it. For himself he had no military ambition. He knew well that his modest military experience did not fit him for high command, though many less qualified, but possessed of vaulting ambition, were to play leap-frog over him in the days to come.

It would be presumptuous to try to assess the thoughts that coursed through the mind of the youthful James Scott. Unlike Marshall, he left no known record, but such was his background that he must have realized that the words he heard were treason. He knew also that men of his station must serve, but how he could not foresee. He must have been deeply moved by Henry's speech, words that had aroused powerful emotions and led to alarming conclusions - enough to make one's head swim. Henceforth he would not falter, though events would tax his mind and body beyond his utmost strength.

That night, alone in his room, Washington wrote in his diary: "Dined at Mrs. Patrick Coote's and lodged where I had done the

---

55. Ivor Noël Hume, 1775, **Another Part of the Field**, p. 116.

night before." If he failed to note the "greatest speech of the century", as some have called it, he was not alone. The "Virginia Gazettes", all of them, while giving details of the resolutions, failed to mention Henry or his speech. Lord Dunmore, writing to Lord Dartmouth, Secretary of the Colonies, simply ignored it.[56]

However the closing days of the Convention were not devoted to undoing their most important accomplishment - the establishment of an independent militia for the defense of liberty. It was recommended to each county that they raise at least one company of infantry and that these should be trained and ready for any emergency. A company of infantry, sixty-eight men, had a captain, two lieutenants, one ensign, four sergeants and four corporals, plus a drum and colours. Each man should be "provided with a good rifle, if to be had, or otherwise with a common firelock, bayonet and cartouch-box (cartridge box) and also with a tomahawk, one pound of gunpowder and four pounds of ball at least, fitted to the bore of his gun."

Meticulous instructions did not stop there. "Every man should also be clothed in a hunting shirt, by way of uniform," and he should "use all endeavor as soon as possible, to become acquainted with the military exercise for infantry." There is little wonder that copies of "The Art of Warr" sold out instantly.

Cavalry troops were each to consist of thirty men, excluding officers, and each man should "be provided with a good horse, bridle, saddle, with pistols and holsters, a carbine or other short firelock, a bucket, (a saddle socket for the gun) a cutting sword or tomahawk, one pound of gunpowder and four pounds of ball at least." Furthermore he should "use the utmost diligence in training and accustoming his horse to stand the discharge of Fire-arms and in making himself acquainted with the military exercise for cavalry."

In the interest of consolidation of the training program, it was decided that the counties should be combined into eighteen military districts. Orange, Culpeper and Fauquier Counties were to form one district.[57]

On Saturday, March 25th, the Convention met to elect its representatives to attend the Second Continental Congress, scheduled to meet in Philadelphia on May 10th. Of those elected Henry, Washington and Lee favored the more radical approach.

---

56. Ibid., p. 118.

57. The present counties of Madison and Rappahannock were a part of this district.

Edmund Pendleton, Benjamin Harrison and Richard Bland were solidly conservative. Somewhere in between were the views of Peyton Randolph but, for reasons of health, there was some doubt that he would be able to attend. A young red-headed delegate from Albemarle County named Thomas Jefferson was chosen to go if Randolph could not. Jefferson's mother came from the conservative Randolph family and he had not yet quite revealed that his own notions placed him squarely among the radicals. Thus the delegation was rather weighted on that side.

On Sunday the Reverend Mr. Selden held divine service at St. John's. By Monday the committee for the encouragement of arts and manufactures had prepared a proposal in which the home manufacture of articles useful in war - woolens, cotton, linen, salt, salt-peter, gunpowder, paper and iron were at the head of the list. Conspicuously absent was any proposal for financing any of these motions. None of the delegates wanted to return to their respective constituencies armed with a proposal to raise taxes too. They had quite enough to deal with.

Late on Monday, March 27th, the Convention was adjourned. Thomas Marshall and James Scott instructed their body-servants to prepare their horses for the long ride home. Scott's servant was a young Irishman named John Riley.[58] He served in the Revolution under Scott as one of his "trusty and confidential soldiers" until it was time to bring his Captain home.

Marshall's man was a young Negro whose name is unknown to us. It was his job to take care of his master's needs, report any kitchen gossip he could pick up and generally make himself useful. He slept where he could because there were no accommodations for his like in the crowded village. Yet it is possible that he would emerge later that year as Fauquier County's first authentic hero.

---

58. From testimony furnished by Christian Riley, his wife, to support a claim made by the Scott heirs, 10 July 1834. (Virginia State Library, Archives Division)

III
The Great Bridge

The road from Richmond to Fauquier County was, in 1775 as in March of any other year, a quagmire. Marshall and Scott goaded their unhappy horses over fallen trees, through treacherous swampland and across streams flooded by the spring rain. It must have been with some relief that they reached Fredericksburg on the Rappahannock. There they could count on a warm bed, a decent meal and, more important, the companionship and advice of some of whose who faced the same problems with more experience and more certainty of the consequences. The center of all concerned with the coming battle for independence was the saloon bar of the Rising Sun Tavern in Fredericksburg.

The Rising Sun was no ordinary country inn. It was, in a sense, the political center of northern Virginia, the gathering point for men of affairs in the upper counties who had come to Fredericksburg to sell their crops and buy necessities for their remote plantations. In these times conversations were heated and the fires of sedition burned fiercely and, fanned by the influence of wine and good fellowship, often spelled the word treason in the heavy smoke-filled air. So at least was the comment of a visiting Englishman at the time.[1]

It was run by George Weedon in partnership with George Washington's younger brother, Charles. The latter's role, however, was minor. He was something of a dilettante and preferred his rather eccentric house then under construction in the Blue Ridge Mountains to his cramped town house in Fredericksburg. He was content to leave the running of the Rising Sun to his gregarious, genial and volatile partner.

There is a great deal more to George Weedon than historians have generally admitted. He was about Washington's age and had

---

1. J. F. D. Smyth, **Smyth's Travels in Virginia in 1773**, condensed from **A Tour in the United States of America**, by John Frederick Dalziel Smyth, London, 1784.

very much the same background in Westmoreland County.[2] He had little military experience but he was an ardent patriot, admired Washington greatly and had followed his career with minute attention. Furthermore he was on intimate terms with his brother-in-law, Dr. Hugh Mercer, who was perhaps, next after Washington, the best equipped man in Virginia for high military rank.

In 1775 Hugh Mercer was fifty and had been in Fredericksburg about fifteen years. He had received his doctorate from the University of Aberdeen in 1744 just in time to serve in the surgeon's corps of the Young Pretender in '45. 1746 found him in Philadelphia. He soon settled near what is now Mercersburg, Pennsylvania where he practiced medicine and became a respected member of the community. He became a Captain in the Pennsylvania Regiment and was witness to Braddock's defeat in 1755, according to some records. More certainly he was a Lieutenant Colonel of Militia on Forbes' expedition to Fort Duquesne in 1758. He was promoted to Colonel of the 3rd Battalion on the 23rd of April, 1759 and made Commandant of Fort Pitt. During these frontier operations he met Washington and it may have been at the latter's suggestion that he moved to Fredericksburg, where he practiced his profession and opened an apothecary shop on the side.[3]

In fifteen years he had inspired confidence in both his medical skill and his knowledge of military matters. Many of the Northern Neck counties had approached Washington to lead them in battle should the occasion arise, notably the independent companies of Fairfax, Prince William, Fauquier, Spotsylvania, Richmond and Westmoreland.[4] As it became increasingly apparent that

2. George Weedon, ca. 1731-1793, is sometimes dismissed by historians casually as a tavern-keeper Washington had known before the war. One offers the curious notion that he was a "German-American saloon-keeper." In fact the first George Weedon came from England and patented land south of Attopin Creek in Westmoreland County, where he died in 1682. This George Weedon was a son of George and Sarah (Gray) Weedon of "Stoney Point", Westmoreland County, almost adjoining the birthplace of James Monroe, to whom he was related by marriage.

3. Hugh Mercer, ca. 1725-1777, married a daughter of John and Margaret (Tennant) Gordon of Spotsylvania County, in 1764. George Weedon married her sister, Catherine.

4. Washington undertook to assume this role in Westmoreland County in a letter to his brother Augustine in 1774. For some reason that county is omitted from a list of such companies to which he sent a letter of resignation dated 20 June 1775.

Washington's time would be taken up with inter-colonial matters, it became important that someone advise those who were attempting to raise and train local troops. Many sought the advice of Dr. Mercer. We have no specific record that Marshall and Scott did so but there is every likelihood that they did. In any event they lingered in Fredericksburg to plan with the leaders of the other Northern Neck counties. In an emergency it was agreed to meet in Fredericksburg with such troops as could be immediately recruited. It was April when they undertook the last lap of their journey home.

The weather was glorious in the Virginia Piedmont in the spring of 1775. The redbud was in bloom on the mountainside and fresh green leaves sparkled in the sunlight against the dark green of holly and pine. Pink and white dogwood cascaded down the mountain ravines and, in the creek beds, young willow shoots were reflected in the ponds from which the ice had fled. The air was fragrant with lilac and honeysuckle mixed with the heady smell of new-turned earth.

Returning to this serene and pleasant land after days of impassioned oratory and heady talk of upsetting the established order must have brought Thomas Marshall and James Scott face to face with the enormity of the task ahead of them. The farmers, busy with their spring planting, could not take time out to talk of future struggles in far away places. In fact, on that account, no court was held in April. It was probably just as well. There must be some groundwork done to prepare the public for the consequences of Convention action.

Naturally Marshall and Scott would turn first to their immediate families and closest friends. William Edmonds,[5] the Sheriff and Colonel of the militia, with his deputies John Blackwell and Elias Edmonds, Jr. could be relied upon. The Chilton brothers, John and Charles;[6] Martin Pickett and his brother, William;

5. William Edmonds, 1734-1816, was a son of William Edmonds of Lancaster County, and his first wife, Judith Sydnor. He married, 16 March 1764, Elizabeth Blackwell, dau. of William and Elizabeth (Crump) Blackwell. They lived at "Oak Spring", near Warrenton. Elias Edmonds, Jr., 1754-1800, was his nephew, son of Capt. Elias and Elizabeth (Miller) Edmonds.
6. John Chilton, 1739-1777, and Charles Chilton, 1741-1793, were sons of Maj. Thomas and Jemima (Cooke) Chilton of Cople Parish, Westmoreland County. John Chilton came to Fauquier before 1765 and married Laetitia Blackwell, dau. of Joseph and Lucy (Steptoe) Blackwell. They lived at "Rock Spring", near Baldwin's Ridge. Charles Chilton married Elizabeth Blackwell, sister of his brother's wife. They lived at "Hereford" on land adjoining "Rock Spring."

Thomas Marshall's own son John and his brother-in-law Thomas Keith [7] were obvious choices to lead the militia in the event of a more general engagement. Recruitment was going to be the problem. There were plenty of chiefs but, so far, no Indians except for the sparsely manned militia. Even then it must have occurred to some that this might lead to a need for troops outside the colony. Fauquier men had gone to the Shenandoah Valley with some reluctance. What would they say if asked to fight in Pennsylvania?

The answers they received from their relatives and friends were, on the whole, reassuring. There was little, if any, Tory sympathy in Fauquier County and the misgivings of those who saw a complete break with England as a threat to their future well-being did not surface immediately. The militia under the command of Colonel William Edmonds was trained and equipped but was not of course expected to furnish the additional troops to the "minute service" who would go to the defense of the colony. It was quickly apparent that there were more men available than rifles, and common firelocks, such as flintlock muskets, were equally in short supply. [8] Men were naturally reluctant to go into battle unless properly equipped and, unfamiliar with the European military tactics which favored musketry, most of them wanted rifles.

It is possible that recruiting efforts might have bogged down in myriad frustrating details and delays had not Lord Dunmore in Williamsburg taken such pains to keep everything stirred up. Fully aware that the shortage of arms and ammunition was hindering the efforts of those attempting to carry out the orders of the Convention and that his own men could not withstand a determined attack on the public magazine at Williamsburg, he sought ways and means of preventing access to some "twenty one barrels and a half of Powder ... three hundred and forty two new Muskets, lately cleaned ... others that want but small repairs and a large number of old Muskets and other small Guns ..." [9]

---

7. Thomas Keith, d. 1802, was a son of the Rev. James and Mary Isham (Randolph) Keith. His older sister married Thomas Marshall. He married, 1775, Judith Blackwell, another dau. of Joseph and Lucy (Steptoe) Blackwell.

8. The inaccuracy and short range of muskets made them of little use in the backwoods. On the other hand a good musketeer could get off five rounds per minute to the rifleman's one.

9. Most of the last had parts missing and were found to be useless. **Journal of the House of Burgesses of Virginia,** 1773-1776, p. 223, (13 June 1775).

Accordingly his Lordship told the Keeper of the Magazine, John Frederick Miller, that he wanted the keys to the arsenal. Miller complied but promptly warned the town authorities that the Governor had ordered the locks removed from the muskets and was about to carry off the powder.

In the early morning of April 21st, Lord Dunmore undertook to remove the gunpowder from the magazine at Williamsburg to the schooner *Magdalen* anchored at Burwell's Ferry, for onward transmission to the man-of-war *Fowey* off Norfolk. The provocative act was immediately detected and the outcry was deafening. Dunmore's reaction was increased belligerence. Having once fought for the Virginians, he roared, "by God, he would let them see that he could fight against them!"[10] Two days later he heard that a large body of men was gathering near Fredericksburg and that they had blood in their eyes.

It was now Dunmore's turn to be alarmed. If word had gone out to the independent companies to assemble in Fredericksburg, then a force of more than two thousand men could swoop down on Williamsburg and flatten the Governor like a swatted fly. That, he heard by a courier from Spotsylvania County on the 28th, was exactly what the council in Fredericksburg proposed to do.[11] It was Peyton Randolph who headed off this violent excursion, but it was a near thing. How many Fauquier men marched to this call to arms is uncertain, but it was now all too apparent that the days on the muster field were no longer innocent fun, but in deadly earnest.

News of the events that took place at Lexington and Concord three days before Dunmore's looting of the Williamsburg arsenal did not reach Williamsburg until April 29th and caused remarkably little stir. Presumably it trickled through to Fauquier a few days later where it caused even less. Later the Virginia Gazette recovered its aplomb and issued an editorial full of sound and fury, but actual bloodshed in Massachusetts was somehow less upsetting than the gyrations of Lord Dunmore. The damage had, however, been done and recruiting in the Virginia counties proceeded apace. There was a great amount of talk in Fauquier County but it was late in May, 1775, before the people had any real awareness of what was really going on.

Monday, the 22nd of May, was the first Court Day in Fauquier after the Convention in Richmond. It was probably the first op-

---

10. Ibid., p. 231.

11. The young courier was Mann Page of "Mannsfield", Spotsylvania County.

portunity that Marshall and Scott had to address a large assemblage of citizens and tell them first hand of the happenings in Richmond two months before. William Grant [12] presided, with Thomas Marshall, James Scott and John Moffett [13], gentlemen, in attendance. There was a long agenda and one searches with mounting dismay for any reference in the minutes to the possible hostilities or any act relating to recent events. There is nothing. In fact a year would pass before there was anything in the Court minutes to indicate that the gentlemen justices had taken notice of any events outside the county.

The only even slightly unusual act was granting permission to the Anabaptists to erect a meeting house on the land of John Kelly, and also permission to erect a meeting house on the land of Original Young, adjoining the Harrison land in the lower part of the county. This was the same Mr. Young who, it will be recalled, we last encountered chasing Elder William Fristoe with a gun. It is evidence that the county officials had at last abandoned any attempt to thwart the growing Baptist movement in the county.

Although the minutes of the May Court in 1775 yield no startling information it can only be assumed that a great deal was going on behind the scenes. The affair of the gunpowder had by that time sputtered out without advantage to either side. The truth was that the Governor realized that, without outside help, he was in no position to carry his point, and cooler heads among the colonists were soon aware that the "minute service" was in no condition to stand up to British regulars, if and when they arrived. The gathering in Fredericksburg had made that situation abundantly clear.

It is not known precisely when the Culpeper Minute Men first assembled and by what method their officers were chosen. It is probable that both had been done before the first of June. Lawrence Taliaferro of Orange was chosen as Colonel, Edward Stevens of Culpeper as Lieutenant Colonel and Thomas Marshall

---

12. William Grant was a half brother of Peter Grant, previously mentioned. He was Sheriff of Fauquier in 1765, vestryman of Hamilton Parish, 1769, and Presiding Justice, 1772. He had been a Justice in Prince William County in 1757.

13. John Moffett was County Surveyor in 1778, Sheriff in 1781. He was a vestryman of Leeds Parish and may have been the Major John Moffett listed as serving with the 2nd Virginia Regiment, 24 March 1778, J. T. McAllister, **Virginia Militia in the Revolutionary War**, p. 201. See also: Mrs. Lee Moffett, **Moffetts of Fauquier County, Virginia**.

of Fauquier as Major.[14] Captaincies would be awarded to any young men who could manage to recruit a reasonable approximation of the 68 men needed to form a company. The captains from Fauquier County who arrived in Williamsburg in October of 1775 were William Pickett, James Scott, John Chilton, William Blackwell and William Payne.[15] Unfortunately we do not have a muster list of any of these companies except the first. Even that one has disappeared since its publication in an unknown newspaper before 1905. The copy is headed: "Roll of Capt. William Pickett's company of the first Minute Batalion of Fauquier of 1776, from the original manuscript for which we are indebted to a friend." It is a payroll for the period between 8 November 1775 to 2 April 1776 and lists a total complement of officers and men of 55, 16 short of the authorized number exclusive of officers. John Marshall was listed as 1st Lieutenant and Isham Keith, his cousin, as Ensign.[16]

It must have been during the early days of training this company that John Marshall, aged twenty, took charge of the company and lectured them on the duties and obligations of a true American patriot. According to somewhat flattering biographers, our hero had walked ten miles from "Oak Hill" to the muster field, wherever it was. The captain (presumably William Pickett) not being present, the men "gathered around their lieutenant, John Marshall, who told them of the news of Lexington and Concord. America was victorious, he said, but added that more fighting was expected. Soldiers would be called for, and as he looked out over the faces of his friends and kinsmen, he said that it was time to polish their firearms and use them in the field." [17]

The writer places this episode in May of 1775, but it must have

14. Field officer rank in the minutemen was not held to be equal to the same rank in the Continental Line.

15. Captain William (?) Payne is not identified in Col. Brooke Payne, **Paynes of Virginia**. He is recorded in the journal kept in the regimental store in Williamsburg thusly: "Culpeper Battn for Capt. Payne's Comp." His purchases were only about one third those of the other company captains. As there is no other record of him, he possibly never reached Williamsburg.

16. This document in National Archives, R 693, Rev. War Rolls, 1775-1783, p. 133, Jacket No. 364, is marked firmly "Not Official." However, every man known from other sources to have served in Pickett's company at the time is listed.

17. Leonard Baker, **John Marshall and the Battle of Great Bridge**.

occurred later. The speech seems somewhat contrived. For instance, not one in ten had firearms to polish. They drilled with sticks. It must have taken them the entire summer to master the manual of arms and the drill, to say nothing of assembling the bizarre uniform they were expected to wear. Of Marshall it was said "Never did man possess a temper more happy, or if otherwise, more subdued or better disciplined." After going through the manual of arms, he lectured them for an hour, challenged them to foot races and walked ten miles back to his father's house.

One cannot escape the impression that it was fun to be playing at war as the golden summer months so rapidly passed. Gradually the nondescript clothing was replaced by hunting shirts made of osnaburg, a coarse, unbleached cotton, supposedly dyed blue but often nearer green or purple as it emerged from the dye-pot. [18] Some had "Liberty or Death" in patchwork on the front, though others asked, half jokingly, if there was not another alternative. They had the common round, black felt hats which fashion dictated should be tacked up on the left brim with a buck's tail as a cockade. As they gloried in being frontiersmen, though most had no frontier experience whatever, their belts bristled with tomahawks, knives and other items of backwoods hardware. Withal they presented a very ferocious appearance, sufficient to cause any British regular to die laughing, if not from other causes.

As the summer progressed bits of news from the outer world reached Fauquier County to add fuel to their ardor. Lord Dunmore, genuinely alarmed at the trend of events, had taken refuge aboard *HMS Fowey*, lying alongside at Yorktown, early in June. Major Marshall and Captain Scott made another long trip to Williamsburg where the House of Burgesses met on the 7th of June. They found that the Governor had fled and had left for their information a long epistle giving his reasons for doing so. [19] The Burgesses then proceeded to pass several bills, none of which the Governor could possibly be expected to sign. Assured by him that he had no intention of doing so, they could only conclude that they were wasting their time in the stifling June heat in Williamsburg. On the 24th of June the Virginia House of Burgesses met for the last time.

Meanwhile the Second Continental Congress that had

---

18. The fact that indigo (tumbleweed), the oldest and most common of natural dyes, grew wild in the colonies probably explains the preference for blue.

19. **Journal of the House of Burgesses of Virginia,** op. cit., p. 202.

assembled in Philadelphia on the 10th of May was still in session. After agreeing initially (15 May) that the colonies should be put in a state of military readiness it took nearly a month for the delegates to take the first forward step toward implementing that plan. On the 14th of June they voted to raise six companies of expert riflemen in Pennsylvania, two in Maryland and two in Virginia to support the Massachusetts troops attempting to relieve Boston.

It was immediately necessary to appoint a commander-in-chief to take over the Massachusetts troops, which on the 31st of May had become the Continental Army and was now being reinforced by troops from other colonies. The choice fell upon Colonel George Washington of Virginia, who was appointed on the 15th and immediately made preparations to leave for Boston. He took command in Cambridge on the 2nd of July.

The Battle of Bunker's Hill had taken place on the 17th of June. It was considered a defeat by both sides. The Americans were naturally disappointed at being obliged to retreat but the British were equally disconcerted by the power and tenacity of the American attack. The engagement, however served to rally the colonies, spur the Continental Congress to action and ended, once and for all, any real hope of conciliation.

For once news travelled fast to the backwoods counties of Virginia. Within less than a week after the resolution to raise two companies of "expert rifflemen" the astonished committees of safety in Frederick and Berkeley Counties were in possession of the resolution. By-passing the House of Burgesses who were trying to placate Lord Dunmore in Williamsburg, the Virginia delegation to the Congress communicated directly with the counties best equipped to furnish men and arms. [20]

Meeting hastily in Frederick County, Charles Thruston, Angus McDonald, Isaac Zane and a few other committeemen elected Daniel Morgan captain from their district, while the committee in Berkeley County chose Hugh Stephenson to lead their company. After General Washington, Morgan and Stephenson were the first two Virginians in the Continental Army. [21]

20. This was the procedure followed in Maryland and Pennsylvania. There is no precise documentation of its use in Virginia but it is very likely that the House of Burgesses was not consulted.

21. Daniel Morgan (1735-1802) was born in Hunterdon County, New Jersey. He was a first cousin of Daniel Boone. He married, 1773, Abigail Curry, dau. of Daniel and ? (Blackburn) Curry. Though Stephenson was considered senior in rank, Morgan managed to reach Boston first and grab most of the notoriety.

Daniel Morgan, a brawny Welsh teamster in the French and Indian Wars, was 39 in 1775 and had come a long way in the twenty odd years since Braddock's defeat. He had served within the militia with courage and resource during the terrible years after 1755, first with Captain Jack Ashby at "Fort Ashby" on Patterson Creek near Winchester, as a commissioned officer in Pontiac's War near Detroit and recently in Lord Dunmore's War. During all of this, after a discouraging start, he had become a prosperous farmer. His many friends knew him as a large (six feet, 200 pounds) fearless, sometimes boisterous but completely disciplined man, a superb rider and a crack shot. At Greenway Court he was held in high regard and he had many friends in Fauquier. Among them were many like Francis Triplett,[22] who would demand that they serve under him though they might have had higher rank in other units.

Morgan immediately set about rounding up rank and file for his company. He had no difficulty; in fact so many crowded to the standard that only the best shots could be taken. Even then, he exceeded his quota and accepted fifteen extra recruits. How many of those came from Fauquier County is not known, but there were several. We do not have a complete roll of company officers, though we do know that William Heth, whom we will meet presently, was among the first. John Austin[23] of Fauquier says that he enlisted in 1775 for three years and, at the expiration of that tour, re-enlisted under Morgan's command under Captain Charles Porterfield, who was a private in the original company.

Morgan raised his company within ten days and, within a month after the original order was issued in Philadelphia, had them ready for the march, fully outfitted and drilled in the rudiments of military duty. The company travelled north by way of the Great Wagon Road, crossed the Potomac at Harper's Ferry and through Pennsylvania by way of York, Lancaster and Bethlehem.

22. Francis Triplett, 1728-1794, was a son of William and Elizabeth (Hedgman) Triplett of "Ship Point", near Dumfries. He was in the Prince William militia in 1750 and was a recruiting officer for Col. Washington in Alexandria in October, 1755. He met Morgan during Braddock's campaign and later financed some of Morgan's business ventures. They remained in close touch, as shown by correspondence.

23. John Austin, 1736-1845, claims the longest service record of any pensioner in the Virginia line. He married, 3 Nov. 1784, Elizabeth Lindsey in Fauquier County. The date of birth claimed in his pension record must be questioned.

They then rode through northern New Jersey, crossing the Hudson at Peekskill, and continued to Boston by way of Hartford. An eyewitness at Frederick, Maryland, said that they were "truly martial, their spirits amazingly elated, breathing nothing but desire to join the American Army and to engage the enemies of American liberty." [24]

Generally the populace lined the streets to see them pass and occasionally treated them to a cold collation of beer, cider, buttermilk and a variety of fruits and vegetables. Despite bad weather they averaged nearly thirty miles a day, completing the 600 mile trip in three weeks. They arrived in Cambridge on the 6th of August, to the immense delight of General Washington and the New Englanders. One nineteenth century historian pictures Washington as so overcome that he went through the ranks with tears running down his cheeks, shaking each man's hand. Possibly, but it does not sound like Washington. [25] Soon, though, they would give him cause to weep.

The rifled gun was unknown in New England at this time and the riflemen were as much of a curiosity around Boston as they would have been around London. They dazzled the rest of the army with their marksmanship and it was a little time before it was fully realized that the length of time it took them to reload coupled with the fact that they could not attach a bayonet rendered them almost useless in any but rather specialized situations. The frontiersmen completely lost their heads in the wave of adulation that engulfed them. They quickly became a disciplinary problem, refusing to stand guard, wasting ammunition in vainglorious displays of marksmanship and inciting mutiny whenever the opportunity offered.[26] Morgan was both mortified and angry. He loved and respected Washington and these disciplinary problems only added to the burden of the Commander-in-Chief. He held his riotous Virginians in check as best he could, meanwhile looking for some way to employ their skills usefully. Washington's enthusiasm for

---

24. John Robert Sellers, **The Virginia Continental Line, 1775-1780**, p. 10.

25. John Esten Cooke, **History of Virginia**, p. 450.

26. Mark M. Boatner III, **Encyclopedia of the American Revolution**, p. 765. Ill-disciplined riflemen are credited with starting the mutiny on Prospect Hill (Cambridge, Mass.) 10 Sept. 1775. Morgan's company was not involved, having left Cambridge on the 9th en route to Quebec.

such troops had certainly cooled and General Charles Lee, with his incredible grammar and spelling, wrote:[27]

> I once was of opinion that some Batalions from the Southward wou'd be necessary—but I have alter'd my opinion. I am now perswaded you have not to the Southward so good materials for common soldiers. Your Riflemen have a good deal open'd our eyes upon the subject, tho' to do justice to their officers They are unexceptional; their Privates are in general damn'd riff-raff—dirty, mutinous and disaffected.

In Williamsburg the Virginia military establishment spent the long, hot summer in that pursuit dear to every Virginian's heart - squabbling over rank. It had been generally assumed that, in the event of war George Washington would command the Virginia forces. Shortly after his elevation to the high command the Independent Company of Fauquier, together with Fairfax, Prince William, Spotsylvania and Richmond, received the following, dated 20 June 1775:[28]

> Gentlemen,
> I am now about to bid adieu to the companies under your respective commands, at least for a while. I have launched into a wide and extensive field, too boundless for my abilities and far, very far, beyond my experience. I am called by the unanimous voice of the colonies, to the command of the continental army: an honour I did not aspire to, an honour I was solicitous to avoid, upon a full conviction of my inadequacy to the importance of the service.
> The partiality of the Congress, however, assisted by a political motive, rendered my reasons unavailing: and I shall tomorrow, set out for the camp near Boston. I have only to beg of you, therefore, before I go (especially as you did me the honour to put your companies under my direction, and know not how soon you may be called upon in Virginia for an exertion of your military skill), by no means to relax in the discipline of your respective companies.

27. Letter, Charles Lee to Dr. Benjamin Rush, 10 Oct. 1775. **Collections of the New York Historical Society,** Vol. I, p. 212.

28. **The Continental Correspondent,** No. 18, August 1, 1775 (Annapolis, Fishergate Publ. Co., 1975).

The Virginia Convention that met on the 17th of July was essentially identical in personnel to the House of Burgesses recently adjourned. Fauquier was again represented by Thomas Marshall and James Scott. So much had happened since the last Convention in March that it was hard to know where to begin. The delegates were under tremendous pressure to create a strong military establishment. They could no longer dodge the problems of finance, recruitment and supply. It was the 8th of August before a bill was presented and the 21st before it was adopted. It contemplated 1,020 rank and file to be divided into fifteen companies of 68 men each. Eight of these companies would form the 1st Virginia Regiment whose commander would also command all Virginia troops. The remaining companies were to form the 2nd Virginia Regiment. Four western districts were asked to recruit only riflemen so that each regiment would have two companies for use as light infantry.[29]

Four names were considered to command the 1st Regiment, Patrick Henry, Thomas Nelson, William Woodford of Caroline County and Hugh Mercer of Fredericksburg. Of them the first two had no military experience whatever. Mercer was easily the best qualified candidate. Woodford's service as an officer in the militia was inconsequential in comparison. However, Mercer was a Scot, without a seat at the Convention, pitted against Henry, one of the most popular figures of his day. Of course Henry won. A touchy pride may have prompted Mercer to withdraw his name from consideration for the command of the 2nd Virginia Regiment. Ultimately Woodford was named for this command.[30]

It must be understood that these two regiments, while raised to defend the colony, were to be on Continental establishment, subject to service outside Virginia. They were thus apart from the "minute men" whose activity was limited to colonial boundaries. Although a high percentage of the minute men later joined the Continental regiments, it is not recorded that any Fauquier men did so until the formation of the 3rd Virginia Regiment in which most of them served.

---

29. W. W. Hening, **Statutes at Large**, Vol. IX, pp. 16-17; **Proceedings of the Convention of Delegates**, 25 Aug. 1775, p. 25.

30. William Woodford, 1734-1780, son of Maj. William and Anne (Cocke) Woodford of Caroline Co. He was a militia officer in the French and Indian War and a member of the Caroline Co. Committee of Correspondence in 1774. He married Mary Thornton, daughter of John and Mildred (Gregory) Thornton of "Fox Spring", Caroline Co.

THE GREAT BRIDGE 73

It was excessively hot and humid in Richmond in August of 1775 and, having organized their regiments and having considered the necessity of issuing the enormous sum of £300,000 in paper money to pay for outfitting and equipping them, as well as paying them for a limited time, the Convention adjourned on the 16th. In doing so they declared, "it is our fixed and unalterable resolution to disband such forces as may be raised in this colony whenever our dangers are removed and America is restored to that former state of tranquility and happiness ..."[31] There were still those who were living in hope that it all would somehow blow away.

In Fauquier the "shirtmen" were drilling through the month of August and seem not to have made a "rendezvous" with their Orange and Culpeper County compatriots until early September.[32] They met in "Major Clayton's old field near Culpeper Courthouse" to drill and await further orders. There they adopted a flag, yellow, showing a coiled rattlesnake ready to strike, with the words "Don't Tread on Me" beneath. Above was inscribed "The Culpeper Minute Men" and on either side "Liberty or Death". The idea of all this propaganda on a banner was not original with them. In fact the first "rattlesnake flag" is said to have been raised in South Carolina.[33]

When sixteen year old Philip Slaughter of Culpeper arrived at "Catalpa", Philip Clayton's home in Culpeper, he found the "old field" churned into a sea of red, slippery mud by the "minute men". Some had tents, others had dug in for a long stay and built huts of plank, to Clayton's annoyance. The Culpeper Minute Men was said to be the largest of the minute battalions but how many there were is not quite clear. It is generally said that there were 150 men from Culpeper and 100 each from Orange and Fauquier.[34]

31. **Proceedings of the Convention of Delegates,** 11-26 August 1775, pp. 14-28.

32. John Marshall wrote that the meeting took place September 1st and that the "express" from Henry was received ten days to a fortnight later. Letter dated 6 Feb. 1832 in the pension file of David Jameson, S 5607, National Archives.

33. It is otherwise known as the Gadsden Flag after Christopher Gadsden, 1724-1805, Revolutionary statesman and general from South Carolina.

34. This statistic appears again and again but it can only apply to the Culpeper Minutemen Battalion just before the Battle of Great Bridge in December. On two previous occasions numbers of surplus men had been sent home.

However, as mentioned previously, a company was supposed to have 68 men and Culpeper is said to have raised five, Orange two and Fauquier no less than seven. Admittedly some may have been under strength, they can scarcely have averaged as few as 25 men each. However, if all were up to strength the total is more than 950 men, exclusive of commissioned and non-commissioned officers. The same source lists the Fauquier captains as William Payne, William Pickett, John Chilton, John Blackwell, George Johnston, Elias Edmonds and Francis Triplett. It is extremely doubtful that the last three were Captains at this time and "John" Blackwell may be in error for William Blackwell, his cousin. It is also rather persuasively claimed that Captain James Scott commanded a company from Fauquier, but, as will be explained later, the records are inconclusive on that point.

We must, therefore, conclude that the total was more than 350 men and was probably more nearly double that number. Of these about 150 had rifles. The rest had whatever firearms they had at home or could pick up along the road.

Late in September Colonel Taliaferro received an "express" from Colonel Henry in Williamsburg ordering him to march there immediately. What particular circumstance prompted Henry's action is not clear. It is true that Dunmore had received some reinforcements both of men and ships but the numbers had so far been small.[35] However, should the reinforcement reach the size expected by Dunmore, as mentioned in an intercepted letter to Sir William Howe, he promised to be a real threat to the colony. Washington urged the Virginians to break his hold on Norfolk as quickly as possible. Henry had only about 400 men in both the 1st and 2nd Virginia regiments and even that number had not enough guns, ammunition, or even blankets and tents to face a winter campaign. Obviously he needed the help of the minute men if he was to take effective action. It took the Culpeper Minutemen several weeks to gather themselves together and make the 150 mile march to the capital.

On October 20th the Virginia Gazette informed its readers that "the Culpeper Battalion of Minutemen, all fine fellows and well-armed (near one half of them with rifles) are now within a few hours' march of this city."[36] Fine fellows they may have been but

---

35. Dunmore's 14th Regiment had 134 privates of whom 60 had been brought from St. Augustine by Captain Charles Fordyce, arriving in Norfolk 20 October 1775.

36. **Virginia Gazette** (Alexander Purdie), 20 Oct. 1775.

well-armed they were not. Their ferocious appearance and rough and ready garb caused a good deal of alarm among the tidewater inhabitants who were not accustomed to having men with tomahawks and scalping knives roaming around. Slaughter says primly, "We took pride in demeaning ourselves as patriots and gentlemen and the people soon treated us with respect and great kindness." [37] It is recorded that such assurances were not always effective.

"Most of us," Slaughter continues, "had only fowling pieces and squirrel guns." Some had not even those. The first thing to be done was to get rid of people like Slaughter, sixteen years old or less, ill-armed and untrained. Furthermore their numbers vastly exceeded authorized quotas. To save face they were told that, since Lord Dunmore had gone on board a British man-of-war, ground troops were no longer needed and half of them were sent home.

Next in order of business was clothing and equipping the men who remained. Almost immediately after arriving in Williamsburg the officers hit William Armistead's regimental store which operated out of Joseph Hornsby's tailor shop. [38] Although they bought miles of osnaburg to make hunting shirts and hundreds of yards of duffel to make leggings for the men it was quickly apparent that the egalitarian spirit that had prompted the officers to dress the same way vanished on reaching Williamsburg. The officers from Fauquier were generous in providing for their men but every order contained materials for officers' uniforms of the best quality.

Thus Captain James Scott bought 9¾ yards of "Broad cloth" for officers' coats, the best blue shroud for leggings and dozens of buttons, large and small. There was buckram for stiffening, twist for working buttonholes and braid for trimming. Daniel Flowerree, who served with Scott, believed that the men were clothed with regimentals from the store of Lackley and Company at Fauquier Courthouse but his memory may not be entirely correct. Scott bought in Williamsburg 90 yds. osnaburg for hunting shirts, 38 yds. for undershirts, 26 for linings, 55 yds. of blue material for leggings for his men. He also bought 12 pairs of shoes.

---

37. Philip Slaughter, **Genealogical and Historical Notes on Culpeper County, Virginia**, p. 47.

38. Apparently most of the Culpeper Minutemen waited until they arrived in Williamsburg to acquire parts of their "uniform.." Hunting shirts could be made up for one shilling sixpence each.

Instead of broadcloth, Captain William Blackwell[39] preferred German serge, lined with shaloon. Captain John Chilton selected blue German serge but the lining was the best linen. Though the color most often mentioned was blue the scene was not monochrome. Captain William Pickett burst forth in a bright green coat lined with green shaloon and Colonel Lawrence Taliaferro was resplendent in claret frieze, faced with buff.

The bills for these items ranged from £30 to £40, a tidy sum in those days, and the men were suitably impressed. Daniel Flowerree, mentioned above, remembered that an old servant of his father had composed a marching song extolling the generosity of Captain Scott, which was sung along the way. Some of the good cheer came directly from the cellars of "Clermont" where Captain Scott had a good supply of whiskey, according to William Payne, a close friend. This statement is affirmed by Christian Riley, wife of Captain Scott's body-servant, John Riley. She recalled at the age of ninety Scott's popularity with his men, his generosity and the fact that "everybody seemed to listen to his talk and like him so much." He was, she said, "a mighty enemy of the English." He was, perhaps, proving himself but, on the other hand, he may have been showing a measure of resentment against his better-educated brothers and their devotion to the British cause.

Williamsburg, of course, looked like an armed camp. The gardens behind the capitol and behind William and Mary College were dotted with tents and trampled into mud. The unpaved streets were so muddy and deeply rutted that they were almost impassable. Colonel Thomas Bullitt, the unconventional brother of Cuthbert Bullitt, the Fauquier attorney, had been appointed adjutant general.[40] With no very clear idea of what he was doing, he was supervising the construction of a system of trenches and chevaux-de-frise around the old powder magazine. Sentries from various battalions, unsure of their purpose, challenged all passers by, each other and any stray cows or pigs. Fist-fights were frequent and the night air was often rent by shots fired accidentally, or through sheer exuberance. The taverns were mobbed and so were the apothecary

---

39. William Blackwell, 1738-1782, son of Col. William and Elizabeth (Crump) Blackwell, married about 1780, Celia Helm, daughter of Lynaugh and Hester (Edrington) Helm and widow of Henry Foote, 1738-1777. She married (3) 1786, Dr. George Graham.

40. Thomas Bullitt never married but openly flaunted a succession of mistresses, one of whom, Martha Bronaunt, gave him a daughter Sarah, whom he acknowledged. The name is spelled interchangeably Bullett.

shops the next morning by searchers for hangover remedies.

Holed up aboard the *Otter* (the *Fowey* had been ordered to rejoin the fleet at Boston) Lord Dunmore brooded fitfully. Reports that shirtmen digging in the Palace garden had found a store of gunpowder did not improve his temper. He did not care much about the gunpowder which he had written off anyway, but if they were digging up the garden he hated to think what was happening to his cherished possessions within the Palace. By the end of October the accumulation of Virginia militia in and about Williamsburg had begun to get on Lord Dunmore's nerves. He decided that it was a good time to show the rebels a thing or two and, if they wanted a southern Bunker Hill, to let them have it. As an appropriate site he selected the little port town of Hampton on the north side of the James River across from Norfolk. Hampton had a measure of strategic importance because it was the patriot's access to the Chesapeake Bay and commanded a sweeping panorama of the Roads. It was necessary that it be in British hands if any attack on Norfolk from the river was to be successful.

Accordingly he dispatched Captain Matthew Squire in a small flotilla consisting of a schooner, two sloops, several tenders and two pilot boats to attack the port. The inhabitants took a rather dim view of the matter and called on Williamsburg for help. As far as they were concerned, they were ready to throw in the sponge and let the British take the town, but the reaction in Williamsburg was more positive.

The Culpeper Minute Men had, therefore, hardly arrived in Williamsburg when part of them found themselves sent to the relief of Hampton under Colonel William Woodford. The contingent included Captain Abraham Buford's[41] company of Culpeper riflemen, a substantial number of Captain William Blackwell's company of Fauquier rifles and some local militia, about 100 men in all. They reached Hampton in the early morning of October 25th. Captain Squire's flotilla had by that time cleared the channel of obstacles planted by the local defenders and had drawn up abreast of the town.

The British gunners immediately opened fire, scattering chickens and raising clouds of dust, but injuring no one. Nevertheless the blast was enough to cause the timid element to contend that the town could not be defended and to urge withdrawal.

---

41. Abraham Buford, d: 1833, Appointed Colonel of the 11th Va. Regiment, 16 May, 1778, and of the 3rd Va. Regiment after the capture of Charleston, May 1780. For notice of him see T. M. Green, **Historic Families of Kentucky.**

Woodford refused to be convinced. He placed his riflemen in strategic spots around town with firm instructions to fire only at specific targets. Just as the British gunners were beginning to enjoy themselves they suddenly realized that carefully aimed bullets were splintering the timbers around their heads and that crewmen were dropping out of the rigging and splattering on deck. They quickly learned what Fauquier County squirrels had been complaining about for a long time—namely that it was dangerous to expose their anatomy too close to those "shirtmen" with their funny hats and long guns.

When Squire reluctantly concluded that he was outgunned and gave the order to retire he discovered a conspicuous absence of volunteers to go aloft to hand the sails or even to man the helm. Most of the crews withdrew to the comparative safety of the holds and the boats drifted rather aimlessly. The two sloops were soon out of control and drifted ashore, where they were captured. Five vessels were sunk and one pilot boat was captured with seven hapless sailors aboard. The schooner got away - but barely.

On November 3rd the Virginia Gazette carried an impudent invitation from the Hampton riflemen to Captain Squire that he renew his visit, or they might have to return it. They further remarked that "if he cannot find the *ear* that was cut off, they hope he will wear a *wig* to hide the mark; for perhaps it may not be necessary that all should know (that) *chance* had effected that which the *law* should have done."[42] As mentioned earlier, the loss of an ear required a bit of explaining.

We have reports from a number of men from Captain Blackwell's Fauquier company of riflemen who had their first baptism of fire in this engagement. One of them was Daniel Orear,[43] or more correctly O'Rear, all of sixteen years old, but nevertheless, equipped by his father with a "rifle gunn". He had been induced to volunteer for three months in the summer of 1775 by Peter Conway, a Lieutenant in Captain Blackwell's company. It was his first venture out of Fauquier County and his first glimpse of a body of water much larger than Thumb Run. They "had an engagement with a party of the enemy 16 or 18 miles below Williamsburg and captured a small vessel belonging to them called a Tender. We killed 6 or 7 & took a number prisoner." When his three months had expired, probably late in November, he was discharged. He did

---

42. **Virginia Gazette** (Alexander Purdie), 3 Nov. 1775.

43. Daniel O'Rear, 1759-post 1834, was a son of John O'Rear. According to his pension record Peter Conway was Blackwell's lieutenant.

not linger around Williamsburg but went straight home, where he remained until January, 1777, when Ensign Isham Keith enticed him to join Captain John Ashby's company of riflemen. We have more about him later.

Jeremiah Brown was eighteen.[44] His term of enlistment was only two months, which barely took him through the skirmish at Hampton. His account of the engagement is limited but he apparently had a good time. However, like O'Rear, enough was enough, and he went home after his experience at Hampton. He did not enlist in the Continental Army but waited to be drafted in September of 1777. He was, though, in the Stafford County militia the following August, 1776, as a volunteer in a company raised by Captain William Phillips for the protection of the plantations along the Potomac subject to depredations by British raiding parties - but more about that later.[45]

Also at Hampton was one of two Joseph Blackwells who lived to confuse Fauquier historians.[46] This one, serving under his first cousin William, was the youngest son of Colonel William Blackwell of Elk Run and his wife, Elizabeth Crump. His father had been a Justice and Colonel of Militia in Fauquier when the county was created in 1759. He was Sheriff in 1766 and died shortly before the Revolution. Joseph was twenty, tall, slender, with the fair hair and blue eyes of that branch of the Blackwell family. He said little about Hampton but he stood on the threshold of a distinguished military career that lasted through the entire war. On the 1st of January, 1776, he ended his tour with his cousin to become a cadet in the 3rd Virginia Regiment under Captain John Ashby. We meet him in almost every major engagement to follow, quiet, responsible and utterly dedicated to the cause.

---

44. Jeremiah Brown, 1757-post 1833, is probably the Jeremiah Brown who married Ann Kelly in Fauquier in 1795. A brother, Jesse Brown, b. 1765, was with him at Yorktown. (S. 6764, National Archives); John Frederick Dorman, **Virginia Revolutionary Pension Applications,** Vol. XI, pp. 44-45.

45. Despite depletion by enlistment in the regular army, the county militias were frequently called out during the entire war to meet local disturbances in their own or neighboring counties.

46. Joseph Blackwell, 1755-1823, of Elk Run, married Ann Grayson Gibson, daughter of Col. John and Mary (Brent) Gibson.

Another of Captain Blackwell's men who lived to tell the tale long after was Samuel Baker.[47] Baker was no youngster. In 1775 he was 35, married and the father of four children. He joined the Culpeper Minute Men in the first flush of patriotism "a very short time after the throwing overboard the tea." He marched to Williamsburg where he encountered "not much fighting except with a boat on the James River ... (where) some were running from the enemy, a good many were running to get to fight them." Thus does he describe the refugees from Hampton and the action that followed.

However Samuel Baker was already beginning to tire of soldiering and worrying about his nestlings in Fauquier. His tour of duty was three months but, according to his friend Robert Rogers, Sr., he hired one John Dickerson to finish it for him and trotted off home. He was thus deprived of his share of the glory at Great Bridge. As a member of the Fauquier Militia he was called up from time to time in the ensuing seven years. Sometimes he served but when it was "inconvenient for him to attend in person," he sent a substitute. During those brief periods nothing ever happened. At the age of 90 he could recall a total of six months service by himself and his substitutes—enough to secure a tiny pension in Alabama.

Baker's military career was not very heroic but it serves to illustrate the fact that the first blaze of patriotism was often quenched early in the game by the stiff wind of practical necessity. It was all very well for young men without responsibility, or rich men with overseers and platoons of slaves, to go off to war for months at a time. For a poor man with six hungry mouths to feed, patriotism was a luxury he could ill afford. There is record later that certain rich men were ordered by the County Court to succour distressed families of Revolutionary soldiers but, in 1775, Baker had no assurance that the county would not just let his little brood quietly starve.

After the fiasco at Hampton Lord Dunmore continued to seek opportunities to teach the rebels a lesson but no feasible plan developed immediately. Meanwhile recruits for the 1st and 2nd Virginia Regiments continued to arrive in Williamsburg. Gradually their numbers approached the total authorized the previous August. By mid-November it was decided that more of the Culpeper Minute Men could be dispensed with, reducing them to

---

47. Samuel Baker, 1740-post 1835, lived on Deep Run where he and Moses Baker had a mill. According to his pension record William Nelson was the lieutenant in Blackwell's company, see note No. 43. (S.10354)

five companies of about 50 men each. Accordingly the companies were consolidated and the surplus men discharged, leaving any good rifles to be used by those who remained. Colonel Taliaferro [48] turned over his command to Lieutenant Colonel Stevens [49] and led the discharged men home. The five Fauquier County companies were reduced to two, under Captains Chilton and Pickett. Captains Blackwell and Payne had presumably already returned home or accompanied Colonel Taliaferro, as there is no further record of them in Williamsburg. Captain Scott elected to remain, though he no longer commanded a company. Captain Pickett, according to the muster list dated 8 November, had in addition to Lieutenant Marshall and Ensign Keith, two sergeants, William and James Withers; [50] two corporals, Moses Allen and Peter Barker; William Bliss, a drummer, and 47 men.

Less is known of Captain Chilton's company. According to David Blackwell, a private in his company, John Keith [51] was second in command. He must have had about the same number of men as did Pickett, making a total a few more than the 100 men usually mentioned. It may be assumed that most of these men were expert riflemen, badly needed as long as Dunmore continued to wage war from his flotilla on the James River.

48. Lawrence Taliaferro, 1734-1798, of "Rose Hill", married (1) Sarah Dade, daughter of Baldwin and Sarah (Alexander) Dade; married (2) Mary Jackson. He was a son of Col. Francis and Elizabeth (Hay) Taliaferro of "Epson." His military record after he left Williamsburg, November 1775, is obscure.

49. Edward Stevens, 1745-1820. Surprisingly little is written about the family of General Edward Stevens of Culpeper in spite of his distinguished military record. Most historians confuse him with General Adam Stephen, 1718-1791, whose military record is disgraceful.

50. William Ramlin Withers, b. 1758 was later a Captain. He married Martha Ann Ashby, daughter of John and Mary (Turner) Ashby of "Greenland" near Delaplane. He was a son of Thomas and Elizabeth (Williams) Withers of "Green Meadows". James Withers, 1745-1791, his brother, inherited "Green Meadows" on Licking Run. He married Elizabeth Nisbett, daughter of James Nisbett, Sheriff of Prince William County. He studied medicine, presumably after the war.

51. John Keith. He was presumably a son of the Rev. James and Mary Isham (Randolph) Keith. He is said to have married (?) Doniphan, but records of him are scarce.

However, by mid-November it was apparent that the Virginians could stop his annoying depredations only by moving troops across the river. Captain Montague, in command of the British shipping, was justifiably apprehensive of fire from the shore rifles but he could still remain out of range by hugging the south side of the channel. What was needed was an effective cross fire. Furthermore, by denying him the use of the south bank landings his supply could be effectively hampered. Patrick Henry was eager to lead a body of troops across the river into Suffolk County. The Virginia Convention approved the plan but had decided reservations concerning Henry's ability to put it into operation.

The command of the troops scheduled to cross the James River eventually fell to Colonel Woodford, commander of the 2nd Virginia Regiment. Colonel Henry finally yielded to the argument that, as senior officer, it was his duty to remain at headquarters at Williamsburg. Woodford was ordered to take six companies from his regiment and five companies of minutemen from the Culpeper Battalion on the march toward Norfolk, about 800 men. The purpose was not to engage the British in any decisive battle, but to move closer to them, secure the south bank of the James and put the fear of God into the loyalist inhabitants of the lower counties.

Reports of troop build-up in Williamsburg and rumors of their intention to cross the James continued to reach Lord Dunmore, to his growing alarm. Though more vessels had come to his aid and the Virginians could not cope with the British by sea, he had no land force sufficient to attempt a march on Williamsburg or even, he feared, protect Norfolk from a land attack. As part of the defenses of Norfolk he ordered the fortification of Great Bridge.

Great Bridge was a flourishing village about 12 miles from Norfolk which served as a shipping point for shingles, barrel staves, lumber, tar, potash and turpentine from the Carolinas. It took its name from a 120-foot long bridge over the southern branch of the Elizabeth River which flowed between marshes which extended about 160 yards on either side. At the southern end of the bridge was an island on which there were a mill and a few houses. North of the bridge, to guard the long dyke or causeway to Norfolk, the British built a wooden stockade, called "Fort Murray". It was defended, according to Dunmore in a letter to General Gage dated 1 December, "by Lieutenant Wallace, one sergeant, one corporal and 25 private men of the Fourteenth Regiment, some volunteers and many Negroes." He added, "Rebels could not easily get possession of that post unless they brought artillery against it, of which by all accounts, they have not at present."[52] He was right. Two four-pound cannon made the position nearly impregnable against anything Woodford had to offer.

However this force was subtracted from the 13 commissioned officers, 3 drummers and fifers and 134 privates Lord Dunmore had at his disposal. He had recruited as many volunteers as possible, but under duress and he doubted their reliability. On the 7th of November he issued a proclamation that was to drive the last nail in the coffin of British rule in Virginia. He offered all indentured servants and Negroes their freedom if they would take arms against their masters "for the more speedily reducing this Colony to a proper sense of their duty to his Majesty's Crown and dignity."[53]

Woodford's initial attempt to cross the James River near Jamestown was prevented by a large, armed British tender. Moving upstream out of reach of the fire from the tender, he prepared to cross at Sandy Point. Here he heard that Dunmore was making punitive raids in Suffolk and sent Lieutenant Colonel Charles Scott[54] and Major Thomas Marshall ahead with 200 mounted riflemen. Scott and Marshall were at Cobham, across the river from Jamestown on the 21st of November and had successfully driven Dunmore's raiding parties out of Suffolk when Woodford arrived with the main force on the 25th.

It was soon apparent that the forces from both sides were converging on Great Bridge. Dunmore's forces were swelled by sailors and marines from the man-of-war, *Otter*, and about 60 volunteer townsmen. They removed the planking from the bridge to lessen the danger of a surprise attack. Along with their two 4-pounders they had some swivel guns and a few other small field pieces. Behind them a force of about 250 men of whom fewer than 100 were regulars (Grenadiers of the 14th Regiment and a body of volunteers known as the "Queen's Loyal Virginia Regiment") waited for a possible siege.

It is difficult to say how long they might have held their position, but they could probably have held on for most of the

---

52. Letter from Capt. Samuel Leslie to General Gage, dated 1 Dec. 1775. **American Archives**, 4th Ser., Vol. IV, p. 367.

53. **American Historical Review**, Vol. XI, p. 64.

54. Charles Scott, ca. 1739-1813, was an N. C. O. under Washington in Braddock's expedition. He raised the first volunteer troops south of the James River. A blunt and practical officer, he offended many but his rise to Brigadier, 2 April 1777, was well deserved.

winter and then executed a strategic withdrawal in relative safety if reinforcement was not provided. Woodford had no artillery and approached the fort with extreme caution. He called for reinforcements from the 1st Virginia Regiment and, characteristically, addressed his plea to the Committee of Safety, by-passing Colonel Patrick Henry. His refusal to acknowledge Henry's superior rank widened the breach between the two men. Under orders from the Committee of Safety, Henry reluctantly sent him three companies of 60 men each under Major Eppes. Though they brought with them 500 pounds of powder and 1,500 pounds of lead, they complained that they were rather coolly received.

Woodford also expected help from Colonel Robert Howe [55] of North Carolina, with a force of over 500 men reportedly well-armed and ready for action. They announced that they were bringing with them three double-fortified 4-pounders, four smaller cannon and 25 or 30 balls. When a small advance contingent arrived it was found that there were no gun mounts, cannon balls or ammunition. Furthermore the men were poorly-armed and had no gunpowder for their guns. Colonel Howe himself did not arrive until five days after the battle and the remainder of the North Carolina troops were in no better condition. The artillery was useless.

Disappointed, but still determined, Woodford had deployed his men before the 3rd of December. For protection they had thrown up breastworks across the road and on an island to the west just out of range of the enemy cannon. A considerable amount of skirmishing took place which was reported by both sides as being more effective than it really was. Lieutenant Colonel Edward Stevens took his Culpeper Minutemen, including most of Pickett's Fauquier company, across the causeway toward the fort on the 4th of December, but was repulsed with minor losses. One casualty, Benjamin Arnold, a private in Pickett's company, had his wrist shattered by a ball. He was one of nine provincials in the hospital on the 10th of December and was doing nicely. Of the other eight, four had merely colds.

Early in the morning of Saturday, December 9th, the Virginians were awakened by a fusillade of gunfire from the fort. As it came almost simultaneously with their own reveille, they were not particularly alarmed at first. Then they beheld an astonishing

---

55. Robert Howe, 1732-1796, was the son of a wealthy planter on the Cape Fear River in North Carolina. He was Captain of Fort Johnson in 1766-67 and 1769-73. Later an artillery Colonel, he was a delegate to the colonial congress at New Bern in August 1774. He became Col. of the 2nd N. C. Regiment, 1 September 1775.

sight. With measured tread and fixed bayonets, a line of redcoats appeared about to cross the bridge. During the night they had replaced enough of the planking to allow six men abreast to cross. They had hoped to surprise the Virginians, but replacing the planking had taken longer than expected. Surprise was further diminished by the premature artillery barrage by gunners from the *Otter*. Incredibly the British were evidently preparing to *attack* across the bridge. Fewer than ninety Virginians were able to reach the breastworks before the fighting began.

Sixty Grenadiers of the 14th Regiment under Captain Charles Fordyce spearheaded the attack. Then followed Lieutenant John Battut with about 30 men from the "Queen's Loyalist Regiment", and finally came the motley crew of Lord Dunmore's "Ethiopians" and Norfolk volunteers under Captain Samuel Leslie. The last group never advanced beyond the bridge.

Lieutenant Edward Travis, in command of Captain Meade's company at the breastworks, ordered his men to hold their fire until the British were within 50 yards. "Believing the redoubt to be deserted, Fordyce waved his hat over his head, shouted 'the day is our own!' and rushed forward toward the breastwork." [56] He fell with fourteen bullets in him. The first volley took appalling toll. Two of his lieutenants [57] fell with him and a third was wounded. The British staggered, stopped, then began to fall back. By this time other Virginians had reached the breastworks and part of the Culpeper Battalion under Colonel Stevens attacked from an entrenched position 100 yards on the British right. The bridge was too narrow for the British to turn quickly under continued heavy fire. In the mad scramble most of the regulars were slaughtered. The entire engagement lasted less than half an hour.

Of the gallant British Grenadiers only eleven survived. Lieutenant Battut was wounded and most of his men were killed or wounded. He and 17 other wounded prisoners were captured. With one mad order Lord Dunmore had thrown away the flower of his little army, earning a niche in Valhalla alongside the idiot who ordered the charge at Balaklava. There was nothing for the British to do but evacuate the fort when night fell, leaving the two spiked cannon behind.

56. B. J. Lossing, **Pictorial Field Book of the Revolution**, Vol. II, p. 534.

57. Lieutenants Napier and Leslie. The latter was a brother of Capt. Samuel Leslie who was at Great Bridge and later was mortally wounded at Princeton. They were sons of the Earl of Levin. Lossing, op. cit., Vol. I, p. 332, says that the name was William, not Samuel, Leslie as stated in **Virginia Cavalcade**, Summer, 1974, p. 10.

Neither the British nor the Virginians could offer logical explanation for Dunmore's insane order. There were some attempts, including the supposition that he had some wild hope of defeating Woodford before the North Carolinians arrived. Colonel Woodford, himself, was responsible for the most amazing and delightful explanation. The tale has everything, a masterpiece of deception, brilliant coordination and a courageous and clever black hero. One wishes that it were true.

In a letter dated 10 December Woodford wrote to the Virginia Convention:

> A servant belonging to Major Marshall, who deserted the other night from Colonel Scott's party, has completely taken his Lordship in. Lieutenant Battut, who is wounded, informs me that this fellow told them that not more than three hundred shirt-men were here, and that imprudent man caught at the bait.

He repeated the story in a private letter to Edmund Pendleton, President of the Convention. It was soon going around that "Lord Dunmore, frantic with rage, swore in his impotent ravings that he would hang the boy who brought the information." Lord Dunmore also blamed Captain Leslie for ordering the gunners of the *Otter* to fire too early. Helen Maxwell,[58] a native of Norfolk, credits Marshall's young body servant with an even more fertile imagination. He told them, she says, "that our men were out of ammunition, had no powder and had been obliged to melt up their shoe buckles for shot." No one seems to have bothered to discover his name or whether Dunmore had taken his gruesome revenge.

Yet, unless Dunmore's ignorance and credulity surpasses belief, the tale does not quite ring true. Attacking six abreast across a narrow bridge, infantry with muskets could not possibly lay down an effective field of fire. Exposed on the bridge they were clay pigeons for expert riflemen, with greater range and accuracy, firing from several directions. Neither could they employ their bayonets effectively after the first volley nor, supposing that they successfully reached the redoubt, could they have held long enough to allow the rest to come up. In fact, it was no less suicidal, under the circumstances, to march against 300 riflemen than against the

---

58. Helen (Calvert) Maxwell and her husband, Capt. James Maxwell (who claimed not to be Tories) nevertheless entertained the British officers in their home. Captain Fordyce, she said, was "not handsome but very genteel."

800 odd in Woodford's command. It took only 90 men to stop them cold in their tracks.

The simplest explanation is that Dunmore was the victim of his own propaganda. He really believed that the Virginians were cowards who would run at the mere sight of a body of British regulars.

There are many accounts of Great Bridge by Fauquier men who participated, but none more complete and accurate than the one given by John Marshall, 1st Lieutenant under Pickett and later Chief Justice of the Supreme Court. However, his story was written long after the war was over, and is curiously colorless. As Chief Justice he was the most distinguished survivor of the Fauquier minutemen still living in 1832 and naturally those who had served with him turned to him for verification of their pension applications under the Pension Act of that year. These he gave cheerfully to the best of his recollection and his replies are often more revealing of his personality than is his dry account of the battle. Significantly he does not mention the escapade of his father's servant nor does he refer to any ruse conceived by his father to deceive Lord Dunmore. Conversely, though, his biographers indicate that he never publicly denied it.

Sergeant William Payne,[59] seventeen, was with Pickett's company under Colonel Edward Stevens on the island to the west of the causeway and to the right of the British crossing the bridge. He felt no danger as he paused to reload his rifle. There was no way that the enemy could come his way. Their musket might strike a man at eighty yards but at 100 yards he was relatively safe. He could pick them off at leisure and he rarely missed. He was going in a day or so to Norfolk and would be there when the city burned. He had seen Captain James Scott a little before but was not sure why he was there or what he was doing without his company on which he had lavished so much money in recent months. It had earned his men's affection but they had not made him a great leader. Later, in the late summer of 1778, Payne joined the Continental Army and served off and on until the end of the war.

Joseph Blackwell, cousin of Captain William Blackwell, who was at Hampton has little to say about Great Bridge. He had been offered a commission as a cadet in a company being raised by John

---

59. William Payne, 1758-post 1832, was a son of John and ? (Floweree) Payne. He was then a sergeant and is not to be confused with Capt. Payne mentioned in note No. 15.

Ashby for the proposed 3rd Virginia Regiment soon to be activated. He had only to wait until the first of the year, when that commission would come through. He knew that he would make a good officer and that the experience gained at Great Bridge would not be wasted.

William Allen[60] of Chilton's company was at the breastworks. The company was directly under the command of Major Thomas Marshall, father of Lieutenant John Marshall. It was an unforgettable experience for a lad of seventeen but it happened so fast he could not remember it in detail. He knew only that he had seen Captain Fordyce go down and he felt almost as if death had brushed his cheek. In 1777 he would march north with Captain Charles Chilton who was bent on taking the place of his brother after Brandywine.

Next to him was David Blackwell,[61] first cousin of Captain William Blackwell. He says specifically that only four minute companies were raised in Fauquier in 1775. His description of the battle is negligible but he was impressed by the consequences. He assisted in burying the British dead. He was among those who then followed Woodford to Norfolk "to protect the place and prevent the enemy from committing depredations." We will soon learn what that amounted to.

For Captain John Chilton December 9th, 1775, marked a turning point in his life. At thirty-six he felt like a father to his men, many of whom were not half his age. The training he had given them had served them well. In their first baptism of fire they did not falter and, thank God, none had received so much as a scratch. He must have wondered vaguely if he could, as Fordyce had, lead them across that terrible bridge to certain death. If so, he must have decided that he could, if he had to, but it was a situation he would try to avoid at all cost.

After the battle Woodford ordered Major Marshall to remain at Great Bridge, to guard the village and keep the road to Norfolk open. Captain Chilton and some of his men remained with him. It was probably there that Chilton received the news from Fauquier.

60. William Allen, 1758-1839, married Frances Pepper in Fauquier Co., 8 August 1781. (Fauquier Marriage Bonds have her name as Hannah, but it is certain that it is in error).

61. David Blackwell, 1750-1841, was the youngest son of Samuel and Elizabeth (Steptoe) Blackwell of "Walnut Lodge", Northumberland Co. He did not enlist in the Virginia Continental Line but returned to Fauquier Co. where 29 May 1776 he married Ann Lewis, daughter of Zacharias and Mary (Brent) Lewis of Fauquier County.

On the 9th of December, the same day on which the British troops reeled and broke before volleys of rifle fire at Great Bridge, John Chilton's young wife died at "Rock Spring", their home near Baldwin's Ridge in Fauquier County.

Laetitia (Blackwell) Chilton was one of the attractive daughters of the Honorable Joseph Blackwell of Fauquier. They were married 10 April 1768, when she was eighteen. He had, though, staked his claim early. Curiously the marriage bond was dated 10 December 1765, when she was only fifteen. They had five children in six years. It is not surprising that it was too much for her, though no one considered that at the time. Suddenly the world that had seemed so golden in the first flush of victory, lay shattered at his feet.

Quietly he ordered his horse made ready. The way was long and treacherous in early winter but, if he hurried, he would be home before Christmas. Then and only then, would he decide what to do next.

At the head of the Virginia and North Carolina troops, Colonels Howe and Woodford entered Norfolk on the 13th of December. It had been determined that Howe's commission predated Woodford's, so Woodford had yielded to him what he would never do to Patrick Henry, command of the forces south of the James. The British, in full flight, had hardly bothered to glance at the defenses of Norfolk, so laboriously built in the months before. They no longer had men enough to man them. Their refuge was on board ships.

"I have just time to inform you that we have at last got possession of the most horried place I ever beheld," wrote Colonel Charles Scott.[62] The occupation was peaceful as many of the "damn'd Tories" cut the British cockades from their hats and substituted buck tails. Howe had 1,275 men under his command whose conduct, on the whole, fell somewhat short of correctness.[63]

---

62. Letter dated 17 Dec. 1775, Charles Scott to Capt. Southall.

63. According to the official list there were:

2nd Virginia Regiment	350
1st Virginia Regiment	172
Minute Battalion	165
2nd North Carolina Regiment	438
North Carolina Volunteers	150
Total strength	1,275

Note: More than half of the Culpeper Battalion had been left at Great Bridge under Major Marshall.

The object of their particular hatred were the Scottish merchants, who suffered rather substantial looting of their stores. Frequently they took pot-shots at the shipping in the harbour, sometimes with effect. Furthermore, they tried to drink the town dry. High living the night before often ended with court martial the next morning.

Lord Dunmore thrashed around on board a vessel which he had re-christened the *Dunmore* [64] in helpless rage and frustration. His letters to Lord Dartmouth were incoherent with invective and self-exculpation. On Christmas day, furious because Howe would not furnish provisions to his fleet, he ordered the ships to fire on the buildings along the shore line. Some fires were started but were soon under control and there were no casualties. At 4 a.m. on New Year's Day the town was rocked by a naval bombardment. Fires were started and a landing party of British marines lighted others to help spread the blaze. The landing party was soon driven off by Colonel Stevens and his Culpeper Battalion. As the fire spread the patriot army, instead of trying to control it, added fuel by taking their revenge on the Tory merchants. Soon the entire town was flaming merrily. Two days later four-fifths of Virginia's largest and most prosperous city was in ashes. What remained was ordered to be destroyed by the Virginia Convention in Williamsburg.

Both sides blamed the other. Certainly Lord Dunmore initiated the action, but the patriot troops could have held the fire in check. The Mayor and Council of Norfolk declared that Dunmore had burned 51 houses, the provincial troops 863 and 416 were destroyed by order of the Convention, to prevent the British from making later use of the prostrate town. [65] He was probably very nearly correct, but the Virginians had control of the propaganda machine, so most of the blame fell on Lord Dunmore.

When the news reached Cambridge on the 31st of January 1776, Washington fulminated with horror at Dunmore's savagery. Dunmore must, he said, "be crushed!" He offered no really practical plan for catching his Lordship in order to perform that operation. He had upwards of 16,000 men outside Boston, but 5,000 British still occupied the city. It was, he said, "an irksome

---

64. Ivor Noel Hume, 1775, **Another Part of the Field.** "The latter vessel appears not to have been a newly siezed prize bearing a fortunate name, but rather an old captive long in preparation and now newly fitted and freshly christened." p. 412.

65. Report of Commission, House of Delegates Papers, 10 October 1777. The commission report omits 32 buildings destroyed by Lord Dunmore late in November.

situation." He had, however, managed to divest himself of some of his rambunctious Virginia riflemen—Morgan's company.

The opportunity came in September with the planned attack on Quebec. The commander, Benedict Arnold,[66] needed three rifle companies. Morgan immediately volunteered his company. A young Danish officer, Christian Febiger,[67] who had served with distinction at Bunker Hill but had had nothing to do since, asked to go along. He was lost in admiration for the tall Virginians with their unerring aim and unfettered minds.

The journey through Maine, conducted in October of 1775, was one of incredible hardship. In cold rain, Morgan and his men, often attired only in Indian leggings and breech clout, struggled through dense underbrush, sloshed through mud and crossed bogs where men sank "half-leg deep." When they reached Point Levi on the south bank of the St. Lawrence about the 6th of November, they were exhausted, battered and nearly starved. Furthermore 100 of their muskets were unserviceable and most of their powder was soaked. Morgan's men had at least kept their powder dry. Of the 1,000 men who had started the journey through Maine, Arnold could muster only about 700. The rest had been lost through accident, illness or desertion.

Help came on the 1st of December with the arrival of Brigadier General Richard Montgomery [68] with about 300 well-

66. Benedict Arnold, 1741-1801, of Norwich, Conn., was a successful business man in New Haven before the war. He was a courageous and often brilliant officer. He served with great distinction at Valcour Island, Oct. 1776 and is credited with much of Gates' success at Saratoga, October 1777. He was much esteemed by Washington until the 25th September, 1780, when the latter had reason to revise his opinion.

67. Christian Febiger, 1746-1796, was born in Denmark, but later, after receiving a military education, joined the staff of his uncle, the Governor of Vera Cruz. Having settled in Massachusetts in 1773, he joined Garrish's Massachusetts Regiment, 28 April 1775 and rendered valuable service at Bunker Hill in June. His wry good humor and conspicuous bravery endeared him to Morgan and his men.

68. Richard Montgomery, 1738-1775, son of an Irish M.P., was born in Ireland and educated at Trinity College, Dublin. After having served with some distinction in the British Army, he abruptly sold his commission in April 1772 and went to America. He married Janet Livingston, daughter of Robert Livingston and settled down to farming near Rhinebeck, N. Y. He accepted a commission as Brigadier in the Continental Army 22 June, 1775, and succeeded General Schuyler when the latter fell ill on the way to Canada.

armed troops, artillery and extra clothing and ammunition. The attack on Quebec, planned for December 30th in the midst of a blinding snowstorm, found the enemy in some confusion but not enough to assure success. Morgan's men were to rendezvous within the city with an advance party, known in the eighteenth century as a "forlorn hope", led by General Montgomery. In this instance the name was singularly apt. The "forlorn hope" was quickly beaten off and its commander killed. The second in command beat a hasty retreat. Finding no one at the appointed rendezvous, Morgan and his men became lost in a tangle of narrow streets in the dock area.

With Montgomery dead the command fell to Arnold who led a charge against the British fortification. Naked courage alone could not carry the day and Arnold fell with a ball through the leg. Arriving on the scene Morgan raced forward and placed a ladder against the enemy work. Mounting it himself, he was forced back by a barrage of musketry. Stunned, his face blackened by powder and his cheek creased by a ball, he scaled the ladder a second time and leaped to the far side. Charles Porterfield and what remained of his Virginia company followed. The British retreated in haste.[69]

They had performed magnificently and suffered heavy losses but eventually the entire British garrison was assembled at the point of attack and Morgan and the survivors were forced to surrender. Weeping with rage Morgan and his men threw down their arms. Threatened with death, Morgan refused to give up his sword. Finally he thrust it into the hands of a startled priest, rather than give it to his captors.

Only twenty-five of Morgan's men survived. John Humphrey, his 1st lieutenant, was among those who died in the streets of the Lower Town. William Heth,[70] his 2nd Lieutenant, lost his right eye. Christian Febiger and Charles Porterfield miraculously emerged unscathed. One historian says that, aside from the officers

---

69. Kenneth L. Roberts, **March to Quebec**. This is an excellent account of this engagement. See also George F. Scheer & Hugh F. Franklin, **Rebels and Redcoats**, pp. 123-158.

70. William Heth, 1750-1807. Very little is written about this man who was to command a large number of Fauquier men later in the war. It is known that he lived at "Wales" after the war and married Eliza Briggs. There is reference to the "Heth-Selden Papers" in the University of Virginia Library, in the **Papers of John Marshall**, Vol. I, p. 98. He was one of three Commissioners appointed to settle army accounts in Illinois, 1781. John Marshall had a number of business dealings with him and is said to have used his "Journal" in preparation of his biography of George Washington.

all of whom later held high rank in the Virginia Line, the members of Morgan's company were "in too poor health or too disillusioned to be of any further use to the Continental Army." "Bosh!" says John Austin of Fauquier County. His health was fine (according to his pension record he lived to the ripe old age of 111) and he wasn't a bit disillusioned. In fact he served longer after he was exchanged than most men served during the entire war.

After the destruction of Norfolk there was no more need for the Culpeper Minutemen. On the 14th of February, 1776, the Committee of Safety sent a message of thanks to Colonel Stevens and ordered Colonel Howe to discharge the companies on guard at Norfolk and Hampton. Later the order was amended to hold some until March, when their duties could be taken over by regulars. The minutemen then turned their equipment over to their replacements and marched home. They were there before the red bud shimmered on the mountainsides. For some the war was over, for most it had not yet begun.

Interlude
Norfolk to Haarlem

On the 10th of March, 1776, after the Americans had fortified Dorchester Heights, the British quietly evacuated Boston. After the British had disappeared out into the ocean, Washington and most of his army advanced overland to New York, half expecting to hear that the enemy was there before them. He was unable to prevent General Howe's landing on Staten Island where he was joined by his brother, Admiral Lord Howe on the 12th of July. Washington expected a landing on Long Island from which an attack could be made on the American position on Brooklyn Heights. If it were captured the enemy would have opened the East River and could also bombard New York.

The spirits of the Americans had been lifted momentarily by the signing of the Declaration of Independence in Philadelphia in July, but that boost did not suffice to turn inexperienced and poorly directed men into trained combatants. The Americans could offer no adequate resistance to the British who charged Brooklyn Heights on the 27th of August. On the 29th of August Washington resolved that the army must be moved across the river to Manhattan, fully aware that New York would no longer be tenable. The evacuation was brilliantly handled but the most brilliant retreat is no substitute for victory. Early in September the American cause was sunk in deepest gloom.

None of this was, of course, known to the Virginia brigades who left Williamsburg on the 16th of August.

The Convention meeting in Williamsburg 1 December 1775, began to prepare more realistically for war with England. They no longer yearned wistfully for immediate "tranquillity and happiness." Fauquier County was represented only by Captain James Scott. Marshall was too busy countering Dunmore's moves in Suffolk to be able to attend.

The Convention voted to increase the size of the two regular regiments to ten companies each. The 3rd Regiment, which had been previously authorized but not activated, would be the first of six additional regiments to be raised. The Convention recognized that the maintenance of such a force would place an overwhelming burden on the local treasury and therefore assumed that all of its regiments would be taken into the Continental service as soon as they were complete. Congress in Philadelphia demurred and replied that only six regiments were needed to defend the colony. On the 13th of February the first six Virginia Regiments were officially accepted. Shortly after Congress relented and accepted three more.

Major General Charles Lee was appointed Commander-in-Chief of the Southern Department. At the same time Colonel Andrew Lewis, the victor at Point Pleasant in Lord Dunmore's War, was raised to Brigadier and Commander-in-Chief of the Virginia troops. When offered a commission to command the 1st Virginia Regiment only, not the entire Virginia force, Patrick Henry abruptly resigned. The Convention selected Lieutenant Colonel William Christian to take his place. Woodford was confirmed in command of the 2nd Regiment.

It was no longer possible for the Convention to ignore the outstanding qualifications of Dr. Hugh Mercer of Fredericksburg to command the 3rd Virginia Regiment. As his second in command Mercer chose George Weedon, the host of the Rising Sun. As Major his choice fell upon Thomas Marshall of Fauquier. This, therefore, was the regiment in which most of the Fauquier troops served early in the war. It was not until 12 February 1776, when Daniel Morgan, recently retrieved from a British prison, was given command of the 11th Virginia Regiment that they gave much thought to any other.

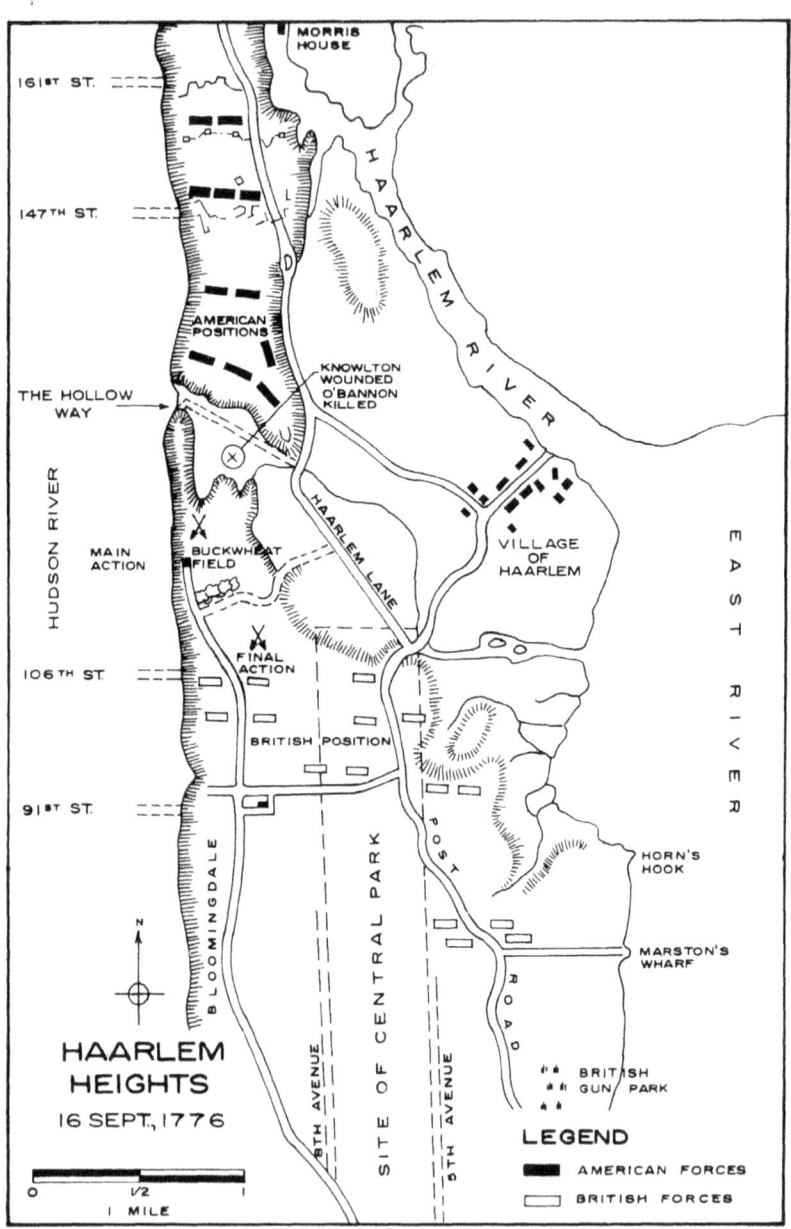

IV

The Heights of Haarlem and the White Plains

During the late spring and early summer of 1776 the regiments provided for by the Virginia Convention of December, 1775, assembled for training. The Convention had distributed the regiments in the colony in four general areas, the northernmost of which, between the Rappahannock and Potomac Rivers, included Fauquier. The tidewater was served by the 5th Virginia Regiment under the command of Colonel William Peachy, with headquarters at Richmond Courthouse (Warsaw).[1] The 3rd Virginia Regiment served the upland counties. Colonel Hugh Mercer, its commander, selected a spot near Dumfries in Prince William County for training.

The Convention had decreed that each regiment have ten companies but the number was soon reduced to eight to conform to regimental usage in the other colonies. Each company, in addition to its captain, had a first and second lieutenant, an ensign, two sergeants, two corporals, a drummer, a fifer and 68 men, 78 in all. The regiment, therefore, was 624 men exclusive of field grade officers and their aides. In addition each regiment was to have a chaplain, a paymaster, an adjutant, a quartermaster, a surgeon, two surgeon's mates and a sergeant major. It is doubtful if any Virginia regiment, at any time during the Revolution, ever achieved this ideal complement.

Leven Powell, an aspirant for high military rank from Loudoun County, observed that the Convention delegates seemed "very desirous of serving either themselves, their Sons, Cousens or

---

1. Proceedings of the Convention of Delegates, 1776. Col. Peachy was succeeded by Col. William Russell, 19 Dec. 1776. William Fletcher Booger, **Gleanings of Virginia History**, p. 131.

Friends..."[2] He was doubtless right, and that proclivity certainly reached down to the company grade officers. Preferment and outrageous nepotism played its part in the selection of officers in Fauquier County as much as anywhere else. However, as it was incumbent upon the captains and their lieutenants to recruit the men under their command, it is obvious that a notably incompetent or disagreeable officer would have little luck in meeting his quota. However, the best recruiting officers are not necessarily the best commanders in the field. Under the circumstances Fauquier fared rather well.

The first captain appointed to the 3rd Virginia Regiment from Fauquier County was John Ashby. His commission was dated 18 March 1776.[3]

John Ashby, son of Robert Ashby of "Yew Hill", was no youth.[4] He was thirty-six in 1776 and had been married for eight years to Mary Turner, sister of Hezekiah Turner of Charles County, Maryland, a prosperous farmer, who had moved to Fauquier. They had five children by 1776 and lived at "Greenland", a place on Kettle Run about two miles west of Delaplane which John Ashby had inherited from his father.

He had been fifteen when his celebrated uncle, Captain "Jack" Ashby had made his remarkable ride through Fauquier to Williamsburg carrying news of Braddock's defeat. He may have taken part in Lord Dunmore's War in which "Captain Ashby", is mentioned in reports but not otherwise identified. The first solid evidence of his participation in the Revolution is in Williamsburg in October of 1775 when he signed a receipt for merchandise from

---

2. Leven Powell, 1737-1810, was a son of William and Eleanor (Peyton) Powell. He married, 1763, Sarah Harrison, daughter of Col. Burr and Ann (Barnes) Harrison of "Chappawamsic". He was a signer of the Loudoun County Resolves, 14 June 1774, and served on the Committee of Safety. In 1775 he was commissioned Major in a battalion of minutemen from Loudoun Co. and in 1777 became Lieutenant Colonel of Grayson's Additional Continental Regiment, sometimes incorrectly called the "16th Virginia Regiment". He was in Dumfries during the engagement at Great Bridge, as shown by a letter to his wife bearing the same date.

3. **Journals of the Continental Congress, 1774-1789.** Ed. by Worthington Chauncey Ford., Vol. VI, 1776, p. 864.

4. John Ashby, ca. 1740-1815, was the third son of Robert Ashby and an unknown first wife. He married Mary Turner about 15 Feb. 1760 (Fauquier Co. Marriage Bond). They had ten children, five born ante 1776.

the regimental store for the Culpeper Battalion.[5] There is no reason to doubt that he served in some capacity at Great Bridge, although existing records do not indicate that he was a company commander.[6] He had, by that time, his eye on a commission in the Continental Army. Joseph Blackwell says that he offered him a commission in the company he proposed to form as early as 1 January 1776.

It appears that Captain Ashby to some extent took over the company that had served under Pickett at Great Bridge. John Marshall, Pickett's second in command, wanted his own company, so Ashby selected as 1st Lieutenant William Nelson,[7] from the southern part of the county. As 2nd Lieutenant he signed on Isham Keith, who had been an ensign with Pickett. The Ensign was his first cousin, Captain "Jack's" son, Nathaniel, his junior by eight years[8] He also signed on most of Pickett's rank and file, although Moses Allen,[9] one of Pickett's corporals, elected to go with John Chilton. Allen was a fine soldier and Ashby was sorry to lose him.

Joseph Blackwell was a cadet. At that time the term implied that he was "a gentleman who enlisted in a regiment as a volunteer private to acquire military skill and obtain a commission." This he did before the year was out in the company being raised by his older brother, Thomas Blackwell,[10] in the 10th Virginia Regiment commanded by Colonel Edward Stevens of Culpeper.

It is a great pity that a complete muster list of Captain Ashby's company cannot be found as it was one of three Virginia

---

5. Armistead's Store Account Book, 24 Oct. 1775, Virginia State Library.

6. According to the unofficial roster of Nov. 1775, he was not in Pickett's company.

7. William Nelson, d: 1776. His commission is recorded incorrectly as "Nielson", dated 18 Mar. 1776. He may have been a son of John Nelson of "Elk Run", died 1784.

8. Nathaniel Ashby, 1748-1811, was the second son of Captain 'Jack' and Jane (Combs) Ashby. He married 3 Dec. 1777 Margaret Mauzy, daughter of Col. John and Hester (Foote) Mauzy.

9. Moses Allen, 1754-1843, after long service which ruined his health and left him destitute in 1818, was refused a pension that year but granted one of $120 per year in 1832 when he was 78 years old.

10. Thomas Blackwell, 1752-1831, married 1781, Judith Grant. He had apparently moved to Culpeper Co. before the war, and died there.

companies to win great acclaim in New York in the early stage of the war. We have the names of some of them, ranging in age from nineteen year old George O'Bannon to thirty-seven year old John Forrester. However, they were generally young, averaging in age under twenty-five, and usually unmarried. Their fathers were almost all farmers and only rarely were they eldest sons. Their term of enlistment was normally two years, though John Forrester[11] mentions that his was for three years. The duration boded ominously for the patriot cause because the enlistments would terminate in the spring and early summer of 1778, when Washington needed every man he could get.

As Captain John Ashby's company was a rifle company it is certain that all were good marksmen, though it was now generally realized that the riflemen were not quite as useful in battle as had originally been thought. Their training was modified to include musketry and a few basic rules of European military tactics. Unfortunately there were few to teach these lessons and fewer still who had ever seen them in practice. There is little doubt that many of the Fauquier riflemen would have preferred to serve under Daniel Morgan but, by early spring of 1776, the news that Morgan was behind bars in Quebec had reached even Fauquier County.

John Chilton's commission as Captain in the 3rd Virginia Regiment was dated 29 April 1776. Quite possibly it took him some time to sort out his manifold domestic problems. In fact it is surprising that he was able to do so at all. Not only did he have five motherless children of his own but his brother William, who had died at "Maidstone" in Fauquier County the previous year, had named him administrator of his estate and guardian of his three children, the oldest of whom was not yet six. A few months after William Chilton's death, John Chilton had learned of the death by smallpox in London of his younger brother, Stephen. Stephen Chilton had been the captain of a merchant vessel in the British trade. He was unmarried but owned a large property in Prince William County, left him by his father, of which some disposition must be made.

All of these responsibilities he placed on the broad shoulders of his brother, Charles and his wife, Elizabeth (Blackwell) Chilton, the sister of his dead wife. To them he left the care of his 590 acre estate, "Rock Spring," his children, his ten servants and all his possessions. After he marched north with the army the following

---

11. John Forrester, 1739-post 1820. He was living in 1820 in Barren Co., Kentucky.

THE HEIGHTS OF HAARLEM AND THE WHITE PLAINS 101

August there is no reason to suppose that he ever saw them again.

Bearing the same date as Captain John Chilton's commission were those of his two brothers-in-law, 1st Lieutenant John Blackwell and 2nd Lieutenant Joseph Blackwell.[12] The Blackwell brothers were in their early twenties and had been raised in a world in which military rank had been accepted as the natural goal of any young men who would amount to something. Their uncles, cousins and in-laws had been Sheriffs, militia officers and Justices of the Peace as long as they could remember. Even their elder brother, Samuel Blackwell, who had studied for the ministry in England but had never served, would exchange his clerical collar for the epaulets of a captain in the Virginia Line. They recruited with enthusiasm in the spring of 1776, and with considerable success.

The earliest muster roll of Captain John Chilton's company that remains was taken over a year later, in June of 1777.[13] Undoubtedly there had been changes in personnel, but a fair percentage of them must have marched north with the original company. Chilton complained that the company was not quite full then, and it was not full in 1777, only 43 men exclusive of officers. What had happened to the rest of them is the tragic story of the winter of 1776-77. In the spring of 1776, however, regimental colors floated high in breeze over the camp at Dumfries, and beneath them some 600 young men strained to perfect their modest talent for killing to escape being killed. As news from the north continued to worsen, they began to take the latter possibility more seriously.

Presumably Captain James Scott was also recruiting, but the commission in the Continental Line for which he yearned continued to elude him. The Fifth Virginia Convention assembled on the 6th of May and, whatever Scott was doing, it was necessary that

---

12. John Blackwell, 1755-1823, married, 1779, Agatha Ann Eustace, daughter of Isaac Eustace of Stafford Co. and widow of Capt. Edwin Hull. Joseph Blackwell, 1752-1826, married, 1783, Ann Eustace, sister of his brother's wife. Stella Pickett Hardy in **Colonial Families of the Southern States of America**, "Blackwell Family", insists that John Blackwell, who had the higher commission, was only 21 in 1776 and three years younger than his brother who served under him. It seems unlikely.

13. Revolutionary War Rolls 1775-1783 (Virginia Jackets, Nos. 62-73, M246, Roll 97, National Archives).

he attend. This time he was accompanied by Martin Pickett[14] instead of Thomas Marshall, who had his hands full as Major of the 3rd Virginia Regiment.

As the months passed it seems that there must have been some reason that prevented James Scott from recruiting an acceptable unit. Regiments continued to be formed without him. He was prodigal in the use of funds, kind and ardently patriotic, but it was somehow not enough. Recruits accepted his rum and whisky from "Clermont", took advantage of his hospitality and then drifted off. They "listened to his talk and liked him so much" when he came from Richmond "for he was very hearty and active in the cause of Revolution."[15] It may be that he was too much so, or it may be that another impediment blocked his path.

It will be remembered that James Scott had a younger brother, the Reverend John Scott, Rector of Eversham and chaplain to Sir Robert Eden, Governor of Maryland. When open revolt came Eden returned to England but John Scott did not accompany him. Though Thomas Gordon,[16] his father-in-law urged him to return to Scotland, he chose to stay in Maryland and fight against separation from England. It took a brave man to breast the flood tide of Revolution, but John Scott was not only a brave man but also an extraordinarily articulate one. He spoke out against independence, both in the pulpit and in private gatherings of his Maryland friends. He was accused of disloyalty and of being in secret correspondence with Lord Dunmore.

Inevitably, in 1776, he was hauled before a committee of the Maryland Convention as a disaffected person with dangerous influence. Specifically he was charged with having tried to dissuade patriots from signing the "association and resolves", a Maryland equivalent of the Fauquier Resolutions. It was also said that he had given encouragement to one Matthew Cannon who proposed raising a force in opposition to the Convention. He defended himself brilliantly, to the secret admiration of some of those sitting in judgement. He admitted his opposition to open rebellion, but

---

14. Martin Pickett, 1740-1809, son of William and Elizabeth (Cooke) Pickett. He was a Justice, Burgess and Tax Commissioner of Fauquier as well as a leading merchant. He married Ann Blackwell, daughter of Col. Joseph and Elizabeth (Steptoe) Blackwell. He was a cousin of Col. Mordecai Buckner of the 6th Virginia Regiment.

15. Rejected Claims, Box 16, Folder 23, James Scott, 1835. (Virginia State Library, Archives Division).

16. Thomas Gordon, Professor of Humanities, King's College, Aberdeen.

declared that he had acted in what he sincerely believed to be the best interest of the colony. Certainly he did not challenge the authority of the Convention,[17] and he had affidavits to prove that most of the charges were false.

The judges were compelled to admit that he had a right to his point of view and that nothing truly damaging could be proven. However they could not leave him in the sensitive area of Somerset County. Consequently, he was banished to a place 100 miles from the tidewater and required to give a bond of £1,000 to the Sheriff of Frederick County, Maryland, that he would remain in that county. Later he was allowed to move to his father's Fauquier County land near Marshall, where he built a modest house which he called "Gordon's Dale" not far from his brother's "Clermont". It is possible that John Scott's troubles affected his older brother's chances for a commission in the Continental Line. It is not the first or last time that "guilt by kinship" has blocked a career.

Entries in The Journal of the Committee of Safety for Fauquier County during June and July of 1776 show that, though James Scott's services were declined, his money was quite acceptable. Warrants issued to "James Scott, Esq." included 16 shillings "for medicines furnished the Culpeper Minute Battalion", 10 shillings "for use of a rifle gun in the Culpeper Minute Battalion", £18 "for arms and waggon hire to the Culpeper Minute Battalion" and £5.10s.3d "for linen to make hunting shirts furnished ditto." Of course there were many such warrants, but Scott seems to have been the one most often called upon when cash was needed.[18]

In the same Journal, in June of 1776, we have an indication of another, usually forgotten, part played by Fauquier County in the Revolution; it was a safe place for the confinement of disaffected Tories. One Charles Neilson of Middlesex County, accused of aiding and abetting the enemy, was "sent to and confined within the limits of the County of Fauquier...and that he do within twenty days repair to the sd County."[19]

17. **The Continental Correspondent**, No. 37, 12 Dec. 1775. The Maryland Convention was also called "The Association of Freemen". In 1775 all able-bodied freemen were ordered to sign the "association" as a method of enrollment for military service. Matthew Page Andrews, **Tercentenary History of Maryland**, Vol. I, p. 582.

18. "Journals of the Committee of Safety in Virginia" in: **Journals of the Council of the State of Virginia**, (Richmond, 1931), Vol. I, pp. 28, 32, 57, 98.

19. **Ibid.**, p. 10.

Also on the 24th of June Colonel Christian, commander of the 1st Virginia Regiment lay before the Board a list of Highland (Scottish) prisoners taken from H. M. S. *Oxford*, including sixteen privates, three corporals, three women and a child who were to be confined in Fauquier County.[20] They were part of a large contingent who were ordered to be distributed among the upland counties. Those destined for Culpeper, Fauquier, Loudoun, Berkeley, and Frederick Counties were to march under regular guard to Culpeper Courthouse. From there the County Lieutenant of Culpeper was to send "those for the other Counties under a proper Guard of the militia, with the Sergeants and Cadets designed for Winchester, to the County Lieutenant of Fauquier, who is desired to secure the lott for that County and to send those for Loudoun, Berkeley & Frederick under a proper Guard of the militia to their respective Counties..."

At sea, Lord Dunmore was probably unaware that potential Scottish recruits had slipped through his fingers. He needed recruits badly. All would be well, he thought, if he could get enough of them so that he could regain a foothold on the mainland of the rebellious colony! His cutters, plying the Chesapeake from the Virginia Capes to the upper tributaries, could not obtain supplies enough by raiding tidewater plantations to maintain life aboard his ships. Short rations and improper clothing added to the misery of the unfortunate passengers and crews. The ships were filthy and crawling with vermin. His only alternative, short of abandoning the colony altogether, was to find a land base.

He first tried a neck of sand near Portsmouth called Mill Point, which could be defended with comparative ease, and was large enough to accommodate his force if supplies could be obtained from the mainland. Unfortunately for him the number of sympathetic Tories willing to furnish them was diminishing rapidly. The Virginians were systematically shipping them off to remote places where they could give no effective help. Smallpox ravaged the garrison, especially among the unhappy "Ethiopians" who were dropping like flies.

On the 22nd of May, Dunmore finally gave up. After setting fire to the barracks, he loaded his men aboard, including the

20. **Ibid.**, pp. 39-40. The British transport ship *Oxford*, with 217 Scotch Highlanders on board was first captured off Boston. While under convoy, the captive and captor were driven apart by rough weather. The ship was picked up by Capt. James Barron of the *Liberty* **and Capt. Richard Barron in the** *Patriot*. Robert Armistead Stewart, **The History of Virginia's Navy in the Revolution, pp. 11, 45.**

shattered remains of the Ethiopian Regiment, and took his ships down river. Dawn found them in Hampton Roads and all Virginia wondered where they would light next. Two days later they were sighted off, of all places, Gwynn's Island, in the mouth of the Piankatank River just south of the Rappahannock. It was not a bad location from which to stage a guerrilla war against the tidewater. Unfortunately, from Lord Dunmore's point of view, it was not far off shore, a fact that was quickly noted by General Andrew Lewis who immediately set about taking measures to "severely & principally chastize the noble Earl." [21]

The defense of the Gloucester Neck had been assigned to the 7th Virginia Regiment commanded by Colonel William Daingerfield. Lewis sent Colonel Hugh Mercer with three companies of the 3rd Virginia Regiment to reinforce Daingerfield. He then ordered two eighteen-pounders sent up from Jamestown. He also called upon contingents from Woodford's 2nd Regiment and the 1st Regiment now under the command of Colonel William Christian. By the 8th of July he had lined up a force of nearly 1,500 regulars opposite Gwynn's Island. There were also at least 400 militia from neighboring counties lined along both sides of the Piankatank River.

On the morning of the 9th, Lewis personally lighted a match to one of the two eighteen-pounders aimed at the British flagship, H. M. S. *Dunmore*. The ball passed straight through the hull of the ship and was quickly followed by several more direct hits. Considerably farther off shore, the *Otter*, Dunmore's largest warship, was also hit "betwixt Wind and Water". So accurate was the fire that, before the rest of the fleet cleared the harbour, three or four more vessels were so badly damaged that they had to be destroyed. When the morning of the 10th of July dawned it was seen that Dunmore had decamped during the night with the remainder of his bedraggled force.

Completely discouraged, Dunmore spent only three more weeks in Virginia. His attempts to find supplies by raiding tidewater plantations were quickly beaten off by Colonel Charles Lewis and his county militia, aided by several companies of the 3rd Regiment. Records are sparse but we have David Blackwell's word that Fauquier militiamen were there. They were also present at another abortive raid which did not reflect much credit upon the

21. Lewis to Gen. Charles Lee, 27 May 1776. "Lee Papers" in: **Collections of the New York Historical Society**, Vol. V, pp. 42-45, 63, 131. New York Historical Society.

militia, though the part played by the Fauquier contingent is unclear. We know of it from the pension record of a Fauquier man temporarily living in Stafford County.

On a high knoll in Stafford County, overlooking the broad Potomac, stood "Richland", the splendid brick home of Captain William Brent.[22] As a parting blow the British landed on the unguarded shoreline and set fire to the buildings on the estate. They were surprised and driven off by three companies of Stafford County militia who were rushed to the scene. The great house was afire when the Stafford militia arrived, but not yet beyond salvage. Jeremiah Brown, whom we first met at Hampton, said that he had volunteered under Captain William Phillips and that they had been joined by two other companies of Stafford militia under Captains John Cook and John James. There were no field officers, and the inexperienced company captains had no control over their men. Instead of attempting to put out the fire the men turned to looting, which was interrupted only by the arrival of the Prince William and Fauquier militia, which the Stafford men mistook for British. They fled, leaving abundant evidence of their misconduct. Captain Brent is said to have remarked ruefully that what damage the British had not completed was cheerfully finished off by his "protectors".

On the 18th of September, it was reported in the Virginia Gazette that:

> "Having heard sundry reports of the Misbehaviour of the Militia of Stafford County at the time Mr. Brent's house was destroyed by the enemy, the Council ordered an investigation."[23]

The investigating committee reported that the action of the Stafford militia was indeed outrageous but declined to fix the blame, citing incompetent leadership and mitigating circumstances.

22. William Brent, 1733-1782, was the son of William Brent of "Richland". He was a member of the Virginia Convention of 1776. He married Elizabeth Carroll, daughter of Daniel and Eleanor (Darnell) Carroll of "Rock Spring", Maryland. Their eldest son, William, was aide-de-camp to Lord Stirling and later Lt. Col. of the 1st Va. Regiment.

23. **Journal of the Council of the State of Virginia**, Vol. I, p. 165. (18 Sept. 1776). On the previous day the record shows a warrant "for Capt. William Brent for £9.12s.7d for the Pay Roll of the Prince William Militia in service at the mouth of Quantico last July."

The raid at "Richland" was the last futile effort of the British in Virginia. During the second week of August Dunmore led such of his fleet as was seaworthy (about 62 sail) toward the capes.[24] About half turned south toward St. Augustine. The rest, with the noble Earl, now permanently chastized, made their way toward New York. For a time the war in Virginia was over.

By mid-June the Virginia regiments had completed the training that could be accomplished without real combat experience. None of them was quite full or completely equipped. In spite of a rather considerable military success against Lord Dunmore, the Virginia high command was in shambles. None of the nine Virginia regiments was quite full but, more important, most of them had suffered or were about to suffer major changes in organization because of endless bickering and jockeying for position among field grade officers. After the situation at New York began to grow critical in the summer of 1776 Congress took a closer look at the Virginia regiments. It hardly seemed right that Virginia "should not contribute a man to an army of 40,000, and an army too on which was to depend the decision of all our rights."[25] To this the Virginia Convention was forced, reluctantly, to agree. It was decided to send two of its Continental regiments north, but which ones? Logic would have called out the 1st and 2nd Virginia Regiments.

General Lewis decided to capitalize on an excellent recruiting opportunity. The terms of service of the men in the 1st and 2nd regiments were about to expire. Lewis directed that the men be reenlisted for three years "to seize the post of Honour as he terms it, hoping that the men's well-grounded Complaints would be thus hushed into peace. But alas! human nature is not so easily smothered and to Col. Woodford's great mortification, the 1st almost to a man swallowed the bait, while his 2nd resisted his eloquent harrangue at their head, and silently rejected the intended honour he proposed doing them by delaying his resignation that he might lead them on the Field of Glory."[26]

24. He tried to land three boatsful of men at Cape Henry in a last futile gesture, but they were quickly repulsed.
25. **Journals of the Continental Congress, 1774-1789**, Vol. V (1776), pp. 597-98.
26. George Johnston to Maj. Leven Powell, 6 Aug. 1776, in: Robert C. Powell, **A Biographical Sketch and Correspondence of Col. Leven Powell**, pp. 37-38.

The dislike that the vain and petty Woodford had inspired in his men had caught up with him. To add insult to injury the men said that they would follow Colonel Charles Scott but not him. When the First and Second Regiments had offered congratulations to Patrick Henry who had been appointed Governor of Virginia on the 2nd of July, Woodford had had the incredible churlishness to write to Purdie's *Virginia Gazette* disassociating himself from this graceful gesture.[27] He was reaping a just reward.

Colonel William Christian, who had replaced Henry in command of the 1st Regiment, now resigned to lead an expedition against the Overhill Cherokees in what is now the western tip of North Carolina.[28] As his successor Isaac Reade, formerly Lieutenant Colonel of the 4th Regiment, was named, by-passing Major Francis Eppes, who had been with the unit since its beginning. Andrew Leitch of Prince William County was promoted to Major.

With the command of the 2nd Regiment in complete disarray, the 3rd Regiment was the most likely candidate to "seize the post of Honour." There were many reasons that made it the most logical choice. It was, at the time, the nearest to being full and was by far the best trained and equipped. Furthermore its intended use exactly fitted its specialized training and talents. It would be an important part of the "Flying Camp", or "camp volant", a military unit designed to serve a somewhat unusual tactical purpose.

When the British had evacuated Boston in March there had been no certainty as to their next move. An obvious one would be a landing on the unguarded coast line between Perth Amboy and Cape May, New Jersey, followed by an immediate march on Philadelphia. It was manifestly impossible to build 150 miles of coastal fortifications. The alternative was the "camp volant", a mobile strategic force capable of reaching almost any point in short order to repel a landing. To be commander of this unit Congress, on Washington's advice, selected the best qualified man they could get, the newly-appointed Brigadier from Virginia, Hugh Mercer, formerly commander of the 3rd Virginia Regiment. Mercer received notice of his appointment while with his regiment before

---

27. Catesby Willis Stewart, **The Life of Brigadier General William Woodford,** Vol. I, p. 682.

28. The Cherokees at the instigation of the Shawnee and other northern tribes but against the advice of British agents attacked settlements in the Watauga and upper Holston Valleys. They were decisively defeated and, as a result, lost their lands east of the Blue Ridge.

Gwynn's Island and immediately reported for duty in New York.

The new commander of the 3rd Virginia Regiment was George Weedon who had come a long way during his six months under the tutelage of his distinguished brother-in-law. He had taken his responsibility seriously, worked hard to make himself fit for command and worthy of the trust placed in him by the great Washington, whom he admired close to idolatry. Aside from that, he was light-hearted and jovial. Because he always kept a gourd handy so that he could offer his men an immediate libation in case of need, he was affectionately known as "Joe Gourd" among the troops. That is not to deny that he may have been shaped a little like a gourd, but he was an excellent horseman and a vigorous leader. Thomas Marshall, of course, moved into the Lieutenant Colonelcy, and William Taliaferro was named Major.

The first regiment to march north from Virginia was the 3rd under Colonel Weedon. They left Dumfries on the 16th of August, 1776 for the long march. The 1st Regiment under Colonel Isaac Reade left Williamsburg about two weeks later. With the 3rd Regiment, possibly through excess of zeal, rode Major Andrew Leitch of the 1st Virginia to his appointment in Samara.

The men had been provided with a suit of clothes consisting of two linen hunting shirts, two pairs of overalls, a leathern or woolen waistcoat with sleeves, a pair of breeches, a hat or leathern cap, two shirts, two pairs of hose and two pairs of shoes, amounting to about twenty dollars. The officers, in uniforms provided by themselves, carried their swords. Company grade officers carried, in addition, a firelock with bayonet, cartouch box, and three rounds of powder and balls. The ranks were equipped with a rifle gun, tomahawk, firelock and bayonet with pouch and horn, or cartridge-box and three rounds of ammunition.[29]

The mood of the men as they left was confident but somber. This was no light-hearted excursion. They knew that some of them, perhaps many, would never see Virginia again. Few, if any, had ever been outside the colony. Perth Amboy was to them what Okinawa was to their descendants, terra incognita. Officers and men were encouraged to make their wills before they left. Some, like John McLain of Ashby's company and Elijah Nash of

---

29. As the officers provided their own uniforms a certain amount of eccentricity was to be expected. Usually their trousers, coats and waistcoats were blue, trimmed with red. They liked to line their coats with white and silver buttons were in demand but usually not procurable. Mary R. M. Goodwin, **Clothing and Accoutrements of the Officers and Soldiers of the Virginia Forces, 1775-1780.**

Chilton's, did so. Others like George O'Bannon did not and later were sorry. Many simply had nothing to leave.

On the 1st of July McLain wrote:

> "This my will if it please God to take me out of this world into an Eternal world. I give to Wm. Sincler my Negro Fellow Henery and as the rest of my properties I give to my two Eldest Sisters and my Eldest Brother if so be that I Never Come up Again—I shall be *very* glad if you will be kind Enough to make———Best Advantage of *hary* Another year. Sir———. I have Got the momps a Comeing on me
>
> I am your most humbled Servant
>
> John McLain." [30]

It was not the "momps" that did Johnny in, but a more virulent disease, in a distant city, under a leaden sky.

Elijah Nash was part way along the road when he wrote his will on the 1st of September:

> "Know all men by these Presents that my will is if I never return from the wars that my Negroe Garl that is now living at James Sanders, should belong to my sister Elizabeth Sanders and her heirs forever.
>
> Elijah Nash." [31]

He must have stopped off home along the way, as the witnesses were close relatives.

Captain John Chilton's will, written the 24th of August, was, as might be expected, crisp and businesslike. He provided estates for all his children, leaving "Rock Spring" to his eldest son, Thomas, along with his surveying instruments. Careful provision was made for their education and maintenance until grown. The executors were Major Martin Pickett and Thomas Keith (both married to sisters of his wife) and his brother, Charles. The witnesses were officers of his own battalion, Samuel Boyd, John Blackwell, John Ashby, Isham Keith and Joseph Blackwell, Jr. It was obviously written en route. The Captain could not permit himself the luxury of stopping home along the way. He signed

---

30. Fauquier County Will Book, 1776-77, discovered in 1954 and filed at the end of Will Book I.

31. **Ibid.**, p. 313.

himself "John Chilton of the Third Regiment of Virginia Regulars."

The route they followed is not absolutely certain but there were sufficient clues dropped along the way to approximate it in general. From Dumfries they took the Dumfries Road to Red House (Haymarket) in Prince William County. Here they joined the Old Carolina Road which took them east of the Bull Run Mountains, past West's Ordinary and through Leesburg to cross the Potomac at Noland's Ferry. Passing through Frederick, Maryland, they crossed into Pennsylvania and stopped near Hanover. Weedon had planned to reach the Flying Camp by way of Philadelphia. However, when they reached York he received a message from John Hancock with vague mention of smallpox in the city and directing him to proceed through the Jerseys by the nearest route.[32] This was the 28th of August.

Two days later, after news of the defeat on Long Island had reached Congress, Hancock sent off another dispatch instructing Weedon to march directly to New York with all possible speed. General Mercer, who had heard that the Virginians were on the march as early as the 19th, sent similar orders.[33] Apparently Washington had asked him for the 3rd Virginia and had written Hancock on the 2nd of September to inform him that he had ordered about 1,000 men intended for the Flying Camp sent to New York. As the 3rd Virginia had not reached full strength and numbered only about 550 men, it may be that Washington was under the impression that the 1st Regiment was with them.

On September 8th Washington was still anxiously awaiting Weedon's arrival and again wrote Mercer of his concern as to the whereabouts of the regiment.[34] In fact they were making as much speed as could reasonably be expected. From York they proceeded

32. John Hancock, 1737-1793, son of a Braintree minister, was an orphan in early life and was adopted by his uncle, Thomas Hancock, the richest merchant in Boston. He was president of the Continental Congress, 24 May 1775 to 29 Oct. 1777. He was possibly apprehensive that, if the real state of affairs in New York was revealed, the Virginians might turn back.

33. Mercer had written to Washington to ask whether the regiment should remain with him or proceed immediately to Manhattan. Washington's reply is lost but he must have asked that the latter course be taken. Mercer to Washington, 19 Aug. 1776, Washington Papers, Library of Congress.

34. Washington to Mercer, 8 Sept. 1776, in: John C. Fitzpatrick, ed., **Writings of George Washington**, Vol. VI, p. 33.

to Lancaster and then, skirting the highlands they passed north of Norristown to cross the Delaware River near New Hope. Across New Jersey, still skirting the mountains, they passed near Plainfield, Montclair and Hackensack. Opposite Dobbs Ferry they halted and prepared to cross the Hudson. At this stage of hostilities Dobbs Ferry, less than ten miles north of King's Bridge, was the most important crossing. Later this ferry was too close to the British defenses of New York for the Americans to use safely and they favored King's Ferry, fifteen miles farther north.

The crossing, though difficult, was made without incident. They then marched south through Yonkers crossing the Harlem River at King's Bridge and encamped at Hellgate 14 miles above New York at that time. The march in the extreme heat of late August had been exhausting and some had dropped by the wayside, but, according to John Chilton, the regiment was "in good spirits and generally speaking healthy, tho' not quite full." "However," he continues, "great joy was expressed at our arrival and great things are expected from the Virginians, and of consequence we must go through great fatigue and danger." [35]

They arrived on the 13th of September having covered well over 400 miles in 26 days, averaging more than 16 miles a day. After leaving Noland's Ferry the terrain had been unfamiliar and the people strange and not always friendly, or so they supposed. What awaited them in New York was largely unexpected. The frantic pleas to come as quickly as possible was their only clue to the serious plight of Washington's army faced with the imminent loss of the city. Colonel Weedon had preceded them by two days, arriving coincidentally, on the same day that Captain Daniel Morgan's rifle company arrived in New York harbor from its long imprisonment in Quebec. [36]

John Chilton's letter to his father-in-law dated September 13th continues: "We are stationed about 14 miles from New York near King's Bridge which is above the place called Hellgate, rather on the New England or Connecticut side...I write in a hurry in the confusion & noise of a camp and the thundering of cannon...I have

35. Letter, John Chilton to Joseph Blackwell, 13 Sept. 1776, Keith of Woodbourne Papers, Virginia Historical Society.

36. Carleton would not agree to exchange of the Quebec prisoners until late July of 1776. The Americans were then placed on transports and sent down the St. Lawrence. They arrived off Sandy Hook on the 11th of September, but Howe detained them until the 25th, when he turned them over to Continental authorities at Elizabethtown, New Jersey.

just this moment heard that the Council of War which sat yesterday have determined to keep New York which we had some expectation of abandoning as it lies immediately under the shipping."[37]

The Virginians were appalled by the conditions they found in the American camp. Gustavus Brown Wallace [38] was amazed that there were only 1,500 troops in the city and only twelve pieces of artillery. He had expected that Washington would have 10,000 men. He also noted with alarm that the army of 58,000 he had supposed was in New York and New Jersey was not above 23,000. What army Washington had, was in a state of shock and utter confusion as the result of the precipitant flight across the East River which had taken place two weeks before. The Connecticut troops were in particular disgrace, having fled in panic from the British at Kip's Bay (34th Street and the East River) on the day the Virginians arrived. Despite the assurances given Chilton, the abandonment of the city was tactically necessary and imminent. Only the military stupidity of the British General Howe had prevented the enemy from charging from Kip's Bay across the island, trapping Washington's men in New York.

While the British waited inexplicably on Murray Hill, Washington was able to evacuate New York by the Bloomingdale Road to the tiny village on the Hudson (about 91st Street) and thence through the "Hollow Way" (a declivity between the Hudson and Morningside Heights near West 125th Street) to the Haarlem Heights. According to Chilton the Virginians were near Haarlem, a Dutch village east of the Hollow Way overlooking the East River. There, on the morning of the 16th of September, a terribly hot and sultry morning, with cannon thundering around him and the air foul with the dust and smoke of battle, the youthful George O'Bannon remembered something he had forgotten to do. George O'Bannon [39] was just an average soldier, one of Captain Ashby's.

37. Letter, John Chilton to Joseph Blackwell, Keith of Woodbourne Papers, Virginia Historical Society.
38. Gustavus Brown Wallace, to his brother, Dr. Michael Wallace, 15 Sept. 1776. A. D. Wallace Papers, 1776-83, University of Virginia. They were sons of Dr. Michael Wallace of Culpeper County. The senior Dr. Wallace had come from Scotland and served as an apprentice to Dr. Gustavus Brown of Port Tobacco, Maryland, before moving to Culpeper County.
39. George O'Bannon, 1757-1776, was a son of John and Sarah (Barbee) O'Bannon who lived on the north slope of the Pignut Ridge near the "waggon road at head of Carter's Run". His mother was a daughter of Thomas Barbee of Stafford Co. Elizabeth Barbee mentioned in his letter was, presumably, his first cousin.

He had spent almost all of his nineteen years at his father's home on the north slope of the Pignut Mountain. He was the ninth son of John and Sarah (Barbee) O'Bannon, so family responsibilities had rested lightly on his young shoulders. Two years before his father had died, leaving him a modest inheritance from the estate granted his grandfather, old Briant O'Bannon who had come to Virginia nearly forty years before.

George remembered his grandfather mostly for his stories of Ireland, especially those about Brian Boru, the great King of Munster [40] from whom the O'Bannons were supposed to be descended. Of that he was no longer certain, but he knew that today he must somehow behave like a descendant of the warrior king, though his hand trembled and his heart pounded with excitement and fear. His brow was furrowed in concentration as he applied the quill he had stolen from an indignant goose, to a torn scrap of foolscap.

> Dear mother and brothers. i writ to let you know that i am in good health thanks be god for it at this present. hoping this lines will find you all in health. remember me to all my friends not forgetting cuzzen Elizabeth barbe, remember my love to her, (i dont expect that i shawl writ ane more), and to let you now that we are not been in know battle yet but wey expect it every day and night. wey are on a iland about fifteen miles long & two miles wid and the innamy is all round the iland. we have know way of get off. we must fite our way off. our men is a fiting every day and night. the other night a battle the other night at kings bridge 3 miles. New Yourk iland were the town is on the iland. i am in grat hopes that i shawl see you all again but wee expect a battle ever day and night. i am grat hope that the town will be burnt in a few days. the english wod have burnt it before this time but they want the town for barracks. but if they dont burn the town wee shawll burn the town ourselves. none more at present but your dutyfull son,
>
> george O'bannon [41]

40. Brian Boru, 962?-1014, King of Munster, became high king of Ireland in 1002 by right of conquest. Shortly after his victory over the Norse at Clontarf, near Dublin, 23 April 1014, he was murdered in his tent. His victory marked the end of Norse power in Ireland.

41. Fauquier County Will Book I, p. 311. Probate 25 August 1777.

THE HEIGHTS OF HAARLEM AND THE WHITE PLAINS 115

All that he had learned in school had seemed to desert him and there was a good deal wrong with the spelling, but it would have to do. His mother and brothers would not be critical, but something was missing, something he had wanted to say -

> it is my desire that brother benjamon O'bannon should have all my astate after my dets is paid. i hope my der brothers you wount think amiss of it for i think he wont it worse.

That would take care of young Benjamin, the tenth son, who had been so far down the line that his father had had nothing left to leave him. He had to stop. His Captain was calling his company together. There was work to be done.

The noise he had heard came from the direction of the Hollow Way where two British light infantry battalions had taken a bit of high ground (near Grant's Tomb today). Washington had ordered an attack together with a flanking movement behind the enemy's right in an effort to cut them off. For the flanking movement he selected Lieutenant Colonel Thomas Knowlton [42] with 150 Connecticut rangers and three of Weedon's rifle companies under Major Andrew Leitch of the 1st Virginia Regiment. The rifle companies, about 230 men, were Ashby's, and those led by Captain Charles West [43] of Loudoun County and Captain John Thornton [44] of Stafford County.

The encirclement started well but was spoiled by an unidentified officer who ordered fire opened prematurely, diverting the column led by Knowlton and Leitch into an attack on the enemy's flank. The British recognized the danger and started to withdraw with the Americans in hot pursuit. About 200 yards to the rear the British reformed momentarily and, in the fire-fight that ensued both Knowlton and Leitch were mortally wounded.

42. Thomas Knowlton, 1740-1776, of Connecticut. Enlisting at age 15, he rose to the grade of Lieutenant in the French and Indian War. As Captain of a militia company, he distinguished himself at Bunker Hill.

43. Charles West, was a son of William West of Loudoun County. The family operated West's Ordinary near Aldie, frequently used by Washington to break his journey to Berkeley Springs.

44. John Thornton, b. ca. 1735, was a son of Col. Francis and Frances (Gregory) Thornton of "Fall Hill", Stafford Co. He married Jane Washington, dau. of Augustine and Ann (Aylett) Washington. His sister, Mildred, married George Washington's brother, Charles.

The fighting, however, continued under the leadership of the young captains until Washington could bring up reinforcements. The heaviest fighting took place about noon in buckwheat fields between Broadway and Riverside Drive at today's West 120th Street. At that point the British had brought up reinforcements to nearly 5,000 men and Washington, immeasurably weaker, had to call a halt.

Writing to General Schuyler, Washington said, "This little advantage has inspired our troops prodigiously..they find that it only requires resolution and good officers to make an enemy (that they stood in too much dread of) give way." [45] The next morning Captain John Chilton wrote to Martin Pickett, Thomas Keith or Charles Chilton: [46]

> Monday morn^g we marched down towards them and posted ourselves near a meadow, having that in our front, N^o River to our right a body of woods in our rear & on our left. We discovered the enemy army peeping from their heights over the fencings & rocks & running backwr^d & forwards. We did not alter our position. I believe they expected we should have ascended the hill to them, but finding us still they imputed it to fear and came skipping down towards us in small parties. At the distance of about 250 or 300 yards they began their fire. Our orders were not to fire till they came near, but a young officer (of whom we have too many) on the right fired and it was taken from right to left, - we made about 4 fires. I had fired twice & loaded again determined to keep for a better chance but, Col$^{o\cdot}$ Weedon calling to keep up our fire (he meant for us to reserve it but we misunderstood him), I fired once more. We then all wiped & loaded and sat down in our ranks and let the enemy fire on us near an hour. Our men observed the best order, not quitting their ranks tho' exposed to a constant warm fire. I can't say enough in their praise. They behaved like soldiers who fought from principle alone. During this three companies of Riflemen from our Regt. West, Thornton and Ashby's with other Comp^{ies} of Riflemen were flanking the enemy and had

---

45. James Thomas Flexner, **George Washington**, Vol. II, p. 130.

46. Chilton's letter was conveyed by Sergeant Beaver of Captain West's company who had been replaced and was going home. The multiple address was to facilitate delivery.

begun a brisk fire on the right of them. On this they began to retreat up the hill, carrying off their dead & wounded, for we had galled them a little ... The enemy retreated about a Quarter & half, when they were reinforced with men and cannon. We had but one field piece in the battle, they had several. The battle began between 8 & 9 in the morning and lasted till about 2. It was rather a skirmish than a battle. However it has taught our enemy that we are not all Connecticut troops, and they are more peaceably inclined than before.

Chilton reports three killed and eight wounded in his regiment. Major Leitch, he says, though wounded badly by three balls, one in the groin and the other two in the side of his belly, "is a man of Spirit and bears it as such. It is dangerous but hope not mortal." Alas, Leitch's "spirit" was no proof against tetanus and he died on the 3rd of October.

'P. S.," writes Chilton, "Tell the old Planters in Fauquier their boys are fine soldiers!" In a previous letter he had written, "Dicky Beale would write but has not an opportunity, he is well, a fine little soldier, remember him to his mother and all his friends as a worthy lad whom I much esteem." There will be more about sixteen year old Dicky Beale,[47] whose warm heart and quick mind would continue to earn him "esteem." "Johnny Blackwell sends compliments", which was par for the course for Johnny, where letter writing was concerned. Somewhere along the line they had left Joseph Blackwell sick with fever and ague. They had expected him to come along with Captain West, but West's company had arrived without him.

One man he did not mention. Though they had lived within a stone's throw of each other, he did not know him. George O'Bannon never left his "iland". Not until the following summer was it realized that his sad little letter must be submitted to probate. It was Benjamin O'Bannon's[48] turn to pick up the torch.

The account given by Gustavus Brown Wallace to his brother the next day closely parallels Chilton's. He adds that the troops that were engaged got General Washington's thanks in public

---

47. The wife of Richard Beale, whom he married late in life, was apparently Mary Elizabeth Grayson, widow of William Grayson. She may have been his second wife.

48. Benjamin O'Bannon, 1759-1839, youngest son of John and Sarah (Barbee) O'Bannon, married 13 Nov. 1780, Eleanor Ash.

orders. "Though I say it that should not say it" he writes in a burst of enthusiasm, "the Virginia Regiment has got great honour in this engagement." Then, pragmatically, "I have sent half my clothes to King's Bridge about 5 miles above here for fear of losing our camp." [49]

It was Friday, September 20th, before George Weedon got around to informing his friend John Page, Lieutenant Governor of Virginia and President of the Council, of the state of affairs in New York.[50] As befitted a gentleman of high rank in writing to another of similar exalted position, he felt that he should begin with a discourse on high-level tactics. He gives a lengthy explanation of the necessity for evacuating New York City and comments briefly on enemy strength. As a side light he gives a description of Washington's temper tantrum at Kip's Bay while the Connecticut troops were running away. His recital of events at the Hollow Way on Monday morning is sketchy though he gives credit to his Virginians, of whom he was justly proud. He says coyly, "I soon got engaged, as did the Major & his party; how we behaved it does not become me to say, but let it suffice to tell you that we had the General's thanks in public orders for our Conduct."

After a rather exaggerated guess as to enemy losses received from highly dubious sources,[51] he comes up with some solid information. The 1st Virginia Regiment has not arrived, but surely they cannot be far off. (They did not arrive until the 27th.) The 3rd Virginia Regiment had had exceedingly hard duty since they had been there, being kept in constant alarm, quite beside the necessary guard, pickets, fatigue parties, all upon the back of a very long march in broiling heat. Yet he believed that they were, "to a man, Noble, Orderly and Brave."

"Believe me to be my Dear Sir, yr^S affectionately

G. Weedon"

---

49. Gustavus Brown Wallace to his brother, 18 Sept. 1776. A. D. Wallace Paper, University of Virginia.

50. Letter, George Weedon to John Page, 20 Sept. 1776. George Weedon Papers, Chicago Historical Society.

51. "the enemy loss was first supposed to be 97 but a deserter that came into...them to have lost between 2 & 3 hundred; this is partly confirmed by an old country man to whose Barn they carried their wounded."

"P. S. Marshall & myself escaped in ye Mondays affair, he with the loss of part of his espantoon [52] & I with part of the hilt of my sword.

G. W."

No, he could not quite stop there. Tucked into the margin of the letter is a bit of engaging naivete:

("Mr. Purdie may say anything modist & not too)
(extravagant for the honor of ye Regt. for in-)
(formation of our Virg^a friends.")

He intended "to have wrote Woodford and Spottswood but cant for my blood find time!" It is just as well. A letter from Weedon at this time and in this vein might easily have caused Woodford to have had a stroke.

Before evacuating New York General Nathanael Greene [53] had advocated putting the city to the torch so that the British could not make use of it for winter quarters. Congress had roundly snubbed him for his pains. Washington, while admitting the tactical advantage of such action, was not in a position to press the point, especially after the noises that he had made when Lord Dunmore was accused of burning Norfolk. Therefore not a single soul in the American high command knew anything about what was going to happen on the night of September 20-21. If they had thought to consult George O'Bannon before it was too late, they might have received a clue.

The fire started shortly after midnight in a wooden house near Whitehall Slip and spread rapidly north with a stiff breeze. A shift of wind about 2 a.m. confined the fire to an area between Broadway and the Hudson River, but 493 houses were destroyed before the British troops and citizens could put out the flames. Confined? Well not quite. Several mysterious fires broke out in other parts of the city. The most beautiful blaze was in the towering shingle steeple of Trinity Church. It made a bonny bonfire as it came crashing to the ground.

52. Espantoon: a shafted weapon having a pointed blade at the head and a crossbar at the base, used by infantry officers in the 17th and 18th centuries.

53. Nathanael Greene, 1742-1786, of Rhode Island. Next to Washington, he was possibly America's most competent general. He was right with respect to New York but his insistence upon defending Fort Washington was probably the most costly blunder of the Revolution.

The British, of course, accused American saboteurs of having set the fires. The Americans were deeply shocked that they could be suspected of such infamy. Washington commented, "Providence, or some good, honest fellow hath done more for us than we were disposed to do for ourselves."[54] For once the marble countenance is suspected of having broken into a slight grin.

A few days after the engagement at Haarlem Heights the 3rd Virginia Regiment moved to Morris Heights on the eastern edge of the plateau about a half mile north of their former camp in the flat area around Haarlem. Chilton, writing to his brother on the 6th of October,[55] seemed pleased with the position and relaxed enough to think of domestic affairs. He asked about his children and urged his brother to help himself to the corn and cattle on his plantation. He asked that care be taken of a colt that he could use "if I am spared" and urged his brother to have the wheat "spiritualized" for sale except a barrel or so which he would have "double stilled & put up to get again, and if I have the happiness to come home free, we may have the pleasure of enjoying ourselves over a good Bowl of it, if I should not come there will be the more for you."

Conditions in Weedon's regiment were not, though, as well as might be inferred from his letter. Exhilarated by the excitement and success after their arrival, he was now running on nervous energy. The truth was that he and his men were exhausted, as Weedon realized. The arrival of the 1st Virginia Regiment had only added to Weedon's problems. On the 5th of October Washington had formed the two Virginia Regiments into a separate brigade under Colonel Weedon, attached to Putnam's division. The 1st Virginia had had a dreadful march, many were sick with fevers and agues and they were quite deficient in both numbers and spirit. The officers were dissatisfied and quarrelsome.[56] News of Major Leitch's death created a commotion as they fought over rank and position. Washington awarded the vacant post to John Fitzgerald,,[57] Weedon's senior captain, but Congress saw fit to go over

54. Flexner, **George Washington**, Vol. 2, p. 131.

55. John Chilton to "dear Friends", probably Charles Chilton or his brothers-in-law as previosuly.

56. Almost on the day the 1st Virginia Regiment arrived the 2nd Lieutenants presented the Commander-in-Chief with a memorial charging that they were being discriminated against under the existing system of promotion.

57. Fitzgerald is described by his contemporaries as unusually handsome and athletic (Flexner). Martha Bland wrote that he was an agreeable, broad shouldered Irishman.

his head and appoint Captain John Green of Culpeper County. Washington was forced to salve Fitzgerald's wounded pride by appointing him to his personal staff.

John Green,[58] son of Robert and Eleanor (Dunn) Green had been a Captain since 6 September, 1775, when he had led his company of Culpeper minutemen to Williamsburg. He was an excellent officer, probably better than Fitzgerald would have been. He was also notably well connected in Fauquier. His wife was Susannah Blackwell, daughter of Colonel William and Elizabeth (Crump) Blackwell. He was, therefore, a brother-in-law of Colonel William Edmonds of the Fauquier militia, Captain William Blackwell, whom we met at Hampton, and Joseph Blackwell, the young cadet with Ashby. As might be expected, though, there was a great deal of muttering in the officers' mess of the 1st Virginia.

Writing to John Page on the 10th of October, Weedon exulted in the "Elbow room" afforded by his new location and voiced regret at the wasted labor and expense in securing their former position.[59] Their lines were now very formidable and, he thought, sufficient for defense against twice their number. However the enemy is busy and the coming and going of shipping in the narrow, deep waterways surrounding his position worries him.

Somewhat surprisingly General William Alexander, Lord Stirling,[60] who had been captured on Long Island, had been exchanged. He arrived looking fit and well-fed. The British had been polite, except our old friend, Lord Dunmore, who had gratuitously insulted him. He was eager to get back to work, and one wonders if the British had not considered that his military abilities would do them more good on the opposite side.

58. John Green, d. 1793, married, 1756, Susannah Blackwell, b:1739. See Mark Mayo Boatner III, Encyclopedia of the American Revolution, p. 450.

59. Letter, George Weedon to John Page, 10 Oct. 1776. Weedon Papers, Chicago Historical Society.

60. William Alexander, 1726-1783, was a son of James Alexander, prominent New York lawyer. The son was on the military staff of Mass. Governor Shirley with whom he went to England. While there he claimed the earldom of Stirling, which was recognized in the Scottish courts but rejected by the House of Lords in London, possibly because of his American birth. He was always known as Lord Stirling in America. He had been captured during the battle of Long Island, 27 Aug. 1776. He was exchanged for Gov. Montfort Browne of New Providence and Maj. Cortlandt Skinner.

The American positions on the high, wooded plateau that extended from Morris Heights to Kings Bridge at the north end of the island, a distance of about four miles, were indeed formidable. About mid-way, on a high eminence near the North or Hudson River, the Americans had built an elaborate earthwork fortification called Fort Washington,[61] intended as the eastern defense of a barrier that would prevent the British ships from access to the river above that point. Opposite, on the Jersey side, was a similar, less elaborate earthwork, called Fort Lee. Between them was a line of sunken ships, too far apart and easily disposed of to form an effective obstacle to shipping. Fort Washington certainly looked strong, unless one realized that it had no ditch, no casemates, no palisade and very limited outworks. It also lacked water, food and fuel. The British had not been close enough to recognize most of these weaknesses, but they had a better idea for trapping Washington's army than an attempt on this imposing landmark.

Howe's manoeuvre was begun at 9 o'clock on the morning of 12 October when a heavy fog in Hell Gate concealed the landing of 4,000 British on Throg's Point, a spit of land jutting out from the Bronx at the entrance to Long Island Sound. The intent was a quick thrust across the neck to the Hudson River, a distance of 16 miles, taking on the way King's Bridge, Washington's only way of retreat from Manhattan Island. Washington was not so obtuse that this possibility had not occurred to him and had moved a body of troops north of the bridge to forestall just such an eventuality.[62] The terrain favored the Americans and they were able to stop Howe in his tracks. Washington had no intention of finishing a brief, inglorious war bottled up on Manhattan Island and quickly realized that he must move the greater part of his army to White Plains, about 17 miles north, to escape entrapment.

Only the garrison at Fort Washington and two divisions under Putnam[63] and Spencer[64] were to remain to guard Fort

61. Fort Washington was laid out by Rufus Putnam and erected in July 1776 by the 3rd and 4th Pennsylvania Regiments under Cols. John Shee and Robert Magaw.
62. Col. Edward Hand's 30-man guard from the 1st Pennsylvania Rifle Regiment stopped the attack. They were quickly reinforced by Massachussetts and New York Continentals with cannon.
63. Israel Putnam, 1718-1790, of Connecticut. Despite a distinguished military career he was, in 1776, too old and fat to be an effective commander. After several inglorious minor engagements a stroke in December, 1779, forced his retirement.
64. Joseph Spencer, 1714-1789, also of Connecticut, was even older than Putnam. According to Freeman, "he discharged routine duties without displaying such scandalous incompetence or slouth as to make his removal a public necessity." "No particular regret is recorded" when he resigned his commission, 13 Jan. 1778.

Washington. As Weedon's Virginia brigade was attached to Putnam's division, it would remain behind. At the last moment, Washington changed his mind and ordered Weedon to join Lord Stirling's brigade and hurry northward to seize the best ground at White Plains. Had it not been for this last minute decision, we might well have ended our book right here!

The British, unable to gain land west of the Bronx River, deployed northward with their backs to Long Island Sound with their extreme right as far north as Rye. Stationed near Mamaroneck was a Tory outfit under Major Robert Rogers [65] called the "Queen's American Rangers", about 500 strong. Lord Stirling thought that it might be interesting to cut this detachment off from the main body and, with luck, capture the lot. He called upon Colonel John Haslet's [66] Delaware regiment, with some Marylanders and 160 men from the 1st and 3rd Virginia regiments (about 750 in all) to try the experiment. The attack was scheduled to take place on the night of October 22nd. With the Virginia troops under the command of Major John Green in the van, they took a crossroad leading to New Rochelle and entered the field just below the Tory camp. Here the Virginians stumbled upon an outpost guard of sixty Rangers. They might have captured them to a man but for the quick thinking of the Ranger Captain who started shouting, "Surrender, you Tory dogs! Surrender!" A melee followed in which it was impossible to tell friend from foe and twenty of the Rangers escaped. The main Tory camp, now thoroughly alerted, proved too strong for the Americans to continue the attack and Haslet was forced to withdraw. Green received a ball in the shoulder which knocked him out for a bit, but his command was quickly taken over by Captain John Thornton of Stafford County (the same Captain Thornton who had distinguished himself at Haarlem Heights) who successfully extricated his men together with his wounded major. Which, if any, of the Fauquier men participated in this particular engagement is

65. Robert Rogers, 1732-1795, of Concord, New Hampshire. A frontiersman with unusual talent for recruiting, he was Captain of an independent ranger company in 1756 which served with distinction during the French and Indian War and in Pontiac's War. A notoriously unprincipled and dissipated trouble-maker, he was soon removed from command of the Queen's Rangers and died in poverty in London.

66. John Haslet was born in Ireland and was a successful doctor in Delaware before the Revolution. He was killed in action at Princeton, 3 Jan. 1777.

uncertain. If any did, it was their only chance for excitement at White Plains. Again the Virginians were heroes of the day with thirty-six prisoners, a pair of colours, sixty stand of arms and as many precious blankets.

However, even Washington must have realized that his Virginia troops had been pushed almost beyond the limits of human endurance. In the punishing heat of the march north some had abandoned heavy clothing in hope of replenishing their store in Philadelphia. That had not been possible and the weather was turning cold. In anguish Weedon wrote to John Page:[67]

> The sufferings of my poor men makes me feel exceedingly, for these five weeks we have been under arms every morning before day, exclusive of the other necessary duties of the army, which has been uncommonly hard, they have been obliged to engage it, entirely naked, some without shoes or stockings several without blankets and almost all without shirts.—

He may have been exaggerating somewhat, but it fell on deaf ears. There is no record that his impassioned plea produced so much as a single shirt. They were on Continental establishment now and as far as Virginia was concerned, the Congress could clothe them.

When the battle at White Plains took place six days later Stirling's brigade was well removed from the thrust of the attack. The Virginia troops were simply spectators, required only to hold their position while Washington withdrew to stronger ground at North Castle beyond the Croton River. To the amazement of all, Howe chose not to pursue. After dark on the 4th of November, the British began their move southward, their objective, as Washington suspected, Fort Washington. Leaving General Lee at North Castle until Howe's destination was certain, Washington ordered Stirling and most of the southern troops to cross the Hudson at Peekskill to meet a possible British attack on the Jersey side. On the 12th Stirling and the Virginians were at Hackensack and on the 17th entered New Brunswick.

---

67. Letter, Weedon to Page, 26 Oct. 1776, Weedon Papers, Chicago Historical Society.

THE HEIGHTS OF HAARLEM AND THE WHITE PLAINS

Some thirteen years later George Weedon wrote of a conversation he had with Lord Stirling after crossing the Hudson River.[68]

> ...his Lordship came to me the morning after crossing and asked me to ride down to a place called English Neighborhood nearly opposite to the fort where General Greene held his Quarters and spend the day with him. I readily agreed to his proposal and instantly took horse. The road by its bends and turns frequently exposed the North River to us, and all the country on the east side, and, at intervals, a full view of the British Columns moving down.
>
> At one of these places, sitting side by side on our horses chatting on the events of the campaign, I observed to his Lordship (that) we had it now in our power to end it most gloriously on the part of America by evacuating Fort Washington before the enemy could set down before it, and leave them an empty shell that had answered every purpose as a place of diversion. My old friend gave me a stern look and, pushing up the cock of his hat with his right hand said,
>
> 'Colonel Weedon, when I was a field officer I never took the liberty of advising my superiors, besides, Sir, do you know the natural strength and importance of that post?'
>
> I begged his Lordship's pardon and observed (that) we were alone, that I did not mean it as a piece of advice, it was only my private opinion. For reasons that were obvious to my mind, I thought it military policy to evacuate it.
>
> While at dinner Lord Stirling observed to Greene with a laugh that 'Weedon was for evacuating his hobby horse.' The General asked me seriously my reasons. I observed to him that General Howe's army was powerful, were well provided with all kind of stores necessary for carrying a siege, that his military fame would be blasted if he retreated into New York and left that post in his rear, - that the fort was not tenable against regular approaches, it had no casemates to shelter the men off duty from the weather and from the enemy's shells, that there was no water in the fort but what was stored in hogsheads.

68. **Ibid.** Letter dated 23 July 1789, to a member of Congress on behalf of the son of General Hugh Mercer whom Congress had voted to educate after the death of his father.

That by cutting off our communication with (the) North River the garrison would be greatly distressed indeed, and further that I conceived it our policy to guard against any circumstances that led to a sacrifice of men and stores.

I was so laughed at for my ideas that, towards the last, I was a little miffed, - Damned the place for a pudding bag and remarked (that) I was sorry I had given my opinion.

20-20 hindsight has been claimed before, but there is a ring of truth in Weedon's circumstantial account of the scene in General Nathanael Greene's mess on that night when he so far forgot himself as to raise his voice in disagreement with a General officer. "Joe Gourd" red-faced and angry, was a figure of fun to the high command. The only difficulty was that he was right and they were not.

For, on the 15th of November, the British took Fort Washington and 2,818 hapless men who would die of disease and starvation in filthy, rat-infested New York prisons, wallowing in their own excrement. General Nathanael Greene, who was largely responsible for the disaster, was "vexed, sick and sorry."[69] Well he might be, for it was one of the costliest blows of the entire war.

As far as we know none of our men from Fauquier was innocent victims of this signal failure in the American command. In helpless rage they watched from the Jersey shore as the fires went out in the ruined fort and British ships ascended the Hudson River contemptuous of the sunken hulks so futilely placed in their path. With the enemy in control of the North River it was useless to try to hold Fort Lee. Greene was in the process of evacuating it on the 19th of November when he learned that Cornwallis had landed about 4,000 men up river to cut off Fort Lee from the main army at Hackensack. Fortunately he was warned in time for him to elude the trap but his men lost their tents, blankets, provisions and artillery. From Hackensack the army retreated across the Passaic and followed the right bank down to Newark. There they were halted for five days by bad weather, but the retreat was resumed on the 28th. The next day the two Virginia brigades met in New Brunswick.

On the 30th John Chilton wrote the sad story of the retreating army to his brother in Fauquier.[70] They were melancholy days,

69. Letter, Greene to Henry Knox, Col. of the Continental Artillery. Greene Papers, William L. Clements Library, Ann Arbor, Michigan.

70. Letter, John Chilton to Charles Chilton, 30 Nov. 1776. Keith of Woodbourne Papers, Virginia Historical Society.

marching in deep mire with so many men to tread it, through the bleak landscape under the dark sky. They rested where they could, always expecting to be called upon to make a stand, but with no certainty where. The enemy was close on their heels and greatly exceeded their numbers. They had expected to be in winter quarters by this time but no safe harbour loomed in sight. The truth was slowly dawning that all of New Jersey was open to enemy attack and that those who stood between the Hudson and the American capital were few and terribly weary.

"You will wonder," Chilton wrote, "what is become of the great Army of Americans you have been told we had. I really cannot tell." They were in some degree imaginary, - only militia, enlisted for two, four or five months. Their terms had mostly expired before the battle of the White Plains, ("if I may call it a battle"). They could not fight the enemy then and they dare not fight them now, though intelligence had the British crossing the river only two miles above the Americans.

"O, God! that our Congress should raise men just for an expense 'till time for them to fight & then their time be out." Howe must have known, as there were many Tories all over the country to tell him. He had timed his landing, significantly, just as the enlistments of a whole regiment were up and they had vanished into the night without looking back.[71] Nevertheless, he had reason to hope that the British would repent their bold step. "Our men are willing to fight them on any terms, - but our Generals are the best judges when it is best to be done.——"

He continues with unaccustomed bitterness, "The appointment of Officers we have just recd by Armistead's Mercenary, (Maddux)[72] which surprises us all. If men were to be particularly preferred for seeing service, where was Isham Keith, John Blackwell & Joe who have seen more service in one month than he, the Captain, could see in Williamsburg in an age? Isham, so old a soldier and so good a one. Don't think me partial when I say that Joe & John are no way inferior to even Isham."

71. The terms of service of the militiamen in General Beall's and General Heard's militia brigades expired 1 December, and they refused to continue in the field.

72. Chilton's meaning is clear but it is not quite certain who "Armistead" and "Maddux" were. Quite possibly the first was Armistead Churchill, a Blackwell relative, and the second Thomas Maddux who later operated an ordinary in Fauquier Courthouse. Certainly Maddux had come from Fauquier as he had brought a message from Charles Chilton to his brother.

His fierce pride in his junior officers is equalled only by his scorn for the supercilious Captain safe in Williamsburg who hired a substitute to fight his battles, yet won the promotion that rightly belonged to a braver man. Poor "Uncle Ishe", (he was thirty-seven and probably full of good advice), was sick in Trenton, as was Captain John Ashby. The latter had been sick on his way home on leave to recruit more men.

The enemy was drawing closer. Already there was the sound of artillery fire across the Raritan. The only bridge in the area had been destroyed but they would soon cross the river in force. That night they camped beside the road to Princeton without food, tents or blankets. Tomorrow things must be better. They could scarcely be worse.

Interlude

White Plains to Trenton

The news of Washington's plight in New York in the autumn of 1776 reached Virginia in the form of an urgent request that three more regiments be sent north. Woodford's 2nd Virginia Regiment was still in no condition to go anywhere. Remembering his friendship of twenty years before, Washington especially asked for Colonel Adam Stephen and his 4th Virginia Regiment. To this General Lewis added the 5th Regiment under Colonel Charles Scott and the 6th under Colonel Mordecai Buckner. On the 4th of September Congress appointed Adam Stephen a brigadier on Continental establishment and formed the three additional Virginia regiments into a second Virginia brigade with Stephen at their head. Command of the 4th Regiment seems to have fallen to Lieutenant Colonel Robert Lawson as acting commander.

On learning of Stephen's appointment, Woodford carried out his long-standing threat to resign. Alexander Spotswood was appointed to command the 2nd Regiment in his stead.

The 4th and 5th Regiments left Virginia in October. In order to avoid the exhausting march, Washington suggested that they travel by water to Head of Elk, Maryland. Progress was slow and, when they reached the Delaware River towns of Chester and Wilmington, Congress halted their march to strengthen the defense of Philadelphia. When General Charles Lee arrived in New Jersey after the battle of the White Plains, he found it so inadequately defended that he begged Congress to allow the 2nd Virginia Brigade to join the 1st Brigade at New Brunswick. The Board of War ordered General Stephen to move as far as Trenton, which left New Jersey as defenseless as before.

The "Flying Camp" under General Mercer had developed into a complete fiasco in spite of Mercer's enthusiasm and personal courage. The Pennsylvania, Delaware and Maryland militia, supposed to supply most of its manpower, was slow to arrive and of poor military quality. The two Virginia regiments intended to join them were, as we have seen, shanghaied along the way. The unit was frequently raided to supply much-needed reinforcements elsewhere. A number of them were captured at Fort Washington. On the 30th of November the organization ended its inglorious existence when over 2,000 enlistments expired.

After White Plains Washington had been compelled to divide his army, much against his better judgement. He had left more than 3,500 men with General Charles Lee, most of them New Englanders, to withstand a possible attack on New England. Late in November, when it was apparent that the British were committed to an attack on Philadelphia, he was in desperate need of these reinforcements. He ordered Lee to rendezvous near Pittstown in the western Jersey highlands with a force under Gates from Ticonderoga and another under Heath from the Hudson Valley. After procrastinating almost to the verge of mutiny, Lee finally crossed the Hudson on the 4th of December and began a slow march through upper New Jersey.

Having placed the greater part of his army in the hands of the faithless Lee, Washington awaited his arrival with mounting anxiety. Providence or fate or luck intervened. On the night of December 12th Lee elected to sleep some distance from his army in an inn kept by an agreeable widow he had previously known. There a delighted detachment of British light horse found him lounging in his shirtsleeves. Captured, Lee wrote that he did not so much mourn for himself as for "a great continent...frustrated in the honest ambition of being free."

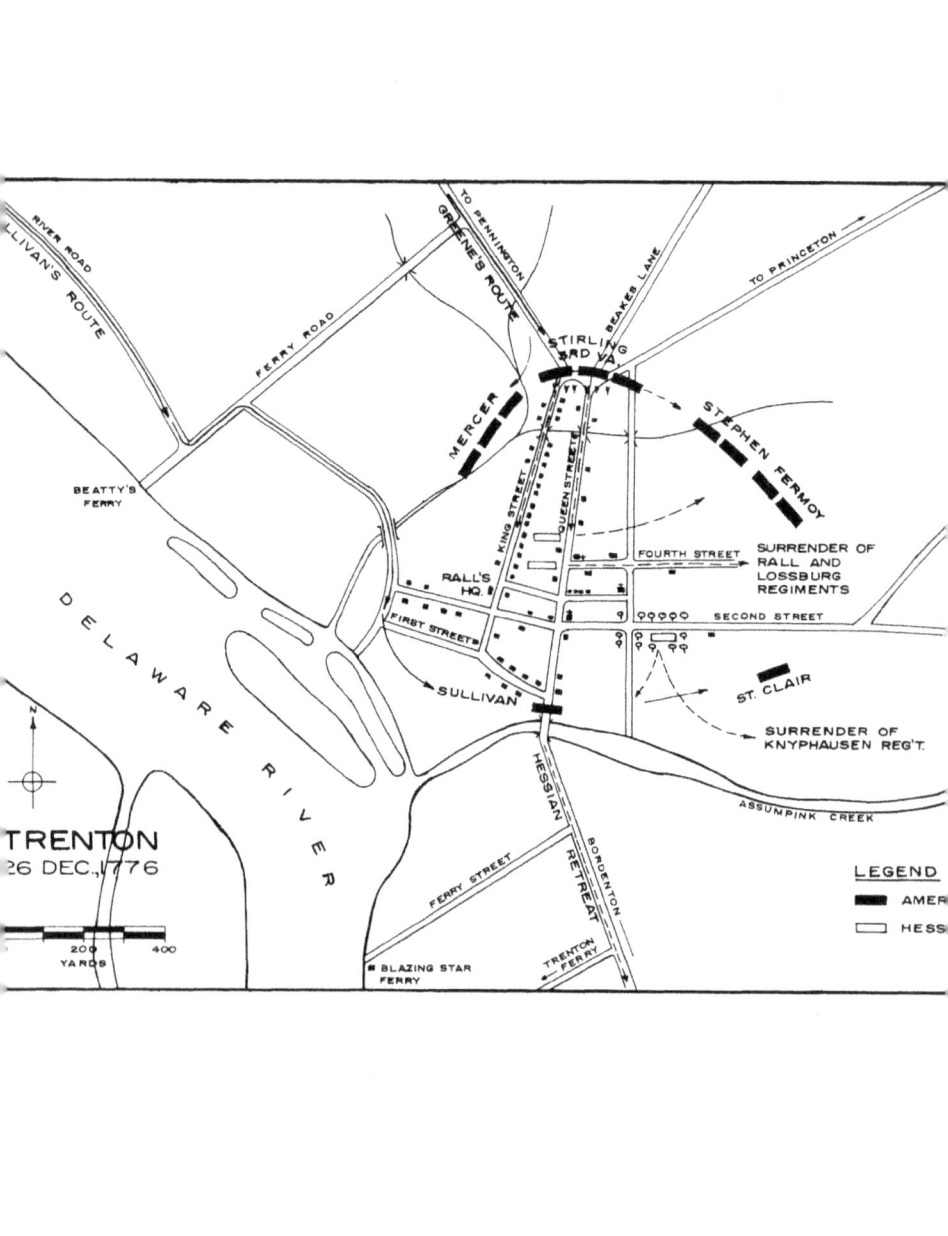

V

Trenton and Princeton

At New Brunswick, New Jersey, on the 1st of December, 1776, the 1st Virginia Brigade, comprising the 1st Regiment under Reade and the 3rd under Weedon, which included the Fauquier men, was down to 575 men of whom fewer than 510 were fit for duty.[1] Most lacked shoes, stockings and shirts and not one in three had a blanket to protect him from the bitter wind. Furthermore they had received no pay for four months and the prospects of having any in the immediate future looked decidedly bleak. Yet, somehow, they were not despondent. They still thought that, given a reasonably advantageous position, they could give the enemy a good licking.

The 2nd brigade, which Congress had finally allowed to proceed to New Brunswick, was in fact not much better off than the first. On the way north they had been forced to leave many men behind because of sickness. Fifty had come no farther than Richmond County Courthouse, others were "convalescent" at Wilmington, and at Trenton 224 men became too ill to march farther. Stephen had only 651 soldiers in his command fit for duty.[2] Together the number of Virginia soldiers in arms during the retreat through the Jerseys could not have been more than 1,240 effectives. There were many reports of forces marching through the Jersey hills to link up with them but there was no shadow of them on the bleak horizon. The appalling truth was that the Virginians at that time numbered more than one third of Washington's entire army between the British and Philadelphia.

There were two factors that operated slightly in favor of the fleeing American forces. The weather, hard as it was on them, was

---

1. General Returns of the Army in the Service of the United States, 3 Nov. 1776, 1 Dec. 1776; Greene to Congress, 1 Dec. 1776. Force, **American Archives** (5th Series), Vol. III, pp. 449-50.

2. Stephen to President of Congress, 16 Nov. 1776. Force, **American Archives** (5th Series) Vol. III, pp. 706, 740.

even harder on the British. Crossing the Raritan was no easy task. The second small boon was that British intelligence was completely fooled as to the size of Washington's army. They simply could not believe that he had so few men under his command.

With the British under Howe and Cornwallis [3] hot on their heels, Washington and his little army could not afford to linger on the road to Princeton. The penetrating wind and rain was still not cold enough to freeze the roads. Soaking wet and caked with mud, the men slogged on, stopping only to try to extricate their baggage wagons from the mire. A pale sun shone fitfully through the heavy overcast as they entered Princeton. Here they paused for a little food, but not for long. Washington detached Stirling's 1st Virginia and Stephen's 2nd Virginia Brigades to act as a rear guard before hurrying the rest of the troops on to Trenton. He hoped that the Virginians could hold the town long enough to allow them time to get their sick and wounded across the Delaware. Dr. David Griffith, surgeon-chaplain of the 3rd Virginia Regiment, was sent ahead to Philadelphia to make arrangements to receive them.

He knew that the Virginians would fight if need be, though hopelessly outnumbered. When he reached the west side of the Delaware on the 5th of December, he found reinforcement by a part of John Cadwalader's Pennsylvania Associators [4] and Nicholas Hausseger's German Regiment. [5] With these and those of his own men fit for duty, about 1,200 men, he recrossed the river on the 7th to support Stirling and Stephen. Intelligence had reached the rear guard that the British were advancing in force and that their numbers made a stand impossible. They could only return to Trenton and, the next morning, withdraw to the west bank of the Delaware. It was not a moment too soon. As they landed they could see that advance units of Howe's light infantry had already reached the town.

3. Maj. Gen. Charles, Earl Cornwallis, 1738-1805, was preparing to return to England when news of the Trenton attack forced him to cancel his plans.

4. Colonel John Cadwalader, 1742-1786, commander of the "Philadelphia Associators" a militia company organized by Benjamin Franklin in 1747. It was reorganized in 1775 as the "Associators of the City and Liberties of Philadelphia" with five battalions.

5. Colonel Nicholas Hausseger, d. 1786, commander of the Maryland and Pennsylvania German Regiment routed 2 Jan. 1777 at Trenton. They "surrendered under somewhat mysterious circumstances." Hausseger apparently joined the enemy.

TRENTON AND PRINCETON

Stirling and Stephen collected their brigades on the Pennsylvania shore to await Howe's next move. They spread out to take positions opposite the river crossings from McKonkey's Ferry nine miles above Trenton to Kirbride's six miles below. As the weather worsened there was no certainty that the river would not freeze over, making a crossing at any point possible.

There were times when Washington had to rely on British phlegm to accomplish what could not be done by American valor. Howe could not bear to spend Christmas on the banks of the icebound river so far from the bed of his Tory mistress in New York.[6] He was in Trenton only a few days before calling off the chase. He left about 3,000 Hessians posted along a line parallel to the river, from Pennington to Mt. Holly. As far as he was concerned, the campaign of 1776 was over.

To guard the river crossings, Washington was forced to spread his weakened force over a wide area. The brigades of Stirling, Stephen and Mercer reached from Yardleyville to Coryell's Ferry nearly ten miles up river. Weedon's regiment was at McKonkey's Ferry, the best of the nine crossings. General James Ewing,[7] with 550 Pennsylvania militia, was to guard the Trenton Ferry and Colonel Cadwalader's Associators were ordered to guard the ferry to Bordentown. While these dispositions were taking place Washington sent the more serious of his sick and wounded to Philadelphia. The bitter weather, fatigue and lack of provisions had taken a dreadful toll. On the 22nd of December, of 1,554 men, the five Virginia regiments were down to only 657 rank and file present and fit for duty.[8] Weedon's regiment, the best of the lot, could count only 196 men able to bear arms. Of the 1st and 3rd Virginia Regiments (Stirling's Brigade) 590 men were sick.[9] In the 4th, 5th and 6th Virginia Regiments (Stephen's Brigade) the sick

6. Sir William Howe, 1729-1814, British commander, had a notorious liaison with Elizabeth Lloyd, wife of Joshua Loring, commissary of prisoners. Loring was detested by the Americans for his brutal mistreatment of prisoners captured at Fort Washington.

7. Brig. Gen. James Ewing, 1736-1806, born in Lancaster, Penna., served with Braddock in 1755 and was with him at his death. His rank was in the Pennsylvania militia. In 1782 he was elected vice president of the Commonwealth.

8. Return of the Forces in the Service of the United States of America Encamped and in Quarters on the Banks of the Delaware, 22 Dec. 1776. Force, **American Archives** (5th Series) Vol. III, pp. 1401-02.

9. Ibid.

list was even longer. It is doubtful that they could muster 500 men among them.

On the 20th of December General John Sullivan,[10] Lee's second in command, reached Washington's headquarters at Newtown, Pennsylvania with the remnants of Lee's command. Though there were only 2,000, not half the number Washington expected, he breathed a sigh of momentary relief. Sullivan, however, was not long in coming up with a shattering bit of information. Washington had every reason to assume that men who had come all this distance had been re-enlisted. To his "great distress and mortification", he found that such was not the case.[11] The incredible fact was that most of their enlistments expired on the 31st of December, less than two weeks off.

Horatio Gates[12] arrived from Ticonderoga the same day with 600 men - all that remained of seven regiments. Including the militia Washington had now 6,600 men, a slightly encouraging number if one did not allow the chilling thought to rise, that, if all left whose enlistments expired, the number would be reduced after the New Year to 1,400 to defend the capital. Yet, somehow, Washington and his men were optimistic. A young Massachusetts major named Samuel Webb wrote:[13]

> ...You ask me our situation. It has been the Devil, but is to appearance better. About two thousand of us have been obliged to run damned hard before about ten thousand of the enemy. Never was finer lads at a retreat than we are...No fun for us that I can see. However, I cannot but think we shall drub the dogs..Never mind, all will come right one of these days.

---

10. Maj. Gen. John Sullivan, 1740-1795, of Irish descent, was an attorney in New Hampshire before the Revolution. He was captured at the Battle of Long Island, but exchanged 25 Sept. 1776.

11. Fitzpatrick, ed., **Writings of Washington**, Vol. VI, p. 417.

12. Maj. Gen. Horatio Gates, 1728-1806, was a son of the house-keeper of the Duke of Leeds. Resentful that he was of the servant class in England, he joined the army and took part in Braddock's campaign. After its failure he settled in the Shenandoah Valley. He owed his advancement to Washington, whom he did not hesitate to betray.

13. Maj. Samuel Webb to Joseph Trumbull, 16 Dec. 1776. Webb, **Correspondence and Journals**, Vol. I, p. 175.

On Christmas Eve the Fauquier men were bivouacked at the edge of a field on high ground above McKonkey's Ferry. A low ridge screened them from the river and the chill wind that swept across the plateau. The sky was overcast with black clouds threatening storm. Below, the Delaware River, choked with ice, flowed sluggishly toward the falls just above Trenton. For the moment they were warm beside their campfires. Their ragged clothes, what there were of them, were dry and the first aching fatigue of the dreadful march had worn off. The fact that some were without shoes was a matter of concern to all and they were wrapping rags around feet that had bled on the icy ground. Yet there was a curious elation among the men. Something was afoot, they knew not what. There was no use asking their taciturn Captain. He knew no more than they did; only that Colonel Weedon had received a hurried message and had ridden off, vaguely in the direction of Newtown, his Excellency's headquarters. Whatever was taking place across the icy river was hidden from them by the hills and the shifting fog, but nothing seemed to be happening. The Hessians set great store in Christmas and would probably leave them alone for a while.

Captain John Chilton sat a little apart, glad for some respite from the responsibilities that had weighed so heavily upon his shoulders for the past few months. The lines of worry had deepened in his face. He felt that the fatigue and strain must show, and that he must overcome. His men depended on him for everything, like children in a way. There were not only his men but others, who had less claim on him but were equally helpless. Captain John Ashby had left them in November on a desperately important recruiting expedition in Virginia, where his name and fame might assure success, if success was possible. Both of Ashby's lieutenants, Nelson and Keith, were sick. The latter, having been ill in Trenton, had recovered enough to go to Philadelphia to see about his and Ashby's sick, of whom there were an appalling number. Nathaniel Ashby was also in Philadelphia, possibly sick or, possibly, trying to secure treatment for his men. Both his and Ashby's companies in the field looked to him for guidance.

Not only guidance but also money was needed. For four months not one shilling had been paid out by the hard pressed paymaster. It was not his fault; there was no money to give. What Chilton had received from his brother, no small amount, had been wisely spent on clothing and extra rations for his men when there were opportunities to buy them. Even at the ruinous prices charged by the flint-hearted Jersey merchants,[14] there had been enough to keep them a little better clad and slightly better fed than most units. It nearly broke his heart to see his proud Virginians as beggars in this hostile land. He could only do his best and that, it seemed, was never enough.

At Christmas his mind must have turned to the silent house on Baldwin's Ridge and his motherless children. There was no lack of affection at "Hereford" where Charles and Betsy Chilton showered on all children a boundless warmth. But it was not quite the same for them and it was certainly not as good for him as the comfort and peace of his own fireside. Young Thomas was nearly eight now and his dark eyes were filled with wonderment when he heard of his father, so far away fighting evil men for a cause he did not understand. Would these children ever benefit from their desperate struggle? He believed that they would. It was the faith that kept him alive, but in the darkest hours there had been doubts, fleeting but not always easily laid to rest in his troubled mind.

Now he and his men stood on the brink of what might well be their last great adventure. Occasionally, in his letters he quoted Shakespeare and it is not unlikely that the lines of Henry V at Agincourt occurred to him:

> He that hath no stomach to this fight
> Let him depart: his passport shall be made,
> And crowns for convoy put into his purse:
> We would not die in that man's company
> That fears his fellowship to die with us.
>
> ...But we in it shall be remembered;
> We few, we happy few, we band of brothers;
> For he today that sheds his blood with me
> Shall be my brother; be he ne'er so vile
> This day shall gentle his condition.[15]

Christmas morning dawned cold and bleak. There was still heavy overcast and fog across the river. The camp was alive with rumor. At Newtown, where his Excellency had conferred with

---

14. **Though** colonial merchants, as a class, generally supported the Revolution, the temptation to reap quick profits on scarce items overwhelmed them in Charleston, Philadelphia and in New Jersey especially.

15. **Henry V**, Act IV, Scene iii.

Generals Mercer, Stirling, Sullivan and Knox,[16] and a few other officers, the lamps had burned far into the night. There had been a great coming and going of couriers; to General Ewing and his militia encamped opposite Trenton, to Colonel John Cadwalader and his much larger contingent of Pennsylvania militia near Pennsbury, six miles down river opposite Bordentown, to various unit commanders upstream guarding the upper ferries. The Fauquier men were sure that an attack was planned but until a plan was received they could only wait. Curiously, no one had sent them any messages.

The reason was quickly evident when, through the lifting fog, they saw the familiar face of Lieutenant Colonel Thomas Marshall. There would be, he said, a grand parade at 2 p.m. on the adjacent open field. They must put their best foot forward, for it would be reviewed by his Excellency, accompanied by Generals Greene and Sullivan. There would be extra rations and, for each man, a tot of rum. They must bank their fires, for they might not be there that night. Above all they must do their best, because they would be joined by the brigades of Stephen, Mercer and Roche de Fermoy [17] and a small troop of Philadelphia light horse. There would also be the troops of St. Clair,[18] Glover [19] and Sargent,[20] mostly Massachusetts regulars and New York militia. Between the Massachusetts regulars and the Virginians there was keen rivalry, in which the Virginians claimed a slight edge. In Massachusetts the story was the reverse.

16. Brig. Gen. Henry Knox, 1750-1806, was in 1775 the proprietor of a book store in Boston. He distinguished himself as a commander of artillery early in the war.

17. Brig. Gen. Matthias Alexis de Roche de Fermoy, 1737-post 1780, was born in Martinique. He arrived in America in 1776 claiming to be a French Colonel of Engineers though no such record has been found in French military archives. "A worthless drunkard," - Wilkinson.

18. Brig. Gen. Arthur St. Clair, 1737-1818, son of William Sinclair grandson of the second Laird of Assery. He married a rich Boston widow.

19. Col. John Glover, 1732-1797, was a wealthy fisherman of Salem, Massachusetts, before the war. He is distinguished as an early advocate of inoculation against smallpox. He and Elbridge Gerry financed a hospital for that purpose in October, 1773. The outraged populace promptly burned it.

20. Col. John Sargent, of the New York Militia.

Fortunately the weather grew colder and the field was frozen solid that wintry afternoon. There were 2,400 men who marched sharply to the beat of muffled drums. There was no fanfare and fifes remained in their slings. They had eighteen cannon which General Knox had somehow contrived to get across the river. At dark, about 6 o'clock, they marched down to McKonkey's Ferry. Here Colonel John Glover and his remarkable group of fishermen from Marblehead, Massachusetts, had assembled the boats. The Marbleheaders were used to extricating the Americans from tough positions, however rough the weather or hot the fire. They had saved the army at Kip's Bay after the defeat on Long Island and had ferried them across the Hudson, even at Fort Washington until British gunboats had forced their withdrawal. Now they were asked to pilot Durham boats,[21] the like of which they had never seen, loaded to the gunwales, across an ice-choked river in the dead of night and in the face of a violent storm. Let Fauquier raise its hat to these men from Marblehead. Without them there would have been no Trenton or Princeton, no American army and possibly no independence.

The plan by then was known to all. The Americans, after reaching the opposite shore would form into two columns. The first, under Major General Nathanael Greene would consist of the brigades of Stephen, Stirling, Mercer and Roche de Fermoy, with part of Knox's artillery including nine cannon. Washington himself would accompany this column. The second column under Major General John Sullivan would consist of Sullivan's own New Englanders, St. Clair and Sargent's brigades, the remainder of Knox's artillery including nine cannon and so many of Glover's men as could be spared from the crossing. After all they might have to get back!

The first column would take the Upper, or Pennington, Road which came into Trenton from the north. The second would follow the River Road which connected with First Street on the south side of the town. In the meanwhile General Ewing would bring his militia across the Trenton Ferry and seize the bridge across Assumpink Creek east of the town, thus cutting off the enemy retreat toward Bordentown. Literally and figuratively General Ewing had cold feet. He never made it. There was just too much ice.

21. Durham boats were developed to carry iron ore, grain, whiskey and other bulk freight between Philadelphia and northern New Jersey. They were 40 to 60 feet long, 8 feet wide and drew only 20 inches when fully loaded. They were usually poled, though some carried sails.

Colonel Cadwalader was to take his Pennsylvanians across at Bordentown where the British had a garrison, to create a diversion that would occupy them sufficiently so that they could not rush to the aid of the Hessians at Trenton. Cadwalader made a small effort in that direction but gave up when he encountered some difficulty getting his artillery across the frozen edge of the river. Fortunately the battle was over before it occurred to the sleepy Bordentown garrison that they might be needed up river.

Stephen's brigade embarked first at McKonkey's Ferry. On reaching the opposite shore they formed a chain of sentries around the landing. As the other units came ashore they formed ranks within this area. The weather became progressively worse. By the time Greene's column was across a high and bitter wind was pelting the half-frozen men with hail and sleet. The boats were nearly unmanageable in the driving storm. This caused a delay of better than three hours. It was not until 3 a.m. that they were ready to resume the march which was to have begun at midnight. There was still nine miles to go, and less than two hours of darkness. Washington pressed relentlessly on, pausing only at Birmingham [22] to let his men catch their breath and eat something. Stephen's brigade was in the van, followed by Stirling's. At Birmingham a message reached Washington from General Sullivan. His muskets were so wet that they were unfit for service.

"Tell General Sullivan that he has bayonets. Use them! I am resolved to take Trenton," came the grim reply.[23]

Two miles short of Trenton Greene's column came to a sudden halt. Rushing forward to find out what was the trouble, Washington discovered General Stephen in conversation with a young captain whom he recognized as Richard Anderson of the 5th Virginia Regiment. Without Washington's knowledge, Stephen had sent a small party under Anderson across the river the previous day, ostensibly to reconnoiter. As he drew closer Anderson blurted out that they had shot a Hessian sentry. The truth of the matter was that they had shot six sentries but had killed none of them. Somehow, Anderson thought, one dead sentry was better than six live ones. Speaking to Anderson but looking with icy fury at Stephen, Washington said:

---

22. Birmingham, N. J. now West Trenton. The present village of Birmingham is twenty miles southeast of Trenton.

23. James Wilkinson, **Memoirs of My Own Time**, Vol. I, p. 129.

"You, sir, may have ruined all my plans by having put them on their guard!"[24]

In fact Washington need not have worried. The British commander of forward units was Major General James Grant,[25] a man of monumental stupidity and utter contempt for Americans. Stirling said that he had heard him tell the Parliament in 1775 that "the Americans could not fight and that he would undertake to march from one end of the continent to the other with 5,000 men." In this view he was in perfect agreement with Colonel Johann Gottlieb Rall,[26] the Hessian commander at Trenton. Speaking no English and after only a few months in America, Colonel Rall was quite an authority on Americans in arms. They were, according to him, a bunch of dirty, half-naked ruffians fit only for skulking around picking off unwary sentinels with their "Gott verdammten Gewehre", a weapon no gentleman would use. Against a trained regiment of his countrymen they would turn tail and run.

When Rall was told about the wounded sentries he barely looked up from the card table. The American raiding parties were always doing that sort of thing. It was Christmas and what real difference did the wounding of a half-dozen sentries make? Bind up their wounds and see that they had an extra ration of grog! Rall felt completely secure in his comfortable headquarters. Besides he was quite drunk. A few hours later they carried him off to bed.

It was 8 o'clock on the 26th when Hessian sentries spotted the first of Stephen's men emerging from the woods a half mile away. After one ineffective volley, they dropped back to the second line of pickets. The advancing Virginians received another harmless volley but they were advancing so fast that the Hessians turned tail and fled. Sullivan, meanwhile, had flushed and routed an outpost of 50 jägers[27] on the River Road. They, too, fled toward the Assumpink Bridge. Greene's column continued so that Stephen's and Roche de

24. William S. Stryker, **The Battles of Trenton and Princeton**, p. 374.

25. Maj. Gen. James Grant, 1720-1806, is a strong contender for the title of least attractive of the British high command in America. He was arrogant, vindictive and utterly contemptuous of American troops.

26. Col. Johann Gottlieb Rall, ca. 1720-1776, of Hesse-Cassel, a veteran of the Seven Years' War. "Noisy, but not sullen, unaquainted with the (English) language and a drunkard", according to one English officer.

27. Jägers (jaegers), "huntsmen", a troop of light infantry originally formed by Frederick the Great from foresters and game-keepers. French "Chasseurs" are a similar corps.

Fermoy's brigades were in position to attack from the northeast and cut the escape roads to Princeton. Mercer's filed off to the right to attack from the west. That left Stirling's Virginians, including those from Fauquier, on a rise north of town where their artillery could rake the two main streets, King and Queen Streets, [28] extending southward to the river.

Locked in alcoholic slumber, Rall was aroused by his aide with difficulty. "Was ist los?" he mumbled sleepily. "Amerikaner!" the aid shouted, they seemed to be everywhere. Rall tried to recollect his addled wits. "Order the men to battle stations," he offered tentatively. "It is too late, sir, the outposts are overwhelmed. They have artillery!" A sudden burst of cannon fire, too close for comfort, rattled the windows on King Street and emptied it of hapless redcoats.

"Gott in Himmel," muttered Rall, to no one in particular.

At the head of King Street Stirling's Virginia battalions, Delaware regulars and a Pennsylvania rifle regiment had covered the artillery being wheeled into place. Soon they were enfilading both of Trenton's main streets with grape and canister shot. The Hessians were trying to form ranks in the streets when the artillery forced them to scatter. Merciless fire between the houses on King Street came from Mercer's brigade to the west. As the Hessians tried to unlimber their own artillery, Rall thought of the two guns flanking, ornamentally, the door to his headquarters. Much good they would do him now! Weedon's men, charging down King Street, drove the Hessians from their guns with a brilliant display of marksmanship.

Captain John Chilton at the head of his Fauquier companies paused for breath where King crossed Second Street. Half-fearfully he looked about him, but his men all seemed to be there, so far undamaged. Lieutenant John Blackwell had outrun him minutes before and he suddenly remembered that John was much younger and could run faster. Dicky Beale's boyish face flashed by him, looking for all the world like a young foxhound just before the kill. He was glad to see that Mose Allen, his platoon sergeant, too was breathless. He was his own age and wheezed like a horse with the heaves. Will Bragg [29] was coming along stealthily, like a hunter

---

28. King and Queen Streets, now Warren and Greene Streets.

29. William Bragg, 1755-1834, enlisted in Chilton's company by Joseph Blackwell 1776. Served until 29 July 1777 when discharged because of an injury. Died in Georgia.

stalking his prey. Isaac Barr,[30] one of Ashby's men, was just standing there, his head bent as though in silent prayer. Looking more closely, Chilton realized that he was simply admiring his feet, on which, miraculously, were a pair of brand new shoes. Chilton smiled ruefully. In theory he disapproved of looting, but at least he would not have to feel sorry for Isaac Barr for a while.

Most of the Hessians seemed to be fleeing to the fields east of the town, probably hoping to find the bridge over Assumpink Creek unguarded. Sullivan must have realized that Ewing had failed his mission because he sent St. Clair forward post haste to close that escape route. This St. Clair succeeded in doing after only a few had crossed. The Hessians could only probe to the northeast. There they ran head on into Stephen's brigade. Now almost completely surrounded and hopelessly out-gunned, they could only ground their arms. Chilton and his men arrived at the end of Second Street to hear shouts of delight from the patriot army. Since 8 o'clock that morning, it seemed that he had lived a lifetime. In fact it was only quarter of ten.

As the Hessian artillery had never really participated in the action, casualties in the 3rd Virginia Regiment were light. The battle had, for the most part, been fought in fog, smoke and driving snow and sleet. There had been little musket fire, only artillery, bayonet and sword. Unable to form ranks, the Hessians had been at a disadvantage from the beginning. They lost 106 men, killed and wounded.[31] Among them lay Colonel Johann Gottlieb Rall, mortally wounded. "Country clowns", he had called the Americans. It had not been an apt phrase, considered in retrospect.

The 3rd Virginia was not, however, completely unscathed. Captain William Washington and his Lieutenant, James Monroe, had both been wounded while leading the capture of the cannon in King Street. On a slight rise east of town, General Washington sat on his horse peering, through the snow that swirled around him, at the dim forms in the field below. A young officer appeared at his side:

"Sir," he shouted, "they have struck."

"Struck?"

"Yes. Their colours are down."

Here Donizetti would have Washington break into a basso

---

30. Isaac Barr, 1751-post 1821, enlisted in Ashby's company 1776-1778. Transferred to Capt. Pike's cavalry spring 1778. Died in North Carolina.

31. Christopher Ward, **War of the Revolution**, Vol. I, p. 302.

aria. Instead Washington wiped his field glasses and stared. With characteristic brevity that concealed his deep emotion, he said, "So they are." [32]

He spurred his horse down Queen Street to the Assumpink Bridge. Sullivan told him that 200 to 300 Hessians had escaped down the Bordentown Road before he had reached the bridge. He then knew that Ewing's mission had failed and suspected that Cadwalader's had as well. Surely he would have received news by this time had it been otherwise. His men were exhausted and the storm showed no signs of abating. Reluctantly he concluded that he must abandon his half-formed plan to push on to Princeton. The storm would soon make re-crossing the Delaware impossible. Then he would be forced to face Cornwallis with half an army. Withdrawal was his only course.

The return was even more arduous than the advance. Three men are said to have frozen to death in the open boats. Some did not reach their camp until noon the next day. Weedon's brigade was fortunate. In honour of their gallant charge down King Street they were entrusted with the prisoners, 900 odd, who must be seen to first.[33] They were in their "old quarters" by nightfall, bone tired but strangely elated. The next morning the ebullient Colonel Weedon was writing to John Page. He had a miserable cold and was unfit for duty but it did not dampen his spirits.[34]

> I can now sit down with some satisfaction to write my Country men, having spent my Xmas this far with much more enjoyment than I ever did one, - and the frolick not yet over as another Expedition into the Jerseys is this night set out in fact.

He describes the battle briefly, in which "The noble Example set by our General made all other difficulties & hardships vanish." The losses were small and he was "honoured with his Excellencies Orders to take charge of the prisoners." In conclusion he writes:

32. James Thomas Flexner, **George Washington**, Vol. II, p. 177.

33. Ward, op.cit., vol. I, p. 302. Ward gives 918 prisoners including 32 officers, 92 NCOs, 29 odd bodies like musicians, etc. 25 servants and 740 rank and file. Estimates of those who escaped range from 300 to 500.

34. Letter, Weedon to Page, dated 29 Dec. 1776, from New Town. Weedon Collection, Chicago Historical Society.

The behavior of our people in general far exceeded anything I ever saw. It's worth remarking that not an officer or private was known that day to turn his back. Should our present Expedition prove equally successful, we shall have these Robbers that have so long lived upon the fat of the New Jersey Farms once more over the Hudsons river ... (I) conclude in wishing you the Compliments of the Season.

I am Dr Sir,
Your most Ob^t Servt
G. Weedon

As usual, Weedon did not tell the full story. Perhaps, at the time, he did not know it. He was ill but he may not have realized that he was far from being alone; fatigue and exposure had decimated his ranks. On the morning of the 30th of December more than a thousand more of Washington's men reported sick. The 3rd Virginia Regiment was so hard hit that Washington thought it best to prolong their "honour" and allow them to continue to Philadelphia with the Hessian prisoners, some of whom could perform useful service as stretcher-bearers. Chilton's and Ashby's companies were especially affected. Joseph Blackwell was gravely ill, as were two of his N.C.O.s and an alarming number of the rank and file. Ashby's company, devoid of officers, was even worse off. Chilton was torn between the desire to accompany his sick to Philadelphia, which he could have done, and the pressing duty to stay with those of his men fit for duty and about to embark on another dangerous mission. In the absence of any field officers (Marshall was needed to command the detachment and prisoners en route to Philadelphia) the 3rd Regiment was placed under the command of Colonel Charles Scott of the 5th Virginia Regiment, a man whom Chilton both respected and admired. This decided the issue. He would stay, counting on Isham Keith to take care of his sick in Philadelphia. He was unaware that Keith, not fully recovered at Trenton, was again ill as a result of the march to Philadelphia.

In Philadelphia those of the 3rd Virginia Regiment who were still able to walk made a brave show. The prisoners were marched through the streets to boost American morale. There were enough of them for a single file on each side, "mostly in light summer dress and some without shoes, but stepping light and cheerful", according to Lord Stirling. They enjoyed it very much and, afterward, it was somewhat difficult to persuade them to rejoin the army.

It is not surprising that they were hesitant. The terrible attrition that Washington had so dreaded was beginning. The losses from illness had been appalling but now the New England troops whose enlistments were expiring were beginning to melt away. It was not unrealistic for the Virginians to foresee a day when the entire war for independence might land squarely on their collective shoulders. What then? The Virginians were brave. They had proved steadfast, they had shown that they could fight, but they were not insane. They were not ready to take on the entire British army.

The most serious loss was the Massachusetts regulars, including especially Glover's Marblehead fishermen whose skills were unmatched in any other unit and could not be replaced. They alone could cope with the angry Delaware in those impossible boats. Washington implored them to stay just six weeks to take advantage of an opportunity that might never again present itself. They refused. He even tried bribery. He offered a totally unauthorized bounty of $10 to each man to whet the edge of their patriotism. The New Englanders pragmatically weighed the bounty against the warmth, food and affection that awaited them at home and decided that it was not enough.

The Virginians were not so generous. They taunted them with cowardice and drew a graphic picture of a day to come when victorious Virginia would bestow upon them an unearned liberty, although they had departed when most needed. That thought began to rankle, for they were not cowards and had fought long and hard for the cause of independence. Shamed by the Virginians with whom they were in endless rivalry, unwilling to accept blame for the defeat of American arms and with their Yankee greed a little stirred by the thought of ten lovely dollars, the Massachusetts men agreed to stay until the 15th of February. About half of the rest followed suit. Asked by an officer if these men should be enrolled, Washington replied with relief, "No! Men who will volunteer in such a case as this need no enrollment to keep them to their duty." He was soon further encouraged by news that Brigadier General Thomas Mifflin [35] of Philadelphia had managed to raise an additional 500 Pennsylvania militia and was on his way.

35. Brig. Gen. Thomas Mifflin, 1744-1800, born in Philadelphia, graduated from the College of Philadelphia (Univ. of Penna.) in 1760. He was handsome, elegant and popular, an excellent recruiting officer and a promising commander. Had he been killed at Princeton his reputation would have placed him among the most honored of patriots.

In fact Washington had no choice but another Delaware crossing. Cadwalader was dismayed that Washington had made a successful crossing on the 25th, whereas he had not. He tried again on the 27th believing that Washington's troops were still at Trenton, and took Bordentown. Shamed by successful crossings both east and west of him, General Ewing, too, eventually got his militia on the other side of the Delaware. Washington had, therefore, 2,500 men east of Assumpink Creek, on the Jersey shore, who could be annihilated by a British attack. A little later he learned that Mifflin had also crossed.

The "Expedition" referred to in Weedon's letter was, therefore, another crossing of the treacherous river. The ice was now so thick that it was extremely difficult to push the boats through, but still too thin to support the weight of a foot soldier. Nevertheless they managed somehow. After occupying abandoned Trenton on the 31st, Washington was confronted with the news that General Grant and Lord Cornwallis were at Princeton with 8,000 men and a large train of artillery. Against such a force Washington was helpless. When all his reinforcements had reached him, he would have, at most, 5,000 men, mostly untrained recruits, and 40 pieces of artillery. [36]

The most that he could hope for was a successful delaying action until he could extricate his army and, if all went well, cut behind the British army and make a dash for the Jersey highlands. To carry out the delaying action, he sent forward a strong force under Brigadier General Roche de Fermoy, including Edward Hand's [37] Pennsylvanians, Haussegger's "German" Regiment and Scott's 5th Virginia Regiment with the remainder of the 3rd Regiment. In one of the most curious actions of the war, Roche de Fermoy inexplicably deserted his men. Promptly the tough, dead-eyed Irish-American rifleman, Edward Hand, assumed command. Under him the force executed a masterly series of delaying feints and withdrawals that left Cornwallis and his men so tired (and over-confident) that, after reaching Trenton on the evening of January 2nd, they postponed attacking the "old fox" until the following day. [38]

36. John Robert Seller, **The Virginia Continental Line, 1775-1780**, p.201.

37. Col. Edward Hand, 1744-1802, born in Ireland, came to Philadelphia in 1767 as surgeon's mate with the 18th Royal Irish Regt. He was practicing medicine in Philadelphia just before the Revolution.

38. Cornwallis reached Trenton at 4:00 p.m. Some of his officers urged an immediate attack but Cornwallis is reputed to have said, "We have the old fox safe now. We will bag him in the morning."

TRENTON AND PRINCETON

At this point the "old fox" was under no illusion that the morrow would be just another day that would take care of itself. He was setting in motion a plan to lead his army back of the enemy pickets and strike Princeton and New Brunswick before the British could recover. Campfires were piled high and a large pick and shovel detail set to dig entrenchments and make enough racket in doing so to cover the noise of moving wagons and artillery. The success of the plan depended on secrecy. Orders were given in whispers, wheels were bound in rags to muffle the sound. The night was bitter cold, enough to congeal the mud that might have slowed the march, but clear. Midnight found the baggage train on the way to Burlington,[39] out of the way and safe from capture by the British. An hour later the main procession filed off toward the northeast, with Mercer's brigade in the van.

At 3 a.m. the column crossed Stony Brook. Two miles ahead lay the little college town of Princeton, wrapped in slumber. Back in Trenton, Cornwallis slept, blissfully oblivious to the fact that the fox had once more escaped his hounds. On the Princeton-Trenton Road at Maidenhead (now Lawrence) General Alexander Leslie's[40] brigade of about 1,200 men was unaware that most of the American army had passed within an hour's march.

At 4 o'clock Captain John Chilton of the 3rd Virginia Regiment, temporarily under the command of Colonel Charles Scott, reached a decision. He would start a new diary. He began impressively:

"1777 January 3 at 4 in the Morn^g"

There for the moment, he ended. There was a burst of gunfire. Contact was made with the enemy. The diary would have to wait.

Princeton had been left with about 1,200 British troops under Lieutenant Colonel Charles Mawhood.[41] At dawn Mawhood left

---

39. Burlington, N. J. a town on the Delaware River about ten miles below Bordentown. Presumably Washington expected to ferry his baggage to the Pennsylvania side if necessary.

40. Brig. Gen. Alexander Leslie, ca. 1740-1794. An experienced but singularly inept officer of whom little has been written in spite of the high rank he later attained.

41. Lieut. Col. Charles Mawhood, d. 1780. His long, undistinguished military career reached its climax when he led his entire regiment against two elderly Tories and 20 militiamen at Handcock's Bridge, N. J. "The affair", says Lossing, "was unmitigated murder."

Princeton with a large body of men to join Leslie at Maidenhead and the move on to Trenton to join in the attack. The last thing Mawhood expected to encounter while crossing Stony Brook Bridge was the entire American army. He thought the men he saw were Hessians or, possibly, Americans retreating from defeat at Trenton. The men he saw shortly before 8 o'clock were 350 of Mercer's, ordered to seize and destroy the bridge. As Mawhood withdrew to defensive positions, Mercer pressed forward with his little band, unaware of the size of Mawhood's force.

Washington, at the time, was on the "Back" or Quaker Road from Trenton with his army under the command of General Sullivan strung out along the road, from the Quaker Meeting House to the outskirts of Princeton. Taking the troops nearest him, Washington rushed to Mercer's rescue. Cadwalader's "Associators" were closest and rashly advanced to within 150 feet of the enemy line. They were immediately repulsed. Washington arrived on the scene as Cadwalader was trying to rally his men and dashed bravely to the foreground of the battle, shouting for others to follow. None did. For a moment it seemed that Washington must be killed.[42] Just then Reade's 1st Virginia Regiment came up with Hitchcock's New England Continentals and Hand's riflemen. Washington led them against the enemy formation. At 30 yards he reined his horse and gave the order to fire. After returning one volley the British line broke and fled in all directions.

Meanwhile Sullivan, at the head of the column on the "Back Road", pressed on to Princeton. The British guard, left by Mawhood to look after supplies, took refuge in Princeton's only sturdy building, Nassau Hall. One round from Colonel Alexander Hamilton's [43] cannon brought all 194 of them tumbling out into the hands of the waiting Americans.

Hearing of the fight at Princeton, Cornwallis rushed reinforcements up from Trenton. The last Americans were leaving the town as the first enemy troops entered from the south. Though the

---

42. George Washington Parke Custis, **Recollections of the Life and Character of Washington.** Custis wrote, "Colonel (John) Fitzgerald, celebrated as one of the finest horsemen in the American army, now dashed his rowels into his charger's flanks and, heedless of the dead and dying on his way, flew to the side of the chief exclaiming, "Thank God! your Excellency is safe!"

43. Col. Alexander Hamilton, 1757-1804. Illegitimate son of James Hamilton and Rachel Faucette, born on St. Croix, B. W. I. He was sent to King's College (Columbia Univ.) in 1773. He was in command of his own volunteer company of New York artillery at Princeton.

opportunity was tempting, Washington realized that his tired men could not then move on the British supply depot at Brunswick.[44] Regretfully he turned his army toward Somerset Courthouse (now Millstone, N. J.) where they made camp about 8 p.m.

The events of the 3rd of January, 1777, had blurred slightly in John Chilton's mind as he took up his pen to continue where he had been so rudely interrupted. Reading further we find, in the past tense:

> The whole Army Marched from Trenton to Princeton engaged a party of the enemy commanded by Major Leslie, defeated them. Leslie was Slain in this battle with other of his officers, as we were obliged to retreat at the beginning of the Battle. The much lamented Genl Mercer had his horse shot under him as he staid too much behind to conduct our retreat and was inhumanly murdered with Bayonets, &c. Maj^r. Fleming [45] was killed in the engagement - Lieu^t. Yates had got a slight wound in the thigh which thrust him into the hands of the enemy who immediately butchered him with the greatest Barbarity. We lost 12 or 14 in this engagement, 7 or 8 wounded slightly. The enemy had 30 or 40 killed and about as many more wounded. We took about 300 prisoners, and should have had it in our power to take many more but, as we had stolen our march from Trenton, expected Genl Grant on our backs from that place with 5 or 6,000 men. Our whole force did not amount to 2500, Pennsylvania Militia included, therefore were obliged to stop pursuit & gather our Men and march with expedition towards the Mountains. (We) got to Somerset Courthouse that night, from Trenton 26 miles. Next morning early marched; got to a small Town called Pluckimin where we got plenty of Beef, Pork &c. which we had been starving for a day or two, not having time to draw and dress Victuals. We staid here a day to refresh, about 14 miles from Somerset Courthouse to this place, from Pluckamin Marched to Morris Town where the 3rd Virg^a. Reg^t. were stationed 4 or 5 days on side of a Mountain without Tents. Ground covered with snow.

44. Washington was to learn that the British had a war chest of £70,000 at Brunswick, enough to have financed him for quite a while.

45. Captain (not Major) John Fleming of the 1st Virginia Regiment.

Such was a soldier's story, not accurate, for he could not be everywhere, but as he saw it, with rumors as he heard them. British General Alexander Leslie lived to fight another day. He was not even at Princeton. General Hugh Mercer was savagely bayonetted but not killed. Washington had him carried to the home of two sisters of the Society of Friends, where he seemed to revive and it was thought for a time that he might pull through. He died, however, on January 12th.

Chilton may have witnessed part of the agony of poor 2nd Lieutenant Bartholomew Yates of the 1st Virginia Regiment. After a slight wound by a musket ball, a British soldier, stopping near him, calmly loaded his musket and shot him through the chest. He then stabbed him thirteen times with a bayonet, "the poor youth all the while crying for mercy." Later a British soldier detected a sign of life in the young man, clubbed him on the side of the head. Even so, Yates lingered a week before he died.

The army reached Morristown on the 6th of January, well ahead of its baggage train, hence the days spent on a windswept hillside without tents. They were lucky to be alive at all.

Weedon, convalescing in Philadelphia, sent John Page a copy of the **Evening Post** with an account of the battle at Princeton. [46] His own story, based on hearsay, is often inaccurate. He fears that the Virginians have suffered heavy losses in men and officers. "Thank God," he writes, "they behaved like men fighting for their just rights and previleges." Yet, despite the optimism shown earlier in the letter, he cautions, "Don't be too much elated with good News; see the infernal tribe that's coming against us next Campaign. Lose not a moment in being prepared for them! Numbers we do not dread, support us, you have the means in your hands and let not slip the Golden Opportunity of establishing your Independence and bidding defiance to British oppression!"

Those of the 3rd Virginia Regiment who faced British muskets at Trenton and Princeton were living dangerously but the odds for their survival were better than for those who braved the horrors of Philadelphia hospitals. Such facilities were, of course, crammed beyond capacity and many sick soldiers lay in private rooming houses without care or medicine except such as could be provided by their companions, many of whom were equally ill. In one such, on the night of January 1st, Nathaniel Ashby, his eyes hollow with loss of sleep, his mouth twisted with suppressed sorrow, sat by the cot on which lay Johnny McLain. The lad who, in July, had feared

---

46. Letter, Weedon to Page, Philadelphia, 6 Jan. 1777. Weedon Papers, Chicago Historical Society.

TRENTON AND PRINCETON   153

"the momps", was now dying of pneumonia caught while crossing the Jersey flats in freezing rain and driving wind. Soon it would be Ashby's painful duty to write, as he had before and would again, a certificate. This one read: [47]

> This is to certify that John McLain of Capt Ashby's Company in the 3rd Virga. Regt. died at Mrs Lefevers near Carpinder Hall in Philadelphia Jany 1st 1777
>
> Nathl Ashby
> Saml Waddy

The Widow Lefevre's commodious house near Carpenter's Hall was filled with soldiers from cellar to attic but the lady was no Florence Nightingale. She gave them little or no attention and charged every farthing that the traffic would bear.

While the soldiers were dying Dr. William Shippen [48] of one of Philadelphia's most influential families was conducting a full scale war against Dr. John Morgan, [49] Director-General of Hospitals. He contrived to bring about Dr. Morgan's removal, without explanation, on the 9th of January. For three months, until Shippen could manage to get his appointment, the hospitals were without any direction at all. In vain men like Joseph Blackwell and Isham Keith struggled to get medical care for their men. By the time they were able to rejoin their regiment at Morristown in the middle of January at least eighteen men were either dead or mortally ill and they could give John Chilton no precise account of their names or condition. Chilton was frantic with worry. On the 11th of February he wrote to his brother, Charles, in Virginia:

> When in the middle of December I brought all my men into Pennsylvania it was then the most healthy Comp^y. in the Reg^t. The weather was extremely cold and duty hard when we encamped at _____ 's Mount, the men very bare

47. See footnote no. 30, Chapter IV. Lt. William Nelson of Ashby's company had died in December, probably of smallpox.

48. Dr. William Shippen, 1736-1808, grandson of Edward Shippen, wealthy Philadelphia merchant. He married, ca. 1760, Alice, daughter of Thomas Lee of "Stratford," and sister of Richard Henry Lee.

49. Dr. John Morgan, 1735-1789, graduated with the first class of the College of Philadelphia (Univ. of Penna.) in 1757. Founder of the medical school at the Univ. of Penna.

of clothes and to a man we all had a surfeit but it wasn't Tom Ransdell's sort. [50]

(What sort of surfeit Thomas Ransdell, his cousin, had, is never explained.) He continues:

> ... Upon application I would not refuse them leave to get clear of it, and advised them to go out into the country to good Farmer's houses and anoint (sic) for it. But by some strange infatuation, tho' contrary to my orders as well as advice, they would immediately push for Philadelphia where Death in every kind of disorder lay in ambush for them; first the Small-pox, Gaol fever,[51] yellow & spotted fever, Jaundice and several other ailments, and this I told them and warned them of. When I heard of their being sick and some dying who had gone before, and sent for those who were well enough to come up, either they never got my orders or did not chuse to leave a place that fate seemed to have sent them to...John Blackwell is being sent home to recruit. Joe and Isham Keith sick, who were not able to join till the middle of Jany The troubles of the whole Comp^y. devolved on me, as well as that of Capt. Ashby's—and as if that had not been enough, (we) marched up to this place where every Officer but one went off.
> Col^o. Weedon was appointed Adjut. Genl., so that I had the trouble and care of the Reg^t. which tho' small yet is equally troublesome in many respects with the whole. The Paymaster not making regular payments distresses me to for, tho' I had money for my own Men and to spare, (of those with me), yet I find it very insufficient for all, and yet they look up to me for Cash on every exigency; and indeed some of their Capt^s. have wrote to me to furnish their Men with money and they at the same time are out at some Town living in Luxury or capering away to Virg^a. while I many times scarcely know how I am to pay for my next shirts being washed. (And I can't see good Soldiers want.)

50. Letter, John Chilton to Charles Chilton, Morristown, 11 Feb. 1777. Keith of Woodbourne Papers, Virginia Historical Society.

51. Usually identified with typhus. However, typhoid fever was epidemic in Philadelphia in 1776-77 and doctors did not distinguish between the two diseases.

> This to me has been a dreadful Campaign. I pray God I may never experience the like. The loss of my men gives me the greatest uneasiness; if I could have been with them in order to have seen them well used I could bear it with greater resignation, but I know they must have suffered many wants, poor young fellows! those that faced death...be snatched from me on the brink...I sometimes blame myself for not going to them for I had leave. But what could I do? The poor Lads who had shared every danger with me begged I would not leave them in the very face of the Enemy. The soldiers of other Companies also chose I should stay if their own went. My own pride, and let me say reason, also told me it was not a time to take pleasure. So I left to those who went to take of my sick. I hope they have done their best. I have not heard. I am told I have lost 18 men. I forbear to mention them because I am not sure who they are. So soon as I can get time I will inquire and get their clothes, Cash, &c. and transmit them to their Sorrowful Friends.

One cannot help feeling compassion for this conscientious, harassed and deeply troubled man. From Captain John Ashby, recruiting in Virginia, the news was not encouraging. The competition offered by officers recruiting for new regiments was fierce. Everyone wanted to serve with Morgan or Edward Stevens of Culpeper. Even Ashby's promising young cadet, Joseph Blackwell of Elk Run, had heard the pied piper. He was transferring to Stevens' 10th Virginia Regiment to a lieutenancy under his older brother Thomas. Who could blame him? There were no promotions to be had in the old line regiments.

The "strange infatuation" that prodded his men to take appalling risks to satisfy their natural desires is no mystery to John Chilton, but he need not spell it out for his brother and he knew that his letters would be circulated in his family. Venereal disease was almost inescapable in Philadelphia if one patronized the many "maisons de joie" which flourished in spite of the Quaker influence.

The post of Adjutant General [52] was one that George Weedon neither sought nor relished. Convalescing in Philadelphia, he received orders on January 9th to leave for Virginia on a recruiting

---

52. The post of Adjutant was important but, as his chief function was to transmit orders of the commanding officer, it required constant attention and left no room for initiative.

mission. As soon as he was well enough to travel he went to Morristown to check on his command before going home. Here he suddenly found himself installed as temporary adjutant-general in place of Colonel Joseph Reed, who had resigned on the 22nd. An effort was made to get General Arthur St. Clair to take the tedious and thankless job, but St. Clair set up such a howl of protest that he was sent to relieve General Horatio Gates on Lake Champlain on February 19th. Weedon was conned into accepting a permanent appointment as adjutant-general by a promotion to Brigadier and promises that he would be given another field command as soon as a replacement could be found. He detested staff work and wanted very much to distinguish himself in the field. In April, impatient that no action to replace him had been taken, though a new campaign was about to start, Weedon asked for a furlough to return to Virginia.[53] Washington was startled. "Surely you meant this by way of Joke or trial only, can you possibly conceive that my consent would be obtained for such an absence as this?" he wrote, "No Sir, it is neither to be done nor expected." He gave Weedon leave until May 10th.

After Weedon's reassignment there were no field officers of the 3rd Virginia Regiment still at Morristown. Marshall was already in Virginia and William Taliaferro probably was also, though no record has been found. Captains senior to John Chilton were also conspicuously absent. John Ashby was in Virginia and another was sick in Philadelphia. The command of the entire regiment was therefore Chilton's. It was small but, as Chilton said, "troublesome." The men begged for leave and ignored Chilton's good advice. There were, of course, few loose women in "good farmer's houses" and fresh eggs and bacon were no adequate substitute. In Philadelphia they were subject to all the dangers Chilton mentions and a few more. Men with minor ailments wound up in hospitals with major complaints, contracted from the other patients. Furthermore many went into hospitals fully clothed and emerged nearly naked, their clothes having been stolen by those who got out before they did. The townspeople, despite their parade, were of little assistance.

---

53. Washington to Weedon, 8 March 1777, Fitzpatrick, ed., **Writings of Washington**, Vol. VIII, pp. 264-65, 322-23.

The situation in Philadelphia was probably best described by Dr. David Griffith,[54] chaplain of the 3rd Virginia Regiment. Dr. Griffith's background gave him a broad field of experience on which to base his conclusions and we would do well to learn more about him. He was not a Virginian but was, in fact, a New Yorker, born in 1742 of a prosperous merchant family. He obtained a medical degree in London and set up a practice in New York in 1763. His strong leaning toward the ministry, however, soon prompted his return to London, where he was ordained by Bishop Terrick on the 19th of August, 1770. On his return to America he served briefly as a missionary in New Jersey before becoming rector of Shelburne Parish in Loudoun County in 1771.

A tall, heavy set man of great dignity, he would seem to have been an unlikely prospect as an ardent revolutionist, but, like the Reverend James Thomson of Leeds Parish in Fauquier, he was among the first to speak out boldly against the British government. He was, in fact, a step ahead of Thomson because he was among the first to volunteer his services as chaplain and surgeon to a Virginia Regiment. The first of his long series of illuminating letters to Leven Powell of Loudoun County was written from a camp called Springfield, near Williamsburg, on the 16th of June, 1776. He marched north with his regiment in August, having tried to get a Curate to take care of the parish in his absence. He offered to give up all his salary and prerequisites, but a qualified man was difficult to find.

He wrote Leven Powell on the 8th of December, having left his regiment at Princeton in order to see that the sick were hospitalized and that the well returned to the army. In Philadelphia he found that "Everything...wears the face of dispondency." He was horrified by the condition of the hospitals and wrote:

> A Strange Consternation seems to have seized every body in this Country; a Universal dissatisfaction prevails, & every body is furnished with an Excuse for declining the Public Service. Publick Virtue seems to be quite extinct; the most excessive extortion prevails among the Inhabitants, and the greatest Peculation & Avarice among the Servants of the Publick.

54. The Reverend David Griffith, M. D., 1742-1789. His letters to Leven Powell are included in **A Biographical Sketch of Col. Leven Powell**, ed. by Robert C. Powell, M. D., 1877. In 1786 Dr. Griffith was chosen as the first Episcopal Bishop of Virginia, but funds could not be found to send him to England for consecration. He was married but mentions no children in his letters.

Such information only added to Chilton's burden.

However there were grounds for some satisfaction. Looking eastward from his camp in the Watchung Mountains, Chilton observed:

> The Conqueror of America finds himself after all his great Conquests in possession of a string of Land inhabited by Starved Tories, of about 14 miles in Length & half in breadth, and but one way to make his escape out, this is by way of Amboy. What will the Ministerial Party say when it comes to be known in England that this is their whole possessions on the Continent? [55]

What indeed? and in addition, where would Howe find food for his garrison? Even the few troops at Washington's disposal could discourage British foraging parties in New Jersey.

Stirling's brigade, which included most of the Virginia troops, was encamped at Quibbletown, a small, oddly-named village some distance southeast of Morristown at the foot of the Watchung Range. Here, on the 23rd of January, a distant drum heralded the passage of about 500 British escorting a supply train along a back road to Amboy. General Adam Stephen was in Morristown, so Colonel Mordecai Buckner hastily assembled about 400 men to skirmish with the enemy. He hoped to take the escort guard by surprise and possibly make off with a few wagons. Lieutenant Colonel Josiah Parker,[56] who was in the van, took off with a few men to locate the British. Parker, a rash, abrasive and offensive officer in more ways than one, only succeeded in alerting the British and getting himself in trouble. When he called with anguish for reinforcements, Buckner sent him about half his troops. Unable to hold his position, even with reinforcements, Parker ordered a retreat. Looking for Buckner, whom he had not seen nor heard from since the firing began, he learned with astonishment that Buckner had fled the field. Collecting what remained of the entire detachment, Parker managed to march them off in good order. He arrived in camp in time to see Buckner ride off toward headquarters to tell his own version of the affair.

---

55. Letter, John Chilton to Maj. Martin Pickett, Hanover Township, N. J., 19 March 1777. Keith of Woodbourne Papers, Virginia Historical Society.

56. Lt. Col. Josiah Parker to Washington, 24 Jan. 1777. Miscellaneous Manuscripts, American Philosophical Society.

Buckner was only too aware that his flight had been witnessed by many and that Parker was not the sort of man to let such a matter rest. Leaving Washington an abject apology in which he hoped that his having become "as contemptable in the Eyes of the Army as it is possible," would be considered sufficient punishment, Buckner took to the hills. He had travelled fifty miles before he was apprehended by a party of light horse sent to bring him back.

As commander of the 3rd Virginia Regiment, it was Captain John Chilton's painful duty to sit on the court-martial which took place at the village of Chatham, near Morristown on February 8th. Though Buckner was a kinsman of Martin Pickett's Chilton seems not to have known him well. He wrote to his brother from Morristown:

> I should have wrote you by John Hall but was summoned to Chatham, a small town about 7 miles from this, to inquire into the conduct of Col^o. Buckner, our Countryman, who you doubtless have heard behaved in a manner unbecoming an American..(sentence illegible)..I returned. Buckner was cashiered & rendered unfit for any Military Post in the Continental army forever...There was but a single circumstance saved him from being shot. It will be to no purpose to inform you what it was unless you had heard the whole trial. [57]

The meaning of Chilton's last statement is uncertain but it might be explained by Buckner's defense. He had served with valor in the French and Indian Wars. Furthermore, some recent distressing news from his family in Virginia had caused him such anguish that it had almost unhinged his reason.

The proud reputation of the Virginia Line was somewhat damaged by this unfortunate affair. There were those who scoffed, "What, can Virginians run too?" The Virginians, who had in the past done more than their share of "scoffing", (witness their scorn of the Connecticut troops at Kip's Bay) went around with their collective tails between their legs. "Great is the scandal Virginians sustained on this unmanly conduct," Chilton wrote, and Weedon "lamented the loss of face" of the Virginia troops. John Page responded to Weedon sensibly and calmly:

> True he is a Virginian, but compare other Virginians with him and they will appear in brighter colours. It is by

---

57. Letter, John Chilton to Charles Chilton, Morristown, 11 Feb. 1777. Keith of Woodbourne Papers, Virginia Historical Society.

comparison only that we judge of men and actions, therefore a few bad men or actions make good men and actions show more conspiciously. [58]

In the Virginia Line there were many good men and actions with which to compare Buckner's regrettable lapse from grace. Two days before Buckner's court-martial, 300 Virginians under Colonel Charles Scott stood off more than 1,000 lobster backs near Amboy. The Fauquier men were not part of this engagement. They could hear the cannon fire all day, at the end of which the British retreated and were harassed by the Americans to their very lines. [59] Colonel Scott had been sick for some days and was far from well during the engagement. About ten days before he had challenged a force of the "much boasted English Grenadiers...backed by a number of Hessians" and had routed them. [60] These and other exploits of Virginia troops had, according to Chilton, "a little wiped out the stain of Buckner."

The Fauquier men were last seen encamped on a snowy hillside on the 10th of January. From this "uncomfortable place" they moved to a house owned by one Samuel Roberts about 2 miles from Morristown where they stayed until the 25th. They then moved to Morristown and were there in cramped, but reasonably warm and dry, quarters on the 11th of February, when one of their number returned from Philadelphia bringing as a souvenir of his travels an incipient case of smallpox. The 3rd Regiment officers then at Morristown, Captain Chilton, Lieutenants Alvin Mountjoy [61] and Joseph Blackwell, and Ensign Robert Peyton [62] were given treatment considered helpful at the time in warding off the

58. Page to Weedon, 5 March 1777 in: **Papers Related Chiefly to the Maryland Line during the Revolution**, ed. by Thomas Balch. (Philadelphia: Seventy-Six Society, 1857) Balch says that this letter was from Mann Page, Jr. but it is more likely that it was written by John Page.

59. Letter, John Chilton to Charles Chilton, Morristown, 11 Feb. 1777. Keith of Woodbourne Papers, Virginia Historical Society.

60. Ibid.

61. Lieut. Alvin Mountjoy came from a family originally from Bristol, England. They settled in Westmoreland County but removed to Stafford County at an early date. Mountjoy was related to Chilton through the Peirce family.

62. Robert Peyton, d: 1777, was a son of John and Seth (Harrison) Peyton of Fauquier. He had three brothers in the Revolution.

disease, including a stiff dose of castor oil. They escaped except Joseph Blackwell, who, weakened by his December illness, came down with a severe case of smallpox and very nearly lost the sight of one eye.

Washington, appalled at the toll taken by smallpox throughout the army, finally ordered that they all be inoculated. The men feared inoculation as much as the disease and, in a day of unsterilized needles and uncontrolled vaccine, they were in some measure justified. Many also believed that such wholesale tampering with God's will was a work of the Devil. Nevertheless, in late February, Chilton marched his men down to Hanover township and had them all inoculated, whether they liked it or not. As a result they "had the Small Pox very lightly generally", he wrote in his diary. From Whippany, in Hanover township, they moved to Chatham, where they waited for spring to come.

There was probably a pub in Chatham. A passer by on a cold night could have been greeted by a rousing song: [63]

> Come on, my brave fellows, a fig for your lives,
> We'll fight for our country, our children and wives.
> Determined we are to live happy and free;
> Then join, honest fellows, in a chorus with me.
>   Derry down, down, etc.
> We'll drink our own liquor, our brandy from Peaches,
> A fig for the English, they may kiss all our breeches.
> Those blood-sucking, beer-drinking puppies retreat;
> But our peach-brandy fellows can never be beat.
>   Derry down, down, etc.
> A fig for the English and Hessians to boot,
> Who are sick half the time with eating of crout.
> But bacon and greens, and Indian corn-bread,
> Make a buck-skin jump up, tho' he seem to be dead.
>   Derry down, down, etc.

---

63. **Magazine of American History** (April 1880) Vol. IV, p. 310.

Interlude
Princeton to Brandywine

Although fresh recruits began to pour into the American camp at Morristown early in the spring of 1777, Washington was still forced to fight a defensive war. Howe in New York had very little territory under his control but he had the advantage of superior mobility because the British fleet under his brother, Admiral Lord Howe, dominated the coastal waters. He could, therefore, attack any place on the Atlantic seaboard, and some distance into the estuaries, speedily and with considerable force.

There were four major plans of attack open to General Howe and he considered each in turn. First, he could march up the Hudson River Valley, make a link with Burgoyne coming down from Canada and cut the New England colonies off from the rest. The two armies could then converge on Philadelphia. The second plan was to let Burgoyne shift for himself and mount a direct attack on Philadelphia by way of the Delaware River or, by sailing up the Chesapeake Bay, attack it overland from the rear. The third plan contemplated an attack through Hampton Roads on the ports of Norfolk and Portsmouth. Having captured them, he could, by a swift thrust westward, hope to cut off the Carolinas and Georgia. He could then turn and attack Washington from the south. A fourth plan involved an attack on Charleston and a broad sweep through the southern colonies defended only by untrained militia. Here he hoped to gain substantial reinforcement from disaffected Tories who would swell his necessarily limited resources in manpower and supplies. Any of these plans might have worked if Howe had been able to settle on one and stick to it.

There was very little that Washington could do to counter the last two plans except to rely on local troops to contain the British until he could assess Howe's commitment and rush in reinforcements. It was necessary that he keep a force on the west bank of the Hudson to prevent, if possible, a link up between Howe and Burgoyne. He felt obliged to defend Philadelphia although he was in some doubt of its strategic importance. Howe, on the other hand, thinking in the European sense, tended to overrate the importance of the capital. In most European countries the fall of a capital marked the end of resistance in the entire nation.

Philadelphia, however, was the capital of only one colony. The Continental Congress could, and did, operate in its own inefficient way almost anywhere, - York, Lancaster, Baltimore, Annapolis or any of a dozen alternatives. The situation is not very different today. Only those who live in the capital of the United States consider it vital to its continued existence. An enemy might wipe it out with a single blow, only to discover that he had accomplished almost nothing. It was after Howe had taken Philadelphia that he realized that he held in his hands a hollow shell from which the kernel had somehow escaped.

Yet Washington was compelled to string out his small army along an attenuated line from Lake Champlain to the eastern shore of Maryland and Virginia, a distance of more than 500 miles. It was manifestly impossible, but Washington counted on Howe's caution and indecision to save him until he could build up his army. Fortunately Howe's caution and indecision were even more than sufficient to accomplish Washington's purpose, even though his marching and counter-marching through New Jersey and New York had little practical effect.

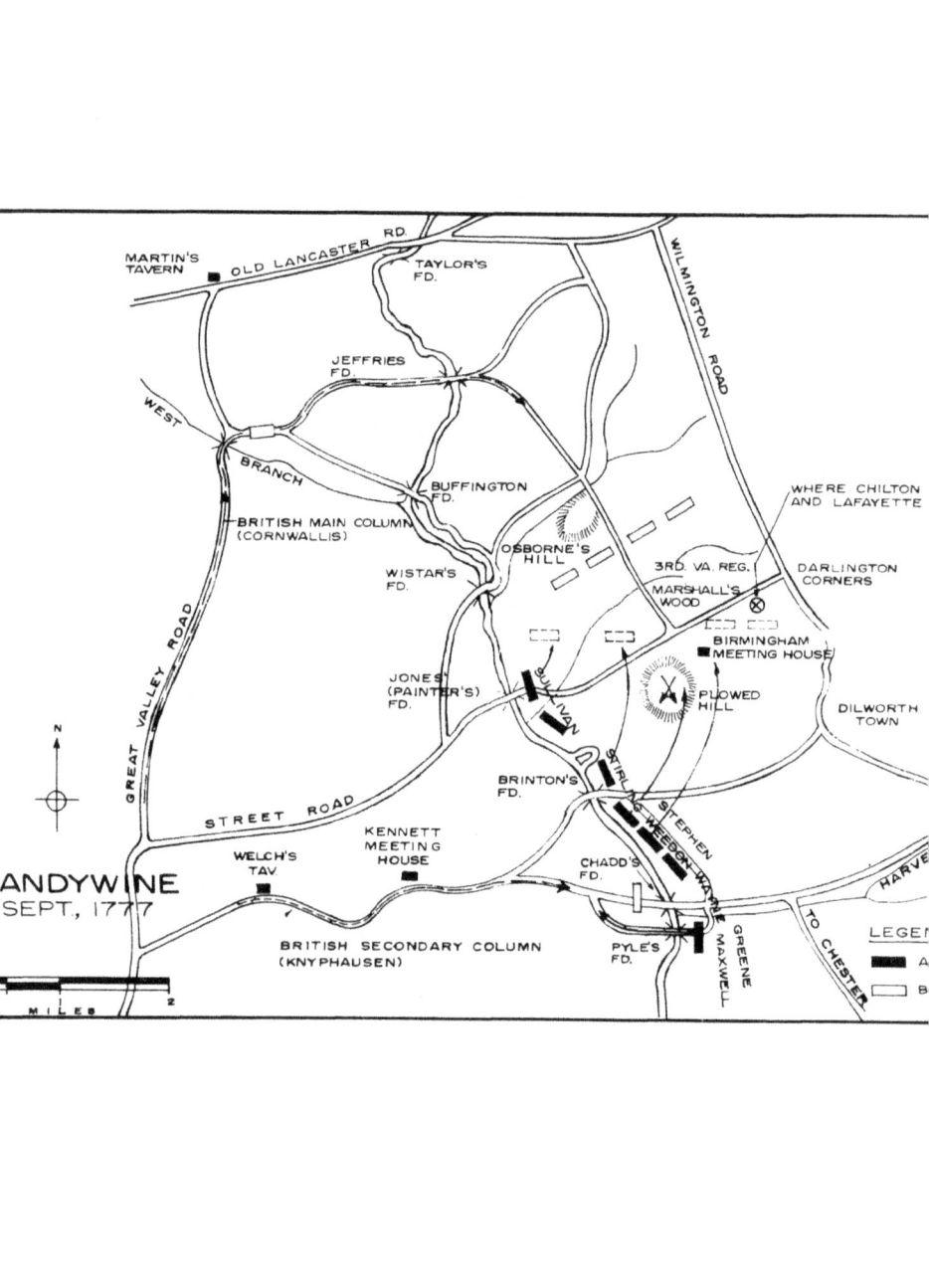

VI
Brandywine

Historians for two hundred years have been complaining about the weather in New Jersey during the winter of 1776-77. In fact it was not especially unusual. It was simply that a great number of men were forced to do, in the dead of winter, things to which they were in no way accustomed, and submit to exposure to a degree that they would not, under normal circumstances, have considered tolerable. In Fauquier County, Virginia, where men sat by their firesides and slept in their own beds, as was their wont, the winter was considered rather mild.

It was also, despite the war raging to the north of them, relatively uneventful. A few, very few, families mourned the loss of sons killed or, more often, dead of disease in Pennsylvania or New Jersey, but casualties among Fauquier men had been light so far. They had not fully realized that they could not remain so if the war was to continue. They still hoped for some miracle that would produce instant victory accompanied by the contrite withdrawal of the British from the American continent.

At Fauquier Courthouse the gentlemen justices met for the first time in 1777 on the 27th of January. William Grant presided, with Jeremiah Darnall, James Scott, John Blackwell, James Bell and Martin Pickett. John Moffett arrived late. Officially nothing much happened. Colonel William Edmonds, having become County Lieutenant in command of the militia, could no longer serve as Sheriff. The Justices felt no hesitancy in submitting the names of three of their number to the Governor for consideration as suitable appointees for the vacant post. They were Jeremiah Darnall,[1] James Scott and James Bell. Captain James Scott was still trying to raise a volunteer company to march north but was

---

1. Jeremiah Darnall was the owner of large tracts of land on Cedar Run, south of the Pignut, patented by Waugh Darnall in 1725. He was named a Justice in 1774 and was a vestryman of Hamilton Parish in 1769. He married a. 1740, Katherine Holtzclaw.

apparently willing to abandon the attempt if the Governor's nod should be in his direction. It was not. The appointment went to Jeremiah Darnall. The remainder of the minutes of the January court are of little interest, although it is amusing to note in passing another of those quaint 17th century court orders:

> It appearing to the court that James Barton has had the misfortune to lose one of his Ears, which was bit off by George Asbury ... it is ordered that the same be Certified.

If the minute books of the Fauquier Court gave no hint of unusual activity in the county it is only because military affairs were not yet subject to judicial notice. In every tavern, ordinary or public place, at every crossroads hamlet or village, recruiting officers were at work. No able-bodied man could escape them and those whose reasons for not joining the colours were somewhat less than compelling, were hard-pressed to justify their position. Attempts were being made to raise no fewer than ten companies in Fauquier County alone, the equivalent of an entire regiment. It was an impossibility, of course, and only those with the most attractive propositions could hope to meet their quotas.

In January, 1777, Washington asked General Adam Stephen to take a long look at the five Virginia regiments already in New Jersey. He found them reduced to a handful of men, and sent all officers not essential to their care in camp back to Virginia to attempt to correct their deficiencies in men and equipment. By that time the two Fauquier companies in the 3rd Virginia Regiment had already sent Captain John Ashby and Lieutenant John Blackwell of Chilton's company to recruit for them. They found the going extremely difficult. The 3rd Regiment had released far too many sick and disaffected veterans, filled with horrendous tales of the sufferings they had undergone and grievances too numerous to count. Naturally the new regiments lacking this past history seemed more attractive. Furthermore the Fauquier men wanted, if possible, to serve in a rifle brigade and neither Ashby nor Blackwell could honestly say that riflemen were wanted in theirs. In fact General Stephen had written to Francis Lightfoot Lee that "Nothing but necessity made me admit so many of them (riflemen) into the regiment." He had advised the Board of War to replace rifles with muskets and bayonets.[2]

---

2. Stephen to Francis L. Lee, 17 Oct. 1776; Stephen to the Board of War, 8 Nov. 1776 in: Force, **American Archives** (5th series) Vol. II, p. 1092; Vol. III, p. 600.

Of the original nine regiment four were still in Virginia and none of them was up to strength. Colonel Alexander Spotswood had whipped the 2nd Regiment into some sort of shape, and started it north by way of Dumfries and Leesburg about the 15th of January. Colonel William Crawford's 7th Regiment was ready to move about the same time.

The 8th Regiment under Colonel Peter Muhlenberg had not recovered from their ill-fated venture into the Carolinas under General Charles Lee in June, 1776. Although they had had little part in the fighting there, they had been victims of coastal fever and agues in such numbers that the burial squad had difficulty keeping up with its customers. As the regiment returned piecemeal to Virginia it is impossible to reckon its losses, but at least a third did not return. Many of those who did were subject to recurrent malaria and were unfit for further service. Nevertheless Congress ordered the regiment to be sent on by companies, beginning the 21st of January. As Muhlenberg had been promoted to Brigadier in command of all Virginia Continental forces,[3] his second in command, Lieutenant Colonel Abraham Bowman took what troops he could assemble in Winchester and marched north. The regiment was deficient in every respect, men, equipment and supplies, but when Bowman arrived in Morristown in mid-March he was given permanent command of the 8th Regiment and promised additional men.

The 9th Regiment under Colonel Thomas Fleming had been ordered north on the 23rd of November, 1776. Fleming had sent four companies to Dover, Delaware, on special duty in November, but the rest were still on the Eastern Shore of Maryland and Virginia until late December. They had been expected in the camp in Pennsylvania before the attack on Trenton. Robert Morris wrote Fleming on the 27th of December urging him to hurry so that he could [4] share the "glory" of defeating the British in New Jersey. Fleming reached Philadelphia on the 30th of January where his entire regiment was inoculated for smallpox. Fleming and his second-in-command immediately succumbed to the disease,

3. General Andrew Lewis had resigned when he was not promoted to Major General In February. It is interesting to note that Muhlenberg had also written to Washington urging him to convert the 8th Virginia Regiment to musketry because where soldiers were without tents and their arms continually exposed to the weather, rifles quickly became useless.

4. Robert Morris to Thomas Fleming, 27 Dec. 1776, in: Force, **American Archives** (5th series) Vol. III, p. 1439.

achieving eternal glory that he had not expected. In early March George Matthews took the regiment to Morristown and was appointed Colonel to replace Fleming.

As none of these four regiments had a contingent from Fauquier their movement north had no measurable effect on the recruiting situation there. Competition to the officers of the 3rd Regiment came from another direction. After Washington's defeat on Long Island Congress had raised Virginia's quota of authorized regiments on continental establishment from nine to fifteen. Authorization for six additional regiments passed the Virginia House of Delegates on the 2nd of November. Filling the top posts in six regiments quickly became a political squabble of major consequence. This was further complicated by the desire of highly qualified junior officers to serve under men whose proven competence might assure them of a reasonable chance to survive.

Only two of these regiments are of special interest to those interested in the men of Fauquier, the 10th and 11th Virginia Regiments. All logic indicated that command of the 10th Regiment should go to Colonel Edward Stevens of Culpeper County, whose competence and gift for leadership had been amply displayed at Great Bridge. The posts of lieutenant colonel and major in his regiment were offered to Christian Febiger and William Heth, Morgan's most gifted subordinates at Quebec. Both declined the honor, saying that "the pecularity and delicacy of their situation will (would) not admit of their immediate acceptance..." This was pure circumlocution. They just wanted to serve with Morgan.

Unquestionably the most famous military man in Virginia next to Washington, and her most authentic hero, was Daniel Morgan. When he was designated commander of the 11th Virginia Regiment the heart of every potential recruit in Fauquier beat a little faster. Certainly Morgan's 11th would be a rifle battalion, if no others were! In this elite corps every man would have opportunity for outstanding performance with a minimum of individual restraint, or so they reasoned. Congress allowed Febiger and Heth to have their way and found replacements for them in the 10th Regiment. Lewis Willis was then named Lieutenant Colonel in the 10th and George Nicholas, Major.

The field officers in these regiments did not, of course, do much recruiting in Fauquier. That was left to the young captains and lieutenants of the Fauquier companies. Both regiments had talented men in that capacity who had been hard at work on their behalf for some time. They had made substantial headway, making it doubly hard for John Ashby and John Blackwell to catch up. For the latter it was especially galling because both Thomas and William Blackwell were his relatives.

Captain Thomas Blackwell[5] of Elk Run, his first cousin, was having rather considerable success in the southern part of the county. As was true of most of those living in the Elk Marsh area, Blackwell had strong ties in Culpeper County and it was only reasonable that he would undertake to raise a Fauquier company to serve under Colonel Stevens. As mentioned before, he had as one of his lieutenants his younger brother, Joseph Blackwell, who had served since the beginning of the war. Regrettably we have not found a muster roll of Captain Thomas Blackwell's company but presumably they marched north shortly after the 12th of March and were inoculated in Philadelphia before joining the main army at Morristown. Lieutenant Colonel Willis remained behind in Culpeper County to try to fill the roster with additional recruits. On the 20th of May Washington organized the Virginia troops into two divisions, one under Major General Nathanael Greene and the other under Major General Adam Stephen, who had been promoted to that rank on the 19th of February. Muhlenberg and Weedon were to command brigades in Greene's division. The 10th Virginia Regiment was assigned to Weedon's brigade, along with the 2nd, 6th and 14th.

Though Lieutenant John Blackwell, recruiting for the 3rd Virginia Regiment found the efforts of Captain Thomas Blackwell in southern Fauquier something of a problem, they were nothing in comparison with those of another first cousin, Captain William Blackwell who was recruiting for Morgan's 11th Virginia Regiment right in his own neighborhood. William Blackwell[6] was the son of Captain Samuel and Elizabeth (Steptoe) Blackwell of "Walnut Lodge", Northumberland County. He had lived for many years in Fauquier on land inherited from his father who died in 1762. As there were two Joseph Blackwells of about the same age and rank so there were two William Blackwells. It is not therefore absolutely certain that he was not the man we have met previously at Great Bridge and historians are divided on the subject. Whether or not he was at Great Bridge he was certainly active in recruiting as early as June of 1776.

5. Thomas Blackwell, 1752-1831, was the fourth son of Col. William and Elizabeth (Crump) Blackwell. He married, 26 Sept. 1781, Judith Grant of Fauquier County. They moved to Culpeper County after the war.

6. William Blackwell, 1736-1777. The surname of his wife, Anne, is unknown. They had two sons, George, b: 1770, and William, b: 1775.

At that time the 11th Virginia Regiment had not been thought of and he apparently had in mind an independent rifle company to serve on continental establishment. We are fortunate in having several complete muster rolls made in the summer of 1777. At that time there were only 38 men and it is probable that the company had never been full. We do know, though, that Captain Blackwell had John Marshall as 1st Lieutenant, James Wright[7] as 2nd Lieutenant and Thomas Ransdell, John Chilton's cousin, as 3rd Lieutenant. The company was raised in August and September, 1776. John Marshall, who had been working on training and recruiting since his return from Williamsburg early in April, was commissioned with James Wright on the 31st of July, 1776.

When Daniel Morgan was appointed Colonel in command of the 11th Virginia Regiment on the 12th of November, 1776, William Blackwell was quick to volunteer the services of his company. The Virginia Convention considered the service of Morgan and his men so important that it was voted on the 1st of November, 1776, to award them additional pay, over and above the pay of the Continental Line. Yet, when they ordered Colonel Morgan to take his regiment north on the 3rd of February, 1777,[8] it was still so far from being full that the order was cancelled. Officers were selected for no fewer than twelve companies but most of them commanded only skeleton units. Blackwell's, designated as Company 6, the only one raised east of the Blue Ridge, was nearer completion than most.

It was soon apparent that Daniel Morgan, whatever his qualifications as a leader of a rifle company, was not at the time in any frame of mind to serve as a regimental commander. He was impatient with recruiting, bored by the details of regimental duty and unwilling to submit to the discipline necessary to effect an orderly chain of command. Furthermore it was simply impossible to recruit whole regiments of men who could meet Morgan's standards of marksmanship. As enlistments continued to lag, Morgan begged to be allowed to join Washington with the men he had, rather than wait until a reasonable facsimile of a regiment could be enrolled. Shortly after the 19th of February, Morgan was

7. James Wright was a descendant of Joseph Wright who patented land on the south side of Watery Mountain in 1727. A James Wright was a vestryman of Hamilton Parish in 1769. He married Mary Duncan, 8 Dec. 1763. His relationship to 2nd Lieutenant James Wright is not established.

8. Journal of the Virginia House of Delegates, 1 Nov. 1776 and 3 February 1777.

allowed to march north with only 180 men, most of them Blackwell's. After stopping in Philadelphia for inoculation, he reached the main army at Morristown early in April.

Several of Morgan's captains remained behind and continued their attempts to raise men in Fauquier and elsewhere, notably Charles Porterfield, who had been with him at Quebec as a non-commissioned officer, Peter Bryan Bruin,[9] also a Quebec veteran, and George Rice. Porterfield had been mentioned by General Arnold in dispatches as the first man to scale the walls of Quebec and was recommended for promotion. Most of his company came from the lower Valley but several were from Fauquier. Peter Bruin had been a lieutenant at Quebec, where he was slightly wounded. Most of his company came from the neighborhood of Ashby's Bent, where he made his home. Rice's men came from eastern Fauquier, Prince William and Stafford. None of them managed to raise an entire company but it is evident that they met with some success. Morgan's name held its magic even when its owner had left the scene.

Captain James Scott's recruiting efforts in the autumn of 1776 closely paralleled those of William Blackwell. We do not know when he or his officers were commissioned, or by what authority but, by January 1777, they were ready to march. His first lieutenant was William Kincheloe. The second lieutenant was a relative newcomer in Fauquier, having moved from Lancaster County in 1772, John Hathaway, then forty, was a tall, heavy set, darkly handsome man of some means. He had built "Hatherage", a substantial stone house about three miles northeast of Marshall. Here he lived with his wife, Sarah Lawson Timberlake, and a rather large family in 1777.

The ensign was John Hathaway's younger brother, James. He had come to Fauquier about the same time his brother had and had married Joanna Neavil, a daughter of George Neavil, who had the ordinary at Auburn. When George Neavil died in 1774 he had left his daughter and son-in-law his mill on Cedar Run, a flourishing operation that continued until 1920.

With his position, wealth and two substantial lieutenants to back him up, it is surprising that, by January 1777, Scott had no Continental Line commitment. He resolved on a bold step. He would take his company north as an independent volunteer company from Fauquier County and take his chances there. As a

---

9. Peter Bryan Bruin married 27 Feb. 1781, Elizabeth Edmonds, daughter of Capt. Elias and Elizabeth (Miller) Edmonds and niece of Col. William Edmonds, County Lieutenant. Her brother was Capt. Elias Edmonds of the Fauquier militia.

member of the House of Burgesses he had known Benjamin Harrison of "Berkeley" [10] a signer of the Declaration of Independence. Harrison was now chairman of the Board of War, a committee of the Congress whose members included, in addition to Harrison, John Adams, Edward Rutledge, Roger Sherman and James Wilson. Scott wrote directly to Harrison in Baltimore, where Congress was then meeting, proposing to bring a company to Washington's assistance under certain terms outlined in his letter. As the letter is lost, we do not know exactly what those terms were, but one of them was that they would "serve where ordered three months from the time of their march." That condition would not have suited Washington but the Board accepted with alacrity as shown by a letter from Harrison to Scott, dated in Baltimore 1 February 1777: [11]

> Sir:
> I recd. your favour by Mr. John Barker and delivered yours to the president to be laid before Congress. They readily comply'd with your request; and Mr. Barker has recd. seven hundred dollars to enable your company to march, which this board have it to command (*sic*) to desire you will do with all possible dispatch. The sooner you arrive at camp to assist our worthy general, the greater will be your merit; and it will certainly add to the pleasure Congress has already recd. from your readiness in hurrying out on this occasion. I am
>
> Your most obed^t. servt.
> Benj. Harrison, chair^n.
> of the Board of War
>
> You must go by Philadelphia to be supply^d. with arms.
>
> B. H.
>
> Capt. James Scott
> Fauq^r. county, Virginia.

While Harrison became somewhat entangled in his sentence structure, his meaning was clear enough for Scott to get his

---

10. Benjamin Harrison of "Berkeley", 1726?-1791, the fifth of that name in direct line, was of the James River Harrisons. No known relationship exists between this family and the Harrisons of the Northern Neck.

11. Rejected Claims, Box 16, Folder 23, James Scott, 1835 (Virginia State Library, Archives Division)

company on the move. A private in his company, James Jones, remembered that at the time of his enlistment at Fauquier Courthouse, Scott's brother-in-law, Cuthbert Harrison,[12] was trying to sign up two Irishmen but he does not say whether they were for Scott's company or for one Harrison was trying to raise on his own. According to Christian Riley, Captain Scott's faithful housekeeper, Cuthbert Harrison was killed in the Revolution. He remains a rather shadowy figure and his recruiting efforts in Fauquier are nebulous. He certainly died between 7 February 1779, and 2 July 1780, but where or why is unknown.

James Jones says that they marched through Leesburg, crossing the Potomac at Noland's Ferry. They then proceeded through Frederick, Maryland and "McCollestown" (probably McSherrystown), Pennsylvania, toward York. On that road Jones was taken sick and the company had to go on without him. They continued on to Philadelphia, where they picked up their arms and were inoculated against smallpox, and arrived at Stirling's headquarters at Quibbletown, New Jersey, about the first of March.

Another officer who was making strenuous effort to raise one or more companies in Fauquier was Lieutenant Colonel Leven Powell of Loudoun County. Powell had been active since the beginning of the war in Virginia and was disappointed when he was not selected for a post as a field officer in one of the Virginia Continental Regiments. As a major of militia he had kept in close touch with the progress of the Virginia regiments in the north through his close friend Dr. David Griffith and was well aware of the latter's deep concern, often despair, for the American cause. As late as the 8th of December, 1776, Griffith had written, "I think that nothing but the most signal interposition of Providence can save our country from destruction." Yet on the 27th, after Trenton, Griffith had written "Things begin to wear a better aspect, Major, than when I wrote you last," and, in mid January, he had a brief note from Griffith indicating that things wore a better aspect for Major Leven Powell. It read in part:[13]

---

12. Cuthbert Harrison, 1747-1779-80, was the second son of Col. Cuthbert and Frances Osborne (Barnes) Harrison of "Fairview", Prince William County. He was unmarried and left his estate to his five sisters.

13. Dr. David Griffith to Maj. Leven Powell, 14 Jan. 1777, in: Robert C. Powell, **A Biographical Sketch of Col. Leven Powell,** ... , p. 74.

Philadelphia, 14 Jany, 1777.

Dear Col: For so it seems I am to call you now. Grayson has a Regiment and you are appointed his second. I congratulate you on the occasion, as I do my Country.

Official confirmation reached him in a letter from Alexandria dated January 25th, from Colonel William Grayson:[14]

Dear Sir: By Express I beg leave to inform you that his Excellency, Gen. Washington, has thought proper to appoint you a Lieut. Col. in one of the 16 additional Continental Regiments, and of which I am to have the command.

If you accept of his Excellency's offer, you will be pleased to meet me immediately in Dumfries, in order to give your assistance in the nomination of the Subaltern Officers, and in other matters relative to raising the Regiment...

With respect to the nomination of Officers, I think you had better not mention it until we have been together and laid our plans, in order to prevent impertinent and improper applications. I am with great Truth,

Yr. Affect. Frd. Willm Grayson.

Faced with what was expected to be the almost total disappearance of the New England troops on the 15th of February and discouraging news of the difficulties in raising additional men to fill the gaps in the old line regiments, Congress had authorized Continental regiments "at large" on the 27th of December. Two of these were to come from Virginia, commanded by Colonel Charles M. Thruston[15] from the Shenandoah Valley and Colonel William Grayson from Dumfries, an old friend of Washington. A third regiment was to be raised in Virginia and Maryland, commanded

14. William Grayson, 1736-1790, was a son of Capt. Benjamin and Susanna (Monroe) Grayson of "Belle Air", Prince William County. He married Elizabeth Wagener. Grayson was an old friend of Washington and had been captain of the Independent Company of Prince William County, organized 11 Nov. 1774. In August, 1776 he was appointed as aide-de-camp to Washington.

15. Charles Mynn Thruston, 1738-1812, was an Anglican clergyman from the Shenandoah Valley. He raised a company early in the war, of which he was Captain. He was badly wounded at Trenton.

by Colonel Nathaniel Gist [16] of Maryland. None of these regiments ever reached full strength. Thruston's was, apparently, never fully organized and was later absorbed into Gist's. Grayson was the only one who, as far as it is known, recruited in Fauquier. His, too, was later absorbed into Gist's regiment but existed as an independent unit from 11 January 1777, until 22 April 1779, during which time it performed with some distinction.

Raising men was, for them also, extremely difficult. In late January Grayson complained that "in every part of this state there is nothing to be seen but recruiting parties." Furthermore those qualified for officer positions were in great demand and all expected rank far beyond anything for which their experience qualified them. As far as rank and file were concerned, the promise of a bounty of $20 and 100 acres of land for a private who volunteered for three years or for the war, failed to find many takers. Those having a sense of patriotic duty had already signed up and those who sought pecuniary gain were waiting for higher offers. One of Leven Powell's friends wrote him that some officers were offering as much as $50 a man.

Although a rich man raising a single company might indulge in such extravagant bounties, it was obviously not possible to raise an entire regiment that way. Grayson, Powell and David Ross, the major of the "Additional Regiment" first promised to have it ready by May first. Even had the men been available, the equipment was in short supply. A promise of 100 blankets in May turned into only 32 in June. Shoes, material for uniforms, leather for stocks and buttons for leggings were hard to get at any price. Grayson wrote Powell on the 25th of June, hoping that they were ready to march and offering to meet him in Leesburg "with money" as soon as he had confirmation. However a letter from Powell to his wife shows that they did not reach Leesburg until the 19th of October and, on the 7th of November, were at White Marsh Church, eleven miles above Philadelphia. They had reached headquarters on the 30th of October as the summer campaign ended and the army was ready to settle into winter quarters.

The original roster of Grayson's Additional Continental Regiment has not been found, so we do not know how many men

---

16. Nathaniel Gist, d: 1796, was probably the son of Christopher Gist, d: 1759, colonial scout from Maryland. His single noteworthy act during the Revolution was to prefer charges against "Light-Horse" Harry Lee for his conduct at Paulus Hook. Weedon called him "the head of the Wrongheads."

from Fauquier were included. Daniel Chumley [17] says that he enlisted in Halifax County for three years in 1778 and was marched to Alexandria, where he was placed under the command of Captain William Triplett, who took the unit to Pennsylvania. Obviously, therefore, Captain William Triplett [18] of Fauquier County was not originally with the regiment, but joined it later with a company of enlisted men or draftees from several counties. Triplett, who was the eldest son of Francis and Benedicta (Sennett) Triplett of Fauquier had returned from Kentucky where he had been surveying with Thomas Bullitt early in the war. He was commissioned in Grayson's Regiment 1 November 1777, but seems to have remained on recruiting duty in Virginia until the following April when he is first reported as having joined his regiment. It is possible that he brought with him the first Fauquier men in the regiment.

While frantic efforts were being made during the spring of 1777 to raise companies in Fauquier County to march north, it might well be asked what, if anything, the Fauquier militia was doing to help the cause. The answer is, - nothing, aside from giving a good deal of moral support. It was certainly not their fault. Though Washington could have made good use of the Virginia militia the Virginia Council of State had no intention of releasing the militia as long as there remained any danger that the British might shift their attention from New Jersey to Virginia. There was a good deal of logic in the belief that they would be well advised to do so. Governor Henry was adamant in his rejection of any plan to leave Virginia defenseless and the hands of Colonel William Edmonds, commander of the Fauquier militia, were tied.

Armistead Churchill presided over the court that met on the 24th of March, 1777. By that time a number of rather important matters had accumulated that merited the attention of the Justices. Certificates were asked for obtaining letters of administration for a number of estates. Two are certainly identified as belonging to men who had died of disease in Philadelphia during the previous winter,

---

17. Daniel Chumley, 1759-post 1833, claimed that he entered service at the age of 16, though his papers clearly show that he was 19, and the unit did not exist in 1775.

18. William Triplett, 1759-1812, according to his own deposition, did not return from Kentucky until the autumn of 1776. His record in Heitman is confused with that of his first cousin of Fairfax County. He married, 12 Dec. 1785, Elizabeth Morehead, daughter of John Morehead, d:1821.

Lieutenant William Nelson,[19] Ashby's 1st lieutenant, who died in December and John McLain,[20] one of his men who, we recall, died on New Year's Day. There were probably more.

There were some militia appointments. Joshua Tullos was to be lieutenant and Daniel Shumate ensign in Captain Nicholas George's company. William Ball was made a captain in place of John Webb, who had died, with James Foley, lieutenant and John Deering, ensign.

However the most important question to come before the court was that of inoculation against smallpox. The heavy losses from smallpox during the Jersey campaign caused Washington to insist on wholesale inoculation for all units joining the Continental army. If the men feared the inoculation as much as the disease, they had reason, and, at home, the opposition was even greater. In Virginia there was a law prohibiting inoculation and those who favored it were subject to fine if caught performing the act.

On the 23rd of April Congress had decided to take some positive measures to counter Virginia's threat to the entire program. It was resolved "that Dr. James Tilton be authorized to repair to Dumfries in Virginia, there to take charge of all Continental soldiers that are or shall be inoculated, and that he be furnished with the necessary medicines." Further it was ordered that inoculation centers be set up at Colchester and Alexandria for the inoculation of troops from the Carolinas. Colonel Grayson wrote Lieutenant Colonel Leven Powell, who had arranged to have the inoculation done at Frederick, Maryland, to escape the Virginia law, to send his men to Dumfries, not to Alexandria. While this placed the military outside the reach of Virginia authorities, there was no help for the private citizen.

When Benjamin Harrison, a private citizen, albeit an influential one, wanted to have his family inoculated at his home, "Glanville", near Marshall, he was forced to ask the Fauquier Court for permission to do so. At the same court Harrison was one of those asked to appraise the estate of Lieutenant William Nelson, who had probably died of smallpox in Pennsylvania. Harrison may well have become alarmed by Nelson's death. The court granted

---

19. William Nelson's estate was appraised by Benjamin Harrison, John Peters, Original Young and George Crosby. John Nelson, probably his brother was the executor.

20. John McLain's estate was appraised by John Wright, Tilman Weaver, John Weaver and John Colvin. He apparently lived near Germantown. William Sinclair was the executor.

him leave to have his family inoculated and, at the same time, began to wonder why all Fauquier families should not be allowed to do so "if they think proper." They passed the necessary resolution.

A storm of protest followed immediately. In the minds of most residents the court had wantonly allowed smallpox to be introduced into the community and there was danger of infecting, not only one family, but their neighbors over a wide area. Furthermore, according to some fundamentalist ministers, smallpox was a manifestation of God's will and, if He chose to punish the wicked in that rather specialized way, man had no right to interfere. A special meeting of the court was called on the 29th of April in which the "gentlemen Justices" executed an about-face. "For reasons appearing to the Court, it is ordered that no person be Inoculated for the smallpox in this County for the Future," they announced grandly, and promptly adjourned. It was the turn of the other side to stage an uprising.

The May Court made another effort to appease the irate inhabitants. While not permitting the introduction of smallpox in any area, leave was granted "to any of the Inhabitants...to inoculate their Families with the smallpox, where any of them shall have the disorder in the *natural way.*" The act made no medical sense whatever but it was no doubt inspired politics. Even after October, 1777, when the Virginia law was repealed, those who wanted to be "immunized" first had to have the consent of a majority of the inhabitants within a two mile radius!

In May of 1777 two other subjects of conversation arose in Fauquier County, as in other Virginia counties, resulting from the difficulty in recruiting and destined to affect the lives of many of the people. The first was the growing realization that the families of those men who volunteered their lives were entitled to some sort of relief and the second was the draft.

Just what was needed to prod the court to act on behalf of the families of soldiers is not known. Certainly John Blackwell and James Bell, Gentlemen, were aware of the problem that faced volunteers without means of supporting their families other than their army pay, and could well afford to come to their aid. Ann Barrett, whose husband is not identified, and Catherine Wise, wife of Samuel Wise, a soldier in the 6th Virginia Regiment were the first of many beneficiaries of this plan. They each received provisions valued at about £12. Enough to keep them for six months.

The nasty subject of conscription, which was only too obviously necessary an enlistments slowed to a halt, was proposed by

Washington with marked reluctance. Governor Henry conceded that the possibility of meeting quotas, especially in the old line regiments, was slim indeed and proposed an act for conscription to the May, 1777, session of the House of Delegates where it was passed. Reporting sometime later, Colonel Humphrey Brooke, then County Lieutenant, said that Fauquier's first quota was 25 men, "which number was delivered a Continent¹ Officer, except 8 or 9 that Deserted."[21] The desertion of one third of the draftees raised under the conscription act was by no means exceptional. What was exceptional is that Colonel Brooke bothered to report at all. Most County Lieutenants did not.

While the people of Fauquier were slowly facing up to their own problems, spring finally reached the heights of New Jersey on which their sons were encamped. It was later than in Virginia and not nearly so spectacular, but it was spring and the army began to come to life. A steady trickle of reinforcements arrived and old friends who had had leave for the winter began to return. John Chilton's letter to his brother-in-law, Major Martin Pickett of the Fauquier militia, is more cheerful than usual.[22] The company had weathered the smallpox inoculation without casualty except that Joe Blackwell's eye continued to trouble him. Blackwell was "sullen" because of temporary disfigurement by the disease which he was afraid would be repulsive in the eyes of Dickie Beale's pretty sister. Chilton had accused John Blackwell of spending his time in Virginia courting instead of the recruiting for which he had been sent. Half-jokingly, he attributed John's failure in the field of Mars to his lack of progress in the field of Venus. He advised him to sue Cocky (Hancock) Lee for having snatched the lovely Winifred Eustace Beale from under his very nose.

There was, as yet, little news from camp except skirmishing. He repeated an unlikely story about General Howe, the British commander, and also some rather heady rumors about the deplorable state of British arms. British deserters were coming over to the American side in droves, he wrote, and six weeks should be enough to trap the British army and end the war. Nevertheless, he was homesick and wanted to see Virginia. As for the Jersey women

---

21. Continental Soldiers; An abstract of men raised under the former laws passed for raising soldiers for the Continental Service. Nov. 1782. **Tyler's Quarterly Magazine,** Vol. IX, No. IV, April 1928, pp. 234-235.

22. Letter, John Chilton to Maj. Martin Pickett, 19 March 1777. Keith of Woodbourne Papers, Virginia Historical Society.

well, "from 16 years old (they) have lost their teeth." Ugh!

In a postscript he writes, "Col⁰ Marshall is to command our Regmt. I am told." Obviously he had not expected to retain command of the 3rd Virginia Regiment once the spring campaign opened up. Colonel Thomas Marshall was at least an old friend to whom, perhaps, he could look for promotion. In consideration of his devotion to duty when others had gone off, leaving their men in his care, he had a right to expect the majority in the 3rd Regiment. Promotion had been a long time coming. Who was better qualified?

The first of the new Virginia troops to reach Morristown was the token detachment from the 11th Virginia Regiment under Colonel Daniel Morgan. Their number was frighteningly small but, presumably, more were to come. The fact that the first group contained a large number of men from Fauquier was a pleasant surprise for Chilton, who numbered Captain William Blackwell among his closest friends, and welcomed a few old drinking companions.

Yet Morgan's advent was not wholly reassuring. Morgan was unhappy as a regimental commander and did not mind saying so. He had no sooner arrived in camp than he began an intensive campaign to be appointed to head a special body of his own choosing, to act under special orders from Washington for reconnaissance and other duties requiring the services of a mobile light infantry. He had in mind a unit of 500 picked riflemen, taken from all Continental Line regiments, that could act very much on its own. No doubt his tongue was given increased eloquence by the fact that the 11th Regiment had been assigned to a brigade commanded by the impossible Woodford. That he finally got his way is indicated by a letter from Washington in June referring to his "Corps of Rangers, newly formed." [23]

From William Blackwell's company he selected sergeant John Morgan, corporal William Sudduth and privates McKinney Robinson, John Straughn, William Dennis and Charles Morgan. He also took the Grant brothers, Daniel and John, who had been with Captain William Pickett at Great Bridge where they had earned a reputation for some rather fancy shooting. His inroads on other Virginia line regiments were certainly discouraging to those who had spent time, effort and probably money recruiting them. For instance Reuben Bryan, a 22-year old Fauquier sharpshooter,

---

23. Washington to Morgan, 13 June 1777, in: Fitzpatrick, **Writings of Washington**, Vol. VIII, p. 236.

whose enlistment had another year to run, had been brought in by Nathaniel Ashby and had been with his company more than a year, was selected. Bryan was pleased and flattered, but it did not boost Ashby's morale a bit. Another such instance was John Austin, who claimed to have been with Morgan at Quebec. Captain Charles Porterfield, apparently with some difficulty, had persuaded him to join the company he was raising in the 11th Virginia Regiment but, at Middlebrook, he was "transferred" to a company headed by Captain Gabriel Long [24] of Culpeper County so that he could serve with Morgan's special corps.

Morgan was willing to spend most of his time in the field with his "Rangers" but he was not especially anxious to relinquish command of the 11th Regiment, as it was the base on which was founded most of his prerogatives at headquarters. As acting commander Christian Febiger did what he could, but regimental affairs in the hands of an acting commander, however capable, tend to fall apart. It was especially true in this instance because the men felt somewhat rejected by Morgan. Officers and men sought other employment. Major William Heth had clamored to serve with Morgan but was unwilling to serve with Morgan away, under Febiger. He demanded and got the Lieutenant Colonelcy of the 3rd Virginia under Marshall, ending forever Chilton's chance of acvancement.

For Captain William Blackwell, past forty and in poor health, it was a matter of bitter disappointment. When young Joseph Parker,[25] his best corporal, told him in May that he had been offered an opportunity to join General Washington's Life Guard, he could only nod absently. Of the men he had so laboriously brought to Morristown, he had lost more than one third and those were the best.

One lovely April day while he was still stationed at Chatham, Captain John Chilton decided to take a week's leave and visit some old friends. It was only the second week he had taken off from his

24. Morgan's Rangers were broken down into four Independent Rifle Companies under Captains Gabriel Long, Shepherd, West and Bradys. All of the Fauquier men whose records have been found served in Long's company.

25. Joseph Parker, 1756-1821, was a son of Thomas and Catherine (Martin?) Parker of Fauquier. His brother Martin also served from Fauquier. He married Elizabeth Duncan, daughter of Joseph Duncan, in 1781.

duties since leaving Virginia and he looked forward to it with pleasure. He had had news that the Fauquier Independent Company, a unit of volunteers under his old friend Captain James Scott, had arrived at Quibbletown, Lord Stirling's headquarters. It was true that he had had some minor differences with Captain Scott before leaving Virginia but surely they would be forgotten in the pleasure of renewing an old friendship so far from home. The little village of Quibbletown lay on the other side of Watchung Mountains, a distance of about eleven miles. With him he took Billy Tomlin, a sixteen year old recruit that John Blackwell had sent up a few weeks before, leaving the lad's widowed mother dissolved in tears. Billy had never mastered the intricacies of reading and writing but his hands were willing and his feet nimble. Chilton was fond of him and wrote his brother Charles to tell Mrs. Tomlin not to cry any more about Billy, as he was a fine soldier. He thought that a rendezvous with his old friends from Fauquier might ease the lad's homesickness.

From the beginning the trip was a disaster. On the way down his heavy boot so inflamed a small infection on his instep that it was with difficulty that he completed the ten mile hike. More than fifty years later Tomlin recalled the noise and confusion of Lord Stirling's headquarters where he had caught only a brief glimpse of Captain Scott before going off to visit his friends in the ranks. They told him that they had been there for some time.

In fact, Chilton and Tomlin could hardly have paid their visit at a more unfortunate time. Captain Scott's command was in complete disarray. The truth is found in the pension record of a 20 year old private named William Reeve. Reeve volunteered in the Fauquier Independent Company on the 1st of January, 1777, for a three month tour. Naturally he expected that enlistment to expire on the 1st of April. However Scott's letter from Benjamin Harrison was dated 1 February, 1777, and clearly stipulated that they would serve "where ordered three months from the *time of their march.*" It seems probable that Scott did not make that fact clear to the men before they headed north in February.

On reaching Quibbletown their company was assigned to Lord Stirling's Division under Colonel Hollinsworth and Colonel Stricker of the "German Troops" (Pennsylvanians). While there they saw some action, a skirmish with British and Hessian troops between Quibbletown and Brunswick. No Americans were killed or wounded but one of the enemy was killed, and several were wounded.

On the 1st of April, Reeve and a number of the men expecting to go home, were confronted with a letter, (Reeve says from Washington, but probably only from headquarters), asking that they remain one week longer. Reluctantly they consented. On the 8th of April, when the week was up, they left without any order, "assuming that Washington's letter was sufficient authorization." Lord Stirling was furious. He promptly sent a squadron of horse to bring them back to camp. He ordered that they remain three weeks longer, serving as his life guard.

It was in the midst of these weeks of enforced and deeply resented extra duty that Captain Chilton elected to visit Captain Scott. The latter's mortification that he had so far lost command of his company that it had attracted the unfavorable notice of both Washington and Lord Stirling explains in large measure his erratic behavior.

At the time Chilton did not say much about his reception at Quibbletown, but, at least from James Scott, it had been cool. Chilton had many friends at Stirling's headquarters and some of them had been his companions during the long winter. He was on terms of easy familiarity with the General and his staff, a familiarity of which Scott was, no doubt, envious. The insecurity of his own position and the labyrinth of internal politics he had met at headquarters baffled and frightened Scott. Through shared experience Chilton commanded their attention and compelled their affection, leaving him, an outsider, frustrated and alone.

Later Chilton wrote that he had not blamed James Scott and had been loath "to break with him, an old friend, for matters that seemed to be more his misfortune than intention." At the time he was hurt and his foot pained him sorely. Long before his week was up he borrowed a horse and returned to Chatham. Billy Tomlin must have found his way back alone. A few days later Chilton wrote to his wife's sisters, Ann Pickett, Judith Keith and Betty, his brother Charles' wife.[26] He was still hobbling about the house in Chatham. He complained that Joseph Blackwell had not returned

---

26. Letter, John Chilton to Ann Pickett. The letter is undated but internal evidence fixes it in April, 1777. Keith of Woodbourne Papers, Virginia Historical Society.

from Hanover and resented his inquiries "after a hearty old grog-drinker." He needed him and Alvin Mountjoy, who was also lame. He was, in fact, lonely and feeling sorry for himself.

The diary that John Chilton had begun so ambitiously on the eve of the Battle of Princeton had almost completely succumbed to the endless repetition of uneventful days during February and March. He lost the part from the 15th of April to the 3rd of July. Trying to remember what had happened, he lost track of time and circumstance. Picking it up where we left off, it reads:

> From Whippany or Hanover went to Chatham 7 miles from Hanover which lies on the Pisiac a smart river not navigable. Here we staid until some time in April when we marched to Newark with an intent to cross over to Bergen where we heard 4 or 500 Tories were assembled but being disappointed in Boats did not cross. Staid at Newark 2 or 3 days, then marched to the Matuchin Lines where we staid till 4th May when we were ordered to join the Grand Army at Middle Brooke.[27]

Undoubtedly Chilton and his men did take part in the fiasco at Newark, but not in April. It is probably just as well that he did not know what really happened to the Bergen operation, as his faith in generals would have plummeted to a new low. For Major General Adam Stephen it was one more step on the road to disgrace.

There was an incident in 1763 when Stephen had been suspected of making a military move of no great value and falsifying reports to make it seem important, but Washington had forgotten about it. He had not forgotten the scene before Trenton when Stephen had sent an unauthorized patrol under Captain Richard Anderson of the 5th Virginia Regiment across the Delaware, nearly upsetting his plans. Nevertheless he had approved his promotion to Major General on the 17th of February, 1777. Anxious to demonstrate his military genius, Stephen had the bright

---

27. The river mentioned is the Passaic. Middlebrook was near present Bound Brook, New Jersey.

idea of surprising the Black Watch, one of Howe's crack regiments, near Piscataway on the 10th of May. His men were soundly trounced. Instead of admitting his misjudgement, Stephen tried to turn it into a victory in his report. When Washington learned the truth he was furious.

A week later Stephen submitted a plan for an attack on a Tory regiment at Bergen, a tiny village at the north end of Newark Bay. To reach it from Newark it was necessary either to cross the bay at its widest point or to cross both the Passaic and Hackensack Rivers. The risk was immense for so slight a gain and Washington laid the plan aside as impractical. When Stephen attempted to press the issue he received a stern rebuke. Washington had no idea that Stephen had already deployed troops in anticipation of approval. Naturally Stephen was unlikely to tell his junior officers that he had been willing to risk their lives on a hare-brained scheme for which he had been roundly snubbed by His Excellency. He blamed the failure on poor communications.

By the end of May the trickle of Virginians returning to join Washington at Morristown had become a steady stream, though far short of the numbers expected. William Woodford arrived to take command of his brigade. After resigning in September, 1776, in anger because Mercer and Stephen had been promoted over him, he had been sulking at "Windsor" until the 21st of February when he had been offered a promotion to Brigadier and command of the 3rd Virginia Brigade, consisting of the 3rd, 7th, 11th and 15th Regiments. At the time Woodford had been gratified but, upon reflection, it occurred to him that he would be outranked by Brigadiers Muhlenberg, Weedon and Scott, who had been promoted during his long period of inactivity. It was true that they had served faithfully and at great personal hazard meanwhile, but that counted nothing with Woodford, who arrived in Morristown shrilly demanding that his commission be back-dated so that he could take precedence over them. Congress wisely refused. Washington rebuked him politely, pointing out that his resignation was of his own doing and implying that only a remarkably petty and insensitive man would make an issue of such "Trifling punctilios" when so much that was important was at stake.

Woodford's regimental commanders had too much on their hands to concern themselves with his problems. Colonel Thomas Marshall of the 3rd Regiment was in somewhat over his head and his new second in command, William Heth, seemed only to be making things worse. Crawford, Colonel of the 7th Regiment,[28] a man of wide experience, disliked Woodford and paid as little attention to him as possible. Because of Crawford's close relationship with Washington, Woodford was afraid to complain. Morgan continued in command of the 11th and 15th Regiments as David Mason, appointed commander of the latter, simply refused to come to New Jersey to serve under Woodford. Only Christian Febiger, acting commander of the 11th Regiment was unperturbed. With his European training he was used to serving under self-centered aristocrats principally concerned with their own preferment.

The company grade officers from Fauquier had returned, bringing with them as many recruits as possible. A muster roll of Chilton's company in June records that both John and Joseph Blackwell were on hand. William More, Joshua Jenkins, Chichester Matthews and Henry Bradford were sergeants. Moses Allen and, surprisingly, Billy Tomlin were corporals and Michael Hynd beat the drum. There were thirty-eight privates but not all ready for duty. William Bailey was sick in Philadelphia and William Bragg in Virginia. The last named had been suffering from a wound on his heel received from a spade while digging entrenchments along the North River in New York. The wound would not heal and Joseph Blackwell was forced to discharge him on the 29th of July. Two of Chilton's men had defected to Pennsylvania and New Jersey regiments and three, William Roach, William Day and Dickson Robinson had been "drafted" into his Excellency's Guard.

Captain John Ashby was back, with Lieutenant Valentine Peyton in place of William Nelson. Isham Keith (Uncle Ishe), in poor health and too old for so rugged an existence, had resigned. This gave Nathaniel Ashby room a little nearer the top as 2nd Lieutenant.

An incomplete muster roll of Captain William Blackwell's company in Morgan's 11th Virginia Regiment dated 1 June, lists the officers previously mentioned and John Morgan, Samuel Philips, John Anderson and Joseph Garner as sergeants. All were from Fauquier although the last may be in error for Charles

---

28. William Crawford, 1732-1782, had known Washington since both were seventeen and was with him at Braddock's Defeat and at Fort Duquesne. He was a Major in Lord Dunmore's War. On the 11th of October, 1776 he was appointed Colonel of the 7th Virginia Regiment. He fought at Long Island, Trenton and Princeton. Heitman says that he resigned 22 March 1777, but Chilton and others mention his service before Brandywine.

Garner, whose pension record shows he enlisted under Blackwell, 14 September 1776.

In the last days of May Washington moved his army from the winter quarters in the highlands to Middlebrook about eight miles from New Brunswick. Weedon, returned from his leave in Virginia, wrote enthusiastically to his friend, John Page, from Middlebrook on the 31st of May. The army was in such splendid shape that "a friendly heart cannot help being highly elated." However he implored Page, "for Heavens sake expedite the completion of your Quotas of men as on the operations of this campaign does in great measure depend the American Cause."

It was the 29th of June when Captain John Chilton next got around to writing his brother Charles in Virginia. He was still stationed at Morristown but had been detached with 50 men to guard Steel's Gap, about two miles from camp. Captain William Blackwell was with him. The men were all healthy and eating regularly. He described with evident satisfaction Howe's last attempt to lure Washington out of the Watchung Mountains and into the open plain between Metuchen and Woodbridge. When Washington refused to take the bait, Howe suddenly withdrew with his entire force to Perth Amboy. Chilton's account was that of a combat soldier some miles from the scene of the battle. Based on largely incorrect intelligence, he drew conclusions as to the enemy's intentions that fell wide of the mark.

From Morristown on the 8th of July he wrote a brief but amusing letter to his close friend Captain William Pickett, Martin's younger brother. He chides him for sitting at home eating "henturkies boiled in a pudding bag", while he, 300 miles from home, is "under the mortifying circumstances of being known to the whole Army by the name of "Old Chilton" [29] and seeing boys whom I would not have made sergeants of every day put over my head for no Earthly reason but that they wear a finer coat, gambol and play the fool more kittenishly than I can." Failure to gain a promotion was beginning to rankle, but he adds with a laugh that his main concern is that these young whipper-snappers are cutting him out with the girls. These he would forego if only he could return to Virginia, but Fort Ticonderoga was under siege and Lt. General Sir Henry Clinton had arrived in New York to reinforce Howe. A leave to go home was impossible.

He had no idea that two days before St. Clair had abandoned Ticonderoga without firing a shot. The strategy being planned at

29. He paraphrases Anthony's comment on Lepidus. **Anthony and Cleopatra**, Act III, Scene V.

Howe's headquarters was beyond his wildest imagining. As action of some sort was obviously about to take place, he decided to resume his diary:

July 3rd 1777 Thursday. His Excellency G. Washington with the army marched from Middle Brook to Morris Town by Whites Tavern where G. Lee was taken, about 10 Miles from M. Brook, within ½ Mile Lord Stirlings seat.[30] To Morris Town from M. Brook 18 m. course NE by N. Staid here till:

Saty. 12th, when the whole Marched and encamped at the Western end of Pumpton Plains crossing Whippony at 4 Miles dist. going thro' a Town of same name in Hanover Township took the Troy road & passed that Township. Crossed the Rockway River at 9 m^s Dist. which makes into Pisiac. This River runs Nearly SW till near its junction with Pisiac & then it runs nearly East. 3 m^s. farther encamped which makes 16 Miles from Morris Town 17 from the encampm^t.

Sunday 13th, Rain, no march. Here I lost my Journal from 15th Ap^l. 77 to this date——

If John Chilton was wrong in his guess as to Howe's next move, he was certainly not alone. The entire American command was bewildered by contradictory reports of British movements. It was not until the first of July, when General Charles Scott and his Virginians of the 4th, 8th and 12th Regiments moved into Perth Amboy, that it was fully realized that Howe had withdrawn his entire army of 18,000 men from New Jersey and was busy on Staten Island preparing for an entirely new operation, the nature of which it was impossible to discern. Howe had several options, all of them perplexing. Since the frontal attack on Philadelphia from the east was apparently abandoned, it might be logical for Howe to attempt a junction with General Burgoyne who was leading a force of 8,000 toward Albany. Hence Washington hurried his troops north toward Peekskill, N. Y. to secure the Hudson River. On the 14th of July the 3rd Virginia Regiment was ordered north on an inland course through the rugged highlands of northern New Jersey and New York. From this point on the entries in Chilton's diary are made almost daily:

---

30. William Alexander, Lord Stirling, had a handsome house at Basking Ridge, New Jersey, which stood until 1920.

14th July 1777 Monday. Genl. beat at day break crossed Beaver Dam Brook at ½ Miles dist. from thence to Paquonac [31] River 7 Miles where there is a regular built fort just below Mount Holly. This fort is not proof against large Cannon—about 300 Yards farther crossed the long Pond River by some called Pumpton R^r. 4 Miles farther crossed a considerable R^r. which is also called Pumpton 3 Miles farther encamped on said R^r in all 15 Miles.

Tuesday 15 Marched up said R^r. 11 Miles to a place called the Clove [32] here they call this R^r. Ramepo which winds thro' Large and Barren Mountains on the right a River not so large as the Ramepo empties into it from the Clove.

18th July we at 9 in the forenoon Marched about 2 Miles back encamped in the Dutch Valley on S^d R^r. Ramepo for the benefit of fresh & good Water Part of our encampment at the clove was in N. York State part in Jersey——

Sunday 20th at Morn^g. Gun the Tents were struck. Marched by the Clove kept the course of Ramepo. through as a road could not have been gotten any other way by reason of the Steep & rockiness of the Mountains. There are very few houses for 16 Miles and then generally mean, the Valley being very narrow and for the most part so stony that no one can live: There are Deer (some say wild Goats) Vermin of various kinds & an abundance of Rattle Snakes. 'twas late brfore we encamped on the Western side of Haverstraw Mount^n within 14 Miles New Windsor—the Mount^ns. to the left of encampm^t. Cheesequakes [33] from this place for near 30 miles back the Country exhibits a very barren prospect, the valley of Ramepo R being generally very narrow. About ½ mile from this encampment the waters Run N. Easterly to North River. the Ramepo empties into Hackinsack being joined by several other Rivers the course Southerly—The Waters emptying into N^o. R^r. is called Murderers Creek. Some of the inhabitants thro' delicacy call it Murdenars.

31. Pequannock.

32. Smith's Clove, a narrow ravine of the Ramapo River in northern New Jersey.

33. The present town of Cheesequake, N. J. does not fit this description. There must have been another place with this odd name.

21st & 22d. Staid here about Mile and half from hence on the Haverstraw Mount is a beautiful Lake near a Mile in Length & 400 Yd^s broad, clear and transparent said to be 30 or 40 feet deep abounding with various kinds fishes. Near this Lake on the Mountain are Garden Gooseberries, Currans & Rasberries, the spontaneous growth of the place.

23d July. March at 9 in Morn^g 2 Miles to Smiths Tavern, from whence crossed Mountains a Westerly course 7 Miles to a place called Oxford where we stopt to refresh. 4 Miles farther Chester, an insignificant place, like Oxford, neither of them Towns passed thro' Chester and encamped.

24th Lay by——

25th Early Marched from Chester 15 Miles on Way Breakfasted at one Wickhams before whose door is a pretty Lake 8 or 900 Yds long & 400 wide said to be very deep; about 8 Miles farther encamped at a place called Warwiendah [34] about a Mile & half in Jersey State where is a fine Spring.

26th Before we March, Capt. Wallace,[35] Capt. Powel,[36] myself, Lt. Mercer,[37] Lieut. Tebbs,[38] Lieut. Baynham,[39] & Ens^n. Payton [40] were denied our Posts in Battalion, for this reason. there was a Genl. order for every Officer to attend Roll Call at Retreat. I had not seen my chest for near a week. I was consequently very dirty with a long beard. I had embraced this opport^y. of Shaving & shifting and was about ½ shaved at the best. I saw the Men turn out and

---

34. Lake Wawayanda.

35. Dr. James Westwood Wallace, a son of Dr. Michael Wallace of Culpeper and brother of Gustavus Brown Wallace. He was a surgeon in the 2nd Virginia Regiment.

36. William Powell, son of William and Eleanor (Peyton) Powell of Dumfries. He was in Morgan's Regiment.

37. John Francis Mercer, of Loudoun County, Virginia.

38. Probably a son of Captain Foushee Tebbs of Dumfries, who was on the Committee of Safety in Prince William County.

39. Joseph Baynham.

40. Robert Peyton of Stafford County. He was promoted about this time.

also saw M^r. Blackw^{ll} [41] go to hear the Roll Call. for this I was arrested—the other Gent. no doubt had their reasons or at least ought to have had, tho' to say truth this order had been too much neglected but to bring in those who had not neglected their duty indiscriminately with those who had, argues a New raised officer grasping any superiority and power. In 15 Minutes our Swords were ordered to be given us again, which all refused to receive but myself. I knew that Col^o. Marshall had been urged to this piece of strict tho' ill timed discipline, that he would act when it came to the pinch as it really turned out, and that it would end in a manner that would do neither party honour. Besides we were on a forced March where I knew we could have no triall untill a battle should be fought as there was at that time the greatest prospect, the report being that the enemy were some distance up the Delaware; and I was very averse to giving my command up to men of their choose^g. to command my Comp^y.

26th (Later) Tents struck at 3 in Morn^g. Marched 11 Miles by 9 Oclock breakfasted in a Meadow by a fine Spring. Encamped at a place called Pettits 25 Miles On our March after breakfast went by Three Lakes all on right hand of road a small River connects them, the first is the smallest, the Middle one near a Mile Long 400 Yards wide, the Last or most Southerly not quite ½ Mile Long 300 Yds wide. the Lakes about 4 Miles back of the encampment, the most Northerly here is also a Furnace.

27th By reason of rain the night past did not move till late this morning passed by a beautiful Lake [42] in cross^g the Mountain about 8 Mile Left hand side somewhat of an oval form about 350 & 300 Yd^s. 3 Miles farther Hackitts Town passed 2 Miles when we were ordered to sit down (in the Sun no water near) to refresh our selves no victuals to eat as the returns of last night was so late that nothing could

---

41. Wm. Blackwell. In Chilton's handwriting this looks very much like "Mr" Blackwell, which may have given rise to the belief in the Blackwell family that Chilton's father-in-law having been Burgess, Sheriff and Commissioner of Peace in Fauquier, was at age 61, commissioned as 2nd Lieutenant in the 3rd Virginia Regiment. However, Chilton on the 14th of August asks his sisters-in-law to give his "respectful compliments" to their "revered father".

42. Lake Budd.

be cooked. No Waggons allowed to carry our Cooking Utensils, the soldiers were obliged to carry their Kettles, pans &.c. in their hands. Cloathes and provisions on their backs. as our March was a forced one & the Season extremely warm the victuals became putrid by sweat & heat—the Men badly off for Shoes, many being entirely barefoot and in our Reg^t. a too minute inspection was made into things relative to necessaries that the Men could not do without, which they were obliged to throw away. Encamped at Musconaconk Brooke 21 mi. The Mountains having the same name of the Brooke the N. Eastern part of the same ledge Mountains are called Pumpton these Mountains were on our Left from Smiths Tavern. near North R^r New York Heights.

28th Marched very early crossed the Masconeconk brooke 4 or 5 Miles below encampment. This days march as well as Yesterday we passed a deal (of) barren Land. 17 Miles to PittsTown, an inconsiderable place which we marched by 12 Oclock. Staid here till about 4 to refresh and draw provisions & moved to Quakers Town 2 Miles encamped.———

29th Marched by Sun got 9 Miles & were ordered to Pitch Tents where we staid that day a small Mile from road.

30th next Morn^g. 30th marched to Howels Ferry on Delaware opposite Brownes on the Pensylvania side 6 miles.[43]

31st about 11 ordered to cross the River. had the misfortune of having our Waggon overset in fording the River This scheme of fording, had like to have proved fatal to several soldiers, two were drowned a day or two before. We with difficulty saved ours. One horse was drowned the Waggon and chief of the Tents were lost. I lost my Tent but luckily the Bed Clothes was wrapped up in M^r. Mountjoys Tent, and the bulk kept the water from soaking through so that they floated—encamped about 2 Miles from R^r our Regt were obliged to take the woods for want of Tents.

Augt 1st Marched overtook Gen. Conways Brigade at 7 Miles dist. breakfasted at Neshaminy Bridge 2 Miles farther Cross road where are a few pretty good houses 2 Miles farther the Crooked Billet passed the Crooked Billet 2 Miles, encamped at forks of the Fall road.[44]

43. Near New Hope, Pa.

44. Camp Crossroads, near Southampton, Pa.

*2d Aug*t Marched to German Town 9 Miles where we stopt about an H^r. Then marched 1½ Miles & encamped near Schuylkill about 5 Miles from Philadel^a. Here we staid till Friday 8th Augt when we were Generally review^d and ordered to March at 2 Oclock. We were told we should not march above 5 M^s. We passed the length of German Town which is 4 or 5 Miles as expected to halt a Mile or two out of Town. Went very slow. Cont^d marching till 9 at night we supposed to get to some fine place but to our great mortification was put in a Stubble field as uneven as a Plough could make Ground and water half a Mile off & that very scarce & mean 11 Miles.

*9*th *Aug*t at 9 Oclock moved a small mile for benefit Ground & water encamped at sandy Brook.

*Aug*t *10th* Marched to Crooked billet. 2 Miles farther encamped at Cross Roads where we staid till Saturday 23 Augt then Marched just before Sun got within 5 or 6 Miles Phil^a encamped rec. Orders for every Man to have clean clothes ready for the Morning, the Arms to be Furbished & bright.

24th The whole was in motion by 4 in the Morning. marched in order a hard rain just as we entered down Water street and up Chestnutt Street crossed the Schuylkill on the floating bridge, then made down the River to the Darby road and encamped at Darby a small Town 12 Mile It is Navigable here for small Craft. in a Creek of the Delaware.

25th Marched early in the Morning at 8 Miles Dist. Chester a smart little but irregular built Town then Marcus Hook at about 3 Miles. encamped within 2 ½ Miles of Wilmington 15 M^s. The road runs within sight of the Delaware whose course is nearly West & sometimes a few points to the Southward. The Land here is not so rich as on the other side Delaware but well cultivated, fine Meadows and better Cattle. the inhabitants too, have not that griping importunate countenance as they have up to the N. Westward especially the Ladies, whose features are more soft, and they also have sound teeth We here saw however a specimen of the dissafection of some of the inhabitants in this County. Newcastle.——Rain this even^g, as indeed there has been, particularly thro' this Month, this whole Summer. Corn and every other vegetable exceedingly fine. The People of these States—Pensylvania Jerseys & N. York, throw 8 or 10 Grains of Indian corn in a hill and never thin it. They don't work their Corn as in Virg, and tho' 6 or 8 Stalks come up they do not give themselves the trouble of pulling the shoots or Suckers away. By tilling of a little Ground they have the Advantage of little Labour, a little Manure and beneficent crops. They don't work so hard as the Virginians. they make as much Money, but they do not live half so elegantly or even Plenteously. Were they to give their corn more distance and thin it I am certain they would find the benefit but they are prejudiced in their own way. They don't allow above 3 feet or 3 ½ feet for corn The little Tob^o they pretend to raise they top at 18 & 20 Leaves———

Tuesday 26 th Marched to Brandywine then took a road which Lead N. Westw^d and marched 2 Miles encamped called camp near Wilmington The enemy it is said have Landed and about 3000 last night took Possession of Iron hill, which is about 12 Miles from the place of their Landing and about 12 M^s. from us. His Excellency the Genl. has gone down to observe their position. Our Light horse took 2 of theirs Lay at this camp 1 day and abundance of rain fell the last night and part of this Morn^g (27th)

28th Gen^{ls}. Greens & Stephens Divisions Marched returning to Brandywine a small Town chiefly consisting in Mills & Taverns 8 or 10 Mills being within 100 Yards of each other a Navigable Creek runs up to the Mills. The Water is brought in canals from Brandywine Creek. There appears to be a smart fall of waters just above the Mills about ½ Mile farther on the South side of a gradual hill is Wilmington the front or Road Street is built irregularly towards the West—they have a Markett house a Navigable creek makes to the Southw^d of the Town (called Christeen) [45] 4 M^s farther an inconsiderable Town, Newport. Here we saw some fine Girls not much unlike our first Virg^a. Nymphs. This day I was Capt. of Rere Guard and stopt about a Mile out. about 12 Oclock Col^o Hollingsworth came by us wounded in the cheek or neck; about 2, the Commisary's Waggons returned by them & some with them heard that the Ministerials were advancing within a few Miles of us (scary creatures) said there were 16,000, which our Soldiers as much believed as they believe George III and his corrupt Ministry have a right to tax

---

45. Christina.

America—here we staid 'till 4.—Marched not more than a Mile, when we stopt till after sunset, when we were relieved and joined the reg^t. lay in the woods without Pitching Tents.

29th Moved about half Mile pitched Tents to dry them at 4 in afternoon moved about 3 Miles to the Eastward pitched Tents and staid this night. Within these three days near 50 Prisoners have been brought in. The enemy seem to be bold but very imprudent. should they continue to act as they have done a few Months will give them into our hands without fighting. We have better than 1000 Men near them who will I expect give a good account of those bloodsuckers who shall be guilty of the temerity of Leaving their Camp for the atrocious crime of robbery, rapine & murder.—

30th Augt. Officer of the day. staid here this day & night.

Sunday 31st continued still in Camp This Camp was in Christeen Hundred. our scouters took 7 Ministerials & one deserted to us. Col^o Heth who was with the advanced detachment came in for provisions &c. [46]

Monday Septr 1st a detachm^t was ordered out this even^g but did not go by reason of Rain till Tuesday Morn^g.

2d Septr. Capt. Ashby [47] L^t. White & L^t. V. Peyton [48] went with the detachment. Col^o Hetn did not sett out 'till this Morn^g this a close cloudy morn^g

3d Septr. The enemy advanced as high as the red Lion they were met with by our advanced party under Col^o Crawford [49] —the engagement was pretty hot. Several on each side was wounded and some slain. Strong reinforcements were sent which obliged our Men to give

---

46. Heth was detached from his regiment to command a detachment of Virginians connected with Gen. Maxwell's light infantry units at Cooch's Bridge, Delaware.

47. Capt. John Ashby, of "Belmont" (later "Greenland").

48. Valentine Peyton, 1755-1781. There are three contemporary Valentine Peytons, all Captains, according to the record. Ashby's 1st Lt., was a son of John and Seth (Harrison Peyton of Fauquier. He may have been the Valentine Peyton who died without issue during the siege of Charleston, S.C.

49. Crawford's status at this time is uncertain. He may have had a special assignment pending acceptance of his resignation of 22 March.

Ground. The enemy returned. Our Division (Genl. Stephens) went to our alarm posts staid a few Hours and returned to camp, pitched our Tents & slept heartily.

4th Septr. staid in camp at Night I was on Guard at a Bridge Red Clay Creek about Mile & half off and near our alarm post with 2 Sub^s. 2 Serjeants 2 Corp^{ls} & 40 privates a peaceable G^d this night—Lieut. Davis of the Pensylvania Troops & Ens^n Westfall both of Scotts Brigade were with me early this Morning came down about 600 men Viz. 200 first with the Q^r. Masters bearing entranching Tools. Col^o. Febiger [50] with 200 & Col^o Willis with 200 they were followed by Waggons loaded with axes with which they felled trees plashing them to form a line by —about 2 in the afternoon Maj^r Genl Sullivans Division came down & took Possession of the lines we had been Plashing. it consists of between 2 & 3000 effective Men. at night was relieved by Capt. Stephen Ashby. [51]

6th Septr. G. Stephens Division Marched by Sun, about a Mile Encamped at Camp near Newp^t. staid here this night as we expected the enemy would be in motion early in the Morning of Sunday 7th. every necessary order was given to be in readiness.—the desserters from the enemy inform that on Saturday Morn^g they drew 5 days provisions which were to serve them to Philadel^a. or Wilmington at least. that their Tents and heavy Baggage were sent back to their Ships.

Monday 8th Sept. the enemy approached as near as Newark. [52] we all lay at our alarm posts.

Tuesday 9th at 2 in the morning we had order to march took the road from Newport to Wilmington 2 Miles then turned to almost North about 2 M^s more we then marched West course 10 Miles S. W. & crossed Brandywine Creek and encamped on the heights of the creek

Here, abruptly, the diary ends. For John Chilton time had almost run out.

50. Febiger, commanding the 11th Regt. and Lewis Willis, commanding the 10th Regt. had only 400 men between them.

51. Stephen Ashby, was a cousin of Capt. John Ashby in the 12th Virginia Regiment. He appears to have come from Hampshire County.

52. Newark, Del. was in the direct line of march but the British turned northward, paralleling the Brandywine, in the direction of Kennett Square, Pa.

Within what is essentially a routine journal we catch occasional glimpses of the day to day struggle. The march north was not easy. The heat was stifling. The rain did not refresh but only served to turn the wretched roads into rocky gullies. Men and horses slogged through the wild and barren landscape under a leaden sky. Sometimes they stopped by a dark mountain lake to clean off the accumulated grime. Usually their baggage wagons were far behind, bogged down in the mire. They were often hungry. They ate more gooseberries and wild raspberries than were good for them.

Torn with indecision, Washington waited until the 22nd of July before he was convinced that the British strike up the Hudson was not in the cards. All reports indicated that the British fleet had sailed out into the Atlantic on a southerly course. The Virginia troops were deployed along the Hudson between Stony Point and Fort Montgomery. Stirling's and Sullivan's divisions had crossed the river to set up a cross fire. After a week of inactivity he determined to give his troops a running start south. It would be a forced march, hoping to reach Philadelphia in time to meet the British coming from another direction.

The order reached the 3rd Virginia Regiment at Chester, N. Y. on the 25th. Stephen, in command of both his and Lincoln's divisions, took a southerly route west of the one on which they had come north. The roads were coated with mud, slippery and treacherous. Horses died in their traces, broken wagons were left abandoned by the way.

Chilton was shaken to the core by the incident on the morning of the 26th. That such a thing could happen to him, who had endured so much, reduced him to cold fury. The author of this "piece of strict, tho' ill-timed discipline" was Lieutenant Colonel William Heth, Marshall's second in command. Heth was much younger than Chilton but one would hardly expect a man who had marched with Morgan to Quebec to have developed the soul of a martinet.

The idiotic rest in the broiling sun at Hackitt's Town was, in Chilton's opinion, Heth's doing, as was the requirement that the men abandon the little things that helped to make life bearable, though they marched without shoes on their feet. Chilton does not blame Heth for the contretemps at Howell's Ferry, but the implication is there.

On the 31st of July Washington had received intelligence confirming the rumored sighting of the British fleet near the mouth of the Delaware, later that it was sailing again out to sea. Twice in one day the troops marched through Germantown. Finally

Washington allowed his men, exhausted by the extreme heat, to collapse at the Falls of the Schuylkill. With the eighteenth century belief that too much bathing was bad for their health in mind, he cautioned them to wash only "moderately".

On August 8th, still worried about the situation in the New York highlands, he sent his Virginia and Pennsylvania riflemen under Col. Daniel Morgan north to watch Burgoyne. Three days later came a dispatch that located the enemy fleet off, of all places, Sineputent Inlet in southern Maryland. Now completely mystified and realizing that his army was encamped in an unhealthy area, Washington prepared to move north.

At Camp Crossroads, about twenty miles north of Philadelphia, John Chilton had begun a letter to his brother Charles on the 11th of August.[53] It was the sort of letter that every junior officer has written or thought of writing since Caesar conquered Gaul. The promotion that never came irritated him to the point of appeal to higher authority. The senior officers agreed that his fortune was hard and wished they had power to give him the rank to which he was entitled by service and hardships endured. But, - and it was the inevitable "but" - "by doing so they would break their Rule of Rising by Seniority of Commissions." It was the old excuse. While other officers left their posts in times of stress and hardship, they still maintained their seniority and so outranked him. It seemed hardly fair.

One need take only a quick glance at the muster roll of field and staff officers of the 3rd Virginia Regiment for August 1777,[54] to understand Chilton's grievance. Charles West of Loudoun County, paid as a company captain in July, had won the coveted promotion to Major. Undoubtedly his commission bore a date earlier than Chilton's but he had certainly not remained with his regiment continuously or served as its temporary commander as Chilton had done. In fact he was even then home in Virginia.

The regiment had a new paymaster from Fauquier, Captain Hezekiah Turner, Ashby's brother-in-law, appointed on the 18th of July.[55] The captains were, in addition to Chilton and Ashby, Philip Francis Lee, Gustavus Brown Wallace, John Peyton, Robert Powell,

---

53. Letter, John Chilton to Charles Chilton, 11-17 August 1777. Keith of Woodbourne Papers, Virginia Historical Society.

54. **Revolutionary War Rolls** 1775-1783 (Virginia Jackets, Nos. 62-73) M246, Roll 97 (National Archives, Washington, D.C.)

55. Fitzpatrick, ed. **Writing of Washington**, Vol. 8, p. 464.

John Thornton, David Arell and William Washington.[56] John Francis Mercer,[57] also of Loudoun County, replaced Charles West as company commander.

Though Chilton felt much abused, he saw no merit in sulking in his tent. He still believed that he was in favor with the generals and was not afraid to argue a point with them when the chips were down. "Old Gen^r Stevens (Adam Stephen) and myself had some very sharp words at Morris Town," he wrote:

> On this occasion I was with two or three officers one evening at the Sutler's (Ramsay's). I had just went up to drink our fill in grog, the retreat beat. I told the Adjutant to step down while I paid the Chit, which I was doing when a Serg^t. and file of men came and informed me (that we) must go to the Genl. I went down very angry making the poor Sergeant and his men keep their distance. "Whew," says the Genl. "Capt. Chilton, is it possible that you should be out of your duty?" I told him it was possible but could not submit that it then was, that the strictest disciplinarians allowed 5 minutes out, and that I had not required two, that I knew my duty and had done it and, admitting I had made a slip, thought it too trifling to be sent for in that manner.
>
> He then said he did not know we were officers, asked our Pardons, asked us to drink grog, which we refused and went very angry away. The next day he called to me quite across a platoon to know how I did and seemed sorry for what he had done. So I even thought it was best to be on good terms again.

Chilton's over-reaction to Stephen's mild rebuke was perhaps indicative of nerves torn thin by fatigue and frustration. His hatred of Heth was festering within him. There is no question that he was jealous of this arrogant, tactless young man who had been raised to a position over him to do a job he knew he could do better. Yet

---

56. William Washington, 1752-1810, son of Bailey and Elizabeth (Storke) Washington. He married 1782, Jane Riley Elliot of South Carolina.

57. John Francis Mercer was a grandson of John and Catherine (Mason) Mercer of Marlborough Point. His father, James Mercer, owned a large tract in Loudoun County on which the present village of Aldie was founded in 1810. He was not related to General Hugh Mercer.

there must be truth in Chilton's complaint that Heth "was overbearing to inferior officers and remarkably mean and cringing to superiors." [58] Heth had a singular talent for making lasting enemies. Chilton's opinion was shared by many. Chilton continued:

> But we have a Gentleman in our Regmt., a Col^o. Wm. Heth, who takes great things upon himself. He entirely rules Col^o. Marshall and will cause him to be as much dispised as himself. Heth does not want sense but is imperious to the last degree. I was never tired of the Service until he joined our Regt. Heth has greatly the ascendency over Marshall which I could not have believed. Anything clever that is done in the Regmt., Heth takes the credit of. What is not well done is thrown on Marshall, which will sink his credit as Heth's rises.

Heth's mismanagement of the forced march, the petty nagging of men trying to do their best against appalling odds, the imperious orders and vituperative criticism he expressed so readily, outraged Chilton. More important was his influence on Marshall. Marshall was a good officer who could be depended upon to carry out orders with intelligence and dispatch, but he was acutely conscious of his lack of military experience. He had not much confidence in his own judgement and was, thus, not an innovative commander. Such a man fell easy prey to one like Heth, ready to pounce on any slip that can be turned to his advantage.

"I have a small notion of entering into the Sea Service," Chilton mused, "if I could have the command of some clever little snug Vessell...If Capt. William Blackwell were not out I should be almost tempted to quit the Service. His tent and mine adjoin so that we are always together when off duty."

A few days later John Chilton wrote to his brother's wife, the gentle Betsy Blackwell Chilton, a heart-warming letter filled with concern for her health and that of the children.[59] "My certain belief of the children being in the best hands," he wrote, "makes the fatigues of the campaign pass off as recreation. Who could not fight, bleed, even dare to die for such valuable friends? My task is

---

58. Letter, Heth to Morgan, 30 Sept. 1777; 2 Oct. 1777. Myers Collection, New York Public Library. These letters are revealing of Heth's characteristic attitude toward his contemporaries.

59. Letter, John Chilton to Elizabeth (Blackwell) Chilton, 14 August 1777. Keith of Woodbourne Papers, Virginia Historical Society.

an easy one compared to yours, - only the many and great obligations you all load me with are too heavy for me."

Through the mist of the sultry August day he tried to recall the faces of his children, but they elude him. "I hardly think I should know Tommy and Joe." Pretty, heedless Lucy, whose "flittering feet" must learn "to tread the paths of prudence and virtue,,' is but a fleeting memory. George and Nancy he had "forgot."[60] He had not seen them in more than a year but so much had happened - so much!

In a recent letter she had given him news of old friends. Information that Dr. Samuel Boyd was to marry Molly Brooke[61] evoked a guarded reply. "She is a fine girl and I shall ever esteem the Doctor for his care and humane usage of the sick and wounded when at Great Bridge. Some parts of his character I confess I am not enamored with, - but all have their foibles." (What foibles?) Joe Blackwell, her brother, was apparently in Virginia, but courting instead of recruiting. Alvin Mountjoy would tell them how Joe cursed the girls when he had smallpox and thus torpedo his chances, or so he promised.

His sister-in-law had also made some references to Captain James Scott. Possibly Scott had already returned to Virginia, ill and verging on nervous collapse. Chilton wrote: "I can't help being very sorry for poor Capt. Scott's afflictions of mind & body. Both are too much to be borne. I once had a tender friendship for him, tho' I confess he had used me in a manner that had cooled it much long before I entered the service." They had not quarreled because he did not think Scott had meant to hurt him.

He was her "ever obliged and affectionate brother" and, by the way, ask Joe to bring some tobacco back with him and ask Charles Chilton to have two or three dozen good twists made up for him for the winter. He would need them - or would he?

Days passed and there was still no news of the British. In the relentless August heat, time seemed to stand still.

Suddenly, on the afternoon of 21 August, Washington had a

60. It is absolutely impossible to reconcile the dates of birth of John Chilton's five children given in the **Bulletin** of the Fauquier society, June 1923, pp. 326-27 and elsewhere, with internal evidence in his letters. The only logical order is contained in his will, i. e. Thomas was the eldest, followed by Joseph, Lucy, George and Nancy.

61. Samuel Boyd, married Mary (Molly) Brooke, bond executed 13 August 1777, Humphrey Brooke, security. Boyd was a witness to John Chilton's will, dated 24 August 1776.

letter from John Page, President of the Council, in Virginia, that the enemy fleet appeared to about to enter the Chesapeake Bay. The army broke camp on the 23rd and within five miles of the capital, Washington called a halt. He wanted to prepare the men for an impressive march through Philadelphia to bring home to the people and Congress the urgent need for supporting American arms.

On the 24th of August, at about seven in the morning of a blistering summer day, with guns cleaned and polished, colors flying and drums and fifes playing a quickstep, 16,000 Continental and militia turned into Chestnut Street in Philadelphia. At the head of the procession rode General Washington followed by twelve light horse. Next came the cavalry and a company of pioneers with axes. Then, at intervals of 100 yards, came the Virginia brigades. Only a sprig of green leaves in their hats gave them some semblance of uniformity in dress. They were not quite soldiers, did not always keep step exactly, but they convinced the crowd that they meant business.

The rumor that Howe had landed 16,000 lobsterbacks at Head of Elk (Elkton, Md.) on the 27th of August was exaggerated, but it was still a formidable number. Howe had about 12,500 men to Washington's 11,000. That the British were "scary creatures" was an opinion that Chilton would live to see refuted.

On the banks of the Brandywine, twelve miles away, the stage was being set.

As a defensive barrier, the Brandywine was of little value. It was deep enough so that troops had to use the fords; but there were many fords. Unfortunately, Washington's reconnaissance failed to establish the number, or even the correct names of those they found. Howe's force made a feint at Chadd's Ford, the obvious crossing east of Kennett Square. His real plan of attack was to outflank Washington by Jeffries Ford far to the north and to encircle the positions guarding Chadd's Ford.

The "heights of the creek" mentioned by Chilton was known as the "Plowed Hill", three miles north of Chadd's Ford. At dawn on Thursday, September 11th two British columns moved out from Kennett Square. The weather was hot and humid. A heavy fog covered them until 7 o'clock, after which the hot sun burned through. On the crest of the ridge Brigadier George Weedon surveyed the panorama before him. To him we owe the account of the battle that follows. Inaccurate in minor detail, it nevertheless gives us a vivid picture of the last hours of Captain John Chilton and some of his valiant men.

The American Army [was] drawn up...opposite to Chadd's Ford; & General Maxwell [62] posted on the Enemy's side in a wood with 800 [63] light Infantry. At ½ past 8 the Enemy appeared & formed on the high grounds in front. They soon engaged Maxwell and he with great Firmness repulsed them twice with much loss. They were reinforced & he retreated in good order about 10 [o'clock], crossed & formed on the banks of the River. The rest of the Army were spectators of the gallantry of this little Corps, who frequently crossed & skirmished with the Enemy in the Course of the Day.

Our Battery was on an eminence which commanded the Ford & the cannonading made the Enemy retire several times; it was better served than theirs.

About 11 o'clock the General received intelligence that a considerable part of the Enemy's Army had filed off to our right & supposing that they meant to cross at Jones Ford Gen[l]. Sterling's & Stephen's Divisions were ordered to march to Birmingham Meeting House (4 miles) by different routes. They had gone about 1½ miles when the General had intelligence that the Enemy had not gone up & ordered the advanced divisions to halt, which they did for two hours; & then received orders to march as quickly as possible. Intelligence from the front repeated the account of the rapid progress of the Enemy, said to be about 1,500 or 2,000, & our troops went on in a Trott to gain the Meeting House Hills before them, which they did, but then discovered the Enemy's Main Body there, amounting to about 6,000.

However, they formed in an agreeable manner. General Woodford's Brigade being to the right, he detached Col. Marshall with his Regiment, (only 170 men) [64] to a fine wood on the right to cover his Field Pieces & right flank.

Thus prepared they discovered General Sullivan's Division marching up & the Brigadiers rode to him to receive Orders, when he directed them to move all to the

---

62. William Maxwell, ca. 1733-1769, a Scotch-Irish emigrant to America with considerable, if not distinguished, military service behind him. He was the unhappy victim of Heth's bitter animosity after Brandywine.

63. Including 200 Virginia Continentals.

64. Of these Chilton commanded about forty.

right to make room for his Division on the *left*.⁶⁵ In making this Alteration, unfavorable ground made it necessary for Woodford to move his Brigade 200 paces back of the Line, and threw Marshall's wood in his Front. The Enemy came on rapidly. Scott, who was next to Woodford was removed to bad ground & from his Brigade to the left...the whole line appeared in some confusion. Woodford's Brigade stood firmly and in good order. Marshall had orders to hold the Wood as long as it was tenable, & then retreat to the right of the Brigade. He received the Enemy with a Firmness which will do Honor to him and his little Corps as long as the 11th of Sept. is remembered. He continued there ¾ of an Hour and must have done amazing Execution. He was called off for fear of being surrounded & retreated in good order.

The Action became general. Woodford was wounded and retired to be dressed. The left wing gave way & the right followed. Woodford's Capt. of Artillery & 9 Lieut[ts] were wounded & more than half his men killed, but his two field pieces would have been saved by the extraordinary Exertions of the remaining Lieut[t] , with Lieut. Col. Febiger, Maj[r] Day & Sergeant Maj[r] Broughton, but that the Horses were shot down & they [were] obliged to quit them. About 6 [o'clock] General Green's Division arrived to cover the Retreat. One of his Brigades [Weedon's] gave the Enemy such a check as produced the desired effect. Nash's Brigade also marched, but too late to be of any service. Lincoln's Division under the command of Brigad[r] Gen[l] Wayne & Maxwell's Corps remained at Chadd's Ford where the Enemy made several violent attacks & were gallantly repulsed & great Numbers of them killed; but they got Possession of the Battery & these Troops joined in the general Retreat in the Evening to Chester where they arrived at 12 at night. They crossed the Schuylkill & encamped at the Falls & Germantown: recruited from the Hospitals a number equal to their losses &, on the 14th recrossed the Schuylkill in high spirits. Our loss in the Battle not more than 600 killed & missing. The

---

65. Because of this ill-considered move Sullivan was known among the troops as "the Evle-genius of America" according to Heth. Letter, Heth to Morgan, 30 Sept. 1777. Myers Collection, New York Public Library.

Enemy's immense! Such another Victory would establish the Rights of America & I wish them the Honour of the Field again tomorrow on the same Terms.

A "victory" that leaves the enemy master of the field is not usually celebrated. After some reflection Weedon wrote to John Page on the 2nd of October,[66] "The misfortune of losing the Battle of Brandywine put us back till the first of the month." General Nathanael Greene estimated that Washington lost 1,200 to 1,300 men of whom about 400 were taken prisoner. The Americans lost 11 guns. Howe lost 577 killed and wounded, and 6 missing. In the 3rd Virginia Regiment Dr. David Griffith counted over forty of its rank and file killed or wounded, three officers killed and four wounded.[67]

Sullivan's unfortunate manoeuvre which forced the 3rd Virginia Regiment into such terrible jeopardy was ill-conceived only because of his ignorance of the terrain. It appears that he simply executed an about-face and wheeled his division about the left wing, which automatically forced both Sterling and Stephen further to the right. Bad terrain caused Stephen to pull back leaving the 3rd Virginia well forward of his line. However Joseph Clark, a Princeton youth, records in his diary an appalling possibility not mentioned in official reports. "...this repulse," he writes, "was the most severe on the 3rd Virginia Regiment, who, through mistake, was fired on by our own men!"[68]

Captain John Ashby was wounded, it is said while going to the aid of the Marquis de Lafayette, who fell from his horse with a flesh wound in the leg. Newly promoted Lieutenant Robert Peyton was killed, as were William White and Apollos Cooper. Captain Philip Francis Lee was badly wounded. Colonel Thomas Marshall was everywhere, encouraging his men. His horse received two balls but he, miraculously, remained unscathed.

Chilton's company, caught in the vortex of this maelstrom during the terrible forty-five minutes before their forced withdrawal, suffered heavy losses. In addition to their captain, Sergeant

---

66. Letter, Weedon to John Page, 2 Oct. 1777. Weedon Papers, Chicago Historical Society.

67. Letter, David Griffith to Mrs. Hannah Griffith, 14 Sept. 1777. David Griffith Papers, Virginia Historical Society.

68. Clark, "Diary" in: **New Jersey Historical Society Proceedings**, Vol. VII, pp. 96-99.

Joshua Jenkins and Robert Coffee [69] were killed. Among the wounded were Lieutenant John Blackwell, Sergeants Henry Bradford and Moses Allen, along with John Brown, John Murphey, and Peter Moore. Michael Hynd, the drummer, was missing after the battle.[70]

The first column of British infantry had just reached the edge of the wood as Captain John Chilton fell with a gaping wound in his side. Fully conscious, he realized that the musket ball that had torn through his vitals had done damage beyond the power of any physician to repair. Around him the battle surged. There were so few against so many, too few to spare any to take him from the field. Here he would stay, under a tree, and watch their valiant efforts. Perhaps his presence might give them greater courage. He had nothing more to give.

As pain dimmed his vision he asked how they had fared. The position could not be held. The retreat had been sounded, they told him. They carried him to an old Meeting House that was being used as a field hospital. Tradition says that it was Birmingham, but Weedon identifies it as Concord Meeting House on the Chester Road near Marshall's Wood. Captain Chilton's work was not finished, but his time had run out. Others would have to finish the course.

---

69. Fauquier County Minute Book, March Court, 1778: It is ordered that the Treasurer pay Charles Chilton gent. L ¾ as an allowance for Mary Coffee the Widow of a Soldier who was killed in the Continental Army.

70. **Revolutionary War Rolls 1775-1783** (Virginia Jackets, Nos. 62-73) M246, Roll 97 (National Archives, Washington, D. C.)

Interlude
Brandywine to Germantown

An interval of only twenty-three days separated the battles of Brandywine and Germantown, but they were twenty-three crucial days in the history of the Revolutionary War. They were days of ambitious planning, furious preparation and burgeoning hope. The army, although it had been forced to leave the field at Brandywine, emerged from the battle curiously elated. In their first pitched battle with the enemy the Americans had not panicked, had inflicted some damage and had retreated in good order. It was true that mistakes had been made. Reconnaissance had been inadequate, intelligence poor and communication faulty. Some of their leaders, they thought, had lacked judgement, Sullivan, Maxwell, (though it is difficult to say what he did to merit Heth's vicious attack) and Stephen. A more balanced appraisal must place most of the blame at Washington's doorstep. His orders had been imprecise, tentative and sometimes contradictory. As Freeman, his biographer writes, "Washington conducted the Brandywine operation as if he had been in a daze."

If so, the next day Washington had fully recovered his facilities and was bursting with energy. The next morning he led his army northward through Philadelphia and encamped on the Schuylkill near Germantown. Fortunately the British did not pursue. As they rested Washington took steps to bolster their morale:

> The Gen[l] with peculiar satisfaction thanks those Gallant Officers & Soldiers who on the 11th Ins[t] bravely fought in their Countrys cause, ... Although the Event of that day from some unfortunate circumstances were not so favourable as could be wish'd, the Gen[l]. has the Satisfaction of Assuring the troops that from every Acc[t] ... he has been able to obtain, the Enemy's losses greatly exceeded ours & he has full Confidence that in another Appeal to Heaven we shall prove successful. The Honb[le].

Congress in Consideration of the Gallant behavior of the Troops on Thursday last, their fatigue since & from a full Conviction that on every future occasion they will manifest a bravery worthy the cause they have undertaken to defend, having been pleas'd to order 30 Hh^{ds}. of Rum to be distributed among them in such a manner as the Commander in Chief shall direct ... to each Officer & Soldier One Gill pr day while it lasts.

Having seen to the comfort of his army, Washington then sent out a flurry of letters in all directions asking for reinforcements and promising, if given them, to crush the British beyond any hope of immediate recovery. He even asked Major General Horatio Gates to give back Morgan and his Rangers "if his situation at all permitted." He wrote Gates on the 24th of September, having no idea that five days before at Freeman's Farm, Morgan had risked his entire command on Gates' behalf and had pulled off a startling coup that set the stage for the battle of Saratoga.

Though Gates could not spare Morgan, Washington's letters produced excellent results from officers of militia in New Jersey, Maryland and Virginia. Brigadier Alexander McDougall marched down from Peekskill with 900 men. William Smallwood came in with 1,100 Maryland militia. David Forman reported with 600 from New Jersey. By the end of the month Washington's strength had climbed to 11,000 men, nearly two thirds Continentals.

When Virginia was heard from, the news was even more exciting. Patrick Henry and the Virginia Assembly, now convinced that Howe was irrevocably committed to an attack on Philadelphia, were willing to release large numbers of militia, many of whom were already on the way. The First Virginia State Regiment under the colorful Colonel George Gibson had already reached York, Pennsylvania. A number of county militia units were on the march by companies and were arriving every day. The losses of Brandywine were severe (over 1,200 casualties, dead, missing or captured, and eleven artillery pieces) but not as large as had been expected. The 3rd Virginia Regiment had received a terrific mauling but many had emerged without a scratch. It is impossible to deny that the Virginia troops had come off the field with considerable honour and their morale was never higher. Lieutenant Colonel William Heth, in an uncharacteristic burst of generosity, said that the 3rd Virginia Regiment alone had prevented the British grenadiers and light infantry from advancing, long enough to save the army from utter ruin. The 11th Virginia Regiment had acted with almost equal valour and had narrowly escaped annihilation but came out with colours flying.

Washington continued to believe that Howe's losses were much greater than they really were. (Weedon's initial estimate of nearly 8,000 casualties had been considerably scaled down but no one dreamed that Howe had lost only 583 men.) When he learned on the 3rd of October that Howe had sent a detachment of 3,000 to the Head of Elk to bring in supplies and a sizeable one down the south bank of the Delaware to lay siege to Fort Mifflin, he felt certain that Howe had so weakened his force near Germantown that he could not resist a sustained assault. Washington called a council of war to decide the feasibility of an immediate attack. The majority of the council, including Muhlenberg, Stephen and Greene, thought such action premature. Five officers, including General Charles Scott, disagreed. Washington, never one to base his action on a consensus, decided to move to attack.

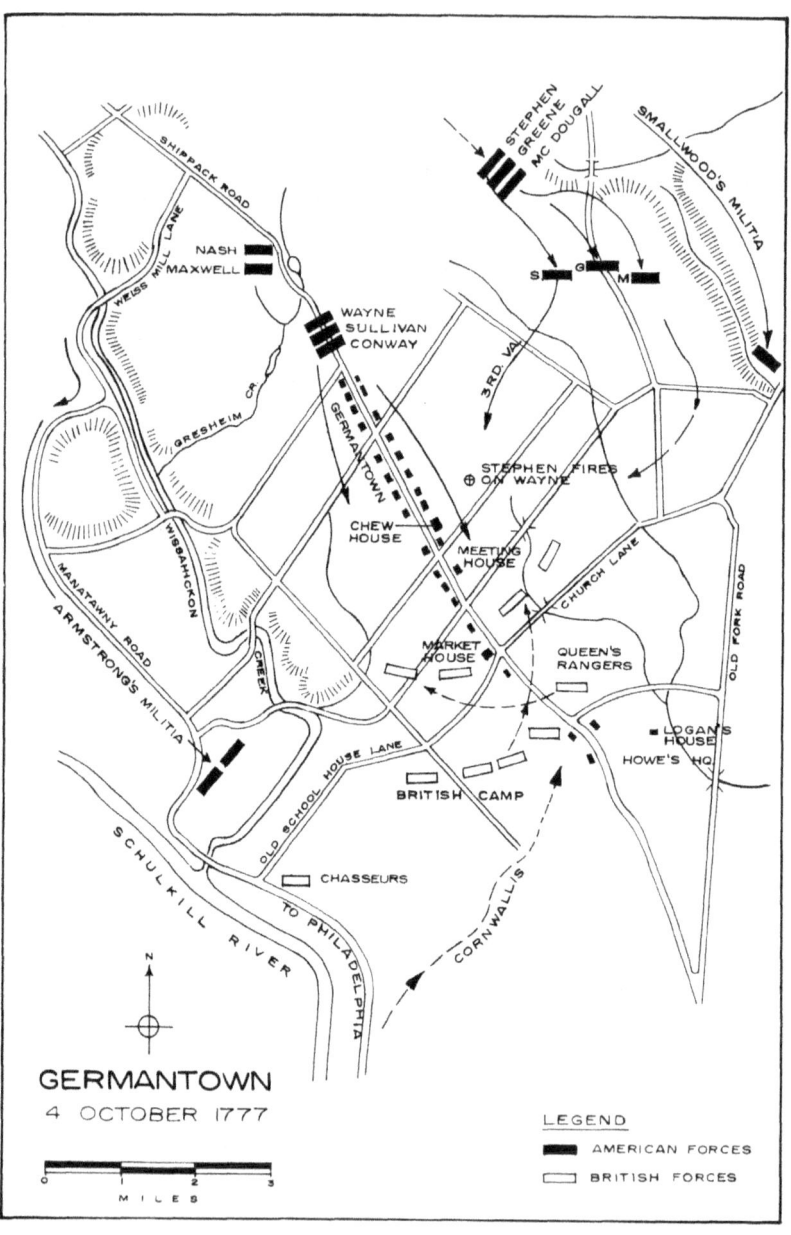

VII

Germantown

The long, golden days of August were over in the Virginia piedmont. The harvest had been good. Charles Chilton had so written his brother John in August. John had been "much rejoiced ... as I was uneasy, having heard that crops were poor in Virginia." Now the barns were bursting with corn and wheat and the farmers could again relax, secure in the knowledge that their families were provided for during the winter. Many of them had promised that, once the harvest was in, they would leave. Now, one by one, those promissory notes were falling due.

So, when Washington's urgent appeal had reached them after Brandywine, they were ready. Some, in fact, were already on their way.[1] Those who had pledged their service to the old companies or regulars departed one by one or in small groups late in August and arrived in Pennsylvania before Brandywine. Their enlistments were for three years as had been customary in the Virginia Line. By far the greater number marched with the County Militia with enlistments of only three or four months. Washington still deplored the short enlistments but, by that time, was willing to take all that he could get. Within three months, with a sufficient force, the war might be won. Without them it could easily be lost.

The pitch of enthusiasm was such in Fauquier that it was decided to send two battalions, an enormous contingent that

---

1. On the 30th of August, 1777, the Governor's Council ordered eight Northern Neck Counties, including Fauquier, to draw out one third part of their militia and march them to Frederick, Maryland, to await the orders of General Washington. They were to be officered as required by law and equipped in the best manner possible. **Journals of the Council of the State of Virginia, Vol. I, Part II, p. 478.**

would, if completed, have numbered over 1,000 men.[2] One who went with them, later claimed that there were nearly that number originally on the march. It seems hardly possible and the same person, whose memory of overall fact is reliable, is often inconsistant in numerical detail. Other sources indicate that the Fauquier militia under Colonel William Edmonds, which crossed the Potomac at Noland's Ferry during the first two weeks of September, 1777, totalled about a fourth of that number. Nevertheless, they were on their way and news of their advent preceded them. For their comrades who awaited them near the White Horse Tavern on the Lancaster Road they could not come too soon.

Still dazed by a battle that had wiped out half their number, officers of the Fauquier companies in the 3rd and 11th Virginia Regiments surveyed what remained of their respective commands. They were a little surprised to find themselves almost leaderless. Brigadier General William Woodford had taken a slight wound in the left hand. That, and the perverse refusal of almost everyone to pay attention to his complaints about his rank, caused him such pain that he retired to Bethlehem, Pennsylvania, to recover. Of his regimental commanders only Colonel Marshall astride his bullet-riddled horse was on hand. Crawford's 7th Virginia Regiment was commanded by Major John Cropper. Crawford himself was on detached service with 300 lightly armed scouts, doing what, is unrecorded. Whatever it was, his biographer says, he was doing it with "his usual bravery and efficiency."[3] Colonel Daniel Morgan, still absentee commander of the 11th and 15th Regiments was, of course, quite busy at Saratoga.

Lieutenant Colonel Christian Febiger had certainly commanded the 11th Virginia Regiment with considerable distinction at Brandywine and had extricated it from a possible trap with masterly skill. His promotion to Colonel on the 26th of September was generally acclaimed, but it made the men of the 11th Regiment

---

2. The British regiment or battalion normally had ten companies of 64 men each with about 90 officers. The Continental regiments, except in Virginia, had only eight companies. As the war progressed the number of Virginia companies was reduced in conformity with the other states. In the summer of 1777 the Council authorized companies of no fewer than 38 or more than 56 men. The size of the Virginia regiment could vary from 350 to 630 men. The average is generally placed at 350 officers and men **fit for duty.** See: M. M. Boatner, III, **Encyclopedia of the American Revolution,** p. 927.

3. **Ibid.,** pp. 303-306.

decidedly uneasy. There was not room for two Colonels in any regiment and the possibility that Morgan would relinquish command unless forced to do so, seemed remote indeed. They expected that Febiger would be given another regiment; and so he was, but not immediately.

The commander of the Fauquier men in the 11th Virginia Regiment was missing, though accounted for. Captain William Blackwell was ill, partly from fatigue and partly from grief at the loss of his best and most faithful friend, John Chilton. He was persuaded to go to the country to recover, which he did with great reluctance. Fortunately his 1st Lieutenant, John Marshall, was alive and well. As acting commander, he signed a payroll dated 1 October containing only 30 names exclusive of commissioned officers. They had, of course sent eight men off with Colonel Morgan to Saratoga. Five were sick or wounded including Sergeant Joseph Garner who had received a musket ball in the groin and would not return.[4]

Brigadier General George Weedon's heart was bursting with pride. The performance of his brigade had brought from Division Headquarters a message from General Nathanael Greene:[5]

> The Genl takes the earliest opportunity to return his warmest thanks to the Officers & Sold^{rs}. of Genl. Weedon's Brigade engag'd in the late Action for their Spirited & Soldierly behavior, a Conduct so worthy under so many disadvantages cannot fail of establishing to themselves the highest Military reputation.

The gallantry of the 10th Virginia Regiment under General Edward Stevens was notable and Thomas Blackwell's Fauquier company shared the applause. Blackwell himself was detached after Brandywine with part of his company to help reinforce the garrison of Fort Mifflin on Mud Island in the Delaware River below Philadelphia. Command of what remained of his company fell to his brother, Lieutenant Joseph Blackwell who wondered what, if anything, he was expected to do in a battle with only seven men fit for duty.

Things were not much better in the 3rd Virginia Regiment. In

---

4. Herbert A. Johnson, ed., **The Papers of John Marshall**, Vol. I, pp. 4-10.

5. **Valley Forge Orderly Book of General George Weedon**, pp. 45-46. MS in the Library of the American Philosophical Society, Philadelphia.

the first place Colonel Thomas Marshall, as acting commander of Woodford's entire brigade, had not much time to give them. Captain John Ashby had been wounded but insisted on remaining with his men. Fortunately Lieutenant Valentine Peyton, his second in command was one of only two company officers in the 3rd Regiment who came through the battle undamaged. Nathaniel Ashby was, for some reason, not about. The state of Ashby's company is not certain from existing records but one of his men, writing after the Battle of Germantown, indicates that their losses had been considerable. Among them was Micajah Farrow, son of Ashby's neighbor in Virginia.

We have a better idea of the condition of the company once commanded by the late Captain Chilton. His brother-in-law and second in command, 1st Lieutenant John Blackwell, had also been slightly wounded but, like Ashby, felt that this was no time to indulge in self-pity. Upon him had fallen full responsibility for Chilton's company. His brother, Joseph Blackwell, had been the other company officer of the 3rd Regiment to emerge unscathed, but his injured eye was becoming progressively worse. Fortunately William Moore, a sergeant who had been recently commissioned as Ensign could carry some of the load. Of the N. C. O.s only Sergeant Chichester Matthews and William Tomlin were fit for duty. The seven wounded were being cared for by Jonathan Crooke on duty in the hospital. Nine new recruits had arrived, but one of those was sick and one had, alas, left without leaving any message. Brandywine had been too much for him.

Robert English, who had been with the company since its beginning, had also had enough. He deserted and, to make matters worse, had foolishly allowed himself to be caught. The penalty was hanging, a prospect that Blackwell hated to think of. The reader will be relieved to know that he talked his way out of it. Two years later he was alive and well in Fauquier County, witnessing a deed.

Six new recruits had been left in Leesburg for smallpox inoculation, including Sergeant Henry Bradford's brother William and Billy Tomlin's brother Stephen. William Moffett, also in Leesburg, was quite ill and it was feared might not be able to continue further. Dickie Beale was present but was expected to leave the company shortly. Most of the administrative duties had fallen to him and his superior intelligence and capability had attracted the attention of Colonel William Heth. After fighting well at Germantown he was appointed regimental sergeant major and, soon afterwards, adjutant.

Lieutenant John Blackwell was promoted to the rank of

Captain of the company on the 15th of September.[6] However, both he and his brother signed a report giving the condition of the company on the 14th of October, 1777, with the customary oath:

> We do Swere that the Within Muster Roll is a true State of the Company Without Fraud to the United States or to any Individual According to the best of our Knowledge.

What had become of Captain James Scott *after* his Fauquier Independent Company went home cannot be easily ascertained from the records. William Payne, "a man of veracity," thought in 1834 that Captain Scott was in the battle of Brandywine. At that time Corporal Billy Tomlin, who certainly was at Brandywine and wanted to be as helpful as possible to Scott's distressed heirs, could not remember having seen him after May. If, as Tomlin says, his company had been more or less attached to Stirling's division and some remained, they may have seen some heavy, heavy fighting. The most reasonable supposition is that part of the company stayed, but under another command. William Kincheloe and John Hathaway were in Fauquier County late in August,[7] but, as we will see later, had certainly returned after the Battle of Germantown.

So things stood during the short interval between two major engagements. The Virginia line, especially the 3rd Virginia Regiment had done itself honour, but at fearful cost. Unquestionably the expected arrival of the militia units from Virginia was uppermost in their thoughts and served to lift their flagging spirits. As days passed without them, anxiety grew.

On the 16th of September Howe started his main column north. Cornwallis moved to link up with Howe at White Horse Tavern. Washington meanwhile had taken refuge across the Schuylkill to avoid being trapped between it and the Delaware. He

---

6. Revolutionary War Rolls 1775-1783 (Virginia Jackets, Nos. 62-73, M246, Roll 97, National Archives).

7. Fauquier County Minute Book, 1773-1780, 25 August 1777: John Hathaway, William Kincheloe, Minor Winn and Thomas Bartlett, or any three, to allot to Elizabeth Rust her dower in the Lands and other estate of John Rust, dec'd.

left General Anthony Wayne's [8] division near Paoli to harass the enemy's left flank. The British rear guard surprised Wayne on the night of September 21st with a bayonet charge. The Americans fled with heavy losses. The next day Howe crossed the Schuylkill at Swede's Ford (Norristown) without opposition. He was then between Washington's army and Philadelphia. There was no way that Washington could prevent the capture of the city.

From his headquarters at Pennypacker's Mill on the Schuylkill about 25 miles above Philadelphia, Washington did not find the outlook entirely black. He knew that the Delaware River forts blocked the British supply ships, and that Howe had been forced to send part of his army to reduce them and also to bring supplies from Head of Elk. Furthermore the remaining force had been split in two: the garrison in Philadelphia under Cornwallis and the main army encamped five miles north on the heights around Germantown. The failure to engage at Swede's Ford had given Howe an exaggerated idea of American impotence. He had not even bothered to erect defenses at Germantown.

On the 29th of September Washington moved to the Shippack Road, five miles from Pennypacker's Mill and on the 2nd of October another three miles to Centre Point, as close as he could get to the British without tipping his hand. His army was now reinforced to 8,000 Continentals and 3,000 militia. The Virginia militia was expected daily but had not arrived. Nevertheless Washington decided to attack the British at Germantown.

The plan of attack has been criticised as far too complicated for execution by experienced regulars, to say nothing of a combination of regulars and raw militia. However upon examination it is difficult to suggest a better one. The terrain was rugged and broken. The roads were horrible. It had been raining for days. The distances to be covered by the four advancing columns differed widely, making coordination difficult. Communication between the columns was nearly impossible. Success depended on perfect timing and perfect timing was simply not in the cards.

The strongest force, under General Nathanael Greene, was to make a wide envelopment through Lucken's Mill to hit the British

---

8. Anthony Wayne, 1745-1796, a prosperous tanner before the Revolution. Appointed Col. of the 4th Penna. Battalion, 3 Jan. 1776, he marched to Canada and fought at Trois Rivieres 8 June. He was later commandant at Fort Ticonderoga. Promoted to Brigadier 21 Feb. 1777, he saw heavy action at Chadd's Ford. He was acquitted of negligence by a court-martial which he requested after the Paoli incident.

right where, it was thought, most of the enemy strength was concentrated. In Greene's three divisions, with Stephen's on the right and McDougall's [9] on the left, was two thirds of Washington's entire force, including the entire Virginia line. Protecting Greene's left were the militia brigades of General William Smallwood's Marylanders and General David Forman's Additional Continental Regiment. They were to follow the old York Road, making a wide sweep around the British right and attack from the rear. If this took place it would be an added bonus. Washington had not much confidence in the militia. As it happened Smallwood's and Forman's troops marched out of the picture. They never even reached the battlefield.

The other main column was led by General Sullivan with his own division and those of Wayne and Stirling. They were to follow the Shippack Road to Chestnut Hill, then drive for the British Center along the Germantown Road. On Sullivan's right was the fourth and last column, about 1,000 Pennsylvania militia under General John Armstrong. Their objective was the British left wing composed mostly of Hessians.

It is probable that Washington had anticipated some problems in coordinating the attack but he must have been wildly optimistic not to have realized that close contact between four widely separated columns marching in the dead of night over fifteen miles or rugged terrain was next to impossible. It was expected that the lead units would be within two miles of Howe's outposts by 2 a.m. on the morning of the 4th of October. Allowing three hours for the remainder to catch up and deploy, the attack was scheduled to begin at 5 a.m.

The rough roads, black night and heavy fog slowed Greene's column considerably. Somewhere along the road Greene took a wrong turn and nearly an hour was lost getting back on course. The Virginia troops slogging along to his right were becoming more and more uneasy. General Adam Stephen was drunk. Marshall and Febiger, seeking direction, were given orders so nonsensical that Febiger, who was closer to the main column, ignored them and followed closely on Greene's right. Marshall, acting commander of Woodford's Brigade, began to lose contact, veering off to the right.

---

9. Alexander McDougall, 1732-1786, was born at Islay, Inner Hebrides but was brought to America at the age of six. A successful merchant in New York before the war, he was imprisoned for writing seditious literature. He was appointed Brigadier just before the start of the New York campaign in 1776 and commanded the forces in the Hudson Highlands during most of the war.

In the blinding fog it was impossible to be sure that the vague shapes ahead were not the enemy.

As the dawn broke there was no sign of the sun, only an impenetrable haze. Suddenly from the right came the sound of heavy gunfire. Bewildered, Marshall halted his men. He now had no idea where he was, as the firing seemed to come from the rear. Then suddenly ahead loomed a massive stone fortified mansion from every window of which poured musket fire. Marshall then knew that he had led his brigade far off course and into some hideous trap.

The explanation was simple. At daybreak advanced units of Sullivan's column had made contact with the enemy. Alerted that something was amiss, the British light infantry under Lieutenant Colonel Thomas Musgrave [10] made a valiant attempt to slow the advance. Falling back before Sullivan's superior strength in the fog, Musgrave was soon aware that Wayne threatened to cut him off. With 120 of his men he took refuge in the large stone house of Benjamin Chew, the late Attorney General of Pennsylvania. Sullivan's troops pressing forward into the center of the British lines dashed by Musgrave's place of hiding without stopping.

Not until the reserves under Lord Stirling, accompanied by the commander-in-chief, came abreast of the Chew house, did Musgrave reveal himself. At almost exactly the same time the 3rd and part of the 15th Virginia Regiments of Woodford's Brigade emerged from the fog in the opposite direction. After Washington was persuaded that it was unwise to leave this enemy strongpoint in his rear, Lieutenant William Smith of the 15th Virginia Regiment approached the fortress under a flag of truce to demand its surrender. He was promptly cut down by enemy musketry. Enraged by this flagrant violation of the rules of war, General Knox moved up several three-pounders. They had no effect on the heavy masonry walls. Attempts at arson were no more rewarding. Finally Washington realized that they could delay no longer and, posting Maxwell's brigade on the grounds to continue the siege, ordered the rest onward.

Sullivan's men were now far beyond the Chew house in contact with the British center. They were unsettled by the firing at the Chew house, well to their rear. Suddenly the left wing under Wayne was fired on from the rear at much closer range. General Charles Scott's Brigade, also far off course, had blundered into

---

10. Thomas Musgrave, 1737-1812, commander of the 40th Regiment of Foot, succeeding Lt. Col. James Grant killed at Long Island.

Wayne's rear in the fog. Mistaking it for the enemy, they launched an attack. Wayne's division broke and fled and Sullivan's soon followed their example.

Much farther north Greene's column on the Lime Kiln Road had lost support from both right and left. Only a part of Stephen's division remained on the right and McDougall, who was supposed to cover his left flank, had veered far to the north. Nevertheless they drove straight into the British right wing with bayonets bared and penetrated the enemy line more than a half mile. With both flanks exposed Greene feared that he would be surrounded and ordered a withdrawal. Most of the Virginia troops managed to fight their way out, but the 9th Regiment, which had advanced to Market Square, was unable to do so. Colonel Mathews and his men were captured along with 100 prisoners they themselves had taken.

Washington was still near the Chew house when his army began to fall back. Attempts to rally the Continentals proved impossible. They jammed the roads and would not stop. What had begun as a retreat became wild panic. A magnificent opportunity for a decisive victory lay in ruins. As it appeared that the enemy was too disorganized to follow up their advantage, the panic subsided, and Washington was able to lead his beaten army back to Pennypacker's Mill in fairly good order. Cornwallis followed them with three fresh battalions from Philadelphia, but made no attempt to contact.

Casualties in the Virginia line in the Battle of Germantown were relatively heavy, 30 killed, 117 wounded and 181 missing. Most of the troops missing and a high percentage of killed and wounded were in the unlucky 9th Regiment.[11] The Fauquier men seem to have gotten off lightly. In the 3rd Regiment Captain John Blackwell's company (formerly Chilton's) had no further losses. Captain John Ashby was still suffering from the wound received at Brandywine and was further disabled by rheumatism as the result of exposure. He was forced to resign his commission on the 28th

---

11. The 9th Regiment was doomed to long captivity. Colonel Mathews, who was wounded but recovered, wrote Washington from his prison on Long Island as late as October, 1780 asking his consideration of the "forlorn state of your Officers of the 9th Virginia Regt. Captured at the battle of Germantown." Col. George Mathews, 1739-1812, was exchanged 5 Dec. 1781 and joined Greene's army in the south. He was "attached" to the 3rd Va. Regt. but Col. Abraham Buford remained in command.

of October. Woodford appointed Valentine Peyton to succeed him according to the following certificate:[12]

> Mr Valentine Peyton, Lieut. in the 3rd Virginia Reg^t. is entitled to a company by the resignation of Capt. Ashby but in order to do Mr. Peyton Justice his Commission should be dated back to the death of Capt. Chilton, 11 Sept. 1777. Certified under my hand this 25th Novr. 1777.
> Wm. Woodford, Brig'd^r. Gen'l.

In the 10th Regiment Lieutenant Joseph Blackwell of "Elk Run" reported three men of his brother's company slightly wounded. He only knew of one officer killed who was well known in Fauquier, Captain John Eustace of Stafford.[13] He was undamaged though his breeches had been cut at the knee by a bullet.

In the 11th Regiment, John Ashby's brother, Benjamin, a 2nd Lieutenant and Regimental Quartermaster, had a slight wound, the first since joining as an ensign when the regiment was formed.

Lieutenant John Marshall, in command of William Blackwell's company in the 11th Regiment, had been in the thick of the fighting around the Chew house and had been wounded in the hand. His report to his father Colonel Thomas Marshall, still acting commander of Woodford's Brigade, on the 13th of October, lists no casualties though four reported sick may have been wounded. Captain William Blackwell was still ill in early November and in January the company is referred to as that of the "late Capt. Blackwell." He had, in fact, resigned his commission because of illness on the 10th of January 1778. Thereafter John Marshall signed the payroll as "Lieutenant commanding".[14]

The 11th Virginia Regiment suffered its most crushing blow on the 9th of October when "Old Denmark", the wily and engaging Christian Febiger, was given the 2nd Virginia Regiment. This regiment in Weedon's Brigade had done much to redeem its previously poor showing by gallant action at Brandywine and

12. Revolutionary War Rolls 1775-1783 (Virginia Jackets, Nos. 62-73, M246, Roll 97, National Archives).

13. John Eustace, d: 1777, was a nephew of William Eustace, Sheriff of Fauquier in 1769, and a cousin of the Eustace sisters who later married John and Joseph Blackwell.

14. **The Papers of John Marshall**, op. cit., Vol. I, pp. 12-13. John Marshall was appointed deputy judge advocate 20 Nov. 1777, but did not serve in that capacity until 16 April 1778.

Germantown, but it badly needed a leader. With Morgan still absent the 11th Regiment was without a field grade officer. In January Captain Charles Porterfield was in command.

The most important casualty after Germantown was the bibulous Major General Adam Stephen. His incapacity had given Marshall the fright of his life and he was justifiably bitter. Febiger was more tolerant since he had ignored most of his drunken orders, but part of his regiment too had wandered off to the right and become embroiled in the siege of the Chew house. Generals Muhlenberg and Weedon had both stuck with Greene after they learned that Stephen's commands were incoherent. It was Brigadier General Charles Scott who had real cause for resentment. It was men of his brigade who had fired on Wayne from the rear, which may have triggered the panic in Sullivan's command. Scott was unwilling to accept the blame for that disastrous misjudgement.

Stephen countered by accusing Scott of cowardice at Brandywine, a monstrous charge without any foundation whatever. In addition he recklessly accused the troops of running from victory. He concluded his letter to Washington on the 9th of October: [15]

> Whereever my Conduct is Suspected I would be obliged to your Excellency to order a speedy & just scrutiny ... I flatter myself that I have given no just cause to the gentlemen I have now the honour to command to find fault with my conduct.

Washington had had enough. To Stephen's dismay he ordered a court of enquiry into Stephen's conduct over the past three months. Stephen flattered himself, but stood alone. The gentlemen he had the honour to command were relentless. He was sentenced to dismissal from the army. Washington quickly approved, ending the military career of his old friend and associate at arms.

General George Weedon, from his headquarters at a place he called "Paulin's Mill", wrote two letters to his friend John Page after the Battle of Germantown. The first, dated incredibly the same day, finds the writer so unnerved by the turn of events that

---

15. Letter, Stephen to Washington, 9 Oct. 1777. Washington Papers, Library of Congress.

his normally legible handwriting is shaky.[16] He gives a clear account of the battle plan and its outcome as he saw it from the van of Greene's column. Having driven the enemy back with considerable loss, he was bewildered and terribly disappointed by the collapse of Sullivan's line on their right which forced their withdrawal. However, he writes, "though the Army arrived here again last night much fatigued having marched all night and all day without halting or refreshing", he was happy to find "that they have no objection to another tryal which must take place soon."

Four days later he had regained his composure and, though laid up with a fever and a cold, we find his handwriting relaxed and his optimism returned.[17] The misfortune, he has concluded, was due to "the most horrid Fogg" he ever saw but "so sportive is fortune and the chances of war so uncertain that when Victory was in our hands we had not Grace to keep it." It especially distressed him that, having overrun the enemy's camp, "Trophies lay at our feet but so certain were we of making a general defeat of it that we passed them by in the pursuit and by that means lost the Chief part of them."

"Such disappointments as these try the Philosophy of a man and happy is he who is so much a predestinarian as to suppose all is for the best." He is truly exasperated that they have only "barren hills for our camps and low Dutch cottages for our quarters ... while the Tyrants of the land are in the most elegant buildings, - even down to a lance corporal." "Patience is a jewel," he writes without conviction.

On the day after the battle Lieutenant Colonel George Gibson arrived with his 1st Virginia State Regiment. This was a special regiment, raised by Act of the Assembly, of 226 experienced men whose tours of duty elsewhere had expired. They were enlisted for three years and were in all respects equal to the Continentals. Temporarily they were assigned to Muhlenberg's brigade to replace the ill-fated 9th Regiment.

On the same day the long-awaited Virginia militia began to come in. Companies from Prince William, Culpeper, Loudoun, and Berkeley Counties were formed into a separate brigade under the command of Colonel William Crawford. A larger group from

---

16. Letter, George Weedon to John Page, letter dated 4 October but written on the following day. Weedon Papers, Chicago Historical Society.

17. Letter, George Weedon to John Page, dated 8 October 1777. Weedon Papers, Chicago Historical Society.

Fauquier was attached to the 3rd Virginia Regiment in Woodford's Brigade.[18]

The make up of the Fauquier contingent merits study because it was neither formed according to plan nor did its performance meet expectations. The reason is obvious. Unfortunately the men were, for the most part, enlisted for only three months. They arrived after the battle of Germantown and, though another major engagement was expected that year, none took place. Not all of them returned to Fauquier County in December, but most did. It is, therefore, not with the hope of discovering unsung heroes that we undertake to determine who they were and why their great expectations came to naught.

In the summer of 1777 the Fauquier Militia was commanded, as it had been sixteen years before, by William Edmonds. He was a stocky, slightly florid man of 43, strong-willed but genial. He loved his 514 acre estate just outside the county seat, called "Oak Spring", his blooded horses and his position in the community. In it he had held a succession of useful offices, Justice since 1771, Sheriff in 1763 and 1774 and, of course, County Lieutenant most of the time. On the 26th of September 1775, he had attained the rank of Colonel by appointment of the Committee of Safety.

Next to him in line was Martin Pickett, his lieutenant in 1761 at the age of 19, and now Fauquier County's leading merchant and man of affairs. Major Martin Pickett had stuck with the militia and certainly deserved to command a second battalion if there was to be one. At 35 he was of medium height, slightly swarthy, with a firm jaw and snapping black eyes. As a member of the Virginia Assembly he was actively trying to give Fauquier effective representation, especially in tax legislation and other matters having to do with commerce.

Of the other militiamen of 1761 not many were still interested, although some had sons who were actively engaged. William Edmonds' brother Elias, who lived at "Ivy Hill" adjoining "Oak Spring," had a son, young Elias, 23 and very promising. There were others, notably John Bayse, William Ransdell and William Bragg, whose sons carried on. One of the original company, John Blackwell, aged 44, was still active as a captain of a company.

The writer is somewhat loath to introduce still another in this army of Blackwells who served in some capacity in the Revolution but John Blackwell, eldest son of Colonel William and Elizabeth

---

18. Lt. Col. Martin Pickett claimed that the Fauquier Militia formed a separate regiment under Woodford, but it is not substantiated in official record.

(Crump) Blackwell, cannot be omitted. Born in 1735, he had married in 1765 his cousin, Ann Blackwell, sister of Captain William Blackwell of the 11th Virginia Regiment and of Elizabeth Blackwell, the wife of Armistead Churchill. He had inherited much of his father's Elk Run property when his father died in 1772. He had long been a Justice, was Sheriff in 1773 and was very active in the community. As far as can be determined, he had no military talent whatever.

In March of 1777 there were in existence six militia companies, commanded by Captains Nicholas George, John Webb, William Settle, Charles Bell, John Blackwell and, possibly, Edward Digges.[19] Between March and August some changes took place. Captain John Webb died and was replaced by Captain William Ball. Captain Nicholas George resigned and William Ball also assumed temporary command of his company until a replacement could be appointed. William Settle also resigned, apparently to accept a commission in a Continental line regiment. He was replaced by Captain Charles Williams. By the end of August two other men who had not previously been associated with the militia were trying to raise companies. They were Benjamin Harrison,[20] son of Colonel Thomas and Ann (Grayson) Harrison, and Samuel Blackwell,[21] eldest son of Joseph and Lucy (Steptoe) Blackwell. At 32, Samuel Blackwell was well educated and darkly handsome. It is said that he had studied for the ministry but had never served. His two younger brothers were Chilton's lieutenants. His four sisters were married to John and Charles Chilton, Martin Pickett and Thomas Keith.

The ambitious plan to send two battalions from Fauquier County to join Washington's army in Pennsylvania must have been conceived during the first week of September, 1777. It could not have been earlier because Governor Henry would not have allowed it. Had it been much later they could not have reached their

---

19. Edward Digges was of a well-to-do Charles County, Maryland family who came to Fauquier and purchased land within the present limits of Warrenton. He and his son, Edward, Jr., hold public office and it is somewhat difficult to distinguish between them.

20. Benjamin Harrison, 1744-1798, youngest son of Col. Thomas and Anne (Grayson) Harrison. He married _____ Rector. His son, Burr Harrison, d: 1842, of "Monterey" m. 1789, Lucy Pickett, dau. of Capt. William and Lucy (Blackwell) Pickett.

21. Samuel Blackwell, 1745-1814. He married (1) Sarah Beale, (2) Margaret (Peggy) Gillison.

destination when they did. It was obviously impossible to enlist anything like the number of men required and it is doubtful if any of them would have enlisted for three years. A three to four month tour of duty was the most that could be demanded. The first battalion under Colonel William Edmonds left Fauquier Courthouse about the 15th of September, before news of the battle at Brandywine had had time to reach them. They followed the usual route, crossing the Potomac at Noland's Ferry and marching in a cold drizzle toward Philadelphia, a distance of some 200 miles.

The clearest and probably most accurate description of the march comes from our old friend Jeremiah Brown, who gave us useful reports on Hampton and Great Bridge. He had been out of service since he took part in the fracas at Colonel Brent's house on the Potomac in August of 1776. He was drafted, he says, in early September of 1777 as a private in a company commanded by Samuel Blackwell of Fauquier in a regiment commanded by Colonel William Edmonds with Armistead Churchill as Lieutenant Colonel and Martin Pickett as Major. They marched through Leesburg, Frederick Town, Maryland, Little York, Pennsylvania, and crossed the Susquehanna River to Lancaster, where the regiment was given arms. They then marched to join the army under General Washington at Pennypacker's Mill near the Delaware River, arriving a few days after the battle of Germantown. There they were attached to Woodford's Brigade composed of the 3rd, 7th, 11th and 15th Regiments. His regiment, the 3rd, was commanded by Colonel Thomas Marshall, with Lieutenant Colonel William Heth and Major Charles West. Three months and two weeks later he was discharged at White Clay Creek, near Germantown, and returned to Virginia. There his brother, Jesse Brown, aged 12, greeted him and two of his buddies, John Jacobs and Thomas Kirk. They said that they had been in Pennsylvania.

This neat and straightforward account indicates that Brown had an excellent memory at 75, and a nice ability to recall what might appear most likely on the official record, which he had probably consulted. He did not include some of the other things that took place of which he must have been aware. He wanted a pension, not controversy. He received it, $25.42 per annum.

It is necessary to go to a less articulate and orderly account to obtain a hint of what really happened along the way and afterward. Reuben Bramblet, 20 years old at the time, volunteered for three months in early September under Captain Samuel Blackwell and just after he had joined his corps he was marched to the battle ground (of Germantown). He then wrote: [22]

> The Colonel of the regiment was Armistead Churchill but he did not command long and went back on the march and the regiment was then conducted to headquarters by Major Francis Triplett. There were two companies, one commanded by Captain Benjamin Harrison and the other by Captain Blackwell.

After his arrival at headquarters they joined the 3rd Virginia Regiment. He turned out under Colonel Innes to fight the Hessians who had landed on their side of the Schuylkill but the Hessians ran and no fight took place. Before trying to reconcile Bramblet's astonishing statement with Brown's, let us consider the equally odd one of William King, about 16 years old, who enlisted as a private for three months in Captain John Blackwell's company. Young King wrote as follows: [23]

> A short time before the Battle of Germantown (we) marched north and joined the main army above White Marsh Creek in the State of Pennsylvania at Pennypacker's Mill. The day after the Battle of Germantown (we) marched by Philadelphia and on to winter quarters at Valley Forge and (were) discharged. Much of his service was spent under Capt. Samuel Blackwell, the said John (Blackwell) having resigned the command. Capt. John Blackwell's Company was under the command of Col. Martin Pickett's Regiment. John and James Hathaway were lieutenants and Francis Triplett was adjutant.

These and other pension records, together with the records of Fauquier Court Minutes of 1777 and 1778, give a murky but comprehensible picture of what really took place. It is evident, and court records bear it out, that the understanding in Fauquier was that Armistead Churchill was to be Colonel of a second battalion and a sort of co-commander with Colonel Edmonds, not subor-

---

22. Reuben Bramblet, 1755-post 1832. He moved later to Gallatin Co., Illinois, where he died. He gives Francis Triplett the rank of Major which he did not hold until Bramblet served under him again in 1781.

23. William King, 1760-post 1833. He and a younger brother, Robert, served again in 1781. He moved later to Bracken Co., Kentucky.

dinate to him. Furthermore Churchill understood that John Blackwell would be his second in command and that their responsibility was toward the two companies raised by men outside the Fauquier militia, Captains Harrison and Samuel Blackwell.

This arrangement, if it existed, could only have been designed to accommodate Churchill's burning desire to hold the rank of Colonel. He was a vain, rather imperious man, fully conscious of the importance of his name and his powerful Carter connections. He had been Justice since 1769 and his attendance record in court was high. When he was present, he usually presided. He had his finger in most pies. Whatever Armistead Churchill wanted of the other Justices on the Court he was likely to get. Just then he wanted to be Colonel of the Militia.

In addition to the companies commanded by John Blackwell, Samuel Blackwell and Benjamin Harrison, Colonel William Edmonds had four companies, none by any means full. The army of 1,100 men which Joseph Oder imagined was, in fact, about 250 according to the most careful estimates. It is not easy to determine who were their commanders on the march. Probably William Ball was along, as was Charles Williams. Both had only recently been appointed as militia Captains. Captain James Bell's company was led by Lieutenant Charles Chilton, John Chilton's brother. It was his singular duty to convey most of the Fauquier County quota of draftees, 47 in number, of whom 26 reached Washington's headquarters. One who did was William Allen, then 19, who had been with John Chilton at Great Bridge.[24]

His account is brief. He was drafted in September, 1777 and marched north in the company of Captain Charles Chilton. They joined the main army two days after the battle of Germantown. He served three months near Philadelphia, then went home. He was drafted again in 1781 and served another three months under the same officer.

William Payne, who had also served at Great Bridge, joined on the 1st of September and marched north under the command of Captain Hezekiah Turner. Martin Pickett was, he thought, Colonel of the regiment. He says that they joined the main army in the city of Philadelphia and he was in the battle at Germantown. He returned to Philadelphia and was discharged after three months and four days. It would be easy to assume that William Payne was talking through his hat, but further research indicates that he was

---

24. See Note No. 60, Chapter III. Allen refers to his half-brother George Shackleford to supply proof of his service.

probably right. Captain Hezekiah Turner, paymaster and adjutant in the 3rd Virginia Regiment, was in Fauquier County just before the battle of Germantown and hurried back. He apparently volunteered to take one of the Fauquier militia companies with him, possibly that of Edward Digges who was detained as a result of complications arising from the death of his father. Turner was in a hurry and probably pushed ahead, arriving before the battle.

Two of Captain Benjamin Harrison's men left accounts which, though brief, help complete the picture. Jesse Moffett marched with Harrison in September under Major Martin Pickett.[25] They reached White Plains (he must mean White Marsh) in Pennsylvania soon after the battle of Germantown. He served until December when they were dismissed in a group. There was no written discharge.

Richard Rosser is a little more specific.[26] He marched with Harrison to Germantown, arriving on the day of the battle. They assisted in burying the dead the next day. After doing so, they joined the main army at White Marsh. Colonel Marshall commanded the regiment. He was discharged at the end of four months.

Joseph Oder's account, for all its erasures, crossing out, and obvious inconsistencies, has a germ of truth not found in others. His deposition is as follows:[27]

> I, Joseph Oder, Sr. ... aged upwards of eighty-one years, having been born in the County of Fauquier, State of Virginia on the 3rd day of August, 1751, who being first duly sworn ... states that he entered the service of the United States under the following named officers and served as hereinafter stated: That in the fall of the year 1777, under Captain Samuel Blackwell, Francis Triplett,

---

25. Jesse Moffett, 1759-1836. He married 27 Dec. 1782, Elizabeth Bailey. His sister-in-law, Hannah Lear, said that when they started to Parson Thompson's (Rev. James Thomson) to get married Jesse dropped the wedding ring in the snow and it took him and several men sometime to find it.

26. Richard Rosser, 1755-post 1832. He testified as to the presence of Andrew O'Bannon at Brandywine. He served later under Captain James Scott's nephew, Capt. Alexander Scott Bullitt, at Yorktown.

27. Joseph Oder, 1741-post 1833. A Joseph Odor was appointed by the first Fauquier Court in 1759 as surveyor of a road from Deep Run to Covington's Ordinary, near present Morrisville.

adjutant, in the Regt. command by Col⁰. Elias Edmunds & Col⁰. Martin Pickett being drafted, this declarent served a tour of two months:—that Col⁰. Martin Pickett also commanded a regiment in company, there being about 1100 troops and that during this tour he marched from Fauquier County, Va. through the intermediate country towards Philadelphia & near the place where the battle of Brandywine was afterwards fought. That when this tour was ended this declarent recd. a discharge from Col⁰. Edmunds which has been long since lost or mislaid.

It is obvious that Joseph Oder, "being very old and unable from bodily infirmity to attend court", was also failing in memory. He confused Colonel William Edmonds with his nephew, Elias Edmonds, under whom Oder had later served at Yorktown. He knew that Major Pickett had been in command and, since he and Edmonds could not have been in command at the same time, he decided that Pickett must have commanded another regiment. He was uncertain whether Brandywine came before or after Germantown.

But the old man did remember that there had been some confusion about the command and that, somehow, Francis Triplett, the adjutant, had played a part. This he remembered though adjutants are seldom remembered fifty years later.

What took place can only be imperfectly reconstructed from a mass of seemingly unrelated material. There was apparently a basic misunderstanding between William Edmonds and Armistead Churchill. There had been no time during the hasty preparation for departure to convene the Fauquier County Court so that they might recommend to the Governor the formation of the second battalion. There was, in fact, no September court in Fauquier. Churchill considered the court action a mere formality, an ex post facto confirmation of an agreement already in effect.

Edmonds, on the other hand, felt that the agreement dealt with future plans. Until the Governor approved the recommendation there was, in fact, no second battalion. He held not the slightest animus toward Armistead Churchill, whom he had known most of his life. It was, however, his responsibility to get the Fauquier militia to Washington's headquarters quickly and in one piece. He only wished that Churchill would not interfere. He understood perfectly Churchill's desire to command a regiment, though he had little experience. He had no objection to his doing so, - someday. However, he believe in taking first things first.

On the march Churchill behaved very much as the commander of a separate unit, issuing orders without coordinating them with Edmonds. Edmonds, through habit and because of Pickett's greater familiarity with military procedure, tended to by-pass Churchill, issuing orders through Pickett. John Blackwell, considered by Churchill his second in command and by Edmonds merely a company commander, was completely frustrated.

Matters reached an impasse when the two companies commanded by Benjamin Harrison and Samuel Blackwell received conflicting orders and, somehow, were separated from the main column. The situation could not continue, and Churchill realized that only by application to the Fauquier County court could it be resolved. Abruptly he decided to return to Virginia, leaving John Blackwell to command a ghostly battalion without any support from above.

John Blackwell's position was manifestly impossible. He was about the same age as Edmonds and Churchill and equally fond of both of them. Furthermore, in the interlocking family relationship peculiar to Virginia, he could not afford to offend either. Edmonds was his sister's husband and Churchill was married to his wife's sister. Under the circumstances he could think of only one solution. Reluctantly he informed Colonel Edmonds that he, too, was returning to Virginia.

Edmonds was in something of a bind, but relieved to have the division in command temporarily settled. He could not spare Pickett to corral the wandering companies and neither he nor Pickett wanted to give the impression that the latter was being promoted as the commander of the second battalion, if it came into being. His solution was to send his most competent staff officer to pick them up and lead them to Washington's headquarters. He sent his regimental adjutant, Francis Triplett.

Those who have attempted biographical notes on the life of Colonel William Edmonds have asserted that he marched his men into Pennsylvania where he received orders from General Washington and Richard Henry Lee (then in Congress).[28] They told him what to do, how to approach headquarters and how to handle the men he could not arm. (Married men who could not be given muskets were to give their blankets to those remaining and return home.) This is probably correct and there may be

---

28. Richard Henry Lee was, at that time, deeply involved in the move to supplant Washington as Commander-in-Chief, known as the Conway Cabal. His approach was characteristically devious so the full extent of his participation is unknown.

documents to prove it. It is certain, however, that Edmonds never reached Pennypacker's Mill. He soon began to wonder what Churchill might do in Fauquier, and whether he might not awe the county court into making recommendations to Governor Henry that they would later regret.

Pleading illness, though there is no mention of such in Pickett's letters, he decided to return to Fauquier County himself. He turned over his command to Major Martin Pickett and his horse's head toward the Virginia mountains. The superfluous "married men" may have gone with him.

Pickett arrived with the Fauquier militia at Pennypacker's Mill on the 5th of October. Triplett may have reached there on the evening of the 4th, at least if we are to believe Richard Rosser's story about burying the dead. Only the company brought north on the double by Hezekiah Turner was in time for the battle. However most of the army believed that another battle was soon to come and they were very glad to see them. Because of their strong affinity for the 3rd Virginia Regiment they were assigned to Marshall's command.

At the time of their arrival everything was understandably in chaos. There was enough distance between Woodford's and Weedon's Brigades so that their arrival was unknown five days later to Lieutenant Joseph Blackwell of the 10th Virginia Regiment. On the 10th of October he wrote to his brother-in-law, Colonel William Edmonds in Virginia, having no idea how nearly he had come to meeting him at headquarters.[29] His brief letter adds little new information, but it does convey the air of expectancy that prevailed in the American camp. Even after Germantown they refused to be discouraged. After a rather terse account of the battle, Joseph Blackwell reports:

> I have not seen either of the Captain Blackwells for two weeks. Captain William Blackwell went into the country sick. I understand he is getting well. Captain Thomas Blackwell [his brother] is at a fort on the Delaware, as I am informed. I think it needless to mention anything about the battle of Brandywine, as I imagine you have a full

---

29. Letter, Lt. Joseph Blackwell to Col. Willlam Edmonds, 10 Oct. 1777. Originally published in the **True Index** (newspaper), Warrenton, Va., 27 Jan. 1877. Fauquier Historical Society **Bulletin**, July, 1924, p. 500.

account of it. Nothing more at present; but I give my love to sister, family and all other asking friends.

I am, sir, your ob't. servant,
Jos. Blackwell

N. B. - Expect every day when we shall have the third battle with the enemy and then I am in hope I shall be able to give you a better account of the times.

J.B.

There were many reunions at the headquarters of the 3rd Virginia Regiment, not all happy ones. Captain John Blackwell, his face white and drawn under his dark hair, awaited the brother of his late Captain. We do not know when or how Charles Chilton received news of his brother's death but the effect had been devastating. In his baggage was whiskey, double-distilled to order, the twists of tobacco and other things in preparation for a joyous reunion. Now there was only his pale young brother-in-law who embraced him in silence, his throat too full for speech. From his uniform pocket he brought forth a tattered notebook which fell open at the last entry. Through tear dimmed eyes Charles Chilton read:

> We then marched 10 miles & crossed Brandywine Creek and encamped on the heights of the Creek.

During the month of October Washington rested his forces in the vicinity of Skippack Creek, preparing for another encounter before cold weather would rule out that possibility. The enemy did not press him, being more greatly concerned with the opening of the Delaware River to their shipping. The full report of Burgoyne's surrender reached the camp causing such elation among the troops as to dim the memory of their own successive defeats. Washington was so encouraged by this new spirit in the ranks that he again thought of taking the offensive. In his report to Colonel William Edmonds in Fauquier, Martin Pickett, commanding the Fauquier militia wrote on the 18th of October:[30]

> Dear Sir: - I congratulate you on the surrender of General Burgoine & his whole Army as prisoners of war. He is allowed the Honnours of war and to be sent to one of the

---

30. Letter, Martin Pickett to William Edmonds, 18 Oct. 1777. Virginia Historical Society.

New England Governments. This news we this moment received. This evening we are to have great Rejoiceing. The firing (of) Cannon, Small Arms, etc. This stroke will have great weight in the political scale of Europe as well as the United States of America. W^m. Howe I think must then soon suffer the same disgrace of Burgoine.

Our army is now very formidable to what it was when I first arrived here. Things at present wares a very good face & I think there will be good account given of those fellows in a little time if they do not move very circumspectly indeed. I think they cannot retreat without the utmost danger as we are near to their heels & a much superior force. If he delays a while our Northern Army will join us & make his ruin certain. Indeed everything wears the most flattering prospect of Victory & certain Independence. The hand of Providence is evidently with us, which the greatfull mind will never forget.

It reads as though Martin Pickett and General Weedon were smoking opium from the same pipe but, in fact, the entire army during those golden days of October, 1777, thought that the war was nearly over and that God, in His infinite wisdom, had already declared in their favor. Doubtless too, Pickett thought that such news would serve to grease the creaking machinery at home. His letter was no private missive, it was intended for general consumption. As such, it is a model of tact and gentle persuasion. Having enlarged rather glowingly on world affairs, he moved rather rapidly from the grand idea to the minute detail.

Our boys are pretty well. We have joined General Woodford's Brigade as a separate redgement,[31] - when I say all (are) well I forgot to tell you that Peter Preist got slightly wounded by accident from one of our own guns which went off. Struck the lower part of his testikles, I think but skin deep, and went through one side of his Peanus, which I hope he will soon get well of without any damage to his Reputation.- If the Northern Army should come to our assistance I suppose I shall have Liberty to return home with our Countrymen, otherways we must be relieved some time in November. I want much to go to the

---

31. Official records show the Fauquier Militia under the command of Col. Thomas Marshall. This may have some bearing on Pickett's abrupt departure on the 7th of November.

Assembly as I have taxation much at heart. I care for nothing that will be done this Assembly but that.
Therefore I hope the Court will not neglect an appointment of Field Officers for the new Battalion in which case there may be officers to relieve me when there comes another detachment out of the County.

As Pickett was writing this letter the surrender of Burgoyne and his army was, in fact, taking place at Saratoga. News of the surrender terms had reached Washington. but not from Gates. The success of Gates at Saratoga presented a stunning contrast to Washington's back to back defeats, and Gates was not loath to exploit it. He had not the slightest intention of marching with the "Northern Army" to Washington's aide. However, Pickett had every reason to expect that, once Burgoyne was out of the way, the two armies would join against Howe in Philadelphia. He expected also that the Fauquier County Court would meet, as was customary on Monday, the 27th of October and name the officers of the second battalion. He was wrong on both counts. Gates refused to march and the Fauquier Court, for the first time in years, failed to convene in October. No relief for the Fauquier militia whose enlistments would expire early in December was therefore possible. Unaware of any of this Pickett continued:

> We have a fort on an Island in the Delaware [32] some distance below Philadelphia which the Enemy have been battering at these two weeks off and on without success, nor do I suppose they can take it by what I have understood, as they can lay all the earth in the fort under water when they please, which is proof against bombs & they cannot bring so heavy mettle against it as we have here, nor can they storm it on account of its being water lockt. Therefore, until the Fort is taken they cannot carry up their ships nor remove the shiver defrises (chevaux de frise). Therefore they cannot keep Philadelphia long if they should attempt it. We hear the troops as well as the Tories are all packed up for a flight. Whether it is true or

---

32. Fort Mifflin on Port Island between Mud and Hog Islands covered the west end of the line of chevaux de frise. There were four block houses of four guns each and a ten gun battery of 18-pounders. The garrison was 450 men reinforced by several small detachments during the siege. Half of them were casualties when the ruined fort was evacuated.

not is uncertain but I think it very likely. - ... before this I mentioned that I did not know what became of Capt. Thomas Blackwell. I have found out that he is in the Fort above mentioned.

He addressed the letter to Colonel Brooke, Mr. Whiting, Colonel Churchill, Mr. Woodford and another person whose name is deliberately deleted, as well as Colonel Edmonds. Had Martin Pickett been around just one month later he might have wondered if *any* information given him during his brief stay outside Philadelphia could be trusted. But, by that time, he was far away. Only two weeks later there was a frown on the "good face" that things had been wearing and the flattering prospects of Victory and Independence had gone into hiding.

The weather turned suddenly cold with flurries of snow. While the snow did not last it threw into sharp focus the woeful lack of adequate clothing, especially shoes. The old line Virginia regiments were particularly destitute and the militiamen were appalled by their condition. From Gates there was no word of any movement to join Washington. In fact he refused to send Washington even formal notice of Burgoyne's surrender. From Virginia came word that no Court had been held in Fauquier and that no prospect of relief was in sight.

The movement to replace Washington with Gates, known as the Conway Cabal, was gaining momentum, though probably without Pickett's knowledge.[33] The rumors, however, could scarcely have escaped his notice. At Saratoga Gates had approached Morgan on the matter. Morgan was horrified.

"I have but one favor to ask of you which is never to mention that detestable subject to me again, for under no other man than Washington will I ever serve," he replied.

Gates, angry but still cautious, saw no merit in trying to keep Morgan against his will. On November 2nd he released Morgan and his men as well as a few Pennsylvania militia. They joined Washington's army at White-marsh on the 18th of November. Washington moved his army to White-marsh, about eleven miles from Philadelphia on the same day Morgan left Albany, in an

---

33. In his letter to Edmonds, 18 October, Pickett complained of the secrecy he encountered at high level. The plot to replace Washington was common gossip throughout the country.

attempt to lessen the pressure on the river forts. On the following day, the 3rd of November, he was told that the Virginia militia was going home, though their enlistments were a month short of fullfillment. Their numbers were not large, but the blow to his pride, at this difficult time, was great. He asked them to stay, and some promised to do so, but not many. He wrote to Congress: [34]

> The Militia from Maryland and Virginia are no longer to be counted on. All the former, except about 200 are already gone; and a few days, I expect, will produce the departure of the whole or chief part of the latter, from the importunate applications which some of them have made.

No record has been found to explain the abrupt and even rude departure of the Virginia militia. In fact there is no record to determine the extent to which the Fauquier militia was involved. Certainly the Fauquier officers were back in Virginia before the 24th of November, and it can be safely assumed that they brought most of the men with them. It is probable that the failure of the court to appoint the officers for the second battalion or confirm the rank of those in the first had a great deal to do with it. Whatever happened had the approval and active participation of Major Martin Pickett. One wishes that he had left some explanation of his conduct.

He must have left after the 7th of November, as he took with him a letter from Lieutenant Colonel Leven Powell of Grayson's Regiment to his wife in Loudoun County. Powell had arrived in camp at White Marsh Church less than two weeks before and had not yet got his bearings. His letter reflects anxiety over the fate of the Delaware River forts and the wish that they had more men. "The militia will not do, they are restless, cannot wait in camp till advantageious opportunities offer for action," he writes. That, in a nutshell, was also Washington's complaint. Powell reports that a detachment from General Gates was near (presumably Morgan and his men) and that he hopes to be home before long.

Undeterred by the defection of the Maryland and Virginia militia, Washington tried to distract Howe from further effort to take the river forts, but they were too vital to Howe for him to raise the siege. Pickett's information that they were virtually impregnable was only someone's wishful thinking. By the middle of November Fort Mifflin, in which Thomas Blackwell and his gallant

---

34. John C. Fitzpatrick, ed., **Writings of Washington**, Vol. IX, p. 479.

comrades wallowed in Delaware River mud, was abandoned. Samuel Burk of Fauquier, who had come north with Captain Rucker of Culpeper, says that there was a shirmish at "Mud Bank Fort" and he took a few prisoners.[35] On the 15th they were all evacuated to Fort Mercer on the Jersey side of the River near Red Bank. After bravely enduring another terrific beating there the spattered garrison withdrew on the 20th. Captain Thomas Blackwell was restored to his 10th Regiment and Samuel Burk went home.

Although he was still not fully convinced that further attack on the British was not wise in 1777, Washington on December 1st asked his Virginia brigade officers to suggest a proper place for the winter cantonment. General Charles Scott suggested Wilmington, Delaware, but Weedon doubted that adequate quarters could be found there. Writing to Washington on the 1st of December, Weedon described the army in Pennsylvania as "the Herculean hinge upon which American Independence turns." He favored placing it in detachments on a line between Reading and Lancaster about 60 miles from Philadelphia. Both Woodford and Muhlenberg supported Weedon's recommendation. Woodford advocated destroying all forage and supplies between the opposing camps, leaving the inhabitants barely enough food for subsistence.

Washington accepted their ideas noncommittally. The destruction of a sixty mile wide swath through some of Pennsylvania's most beautiful and fertile farmland aroused the spirit of Cincinnatus in him. There *must* be a better solution. Brigadier General James Irvine, a Pennsylvania militia officer, had another idea. There were no ready-built quarters, but there was plenty of timber, the ground was well drained, topographically advantageous for defense and far enough from the enemy to avoid a surprise attack.

On the 4th of December Howe made one last effort to end the war in 1777. About 10,000 redcoats moved to the vicinity of Chestnut Hill, only two or three miles from the American lines. There, according to George Weedon, "the two armies lay like Saul and the Philistines with only a small valley between." [36]

---

35. Samuel Burk marched north under Major Robards of Col. James Pendleton's detachment of Culpeper militia. Robards succeeded Pendleton when the latter returned to Virginia soon after arriving at camp.

36. Letter, George Weedon to John Page, 17 December 1777. Weedon Papers, Chicago Historical Society.

Washington was ready for him and Howe, apprised of the fact, thought better of the idea. He spent the next two days reconnoitering the situation. Morgan's riflemen gave his reconnaissance parties such a bad time that Howe got little useful information. Again according to Weedon, on the 7th of December, "These mighty men retreated back to their strong lines with precipitation, leaving us masters of the Ground."

Reluctantly Washington then gave up any thought of further action. With the Delaware River open to enemy shipping, supplies were pouring into Philadelphia. The generals, especially those of the Virginia line, had good reason for not wanting to fight in the snow. Half of their men were already in the hospitals, many of the rest were half-naked, hungry and shoeless. On the 11th of December Washington broke camp, crossed the Schuylkill and, on the 19th, brought his army to a place called Valley Forge.

Under lowering gray skies, through woods bare of leaves, over roads encrusted with ice, Fauquier horsemen converged on the County Courthouse on Monday, the 24th of November, 1777. It would be, they knew, the day of reckoning from which none was immune. The militia was home and some had interesting tales to tell. Not all were happy and some, - well, some were pretty sore.

The decrepit brick courthouse, the defects of which no amount of repair ever seemed to cure, was bleak without and uncomfortably cold within. The voice of the County Clerk could barely be heard above the hubbub of the excited crowd. In vain he rapped for order as the Gentlemen Justices filed in. Surprisingly only four were present but they were key figures in the proceedings about to take place. They were William Grant, Colonel Armistead Churchill, Lieutenant Colonel John Blackwell and Captain James Bell, to give them the military titles they so assiduously sought. However the military matters were reserved until last. A long agenda came first. [37]

Almost the first order of business was a petition by Colonel William Edmonds to build a water mill on Blower's Run. The Court ordered the Sheriff to summon a jury to examine the land and submit a report. The matter was unimportant but Edmonds made his point. He was not only present but would remain to contest any later action that might adversely affect his interests.

Following came a long list of leases, inventories, deeds to be recorded and roads to be viewed and reported upon. After a while another Justice elbowed his way through the crowd. He was Martin

---

37. Fauquier County Minute Book, 1773-1780, 24 Nov. 1777.

Pickett, fresh from the camp outside Philadelphia and late as usual. Edmonds may have sent for him. Pickett took his place on the bench with the other Justices.

The next order of business involved provision for the subsistence of the wives and families of soldiers in the Continental Army. Two of them, Elizabeth and Lydia Morrison, were widows of soldiers who had been killed or died of wounds in the Continental service. The sums varied from £ 3 to £ 6 which, judging from the incidence of such grants, was supposed to last them six months. The widows were given £ 10 and £ 12, or about three month's pay for their late husbands.

Next came the question of the distribution of salt. It was one commodity that Fauquier County had to import and it was in such short supply that rationing was necessary. William Grant was empowered to receive and distribute forty bushels among the inhabitants. The salt was in the hands of Richard Adams, Esq'r at Richmond. Armistead Churchill, Henry Peyton and John Moffett, all justices, were similarly charged.

There were several wills to be submitted to probate but only two of interest. The first was that of the late Joseph Smith [38] who probably died in the service, though the fact is not made clear. He left a widow, Mary (Pepper) Smith, and three children, Ruth, Wilhelmina and Abner. Subsequently, Mary Smith had married Andrew O'Bannon, [39] elder brother of George O'Bannon who died at Haarlem Heights. Andrew O'Bannon was a teamster who had served at Great Bridge. He was later wagonmaster in the 3rd Virginia Regiment and had care of the baggage of Captain Chilton's company among others. The British captured his wagon and team after Brandywine, but let him go home. He had married Mary Smith on the 10th of October and asked to be appointed guardian of her children. The Court agreed and appointed William Nash, Edward Ball, William Smith and Thomas Maddux, or any three of them, to set aside her dower and divide the rest among the children. They did not, apparently, try very hard. The May 1778 Court appointed Aylett Buckner, William Pickett, Francis Attwell and Moses Johnson to do the job for them.

The other will of interest is that of Captain John Chilton. It

---

38. Joseph Smith, d: 1777, is said to have been the son of Capt. Joseph Thomas Smith of "Mt. Eccentric".

39. Andrew O'Bannon, 1745-1813, Garrard Co., Ky., fifth son of John and Sarah (Barbee) - O'Bannon, m: 1777, Mary Pepper, 1754-1839, widow of Joseph Smith.

was proved by the oaths of Dr. Samuel Boyd, Captain John Ashby and Lieutenant Isham Keith. Charles Chilton and Thomas Keith were granted certificate for obtaining probate. Martin Pickett, the third executor, declined probably feeling that two were enough. Charles Morehead, James Hathaway, Ambrose Barnett and George Rogers were asked to appraise the estate. The inventory returned in September, 1778, gives no total but the estate was apparently relatively large.

Two more Justices arrived, raising the total of those present to eight. They were Henry Peyton [40] and Charles Chinn.[41] The main issue could be postponed no longer. The County Clerk announced

> Armistead Churchill, Gentleman, is recommended to his Excellency the Governor as a proper person to be appointed Colonel of the second Battalion of Militia in this County.

There was no mention of William Edmonds who was already Colonel of the first battalion and needed no further recommendation. If there was objection to the Clerk's announcement, it is not recorded. He continued:

> Martin Pickett, Gent. is recommended ... to be appointed Lieutenant Colonel to the First Battalion ...
> John Blackwell, Gent. is recommended ... to be appointed Lieutenant Colonel to the Second Battalion ...
> Samuel Blackwell, Gent. is recommended ... to be appointed Major to the First Battalion ...
> Edward Digges, Gent. is recommended ... to be appointed Major to the Second Battalion ...

There is no recorded objection. Churchill had his way. It remained only to replace company commanders who had been promoted or had resigned. The Clerk droned on:

---

40. Henry Peyton, 1744-1814, was a son of John Peyton of "Stony Hill", Stafford Co., and his second wife, Eleanor   . He lived on Broad Run on the north slope of the Pignut adjoining Gordonsdale. He married, 1764, Susanna Fowke, daughter of Capt. Chandler and Mary (Fossaker) Fowke.

41. Charles Chinn, d: 1788, natural son of Rawleigh Chinn by Margaret (Ball) Downman, widow. He married Scytha (Seth) Davis, dau. of John and Mildred (Higgins) Davis.

Francis Attwell,[42] Gent. is recommended ... to be appointed Captain in the room of Captain Charles Bell, who has resigned his Commission.

To serve in Atwell's company William Norris was recommended as 1st Lieutenant, Joseph Taylor, 2nd Lieutenant and Thomas Edwards, Ensign.

Joseph James,[43] Gent. is recommended ... to be appointed Captain in the room of Samuel Blackwell, Gent. promoted.

Presumably junior officers under Blackwell continued to serve in Captain James' company.

Thomas Bronaugh,[44] Gent. is recommended ... to be appointed Captain in the room of John Blackwell, Gent. promoted.

The junior officers recommended to serve under Thomas Bronaugh had a problem. The 1st and 2nd Lieutenants had the same name, James Withers, (written Weathers). One was the son of James and Catherine (Barbee) Withers[45] and the other a son of Thomas and Elizabeth (Williams) Withers.[46] With the confusion in names it was probably easier to deal with their cousin, Berryman Jennings, Ensign.

42. Francis Attwell, ca. 1750-1781, was of an old Westmoreland Co. family where an ancestor, Thomas Attwell, patented land on Machodock River in 1661. He married 1768, Mary McDonald, dau. the Rev. Daniel and Ellen (Barret) McDonald. The Rev. McDonald was Rector of Brunswick Par. until his death in 1762.

43. Joseph James, b: 1746, son of George and Mary (Wheeler) James of Stafford Co.

44. Thomas Bronaugh, died post 1811, son of Samuel Bronaugh (died 1741) and his wife Catherine   . married Elizabeth Newton, dau. of Maj. William and Elizabeth (Kenyon) Newton of Little Falls, Stafford Co.

45. James Withers, 1743-1808. He married in November, 1773, in Fauquier, Sarah Pickett, d: 1825, daughter of William and Elizabeth (Cooke) Pickett. He was therefore a brother-in-law of Martin Pickett.

46. James Withers, 1745-1791. See Chapter III, Note No. 50.

Charles Chilton, Gent. 1st Lieutenant; James Hathaway, 2nd Lieutenant and George Rogers, Ensign, are recommended ... to be appointed to the said offices in Captain James Bell's company.

Though Charles Chilton had taken the company to Philadelphia as acting Captain, James Bell did not step aside. John and James Hathaway were in camp outside Philadelphia, with a few of the Fauquier Independent Company. According to William King, they were relieved to turn their company over to Captain John Blackwell. When Blackwell returned to Virginia, they attached themselves to Charles Chilton, half of whose draftees had, as previously reported, gone over the hill. Captain Bell agreed to take 2nd Lieutenant James Hathaway at Chilton's urging, but had no room for John. The latter raised a company of his own in 1779, which saw service in the southern department.

With the future of the Fauquier Militia decided, they thought, the Gentlemen Justices called it a day. In fact, they had fought only the first round in a battle that never really ended. They had, thus far, accomplished nothing. Snow was falling in the Blue Ridge, the fires of home burned brightly and no one suggested that they return to Valley Forge.

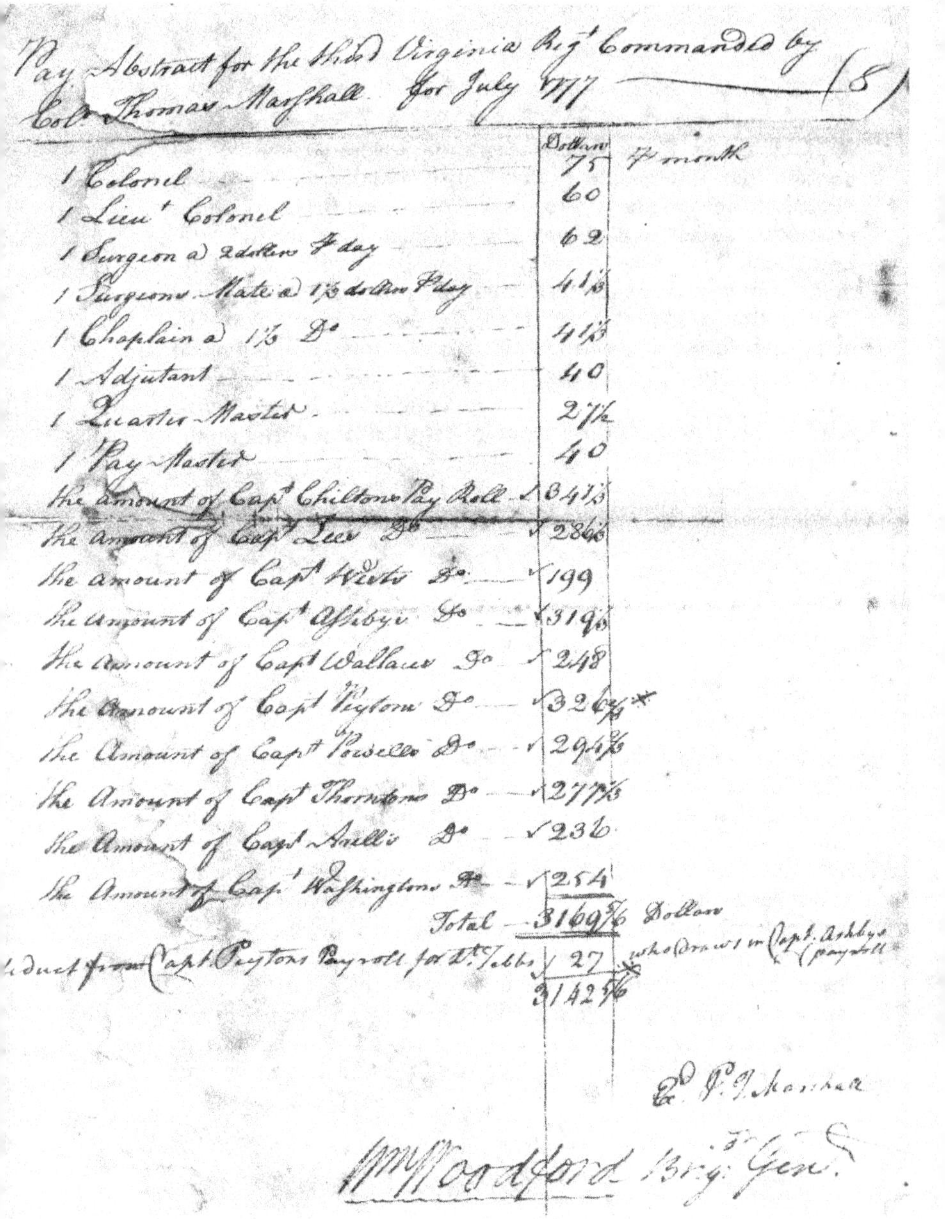

Pay Abstract for the third Virginia Regt Commanded by Colo Thomas Marshall for July 1777 (8)

	Dollars	
1 Colonel	75	⅌ month
1 Lieut Colonel	60	
1 Surgeon @ 2 dollars ⅌ day	62	
1 Surgeons Mate @ 1⅓ dollars ⅌ day	41⅓	
1 Chaplain @ 1⅓ Do	41⅓	
1 Adjutant	40	
1 Quarter Master	27½	
1 Pay Master	40	
the amount of Capt Chiltons Pay Roll	√ 341⅓	
the Amount of Capt Lees Do	√ 286⅓	
the amount of Capt Wests Do	√ 199	
the Amount of Capt Ashbys Do	√ 319⅓	
the Amount of Capt Wallaces Do	√ 248	
the Amount of Capt Peytons Do	√ 326⅔	*
the Amount of Capt Powells Do	√ 294⅔	
the Amount of Capt Thorntons Do	√ 277⅓	
the Amount of Capt Arells Do	√ 236	
the Amount of Capt Washingtons Do	√ 254	
Total	3169⅚	Dollars
deduct from Capt Peytons Payroll for Lt. Tebbs	27	who draws in Capt. Ashbys payroll
	3142⅚	

E. P. T. Marshall

Wm Woodford Brig. Gen.

"Pay abstract for the third Virginia Regt. Commanded by Colo. Thomas Marshall...for July 1777."

I *Thomas Blackwell Capt. 10th Va. Regt.* do acknowledge the UNITED STATES of AMERICA to be Free, Independent and Sovereign States, and declare that the people thereof owe no allegiance or obedience to George the Third, King of Great-Britain; and I renounce, refuse and abjure any allegiance or obedience to him; and I do *swear* that I will, to the utmost of my power, support, maintain and defend the said United States against the said King George the Third, his heirs and succeffors, and his or their abettors, affiftants and adherents, and will ferve the said United States in the office of *Capt.* which I now hold, with fidelity, according to the beft of my fkill and underftanding.

Blackwell Capt

Sworn before me at Camp 12th May 1778

P. Muhlenberg B.G.

Capt. Thomas Blackwell

I *Joseph Blackwell Lt. 10th Va. Regt.* do acknowledge the UNITED STATES of AMERICA to be Free, Independent and Sovereign States, and declare that the people thereof owe no allegiance or obedience to George the Third, King of Great-Britain; and I renounce, refuse and abjure any allegiance or obedience to him; and I do *swear* that I will, to the utmost of my power, support, maintain and defend the said United States against the said King George the Third, his heirs and succeffors, and his or their abettors, affiftants and adherents, and will ferve the said United States in the office of *Lieutenant* which I now hold, with fidelity, according to the beft of my fkill and underftanding.

Jo. Blackwell

Sworn before me at Camp 12th May 1778

P. Muhlenberg B.G.

Lt. Joseph Blackwell

Oaths of Allegiance to the United States of America signed at Valley Forge by order of Congress, 3 February, 1778. (Courtesy National Archives)

COL. JOSEPH BLACKWELL
of Elk Run (1755-1823)
(after an old profile
by G. Pargellis)

COL. WILLIAM EDMONDS
(from portrait in
Clerk's Office)

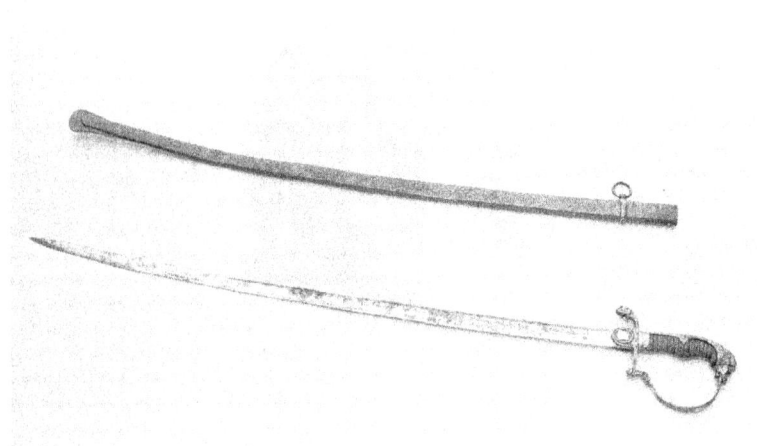

Courtesy Mason County, Ky. Museum

Sword presented to Col. Thomas Marshall, for distinguished service at Brandywine, by House of Burgesses. This heirloom descended to Capt. Thomas Marshall, Jr., who by his will bestowed it to his son, Gen'l. Thomas Marshall III. The latter left no male issue, and, on his death, his daughter, Mrs. Julianna W. (Marshall) Bland, presented it to the Maysville and Mason County Library, Historical and Scientific Association.

JOHN O'BANNON
(ca. 1760 - 1810)
(see Note # 7, Chap. XI)

JOHN MARSHALL

MARY R. KEITH MARSHALL

COL. THOMAS MARSHALL

"THE HOLLOW"
built 1765

"OAK HILL"
built about 1773

Interlude
Valley Forge

The suffering of the American Army at Valley Forge during the winter of 1777-1778 is legendary and there is no need for us to dwell further upon it here. Those who survived it deserve all possible credit but, in simple truth, not many of them came from Fauquier County, Virginia. The militia had returned home in November and regulars in the first nine Virginia regiments soon followed.

As the terms of service of the men in the first nine regiments were due to expire between January and April of 1778, Washington was faced with almost certain loss of many of his experienced troops. The Virginia officers believed that, if the men were allowed to spend Christmas at home, they might be induced to re-enlist in the spring. They also proposed an increase in the Continental bounty for re-enlistment, as state militia units were offering amazing sums.

Washington readily accepted the proposal for a bounty increase but hesitated at further reduction of his meagre force. However, when Virginia soldiers began applying for discharges, he knew that, unless something was done, he would lose them all. On the 4th of January, 1778, only forty Virginians had signed up for another tour of duty. When the trend did not alter in the next two weeks, he released all soldiers whose terms of service had expired or would expire in the next two months. On the 21st of January they started home, leaving their arms and gear behind for those who remained.

While the rank and file were leaving camp by platoons, Washington was plagued by requests for furloughs by the line officers. Furthermore, "preceiving that this passion is more prevalent among my countrymen than in any other troops in the whole army," his native pride was wounded. He wrote to Weedon:

> Muhlenberg is now gone, you think it the hardest case imaginable that you are here, Woodford and Scott are also

applying, the field officers of all your Brigades are, in a manner, absent ... I can see clearly that instead of having the proper officers to assist in arranging, training and fitting the Troops for the field against the next Campaign, that we shall be plunged into it as we were last year, heels over head ...

Nevertheless he gave his consent for Weedon to leave, and Scott soon followed. At the end of March none of the four Virginia Brigadiers was on duty at Valley Forge. Washington hoped against hope to derive some benefit from their absence. On arrival in Virginia he expected them to forward all draftees, recruits and re-enlisted men. The result was disappointing. By the middle of May only 800 men had marched out of the state. Of these 41 were left on the road and 42 deserted.

On the 4th of December, 1777, a replacement was named for Major General Adam Stephen who had been so ingloriously dismissed. As commander of the division that included Woodford's and Scott's brigades, Congress named Marie Joseph Paul Yves Roch Gilbert du Motier, Marquis de Lafayette. He was barely twenty, had very little military experience and was struggling with the English language. Any reasonable application of logic would have indicated that the appointment of this exotic specimen to command the Virginia Line would be a disaster. It was not.

The young "Markwiss", as the Virginians like to call him, had many qualities going for him besides age and experience. He was hard-working, willing to learn, naturally brave and completely loyal. He sought good advice and took it. He mastered English quickly and thereafter rarely spoke French, to the annoyance of his compatriots. In addition, he was utterly unassuming. Having no close competitor on the social scale, he could afford to treat everyone with equal courtesy and tact. The junior officers had a champion and, to their delight, one who had the ear of the Commander-in-Chief.

Though half of the Virginia troops were discharged during the winter at Valley Forge, new recruits failed to make up the deficit by more than 1,000 men. Nevertheless, owing to the appearance on the scene of another European officer, a Prussian drill master, those that remained were in better condition and better trained when spring came than they had ever been previously. Now, they thought, they would put an end to the insolence of Sir William Howe.

VIII

Monmouth

The snow that fell gently on the rough wooden huts being built at Valley Forge also blanketed the foothills of the Blue Ridge. At camp the wind whistled through jerry-built walls and poorly designed chimneys poured acrid smoke into the bleak interiors. In Fauquier all was snug and warm by the fireside. Though much food had gone to provide the army, there was plenty left, - old hams, well-cured bacon, potatoes and corn in abundance. Warm feather beds piled high with eiderdown quilts offered a marked contrast to the hard ground on which soldiers had slept in cold rain and biting wind. To return to a land of warm clothes, good food, horses to ride and serving people to anticipate every need, was balm to men wracked by hardship and privation. For a while they counted their blessings, - but before long they would grow restless. The war was far from being over.

The return of the 3rd Virginia Regiment was a cause for special rejoicing for they had been in the field for a long time. For many of them enlistments had expired and another tour of duty depended upon their ability to repair their health and fortunes during the winter. Of one thing they were certain, Colonel Thomas Marshall would not return. Late in November the Governor had picked him to command the Virginia Regiment of State Artillery. The lack of a Continental artillery had seriously handicapped Washington early in the war. However, in the spring of 1778 the field artillery under the indefatigable Henry Knox, had developed from a make-shift organization of inadequate weapons and inexperienced men to a combat arm that had performed well at Germantown.

Virginia had not been remiss in her contribution to that service. In fact the 1st Continental Artillery Regiment under Colonel Charles Harrison was largely made up of Virginia volunteers, among whom some were from Fauquier. That did not solve Virginia's problem, however, The Assembly was all too conscious of the need to have its own artillery to ward off an attack by Howe, if he should direct his attention toward Virginia's undefended coast. Marshall's command was, therefore, essential to their peace of mind. Marshall was delighted. As regimental officer under Woodford, he had been acting Brigade commander most of the time, without the rank to go with it. Now, he thought with some amusement, it might be fun to let Woodford shift for himself at Valley Forge. As soon as his men were in winter quarters, toward the end of December, he resigned his Continental commission and set out for his hilltop house in Fauquier County. Lieutenant Colonel William Heth assumed command of the Regiment.

Later Marshall wrote that it was "a command he was only induced to take by the preference he (had) ever felt for the Artillery service."[1] Although he may have been relieved to escape from Woodford's clutches, he was probably quite sincere. Certainly he threw himself into his new job with gusto. Soon "Oak Hill" was a center of feverish activity. Captain Elias Edmonds,[2] Colonel William Edmonds' nephew, had been working since the previous August in anticipation of some such eventuality. We have the word of Charles Kemper, who had served under Edmonds as a gunner during that period. When the time came to leave Fauquier in February, Kemper declined with thanks, but he did enlist in the same unit later and was eventually commissioned.

Through January and early February most of the men of the 3rd Regiment drifted home, one by one or in small groups. Some of the officers came a little sooner, charged with the responsibility of persuading their men to re-enlist if possible. Captain John Ashby of the 3rd Company had been home since November and was nursing his rheumatism at "Belmont". His successor in command, Captain Valentine Peyton, arrived in December, badly in need of a 1st Lieutenant. It seems that Lieutenant Nathaniel Ashby had resigned in November and had returned to his home in the southern part of the county for the wholly frivolous purpose of getting married. On the 3rd of December he married Margaret (Peggy) Mauzy.[3] Her step-father, Original Young, handed over

1. Fauquier Historical Society, **Bulletin**, No. 1 (1921), p. 141, "Memorial of Thomas Marshall for Military Emoluments."

2. Elias Edmonds, 1754-1800, son of Captain Elias and Elizabeth (Miller) Edmonds of "Ivy Hill", Fauquier Co. He married his cousin, Frances Edmonds, daughter of John Edmonds of Lancaster Co.

3. Chappelear and Gott, **Fauquier County, Virginia Marriage Bonds, 1759-1854**, p. 5.

her dowry, of which he had been forced by the Fauquier Court to keep meticulous account, probably with some relief.

Captain John Blackwell of the 4th Company arrived in Fauquier in January, bringing with him his brother Joseph. Joseph Blackwell's eyes were still troubling him and his sister, Judith Keith, believed that he left the 3rd Regiment that winter and later served in the Quartermaster department in Richmond. John Marshall, a close friend, also thought he left the service early in 1778. His name appears on the roster of the 4th Company of the 3rd Virginia Regiment as late as 1 April 1778, but it is doubtful that he returned to Valley Forge.

Most of Chilton's old company did not re-enlist. Those who had been wounded at Brandywine were discharged, including Sergeant Henry Bradford[4] and privates John Brown, John Murphy and Thomas Kelly. Colonel Marshall also discharged some whose terms of enlistment had long since expired. Among them was John Dulin who had served with Chilton since Great Bridge. Marshall also discharged Dulin's friend, Samuel Cox, who had been with Ashby about the same length of time.

Amidst the rejoicing there were a few families left desolate. The gaps in the ranks were not many but were not less deeply felt. Some had to remain to hold the regiment together at Valley Forge. One of those was Dickie Beale, who had no one to blame but himself. His zeal and superior intelligence had won him the post of sergeant-major and regimental adjutant. Naturally he could not be spared. He stayed through the winter at Valley Forge but, when he left in March of 1778, he left for good.

Of course officers of regiments other than the 4rd were given furloughs that winter, ostensibly for recruiting purposes. The rank and file of the younger regiments, as the 10th and 11th, whose enlistments had another year to run, had no such luck. They were among those who sat around campfires on the bleak hillside and bemoaned their fate. The fact that the Fauquier militia had arrived

---

4. Henry Bradford, 1757-1815, was a son of William and Mary (Morgan) Bradford of Marr's Run. When William Bradford died 1759-60 (Fauquier Co. Will Book I, pp. 8, 9) his will mentions a son Henry and daughter, Ann. He also mentions an unborn child who, if male, was to inherit ½ his 206 acre farm. This child, born in March 1760, was a son named William for his father. When Henry Bradford was seven his mother married William Nash and, when he was 13, he was apprenticed to John Cook, a tailor, to learn his trade. He married, near Nashville, Tenn., 1785, Elizabeth Payne, daughter of Josias Payne and widow of (?) Blackmore. He died in Sumner Co., Tenn.

after the action was over and had departed before the winter set in did not go unnoticed. However, though the militia was back in Fauquier County, it had troubles of a different sort.

They must have arrived early in December, because it is recorded that Martin Pickett got his wish and was able to attend the Virginia Assembly in Williamsburg before the middle of the month. He was accompanied by Hugh Nelson [5] in place of Captain James Scott. Little is known about Nelson, who had never previously held public office in Fauquier. Although he had been named by Governor Henry as one of the new Justices on the 27th of November, he apparently never bothered to take the required oath. What transpired at the Assembly is a matter of record, but neither Pickett nor Nelson is mentioned as having uttered a word.

For some reason there was no court held in Fauquier in January of 1778. The Governor had appointed the Justices late in November but the list was not presented to the Court until the 23rd of February. [6] There was nothing surprising about the quorum except possibly that the Governor had not been advised that John Chilton had been killed at Brandywine. The rest had long service in the court. The names of the new Justices, however, held some surprises. They were William Pickett, [7] Thomas Bronaugh, Thomas Keith, Hezekiah Turner, Aylett Buckner, Zacharias Lewis, Charles Chilton, William Blackwell, Peter Grant, Hugh Nelson, Landon Carter, [8] Edward Digges, Benjamin Harrison, Thomas Digges, Francis Triplett and William Heale. It was the same list

---

5. Hugh Nelson must be the most mysterious person ever to have held high office in Fauquier Co. Appointed Justice in Nov. 1777, he seems never to have qualified. He appears once in the Marriage Bonds, as security for the marriage of Nathaniel Nelson and Jane Byrd-Page, 2 June 1778. He appears once in the Will Books, 1759-1800 when he was paid by the estate of Mary Bland for a wolf's head in 1783. That is all.

6. Fauquier County Minute Book, 1773-1780, 23 Feb. 1778.

7. William Pickett, 1742-1814, son of William and Elizabeth (Cooke) Pickett, was a brother of Martin Pickett. He m: 1769, Lucy Blackwell, daughter of William and Elizabeth (Crump) Blackwell and widow of Moses Green.

8. Landon Carter, 1751-1811, son of Col. Charles Carter of "Cleve". He inherited "Ludwell Park" on Tin Pot Run. In 1785 an attempt to establish a town to be called Carolandville, on 53 acres of his land near Norman's Ford. John Blackwell, Humphrey Brooke, George Fitzhugh, William Pickett and Thomas Helm were named trustees, but the enterprise failed.

that had been recommended to the Governor in July, but a lot had happened since. Fifteen of the justices including seven of the new men were immediately sworn into office. Others took their oaths at later sessions but it appears that, of the new justices, Zacharias Lewis, Peter Grant, Hugh Nelson and Benjamin Harrison never took an oath and, consequently, did not serve on the court.

From a casual inspection it is evident that the appointment of new justices was largely confined to men who had a particular interest in the Fauquier militia or the Continental army. Turner and William Blackwell were in the army. Peter Grant had started as a captain in Grayson's Additional Regiment but had switched to the 11th Virginia Regiment in hope of serving under Morgan. Charles Chilton and Bronaugh had been recommended for the militia in the November Court. Harrison and Edward Digges were already militia Captains. Three men, William Pickett (brother of Martin Pickett), Francis Triplett and Thomas Keith, had not been on the November list but were actively engaged in the training program and expected to be commissioned. Aylett Buckner held similar expectations.

The Governor had not acted on the list of officers recommended in November and it was obvious that, if all these hopefuls were to be accommodated, a new and more comprehensive list must be filed. This was naturally opposed by all of those for whom the old list made ample provision. They saw nothing to be gained by rocking the boat. A showdown between the two factions in the February court was headed off by the presiding Justice, Joseph Blackwell. Fewer than half the Justices were present and a vote among those few who were, whatever the outcome, would be subject to criticism.

Not much happened, therefore, at the February Court. The will of Colonel Thomas Bullitt, the old Kentucky hand who had been the Adjutant General in Williamsburg, revealed the startling fact that he had left a substantial part of his estate to his mistress and her illegitimate daughter, to the almost complete exclusion of his heir-at-law, his brother Joseph.[9] It was also revealed that William Allason still had to get the Court's permission to inoculate his family for smallpox, although the law had been repealed. The County Treasurer was ordered to pay toward the support of Winny Elliot and Martha Mattox, both wives of soldiers in the Continental Army.

The new County Surveyor, commissioned by the College of William and Mary to replace John Chilton, dec'd., was John Moffett.

9. Fauquier County Will Book I, pp. 321-22.

The most interesting matter to come before the February Court was a motion by Captain James Scott that an acre of land on Mill Run be laid off so that he could build a water grist mill. Scott, who was last found in Lord Stirling's headquarters in New Jersey, had returned home either before or after Brandywine, it is uncertain which. He had originally proposed the mill in September, 1774, but he "could not have a Jury on the land as William Edmonds, the proprietor thereof, was Sheriff and no Coroner being sworn after Independency was declared in this State." Just why his reasoning had bearing on the issue in unclear, but not the court action. They turned him down flat. He had had, they said, plenty of time to execute the order before Edmonds became Sheriff. Apparently Colonel Edmonds objected to Scott's mill because it offered competition to the one he was building on Blower's Run. [10]

And finally William Pickett, Aylett Buckner and Edward Digges were appointed to agree with workmen to repair the Prison, the "insufficiency" of which was truly appalling.

It must have been extremely difficult for the young men of Fauquier in the winter of 1777-78 to decide which of the many opportunities offered them to "seize the post of Honour" afforded the best hope of fulfillment without losing one's precious life. Quite apparently service in the old Virginia line regiments had lost its appeal. It had been proved to be not only dangerous but quite uncomfortable. The recruiting efforts of Captains John Blackwell and Valentine Peyton met with small success. Captain Peter Grant appointed Thomas Kincheloe [11] as recruiting sergeant to try to round up enough men for the 11th Virginia Regiment to justify his rank. Kincheloe's success was negligible and Grant finally gave up. Apparently, according to his pension record, Kincheloe never left the county before his discharge a year later. Only one young recruiting officer was doing well. He was 18 year old Benjamin O'Bannon, younger brother and heir of George O'Bannon who had died on Haarlem Heights.

O'Bannon had marched north in the autumn with Captain

10. John Blower was an early settler in Fauquier who patented 807 acres north of Cedar Run "on some of the small branches adjoining Col. Carter, Col. Tarpley and Parson Scott" and 159 acres "on the branches of Ceader Run on the south side of the Pignut adjoining Waugh Darnell", 1727, 1729. The site is on Mill Run three miles east of Warrenton.

11. Thomas Kincheloe, 1761-post 1832, was born in Fairfax but his father moved to Fauquier when he was one year old. He died in Breckinridge Co., Kentucky, survived by his wife, Nancy.

John Blackwell and had served out his three month tour. Returning to Virginia fired with patriotic fervor, he managed, he said, to raise a company of "about 100 men" for whom the militia offered too little excitement. "About 100 men" is about twice the number raised by any captain in Fauquier before him so, when he delivered them to Washington at Valley Forge, he received a well-deserved captaincy. Probably the secret of his success lay in the fact that he had not committed them to any regiment. Washington turned them over to Morgan who stood in desperate need of reinforcement. That suited them quite well.

Colonel Thomas Marshall and Captain Elias Edmonds were busily organizing their artillery regiment, signing up all who would stand still. The Assembly even voted him £ 100 for recruiting on the 13th of February.[12] It did not go far. Marshall exhausted most of his personal fortune on the enterprise. In February he, with Edmonds' Fauquier company, departed for Yorktown where, according to the pension record of Elijah Clay[13] of Cumberland County, a body of men including himself, was already in training for Marshall's command. Elias Edmonds was soon promoted to Major in command of a battalion. The table of organization of an artillery regiment was something new to the Virginia Assembly and it took some time before it could be worked out, during which several Fauquier aspirants bided their time with increasing impatience.

For many the most exciting possibility for assuring one's future seemed to lie in following the footsteps of Captain Lynaugh Helm.[14] Lynaugh (or, as he preferred, Leonard) Helm was a son of Thomas Helm who had patented 283 acres "on Dorrell's Run adjoining John Catlett" in 1727 and had followed it with several other grants on the branches of Cedar Run. However Lynaugh

12. Journals of the Council of the State of Virginia, Vol. II, p. 81.

13. Elijah Clay did not serve very long. His health was "somewhat bad" in October, 1779, and he was discharged with credit for a full three years' service. When asked to explain he replied naively that he had had a negro boy with him at Yorktown and Williamsburg who waited on the officers. It might have made some difference.

14. Lynaugh Helm died soon after the war. In 1796 his son, Achillis Helm, deeded 750 acres of his Illinois grant to Colonel Simon Triplett of Loudoun County "in consideration of the trouble and expense of the said Triplett in getting a law passed by the Virginia Assembly to carry into effect his claim of 3,334 acres to which Leonard Helm, father to Achillis, was entitled in right of his command in the Illinois Regiment."

Helm's heart was in Kentucky which he often visited as a member of the frontier border patrol. He was skillful in dealing with the Indians and a resourceful frontiersman. Somehow he had come to know the intrepid Major Clark of Kentucky and though nearly twice his age, had formed a fast friendship. In January under Helm's sponsorship Clark had fired many in Fauquier with visions of manifest destiny.

George Rogers Clark [15] was then 26, a strong, red-headed frontiersman with a compelling manner and penetrating black eyes. Born in Albemarle County, he had been in Kentucky for seven years. He was a captain in Lord Dunmore's War at the age of 22, and had never stopped pressing for further action to win control of the Ohio and Mississippi Rivers. Late in 1777 he had carried his arguments to Governor Henry. Henry had been intrigued but hesitated to lay the matter before the Assembly for fear that news of the project might reach the frontier and alarm the Indians. Instead he had "several private councils, composed of select gentlemen" who, to encourage those who would engage in such service, "promised to use their influence to procure from the Assembly three hundred acres of land for each in case of success." They then provided Clark with a Major's commission, £ 1,200 for the expedition, and an order on Fort Pitt for boats and ammunition. He was authorized to raise seven companies. Publicly his orders were to defend Kentucky, but his secret orders were to take Kaskaskia, an outpost on the Mississippi, Vincennes and, if possible, Detroit where there was a British garrison. Note that Clark was leading an expedition for the State of Virginia without the knowledge or consent of the Continental Congress. In his *Memoirs* Clark wrote: [16]

> on the 4th (of January, 1778) I set forward, clothed with all the authority that I wished. I advanced to Major William B. Smith £ 150 to recruit men on Holston and to meet me in Kentucky. (He never joined me.) Captain Leonard Helm of Fauquier and Captain Joseph Bowman of Frederick

---

15. George Rogers Clark, 1752-1818, born near Charlottesville, Va., had little formal education when he started studying surveying at the age of 19. His wide knowledge of history and geography is evident in his **Memoirs**. He was unmarried.

16. Clark's "Memoirs", from English's **Conquest of the Country**, p. 469. Governor Henry's "select gentlemen" were George Mason, George Wythe and Thomas Jefferson.

were to raise each a company and on the 1st of February I arrived at Red Stone. [Brownsville, Pennsylvania, on the Monongahela]

Captain Helm did not have an easy time recruiting. He wrote Clark that several gentlemen in that quarter, (Fauquier) "took pains to counteract his interest in recruiting, as no such service was known of by the Assembly." Consequently he had to send to the Governor to get his conduct ratified. However, on the 29th of March Clark had information that Helm's and Bowman's companies were on the way.

Clark admitted that most of the Fauquier recruits either had interest in Kentucky or relatives already living there. The promised three hundred acres was an effective lure to landless younger sons and those living on leases which would soon expire. None of them knew the real purpose of the expedition except Clark and his captains. Though Major Smith sent only a token force, he had two other companies under Captains John Montgomery and William Harrod. Early June found them on a little island[17] in the Ohio opposite Louisville about to start on their great adventure.

The expedition caused a sensation in Fauquier, not only that spring but in those to follow. One has only to read John Filson's *The Discovery, Settlement and Present State of Kentucke*[18] to understand the lure of that distant, unmatched El Dorado. Many of those who lived on leased land in Fauquier and saw no hope of having their own broad acres, avowed that as soon as the war was over they intended to move to Kentucky, lock, stock and barrel. If George Rogers Clark was successful, it was theirs to own, to love and to *exploit*. Conservation had not then entered the American vocabulary.

Another enterprise of Governor Henry and his Council designed to attract volunteers from Fauquier and elsewhere was announced on the 26th of February. According to the Journal of the Council

> The Board further proceeded to appoint Colonel John Smith of Frederick to command a Regiment of Volunteers - Lewis Burwell of Mecklenburg to be Lieutenant Colonel - William Pickett of Fauquier, Dandridge Claiborne of King William & John Nelson of York to be Majors.

17. Corn Island.

18. John Filson, **The Discovery, Settlement and Present State of Kentucke**, published Wilmington, 1784.

This was to become the 2nd Virginia State Regiment. In the light of subsequent events it appears that William Pickett of Fauquier must have declined this appointment, preferring to serve with higher rank in his own county militia if possible.

The cauldron of political intrigue seethed and bubbled in Fauquier during March. The issue was the command of the militia. By the 23rd it was about to boil over. The Court proceedings on that day began innocently enough, with James Bell, John Blackwell, William Pickett and Edward and Thomas Digges on the bench.[19] James Scott was much in evidence and soon joined them. Even Bryan Martin was on hand on the matter of a deed between himself and Lord Fairfax. Witnesses were David Allason, Captain James Scott and his younger brother, Robert Scott.[20]

Thomas Bryan Martin was maintaining a low profile in 1778. The Assembly had abolished quit rents but, in recognition of Lord Fairfax's loyalty, had excepted those on the Northern Neck lands. Property belonging to "British subjects" was, however, sequestered. Lord Fairfax had been seriously ill that winter and, as Washington wrote from Valley Forge, had "in a manner (shook) hands with death." However, in the spring of 1778, was "perfectly restored" and had "as much vigor as falls the lot of ninety".

There were the usual wills to be submitted to probate, inventories arranged for, deeds to be recorded and even an ear bitten off. This time William Berry was the bite-ee and John Cantwell the bite-or. The proceedings were routine and dull.

Interest began to pick up when John Moffett, a new Justice, arrived and silently took his seat. In addition Hezekiah Turner and Francis Triplett, who had been absent in February, took their oaths. Martin Pickett and Thomas Keith arrived. William Grant then took the prescribed oath. There were then twelve Justices present, a most unusual number, but the Court continued its routine work. Neither side, apparently, had the advantage.

Cuthbert Bullitt was granted permission to inoculate his servants and slaves for smallpox. Various citizens were ordered to pay wives of soldiers in the Continental army amounts ranging from £6 to £12: Frances Butler, Jemima McGraw, Mary Coleman,

---

19. Fauquier County Court Minute Book, 1773-1780, 23 and 24 March, 1778.

20. Robert Scott, ca. 1749-1782, was a son of the Reverend James and Sarah (Brown) Scott. He married Catherine Stone. He died at sea at the age of 33. His only child, Alexander Scott, married the only child of Captain William and Celia (Helm) Blackwell.

Hannah Elliot and Mary Coffee, whose husband Robert had lost his life at Brandywine. William Pickett, Aylett Buckner and Edward Digges reported that the prison was indeed a scandal and quite beyond repair. They recommended a new one. After considerable discussion during which conservatives protested spending good money to house miscreants, it was finally agreed that William Edmonds, Armistead Churchill, Thomas Keith and Edward Digges were to "agree with Workmen" to build a new one.[21]

Thomas Bronaugh arrived. Rather surprisingly William Edmonds and Armistead Churchill, though present, made no move to take the qualifying oath so that they could vote. Their presence, though, was sufficiently inhibiting so that no one was willing to raise the major issue. The day had been long and tense but the real action had taken place outside the courthouse. About 4 p.m. four of the Justices had had enough and abruptly departed. James Scott, presiding Justice, adjourned the court until 10 o'clock the next morning.

Promptly at the appointed hour on the 24th of March, James Scott raised his gavel. From the composition of the court it was apparent which side had won the battle. Ranged beside Scott were Martin and William Pickett, Thomas Keith, Hezekiah Turner, Aylett Buckner, Charles Chilton, Edward Digges and Thomas Bronaugh. All of them were militia officers, or expected to be, except Turner who favored the new men. Only James Scott and Martin Pickett were of the quorum. Together they were prepared to overturn the November recommendations to the Governor and substitute a new list from which Armistead Churchill was conspicuously absent. Only Edward Digges dissented, not without reason. Along with Churchill, he too, would be retired to his farm. His excuses for not leading his company north in October had not been quite adequate.

Humphrey Brooke, County Clerk, arose and announced that these were the recommendations to his Excellency the Governor for officers of the Fauquier militia. He forbore mentioning that there had been a previous list. The first name was easy:

> William Edmonds, gentleman, is recommended to his Excellency the Governor as a proper person to be appointed Colonel to the first Battalion of Militia in this County.

---

21. This is the building recently restored.

This was implied but not stated in the earlier list. There was no question that Edmonds was entitled to the office he had held so long. Approval was unanimous. Brooke then continued.

> Martin Pickett, gentleman, Colonel to the second Battalion.

Then the storm broke. The Edmonds-Pickett faction had obtained control of the militia, it seemed. Edward Digges rose from his seat, flushed with anger, and strode from the courthouse.

> John Blackwell, gentleman, Lieutenant Colonel of the first Battalion. William Pickett, gentleman, Lieutenant Colonel of the second Battalion.

In ousting Churchill, Edmonds did not want to deprive his wife's brother, John Blackwell, of the Lieutenant Colonelcy he had been promised so long. William Pickett was the Captain who had commanded the Fauquier troops at Great Bridge and only a month before had been proposed as a Major in the 2nd Virginia State Regiment. It is not very clear whether or not he had refused that appointment.

> Samuel Blackwell, gentleman, Major to the first Battalion.
> John Moffett, gentleman, Major to the second Battalion.

Samuel Blackwell had no taste for this family quarrel and was trying to extricate himself. Moffett replaced Digges to the latter's considerable chagrin.

Four companies had been mentioned in the November list, those of Captains James Bell, Francis Attwell, Joseph James and Thomas Bronaugh. They were allowed to remain virtually intact. Four other companies had existed previously, those of Captains Nicholas George, William Ball, Charles Williams and Edward Digges. All of these company commanders were replaced. Nicholas George resigned. His company was taken by William Blackwell,[22] (not Morgan's company commander in the 11th Virginia Regiment but his cousin) with Daniel Shumate,[23] 2nd lieutenant

---

22. William Blackwell, 1738-1782, see note No. 39, Chapt. III. He had been wounded at Germantown but had recovered.

23. Daniel Shumate, was a son of John Shumate, d: 1784, of Elk Run. Their land adjoined that of John Crump and the families intermarried.

and Rodham Tullos, ensign. William Ball was replaced by Francis Triplett, with John Deering, 2nd lieutenant and William Seaton, Jr., ensign. It is not clear what happened to Williams' and Digges' companies. These men seem to have been distributed among the other units.

The company raised by Captain Benjamin Harrison was apparently broken up. An undated roster has been found [24] showing James Key as 1st lieutenant, Linsfield Sharp, 2nd lieutenant and Thomas Conway, ensign. In March, 1778, Sharp was with Captain Joseph James and Conway, promoted to 1st lieutenant, was with Captain William Pope. The men were scattered. William Jeffries joined the 11th Virginia Regiment; William Smith the 1st and William Wickliff [25] the Westmoreland County Militia under Captain William Nelson. A number did not re-enlist immediately but saw service with the Fauquier militia in the southern campaign. Exclusive of officers, Harrison's company had numbered sixty, almost all of whom saw later service in some capacity.

Captain James Scott's company roster is contained in Gwathmey's *Historical Register of Virginians in the Revolution* although the original has not been located. It, too, is undated but was obviously taken before May 1777. Lieutenant William Kincheloe [26] held part of the company together until the spring of 1778 at Valley Forge. He was promoted to Captain before being mustered out. William Ford served under him in November and December, 1777 guarding British prisoners taken at Saratoga. Scott's men also scattered through the Continental Line and other militia com-

24. John H. Gwathmey, **Historical Register of Virginians in the Revolution** (Richmond, 1938) p. 860.

25. Charles William Wickliffe was a son of Robert and Elizabeth (Arrington) Wickliffe. His father was a vestryman of Hamilton Parish. He married Lydia Ann Elizabeth Hardin, dau. of Martin Hardin of Hardin's Ordinary on Elk Run. They moved to Kentucky in 1780.

26. William Kincheloe, 1736-1797, was a son of John and Elizabeth (Canterbury) Kincheloe and an uncle of Thomas Kincheloe (see Note No. 11). Born in Prince William Co., he moved to Fauquier in 1762, where he bought 400 acres of the Burgess patent of 1731. He moved to Kentucky after the war and built Fort Kincheloe ("Burnt Station") on Simpson's Creek in Nelson Co. He and his family had left the fort when the occupants were massacred by Indians under the renegade Simon Girty in 1781.

panies. James Bryan went with the 11th Virginia Regiment, John Hogan with the 5th and Jesse Smith was a corporal in the 3rd. Samuel Humphries marched off with Leonard Helm and wound up in George Rogers Clark's Illinois Regiment. John Thomas [27] Chunn, a private under Scott, became, in August of 1781, a Major in the Fauquier militia. Wharton Ransdell and John Barker, also privates, were commissioned as ensigns on the March list, but were not assigned to specific companies.

Scott's sergeant, Turner Morehead,[28] was named Captain of a company in March of 1778 and it would not be surprising to find that most of Scott's 43 rank and file served under him. Of the four companies added in March, Turner Morehead was to command the first with Robert Layton as 1st lieutenant, Thomas Keith, 2nd lieutenant and William Ransdell, ensign. The second was to be commanded by Tilman Weaver,[29] with James Blackwell,[30] 1st lieutenant, Hubbard Prince, 2nd lieutenant and Lewis Ashby,[31] ensign. William Pope was named captain of the third, with Thomas Conway, 1st lieutenant, William Kenton, 2nd lieutenant and John Combs,[32] ensign. The last of the new companies was to

27. John Thomas Chunn, 1749-1804, bought 1,000 acres of the James Ball tract in 1776, part of which was Captain John Ashby's "Belmont". He lived at "Mt. Independence" on Crooked Run, 3 miles north of Delaplane. He later bought Woolf's Mill on Goose Creek, near Rectortown. He left a large estate at his death.

28. Turner Morehead, was a son of Charles and Mary (Turner) Morehead. He married, 14 June 1779, Ann Ransdell, daughter of Wharton Ransdell, d: 1786.

29. Tilman Weaver, 1746-8-1809, was a descendant of one of the twelve German families from Nassau-Siegen who founded Germantown on Licking Run. He was the eldest son of Tilman (d: 1760) and Ann Elizabeth Weaver.

30. James Blackwell, b: 1743, was a son of Samuel and Elizabeth (Steptoe) Blackwell of "Walnut Lodge", Northumberland Co. He married his cousin, Ann Blackwell, daughter of Col. William and Elizabeth (Crump) Blackwell.

31. Lewis Ashby, 1746-1806, was the eldest son of Captain John and Jane (Combs) Ashby. He was a brother of Nathaniel Ashby of the 3rd Virginia Regiment. He married, 1778, Leannah Darnall, dau. of Jeremiah Darnall, d: 1795.

32. John Combs may have been the son of John Combs, Jr. whose curious nuncupative will was proved in Fauquier Co., 28 May 1781 by Original Young and Ennis Combs by "oath of the holy Evangelist."

be commanded by William Grigsby[33] with Burr Harrison, 1st lieutenant and William Nash,[34] 2nd lieutenant. In addition it was recommended that eight extra 2nd lieutenants and seven ensigns be appointed to provide for additional companies if recruiting should prosper.

It is probable that no word had been received from Governor Henry in April. There was no April Court. Armistead Churchill was probably working feverishly with his powerful connections in Williamsburg to restore the status quo. When the court convened on the 25th of May there was a shock in store for the Edmonds-Pickett camp. The Governor ignored the March recommendations for field officers in the 1st and 2nd Fauquier Battalions and returned to the recommendations on the November list. He appointed Armistead Churchill Colonel of the 2nd Battalion with John Blackwell as Lieutenant Colonel. Instead of Edward Digges, he appointed Aylett Buckner as Major. William Pickett's high hopes were again dashed, as were John Moffett's. Both Churchill and Buckner were on hand to take the oath. So were the captains of three new companies, Pope, Bronaugh and Morehead, with their junior officers.

It appears that the Governor appointed most of the company grade officers as recommended on the March list. His letter of appointment has not been found, so we cannot be certain that all were made. Neither can we be certain that all who were appointed were sworn into office. It is a surprising fact that a high percentage waited until September or even November before taking the required oath. Presumably they continued to function meanwhile, considering the oath a mere formality. In fact it is not recorded when William Grigsby, brother-in-law of attorney Cuthbert Bullitt, took his oath. Possibly it could be done privately. That he did so is shown by the pension records of Jesse Moffett and John Murphy. Toward the end of the year James Bell finally resigned command of his company and Charles Chilton, long his second in command, was raised to Captain.[35]

33. William Grigsby, d: 1782, may have been killed or died of wounds near the end of the war. He was a son of John Grigsby, d: 1772, in Fauquier Co. He married 8 Feb. 1771, Elizabeth Bullitt, daughter of Capt. Benjamin and Elizabeth (Harrison) Bullitt. She m: (2) 2 Sept. 1782, Joseph O'Bannon, brother of George and Benjamin O'Bannon.

34. William Nash married 23 Feb. 1764, Mary Morgan, the widow of William Bradford of Marr's Run. He was the step-father of Henry and William Bradford of the 3rd Virginia Regiment.

35. Fauquier County Court Minute Book, 1773-1780, 28 Sept. 1778.

However the Fauquier militia, despite all the furor, performed no military service in 1778. It was, in fact, never to appear on any battlefield north of the Mason and Dixon line. If the British wanted to meet these military gentlemen, they would have to move south. That time was not far off.

We have anticipated a little in order to conclude the affairs of the Fauquier militia. However there were many from Fauquier still in the Continental Line, both in Virginia and at Valley Forge, of whom the last has not been heard. From Valley Forge, as the winter progressed, the news was increasingly dull. Once the huts were built, the wood supply secured and the food supply reasonably stabilized, time hung heavy on their hands and they were bored. Thus Brigadier General George Weedon began a letter to his friend John Page, dated the 25th of January, 1778: "For fear that you should think I have forgot you, I sit down to convince you otherwise, but so barren is the camp of news that I fear I shall not give you the worth of postage." [36]

He does go on to describe in some detail an incident at Scott's farm about 5 miles SE of camp during which Captain Henry (Lighthorse-Harry) Lee [37] and eight men beat off a raid by 200 British horse. Captain Lee belonged to Colonel Theodoric Bland's 1st Virginia Regiment of Light Dragoons. The regiment needed a lift. Theodoric Bland, a kinsman of Lee whose grandmother was a Bland, was described by him as "noble, sensible, honourable and amiable; but never intended for the department of military intelligence." In other words, he was not very bright, and was largely to blame for the conflicting intelligence that had robbed Washington of any chance for victory at Brandywine.

---

36. Letter, George Weedon to John Page, 25 Jan. 1778. Weedon Papers, Chicago Historical Society.

37. Henry ("Lighthorse Harry") Lee, 1756-1818, was the eldest son of Lt. Col. Henry and Lucy (Grymes) Lee of "Leesylvania" on the Potomac above Dumfries. He married (1) Matilda Lee, daughter of Philip Ludwell and Elizabeth (Steptoe) Lee and (2) Ann Hill Carter, daughter of Charles Carter of "Shirley". Robert Edward Lee was a son of his second marriage.

Too many pretty things cannot be said of this Gallant *little* officer. He and his Lieutenants (Linsey [38] and Payton [39]) with a very small troop of Horse has during this campaign taken themselves 132 prisoners before they lost a man. In two little affairs that has happened lately he has lost eight, which is all the enemy has for their 132.

Congress, too, was charmed by Lee's "little affair" at Scott's Farm and, on the 7th of April: [40]

> RESOLVED: That Captain H. Lee be promoted to the rank of Major-Commandant: that he be empowered to augment his present corps by enlistment of two troops of horse to act as a separate corps.

This later addition of three infantry companies resulted in the creation of Lee's Legion, one of Washington's elite units in which membership was assiduously sought and proudly cherished. We will meet them later when Charles Morehead [41] of Fauquier and several of his friends had joined their ranks.

However, "little affairs" did not make a winter and Weedon was still bored. He wanted to go home. He should have sensed that events at Valley Forge were building to a climax that would adversely affect his fortunes. Brigadier General William Woodford was implacable in his demand for precedence over the other three Virginia Brigadiers and was constantly intriguing to bring it about. Washington would have none of an issue he considered too petty for serious thought, but Woodford's friends in Congress worked

---

38. William Lindsay (not Lindsey) d: 1792 was a son of Col. Robert and Susannah (Austin) Lindsay of "The Mount", Fairfax Co. He married, 1766, Ann Calvert of Culpeper Co. They lived at "Laurel Hill" near Colchester.

39. Henry Peyton (not Payton) appears to have been a son of Henry and Ann (Thornton) Peyton of Prince William Co. He died without issue during the war.

40. Heitman, "Lee", quoted in Boatner's **Encyclopedia of the American Revolution**, p. 608.

41. Charles Morehead, son of Capt. John Morehead of Fauquier, married, 3 Oct. 1786, Margaret Slaughter, daughter of Cadwallader and Margaret (Ransdell) Slaughter of Culpeper. He was a cousin of Turner Morehead and a brother-in-law of Capt. William Triplett.

like beavers on his behalf.[42] Congress appointed a committee to look into the matter. It was then that Weedon committed a capital blunder, - he left camp on furlough on the very day on which the committee arrived. Woodford had their undivided attention.

Weedon's last appearance as officer of the day was on the 7th of February.[43] His departure was poorly timed. He may have believed that the tide of opinion was turning against him, but, if so, he was mistaken. The civilian committee, unwilling to make a decision of purely military nature, placed the matter in the hands of a board of general officers. They met on the 4th of March, 1778, and rendered a decision in Woodford's favor. On the 19th Congress resolved:[44]

> That General Washington call in and cancel the commissions of Brigadiers Woodford, Muhlenberg, Scott and Weedon: and that new commissions be granted them; and that they rank in future agreeable to the following arrangement: Woodford, Muhlenberg, Scott, Weedon.

On the 31st of March Weedon was in Fredericksburg unaware of what had taken place. He wrote to John Page in Williamsburg reporting that his last letters from camp contained nothing of interest.[45] Colonel Smith[46] of the 2nd Virginia State Regiment had arrived in Fredericksburg on the 29th but the wind was so high that he could not cross the river. The Governor had instructed him to have the troops inoculated in Alexandria or Georgetown, but Weedon ordered them north by way of Noland's Ferry in response to Washington's order to send them with all possible speed,

---

42. Notably Joseph Jones of Fredericksburg, Woodford's cousin, who apparently made the matter of Woodford's rank his major concern while in Congress.

43. **The Valley Forge Orderly Book of General George Weedon**, Dodd, Meade & Co., 1902, p. 224.

44. Ford, ed., **Journals of Congress**. Vol. X, p. 269.

45. Letter, George Weedon to John Page, 31 March 1778. Weedon Papers, Chicago Historical Society.

46. John Smith of Frederick Co., according to the Journal of the Council. However, Dr. J. Dallas Robertson in his brief biography (Winchester-Frederick Historical Society **Papers**, Vol. IX, p. 17) does not mention his command of the 2nd Virginia State Regt. He is credited only with the care of British prisoners after Saratoga.

without inoculation. The detachment fell far short of the numbers expected, having only 202 State troops and 228 draftees. Colonel Smith told him that 300 more men were left for inoculation at Yorktown. He ended heatedly: "Col⁰ (Charles) Harrison with his Regiment of Artillerists have been long expected, - for God's sake what keeps him? The season is advancing fast and much depends on Early operations either offensive or defensive."

There was then no hint of the blow that must have fallen a few days later. Washington wrote him a friendly letter attempting to soften it and keep him in the service.[47] Greene also wrote to the same purpose. However Woodford successfully defeated their ends. Having obtained all that was important to him in the war, rank, he happily departed for two months' vacation in Virginia. He was not so hurried, though, as to neglect to send Weedon a copy of the resolution with a curt note. It was ample reason for Weedon to foresee that his further service in the army would be attended by unremitting humiliation. With great reluctance he offered his resignation.

Congress was not without sympathy but saw no way to resolve the issue. They permitted him to retain his rank and retire without pay or prejudice until such time as the obstacle was removed from his path by the British or some other kindly agent. Scott really had no cause to complain, because Woodford clearly outranked him, but Muhlenberg was similarly troubled. He wrote to Washington with some bitterness but, after much brooding, finally decided to settle for an assurance from Congress that, in ranking him below Woodford, nothing prejudicial to his character or service had been intended:[48] Congress gladly complied.

Boredom at Valley Forge produced other results even more dismal than the loss of good officers through petty jealousy and bickering. The needless death of young Duff Green is an example. Duff Green was not from Fauquier. His father was Colonel John Green of Culpeper was had been named in January to take command of the 10th Virginia Regiment in place of Colonel Edward Stevens who was resigning. His mother was Susannah Blackwell, sister of Thomas and Joseph Blackwell of Elk Run. His connections in Fauquier County were almost endless.

He was a handsome, headstrong lad who, only with difficulty, had been persuaded to wait for his eighteenth birthday before

---

47. Letter, Washington to Weedon, 15 March 1778, in: Fitzpatrick, ed., **Writings of Washington**, Vol. XI, p. 88.

48. Ford, ed., **Journals of Congress**, Vol. XI, p. 807; Vol. XV, pp. 1418-19.

joining a Continental regiment as a subaltern. Valley Forge in February of 1778 was not the best place for a boy with a well-developed combativeness, and a prickly, cavalier sense of honour. Duelling was strictly forbidden but, partly because of the risk involved, continued to tempt the young lions. When spirits ran high and grog flowed, tempers flared and too often a meeting on a bleak hillside in the wintry dawn followed. The usual result was one or two flesh wounds, but on one such morning Duff Green died in a pool of blood that stained the snow around him.

Such incidents emphasized the need for some diversion to engage the attention of the men if there were to be any left to shoot at the British instead of each other. Happily the solution was at hand. The man responsible for this was introduced in the orderly book of Weedon's brigade on the 28th of March: [49]

> Baron Steuben, a Lieutenant General in Foreign service, and a Gentleman of great Military experience, having obligingly undertaken to exercise the office of Inspector General in this army ... The Commander in Chief ('till the pleasure of Congress shall be known) desires that he may be respected and obey'd as such; and hopes & expectes that all officers of whatsoever Rank in it, will afford him every aid in their power, in the execution of his office.

Friedrich Wilhelm Augustus, Baron von Steuben was about as much a Lieutenant General in the foreign service as Lafayette was a General in the French army. He had served under Frederick the Great as a drill captain until he was discharged in 1763 for rather obscure reasons. He was then chamberlain to the petty court of Hohenzollern-Hechingen, where he became a Baron, titled but penniless. After several unsuccessful attempts to secure posts in foreign armies, he ran into Benjamin Franklin in Paris. Franklin, whose hearing was only as good as he wanted it to be, wrote to Washington, introducing him as a former "Lieutenant General in the King of Prussia's service."

If Steuben had really been a Lieutenant General he would probably not have known enough about army discipline to be much good to Washington. Lieutenant Generals left such duties to their drill captains, and a good drill captain was exactly what the American army needed. Steuben was a good drill captain and also an unforgettable personality. Standing before his shivering, half-starved provincials in a magnificent uniform he put on a show

---

49. **The Valley Forge Orderly Book of George Weedon**, p. 273.

worth paid admission. When he ran out of curses in German and French he called on his French-speaking aide, Captain Benjamin Walker [50] to swear at them in English.

"*Viens, Walker, mon ami* ... Goddam de *gaucheries* of dese *badauts*,[51] he would roar, "*Je ne puis plus.*" The results were marvellous to behold. He started with a model company of 100 picked men. He instilled in them pride in their unit and spread his instruction in a sort of geometric progression through the little army. After hours of tedious drill there emerged real soldiers out of men whose only military talent was a will to fight.

The Fauquier companies in the Virginia Line on the 1st of June 1778 were small indeed, but they were trained veterans.

During the spring Washington asked Elias Boudinot,[52] Commissioner of Prisoners, to arrange the exchange of General Charles Lee. Just what Washington saw in this conceited, dirty and treacherous man is a mystery, but he had certainly impressed him with the extent of his military ability. Baudinot offered General Richard Prescott in return and the exchange was arranged to take place on the 5th of April. He was met personally by Washington who had staged an elaborate parade in his honour. After a sumptuous dinner he was quartered in a room adjoining Mrs. Washington's sitting room. He promptly smuggled a prostitute in through the back door. His only recorded comment was that "he had found the army in a worse situation than he expected and that General Washington was not fit to command a sergeant's guard."[53]

In April the red bud bloomed again on the mountain side, heralding another spring in Fauquier. It was time for the officers and men of the Continental Line to march north again and rejoin their regiments. The two captains of Fauquier troops in the 3rd Virginia regiment did so with mixed emotions. Resignations had depleted their numbers and had created vacancies that made promotion possible. At the same time it was apparent that the

50. Benjamin Walker, Steuben's aide, inherited, with William North, Steuben's estate on his death in 1794.

51. *Baudauts*, Paris argot for idlers who hang around fairs, whose attention is only briefly engaged before they turn to something else.

52. Elias Boudinot, 1740-1821, wealthy and prominent New Jersey lawyer of Huguenot descent; described as tall, handsome, "elegant, eloquent and emotional." He married Hannah Stockton.

53. Elias Boudinot, **Journal of Historical Recollections...** Philadelphia, 1894, pp. 77-78.

Virginia Continental Line was short more than 1,000 men. In fact, as late as June, 1778, only 3,241 were fit for duty, all ranks included. If this trend continued some consolidation must take place and many officers would be supernumerary.

Captain John Blackwell counted a few old friends. Faithful Sergeant Moses Allen was on hand, as were William Bawcut (promoted to sergeant in place of Henry Bradford), Johnathan Crook, Benjamin Hamrick, John Walton, Daniel Pennington, William Bailey and George Russell. William Davidson, who had considered re-enlisting in a New Jersey company, had had second thoughts and was back with his old outfit. Billy Tomlin's brother Stephen and Willie Moffett, who had been inoculated in Leesburg, were now ready to serve. Richard Bayse,[54] who had signed up the previous summer and had fought at both Brandywine and Germantown was on his way but had not arrived on April 1st. The rest, totalling only thirty, were draftees and short-termers from other disbanded units.

Valentine Peyton's unit was no better off. Still lacking a Lieutenant, he carried Isham Keith's name in that rank, though Keith had long since resigned. He had only 34 men in March and only a handful of recruits came later. They remained about 40 in all. Also in Woodford's brigade Colonel John Cropper was given permanent command of the 11th Virginia Regiment on the 29th of April, ending Daniel Morgan's absentee tenure of that office. John Marshall was promoted to captain of his company, with Robert Porterfield, 1st lieutenant and John Barnes, recently promoted, 2nd lieutenant. As Marshall was usually on detached service as Deputy Judge Advocate and Porterfield was acting aide to General Woodford, it was left to Barnes to run the show. There were 53 men but, when staff clerks, guards and orderlies for high-ranking officers were subtracted, only 37 remained to fight the enemy.

Colonel Daniel Morgan still held on to his special rifle unit but their number is difficult to determine because most of them appeared on the pay rolls of other regiments, especially the 11th and 15th. Colonel Christian Febiger was still in command of the 2nd Virginia Regiment. In his second company under Morgan Alexander were a scattering of men from Fauquier: Aaron

---

54. Richard Bayse, 1758-1822, m: 4 Dec. 1781, Nancy Taylor. No known issue.

O'Bannon,[55] Alexander Keith,[56] another John Ashby [57] and the Blackmore brothers, George and Thomas.[58] This company had 33 men in March and only four more in June.

Captain Thomas Blackwell of the 10th Virginia Regiment was also at a loss for men. Colonel John Green soon after his son's death left for Virginia and did not return until early April. On the sixth of April he took command of his regiment. He had hardly done so when the news reached him that his second son, John Green, aged 20, a Lieutenant in the 1st Virginia Regiment of Artillery under Colonel Charles Harrison, had died suddenly of unknown cause before the regiment had left Virginia.

Joseph Blackwell had remained on duty at Valley Forge through the long winter, though an old bayonet wound in the leg given him in a skirmish by one of Howe's Scotch Highlanders continued to give him pain. Colonel Green had readily consented to his furlough in April, especially because his brother William was getting married in Fauquier. Months before he had come upon his badly wounded brother after a battle and had managed to get him medical assistance before he bled to death. Now, almost fully recovered, Captain William Blackwell was ready to end his bachelor career. For Joseph Blackwell it would be a welcome break in the almost unremitting gloom of the past two years. Furthermore, the wedding would take place at Brent Town.

Even in 1778 the immense, half-feudal principality of Brent Town retained the tidewater tradition of landed estates presided over by aristocratic owners who lived in some splendor despite being a bit short of cash. It lay about eight miles northeast of Elk Run, straddling the Fauquier-Prince William line. Though it had

55. Aaron O'Bannon, was an illegitimate son of Bryant O'Bannon by Margaret Johnston. In his will he left 257 acres in Frederick (later Berkeley) County to Aaron and Francis Johnston, to revert to his grandson, Bryant O'Bannon, if they should die without heirs. An Act of Assembly dated October 1778, ordered his lands sold and Bryant O'Bannon had the Assembly pass another act in May, 1782, establishing his right to the property. Aaron O'Bannon may have died in the Battle of Monmouth.

56. Alexander Keith, 1748-1822, son of the Reverend James and Mary Isham (Randolph) Keith. He married (1)   Yancey, (2) Mary Ann Callihue, widow of Charles Thornton.

57. John Ashby, 1753-1841, son of Stephen Ashby. He married, 10 April 1797, in Mercer Co., Ky., Mary (Polly) Hardin.

58. George and Thomas Blackmore appear to have enlisted in Frederick County. Thomas Blackmore was killed at Germantown.

not lured Huguenot settlers at the end of the 17th century to establish themselves beneath its towering trees, as mentioned before, it had proved attractive to the descendants of the Chotank [59] aristocracy from Westmoreland County. It had, at some time, been divided between the heirs of the four original owners, Robert Bristow, Nicholas Hayward, George Brent of "Woodstock" and Richard Foote of "Cedar Grove." In the division the portion that lay in Fauquier County had been acquired by the heirs of Richard Foote and his wife, Hester, who was Nicholas Hayward's daughter. Much of the Hayward tract had been sold in 1734 to Colonel Henry Fitzhugh of "Bedford".[60] The Foote and part of the Hayward dividends had descended before the Revolution to Richard Foote,[61] who built "Truro" in Prince William County and to George Foote,[62] his brother, who lived on Cedar Run in Fauquier. They married sisters, Margaret and Celia Helm, daughters of Captain Lynaugh and Hester (Edrington) Helm.[63] Captain Helm was something of a power in Prince William County, Justice, Sheriff and member of the Committee of Safety. Contemporary accounts agree that his daughters were unusually attractive, lively and strong-willed. Elizabeth Foote [64] considered them "worldly" and "devoted to fashion". She disapproved of them heartily, but then Elizabeth Foote disapproved of most people.

59. Chotank, an old name for St. Paul's Parish, a notably rich parish in Stafford and King George Counties.

60. "Bedford", the great plantation of Col. Henry Fitzhugh in Stafford Co. Henry Fitzhugh, 1687-1758, m: Susannah Cooke, daughter of Mordecai Cooke, grandfather of John and Charles Chilton.

61. Richard Foote, 1729?-1779, son of Richard and Katherine (Fossaker) Foote of "Cedar Grove", St. Paul's Parish. His wife, Margaret (Helm) Foote m: (2) John Thornton Fitzhugh.

62. George Foote, 1750-1775, brother of Richard Foote, above. His wife, Celia (Helm) Foote m: (2) Capt. William Blackwell, m: (3) Dr. George Graham.

63. Lynaugh Helm, 1715-1789, owned land in both Prince William and Fauquier Counties. He married Hester Edrington, daughter of Christopher Edrington of Richmond Co. A third daughter, Lucinda, married Thomas Fitzhugh, 1753-1829.

64. Elizabeth Foote, 1746-1812, sister of Richard and George Foote, whose devotion to the established church was extreme. In November, 1779, she married Lund Washington and moved to Mount Vernon, where her piety almost drove the Custis children to open mutiny. She left no survivng issue.

It would, perhaps, be unfair to say that the Helm sisters had married for money, but we may take note that both George and Richard Foote were considerably older than their wives. When George Foote died in the autumn of 1775, he left a large estate to his young wife and two children, Richard Helm Foote, aged 3, and Hester, 1. [65] Captain William Blackwell had found the vivacious young widow irresistible during the months of his convalescence.

No account of the wedding which took place sometime after the 6th of April, [66] has come down to us but we can visualize an occasion of some rural elegance. George Foote's house was, no doubt, larger and finer than the house of Thomas Marshall near Markham, but it probably fell far short of being able to hold all the Blackwells, Edmonds, Footes, Helms, Fitzhughs, Crumps and their kinfolk and friends. Most of the festivities must have taken place out of doors under the spreading trees on the banks of Cedar Run.

There may not have been much grandeur in the surroundings, except that derived from nature, but the lovely blond bride and the tall, fair haired, blue eyed groom and their guests did not lack elegance. Joseph Blackwell was struck by the preponderance of young men resplendent in a variety of handsome uniforms and their ladies, - well! they were simply stunning. While travelling in the area in 1774 Dr. Johann Schoepf remarked that, even though the houses were plain and not too well kept "it is nothing extraordinary to see the lady of the house and women generally clothed and adorned with great fastidiousness: for the fair sex in America cannot resist the propensity to make themselves fine, even when remotely situated they must forego the pleasure of being admired except by the casual traveller." [67]

Though the conversation was light, it was remarkably well-informed. Many of those attending were from the area around Philadelphia and Williamsburg. There was plenty of heady speculation about the end of the war, so much so that Colonel Robert Ballard had complained to Washington that the Governor and Assembly were almost convinced that the British had given up. "I was never so trifled with by Gent[n] [68] in all my life," he declared.

65. Richard Helm Foote, 1773-1818, married, 1795, Jane Stuart, daughter of the Rev. William Stuart. Hester Foote m: 1799, William Edmonds of "Edmondium" (now "Loretta") Fauquier County.

66. Chappelear & Gott, **Fauquier County Marriage Bonds**, p. 12.

67. Johann David Schoepf, **Travels in the Confederation**, Vol. II, p. 33.

68. Letter, Ballard to Washington, 24 July 1778. Washington Papers, Library of Congress.

Joseph Blackwell wondered if their confidence was not the outgrowth of too much toddy and Madeira, but it was fun to dream, if only briefly.

There was much talk of Kentucky and the name of the bride's cousin Leonard Helm was on everyone's lips. Joseph Blackwell probably got an earfull from a relative who probably knew more about Kentucky than most men in Fauquier. He was Captain Francis Triplett whose eldest sister, Elizabeth, was the wife of Helm's uncle John Crump. Captain Triplett's son, William, had been one of the surveyors with Colonel Thomas Bullitt in May of 1775 and held a preemption patent on 1,000 acres, "improved and marked, lying on the south side of the east fork of Licking Creek, N^O. W. of Water's land on the Buffalo road."[69] The land was near Limestone, later Maysville, on the Ohio River. Francis was already planning to move there after the little business with Lord Howe was finished. He might have gone with Helm had he not just been appointed captain of a militia company.

It was a good party. Lieutenant Joseph Blackwell of the 10th Virginia Regiment was sorry when it was over. After that brief glimpse of the world as it should have been, he returned to Valley Forge. Riding through the fertile countryside of Maryland and Pennsylvania burgeoning with spring, his heart was somehow lifted. Perhaps some of the rumors were true. Perhaps Howe really was being recalled to England. Perhaps the British were ready to call it quits. Perhaps; well perhaps anything!

The morning of May 1st was one of those brilliant and beautiful spring mornings. The troops with dogwood wreaths in their hats paraded to fife and drum around their regimental Maypoles. The long and terrible winter was over. Then came the joyous news, France had recognized the United States! "I believe no event was ever received with more heartfelt joy," Washington said.[70] On the 5th official notice was given and the 6th was a day of "Universal Happiness & the strictest Propriety."

There was a *feu de joye* and a great parade in which Baron Steuben doubtless had a chance to appreciate the task before him. After a cold collation in a wooded amphitheatre near camp, the officers were invited to an entertainment by his Excellency. As the General stood to take his leave: [71]

---

69. Cliff, **History of Maysville and Mason County, Kentucky**, p. 31.

70. Scheer & Rankin, **Rebels and Redcoats**, p. 364.

71. **Ibid.**, p. 365.

There was a universal clap, with loud huzzas, which continued till he had proceeded a quarter of a mile, during which time there were a thousand hats tossed in the air. His Excellency turned round with his retinue and huzzaed several times.

There were "claps" and "huzzas", toasts and speeches and most everyone got a little tipsy on grog but there was always May 2nd to think of, the morning after, when a thousand hats must be retrieved and placed on a thousand aching heads. Nothing had really changed. The British were still in Philadelphia and the French were - in France.

The atmosphere at Weedon's headquarters on the banks of the Schuylkill on Saturday May 2nd was gloomy. The four regimental commanders, Febiger of the 2nd, John Gibson of the 6th, Green of the 10th and William Davis of the 14th, were frankly worried. They had heard only indirectly of the action of Congress with respect to Woodford's rank. That both Muhlenberg and Weedon might resign loomed as a possibility. They did not know of Muhlenberg's bitter letter to Washington dated 10 April, in which Muhlenberg said candidly that most officers believed "that the change would have taken place if General Woodford had had no claims, as Congress were determined to put him into a post where he might have the first chance of promotion." Weedon's resignation was submitted to Congress on the 13th of April. Rumors were rife but there was no solid information on what might happen to the commands of either Brigadier.

To add to their burdens, his Excellency took the occasion to deliver to them a stern lecture on religion, of all things, and ordered them to attend Divine service on Sunday and give thanks!

General Weedon's orderly book was continued in his absence into May. By that time it was apparent that he would not return. Considering the dearth of new recruits, his officers were justifiably apprehensive that his brigade might be combined with Woodford's. On the 7th of May the orderly book ends in mid-sentence:

The Honorable Congress have been pleas'd by the Resolution of 3.d. of Feb[r]. last to require all Officers, as well as Civil as Military holding Commissions under them, to Take & Subscribe the following oath or affirmation, according to the Circumstances of the parties

The text of the required oath is omitted but read as follows: [72]

> I, _____ do acknowledge the UNITED STATES OF AMERICA to be Free, Independent and Sovereign States, and declare that the people thereof owe no allegiance or obedience to him: and I do _____ that I Great-Britain: and I renounce, refuse and abjure any allegiance or obediance to him: and I do _____ that I will, to the utmost of my power, support, maintain and defend the said United States against the said King George the Third, his heirs and successors, and his or their abbettors, assistants, and adherents, and will serve the said United States in the office of _____ which I now hold, with fidelity, according to the best of my skill and understanding.

As Washington later pointed out, there was nothing in this oath that was either unusual or cause for alarm. However, when it was placed before the officers of Weedon's and Woodford's brigades, they flatly refused to sign. In the entire army they were the only ones to do so. [73] Washington was mystified. General Lafayette was not. With consummate tact he explained to Washington the cause for their concern. They had no objection to the oath except to the last two lines: "and I will serve the said United States in the *office* of ... *which I now hold,* with fidelity, according to the best of my skill and understanding."

A "memorial" signed by 26 officers of the two brigades contained mostly window dressing, but included one pertinent question:

> (3) Would not the oath debar an officer from the privilege of resigning when circumstances might render it indispensibly necessary that he should quit the army?

---

72. Hundreds of these forms may be found in the National Archives. Those of Capt. Thomas Blackwell, Capt. John Gillison and Lieut. Joseph Blackwell, all of the 10th Va. Regt., dated 12 May 1778, are endorsed: "Sworn before me at Camp - P. Muhlenberg, B.G."

73. Washington to Lafayette, 17 May 1778. Washington writes: "At the same time I cannot but consider it as a circumstance of singularity that the scruples against the oath should be peculiar to the officers of *one Bridgade and so very extensive*." He was referring to Woodford's brigade.

In a nutshell, they did not trust Woodford. They thought of resignation as a last resort if serving under his command should become unbearable. Would not this oath be a weapon he could use against them if they decided to resign or, more important, seek a more agreeable post under another commander? Washington assured them that it would not. With thanks to the young Marquis for his good offices, they signed the oath without further demur. No successor to Weedon was appointed but, to their immense relief, Muhlenberg decided to remain.

It had been rumored in April that General Howe was returning to England, to be replaced by Sir Henry Clinton. In early May an even more heady rumor was going the rounds, - that the British planned to evacuate Philadelphia.[4] Washington was baffled and decided to detach a strong force from Valley Forge to gather information that would indicate the time of the enemy withdrawal. They could harass the foraging parties that they would have to send out to prepare for any change of base. Lafayette was given command of the operation, probably as a way of honoring the new French alliance and to gratify the young Major General's burning desire to command troops in combat. He assigned 2,200 men and five guns, most of Lafayette's division which included the entire Virginia Line.

The whole enterprise was a risky and ill-advised one to entrust to an inexperienced general. The force was too large for reconnaissance and too small for battle. Lafayette left camp on the 18th of May with the brigades of Enoch Poor of Massachusetts and the two Virginia brigades of Muhlenberg and Scott. In addition to his own, Muhlenberg had command of Woodford's and Weedon's. They took up a strong position at Barren Hill, near Matson's Ford [75] on the Schuylkill about midway between the two armies.

The British were living it up in Philadelphia and, on the night of the 18th were celebrating in a grand gala on the occasion of Lord Howe's departure. The next morning they were a bit hung over but not exactly asleep when spies brought news of Lafayette's position. As a sort of rousing farewell gesture to Lord Howe, they decided on a large scale attack. 5,000 men under General Grant

74. The British decision to leave Philadelphia in which they were strongly entrenched was based on a realization by the King and the North Ministry that a land war against the colonies was difficult, if not impossible, while fighting France and, probably, Spain as well. When peace proposals that did not include independence were rejected, the Ministry hoped to reduce them by naval blockade.

75. Conshohocken.

with 15 guns and 2,000 grenadiers under General Grey would spearhead the engagement. Clinton and Howe would lead a strong force against the center. They set their trap carefully and, on the morning of the 20th prepared to catch their prey.

They reckoned without Captain Allan McLane. [76]

Allan McLane was a young Philadelphian who, by the unlikeliest of coincidences, had served as a volunteer with the Virginians at Great Bridge. He had been visiting relatives. Returning to Philadelphia he had raised his own company and had dedicated his personal fortune to maintaining and equipping about 100 men. At Valley Forge his troop had so successfully harassed British foraging parties that they were known as "the market-stoppers." In May of 1778 his company, reinforced by a company of dragoons and about 50 Oneida Indians, nearly drove the British to distraction by simulated attacks designed to ruin their sleep. They dropped iron pots full of gunpowder and scrap metal which exploded with a loud bang and flung hardware in all directions.

It was McLane's men who nabbed two British grenadiers at Three Mile Run and learned of the British plan. After sending a small detachment of riflemen to fight a delaying action, the young Captain raced to Lafayette at dawn to warn him. McLane had a lifetime's intimacy with the terrain around Barren Hill. He knew of a little-used sunken road to Matson's Ford. Putting to dramatic use the training his men had received from Baron Steuben, Lafayette formed his men into compact platoon columns and, after setting up a small rear guard to simulate a defense, coolly slipped away with only minor casualties. On the morning of the 20th Clinton moved from the south on Barren Hill, only to meet the scouts of Grey's column moving cautiously down from the north. The birds had flown.

So, due to Lafayette's presence of mind, McLane's special knowledge and Steuben's applied profanity, the Virginia line escaped annihilation. But it was a very near thing, and Washington must have realized that he was lucky not to have paid dearly for his lack of judgment. To the men from Fauquier, Lafayette was a hero, closely followed by the Baron with his marvelously expressive vocabulary.

By the 1st of June, 1778, Clinton's intention to leave

---

76. Allan McLane, 1746-1829, son of a Scottish merchant from the Isle of Coll, inherited a substantial fortune on the death of his father. After Great Bridge, he joined Washington's army in New York and captured a British patrol at the battle of Long Island. He fought at White Plains, Trenton and was promoted for gallantry at Princeton.

Philadelphia was no longer a rumor. The British had begun to level their defensive fortifications. On the 29th of May a notice had appeared in the *Virginia Gazette:*

> The Commander in Chief positively requires all officers of the State of Virginia, except those who are detained on public service by his Excellency, the Governor of the State, or any General officer of the same, or those who have furloughs not yet expired, immediately to join their respective Corps.
>
> By his Excellency's command
> Alexander Hamilton, Aide-de-Camp

Though he wanted the largest possible force available, Washington was determined to take no more risks. He would wait until Sir Henry Clinton had committed himself to some course of action before attempting to thwart him.

Colonel Charles Harrison finally got his 1st Continental Regiment of Artillery under way, crossing the river at Fredericksburg on the 9th of June, more than two months after Weedon had asked "for God's sake" what had happened to them. They had been training at Yorktown with Marshall's Virginia Regiment of Artillery and travelled north by the usual route across the Potomac at Noland's Ferry, reaching Valley Forge in record time. Sylvester Welch of Northumberland County, who had enlisted there in 1777 under Edmund Denny, described the march. His closest friends, Edward Shacklett, John Roach, Dale Carter and James Bailey, among others, appear to have come from Fauquier, which probably influenced his decision to settle there after the war.

One Fauquier man did not accompany the regiment. He was Gideon Johnston. He had started out in 1775 or 1776 as a private in Captain Richard Meade's company of the 2nd Virginia Regiment. He was transferred to Harrison's artillery early in 1778 where he was commissioned as a lieutenant. He was a fine officer and Colonel Marshall offered him a captaincy, which he accepted and served throughout the war.

Marshall was still battling with his organizational problems. In June the Assembly threw up its collective hands and [77] ordered, "that Colonel Marshall, with the Advice and Assistance of the other field Officers of the State Regiment of Artillery, do report their Opinion, specially how the Rank of the other officers in the

---

77. *Journals of the Council of State of Virginia,* Vol. II, p. 144.

said Regiment ought to be settled as soon as may be." The odd rank of Captain-Lieutenant, whose responsibilities related to guns, not men, peculiar to an artillery regiment seemed to baffle them. The Journal of the Council of State reports, 27 June 1778: [78]

> The Governor with the Advice of the Council appointed the following Persons Captains Lieutenants ... according to seniority, viz: William Jennings, Thomas Clay, Richard Booker, Samuel Blackwell, Gideon Johnston, Edwd Valentine, Richard Crump & Stephen Turnbull. And Colonel Marshall having made out a List of Cadets ... recommending them as proper Persons to be appointed Second Lieutenants, - The Governor ... issued Commissions ... as they stand below, viz: John Williams, William Thomson, Peter Kemp, Thomas Marshall, Jr., Humphrey Marshall, Robert Coone, John Quarles, Yancey Lipscomb, Daniel Lipscomb and Thomas Weeks.

How many of these men were from Fauquier is difficult to tell, though some names are easily recognized. Samuel Blackwell had found an escape from the Fauquier militia, at reduced rank but without the attendant in-fighting. Richard Crump, Peter Kemp and the two Marshalls were from Fauquier. Thomas Marshall,[79] Jr., was Colonel Marshall's sixteen year old son and Humphrey Marshall [80] was his nephew. Thus fully organized, the Virginia Artillery sat down to await developments.

At Valley Forge the game was also one of watchful waiting. For Colonel John Green it was one of continued anguish. His eldest son, William, only 21, had gone to sea, influenced by some of his tidewater relatives. In May he was Captain of the American sloop *Defiance* off the Virginia capes. The *Defiance* was captured by a British frigate and Captain Green was reputedly lost at sea. He escaped and turned up three years later, but in June of 1778 Colonel Green had lost, or thought he had, his three eldest sons. He fought grimly on, the war was not over and he could usually be

---

78. **Ibid.**, p. 156.

79. Thomas Marshall, Jr., 1761-1817, moved to Washington, Mason Co., Kentucky in 1790.

80. Humphrey Marshall, 1756-1841, son of John and Mary (Quesenbury) Marshall. He married his 1st cousin, Mary Ann Marshall, daughter of Col. Thomas Marshall. He moved to Kentucky about 1785 and lived at "Glenwillis", near Frankfort.

found where the battle raged hottest. The Greens did not give up easily.

On the 18th of June Washington received a message that the enemy was on the move. Quickly he put his army in motion while detachments of militia and regulars in New Jersey attempted to slow the redcoats on their march. He had 12,200 Continental and militia troops when they crossed the river at Coryell's Ferry. General Maxwell's Brigade of about 1,300 was at Mount Holly.

Major General Charles Lee commanded the right wing with the brigades of Generals William Woodford, Charles Scott and the Massachusetts and North Carolina troops. Stirling's left wing was composed of the rest of the New Englanders and Pennsylvania troops. Lafayette's division included the Maryland troops and the brigades of Muhlenberg and Weedon under the command of Muhlenberg. They formed the second line which left Valley Forge on the 19th. Anthony Wayne and his Pennsylvanians had gone on ahead. On the 23rd Washington brought his army to a halt at Hopewell, New Jersey, twelve miles northwest of Princeton, to survey the situation. Rain and intense heat had hampered his progress and there was still no word as to the specific route Clinton intended to follow to reach New York.

There were two possibilities, a more northerly course to embark his troops at Amboy; or to turn sharply to the east and embark at Sandy Hook. He could, of course, strike south along the Delaware to meet his fleet near the capes, but that seemed unlikely. While Clinton moved slowly up to Allentown over roads deep with sand, in 100^0 heat, Washington called a council of war, to decide whether or not they should hazard a general action. What Alexander Hamilton contemptuously called "the most honourable society of midwives" decided against it. Greene, Wayne, Steuben and Lafayette dissented, but were outnumbered. Wayne [81] even wrote in protest, as did Lafayette and Nathanael Greene, to no avail.

Consistent with the recommendations of the council, Washington detached 1,500 men under Colonel Charles Scott to harass the enemy's left flank. Bewildered, Scott wrote, "I have not the most distant Idea of having it in our power to annoy the Enemy on their march to Amboy, if that should be their route." [82] Again

---

81. Letter, Wayne to Washington, Hopewell, 24 June 1778, from Stille, **Major-general Anthony Wayne and the Pennsylvania Line**, p. 143.

82. Letter, Scott to Washington, 18 June 1778. Washington Papers, Library of Congress.

the detachment was too large for reconnaissance and too small for battle. Fortunately Washington then discovered that Clinton had put his entire army on the one road from Allentown to Sandy Hook. Now his objective was obvious. Washington sent Wayne on with 1,000 Pennsylvanians to reinforce Scott. The main army stopped at Cranberry on the night of June 25-26 to wait out a severe rainstorm. Lafayette had gone forward with Wayne to command the advance. Lee had been offered the opportunity but had condescendingly declined.

Upon realizing that the van now numbered more than 4,000 men Lee changed his mind. Washington, unwilling to offend Lafayette, suggested a compromise which resulted in some ambiguous orders that would later rise to haunt him.

After a grueling 19 mile march in stifling heat, Clinton reached Monmouth Courthouse on the afternoon of June 26th. There he paused to rest his men, choosing his ground with care as he knew that the Americans were constantly looking for an opening to attack. Washington sent Lafayette forward to Englishtown, five miles west of Monmouth. The next day Lee went forward to command the van, which was further reinforced by Grayson's Additional Regiment of Virginians and Massachusetts regulars under the immediate command of Colonel William Grayson. Some time before Washington had sent Morgan and his rangers to harass the British right.

As soon as Grayson reached Englishtown in the early morning of the 28th Lee ordered him to Tennant Meetinghouse, two miles nearer Monmouth. About 5 a.m. Lee followed with Lafayette's, Wayne's and Scott's detachments. Clinton was already on the move but had left Cornwallis to guard the rear, with 2,000 elite troops and most of his dragoons. On learning that the enemy had resumed their march, Lee ordered Grayson to attack. As he was preparing to do so he encountered the New Jersey militia under General Philemon Dickinson[83] in full retreat. They had come upon Cornwallis' rear guard in their reconnaissance and had mistaken it for the entire enemy force. Grayson and Dickinson were discussing their problem when Lee arrived. Lee concluded that the main British force must have left Monmouth, and sent his advance troops across a causeway flanked by swampland to rout the enemy covering party on the other side. About 1 p.m. Clinton realized that

---

83. Philemon Dickinson, 1739-1809, as commander of the New Jersey militia, was expected to destroy roads and bridges, as well as gather intelligence. He was not expected to hold any position, so he was really not "retreating" when Grayson met him.

the American harassment had reached dangerous proportions. He detached the 17th Light Dragoons and a brigade of foot to re-enforce Cornwallis and face about for a flanking manoeuvre.

What happened after that has become no clearer in the last two hundred years than it was the day after. In general, when Lee's 5,000 men encountered this increased opposition, they began to fall back in disorder. Lee completely lost control. Isolated units under Wayne and Scott in strong positions were abandoned without support. Grayson's gallant regiment was almost wiped out. Rushing forward with his main force to support Lee, Washington met the retreating men with stupified disbelief. Suddenly he remembered that Lafayette had suspected Lee of treachery and had warned him. Coming abreast of Lee still floundering in a morass of conflicting orders, he demanded an explanation. Lee muttered something about false intelligence and an attack against his better judgement. Washington peremptorily ordered him to the rear and took over his command.

Clinton, encouraged by his initial success, was now trying to bring about a general engagement. He got more than he bargained for. As the American lines stiffened the training given them by Baron Steuben began to show to advantage. Colonel Henry Livingston's New Yorkers checked the enemy advance, a pause that allowed time for Colonel Eleazer Oswald to bring his Second Continental Artillery into effective action. Livingston was further reinforced by General Knox with several additional guns. Greene's artillery and the First Continental Artillery under command of Lieutenant Edward Carrington in Harrison's absence, assisted by covering fire from Woodford's brigade enfiladed the enemy left wing and center.

Although the Americans were driven from some advance positions, they soon consolidated their lines on more suitable ground behind the "west morass" that had inhibited troop movement west of Monmouth. Greene's division held the right wing. Wayne's five Pennsylvania regiments were posted along a hedge row slightly forward of center. Stirling was on the left. Clinton first attempted to overrun the left. Stirling held and, as the attack faltered, two New Hampshire regiments and the 1st Virginia charged down on the extreme right flank of the British, who fell back.

Clinton next hurled Cornwallis' guard against the right wing of the American line. They were thrown back. Wayne's Pennsylvanians were performing magnificently in the center. A determined charge by Lieutenant Colonel Monckton on Wayne's position with the 2nd British Grenadier Battalion was thrown back with heavy casualties, leaving Monckton mortally wounded almost at Wayne's feet. The hour was late and the men exhausted. Clinton withdrew to a strong position. The Continentals were too worn out to follow and fell on their arms a few yards beyond their lines.

When morning dawned Clinton led his army silently away. Before Washington realized it they had reached a point where further pursuit was hopeless. He remained on the battlefield long enough to bury the dead of both armies. He then started north toward the New York highlands.

The casualty reports for the battle of Monmouth are unreliable. Washington gave his losses at 60 killed, 130 wounded and 130 missing. There must have been more American dead, as Grayson's Additional Regiment had been all but annihilated at the beginning. Clinton's figure of 1,200 casualties is more likely, but does not include 600 or more Hessians who simply ran away.

Individual participation by the men of Fauquier in the Battle of Monmouth is somewhat difficult to evaluate. Whereas in most engagement they had interesting details to offer, most of them were content to say of Monmouth merely that they had been there. The simple reason is that, for the most part of the day, they had very little idea where they were, which way they should go or what they were supposed to be doing. Many noted that they had met friends running in the opposite direction, each convinced that the enemy was ahead or, possibly, behind. We can only attempt to locate the various units and conjecture what their experiences must have been.

Muhlenberg's two brigades, his and Weedon's, seem to have been held in reserve in the second line of Greene's right wing until the final phase of the battle. Consequently Febiger's 2nd Virginia and Green's 10th Virginia Regiments had a relatively easy time. Colonel Daniel Morgan and his Rangers seem to have become bogged down in the "west morass" and had only intermittent and unproductive contact with the enemy. Captain Benjamin O'Bannon managed to get himself wounded but makes light of the matter. His brother, Andrew, was with him as was John Austin, serving now under Captain Charles Porterfield. Neither commented on the battle except to say that they were present. [84]

Woodford's and Scott's brigades under Lafayette were in the thick of the battle and both behaved with distinction. The Fauquier men in the 3rd Virginia Regiment under Heth, and John Cropper's 11th Regiment, bore the palm and, fortunately, casualties were

---

84. Although Morgan was not effectively engaged in the Battle of Monmouth he did conduct a vigorous pursuit after the action.

light. Colonel William Grayson's regiment was attached to Scott's brigade and there the story was far different. Captain William Triplett and Daniel Chumley, who served under him, survived. For Chumley, who was only sixteen, it was a shattering experience. If veteran soldiers like Moses Allen, William Bradford, Isaac Barr, Alexander Patton and Henry Allen of the 3rd Regiment were caught in the maelstrom of Lee's precipitate retreat, they never mentioned it and more than made up for it later as they covered the artillery regiments who raked the British flanks. Men like Sylvester Welch, a gunner in Harrison's 1st Virginia Artillery, were in their glory. It was one big battle and he made the most of it. He wished that Gideon Johnston had been there to see the dust fly.

In the heat, humidity, noise and stench of Monmouth Washington's army had shown that it could stand its ground in the face of attack by European troops. Tactically historians might call the battle a draw but American confidence reached a new high. An added bonus was that, once and for all, General Charles Lee was eliminated from their ranks. It may not have been, as Trevelyan says,[85] "the most scorching summer day ever known in America," but it was not far off. In addition to other casualties 37 Americans and 60 British died of sunstroke. There was no relief in sight. Washington led the Continental force to White Plains in New York by way of New Brunswick, Aquackanock and Paramus. Things had come full circle, with the British in New York and the Americans at White Plains, as they had been two years before. The difference was that the Americans had, since Germantown, forged an army.

---

85. George Otto Trevelyan, **The American Revolution**. The English are staggered by the summer heat in the northeast United States and frequently exaggerate it.

Interlude
Monmouth to Stony Point

The campaign in the summer of 1778 began and ended with the Battle of Monmouth Courthouse. Afterwards Clinton was busy settling his troops in and about New York. At White Plains Washington reviewed the situation without arriving at any feasible plan for dislodging them with the forces at his command. A French fleet under the command of Admiral d'Estaing left Toulon in April and, after an incredibly slow crossing, arrived off Sandy Hook on the 9th of June. d'Estaing easily convinced himself that his deep-draught vessels could not manoeuvre to attack the English fleet in the port of New York. He then moved to Newport, Rhode Island, and Washington sent a large force under Lafayette and Nathanael Greene to meet him. The French landed but, on the approach of a British fleet, withdrew their troops and re-embarked. Both fleets were severely damaged by a gale and limped back into port without engaging. While repairs were being made d'Estaing was the object of a bitter attack by General Sullivan which only increased his determination to do nothing. His secret orders from Vergennes, the French foreign minister, were to avoid any risk to the fleet under his command. On the 4th of November he set sail for Martinique.

Clinton remained oddly inactive in New York. Washington did not know that when he had taken command in May, it had already been decided in London to abandon further operations in the north. He was deeply concerned about his still-dwindling army. While on the march to White Plains he had heard that Virginia was determined to fill up her regiments. He ordered Lieutenant Colonel Holt Richardson and such officers as could be spared from the 3rd, 7th, 11th and 15th regiments to Virginia to superintend the recruiting service. They found the task near to impossible. When Colonel James Wood of the 12th Virginia Regiment arrived in Williamsburg early in November he listened incredulously to reports that the British were embarking, and would probably not land on the Continent again. In addition he was told by Thomas Nelson, Jr., who was then trying to raise a cavalry unit, that "So great is the aversion of the Virginians to engaging in the army that they are not to be induc'd by any method." The truth was that they were too busy making money. Officers who had returned to recruit resigned when they found "that every man who remains at home is making a fortune, whilst they are spending what they have in the defence of their Country."

In September at White Plains, Washington rearranged the organization of his army. Naturally the Virginia Line, which still lacked 2,731 men to complete its quota, underwent extensive reorganization. The 9th Regiment which had been so badly mauled at Germantown was combined with the 1st under Colonel Richard Parker. Similarly the 6th Regiment was combined with the 2nd under Colonel Christian Febiger; the 5th with the 3rd under Colonel William Heth; and the 8th with the 4th under Colonel John Neville. The 7th Regiment under Colonel William Russell then became the 5th. The later units 10th through 15th, were redesignated as the 6th through 10th. Colonel John Green's 10th Regiment became the 6th, and Lieutenant Colonel John Cropper's 11th Regiment became the 7th. Cropper, however, was on leave in Virginia, so Colonel Daniel Morgan resumed command.

The officers in the eliminated regiments, of course, became supernumerary unless a vacancy of equal rank existed in the regiment with which theirs was combined. Many quit in disgust when officers they had formerly commanded were placed over them. The dissatisfaction was general. Even those who had retained choice posts were upset because Congress had made the new assignments in so whimsical a manner that they feared like treatment on the next go-round.

With the failure to link up with d'Estaing and the French troops, the reason for remaining at White Plains disappeared. Washington split his force into three parts. General Gates and McDougall led their forces to Danbury, Connecticut, and General Israel Putnam conducted the Virginians to the left bank of the Hudson near West Point. In November Washington sent them to the Jersey highlands around Middlebrook. The men fared reasonably well. Despite some shortages it was the easiest winter since the war began.

Well before the Virginia Line was settled for the winter the Virginia brigadiers began to plague the Commander-in-Chief with demands for furloughs. Scott said that he would have to resign if he were not allowed to take care of some pressing domestic affairs. Woodford left for home on the 21st of October. Washington begged him to return in February so that Muhlenberg could have some time off before the next campaign. Woodford, who was his "Excellency's Most obedient, humble servant," refused. He arrived at headquarters about the middle of April, complaining of fatigue owing to the bad roads.

In October Lafayette asked permission to return to France to try, if possible, to stimulate his countrymen to more effective assistance to their allies than had been achieved in d'Estaing's abortive efforts. After a bout with fever which delayed his departure until the 11th of January, 1779, he reached France to receive a hero's welcome. The Virginians missed him. General Israel Putnam, "Old Put", was a nice old has-been but not very sympathetic to the "delicate sensibilities" of the Virginia line officers. In fact he considered them a bunch of children, and so, in some respects, they were.

IX
Stony Point

After the Battle of Monmouth a singular apathy settled upon the land. The British, bottled up in New York, seemed content to stay there, threatening no one. That Sir Henry Clinton's strange inactivity was the result of high level policy shaped by the North ministry was unknown to the Americans, but they were satisfied to let sleeping dogs lie. In Philadelphia the members of Congress bickered among themselves to little useful purpose. In Williamsburg Governor Henry and his Council pondered such weighty questions as whether or not to alter the rations issued to Colonel Marshall's troops.[1] Some insisted that 14 ounces of bacon and one quarter pound of pork or beef per day with a quarter pound of flour and 1½ pounds of Indian sifted meal was quite enough. It was not exactly a balanced diet, but that point was not raised. They were lucky to have that much.

In Fauquier County the crops were good and, to everyone's surprise and delight, were bringing steadily higher prices. The farmers happily pocketed their paper currency, oblivious to the fact that they were experiencing no boom, but merely the first dire portents of what would become rampant inflation. It was not until they tried to spend their money and found out how little it would buy, that the truth dawned. The soldiers at White Plains, engaged in routine duty around camp for low army pay which was becoming increasingly worthless, were green with envy.

In order to provide some useful work for his Virginia troops and to keep them out of mischief, Washington sent most of them to the west side of the Hudson to finish the fortifications of West Point. This towering natural formation dominated the Hudson River Valley and was considered by many the "Key to the Continent." Certainly Sir Henry Clinton felt that its reduction was necessary to British operations in the north, as witness his later attempt to secure it by bribery when he knew that he could not

---

1. Journal of the Council of the State of Virginia, Vol. II, p. 179.

take it by force of arms. We owe the knowledge that Fauquier men worked on completing this massive fortress to William Baylis [2] of Frederick County.

William Baylis was 18 when he enlisted as a cadet in Captain William Vass' company of the 12th Virginia Regiment under Colonel James Wood. He was soon promoted after fighting well at Brandywine. He was in the Monmouth engagement and followed on to White Plains. At West Point he was asked to take command of Captain Presley Neville's company when the latter was appointed aide to General Lafayette. Baylis was a close friend of Captain John Marshall who said that he did not believe that Baylis lost a day's duty in three campaigns. When the remnants of the Virginia line finally were dismissed as supernumerary in the autumn of 1779. Marshall and Baylis "walked in" to Virginia together with four or five others.

Baylis, who apparently had engineering experience of some sort, was remembered by the Fauquier men as an efficient and practical officer whose leadership at West Point, despite his extreme youth, was exceptional. Later he was given command of a company of Fauquier volunteers, a rare assignment for a man born outside the County. We will hear of him again.

After the works at West Point had been completed, insofar as it was possible, the Virginia troops were dispatched to the Jersey highlands for the winter. For a change they appear to have been reasonably light-hearted, well-fed and warmly clothed. Their mood is reflected in a letter from Mace Clements, a surgeon's mate, to Colonel John Cropper on leave in Virginia,—well, not *exactly* "on leave." Colonel Cropper had a drinking problem and he had been suspended to give him a chance to dry out.[3] Mace was lost in admiration for Major Gustavus Brown Wallace of the 3rd Virginia Regiment, whose earnest biographer has this to say of him: [4]

---

2. William Baylis, 1759-1844. After the war he moved first to Union Co., Kentucky and later to Rives Co., Missouri.

3. John Cropper's home was on the eastern shore of Virginia. While in Virginia he was one of the victims of British raiders who, in February of 1779, landed at his plantation and destroyed or carried off a great part of his property. Letter of resignation from Lt. Col. John Cropper, Jr. to John Jay, Esq., President of Congress, 16 Aug. 1779.

4. Alvin T. Embrey, **History of Fredericksburg, Virginia.** (Richmond, 1937), p. 127.

It is said that the soldiers under him found no task too severe, no service too irksome, because he shared with his men whatever befell them. He was a mild but firm disciplinarian and was several times transferred to build up the morale of new regiments to which he was assigned.

Mace had a slightly different point of view, (or did he?) He wrote from Pompton Plains, New Jersey, 14 November 1778: [5]

> I am satisfied it would give you great pleasure to hear that our Brigade had agreeable station, and I assure you old fellow, we are as happy at present as men can be—we are now stationed at Pompton Plains, in sight of the Fort, in as fine a naberwhod for the Females as any in the world non accepted—We can in one half hour collect upward of Thirty, and as good GAME as ever fluttered, that you must think will make great satisfaction for our former hardships & long sufferings. You may depend if Pompton should be our Winter Quarters, I should not see the Old Dominion this winter, but as we expect not to stay long, I shall try to obtain a furlough as soon as possible.
> But halt for awhile, and let me give you a short detail of your old friend Wallace . . . He is now one of the first men in the Parish, next to the Minister. He lives in a house, where there is a fine little Dutch girl, and he is determined to lay close seage to her. He says he thinks he shall be able to starve her out in four or five days—but if he should fall through in that manoeuvre, he is determined to raise a light apron and harass her parties in that way; which he thinks will most certainly complete his designs.
> I think that such a manoeuvre as that would do honour to any Genl in our line, and with a small recommendation to Congress, he would at best get a Brigdr commission.

Major Wallace was apparently the sort of man who would make any sacrifice to share whatever befell his men in order to build up their morale. Alas, Pompton Plains was not decided upon for winter quarters, but it wasn't very far away and undoubtedly a satisfactory line of communication was established.

Brigadier General William Woodford took off for Virginia on the 21st of October leaving something behind for the junior officers

---

5. Letter, Mace Clements to Col. John Cropper, Accomac, 14 Nov. 1778, Executive Papers, Virginia State Library.

to mull over in his absence. He had been appointed to a committee to draft a set of regulations as to rank and right to command. The committee was chaired by General Gates, but the ineffectual Gates was putty in his hands. After all Woodford was perhaps the greatest authority on the use of rank as a lethal weapon. The result, as might have been expected, was a document in which Woodford would effectively control the rank and promotion of all officers in the Virginia Line. Promulgated on the 15th of September, it struck the headquarters like a bombshell.

Dr. James Westwood Wallace, brother of "Gusty", writing to another brother, Michael, said:[6]

> All the officers in the Virginia line were much displeased with the establishment, as it was thought by them improper that they should be discriminated by one person, who perhaps might, from a partial disposition, leave out valuable officers and appoint others less worthy. They unanimously opposed it and, from Colonels to the ensigns, all sent their resignations to Headquarters.

Washington refused to accept the resignations, of course, and wearily set up a Board of Review in each brigade to deal with the matter. When Woodford applied for furlough, Washington granted it, glad to rid himself of this pompous fool. Colonel Daniel Morgan was left to conduct his brigade to winter quarters. He supposed that General Woodford "forgot" to leave necessary instructions concerning certain routine brigade matters with which he was unfamiliar. General Scott felt that, unless he was permitted to return to Virginia to meet some unexplained family crisis, he would be forced to resign. This left Muhlenberg, visibly disappointed but, to Washington's relief, "determined to wait until the service will admit your absence with convenience."[7]

Fortunately others were exerting themselves toward holding together the Virginia line, rather than tearing it apart. Conspicuous among them was Colonel Christian Febiger, who not only worried about the welfare of his men but used a lively imagination to see that they were as well-supplied as possible. It was Febiger who,

6. James W. Wallace to Michael Wallace, 15 Sept. 1778, in: H. E. Hayden, **Virginia Genealogies**, p. 708. 213 officers of the Virginia Line signed a protest to this high-handed document.

7. Washington to Muhlenberg, 28 Oct. 1778 in: Fitzpatrick, ed., **Writings of George Washington**, Vol. 13, p. 173.

after hearing that there were large stores of clothing belonging to the State of Virginia in Philadelphia, bogged down in army red tape and inefficiency, raced to the capital to see if something could be done to liberate them. Using great charm and a certain amount of appropriate palm-greasing, the big Dane came back to camp with an enormous quantity of spoil; enough to clothe the entire brigade.

He had perhaps been a little over-zealous. Washington, quite pleased but cautious, wrote to Morgan: [8]

> Colonel Febiger informs me that the State has sent up a number of Waistcoats, Breeches, shirts & Blankets to their Agent, to be sold out to their troops at moderate prices. It would be well to deliver out the two latter Articles immediately as the troops are in great want of them, but . . . I would recommend you not to permit (sale of the rest) until they are really wanted . . . as they are too apt to dispose of anything more than what they have in wear, for liquor or for some trifling Consideration.

When the 2nd Virginia Regiment outdid the others in re-enlistments that winter, Woodford modestly admitted that it was because of their devotion to him. He may have thanked Febiger, but the letter has not survived.

The winter of 1778-79 was mild in Fauquier County and, in contrast to the previous ones, probably rather festive. There was much activity in the Fauquier County Courthouse but the Court minutes are exceptionally dull.[9] The militia had no occasion to air its internal friction in court and, aside from a murder or two of very inconsequential folk, there is no excitement. William Blackwell and Armistead Churchill undertook to get workmen to repair the bridge over Marsh Run and William Pickett, Aylett Buckner and Francis Triplett to find a contractor to build a Bridge over Thum Run. Public work throughout the county had been badly neglected.

In January the Court ordered the Gentlemen in the Commission of Peace for the county who had neglected to take the oath of office to appear at the next court and explain why. None did or,

---

8. **Ibid.**, p. 249.

9. Fauquier County Minute Book, September 1778 through March 1779. The court met every month but in October, December and January very briefly.

if they did, it is not recorded. In February the bridge over Marsh Run became a casualty and John Blackwell was added to the committee to find a contractor to build a new one.

In March some new militia officers were recommended to the Governor, probably to replace some who had fallen by the wayside, but in most instances there is no indication as to whom they replaced. They were Alexander Bradford,[10] 1st lieutenant, William Ball, 2nd lieutenant and William Smith, ensign, in one company, probably under Captain Joseph James. Benjamin Ball, 1st lieutenant, Thomas James, 2nd lieutenant and Peter Kemper [11], ensign, were recommended for another company. Matthew Neale was recommended as ensign in Captain Triplett's company in place of William Seaton. Captain Attwell's two lieutenants, were moved up a notch and John Ball was recommended to replace Thomas Edwards as ensign. Most of these were promotions or reappointments in grade.

And, in March, James Bell, Charles Chilton and Thomas Digges, gentlemen, or any two of them, were appointed to settle John Green's account of the administration of the estate of Duff Green, deceased. The estate was not finally settled until 1784. [12] Young Green had inherited a substantial amount of property in Fauquier.

The county levy laid on the 23rd of November, 1778, was the second in seven months. It was made in pounds of tobacco, as was usual, but possibly also more practical, since it was impossible to tell what was happening to Virginia currency. There was plenty of it but it was depreciating at lightning speed. A straw in the wind was the amount of cash required to support the families of men in the Continental army. Through 1778 the amount paid semi-annually averaged about £12. By February, 1779, that sum had risen to £20. In June that had doubled, and in August, grants of £50 were not unusual. In October the amount paid one Ann Keirnes was £80. Soon after the Court abandoned any attempt to furnish the wives of soldiers with cash allowance and substituted

10. Alexander Bradford, 1728-1795, son of John and Mary (Marr) Bradford is identified in **The Bradfords of Virginia** by Nelle Rhea White as the man who served in the Fauquier Militia in 1779. It is possible but logic would suggest that he was of the next generation.
11. Peter Kemper (or Kamper) was a descendant of one of the original families who settled Germantown. The first John Kemper and his son, Peter, took a grant of 264 acres on the branches of Great Run about two and one half miles south of Warrenton in 1727, known as Cedar Grove (now Clovelly). A succession of John and Peter Kempers followed and, at the time of the Revolution there were at least three of each. Distinguishing between them is difficult.
12. Fauquier County Will Book II, 1783-1796, pp. 33-35.

food instead. The currency was depreciating so rapidly that any given amount might be worthless at the end of six months.

We can assume, the nature of public bodies being as they are, that these amounts given to soldiers' families were not generous, and that they were only increased as a result of proven necessity. The Fauquier soldier serving in New Jersey, and, himself, having difficulty getting by on his army pay, must have been deeply worried lest his family in Virginia be fast reduced to beggary. One wonders why he did not give up and go home. Of course many did, but a glorious few remained.

As the poor grew poorer and the rich richer all was gaiety in Philadelphia and Williamsburg during the Christmas season. Washington shook his head, but there was nothing he could do about the continuous round of festivities. At Camp Middlebrook, having abandoned all hope of going home, the "Reverend General" Peter Muhlenberg gave a ball on New Year's Day. "Not one of the company was permitted to retire till three o'clock in the Morning" according to the Virginia Gazette.

While they danced at Middlebrook, far away on the coast of Georgia, the British had landed on the 29th of December and, after a brief skirmish, had captured Savannah!

When this bit of news crept at a snail's pace to Philadelphia the Americans simply refused to believe it. They had been well aware that Colonel Archibald Campbell with some 3,500 men had sailed from Sandy Hook on the 27th of November, escorted by a squadron under Commodore Hyde Parker. They had decided quite firmly that they must be headed for the West Indies. Therefore this unpleasant gossip from Savannah must be wrong. Unfortunately Colonel Campbell had not adhered to the course selected for him by the Americans.

Savannah was supposed to be defended by General Robert Howe (whom we last met at Norfolk) with some 700 Continentals and 150 Georgia militia. General Howe was a nice fellow but his abilities as a commander fell somewhat short of those of Colonel Campbell. After being thoroughly outgeneraled, Howe was forced to take to his heels, leaving the city in the hands of the enemy.

It is not quite fair to say that the capture of Savannah came as a complete surprise to the American high command. The greater manoeuvrability that the British had by reason of their domination of the coastal waters was a fact of life they had been living with for a long time. The southern coast from the Virginia capes to Florida was vulnerable and the only question was where the enemy might strike first. The ponderous, dependable General Benjamin Lincoln had been named commander of the southern department and had arrived in Charleston on the 7th of December.[13] His mission was to assemble an army that could defend the southern coast, from Cape Fear to the Rio Santa Maria on the Florida border. He had hardly time to get his bearings in Charleston before the blow fell. Gathering 1,500 men, Lincoln marched on Savannah. About 15 miles north of the city he came upon Howe's fleeing remnants, who convinced him that the British were by then so strongly entrenched as to make an attack impossible.

The news, when it was accepted in the north, radically altered plans for the next campaign. To the Virginians it was abundantly clear that, with Savannah in their pocket, the British would turn next to Charleston and Portsmouth. Sending the militia regiments out of the state could not be considered, and the recall of the State regiments was contemplated. Enlistments in the Continental line regiments plunged to zero.

Before allowing the rank and file in the Virginia line leave to return to Virginia for Christmas of 1778, Washington had shrewdly insisted that they reënlist. A case in point was that of Joseph Goddard, who had been in the army about a year.[14] Though Goddard was from Fauquier, he had enlisted with Captain Thomas Blackwell in Green's 10th Virginia Regiment. In December he was in a company commanded by Captain James Williams at Middlebrook and reenlisted for the war in order to go home on leave. He went home with Captain Williams, arriving on Christmas day. Once there, he began to have second thoughts about returning, as many did.

He inveigled a man named Harris to serve in his place, whom Captain Williams agreed to accept, *if* Harris arrived in camp. Goddard gave Harris money and clothes, with which Harris, of course, absconded. In April Goddard was ordered to return to the Grand Army at Middlebrook,—or else! Goddard returned promptly.

If the news from Georgia was disquieting and that from New Jersey merely dull, the news from the west was neither. It was, in

13. Benjamin Lincoln, 1733-1810, of Massachusetts, was a moderately prosperous farmer before the Revolution. "An able and more industrious man than his great bulk and loose jowls would indicate." (Freeman, **Washington**)

14. Joseph Goddard, 1761-1845. He enlisted at the age of 16. He married 10 Oct. 1779, Frances Rector, dau. of Henry Rector. He later moved to Fleming Co., Kentucky, with Burtis Ringo, whose wife, Hannah Rector, was a cousin of Frances. Ringo also served in the 10th Virginia Regiment.

fact, highly satisfactory. Major George Rogers Clark with four companies under Captains John Montgomery, Joseph Bowman, Leonard Helm and William Harrod had left Corn Island on the 24th of June 1778 and reached the French town of Kaskaskia on the 4th of July. The town was taken completely by surprise and surrendered without firing a shot. Once the terrified inhabitants were convinced that the Americans were not barbarians and had no intentions to take their lives or property, they proved quite helpful. Captain Bowman even pressed on to Cahokia, a French river town opposite the Spanish trading post at St. Louis, and, with the help of Frenchmen from Kaskaskia, persuaded them to surrender.

There remained Vincennes, but a friendly French priest, Father Gibault, suggested that he would take care of that post. Clark agreed and Gibault returned to Kaskaskia early in August to report that the townsmen would welcome an American garrison. Clark wrote: [15]

> I plainly saw that it would be highly necessary to have an American officer at that post. Captain Leonard Helm appeared calculated to answer my purpose. He was past the meridian of life and a good deal acquainted with the Indian. I sent him to command at that post and also appointed him agent for Indian affairs in the department of the Wabash...

Captain Helm easily won the confidence of the inhabitants of Vincennes and, in addition, the firm friendship of the local Indian chief who bore the perfectly splendid title, "The Grand Door to the Wabash." The Grand Door assured Helm that he was happy to see one of the chiefs of the long knives in his town and would take upon advisement the proposal that he support the American cause. A few days later Helm was invited to attend an Indian council where the Grand Door jumped up, struck his breast; called himself a man and a warrior, and announced that he was now a big knife and Captain Helm's brother. Helm was deeply touched.

Helm and his "garrison" settled down in Fort Sackville, as the blockhouse at Vincennes was called, for a pleasant winter. However Govenor Henry Hamilton, the British commander at Detroit was more enterprising than Helm expected. In December, with 30 regulars, 50 French volunteers and about 400 Indians, he recaptured Vincennes and the garrison of Fort Sackville (Captain Helm

---

15. George Rogers Clark, **Clark's Memoir**, from English's **Conquest of the Country**, p. 490.

and two soldiers). On hearing the news, Clark at Kaskaskia braced himself for an attack. When nothing happened he determined to mount an attack himself. Winter floods had widened the Wabash to something like eight miles and the British at Vincennes felt quite secure. It was their turn to be surprised. Clark, with about 170 men, made an incredible march, much of it through icy water breast high, and on the 22nd of February camped outside Vincennes. Hamilton was caught. His Indian allies and French volunteers had returned to their homes. He could expect no help from the French inhabitants of Vincennes, and he was not unmindful of the Grand Door who was perfectly capable of loosing a mob of howling warriors to help the "big knives." After some aimless argument to maintain his dignity, he capitulated.[16]

Henry Hamilton had a bad reputation for offering rewards to the Indians for scalps, which earned the sobriquet "Hair-buyer", but he was kind to Leonard Helm. In return Helm argued so persuasively for lenient terms that Clark was obliged to remind him that he was a British prisoner, and therefore had no say in the matter. Hamilton was sent under heavy guard to Williamsburg and after several months was paroled and sent to New York. The Grand Door, who had asked to share his brother's captivity, returned to his people. All was serene again along the Wabash.

The stories of success in Illinois lost nothing in the telling when the men reached Fauquier. One of those who returned was Tilman Kamper[17] who enlisted under Captain Helm for six months and marched with him to Redstone. He was with Clark's army that captured the Chevalier de Rocheblave (he calls him "Governor Roseblank") the French commander at Kaskaskia. When his term of enlistment expired he volunteered to go with Captain Bowman to Cahokia, where he stayed for seven months. After the fort at Vincennes was re-taken he volunteered to stay two and a half months beyond his second tour to help in holding the posts and treating with the Indians until more troops came. He then returned to Fauquier.

Men like Tilman Kamper and others who returned from the west were listened to with growing interest in Fauquier, especially

16. Henry Hamilton, d: 1796, had served under Amherst at Louisburg and under Wolfe at Quebec. He was Lieutenant Governor of Canada and Commandant at Detroit, 1775-79.

17. Tilman Kemper (or Kamper) may have been a brother of Peter Kemper (see Note 11). Tilman, 1759-1836, and Peter are named as sons in the will of John Kemper, proved in Fauquier Co., 25 Feb. 1799.

in the southern part of the county. Here land too long in intensive cultivation, was beginning to wear out and successive generations had partitioned it so often that the remaining tracts were too small to return a profit. What they needed was more land, and it seemed reasonable that those who fought to defend Kentucky would be in on the ground floor when it came to obtaining Kentucky land grants. It was a disturbing thought for those engaged elsewhere, and hasty assurances had to be given that all who fought for Virginia in any combat area, would share equally in the rich bonanza that was Kentucky. Not all were convinced. The scramble to get to Kentucky is mentioned in a letter from Daniel Morgan to Woodford in early October. Writing from "Saratoga" in Frederick County, Morgan says:

> The people are going to Kentucky so fast that that really surprises me. The roads are crowded with them from all parts—I am apprehensive that some of them will starve this winter.

So the Fauquier regulars in the Continental line left for camp at Middlebrook in the spring of 1779 with decidedly mixed emotions. Eager as they were to get the war over with, they knew that a long, hard struggle still lay ahead. The attrition in the Virginia line worried them as it curtailed both the opportunity for advancement and influence at headquarters. For most the financial plight of their families and their own inability to combat inflation threatened their peace of mind. They were justifiably apprehensive of the widespread changes in command and its effect on the quality of leadership. Congressional meddling, in which merit and length of service in the field were ignored and politics secured promotions, disgusted many valuable officers and left the men bitter and insecure.

Far more important, however, was the growing realization that unless General Lincoln was heavily reinforced in Charleston, South Carolina must soon be in British hands. On the 5th of May, Washington wrote Brigadier General Charles Scott, who was in Virginia collecting recruits for the Virginia line:

> I am now to inform you that the original intention of bringing those levies to reinforce the Army here is changed and that they are destined as a reinforcement to the Southern army.

Scott read the order in dismay. Washington was referring to the 2,216 men voted by the last Assembly. So far the force existed only on paper. It had been impossible to clothe and equip the few Scott had managed to sign up. There was no force to reinforce Lincoln, no force to defend Virginia if necessary.

It appeared to be necessary. On the 10th of May Vice Admiral Sir George Collier sailed into the Elizabeth River with 22 transports and several escort vessels. On them were 1,800 grenadiers, light infantry and artillery under Major General Edward Matthews. They quickly took Portsmouth and marched against Suffolk and Gosport, laying waste the plantations along the way. Scott quickly positioned his thin line across the peninsula between the York and James and began to throw up earthworks around Williamsburg. However the British had intended only to create a diversion and soon sailed away with 3,000 hogsheads of tobacco. The Virginia Assembly had been scared out of its collective wits.

If the Virginia regulars were worried about the safety of their own State, it is not surprising. General George Weedon, in Fredericksburg in poor health, wrote John Page on the 12th of April:[18]

> Nothing astonishes me more than to find such a deficiency in the means of defence (after so long a war) as appears in this and every other State on the Continent . . . every day teaches us to be aware of ourselves and yet I fear was the Enemy to make a descent on Virginia we should find we were inadequate to proper opposition till our Country was spread with ruin and devastation. . .
> The situation of this country requires four Magazines, one at the head of your principal rivers and one at Williamsburg; from these supplies might be drawn with conveniency to furnish your militia when called for . . . Establish these magazines, fortify your principal seaport towns and put your militia on a proper footing so as to be able to call out eight or ten thousand if necessary and be provided to accoutre them at short notice and your country is Secure.

The plan was not without merit, but Page had not the means with which to implement it. Weedon found inactivity in such a crisis most irksome and offered to do anything he could to help, short, of course, of serving under General Woodford.

---

18. Letter, George Weedon to John Page, 12 April 1779. Weedon Papers, Chicago Historical Society.

When Woodford finally reached Middlebrook, he found that still another consolidation of Virginia troops had taken place. The 3rd and 4th Regiments were combined under Colonel William Heth, with Gustavus Brown Wallace as second in command. Wallace had, however, been sent south to help General Scott. He had volunteered for the assignment and was not a bit reticent in underlining for his old friend, John Cropper, the nobility of his act. In his opinion he had not one chance in ten of ever returning from Charleston.

The 5th and 11th Regiments were combined under Colonel Abraham Buford, former commander of the 11th, with Robert Ballard as Lieutenant Colonel. Heth's and Buford's regiments, with the 2nd, 7th and 8th under Febiger, Morgan and Wood, would form Woodford's brigade.

Muhlenberg's brigade was to include the 1st and 10th Regiments combined under Colonel Richard Parker; the 6th under Colonel John Green; Colonel Nathaniel Gist's Additional Regiment and the 1st and 2nd Virginia State Regiments. If the reader wonders in this turmoil what had become of the men from Fauquier, let it be said that *all* were now in Woodford's brigade except the few who had been with Grayson's Additional Regiment, now combined with Gist's; the two State regiments, and those who had, since the beginning, been with John Green. Even in the last, the company commanders had changed. John Gillison was now commander of the 1st company. Captain Clough Shelton of Albemarle County[19] commanded the 2nd company in place of Thomas Blackwell, who was declared supernumerary. Joseph Blackwell, his brother, however, remained as Shelton's 1st lieutenant.

Much of this would be of only academic significance were it not for the fact that Woodford's brigade was moving with grim, irrevocable steps toward Charleston and Waxhaws.

Most of the attention in the north was now being focussed on the newly organized Light Infantry Brigade under the command of Brigadier General Anthony Wayne. Washington had had in mind for a long time the creation of a special elite unit of about 1,200 men arranged into four regiments of two "battalions" each. The men were to be selected from the most daring veterans in the army, led by its most intrepid officers. Daniel Morgan would have given his right arm to have led such a unit but, to his utter dismay, he

---

19. Clough Shelton, commander of a company in Green's Regiment, is named in a number of Fauquier pension records and it is frequently assumed that he was related to the Chilton family. There was no connection.

was passed over in favor of the younger Wayne. As a result, on the 18th of July, Morgan resigned. His stated reason was ill health, but his disappointment was evident to all.

In the entire American army it would have been hard to find five more capable men than those selected to command Wayne's four regiments. They were Colonel Christian Febiger of Virginia for the 1st, Colonel Return J. Meigs [20] of Connecticut for the 2nd, Colonel Richard Butler of Pennsylvania,[21] for the 3rd, Major William Hull of Massachussetts [22] and Major Hardy Murfree of North Carolina.[23] Hull and Murfree held joint command of the fourth regiment. All had served with great distinction but were relatively young and wholly dedicated. All six companies of the Virginia Continentals attached to the brigade were, of course, assigned to Febiger's regiment. Ranging through Woodford's brigade, Febiger took the best men he could lay his hands on. His choice was unerring.

The British fired the first shot that opened the military campaign of 1779. On the 28th of May, Clinton assembled an elite force of about 6,000 men at King's Bridge and, embarked aboard a fleet of 70 sailing vessels and 150 flat-bottomed boats, started up the Hudson River. Washington thought that they were headed for West Point but, on the 2nd of June, Clinton landed his army on both sides of the river at King's Ferry and prepared to attack the forts on Stony Point and Verplanck's Point at opposite ends of the ferry.

There was not much that the American garrisons could do to

20. Return Jonathan Meigs, 1740-1823, Connecticut pioneer and General, served at Lexington and Concord. His **Journal** describing Arnold's march to Quebec is a classic of military reporting. A brilliant raid at Sag Harbor, N. Y., 23 May 1777, won for him one of Congress' "elegant swords".

21. Richard Butler, 1743-1791, a Pennsylvania officer of Irish descent, served in Pontiac's War and as an Indian trader at Fort Pitt. As Lt. Col. with Morgan's Riflemen, he performed well at Saratoga. He was commander of the 9th Pennsylvania Regiment.

22. William Hull, 1735-1825, a fifth generation American, was born at Derby, Connecticut. After graduation from Yale, he practiced law before the Revolution. He was Lt. Col. of the 3rd Massachusetts Regiment and had served at White Plains, Trenton, Princeton, Saratoga and Monmouth.

23. Hardy Murfree of North Carolina had won his spurs at Germantown and Monmouth. His fame has been somewhat dimmed in history because Wayne never spelled his name correctly. As "Major Murphy" he is a little hard to identify.

ward off the attack. The 40 man garrison at the unfinished work at Stony Point stopped long enough to burn a blockhouse before prudently withdrawing across the causeway to solid ground. The 70 men of the 5th North Carolina Regiment made a valiant effort to hold Fort Lafayette, a small but complete work on Verplanck's Point, but it was, of course, impossible. Washington expected that the British would then press on to West Point but, oddly enough, Clinton set his men to completing the fort at Stony Point which had, of the two, the strongest natural position. Having done so he returned with his troops to New York, leaving a fairly strong garrison to hold any American attack.

The reason for Sir Henry Clinton's strange behavior was not of his own making. Instructions from the War Office in London had been explicit: "bring Mr. Washington to a general and decisive action at the opening of the campaign", they advised, following their advice with a number of wholly impractical suggestions for doing so, and promises of reinforcements they never sent. To Germain, Clinton wrote, "For God's sake, my Lord, if you wish I should do anything, leave me to myself," continuing with weary sarcasm, "to force Washington to action upon terms tolerably equal has been the object of every campaign during this war." [24]

Washington sat tight, but he was not idle. To him a continued defensive, while the country expected action and his army faded away, was humiliating in extreme. He asked Major Henry Lee and his Virginia dragoons to bring him every morsel of information he could gather about Stony Point. Lee promptly turned to the ever-resourceful Captain Allan McLane who had, since Barren Hill, detached himself from the Delaware partisans and joined Lee. McLane, disguised as a poor countryman escorting "the widow Calhoon and another widow going to the enemy with chickens and greens," [25] managed to get into the fort. He emerged with an accurate plan, a good description of the still-uncompleted portions of the work and a close estimate of the number of those defending it. In fact, he had just about everything needed for an attack but the countersign.

Washington listened to McLane's report and Lee's overconfident advice, but he was really waiting for Wayne, whom he had recalled from leave. Meanwhile he had moved the main army to Smith's Cove. The Virginia troops under Lord Stirling were the

---

24. George F. Scheer and Hugh F. Rankin, **Rebels and Redcoats**, p. 414.

25. Allan McLane, **Journal**, McLane Papers, Liber II, New York Historical Society.

last to arrive, owing to a shortage of wagons, and it was only after a fatiguing march that they joined the rest on the 7th of June.

The enemy action after taking Stony Point was, Washington admitted, a source of "great perplexity to us" but he was further puzzled to learn that the press was blowing up this minor coup into a major victory in New York and, presumably, London. From his headquarters in New Windsor he rode down to Stony Point and stared at it through his spyglass in an effort to discover some strategic value he had overlooked. Certainly if the enemy thought that winning this anthill was a useful propaganda ploy, then retaking it could be similarly exploited by the Americans.

What he saw may have surprised him. Certainly the fort was formidable. Stony Point jutted over a half mile out into the Hudson River and rose some 150 feet above the water on the east side. The only practical approach to the fort was from the west across a marsh which was inundated at high tide. In addition the 600 man garrison that Clinton had placed on the promontory, according to McLane, had the advantage of two series of works. On the summit near the river were seven batteries connected by trenches and enclosed to the westward by a line of abatis running across the point from one side to the other. Below and farther west were three smaller batteries and another line of abatis. On the other three sides the river swirled beneath the jagged, wooded cliffs. Yet to Washington there seemed to be a way to attack, risky, - yes, but in the hands of highly trained troops, possible. Wayne, having returned from his home near Radnor, Pennsylvania, considered his plan and agreed.

Preparations were made with care and secrecy. On the afternoon of July 15, Wayne made a secret march south from Fort Montgomery, securing the mountain passes en route. About 8 o'clock in the evening the brigade stopped at the farm of David Springsteel, a mile and a half west of the point. That Wayne was not completely without misgivings may be deduced from a letter he wrote to his closest friend, Sharp Delany:[26]

---

26. Charles J. Stille, **Major General Anthony Wayne and the Pennsylvania Line in the Continental Army**, pp. 192-193.

> Springsteel's 11 o'clock
> 15 July 1779, near the
> hour & scene of carnage.

Dear Delany:- This will not meet your eye until the writer is no more . . . I know that friendship will induce you to attend to the education of my little son & daughter. I fear that their mother will not survive this Stroke . . . Then farewell my best and dearest friend and believe me to the last moment

> Yours most sincerely
> Anth'y Wayne.

He then had supper, and was on his way.

As for Christian Febiger, when he first beheld Stony Point and realized what was expected of the light infantry, he simply sat down and made out his last will and testament. Characteristically and to the point, he began:[27]

> Whereas there is . . . some danger of my taking a place among the deceased heroes of America . . .

The battle plan had been worked out with the greatest care. The right wing was composed of the 1st Regiment under the command of Colonel Febiger, whose battalion commanders were Lieutenant Colonel Francois Louis de Fleury[28] and Major Thomas Posey.[29] The men were almost all Virginians. The van was led by a

---

27. Christian Febiger Papers, Harvard University, microfilmed for the Virginia State Library.

28. Francois Louis, Sieur Teissedre de Fleury, 1749-1794?, was, like Lafayette, a French volunteer who was popular in Virginia. He served at Brandywine with such distinction that, when he had a horse shot out from under him, Congress in a rare burst of generosity, voted him a new one, "as a testimonial of the sense the Congress have of Monsieur de Fleury's merit." He is said to have been executed during the French Revolution, but that is uncertain.

29. Thomas Posey, b: 1750, was a son of Capt. John and Martha (Price) Posey who were neighbors of Washington at Mount Vernon. Washington is said to have shown him marked favoritism during the war which excited the envy of other junior officers. He married (1) in 1775, the daughter of Sampson Matthews (2) Mary Alexander, daughter of John and Lucy (Thornton) Alexander. He was later Governor of Indiana.

forlorn hope, 20 picked sappers under Lieutenant George Knox.[30] Then followed an advance party of 150 carefully selected men under Lieutenant Colonel Fleury. Following that came the main body consisting of Colonel Return Meigs' Connecticut Regiment, part of the 4th Regiment under Major William Hull of Massachusetts and the remainder of Febiger's 1st Regiment.

The objective of the right wing was to cross the marsh on the south side of the point where the abatis were closest together and scale the height in complete silence and without firing a shot. Here the defenses were closest to the main enemy works and, though there were three lines of abatis to penetrate, it was expected that enemy resistance might be less. Because the right wing was the main effort, Wayne, himself, accompanied it.

The left wing had an almost equally dangerous mission. It was made up of Colonel Richard Butler's 2nd Regiment of Pennsylvanians. Its 150 man advance party was commanded by Major John Steward of Maryland,[31] with Lieutenant James Gibbons[32] commanding a 20 man forlorn hope in the van. They had farther to go across marshy land and, because the ferry was on that side of the point, it was expected that resistance would be stiffer. The terrain was somewhat less rugged and there were only two lines of abatis. It was not, however, an appealing prospect.

The center was composed of about half of the 4th Regiment under Major Hardy Murfree; mostly North Carolinians. They were to advance across the causeway, supported by Major Henry Lee and his Light Horse including McLane and his Delaware partisans. Only the center was allowed to use musketry and they were expected to lay as heavy a barrage as possible to concentrate the attention of the garrison.

The Fauquier men who participated in the attack on Stony Point and lived to tell of it, were all in the advance party of the right wing under Colonel de Fleury, or with Lieutenant Knox in his forlorn hope.

The dark night favored the attackers as they started forward

30. George Knox, Lieutenant of the 9th Pennsylvania Regiment. Colonel Return J. Meigs accused Wayne of having favored the Pennsylvanians in selecting leaders for the forlorn hopes. Wayne replied that they obtained their positions by lot and that he had not known that they had volunteered until they had taken their posts.

31. John Steward (Major "Jack") of the Maryland Continental Line.

32. James Gibbons, Lieutenant of the 6th Pennsylvania Regiment. (see supra, Note 30).

about 11:30 p.m. on the 15th. The countersign had been obtained by a young Negro named Pompey who belonged to a local farmer. Earlier in the evening Pompey had taken a load of strawberries to the fort, having said that it was hoeing time and his master would not allow him to absent himself in the daytime. He therefore could only come after dark. The first sentries were given the countersign and silently garrotted by the Americans as they passed by. An alarm was soon given, though, and the British opened fire. The Americans pressed forward without shooting back. The forlorn hope chopped and clawed through the first line of abatis and rushed for the second ones, as the advance parties crowded forward on their heels. Murfree started his demonstration of musketry in the center.

The ploy worked. The British commander, Lieutenant Colonel Henry Johnson,[33] did not consider the possibility that any sane commander would attempt to ford the marshes to the right and left. With half his garrison, he charged down the hill in the center to meet what he thought was the main threat. On the right Wayne was taken out of action momentarily by a head wound, but revived and pushed on. Febiger and Lieutenant Colonel Samuel Hay, one of Butler's battalion commanders, were also wounded. Both of them refused to stop.

By that time the fiery de Fleury had joined Knox's party and was hacking at the heavy abatis surrounding main enemy works. Suddenly they were through! De Fleury raced to the enemy flag and tore it down with his own hands. Lieutenant Knox was next within the enclosure, followed by Sergeant Baker of Virginia, who had been wounded four times in the assault. Baker was followed by Sergeants Spencer of Virginia and Dunlop of Pennsylvania. Almost immediately after them was Major Thomas Posey of Virginia. Within a few minutes came Henry Allen[34] and Peter Hedgman Triplett,[35] both of whom were from Fauquier. There was also Joseph

33. Henry Johnson, 1748-1835, Lt. Col. of the 17th Regiment of Foot. He was court martialed after Stony Point but evidently acquitted as he was in command subsequently in Virginia and the Carolinas.
34. Henry Allen, 1758-1831, married 14 Dec. 1781, Catherine McConchie, (McKonkey) in Fauquier Co. After his marriage he was transferred to the public arms factory in Fredericksburg, where he remained until the factory was abandoned after the war. This was the factory started by Fielding Lewis, Washington's brother-in-law, in which he had lost most of his fortune.
35. Peter Hedgman Triplett, 1755-1851, married 1785, Catherine who survived him. His brother, George Triplett, 1753-1833, was a 1st Lieutenant in the 1st Virginia State Regiment under Col. George Gibson. He married, 1816, Sarah Birkhead.

Goddard, previously mentioned. By absconding, Mr. Harris had given him the proudest and probably the most frightening time of his life.

Both Henry Allen and Peter Hedgman Triplett were old soldiers who had fought in many a weary battle before ascending the heights at Stony Point. Allen came from the southern part of Fauquier where his ancestor William Allen and John Brown had patented 713 acres between "the Great Marsh and the river (Hedgman's)", as early as 1710. This had been followed by several subsequent grants which placed the Allens among the largest landowners in the Marsh Run area. As did many of the young men in this locality, he enlisted in Culpeper County in the 3rd Virginia Regiment under Lieutenant Armistead Minor. He had fought at Brandywine, Germantown and Monmouth. He had weathered Valley Forge without pleasure but with impunity, and had been in a number of lesser skirmishes. He was only twenty years old, but he was tough and dependable.

Peter Hedgman Triplett was even more experienced and equally indestructible. He was born in Culpeper County, the son of Thomas and Hannah (Crump) Triplett. His great uncle was Major Peter Hedgman, Burgess from Stafford County, whose huge Fauquier County estate was later sold to Hancock Lee and became Fauquier Springs. Peter did not inherit any of that, but he did inherit the farm on Elk Run that belonged to his uncle, George Crump. He was also a nephew of Captain Francis Triplett.

He had started out in the marines in 1776 and had served on the eight gun sloop *Liberty*, commanded by Captain Walter Darrell Brooke. Tiring of that, he was mustered out of the marine service and enlisted in the infantry under Captain John Lee in the 1st Virginia State Regiment commanded by Colonel George Gibson. Arriving outside Philadelphia before Brandywine, he had also been at Germantown, Monmouth and Barren Hill. Peter was twenty-five and was reaching the end of a three year tour of duty with Colonel Gibson when Colonel Febiger (he calls him "Colonel Quebecker") collared him for John Knox's forlorn hope. He was soaked to the waist after crossing the marsh and was working frantically with his axe on the abatis near the "Brave and Gallant Genl. Wayne" when he received his wound. Moments later Peter, too, was wounded but continued up the rocky cliff. His was no flesh wound, though. Invalided home, he barely allowed himself time to recover before he was off to see what George Rogers Clark was doing in Kentucky.

Within the Fort at Stony Point all was chaos. Within minutes after de Fleury snatched down the flag, Lieutenant Gibbons, muddy to the neck, his clothes torn to ribbons on the abatis, arrived with three of his twenty men. Steward and his advanced party was right behind him. In the center the British commander, realizing his mistake, attempted to regain the heights. He was cut off and captured by Febiger's men. Other British pockets, vainly trying to resist, were overwhelmed and they soon began throwing down their arms. The entire garrison was taken, 624 men including 20 killed, 74 wounded and 58 missing. Even more important were 12 cannon and some $180,000 worth of stores. Wayne reported 15 Americans killed and 83 wounded. Among those killed was Alexander Maddox of Fauquier.

Rather relieved at not having taken a place among the deceased heroes, Christian Febiger wrote to his American bride on the 17th of July: [36]

> My Dear Girl: I have just borrowed pen, ink and paper to inform you that . . . at 12 o'clock last night we stormed this confounded place . . . A musket ball scraped my nose. No other damage to "Old Denmark". God bless you. Farewell,
> FEBIGER.

A few hours before Anthony Wayne had also a few words to say. To Washington, at 2 a.m. he had written: [37]

> Dear Genl —The fort & garrison with Col^o Johnston are ours. Our officers and men behaved like men who are determined to be free.
> Yours most sincerely,
> Anth'y Wayne.

The bravery, discipline and stunning tactical planning displayed in the capture of Stony Point was impressive both in America and abroad. Baron Steuben, who had taught the Americans the use of the bayonet was understandably delighted to learn that the fort had been taken without the use of musketry. However Washington faced the fact that he could not spare men and ordnance to hold the fort. He pointed out to Congress the damage inflicted on the enemy and a possible depressant effect on the enemy's spirits, but he did not describe it as a major victory. In reality he understated

---

36. Magazine of American History, Vol. VI, p. 194. Quoted by Boatner, **Encyclopedia of the American Revolution**, p. 363.

37. Stille, **Antony Wayne**, p. 196.

the case. The assault, in effect, paralyzed Clinton. He dared not make another offensive move without reinforcements and was so completely discouraged that he tried to resign the service and return home. However he did not communicate his state of mind to Washington.

The plaudits that fell upon Wayne as a result of the capture of Stony Point were as gall and wormwood to "Lighthorse Harry" Lee. He had provided the reconnaissance, for which Wayne had thanked him profoundly, and, in his own eyes, had planned the attack. Yet he had been assigned to a relatively minor role, supporting a column whose only function was to keep the enemy amused while others did the real work. The only thing that could restore Lee's deflated ego was another Stony Point in which he, himself, was the hero. Casting around for such an opportunity, his eye fell on Paulus Hook.

Paulus Hook was near Bergen, which had been the object of General Adam Stephen's abortive plans before Brandywine. In some respects it resembled Stony Point. It was a low-lying sand spit thrusting itself out into the Hudson River opposite New York. The tip was fortified by two redoubts protecting several blockhouses, barracks and a powder magazine. Six heavy guns were mounted in the center redoubt, which was about 150 feet in diameter. There were 3 twelve-pounders and an eighteen-pounder in the larger oval redoubt nearby. The enemy camp was separated from the mainland by a tidal salt marsh. There was also a moat running across the peninsula north of the camp and the usual line of abatis. A single road on a causeway crossed the marsh but final access to the camp was controlled by a drawbridge across the moat.

On the night of the attack there were about 200 redcoats on the spit commanded by Major William Sutherland.[38] This did not include women and children who had been allowed to live with the troops and a foraging party roaming nearby, which had been replaced by a company of Hessians and a few light infantry. The attack planned by Lee closely resembled the strategy used at Stony Point.

Lee placed his plan before Washington privately and the latter, at first, looked upon it with serious misgivings as involving too much risk to obtain relatively slight advantage. He yielded to Lee's persuasion, though, and authorized him to proceed with 100 men each from Muhlenberg's and Woodford's brigades, plus two

---

38. William Sutherland may have been aide-de-camp to Sir Henry Clinton in 1778. There were several British officers with the same name. See Boatner, **op. cit.**, p. 1084.

Maryland companies and Captain Allan McLane's corps of dragoons (dismounted) to augment Lee's own force. In all, Lee had about 400 men.

4:30 on the afternoon of the 18th of August found Lee and his army leaving New Bridge on the Hackensack River for Bergen, about two miles from Paulus Hook. Lee timed his march to reach the hook under the cover of darkness to begin an assault at 12:30 on the 19th. This would give him an hour and a half to storm the redoubts and get his men back across the moat before the tide ebbed.

Things began to go wrong early in the game. The first untoward incident came when Major Jonathan Clarke,"[39] at the last moment, questioned Lee's right to command, claiming an earlier date of rank. Lee heatedly gave him the date of his commission, incorrectly as it turned out. Then, as the column passed Bergen, the principal guide took a round-about way, supposedly to avoid a British out-post. Whether or not this was deliberate, it cost Lee three hours and left the troops in the rear, mostly from Woodford's brigade, wandering aimlessly in the darkness.

Lee sent Lieutenant Michael Rudolph[40] ahead to find out if he could still cross the water barrier. He was arranging the forward units for the attack when he was told that nearly half the Virginians had failed to reach the point of rendezvous. Rudolph reported that the moat was full but could be forded at the drawbridge. Hastily modifying his plan of attack, Lee sent two columns instead of three across the salt marsh, ordering them to keep their muskets from getting wet.

Even when the Americans reached the drawbridge there was no alarm from the enemy. After a brief pause the forward units plunged into the moat. It was fordable, - but barely. There was no way to keep their powder dry. However, on reaching the opposite side they found an opening in the abatis and, hardly breaking their stride, caught the enemy completely off guard. About 160 of the enemy surrendered immediately. Many others who tried to resist were left with bayonet wounds. About twenty-five Hessians in the circular redoubt refused to give up. Dawn was breaking, alarm

39. Jonathan Clarke commanded men from Woodford's brigade forming Lee's right wing. His charge that Lee had lied to him about the date of his commission was not among those printed in the **Virginia Gazette**, 16 October 1779.

40. Michael Rudolph was from Lee's own dragoons. He later covered the retreat so ably that the pursuing British were unable to attack Lee's rear at Liberty Pole.

guns sounded across the river and the Hessians in the redoubt had 12 cannon. Lee had no choice but to retreat, not even pausing to spike the cannon they had captured in the oval redoubt. He could not burn the barracks because of the women and children lodged inside.

They got back across the marsh in record time and made their way to the Hackensack River where Captain Henry Peyton was to have boats ready to ferry them to Newark. Neither Peyton nor the boats were to be found. After sending a hasty message to Stirling asking for support, Lee started his column north with the prisoners. At Weehawken crossroads he caught up with Captain Thomas Catlett [41] with fifty men, completely lost since the night before. At least Catlett and his men had some dry powder, so Lee felt a little more secure. Shortly after Lieutenant Colonel Burgess Ball [42] came up with a relief column from the 1st Virginia Regiment. Lord Stirling had his message and had acted promptly.

The raid was not an unqualified success. They had failed to damage the installation or bring off any much needed stores of arms or ammunition, but they had 158 prisoners and had given the British a nasty jolt. Furthermore Lee had brought the whole thing off with the loss of only three or four killed and perhaps seven captured. To Lee's immense disgust, the man who claimed to be the commanding officer turned out to be a private masquerading as such. Sutherland had been in the circular redoubt with the Hessians.

Samuel Courtney, [43] a Fauquier man under Captain John Gillison in Colonel John Green's 6th Virginia Regiment (formerly the 10th) was among the Virginians who reached the fort. It is too bad that he did not tell us more about it, but his pension record is notably laconic. Captain William Baylis is more communicative. He was then commanding Captain Presley Neville's company under

41. Thomas Catlett was in temporary command of 50 men from the 2nd Virginia Regiment. He appears to have been a son of Lawrence Catlett of Culpeper Co. d: 1782.

42. Burgess Ball, 1749-1800, son of Jeduthan and Elizabeth (Burgess) Ball. He married (1) 1770, Mary Chichester, (2) 1781, Frances Washington, dau. of Col. Charles and Mildred (Thornton) Washington. She was a niece of George Washington.

43. Samuel Courtney, 1755-post 1820, enlisted from Caroline Co., but, apparently, lived in Fauquier where, 17 May 1779, he married his cousin, Sarah Courtney. He re-enlisted at Middlebrook in 1779 to obtain leave before marching to Charleston.

the orders of Colonel James Wood of the 8th Regiment. Although the 8th Regiment was now in Woodford's brigade, Baylis and his men had kept up with the forward section and had forded the moat with the main body. Baylis had received a slight wound in the arm, but it had not slowed his pace or cooled his ardour.

Naturally Lee felt that, considering the mishaps along the way, he had not done too badly. He expected to be received in camp with cheers, a band or two, and possibly the glad tidings of a promotion. Instead there awaited him - a court martial. His first reaction to this preposterous turn of events was to laugh. However, when he realized who was at the bottom of this, he knew that it was no laughing matter. It was Brigadier General William Woodford.

Woodford was angry that Lee had communicated his proposal privately to the Commander-in-Chief without his prior knowledge. He was annoyed that the decision to use 100 men from his brigade was made by Lord Stirling at division headquarters without consulting him. While openly stating that he would not have sanctioned the mission, he was outraged because he had not been chosen to command it. Finally his petty jealousy and unchecked malice toward the young officer made him look ridiculous. All of that he blamed on Lee.

He could not, of course, bring charges himself. Lee's immediate superior was Colonel Nathaniel Gist. Gist did not like Lee, but he was no fool. It is extremely improbable that he would have preferred charges had he not been pressured from above. He placed Lee under arrest and ordered a court martial, for the 11th of September, 1779. The charges were as follow: [44]

1. Withholding a letter from Stirling to Col. Gist of the 16th Virginia Regiment.
2. Obtaining 300 men from Col. Gist.
3. Marching to "Powles" Hook in so much disorder that almost the whole of the 1st Battalion was lost.
4. Ordering a retreat before taking prisoners.
5. Bringing off the party in confusion.
6. Behaving in a manner unbecoming an officer and a gentlemen.

The 2nd, 4th and 5th were obviously untrue. The 1st was a matter of no concern to Lord Stirling who had the only cause for complaint. The 3rd was unfortunate, but hardly within Lee's control

---

44. **Virginia Gazette** (Dixon & Hunter), 16 October 1779.

and the 6th was a silly catch-all, intended to be insulting rather than serious.

Washington was both angry and embarrassed. It was he who had given Lee the command and had instructed Stirling as to the composition and number of troops. He considered the detachment too small for the command of a general officer and he felt that depriving field grade officers of responsibility for such tasks was insulting to both their intelligence and competence. Stirling, who had given the enterprise his full support and careful attention, was similarly irked. Woodford tried to bring Muhlenberg into the act, as he was the only other Virginia Brigadier at headquarters (Scott was in Virginia recruiting for the southern department). Muhlenberg would have none of it. Even Major Jonathan Clark tried to disassociate himself from the proceedings. He stated flatly that he believed that the wrong date of his commission given him by Lee was an honest mistake. Certainly his actions proved it. He had served bravely and conscientiously under Lee's command and, in fact, was the first to breech the walls of the redoubt.

The court martial is said to have been presided over by "Colonel" John Marshall as deputy Judge Advocate, with great partiality for Lee, who was his friend. John Marshall was not a Colonel, as is shown by a muster roll he signed as a Captain on the 7th of September. Also, in the voluminous Marshall papers there is no mention of his having acted in the capacity of deputy Judge Advocate in this or any other court martial about this time. In fact Lord Stirling presided over the trial and the largest role that John Marshall could have played is that of Lee's attorney. Be that as it may, it requires no partiality to assess the charges against Lee as a lot of trumped-up nonsense. Lee's coldly furious testimony in his defense practically annihilated the hapless Gist. Lee was acquitted on all counts. Congress conveyed its thanks to Major Lee for bravery in action. Woodford took modest satisfaction that his friends in Congress were able to block Lee's recommended promotion.

At the end of August, for the Fauquier men as well as those from the other Virginia counties, the campaign in the north had ended and that in the south had just begun. In Fauquier County the war had receded again in men's consciousness, as they grappled with local problems, the greatest of which was the mounting inflation. In June Sheriff Jeremiah Darnall had refused to give bond for the collection of taxes, "agreeable to the Acts of the last Assembly," for the simple reason that he knew that many could not pay the enormous levies or would refuse to do so.[45] The surprised Court recommended James Bell, John Moffett or John Blackwell in his place. However Joseph Nelson objected, saying that he subcontracted the shrievalty as a sort of concession. This unorthodox transaction baffled the Court. Nelson, a braver or perhaps more foolhardy man than Darnall, insisted on his rights, but the Governor appointed Bell.

There appears to have been a neat little gambling den operating in the county that summer at John Cornwell's [46] ordinary. Furthermore it flourished on the Sabbath. It is not quite clear whether or not it flourished on week-days as well, or if that was against the law. John Rust,[47] who operated "in a booth" (whatever that implies) was a partner in crime and William Strange a willing accomplice. All were fined. One Richard Green [48] of Leeds Parish was the kill-joy who brought the matter to the attention of the authorities.

Bootlegging, or at least "retailing Spiritous Liquors contrary to law" was also a problem. A sudden crack-down brought to light four from Leeds Parish and seven from Hamilton Parish who were indulging in this nefarious pastime. Most of the fines went to the State. Fines for gambling went "for the use of the poor" except some "for the use of the Informer." One had the feeling that the "Informer" would have been well-advised to remove to Kentucky without delay.

A further reflection of hard times was the inordinate number of lawsuits in progress involving claims for varying amounts of money owed by some of the most substantial, as well as the least substantial planters. No fewer than sixty were pending in July. Some defendants had died but more had left the county, probably for Kentucky where old obligations had a marvellous way of being mislaid.

45. Fauquier County Court Order Book, 28 June 1779. Darnall's accounts were in some disorder, as he was summoned to appear before the Court in November to answer unexplained charges brought by Cuthbert Bullitt, Commonwealth Attorney.

46. John Cornwell kept an ordinary at his home on Crooked Run.

47. John Rust was a son of John (d: 1776) and Sarah (Singleton) Rust of Cedar Run. He married Sarah Mason according to Ellsworth Marshall Rust, **Rust of Virginia.**

48. There are many Greens in Fauquier Co. but diligent search fails to uncover another contemporary record of Richard Green. He may have died young.

Between the July and August Courts the troubled life of Captain James Scott came to an end. In July a lease was executed in his name with his brother, the Reverend John Scott of "Gordonsdale" as witness, but had been almost a year since James Scott had officiated on the Court. Even then this still-young man (he was only 37) looked old and ill. The "sickness in the breast and stomach from marching and fatigue and laying out of nights" had taken its toll. Yet to all who would listen he said that he must go back to his men "at all risks, even if he lost his whole estate by it, and his life."[49] His friends exchanged glances in pity. There were no men and, if there were, it was evident that James Scott would not see them again.

That he might lose his whole estate was no idle threat. His wife, Elizabeth (Harrison) Scott was frantic with worry that his debts incurred for the Fauquier Independent Company might ruin his family. In fact the story of James Scott's estate is an excellent illustration of the effects of inflation and it is worth anticipating a little to tell it.

One month after James Scott's death, the will of Captain Nicholas George was submitted for probate. Captain George was not a poor man. He was a militia Captain, briefly a Justice, and owned an average amount of land and a dozen or so Negroes. Not much is known about him, but there is certainly no reason to expect that his personal estate, exclusive of land, was worth four times that of the richest men in the county two years before. Yet his inventory, returned in March of 1780, indicated a valuation of £8,450.

More is known about John Peake,[50] the inventory of whose estate was returned three months later. Like Nicholas George, Peake was a man in secure but not affluent circumstances. His estate was valued at more than £17,500. Continuing this trend, it is not surprising that the estate of Captain James Scott, two months later, was valued at nearly £59,000. Obviously Elizabeth Scott would have had no worries if this appraisal had been made in real money. In fact Virginia currency had sunk in value to the point

---

49. Affidavit of Christian Riley, 8 Feb. 1834. Virginia State Library, Archives Division.

50. John Peake, ca. 1715-1780, son of William Peake of "Bradley" near Colchester, Fairfax Co. He sold "Bradley" 1768 to the Rev. Lee Massey, Rector of Truro Parish, having moved to Fauquier Co. He married Mary Harrison, dau. of Capt. William and Sarah (Hawley) Harrison of Neabsco Creek, Prince William Co. She was the widow of John Brown, d: 1744.

where it no longer served as a valid medium of exchange. An extremely detailed inventory of an estate of approximately the same size filed in Fairfax County a month later,[51] compared with an equally detailed inventory filed three years before shows that the Virginia pound was less than one fortieth the value of the pound sterling. Captain James Scott's estate was worth, therefore, less than £1,500 in prewar currency. He was still rich, but he owed thrice that amount.

The *reductio ad absurdum* in Fauquier came in August of 1781, with the inventory of the estate of Dixon Brown[52] of Brown's Run. Brown was doubtless a nice fellow and a solid citizen, but he was certainly no Croesus. He was, in fact, relatively poor. Yet his bewildered family were handed an appraisal of nearly £102,000. The abashed appraisers explained that the appraisal was made in specie (gold coin) and that, to allow for the depreciation of Virginia Currency, they had multiplied the total by 600! In pre-war money Dixon Brown was worth about £170. One can understand why Elizabeth Scott had trouble sleeping at night.

The only explanation for the relative calm with which court proceedings were carried on during the autumn of 1779 is that the people of Fauquier did not realize what was happening to them. The Court minutes record the usual transactions with little reference to an economy gone haywire. In September William Grant and Hezekiah Turner were appointed to a commission to enforce "An Act for laying a Tax payable on certain enumerated Commodities." The commodities were essential, the tax exorbitant.

In October a new list of recommendations went to the Governor for officers in the militia. New Captains were Joseph Wheatley, James Foley, Jr.,[53] John Hathaway and John Ball. First Lieutenants were Augustine Jennings, Minor Winn,[54] Henry

51. Fairfax Co. Will Book D-1, 1776-1782, pp. 209-214.

52. Fauquier Co. Will Book I, 1759-1783, p. 442.

53. James Foley, d: 1797, m. (1) Sarah O'Bannon, 1737-ante 1786, dau. of John and Sarah (Barbee) O'Bannon, m: (2) 1786, Elizabeth Oglevie.

54. Minor Winn and his brother, James Winn, both Captains in the Fauquier Militia, were sons of Minor Winn, d: Fauquier 1775. Minor and James Winn married sisters, Elizabeth and Hannah Withers, daughters of Col. Thomas and Elizabeth (Williams) Withers of "Green Meadows", Fauquier Co. Minor Winn, Jr., was T. J. "Stonewall" Jackson's grandfather.

Peyton, and John Barker. Second Lieutenants were John Fletcher, Joseph Smith and William Heale. Ensigns were Baylor Jennings, Thomas Nelson, Ambrose Barnett and Joseph Nelson. It is not clear whether this meant four new companies or whether the men were simply replacements for men who had resigned. Many of these names are later found on rosters of companies actively engaged in the Southern campaigns.

A measure of interest in self-protection against future military demands prompted soldiers who had been discharged after three years service to record these discharges in the county courthouse. Thus we find that John Barbee, a sergeant of the 1st Virginia Regiment and William Barber, a private in the same regiment, registered certificates signed by General Muhlenberg. Similarly John Jones, a Sergeant in Washington's Guard, produced a certificate signed by Captain Caleb Gibbs, commander. Daniel Grant, a soldier in Captain Gabriel Long's company of Morgan's Rangers had one signed by General Woodford. Woodford also signed a certificate for William Keirnes, a soldier in the 7th Virginia Regiment. Many who lost their discharges and were later in desperate need of pensions must have bitterly regretted not having taken this sensible precaution.

In the north there was not much more that the Virginia line could do during the rest of the year except wait and complain. They did both. Washington kept his army near West Point in vain hope that the French fleet would appear off Sandy Hook. d'Estaing chose to lay siege to the British garrison at Savannah. When that failed part of the fleet sailed to the West Indies, the rest home. While waiting the Virginia troops were encamped around Fort Montgomery on the Hudson between West Point and Stony Point. Christian Febiger wrote wearily: [55]

> we are stationed on the banks of Hudsons River 2 miles above Montgomery and 4 below West Point in a hollow Front & right Flank and rear cover'd by almost insurmountable Mountains and our left by the River. Our Neighbours are Batts, Screetch Owls and Rattle Snakes, and the produce of the country is a great variety of Rocks and Stones here and there interwoven with desponding Cedars, Oaks and other Scrubs. Our diet consists chiefly of Salt Beef and Biscuit & Beef, - now and then a Drink of

---

55. Letter, Febiger to Heth, 3 Sept. 1779. Christian Febiger Papers, Harvard University Library.

Grog. Thus my Friend we fare yett we sometimes creep out of our lurking holes and play Mr. Britton some bold pranks.

The letter was directed to Colonel William Heth on the 3rd of September. Heth was home on leave following the tragic death of his wife.

By November the weather in the New York highlands was so bitterly cold that the distribution of blankets and winter clothing was ordered and the army was on its way to winter quarters. They did not know where they were going. Vague rumors were circulating that the Virginia line would be sent to Charleston to reinforce Lincoln but daily the orders seemed to grow more confusing. Lee and his dragoons were detached and sent to Monmouth. The special unit that had served under Wayne was held together, though they rightfully belonged in many regiments to which the men wished to return for winter quarters. Febiger, who commanded the 1st Regiment under Wayne was away from his 2nd Virginia Regiment, for which he felt the greatest responsibility. On the 16th of November General Greene ordered them south by way of Haverstraw, Pompton and Rockaway in the direction of Morristown.

Febiger wrote to Woodford on the 30th of November in part: [56]

> Lt. Coleman of the 1st State Regiment has for more than two months been unfitt for Duty and still continues so and no prospect of his getting better. It will make it necessary if we are continued to have another Officer in the Company as Captain G...t who commands it is a perfect Cypher,...We are very anxious to know where our Winter Quarters is to be and whether we are to be continued or not, our inclination is uannimously to be separated and join our respective Regiments in Winter Quarters.

On the same day he showed his real feeling in a letter to Captain John Stokes, a friend at headquarters: [57]

---

56. Steward, **Life of Woodford**, referenced as a MSS in the Chicago Historical Society. Febiger to Woodford, 30 Nov. 1779.

57. Letter, Febiger to Stokes, 30 Nov. 1779. Christian Febiger Papers, Harvard University Library.

here we are in the damndest hubbub about Cloaths, Shoes, Winter Quarters, Continuance or breaking up, jumping from one Subject to the other in the most barbarous manner. We see neither man, Beast or Devil but ourselves and sometimes a Girl from Newark: - God damn all your heads and Tails, not meaning Treason, for not informing us of our Destination.

The prospect of going to Charleston filled the Virginians with natural alarm. They would never forget what had happened to Muhlenberg's hapless 8th Virginia ("German") Regiment under General Charles Lee in the summer of 1776 when malaria had decimated their ranks. Possibly another reason for apprehension was the growing certainty as to the identity of the man who would lead them. It was only too evident that Washington could not possible send Stirling, even had the latter wished to go, because he outranked Lincoln. However Woodford outranked both Muhlenberg and Scott and Scott, at least, was already heavily committed. It was about this time (9 November 1779) that Colonel John Nevell wrote to Daniel Morgan:[58]

Genl. Woodford has had Command of the Division for some time past and I am sorry to inform you (that) he is very Much Disliked in Particular by his old Brigade, much more than by those that joined him in this Campaign.

He goes on to say that he had, himself, no personal quarrel with Woodford and would even support his promotion if it would make room for Morgan to return to the army as a Brigadier. Many disagreed. Colonel William Davies of Petersburg, whose long and useful career had been continuously thwarted by Woodford's unrelenting animosity, simply refused to accept the appointment as sub-inspector under him without "any acquaintance or interest with the commanding General which could avail me against any arbitrary or unjust act of his, should he attempt any."[59]

58. Letter, John Nevell to Daniel Morgan at "Saratoga", his Virginia farm, 9 Nov. 1779. Col. John Nevell (Neville) was of the 4th Virginia Regiment. Myers Collection No. 1000, MSS. Div., New York Public Library.

59. William Davies to Robert Hanson Harrison (Washington's secretary) 20 March 1780. Correspondence with Officers, Washington Papers, Manuscript Division, Library of Congress.

If the officers under Woodford felt threatened, the rank and file had no reason to feel less so. Courts-martial held in his command were notably harsh and punishment for trivial offenses severe in extreme. Yet it made very little difference what the officers or the rank and file of the Virginia line thought of going to Charleston under Woodford or anyone else. Early in December the matter was decided.

The predicament of Major General Benjamin Lincoln in Charleston was growing increasingly desperate. He had, at most, about 3,000 men with little prospect of getting more either from Virginia or the Carolinas. Brigadier General Charles Scott had, thus far, made little headway in recruiting and equipping the 2,200 men that Washington had asked him to send to Lincoln in May. During the second week of October he had 300 men ready. Washington released Colonel Richard Parker of the 1st Virginia Regiment to lead them with Lieutenant Colonel Gustavus Brown Wallace as second in command. The latter's deep misgivings had not abated. He was, he considered, a dead man. The detachment arrived in Charleston on the 5th of December.[60] When Lincoln counted them he did not bother to be polite. He sent off a hot letter to Congress demanding more than token reinforcement if they did not expect him to evacuate the city.

Congress had anticipated some such reaction. On the 29th of November they ordered Washington to release the North Carolina Brigade and all of the Virginia troops at headquarters, if they could possibly be spared. The General replied, "I have determined illy as they can be spared, to put the whole of the Virginia Troops in motion..."[61] In the same dispatch, however, he asked the Congress to provide water transport from the Head of Elk to Charleston for the Virginia soldiers. Washington knew more about his Virginians than he was willing to admit.

Excluding the sick and those already on furlough, there were about 2,000 Virginians at headquarters, but the number was misleading. Possibly a third of them had signed up for three years in the winter of 1776-77. Their terms of enlistment would soon expire. Washington wrote Woodford on the 6th of December

---

60. Gustavus B. Wallace to Michael Wallace, 7 Dec. 1779. A. D. Wallace Papers, University of Virginia Library. Wallace was second in command to Heth in the 3rd Virginia Regiment. He accompanied Parker to Charleston.

61. Letter, Washington to the President of Congress, 29 Nov. 1779. Fitzpatrick, ed., **Writings of Washington**, Vol. XVII, pp. 208-209.

alerting him to keep the proposed move secret and continue building huts as usual. The following day Woodford received a letter from the Commander-in-Chief that revealed his real concern: [62]

> Dear Sir:
> It is my wish that we should endeavor by every practicable means to reenlist the Old Troops for the War. I therefore request that you will inform the Cols. and Commanding Officers of the Regiments in the Virginia line that they may enlist promiscuously throughout their line any of the Soldiers whose present terms of service will expire by the last of Feb. The men re-enlisting for the War shall be furloughed to the first of April...and a warrant shall be granted for the Continental bounty of Two Hundred Dollars to each and of 10 Dollars to the Officers for every one re-engaged...
>
> G. Washington.

In three years the Virginians had fought in many battles, often against fearful odds. They had suffered great hardship and had often made sacrifices far beyond the call of duty. They were tired beyond endurance, some beyond the will to suffer more. Why should they re-enlist? The lavish bounty in worthless currency was no inducement. They could leave the service with honour. Who could find fault? Few rose to the bait.

Colonel Christian Febiger, who was not at all eager to go to Charleston, stayed behind in Philadelphia to issue proper papers to retiring soldiers and settle their claims for pay and compensation. In fact "Old Denmark's" fighting days were about over. He had served his country long and well. He remained in Philadelphia to forward arms and supplies to the South, in which duty he was highly efficient and immensely persuasive.

Among the rest of the Virginians, Washington knew, were others who had reached nearly to the end of their capacity to bear danger, hardship and, as they fully believed, possible death from the diseases that lurked in the fetid marshes of the Carolina lowlands. They, he thought, would desert. Hence his request that the Congress send them by water. He doubted that, even in their misery, they would jump overboard.

On the 8th of December orders arrived from Congress for the Virginia line to march to Philadelphia, where further orders would

---

62. Letter, Washington to Woodford, 7 Dec. 1779, **ibid.**, p. 228.

await them. On the following day the 1st and 2nd Virginia State Regiments started toward the Delaware. On the 10th Woodford's main body followed. On the 11th Colonel Nathaniel Gist brought the final detachment of two regiments. A number of men had to be left behind for want of shoes. [63]

At Trenton Woodford received orders to detach 213 men whose commissions expired in December as a guard over a large number of prisoners, mostly from Stony Point and Paulus Hook, who were being sent to Fort Frederick in Maryland. [64] Arriving in Philadelphia on Christmas, Woodford found to his dismay that, rather than an easy voyage, he would have to march the entire distance to Charleston. The Board of War had been unable to find enough ships to transport his men. The weather was unbelievably cold and stores of every sort almost unobtainable at any price. Furthermore a large British fleet sailed out of New York Harbour on the day after Christmas headed southward.

The land route proposed by the Board of War must have chilled Woodford to the marrow of his bones: Lancaster, York, Frederick, Leesburg, Red Store (Haymarket), Dumfries, Fredericksburg, Petersburg and Camden. The weather was some of the worst on record, even in Virginia. The James River was a solid block of ice. "A Gentleman from York" said that the ice at Gloucester was such as was not remembered by the oldest person then living. Four feet of snow blanketed the Piedmont. Even Woodford wondered how he could be expected to lead his men by their own firesides without losing half of them. In Philadelphia even the Board of War dared not let Woodford take the road with his ill-clad, ill-shod troops.

There was another and even greater problem. Richard Peters of the Board of War wrote to the President of Congress: [65]

> The Board on Application of General Woodford have drawn Warrants on the Paymaster General to the amount of $150,000 to enable him to move the Troops which could not be done before the men received their pay and arrearages of Cloathing. The Monies due them...according to an estimate by the clothier General in our opinion is not immoderate (but) amount so much beyond our ex-

63. Letter, Washington to Lincoln, 12 Dec. 1779, *ibid.*, pp. 257-258.

64. Journals of the Continental Congress, Vol. XV, p. 1382.

65. Papers of the Continental Congress, 148 I 9.

pectations that the Board has deemed it prudent & proper to take the advice of Congress on the Subject. The monies due on this account alone will amount to half a million dollars and we are of the opinion that unless it is paid great dissatisfaction & perhaps Mutiny will ensue...

Despite the weather and the continued lack of adequate clothing, the Virginians left Philadelphia on the 13th of January 1780. It is said that the Liberty Bell in the high steeple of the State House spoke in solemn tones through the frosty air.[66] They did not send to see for whom the bell tolled. Some may have wondered if it was not for the Virginia line.

---

66. The bell tolled for the funeral of a member of the Congress who had died three days before. Burial was postponed because of the frozen ground.

Interlude

The War Moves South

Sir Henry Clinton sailed from New York Harbour after narrowly escaping being trapped by ice, on the 26th of December, 1779. His fleet under Admiral Marriott Arbuthnot included 10 warships on which were mounted 530 guns, 18 transports on which were carried 396 horses, materiel and supplies, and 72 on which were carried 8,700 troops. More than 5,000 sailors manned the rigging.

It was a formidable armada, but all was not well on the bridge of Sir Henry's flagship as it cleared the straits off Sandy Hook. The Commander paced the deck with helpless rage. Just before leaving he had fired off to the War Office another in his series of resignations. The orders framed in the comfortable London office of Lord Germain had, against Clinton's better judgement, launched this expedition in the dead of winter and in the teeth of the raging Atlantic that flung its towering waves against a rock-bound coast. To help him on this suicidal mission the Admiralty had sent him Arbuthnot, a cantankerous old naval mediocrity, instead of a competent and cooperative admiral he had begged for.

As second in command, he had Cornwallis. Cornwallis was not incompetent but he was ambitious, domineering and at times insufferable. In addition he held a "dormant commission" to take command in the event something should happen to Clinton. It is true that Clinton had been pressing for retirement, but Cornwallis' tactless reminders of his position were beginning to get on his nerves. There was not much time for Clinton to brood over the wrongs that had been done him. When the convoy was two days out of New York Harbour they met the full fury of the Atlantic head on. There followed thirty-eight days of pure horror.

The tempest that struck on the 2nd of January was one of the worst in Atlantic history. Clinton said that scarcely a day passed unmarked by the foundering of a transport or the further dispersion of the fleet. On the morning of the 4th of January only 48 ships were in contact. Three of the largest warships, the *Russell*,

Renown and *Robust*, were nowhere in sight. The *Renown* had in tow the demasted transport *Anna* with 200 Hessian chasseurs aboard. The *Anna* finally broke loose and was blown clean across the Atlantic. If the ships got too far from land to avoid being blown ashore by the stiff nor'wester, the Gulf Stream threatened to sweep them into mid Atlantic. Terrified horses had to be thrown overboard to prevent their breaking ships apart in wild stampede. For days the shifting gale prevented any forward movement whatever. Almost all the horses, much of the artillery and tons of supplies were lost. Although headed for Charleston, the fleet had to go to Savannah for repairs. It was well into February before the British could turn their eyes toward Charleston.

The Americans derived some comfort from the realization that the enemy was having a rough time at sea. In fact, it was their only comfort. From Morristown, Richard Kidder Meade wrote to Woodford in January:

> We have no certain accounts of the Fleet, destined by report for the Southward—Some of them it is said are on Shore on the Jersey coast—but I fear our chief dependence is on their being dispersed at Sea—from the violence of the storm. The old Seamen in this neighborhood give it as their opinion that they must have received immense damage. Nothing but so happy an event can possibly give you time to arrive in Season.

Not even the fury of the Atlantic, though, could offset the brutal force of old man Winter operating on land to delay the reinforcement of the beleaguered garrison at Charleston.

X
Charleston

Because of the extreme weather, it was necessary for General Woodford to march the Virginia line from Philadelphia to Fredericksburg in three divisions. Accommodations along the way were not sufficient to house them at night and men left out-of-doors would be frozen stiff by daybreak. Noland's Ferry was not operating because of the ice. The men could easily cross, but getting the horses and heavy artillery across the Potomac on ice was a frightful task. Wagons were continually breaking down and the terrified animals refused to venture on the slippery surface or down the precipitous banks of the river. On the opposite side heavy snowdrifts and fallen timbers blocked the old Carolina Road through Leesburg, past West's Ordinary and along the east slope of the Bull Run Mountains. Some wanted to cross the Rappahannock at Norman's Ford but rumors of the conditions of the roads through Orange and Spotsylvania Counties decided Woodford to remain on the Dumfries Road and cross at Falmouth.

The first two divisions under Colonels William Russell and John Neville, who were at Lancaster, Pennsylvania on the 13th of January, arrived with the artillery in Fredericksburg on the 8th of February, 1780.[1] Woodford had gone ahead to prepare for their reception. Desertions had been fewer than he had anticipated, but his ranks were, nevertheless, notably thinner. Men who had enlisted for the war late the previous spring, had been denied a furlough at that time, but had been promised one during the winter. Now they claimed it, and the Board of War "had directed that the public faith should not be violated." Reluctantly, Woodford had let them go but, "from the great number of inducements they (would) meet with in the state to violate their furlough,"[2] he apprehended a bad account of them in the spring.

1. Letter, Woodford at Fredericksburg to Washington at Morristown. Washington Papers, Library of Congress, Manuscripts Div. General Woodford then thought that the British fleet was destined for St. Augustine.
2. Letter, Woodford to Washington, 13 Jan. 1780. Historical Society of Pennsylvania Mss.

The third division under Colonel Nathaniel Gist was five or six days behind, picking up stragglers and trying to repair broken wagons and retrieve abandoned stores. Woodford rested his men in Fredericksburg and waited for Gist to catch up. There had been few recruits and he was at a loss to know what to do with some forty extra field and company grade officers who accompanied him. He wrote Washington that he was going to Williamsburg to consult the new Governor, Thomas Jefferson, about it. At least his old enemy, Patrick Henry, was no longer in office. Henry, ill and disillusioned by his inability to cope with the British raid under General Matthew the previous May, had retired to "Scotch Town" to recover.

Woodford found utter chaos in Williamsburg. The government was being moved to Richmond and no one had time for him. The Governor was away. He learned that the Assembly had adjourned without making provisions for filling the regiments, and could give him no idea of the number of officers that might be needed. He had started his Virginians on the road from Fredericksburg to Petersburg on the 12th of February, a distance of less than 150 miles. Nearly a month went by before they reached their destination. The mud, melting snow and alternate rain and sleet had almost finished them off. On the 8th of March Woodford wrote to Washington, a letter in which a new Woodford emerges. For the first time he shows concern, a feeling of responsibility, a sense of imminent danger, and, most surprising of all, humility. For once he names no scapegoat, offers no lame excuses, attempts no cover-up of past neglect. It reads as follows:[3]

Petersburg, Va. March 8, 1780.
Dear Sir: My last to your Excellency was from Fredericksburg the 8th of February. You will no doubt be surprised that we should be near a month in getting so short a distance ... but you may be assured it was not possible to get the artillery and baggage on one day sooner and if it had not been for the assistance we received from the Gentlemen upon the road, they would not have reached this (place) till the Earth was settled.
The day I arrived here I received a letter from Gen'l. Lincoln (a copy enclosed) this determined me to leave my military stores and baggage to follow on. The troops

---

3. Letter, Woodford to Washington, 8 March 1780. Washington Papers, Library of Congress, Manuscripts Division.

marched this morning. I took a few waggons to carry our tents as I could not think it prudent to expose the men upon so long a march. The artillery will leave this in a few days ... escorted by 140 men of Colo. Buford's regiment, which is all of that corps that can be marched at present; about 300 of them will be left and I see no probability of them being equipt for a march in any short time. The Colo. is now at Williamsburg upon that business. General Scott is here at present, but will go without the men in a few days. The Board of War in Virginia have advised me by letter that about 600 of the State troops would march in about two weeks to the aid of Carolina, including two troops of Dragoons, and requested I would give the necessary orders to the qr. Master and commissary for their accomodations. I have accordingly done so but fear they will not be ready to move as soon as the Board expected ...
I am sorry to inform your Excellency that our numbers are much reduced by desertion and sickness together with the furloughed men already mentioned. Another thing is the men who have been all along mustered and returned for the war ... a number of these have produced certificates from the officers who enlisted them that their time was expired ... I have taken the repeal method of submitting these cases to the further consideration of a board of officers. In most instances they have judged them entitled to a discharge and when it has been other ways ... desertion was the consequence, not only of the man in question, but he has generally carried off others with him. This mischief will continue and a general dislike of the southern service will, I fear, reduce us still more.

General Lincoln's letter had virtually guaranteed the fall of Charleston unless he received immediate reinforcement. His letter reached Woodford on the 5th of March. On the 6th the Virginia line was on the march. On the 11th the *Virginia Gazette* announced grandly:

General Woodford's brigade consisting of 2,000 hearty young fellows, well equipped and three companies of Col. Harrison's artillery, with 6 brass field pieces, marched from Petersburg last Monday on their way to Charleston.

On Monday, the 6th of March, 1780, General Woodford's Brigade in fact numbered only 737 men fit for duty.

Brigadier General Charles Scott set out a few days earlier with a few recruits and detachments from the 1st and 2nd Virginia State Regiments. Colonel Buford remained behind to bring the last regiment of his brigade, about 440 men,[4] for whom he had been unable to get clothing and arms.

Woodford's column travelled southward at a rate of twenty miles a day, except on days when they were "plagued with a Ferry". On the 31st of March they were at Camden, South Carolina, having left only 13 sick along the road. Scott, unencumbered by artillery, had already reached Charleston. By that time Charleston was all but surrounded. Colonel Neville, riding ahead, found only one way open, from Hobcaw Ferry down the Cooper River. On the 6th of April they arrived in the city to be greeted by the firing of a *feu-de-joie* and ringing of bells at night. They had covered 505 miles in 30 days! Charleston was overjoyed.

Their joy was short lived, however, when they fully realized that 700 were all of the Virginia line, of the 3,000 they had been promised would reach them in their extremity. Although justifiably proud of the speed with which his men had completed the forced march, Woodford wrote to Washington on the 9th of April predicting that the last escape from Charleston would soon be cut off. Their arrival had seemed to give the garrison fresh confidence, a confidence that obviously Woodford did not feel. With a rare burst of candor, he wrote: "My want of experience in the defense attack of a place will not enable me to give your Excellency my opinion upon the whole of the situation with any degree of precision."[5] Some of his Virginians were not so guarded in their reactions. They knew that they had marched into certain captivity, and said so. The Chief Engineer of the Continental Army, General Duportail, agreed. The situation was hopeless.

Outside Charleston the only operative American military unit was one under Brigadier General Isaac Huger[6] at Monck's

4. The number of men in Buford's regiment is variously reported. Woodford expected him to march about March 15th with the artillery escorted by 140 men, leaving 300 behind without arms or equipment.

5. Letter, Woodford to Washington, 9 April 1780. Washington Papers, Library of Congress, Manuscripts Div. Quoted by Sparks.

6. Isaac Huger, 1743-1797. One of the celebrated Huger brothers of South Carolina. They were sons of Daniel and Mary (Cordes) Huger (pronounced u-gee) of "Limerick". Well-educated and comfortably circumstanced, all five performed valuable service during the Revolution and afterwards in public office.

Corner, 30 miles north of the city. Huger's command consisted of militia and about 400 Continental cavalry. The latter comprised remnants of Baylor's Horse,[7] some men from Theodorick Bland's regiment of Virginia dragoons, Hugh Horry's[8] South Carolinians, a few of Stephen Moylan's[9] cavalrymen and what was left of Pulaski's ill-fated legion. The cavalry units were commanded by Colonel William Washington, who had been sent south early in 1780.

Monck's Corner was not the first encounter between William Washington and Banastre Tarleton,[10] nor would it be the last. The cocky, red-headed, ruthless cavalry leader was the new comet in the British sky. He was two years younger than Washington, and a relative new-comer to the American scene. He had come with Clinton and had obtained his permission to forage for horses to replace those lost in the storm off Cape Hatteras. On one of these foraging expeditions, after having picked up a few dispirited nags, he had run into a body of militia and dragoons at Bee's Plantation on the 23rd of March. Here he killed or captured fourteen cavalrymen and picked up a number of desperately needed mounts. This had encouraged him to move against Washington's Horse at Governor Rutledge's plantation on the 26th, but there he was driven back with some loss.

On the evening of the 13th of April, Tarleton moved toward Monck's Corner with his cavalry and a body of Loyalist American

7. After the Tappan Massacre, 28 Sept. 1778, the 40 men who escaped stayed together as "Baylor's Horse" and volunteered their services in the Southern Department.

8. Hugh Horry (pronounced O'Ree) was another South Carolinian of Huguenot descent who, with his two brothers, performed valuable service much as did the Huger brothers to whom they were related. He later commanded the foot element of Marion's Brigade.

9. Stephen Moylan, 1737-1811. An Irish born Pennsylvanian of considerable means, Moylan undertook several important jobs for the Continental Army, and failed at most of them. In January, 1778 he became Colonel of the 4th Continental Dragoons. His "Virginia Regiment of Horse" may have been a detachment of that unit serving under Washington, but Moylan himself, was not there.

10. Banastre Tarleton, 1754-1833, son of the Mayor of Liverpool, was well-educated, ambitious and completely ruthless. His odious reputation and boundless conceit have to a large extent obscured the fact that he was a brilliant tactician and a fearless leader. He was knighted in 1820 and married Susan Pricilla, illegitimate daughter of the 4th Duke of Ancaster. They had no children.

Rangers under Major Patrick Ferguson.[11] A captured Negro messenger guided them and provided complete information about Huger's dispositions. About 3 a.m. on the 14th, the British surprised Washington's cavalry, posted to screen Biggins Bridge, and scattered the militia guarding the bridgehead. The engagement turned into a complete rout for the Americans, with Huger and Washington fleeing into the nearby swamps on foot to escape capture. Tarleton captured over 300 precious horses to replace the swamp tackies and more than 40 loaded wagons. About 100 Americans were killed or captured. Tarleton reported three men wounded. The last escape route from Charleston was slammed shut in the face of its defenders.

After the 14th of April, the situation within the beleaguered city deteriorated rapidly. By the 19th Clinton's men had pushed their approaches to within a thousand feet of the American lines in spite of almost unbearable heat and the artillery fire directed against them. Lincoln knew that the fall of the city was inevitable. He had within his lines 5,684 men against Clinton's 12,700, exclusive of Arbuthnot's 4,500 sailors held in reserve. The defense positions around Charleston were in wretched condition owing to the criminal neglect of the townspeople. Yet when Lincoln proposed surrender, Lieutenant Governor Gadsden,[12] backed by his council, threatened to side with the enemy and attack the regular troops if they showed any sign of withdrawing. A heated council of war ended in adjournment without decision.

Lincoln's garrison comprised about 2,000 South Carolina troops, 1,200 North and South Carolina militia, 800 North Carolina Continentals and about 250 miscellaneous and civil officers, for a total of 4,250. The rest, about a fourth of the whole, were Virginians under Brigadier Generals Woodford and Scott. The 700 men Woodford had brought, together with those of Colonel Richard Parker's regiment already there, totalled about 900. Scott

---

11. Patrick Ferguson, 1744-1780. Scottish graduate of the London Military Academy at 14, he was intrigued with the possibilities of the rifle and, on 2 Dec. 1776, secured a patent on the first breechloading rifle used in the British army. Howe successfully thwarted his attempts to form a rifle brigade, but he came south with Clinton and 150 British "rangers" of the 71st Highland Regiment.

12. Christopher Gadsden, 1724-1805. Charleston merchant and acknowledged leader of the South Carolina radicals, Gadsden was among the first to move for independence and for the disestablishment of the church. He had been a Brigadier in the South Carolina militia but a dispute over the command led to his resignation and a duel with Robert Howe.

had about 500 from the 1st and 2nd Virginia State Regiments. There were also 47 supernumerary officers from the 4th, 5th, 6th, 7th, 8th, 10th and 11th Virginia Regiments. Their reason for being in Charleston is incomprehensible.

On the 24th of April Lieutenant Colonel William Henderson led about 300 Virginia and North Carolina Continentals in a surprise attack on the enemy approaches. Caught off guard, the British retreated to the second line where the Americans faltered. They withdrew with minor losses but there remained no hope that a break-through was possible.[13] On the following morning the British opened a heavy artillery barrage, in which Colonel Richard Parker and two privates were killed while looking out over the parapet. Shortly after the 200 man garrison at Fort Moultrie on Sullivan's Island was forced to surrender to Arbuthnot's marines and seamen.

In Charleston, General Moultrie[14] saw "fatigue so great that, for want of sleep, many faces were so swelled they could scarcely see out of their eyes." Yet there was nothing really for the garrison to do but await the inevitable. Food was growing short. The defensive walls were crumbling under the enemy cannonade. The canal, that Lincoln had dug across the Neck outside the lines as a last desperate measure of defense, had been drained. It made an excellent ditch for British fatigue parties to plant new works.

On the 7th of May Lincoln opened negotiations to discuss terms. When no agreement was reached by the evening of the 9th, Clinton renewed the bombardment. After another day and a half of horror, with the town militia having thrown down their arms, provisions exhausted except for a little rice, Lieutenant Governor Gadsden admitted defeat and asked Lincoln to renew the negotiations. There were no terms to speak of. A contemptuous Briton wrote to his father:[15] "They were indulged with beating a

13. It is not possible, from the record, to single out those of Woodford's command who participated in Henderson's rash gamble. Its failure, though it was one of the most courageous acts of the war, doomed its participants to obscurity.

14. William Moultrie, 1730-1805, son of a prominent Charleston physician, was a recognized leader of military affairs in South Carolina before the Revolution. He was appointed a Continental Brigadier 16 Sept. 1777 but had no opportunity to serve until after the capture of Savannah. Criticized as "too easy-going" he nevertheless commanded several successful actions, notably one at Beaufort, S.C., 3 Feb. 1779. His brother, John, was a prominent Loyalist.

15. Quoted but not identified by Franklin B. Hough, **The Siege of Charleston,** Albany, 1867.

drum and to bring out their colours cased." The militia, he wrote, could not be prevailed upon to come out; they began to creep out of their holes the next day. They, poor creatures, were allowed to go home and plow. There they could be useful, he remarked sarcastically.

General Moultrie found one Englishman who was more generous. He had returned to the Citadel to go over artillery stores with one Captain George Rochefort. While they were inside together, Rochefort said, "Sir, you have made a gallant defense, but you had a great many rascals among you who came out every night and gave us information of what was passing in your garrison."[16]

For the Americans the surrender of Charleston was the worse blow of the war. Following the capitulation, Clinton held the Continental troops as prisoners of war. This meant the end of the Virginia Continental Line as an effective fighting unit, yet their spirit was not completely quenched. Some would fight again as state troops or militia. We know of some Fauquier men who were captured at Charleston, but probably not a tenth of the number there. As they marched out of the town to the tune of the "Turk's March" at 11 o'clock in the morning of the 12th of May, 1780, and grounded their arms near the Citadel, let us look at them one by one. They were not an impressive lot. Tired, hungry, tattered and dirty, they struck our unpleasant British friend as "the most ragged rabble (he) ever beheld." (One hopes that he got his come-uppance after Yorktown.) Although the officers were allowed to keep their side arms, the capitulation terms were generally harsh. Continental officers and men were sent to Haddrel's Point (now Mount Pleasant) which had been occupied by the British on the 25th of April. This low, swampy peninsula had been fortified before the British attack on Charleston in 1776, but there was little habitable shelter. In this wretched place they were to remain for more than a year.

Captain John Blackwell of the 3rd Virginia Regiment had come a long way to meet his final defeat. He was now 28 years old and had served a quarter of his life in the cause of freedom. Behind him lay all the major battles in which the Virginia line had been embroiled. Just before the long march to Charleston he had been married. His bride, Agatha Ann Eustace, daughter of Captain Isaac Eustace of Stafford County, had been only fourteen. One wonders now why such marriages took place in that remote time,

---

16. William Moultrie, **Memoirs of the American Revolution**, New York, 1802.

but they were not uncommon. The child bride who awaited him in Virginia could have had no concept of the situation that faced him during the long bleak months that stretched ahead.

Faithful to the last, his 1st Sergeant, Moses Allen, was with him. The tall, lanky Virginian had re-enlisted for the war at Middlebrook. As a 1st Sergeant in the Continental line, the British would not let him go, but as an N. C. O. he as not exempt from work detail. Part of the time they kept him confined in a filthy prison ship in Charleston Harbour. From that a wretched work gang issued forth to work on a fort being built on a small island, which was under water at high tide. He was always wet, always covered with slime, always miserable. Broken in health, they finally sent him home. In Virginia he was given forty days leave with his family. However forty days was not enough to cure him of the effects of his imprisonment. In March of 1782, General Muhlenberg, who happened to be in Fauquier, signed his discharge upon the advice of his doctor. He had served his country one month less than six years.

Captain Joseph Blackwell of Elk Run had no business being in Charleston, but he was anyway. As an officer in Green's 6th Virginia Regiment, he had no command. On the way to Charleston he had visited his home on Elk Run for a few days, according to his 15 year old nephew, William Edmonds, Jr., but had said that he must not linger.[17] He was finally exchanged in June of 1781 when "a general cartel took place and exchanges were made according to superiority of rank, and the rest sent home on parole, not to be within 40 miles of a British Camp." His military career was over.

Daniel O'Rear had been in John Ashby's company in the 3rd Virginia Regiment but, according to his pension record, never served outside Virginia until he moved with his father to Wilkesboro, North Carolina in September, 1779. There he joined Captain Richard Allen's Company in Wade Hampton's Regiment and marched to Charleston. He was in the skirmishing along the Ashley River at the end of March, attempting to prevent Clinton's crossing. However he was an orderly sergeant in Captain John Loman's company of Colonel Williams' Regiment when the city was taken. He was paroled and sent home during the summer. In October, while still on parole, his father's house was attacked and looted by Tories. Among other things, they took his father's trunk containing his discharge and parole papers.

17. William Edmonds, Jr., 1765- , was chiefly concerned that the war might be over too soon for him to participate. It was. He married, 12 Jan. 1799, Hester Foote, daughter of George and Celia (Helm) Foote.

Samuel Courtney had been in Green's 6th Virginia Regiment. He re-enlisted at Middlebrook in the winter of 1779-80. Having served both at Stony Point and Paulus Hook, he marched south and participated in skirmishes with Indians along the Savannah River in the early spring. It would appear, therefore, that he marched with Colonel Richard Parker. Undaunted by his capture at Charleston, Courtney, after the expiration of his parole, joined Captain Alexander Parker's Virginia company and served until the end of the war.

Daniel Chumley, who had been in Grayson's ill-fated regiment under Captain William Triplett at Monmouth, remained with Scott's Brigade. He marched south with Scott in Captain Mitchell's company, through Halifax on the Roanoke River, and Fayetteville, North Carolina. His term of enlistment expired while he was a prisoner, and General Lincoln discharged him. The British allowed him to go home. After three years in the army, he had not yet reached twenty-one.

Lieutenant Colonel Gustavus Brown Wallace proved impervious to the agues and diseases of Charleston's subtropical climate but he was captured anyway, along with his 19 year old brother. He wrote from Haddrel's Point on the 7th of June to one of his brothers, "I am now a prisoner with our brother Tom, we capitulated on the 12th of May." He sounds discouraged but Gus Wallace was never long without an angle. Somewhere he had learned that money talks and the prospect of getting money will move many obstacles. He soon got in touch with Brigadier General Thomas Nelson of Virginia, who suggested that he be allowed to return to Virginia and arrange for the payment of debts incurred by officers of the Virginia line while in Charleston. Lord Cornwallis took the bait and sent the necessary passport in exchange for 300 to 400 hogsheads of tobacco.

Just how successful Wallace was in prying loose hard cash from the Virginia line officers is a moot question. For whatever happened he very probably had a plausible explanation.[18]

---

18. Despite (or possibly because of) his reputation as a great ladies' man, he never married. He died in 1802 of typhus contracted on a ship returning from Scotland, where he had gone to investigate an inheritance. Put ashore alone in the swamp grass of Potomac Creek about five miles below Fredericksburg, he was found dying by a servant of his cousin, Frances (Moncure) Daniel of "Crow's Nest". So lethal was the disease considered, that he would not let her approach him but did consent to be taken to Fredericksburg in her carriage. He died a few days later.

It was given to Brigadier General William Woodford to drain the dregs of defeat to the bottom. The humiliation of defeat, the unhealthy climate and the wretched living conditions at Haddrel's Point were too much for him. The nature of his malady is uncertain but, by the middle of September, the doctors gave up hope of cure and recommended sea air and a change of living conditions as the only remedy. He prevailed upon the British to send him to New York, but died almost immediately upon arrival. He was buried 13 November 1780, in Trinity Churchyard. His grave was unmarked and cannot now be exactly located. There is no tombstone on which to engrave the rank that meant more to him than glory, or the affection of his countrymen.

After the surrender of Charleston there existed only one small remnant of the Virginia line. It was that part of the 3rd Virginia regiment that General Woodford had been forced, for want of clothing and arms, to leave behind at Petersburg under Colonel Abraham Buford. Its end came swiftly.

It had been the 20th of March, 1780, before Buford had been able to secure the necessary equipment to set his regiment in motion. Even then their progress was slow, partly because of the weather and partly because of the fact that they were encumbered with a large part of Woodford's artillery which, in his haste, he could not take with him.

A young soldier named Richard Bailey [19] tells the tragic story. Richard Bailey of Fauquier, an 18 year old recruit, had entered service in March of 1779 for a tour of 18 months as a substitute for a Fauquier man he does not name. He went first to Alexandria under Captain George Wales of the 4th Virginia Regiment, who had appointed him orderly sergeant. He went then to Fredericksburg where the substitute militiamen were "ordered out and mustered into actual service." Presumably he meant the regular army on Continental establishment. After drawing regimental clothing, they moved to Williamsburg, where they awaited orders. On the 3rd of June, 1779, they moved to Petersburg, where Colonel Abraham Buford took command. On the 29th of March Bailey's company was ordered to Charleston, others having preceded them. They soon caught up with the rest who had been delayed by efforts to get heavy artillery across rivers swollen by spring freshets.

19. Richard Bailey, 1762-post 1843, apparently never married. His wanderings after the war are noteworthy—first to Mecklenburg Co., N.C., then to Jefferson Co., Tenn., Smith and Lawrence Cos. in Tenn., then Lauderdale and Lawrence Cos. in Alabama. He was never anywhere long enough to put down roots and left no heirs.

On the 1st of May they reached Lenud's (or Lanneau's) Ferry on the Santee River about 40 miles from Charleston.[20] There Buford rested, having heard of the precarious situation at Charleston. With him were 200 men of the 3rd Virginia Regiment and about 150 men like Bailey, from a variety of other units. They were soon joined by a small body of Colonel William Washington's dismounted cavalry, refugees from the unfortunate encounter at Monck's Corner three weeks before.

It appears that the 6th of May was one of those sultry, lazy spring days along the Santee, when activity seems repulsive and problems seem remote. Certainly the men who lounged about the ferry and plunged aimlessly into the sluggish river were not thinking of the British or of any immediate danger. About 3:00 o'clock the afternoon stillness was shattered by frantic shouts from south of the river. As they learned later a small contingent of American cavalry under Colonel Anthony White had captured an officer and 17 light infantrymen of Tarleton's command who were foraging at "Wambaw", the plantation of Colonel Elias Ball near Strawberry, about ten miles south. They had made a bee-line to Lenud's Ferry with their prisoners and with Tarleton in hot pursuit. Just short of the river Tarleton and his 150 dragoons attacked. There was no contest. White's troops were surprised and outnumbered. Buford's were unprepared to offer effective help. Colonel William Washington and a few men who crossed the river to reinforce White, escaped only by swimming the river. A number were drowned in the attempt. Tarleton liberated the British prisoners just as they were about to be ferried across the river. He reported 5 American officers and 36 men killed or wounded, 7 officers and 60 dragoons captured. Tarleton's casualty figures are usually exaggerated but his claim that he captured all the rebel horses is probably correct. There were, apparently, no British casualties. At Monck's Corner Colonel William Washington had fled into a swamp, at Lenud's Ferry he swam the river to escape Tarleton. He would simply *have* to think of a better exit!

Buford's men, the enthralled, if not exactly enthusiastic spectators of the catastrophe across the Santee, no doubt developed a healthy respect for Tarleton's dragoons, now superbly mounted on rebel horses. The report of the surrender of Charleston was a reasonable excuse for Buford to reverse his course and head for Hillsborough in North Carolina. Marching along the Santee, he

---

20. Located near where U.S. Hwy. 17 crosses the Santee, the Huguenot name for the ferry is pronounced Le-noo.

soon fell in with General Richard Caswell[21] and 700 North Carolina militia on their way to Charleston. He advised Caswell of the melancholy news and, together, they reached Camden. At this point Caswell turned west toward Greenville and Buford took the northerly route toward Salisbury, North Carolina.

British reconnaissance quickly learned of Buford's position and reported it to Cornwallis. Cornwallis followed post-haste but quickly realized that his large force with five heavy field pieces could not possibly catch up with Buford, who had a ten day lead. He turned the mission over to Tarleton, who with 40 dragoons, 130 cavalry and 100 infantry, riding double with his horsemen, set out after them. Even though the weather was hot and sultry and his men and horses nearly worn out from previous exertion over a wide territory, Tarleton reached Camden on the 28th of May. There he learned that Buford had left Rugeley's Mill, only 12 miles to the north, two days before.

Tarleton rested his men and horses until the early morning of the 29th of May and by mid-afternoon his van had closed in on Buford's rear. They had ridden 105 miles in 54 hours. Buford had sent his supply train and field artillery ahead and his 350 Virginia Continentals were moving on the double along the Catawba River. Tarleton's horses, under their double loads, were nearing exhaustion. Having come this far, Tarleton was not ready to give up the chase, and, to slow his prey, sent Buford peremptory demands for surrender. The gambit was successful. While Buford pondered the demand, Tarleton pressed steadily forward.

About 3 o'clock in the afternoon there was a brief skirmish between Tarleton's van and a small rear guard of Virginians, commanded by Lieutenant Pearson. The Virginians were chopped to ribbons in a particularly brutal attack. Furiously angry, Buford returned a defiant answer and formed his available infantry and cavalry in a single line along the road in an open wood, to meet an attack. There was no time to bring his field pieces into position. Consequently the British were able to form within 300 yards of Buford's line without drawing fire.

The story of Waxhaws,[22] the name commonly given to the

21. Richard Caswell, 1729-1789, was born in Maryland but moved to Wake (now Raleigh) N. C. when he was 17. After a long military and political career, he was Governor 1776-1780. In 1780 he became Maj. Gen. of N. C. Militia.

22. Waxhaws takes its name from a wide place in the road through beautiful green country near the Carolina line called "the Waxhaws", the meaning of which is obscure.

place, is one of appalling horror. Buford foolishly ordered his men to hold their fire until the enemy had advanced within fifty paces. "The mistake, though gallant, was fatal," wrote Fortescue, "the volley was fired too late to check the rush of horses, and in an instant the American battalion was broken up and the sabres went to work." Tarleton had ridden around the American flank and made a dash for the colours in the center of the line. The officer who raised a flag of truce was slaughtered and Tarleton's horse was killed under him. Belief that he had been killed stimulated a vindictive fury in the British cavalry. Every man who had fallen was ruthlessly bayonetted, despite cries for quarter. Remounted, Tarleton surveyed the scene without any attempt to halt the action.

Thus perished in a sea of blood, along a lonely road in South Carolina, the last remnant of the gallant Virginia line. 113 were killed outright and 203 captured. Of the latter, 150 were bayonetted on the battlefield and were too badly wounded to move. Most of the other 53 prisoners were wounded and many died before an exchange was arranged. Buford and a few other mounted men escaped, along with 72 men who were in a forward column. One of these was Richard Bailey. How many from Fauquier died, we do not know, but he alone remained to tell the story in the years to come.

After the battle of Waxhaws, Bailey was sent to Chesterfield Courthouse near Petersburg on recruiting duty until the first of September. It seems improbable that his story lured many into the Virginia line, but he tried. In September Colonel Buford was ordered to take his men and such recruits as they had secured to Hillsborough, North Carolina, where the main army was collecting. At Hillsborough Buford signed a discharge for Bailey and gave it to Captain Smith of the Maryland line who had charge of a party of British prisoners, (one wonders where they came from) destined for Richmond. Smith delivered his prisoners and gave Bailey his discharge on the 25th of October. However, young Bailey had just begun to fight. By the following April he was back in the army again as a substitute for Benjamin O'Rear who was drafted for three months. He was a smart lad and usually wound up as orderly sergeant. It was this non-commissioned rank that had earned him a position with the supply train at the head of Buford's column. He decided that it was a good place to be.

With the battles of Charleston and Waxhaws, the British had eliminated almost all organized resistance in the Carolinas and Georgia. The disaster to the Virginia line left only the 9th Virginia Regiment, destined to sit out most of the war at Fort Pitt. When news of the two defeats little more than two weeks apart reached

Virginia the people, at first, refused to believe it. When it could no longer be denied, the deepest gloom settled over the state. In Fauquier County the people to whom the war had seemed remote, now realized that little stood between them and the surge of British conquest. So far the militia had been idle. The time had now come when Virginia must, itself, be defended.

Surprisingly one searches in vain for any reflection of mounting anxiety in the Minutes of the Fauquier County Court. It is true that a great many soldiers sought certificates for military service, but that was for enlistments expired and battles long since fought and mostly lost. Significantly not a single one of these requests was made by a member of the 3rd Virginia Regiment. Of them few were left, and those few continued on. Those who lived in Fauquier County but had served in regiments not usually associated with the county were more anxious to have their service recorded. Thus we find that Richard Wilson and William Smith produced certificates signed by General Edward Stevens of the Culpeper militia. William Smith also presented a certificate for his brother, Robert, who had died in the service. He was his brother's heir-at-law. The Fauquier men who had served in the 2nd Virginia Regiment in Captain Eustace's company under Colonel Charles Mynn Thruston,[23] asking that their discharges be recorded included William Wright, William Prove, Vincent Rollins and Robert Sherrington. Most of Thurston's regiment had come from Frederick County.

A number of certificates were signed by a Colonel Byrd, whose regiment is not named. They were Sergeant Swanson Brown, Stephen Connor, John Nicholson and William Hall. There were two from the 1st Virginia Regiment of Artillery signed by Lieutenant Colonel Edward Carrington. They were Sergeant Edward Shacklett and John Hopper. The record of John Marr of Marr's Run, who was killed, was presented by his heir, Daniel Marr.[24] Colonel John Green of Culpeper signed a certificate for Samuel Wise of the 6th Virginia Regiment, whose wife had long been supported in Fauquier.

Certainly the most curious request for certification of service

---

23. Heitman says that Thruston lost an arm at Amboy, 8 Mar. 1777 and resigned 1 Jan. 1779. The soldiers were apparently careful to obtain their certificates before the resignation became effective.

24. The Marr family of southern Fauquier laid costly sacrifices on the altar of liberty. Captain John Quincy Marr was the first to die for the Confederacy.

came from Thomas Muccaboy, who had served under Colonel William Russell in Scott's Brigade and had been discharged as unfit for duty. Muccaboy not only wanted recognition for that, but also for service in the 47th *British* Regiment. This was apparently in order to qualify for land bounties offered for service in British units at the end of the French and Indian Wars. Such bounties were offered along the Great Kanawha River. If Muccaboy was claiming one of these bounties his "unfitness for duty" must have been due to his advanced age.

It would seem probable that the number of those killed at Charleston and especially at Waxhaws, would have produced a number of soldiers' wills submitted for probate in the Fauquier Court. Such however is not the case. The young men who died were usually unmarried and had not yet inherited family lands. They left no wills in most instances. When they did there is seldom anything in either wills or inventories to identify them specifically as military casualties. In fact only two or three are likely possibilities.

Of more interest is the list of those named during 1780 to fill posts in the expanding militia. Two new Captains were named, Richard Rixey [25] and Thomas Conway.[26] In addition it is noted that Eppaphroditus Timberlake was named 2nd Lieutenant to replace Thomas Edwards, promoted to Captain in Daniel Floweree's company, presumably to take Floweree's place. John Garrington and Rolly Smith were new 1st Lieutenants, Samuel O'Bannon,[27] William Ball and John Hogains, 2nd Lieutenants; and Jeremiah Boggess, Richard Luttrell and John Craine, ensigns.

25. Richard Rixey, Jr., married 15 Nov. 1764, Elizabeth Morehead, daughter of John Morehead. Her brother, Charles, was with Washington's Horse and another brother, John, was a Captain of militia.

26. Thomas Conway married, 22 June 1778, Lydia George, daughter of Capt. Nicholas and Margaret George. Thomas Conway was a son of Thomas Conway who died in Fauquier County in 1784, leaving his son, Thomas, Jr., a tract of land on Town Run on which the younger man was already living.

27. Samuel O'Bannon, 1751-1830, was another son of John and Sarah (Barbee) O'Bannon. He married, 1775, Sarah (Sally) ? In his will, dated 18 Nov. 1773, John O'Bannon left his son Samuel a tract of 139 a. "beginning at Nelson's third Corner and binding on the lines of the said Nelson, The Rev'd Mr. Scott and Gibson line 150 yards above the old ford on Broad Run."

Samuel Pearle, who was recommended in June as an ensign, was again recommended in November as a 2nd Lieutenant.

The county was paying toward the support of at least ten families of soldiers in the Continental Army or their widows. Some had been on the list since July of 1777, but inflation had raised their stipend enormously. Jemima McGraw, who received £ 10 for necessities in 1777, received £80 in May of 1780. Patty Ballance had had £7 in 1777. In November of 1780 she set some sort of record with £360. In August the weary appraisers of Captain James Scott returned an inventory "allowing for a depreciation from fifty to sixty for one."

Another manifestation of inflation was even more dramatic. The Justices decided in May that something had to be done to halt the appalling flight of charges by ordinary keepers, beyond the bounds of reality. It was rapidly becoming so that a traveller could not carry enough money with him to assure his safe return. Good West Indies Rum, which had sold for about £1 before the war, was pegged at £40 per gallon. Brandy, whether imported from France or domestic, was fixed at the same amount. Breakfast or a hot dinner was £1.16s; a night's lodging with *clean* sheets was 18 shillings. Whiskey, apparently less popular than rum, was £24 per gallon. If one could get by on beer or cider at £1.10s the quart, do without coffee or tea for breakfast at a saving of six shillings and, presumably, settle for slightly soiled sheets, the tariff was less but still pretty expensive.

However the ordinary keepers were outraged beyond endurance. At such prices they could not make a profit, nay, Goddamit, if they were compelled to submit, they would shut up shop! Then, what? In May the gentlemen Justices hastily reconsidered. Good West Indies rum and French brandy could be raised to £65 per gallon. A quart of beer rose to £2.2s, though Virginia cider could be had for 12s a quart (there were plenty of apples). Breakfast with tea or coffee or a hot dinner cost a hefty £3. However one could save £1.4s by going without tea or coffee. The night's lodging with clean sheets had risen to £1.4s, a rise of 25 per cent. However for that princely sum, one slept, not only between clean sheets, but also *one in a bed*.

In the spring of 1780 John Marshall, then a Captain in the 7th Virginia Regiment was feeling very supernumerary and rather forlorn. He was visiting his father, who was stationed at Yorktown with his regiment of Virginia Artilllery, when he learned that George Wythe had been appointed professor of law and police at William and Mary College. He decided to attend his lectures and, during May, June and July, 1780, received his entire formal education in the law.[28] On the 28th of August he was waiting on the doorstep of the Fauquier County Court clutching his license to practice law and demanding to be sworn. The Justices were pleased to oblige him. His military career was over.

A review of all the Virginia military units in which men from Fauquier County might have been serving in the summer of 1780 is necessary in order to determine which, if any, were engaged in the next almost total disaster that was to befall American arms on the 16th of August. We have found only one pension record in which anyone from Fauquier so much as mentions the Battle of Camden, South Carolina, which took place on that awful day. Quite possibly others were they but equally possible is the supposition that, had they been, they would have maintained a discreet silence. At Camden the Virginians, whoever they were, disgraced themselves.

On the 16th of April, before the fall of Charleston, General Kalb[29] had started south with a body of Maryland and Delaware Continentals and Colonel Charles Harrison's Virginia Artillery Regiment. With the last unit, under circumstances not fully explained, rode Captain Gideon Johnston of Fauquier. Quite possibly he commanded a detachment from Colonel Thomas Marshall's 1st Virginia State Artillery, sent to swell the ranks of his old commander.

Kalb was at Parson's Plantation, about 35 miles northeast of Hillsborough, North Carolina, on the 20th of June when he received word of the surrender of Charleston five weeks before. As the purpose of his expedition was to help defend Charleston, he was in something of a quandary as to what he should do. Pressing forward in spite of heat, insects and lack of equipment and provisions, he had reached Buffalo Ford on Deep River when news caught up with him that Congress in its infinite wisdom had replaced him with the ineffable little toady, General Horatio Gates. He had

28. Herbert A. Johnson, ed., **The Papers of John Marshall**, pp. 37-87. The brevity of John Marshall's formal education in the law seems hardly credible but it is amply documented in his papers.

29. Johann Kalb, 1721-1780, was a Bavarian peasant who served under the great Marshal Saxe in the War of the Austrian Succession (1740-48) and with distinction in the Seven Years' War (1756-63). In 1764 he married an heiress and retired from the army. He returned under the Comte de Broglie in 1776 and was commissioned a Brigadier. He came to America with Lafayette in 1777. He was a remarkable soldier, tall, handsome, intelligent and brave. His bogus title was adopted simply because it seemed to be what the Americans expected of foreigners of high rank.

in the meantime been joined by 120 survivors of Pulaski's Legion.³⁰ On the 25th of July he turned over his command to Gates at Coxe's Mill on Deep River.

Aside from Harrison's Artillery, the only other Virginia units in North Carolina at the time were 700 militia under General Edward Stevens of Culpeper, and 100 militiamen whom Lieutenant Colonel Charles Porterfield of Frederick County had managed to keep in the field after the surrender of Charleston. Stevens, who had resigned the colonelcy of the 10th Virginia Regiment to become a Brigadier General of militia, commanded raw recruits from all parts of Virginia. Some may have come from Fauquier or Culpeper Counties, but none has been identified as such. Porterfield, on the other hand, had experienced men, some of whom had, like himself, served in the Continental Line, but had not rejoined after Morgan resigned. Kalb was unable to make contact with either Virginia unit at the time.

When Gates relieved Kalb he announced that the "Grand Army" would march at a moment's notice. "The ... Order was a matter of great astonishment to those who knew the real situation ... but all difficulties were removed by the general's assurances that plentiful supplies of rum and rations were on the Route," wrote Colonel Otho Williams.³¹ Those who knew the country urged that the "Grand Army" circle westward through Salisbury and Charlotte, a route that would take them through fertile country

---

30. Pulaski's Legion was a cavalry unit under the command of Casimir, Count Pulaski, which Washington sent south in February, 1779. Pulaski was mortally wounded in a gallant but fool-hardy charge against the British at Savannah, 9 Oct. 1779. Boatner says that he died aboard the U. S. brig **Wasp** and was buried at sea. According to the records of the Glascock family he was rescued from the British by Capt. Thomas Glascock, a Georgia relative of the Fauquier Glascocks, and died in his arms. He is buried in at least two places on land, according to records of almost equal validity. Capt. Glascock later joined a Virginia Regiment as a Lt. and is often confused with Thomas Glascock of Fauquier County, d. 1793. Northen, W. J., ed., **Men of Mark in Georgia**, 1910. Two vols.

31. Otho Holland Williams, 1749-1794, was born in Frederick, Md. shortly after his parents emigrated from southern Wales. He was commissioned a Lieutenant in Capt. Thomas Price's rifle corps and succeeded to command of Col. Hugh Stephenson's regiment of Virginia and Maryland riflemen after the latter's death before Sept. 1776. He was wounded at Fort Washington but was released from prison in time to march south with Kalb. He was an outstanding combat commander and also the author of a splendid **Narrative** which is much used and quoted by historians.

where the local inhabitants were sympathetic. Gates, immune to good advice as always, chose a more direct route through pine barrens and swamps, infested by Tories. When the promised rum and rations did not materialize, Gates assured the troops that they would find abundant corn on the Peedee River. They did, but the corn was still green. From a diet of green peaches they changed to a diet of green corn, and got equally sick on both.

After crossing the Peedee on the 3rd of August, they were joined by Porterfield's militia and Francis Marion's "swamp fox," as sad-looking an outfit as one could imagine. Gates was disgusted with their appearance and, when Marion suggested that they go to the interior on reconnaissance, Gates agreed. It was one of his few intelligent decisions.[32] Considerably less brilliant was his reply to Colonels William Washington and Anthony White, who were trying to build a cavalry unit around the survivors of Lenud's Ferry and Monck's Corner. When they asked Gates' support in recruiting horsemen and mounts and offered to join him, Gates refused help and offered the opinion that he did not think the south good cavalry country![33] Since Washington and White could not have saved the day at Camden by themselves, they could soon count their blessings; fate in the form of an idiot general had intervened to protect them.

Although the British controlled Georgia and South Carolina, the situation of Cornwallis was somewhat precarious. His 8,300 men were widely scattered and many were sick. There were 800 in hospitals in Camden alone, who must be abandoned if the place

32. Francis Marion, ca. 1732-1795, and his "swamp fox", may not have been much to look at but their performance was terrific. Marion was a Lieutenant Colonel of militia when a lucky break enabled him to escape from Charleston just before the surrender (see Lossing). As a guerrilla leader he was audacious and imaginative. Tarleton, dispatched by Cornwallis to take him reported, "as for this damned old fox, the devil himself could not catch him." Colonel John W. T. Watson complained that Marion "would not fight like a gentleman or a Christian." In short, he kept the British in a state of perpetual apprehension.

33. William Johnson, **Sketches of the Life and Correspondence of Nathanael Greene**, Vol. I, p. 506. "He did not conceal ... that he held cavalry in no estimation in the southern field."

was not defended. As the youthful Lord Rawdon,[34] who commanded at Camden, learned that Gates with an estimated 7,000 troops was headed in his direction, he sent frantic appeals to Cornwallis in Charleston. He dared not remove the garrisons from Hanging Rock and Rocky Mountain, which had been held with difficulty against Thomas Sumpter's[35] South Carolina Partisans.

On the 11th of August Gates found Rawdon strongly entrenched 15 miles N. E. of Camden. Though his troops outnumbered the British at least three to one, nothing could be gained by an attack across a broad marsh in front of the British stronghold. If he had bypassed them and made a dash for Camden, he could easily have taken it with near fatal consequences to the enemy. Instead Gates attempted an elaborate flanking movement which wasted time and allowed Rawdon an orderly withdrawal to Camden, covered by Tarleton's dragoons.

Gates had reached Rugeley's Mill (now Clermont) on the 14th of August when General Edward Stevens joined him with 700 Virginia militia. This swelled Gates' force to about 4,100. Cornwallis thought he had 7,000, and so apparently did the "Hero of Saratoga" who waved aside efforts to tell him otherwise. "There are enough for our purpose," he said grandly, though not entirely sure what that purpose was. Cornwallis reached Camden on the evening of August 13th. He had, at most, 2,250 men fit for duty, but they were seasoned veterans. Believing himself outnumbered three to one but unwilling to abandon the sick and the quantity of stores in Camden, he decided to fight.

34. Francis Rawdon-Hastings, Lord Rawdon, 1754-1826. Irish nobleman, served at Bunker Hill and was aide-de-camp to Clinton and later on the staff of Cornwallis, with whom he came to the southern theatre. Rawdon had "a curious reputation as the 'ugliest man in England' " (Peckham, **War for Independence**, p. 136) but he was tall, vigorous and had a fine bearing. He was also humorous, as witness his letter from Staten Island, Aug. 1776: "The fair nymphs of this isle are in wonderful tribulation, as the fresh meat our men have got here has made them as riotous as satyrs. A girl cannot step into the bushes to pluck a rose without running the most imminent risk of being ravished, and they are so little accustomed to these vigorous methods that they do not bear them with the proper resignation, and of consequence we have most entertaining courts-martial every day."

35. Thomas Sumpter, 1734-1832, was a son of a Welsh redemptioner, born near Charlottesville, Va. He was with Braddock. He was jailed in Staunton, Va. in 1762 for some unexplained peccadillo, but escaped to South Carolina. As an effective leader of partisan militia in the Revolution, he was known as the "Carolina Gamecock".

At this stage in the game Gates' councils of war were merely announcements to his staff of his intended course of action. When Gates informed them on the 15th of August that he proposed to march his starving troops through the woods at night to Saunders Creek, five miles from Camden and attack at dawn, they were too stunned to protest. Gates clearly implied that he was not interested in their views. Armand, who commanded the remains of Pulaski's Legion, learning that they were expected to lead the van, pointed out that mounted troops were wrong for such a mission, Gates brushed him aside. Some rations had been corralled to give the men something to eat that night, to which Gates added a touch that might have been hilariously comic if the result had not been so serious.

The men were so hungry that they wolfed the half-cooked rations. There was no rum, but there was plenty of molasses. Gates had the brilliant idea of issuing each man a gill of this delicacy as a substitute. The combination of half-baked bread, raw meat and a mixture of molasses and corn meal mush produced an effect on the men's digestive apparatus little short of disastrous. Sparing the reader the scatologic detail of contemporary accounts, it is enough to say that the men were "breaking ranks all night and were certainly much debilitated before ... morning."[36]

Gates started from Rugeley's Mill toward Camden about 10 p.m., coincidentally, just as Cornwallis left Camden to attack *him* at Rugeley's Mill. The advanced cavalry clashed about 2:30 on the morning of the 16th of August, but broke off contact after fifteen minutes of hot encounter. Gates called a council of war. Having by then realized that he had committed his entire army to an engagement for which he had no plan, he hoped that someone would propose a retreat, which he could then blame on the others. He was met with a painful silence. Finally General Stevens broke the ice. "Gentlemen, is it not too late *now* to do anything but fight?" he asked tentatively. He was thunderstruck by Gates' response. "We must fight then," said Gates, "To your commands, gentlemen."[37] The council gasped. Thus the strategic planning of the Battle of Camden was begun at the eleventh hour,

---

36. Otho Williams, **Narrative**.

37. Modern historians generally agree that Stevens was merely asking an honest question, normal to an experienced general only lately arrived at the scene of action. It is no reflection on Stevens' unquestioned bravery to doubt that the accolades bestowed upon him in this instance were really justified.

based on a simple question asked by an officer who had joined them only the day before yesterday.

Gates had, in addition to superior numbers, slightly more favorable terrain. Cornwallis, with his back to Saunders Creek had no depth in which to manoeuvre. Believing himself hopelessly outnumbered and well aware that defeat would amount to annihilation because of the obstacle at his rear, he prepared to attack. The American line, as arranged by Gates, was ample evidence that he knew nothing of the capabilities of his troops or even how many there were. On the left, where the terrain favored an enemy flanking movement, he placed Stevens' terrified Virginia recruits. North Carolina militia made up most of the center and Gist's Maryland Brigade formed the right wing. The six remaining guns of Harrison's 1st Virginia Artillery were grouped forward of center. Two guns had been loaned to Sumpter and ten had been left behind for want of horses.

Settled in a command post well to the rear, Gates waited for the battle to happen. As he apparently intended to give no further orders, the conduct of the battle was taken over by Otho Williams, the brilliant Welshman, who was his Adjutant General. If anything could have saved the situation, Williams would have done it, but it was past saving. Half of Gates' regulars were kept in reserve and the rest were with Gist, far from Stevens' hapless recruits. When the British charged the American left, the latter threw down their *loaded* arms and fled in panic. The North Carolinians in the center immediately followed suit. There were isolated pockets of resistance but most of the militia (at least two thirds of the army) fled without firing a shot.

Having put the American left to flight, the British wheeled to roll up the exposed flank of the American right. There they met stiff resistance. The fog and smoke of battle isolated the right from the realization that they stood alone against the entire enemy army. They were soon engaged in hand-to-hand combat and the Continentals refused to budge. Kalb, in command of the right wing, was sufficiently hard pressed to call for the reserve when his flank was attacked, but he would not retreat without orders from Gates. Unhorsed and bleeding from multiple wounds, he attempted a counter attack, but soon fell mortally wounded. Tarleton's horse then struck from the rear, having abandoned pursuit of the left wing. The battle was over.

The wave of panic that struck the Virginia militia was not long in reaching headquarters. Gates, incoherent and shaking with fear, fled the scene without looking back. He paused briefly at Rugeley's Mill, but not long enough to prevent his reaching Charlotte, 60 miles north, on the day of the battle. Two days later found him at Hillsborough, North Carolina, 120 miles farther from Camden. On the 22nd of August, Gates wrote to Governor Caswell of North Carolina, "I therefore resolved to proceed directly thither to give orders for assembling the Continental Troops on the march from Virginia." Apparently, as the battle raged on the morning of the 16th of August, it had suddenly occurred to Gates that he should be somewhere else doing something quite different. That was his story, and he would stick to it.[38] Fortunately the military reputations of the Virginia commanders were not lost on the field at Camden. The personal courage of General Edward Stevens in his attempts to rally his terrified men, was widely applauded. Congress was pleased to commend, among others, Colonel Charles Porterfield and his corps of Light Infantry for their bravery and good conduct. Porterfield did not really care. The heroic Virginian from Frederick County, who had climbed the heights of Quebec with Morgan and had emerged unscathed from countless battles since, was mortally wounded.

The day before Camden, Gates had imprudently loaned Thomas Sumpter not only two badly needed field pieces, but also 100 Maryland Continentals and 300 North Carolina militia. With them Sumpter achieved a modest success at Wateree Ferry, capturing 30 men and a rather considerable number of stores. As soon as Tarleton had Camden under his belt, he set out in pursuit of Sumpter. He found him and his men resting at Fishing Creek, North Carolina, their arms stacked, some asleep, some cooking and others bathing in the creek. Wasting no time, Tarleton attacked, killing 150 of Sumpter's force, capturing 300, and releasing the British prisoners. He also recaptured most of the stores. Sumpter escaped, but barely. Coatless, on an unsaddled horse, he reached Hanging Rock two days later.

For the first time in the controversial career of General Horatio Gates he found no one who would listen to his excuses. Even Congress had had enough. The news of the defeat at Camden burst like a thunderclap over the north and reverberated ominously in the Virginia mountains already wrapped in the dark cloud of Charleston and Waxhaws. Two armies had been thrown away in the South, armies that had contained many of Virginia's sons, ill-equipped and, many of them, hopelessly unprepared for battle. The

---

38. Contemporaries, among them "Lighthorse Harry" Lee and Nathanael Greene, have been remarkably kind to Gates. Montross in **Rag, Tag and Bobtail,** says that it probably did not occur to Gates that his political foes would "insinuate cowardice."

time was fast approaching when only the State troops and the militia could offer a buffer against Cornwallis and his marauding army.

Watching in helpless agony were two Virginians who had served their country well but were, through the machinations of army politics, denied the opportunity to exert their talents to stem the tide of British victory. Congress had not forgotten them, though it seemed little disposed to grant them any balm for their wounded pride. On the 16th of June Brigadier General George Weedon and Colonel Daniel Morgan were summarily ordered by Congress to join Gates, in what capacity Congress did not stipulate.

After the fall of Charleston, Weedon had actively sought a command, but Virginia offered him nothing. His old friend John Page was no longer Lieutenant-Governor and the new Governor, Thomas Jefferson, seemed to be lost in the fog of his own ineptitude and bewilderment with military matters. Washington, himself, threw cold water on his request for a command outside Virginia, pointing out correctly in a letter to Joseph Jones that every State with troops enough of its own to form a Brigade wanted it commanded by one of its own officers. Nevertheless, pocketing his pride after the defeat at Camden, Weedon offered to help train the raw recruits in whom Virginia's last hope rested. He hurried to Richmond to help bolster the morale of the distraught Governor.

The order of Congress made no mention of giving Daniel Morgan the promotion he deserved, or even of restoring him to the relative rank he held at the time of his retirement. He was badly crippled with rheumatism or sciatica (more recently diagnosed as arthritis) and riding was agony for him. However, when he heard of the disaster at Camden he forgot his aches and pains, as well as his personal grievances and hastened to join Gates at Hillsborough. Having served under Gates at Saratoga, he knew only too well how desperately leadership was needed there. He arrived late in September.

It is not improbable that, on his way south, Morgan passed through Fauquier. How else can we explain the sudden burst of patriotism that impelled a single county in the Virginia piedmont to send in his wake a revitalized militia unit that would turn the tide of battle when it was most needed? Yet that, by and large, was what happened. The men of Fauquier were approaching their finest hour.

The Fauquier militia had not much but blisters to show for five years of marching up and down again. Its history, after the Battle of Great Bridge has been told, is best recapitulated in the pension application of Benjamin Martin,[39] who had served since the first gun. Benjamin Martin was a true son of Fauquier. His ancestor, John Joseph Martin, had been one of those stalwart German pioneers, who had headed one of the twelve families that had settled Germantown in 1720. Through thrift and imagination the Martins had prospered, but they had never held public office or taken much interest in public affairs. They were always interested in the militia, though, and most early rosters contain their name.

Young Benjamin was seventeen when he quit the house of his father, Henry Martin, in September of 1775 to join Captain William Pickett's company of minutemen on the march that led to Great Bridge. He was a guard "off to the left of our works" at the end of Great Bridge when Captain Fordyce made his gallant and foolish bid for glory. He had watched in bemused silence as Norfolk went up in flames and continued his guard duty until the end of March, 1776, when he was discharged in Suffolk County until further orders. At that time Colonel Marshall and Colonel Scott had enlisted each a regiment of regulars for Washington's army, and John Marshall commanded a company. They had, he wrote, "nothing more to do with the minute men." Nearly 60 years later, there is still a hint of disappointment.

As the Virginia Line moved north in the summer of 1776, with banners aloft and bugles blowing, the minutemen were called upon to protect the mouths of the rivers against British raiding parties intent on plunder and destroying the salt works. Captain James Winn commanded their company under Colonel Elias Edmonds, Sr. For convenience they were stationed at Springfield Camp[40] near Williamsburg. After three months the raids had subsided and most of the men were sick. They were again discharged until further orders, but that was the last call they received as minutemen.

Benjamin Martin was among those who marched north to no useful purpose in the autumn of 1777, only to arrive after the Battle of Germantown. He was a corporal by then, in Captain Benjamin Harrison's company, with James Key as Lieutenant. On the way through Lancaster County in Pennsylvania they encountered Anthony Wayne's men wounded at Paoli, grimly

---

39. Benjamin Martin, 1758-1838, married, 20 June 1781, Nancy Kemper, 1760-1841, probably a sister of the man for whom he substituted. They moved to Barren Co., Kentucky.

40. Springfield Plantation, near Williamsburg, had been the training ground for the Virginia Continental Line since early in the war.

trudging toward Lancaster. Upon arrival they encamped near Marshall's 3rd Virginia Regiment. The next day they marched over the battlefield of Germantown. "I noticed a gate below a house they called Chew's house. The gate was very much shattered with grape or canister shot and the Blood of the men that had been killed was plainly to be seen on the ground." It was a sobering experience, but not discouraging. At least it did not prevent his thorough satisfaction when the Americans blew up the 64-gun British ship *Augusta* in the Delaware River. "Tremendous was the explosion it made," he wrote enthusiastically. About the middle of December he went home with the rest of the Fauquier troops.

He was twenty-two in the summer of 1780 when the bugle again called. In reality the call was not for him but for his friend and relative, James Kemper,[41] but Kemper was married and he was still single. He had seen enough of war and heard enough of the danger that threatened to realize that this would be no idle tour of a deserted battlefield. The blood that would be spilled might be his own. Yet he volunteered under Captain Francis Triplett in a company with John Combs [42] as 1st Lieutenant to march to Hillsborough to join Gates and the new army.

There was not much in the previous known history of Francis Triplett that would lead one to expect him to lead this adventurous expedition. He was not young (52), had been a cadet under Braddock and a recruiting officer under Washington in Alexandria, but he had little combat experience. He had, as far as is known, commanded troops only briefly, before the Battle of Germantown, but they had been miles from the scene of action. His only known military asset was his long and enduring friendship with Daniel Morgan. Morgan thought he could do anything and, under Morgan, he believed he could also. Apparently Captain James Winn believed so too. At any rate, Winn undertook to raise a company and march with him.

James Winn, a younger son of Minor Winn who died in Fauquier County in 1778, had been a militia captain a long time. After returning from Williamsburg in the winter of 1776, he dropped out of sight and one wonders why he was not embroiled in the internecine war that engrossed the Fauquier militia in the spring of 1778. The answer is given us by William Ramlin Withers [43] who was with him. They were in Colonel William

---

41. James Kemper was possibly a brother of Peter Kemper, See note No. 11, Chapter IX.

42. John Combs, see note No. 32, Chapter VIII.

43. William Ramlin Withers, see note No. 50, Chapter III.

Crawford's Virginia Regiment at Fort Pitt. Withers enlisted under him in the autumn of 1777 and served two years.

Colonel William Crawford, whom we last met at Brandywine, had been asked by Washington to serve at Fort Pitt under General Edward Hand. In May of 1778 he took command of the new Virginia regiment formed by General Lachlan McIntosh,[44] in which Winn was then serving. When General Hand resigned in August, McIntosh took over at Fort Pitt and Crawford led a number of punitive raids against the Indians, who were pushing deeper into the white settlements of the Ohio country. Winn saw hard duty under Crawford and, in the autumn of 1779, returned to Fauquier. Withers returned with him.

It is reasonable to suppose that the companies raised by Triplett and Winn included some men from the militia they had previously commanded, but both of them tried hard to secure enlistments from Fauquier men who had had earlier service with the Continental Line. They were apparently successful, because the record shows that they were customarily given the responsibility and treatment of trained veterans. Unfortunately this cannot be proven from pension records, since only the youngest survived until 1833 when most of the pension applications were filed. In some instances the pension applications fail to mention previous service, though it is clearly implied. Spencer Withers, for instance, who enlisted under Captain Francis Triplett, was immediately appointed orderly sergeant, a post he could hardly have held without some previous experience.

It appears also that many of the men who were obligated to serve sent substitutes instead who were more experienced. Benjamin Martin, as mentioned before, was a substitute for James Kemper. Peter Bashaw,[45] a veteran at 17, substituted for Joseph Jones for three months when his tour of duty expired and he was

---

44. Lachlan McIntosh, 1725-1806, was born in Inverness, Scotland and came to Georgia with his parents at the age of 11. He had a chequered career which culminated in the killing of Button Gwinnett, the Signer, in a duel. Although considered "the handsomest man in Georgia", he was lazy and incompetent. After commanding the North Carolina troops at Valley Forge he was ordered to the Western Department in May of 1778.

45. Peter Bashaw, 1763-post 1864, son of James and Frances (Taylor) Bashaw, was around when most Revolutionary veterans had quit the stage. In 1809, apparently still unmarried, he moved to Davidson Co., Tenn. On the 26th of March 1864 one Nathaniel Cross wrote from Nashville that Peter Bashaw, aged 101, was still living in a somewhat indefinite area known as White's Creek.

discharged at Charlotte, North Carolina. He was something of a professional substitute and had as later clients Harmon Utterback [46] and Josiah Holtzclaw. [47]

Captain Francis Triplett sat on the Fauquier County Court held on the 28th of August, 1780, and returned a list of tithables taken by him. Other lists of tithables were not returned until September, indicating an interest on Triplett's part in getting that bit of business out of the way before his departure. At the same court one of his men, James Bailey, was placed under a £250 bond for behaving himself "til he joins the troops at the general Rendezvous." Captain James Winn and his wife Hannah (Withers) Winn are joined in a deed recorded in the September Court, but it may well have been executed earlier, before his departure.

We learn from the pension record of the obstreperous James Bailey that the two companies numbered 170 men. The exact day of their departure is somewhat up in the air. Benjamin Martin says that they left Fauquier Courthouse on the 1st of September, passing through Fredericksburg, Richmond, Petersburg, thence to Hillsborough, North Carolina where they joined the Maryland troops under Colonel Howard. Thomas O'Bannon, one of Winn's men, says that they left after the 4th of September, to his later regret when his pension application was not accepted because he had served four days less than the required six months. John Fishback [48] the 23 year old son of Philip Fishback, who lived a short

46. Harmon Utterback, 1746-1826, was a descendant of the first of his name to come to Virginia from Musen in the province of Nassau, Germany, at the invitation of Governor Spotswood in 1714. He was born at Germantown and married (1) Elizabeth Crump; (2) Margaret Strumatt. At the time of the Revolution a Harmon Utterback was a prosperous farmer and large landowner in Fauquier. Another Harmon Utterback, 1755-1854, served as a Private in Captain Wm. McClanahan's "Baptist Company" from Culpeper County.

47. Presumably Josiah Holtzclaw, ca. 1745-1816, son of John and grandson of the Emigrant, Jacob Holtzclaw who settled in Fauquier County in 1720. Although he hired a substitute, he furnished supplies (beef) to the Fauquier Militia.

48. John Fishback, 1757-post 1839, was a descendant of another Germantown settler, John Fishback, who, with his son John Philip, later took up large grants on the slopes of the Pignut and on "Fishback's Ridge" a spur of the Bull Run Mountains. John Fishback married Martha (Patty) Pickett, b. 1760, daughter of William Sanford and Elizabeth (Metcalf) Pickett. They moved to Bracken Co., Ky., soon after their marriage in 1785.

distance down the road from Winn, told his sister, Mary Strother, that they marched around the 1st of October. George Rogers,[49] drafted in August, gives the same route as Martin and tends to confirm his dates.

Through the last golden days of Indian summer the Fauquier men marched south. They had thought to stop in Richmond to pick up tents and other much-needed items of clothes and equipment, but found the shelves of the commissary empty. Governor Jefferson, frustrated and helpless, told them that "the situation as to clothing is desperate" but he hoped to send them some later.[50] They continued undiscouraged. As old line veterans, they had not really expected much.

On the 7th of October Gates announced a new arrangement of his troops, modelled to a large extent on the elite battalion of light infantry that had served under Wayne at Stony Point. At last Morgan would have what had been denied him in New Jersey, command of a special force, picked to suit his own specifications. Selected men were drawn from the Maryland, Delaware and Virginia Continentals and made into three companies of light infantry to which were added some expert riflemen and cavalry. A few veterans from Buford's corps of the 3rd Virginia Regiment formed the nucleus of the 1st company under Captain Peter Bruin, one of Morgan's stalwarts who came from Ashby's Bent. The 2nd and 3rd companies were chosen from Maryland and Delaware Continentals under the command of Captains Benjamin Brookes and the gallant Robert Kirkwood[51] of New Castle, Delaware. To these were added 70 horsemen under Lieutenant Colonel William Washington and 60 Virginia riflemen under Captain James Tate.

49. George Rogers, 1764-1858, was a son of Henry and Elizabeth (Lankford) Rogers of Somerville, Fauquier Co. He married 27 October 1791, Elizabeth Randall, 1772-1861. His father is listed among those who furnished supplies to the army.

50. Gen. Nathanael Greene, passing by in mid-November, fared no better. He was obliged to leave Baron Steuben behind in Richmond to forward whatever he could beg, borrow or steal. Virginia pleaded poverty so great that they could not even furnish forage for the horses. See Ward, **The American Revolution**, p. 479.

51. Robert Kirkwood, 1730-1791. Called by Greene "the American Diomedes" after the legendary Greek hero at the siege of Troy, and by Lee "the gallant Kirkwood", the brave Delawarian was killed in action in 1791 fighting Indians in Ohio. "It was the thirty-third time he had risked his life for his country," wrote Lee, "and he died as he had lived, the brave, meritorious, unrewarded Kirkwood."

The infantry of this new *corps d'elite* were commanded by Lieutenant Colonel John Eager Howard [52] of Maryland.

It was into this splendid company that the Fauquier men under Triplett and Winn were received with joy on both sides. In spite of the deplorable lack of stores of any kind, the light infantry fared rather better than the rest of Gates' army. The State of North Carolina, though its resources were almost exhausted, managed, "to collect a suit of comfortable clothing for each one of Morgan's command before they entered upon the severe and active duties before them." Each man got one new shirt, a short coat, a pair of woolen overalls or trousers, a pair of shoes and a hat or cap. The state also "supplied the other troops, but not so comfortably as Morgan's." [53] There were not enough blankets to go round but, wise to the ways of the commissary, the Fauquier men had brought their own.

So Morgan's command was the heir and successor to the old Virginia Continental Line. The spirit of Trenton and Brandywine was not lost, merely sleeping. What is really astonishing is the high percentage of them who had been born in the foothills of the Blue Ridge and had watched at nightfall its long purple shadow creep across their father's farms. Once more they served under a leader who, like Thomas Marshall, was one of their own. Morgan, they thought, would see to it that theirs was a post of honour. Morgan would not let them down.

On the 13th of October Congress, at long last, raised Morgan to the rank of Brigadier General. For the "Old Waggoner" fortune's wheel had turned full circle. General Horatio Gates now looked to him to repair the tattered fabric of his once-great reputation.

52. John Eager Howard, 1752-1827, was a well-educated son of a rich Maryland planter when he became Captain in the 2nd Maryland Battalion of Gen. Hugh Mercer's "Flying Camp" in July, 1776. He fought with distinction at White Plains, Germantown and Monmouth. As Lieutenant Colonel of the 2nd Maryland Regiment, he even came through Camden with his reputation intact. Greene said that he was "as good an officer as the world affords" and Lee wrote "He was justly ranked among the chosen sons of the South." He married, 18 May 1787, Margaret (Peggy) Oswald Chew, daughter of Chief Justice Benjamin Chew of Pennsylvania, whose mansion at Germantown he had helped to wreck.

53. William Johnson, **Sketches of the Life and Correspondence of Nathanael Greene**, Vol. I, p. 508.

54. In Fauquier it is considered irrelevant and immaterial that Morgan's estate "Saratoga" happens to lie in Clarke County. He was their man, and you had better believe it.

Interlude
Kings Mountain

Lord Cornwallis had every reason to be pleased with himself after the Battle of Camden. Having vanquished his only formidable opponent in the South, he confidently expected the rich province of North Carolina to fall into his lap like a ripe plum. Nevertheless he planned his strategy carefully, relying heavily on expected help from Tory sympathizers, whom he imagined existed in large numbers, waiting only for a little encouragement from him.

Toward the end of September he advanced the main army to Charlotte, North Carolina, detaching his right wing to move up along the coast to secure Wilmington and the Cape Fear River as a supply route. His left wing, composed entirely of American loyalists under Major Patrick Ferguson, who were already operating in the back country of South Carolina, was to strike northward under the shadow of the western mountains, picking up Loyalist recruits along the way. On the 23rd of September Ferguson was at Old Fort, North Carolina, near the source of the Catawba River in the Blue Ridge Mountains.

Ferguson, without knowing it, was tempting fate. West of the mountains in the valleys of the Holston and Clinch Rivers in what is now eastern Tennessee and southwestern Virginia, had settled a hardy group of pioneers from western Pennsylvania, Maryland and Virginia, who had moved from more populous regions to enjoy the freedom for which the colonies were now fighting. They were beholden to no man, paid no taxes and, in short, needed no Declaration of Independence. They *were* independent. Furthermore, they were ready to defend that independence from the inroads of any British *or* Americans who dared dispute it.

On the 10th of September Ferguson paroled one Samuel Phillips and sent him across the Blue Ridge to tell the "over Mountain men" to "desist from opposition to British arms and take protection under his standard." Otherwise he would "march his army over the mountains, hang their leaders and lay their country waste with fire and sword." Young Phillips carried his message and to it added a few embellishments. He had heard of "Tarleton's Quarter", the burning of plantations along the Catawba and Broad Rivers and the sorry plight of the women and children who had stood in the way of the British.

The "over Mountain men" were very literal-minded. It did not occur to them that Ferguson's threat must be an idle one. No commander in his right mind would try what Ferguson proposed, and Ferguson was no fool. They decided that they had better go and get Ferguson before Ferguson got them. That is what they did.

The rendezvous was set for 25 September at Sycamore Shoals on the Watauga near present Elizabethton, Tennessee. More than 1,000 men showed up, most of them mounted and carrying the long hunting rifle of the frontier. From Virginia came the giant Indian fighter, Colonel William Campbell, with 400 men. A week or so later they were joined by several hundred South Carolinians. Though the "over Mountain men" were in the minority, they gave their name to the little army.

When Major Ferguson learned that this rabble was on his trail he was not greatly worried. He began a slow retreat toward Charlotte and, on the way, espied a natural fortification which seemed to him ideal for defense. He did not particularly relish the idea of marching to Cornwallis' headquarters with this tatterdemalion crew at his heels. It might appear as though he was afraid of them. He decided to make a stand at King's Mountain.

Rising 60 feet above a relatively flat terrain, the rugged slopes of King's Mountain looked impregnable. The sides were boulder-strewn and heavily wooded but, at the top, was a treeless ridge on which Ferguson could deploy his forces in classic British style. He had with him about 800 Loyalist militia and 100 picked men from the King's American Rangers, the Queen's Rangers and the New Jersey volunteers. He was the only Englishman on King's Mountain.

For the man who had invented the breech-loaded rifle, Ferguson was curiously myopic in one respect. He failed to realize that God, in his infinite wisdom, had especially designed King's Mountain to favor exactly the sort of force that was marching against him. As an example of efficient encirclement and precision in attack, the "over Mountain men" and their allies set some sort of record. The trees, boulders and ravines of the slopes did not constitute an obstacle to the attackers but provided marvellous defensive positions for riflemen. Suddenly aware of his first fatal error, Ferguson, possibly the best marksman in the British army, promptly made a second worse one: he decided to defend King's Mountain with the bayonet! After a number of useless sorties his men were driven back into the open camp area where the surrounding sharpshooters, safely ensconced in trees and almost impossible to see, could pick them off one by one. Some death-wish impelled Ferguson to insist on wearing a checked red shirt. He was a neat target for no fewer than nine squirrel-hunters. The "over Mountain men" showed some disposition to visit "Tarleton's Quarter" upon the hapless Loyalists but wiser heads soon prevailed. None, however, escaped capture.

No Fauquier men participated in the Battle of King's Mountain but their spirits were lifted by the first ray of light to penetrate the gloom of defeat. It altered the course of war in the South. It tipped the balance of Loyalist support in favor of the patriot cause. It forced Cornwallis to withdraw from Charlotte, which he found "an agreeable village, but in a damned rebellious country," to Winnsboro, South Carolina, and delayed his offensive three months. It was, according to Sir Henry Clinton, "the first link of a chain of evils ... that at last ended in the total loss of America."

After the Battle of King's Mountain the "over Mountain men" went home, their mission accomplished. As a fighting force, they were never heard of again, but then it is not recorded that anyone ever again tried to obtain their submission by idle threats.

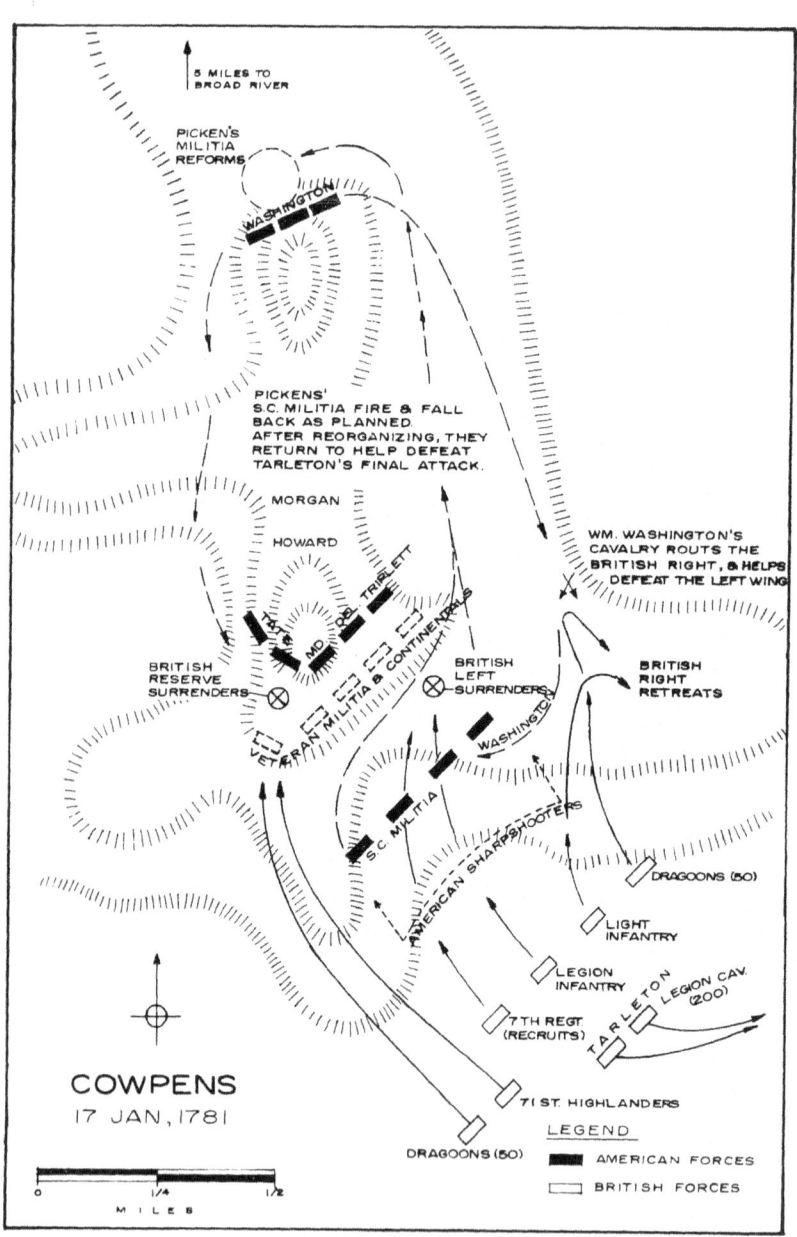

XI

Cowpens

Washington honestly believed that Major General Nathanael Greene of Rhode Island possessed the finest military mind that had flowered in American since the war began. He was entirely correct, but he had great difficulty persuading Congress to see it his way. The blunt, 38 year old New Englander was too apt to confront the Congress with unpleasant truths for him to win wide popularity amongst them. However, in the autumn of 1780, Congress was at its collective wit's end. They had appointed Robert Howe, who had lost Savannah for them, as well as the rest of Georgia. Next they named Benjamin Lincoln, who lost Charleston and most of South Carolina. They had then called on Gates who lost the whole army and the rest of the south. They decided to throw the choice of Gates' successor in Washington's lap. Washington selected Greene without the slightest hesitancy.

Greene was at West Point wondering vaguely whether his recent refusal to continue as Quartermaster General would tempt Congress to dismiss him from the army.[1] He did not much care. The Continental Congress had been a wretched and ungrateful employer. Only one man had his respect and could galvanize him to action. That man was his Excellency, George Washington. He accepted the command modestly, and promised nothing. After exhorting Congress, the new Quartermaster General, Timothy Pickering, and the Board of War to obtain clothing and supplies, and receiving little or nothing, he went on his way. Congress gave him $180,000 in Continental currency, which was virtually worthless.

---

1. Thomas Mifflin, the man who had failed so miserably as Quartermaster General, had presented a plan for reorganizing Greene's department on the 27th of March, 1780. Congress approved the plan on the 15th of July, and Greene announced that he would no longer serve in that capacity. Some delegates made an unsuccessful attempt to have him expelled from the army.

At Annapolis, Greene pleaded with the Maryland Board of War for clothing and left General Mordecai Gist[2] in Baltimore to arrange for forwarding whatever he could collect. Similarly he appealed to Jefferson in Richmond for clothing and supplies. Jefferson could offer little hope that anything would be forthcoming. There was not even forage for his horses. He did, however, obtain a promise of reinforcements as soon as they could be equipped. General Edward Stevens had 400 new recruits under his command, among whom were some experienced men who had re-enlisted.

In addition the 1st Virginia Regiment of Artillery was encamped at Yorktown and, although it had been much reduced by the expiration of enlistments, he might still obtain help there. His old friend, Colonel Thomas Marshall, though still in command, had been encouraged by the Virginia House of Delegates to go to Kentucky during the previous summer to arrange for the survey of bounty lands to be granted to the Virginia troops. This was a crucial issue on which the success of recruitment depended. Marshall's surveying experience together with a military record that had earned him the confidence of the Virginia line, made him an ideal man for the job.[3]

Lieutenant Colonel Elias Edmonds was in command at Yorktown. He was ready and willing to move south with Greene, provided, of course, his regiment was released by the Board of

---

2. Mordecai Gist, 1743-1792, was a nephew of Christopher Gist, the Maryland colonial scout, and probably a cousin of Nathaniel Gist (see note No. 16, Chap. VI). He was a Baltimore business man before the war. After distinguishing himself at Long Island, he was promoted to Colonel and commanded the 3rd Maryland Regiment at Germantown. He came south with Kalb and fought brilliantly at Camden. Thereafter he returned north and joined Greene who employed him in gathering supplies, especially in Maryland, where he was widely respected.

3. By 1780 the influx of settlers in Kentucky had reached such proportions that the Virginia troops who had been promised land bounties became decidedly apprehensive that all the best land would be grabbed by speculators.

War. Although the number of rank and file was greatly reduced, the Board was unwilling to part with the entire unit. They did, however, release one artillery company under Captain Christopher Roan, with John Watlington as Captain-Lieutenant and Cary Wyatt as 1st Lieutenant.[5] It is probable that they took one or two light artillery pieces also, if they were able to liberate them from the Board.

Another of Greene's valuable acquisitions was Lieutenant Colonel Edward Carrington, formerly second in command to Colonel Charles Harrison, of the 1st Continental Artillery. Greene was greatly impressed with the intelligence and ability of this dedicated officer when he met him in Richmond. As Carrington was a Continental line officer, he was at liberty to join Greene.

Greene left Baron Steuben in Richmond to forward any supplies he could get and possibly help Stevens with his training. On the 27th of November he was at Hillsborough, North Carolina, only to find that, after the enemy defeat at King's Mountain, Gates had moved cautiously to Charlotte. On the 2nd of December he arrived at Charlotte to take over Gates' command.

Meanwhile Gates had not been idle. His single talent was for organization and, though his material was meagre, he had put together, at least on paper, a "shadow of an army." He had 90 cavalrymen under Lieutenant Colonel William Washington, 60 artillerymen and 2,307 infantry, of whom only 1,482 were present and fit for duty. Only 949 of his foot were Continentals. The rest were militia, of whom only a few hundred were trained and could be counted on. The rest were local militia who came and went as they pleased, disputed orders and plundered the civilian population. Fewer than 800 of all ranks were properly clothed and equipped.

4. "The Board of War, although entrusted with important executive functions, consisted of an unpaid commission of three men. This body, aware of the growing criticism of military management, asked the House of Delegates in December, 1779, for pay and authority. Thereupon the legislature voted the Board of War salaries and ordered it to report to the governor ... these changes do not seem to have resulted in any improvement and the board was abolished at the most critical period of 1781." (H. J. Eckenrode, **The Revolution in Virginia**, pp. 206-7)

5. Colonel Thomas Marshall, 4 Feb. 1781, listed those under Captain Roan's command "to ye south". In addition to those named, Josiah Vallentine was 2nd Lieutenant and "according to the best accounts I am able to get of them" there were 26 rank and file enlisted for the war and between 30 and 40 whose terms of enlistment were nearly expired.

Brigadier General Daniel Morgan, working hard to build up the strength of his new light infantry, was delighted when new recruits from Virginia came in to join him. Augusta County sent an entire company. County Lieutenant Samuel McDowell of Rockbridge County, writing to Jefferson in April, mentioned that he had sent Captain James Gilmore, who had been with Colonel William Christian in the expedition against the Cherokees, to join Morgan with upward of 40 men. When the Augusta and Rockbridge men arrived Morgan had the happy idea of a complete Virginia battalion made up of Triplett's and Winn's Companies and the two new ones. He promoted Francis Triplett to Major to command it and raised John Combs to Captain to take over Triplett's company.[6] Lieutenant Colonel Howard remained in overall command of the infantry.

The record shows that Francis Triplett had brought a number of horses with him on his march to Hillsborough. Some were his own or had been wangled from his neighbors. Others were certainly ridden by their owners who had no intention of serving in the infantry if they could avoid it. It would appear that they had very probably joined in response to an urgent plea from Francis Triplett's son, Captain William Triplett. This young man, after the near-annihilation of Grayson's Additional Continental Regiment at Monmouth, had found his niche with Colonel William Washington's Horse. He had been with Washington at Monck's Corner and Lenud's Ferry, and took no pride in either engagement, but he was not discouraged. His faith in the cavalry was unbounded and he had no hesitancy in committing his own and his father's most precious possessions, their horses, to the cause. Slender, fairhaired, the 21 year old William Triplett was called "the Kentuckian" because he was one of few who had visited that distant land of promise. His year on the frontier had given him a pioneer's hardiness which combined well with his skill with a sabre and his passion for horses.

6. This information is from the very detailed pension claim of Benjamin Martin (R.6965) supported by a number of other pension records. No contradictory evidence has been found except that the Auditor's Account Book VII, p. 299, lists: "Saturday, the 17th of March, 1781, warrant to Captain Francis Triplett for pay of his company and Capt. James Winn's of Fauquier Militia on duty to the southward, Pay Rolls and certificates 85431-7." It is believed that Major Triplett was in Richmond on that date. News of his field promotion had not reached the auditor's office, but all official dispatches name him as "Major".

On reaching Hillsborough the young Fauquier centaurs had no difficulty transferring into the cavalry. Among them were John O'Bannon,[7] James Rogers,[8] William King[9] and several others. The fact that they were loved more for their splendid mounts than for themselves did not worry them. Of one thing they were certain. If Tarleton tried to take them, as he had so many, he would have a fight on his hands.

When Greene met Gates at Charlotte on the 2nd of December he was not disposed to embarrass the defeated general with any reference to what had gone before. He treated him with tact and courtesy, to which Gates replied with dignity and an earnest desire to be helpful. When Gates issued his last orders on the day following, announcing the change of officers, he courteously chose "Springfield",[10] scene of Greene's latest battle, for the parole and "Greene" for the countersign. It was a small thing, but graceful. When Greene addressed the army he paid Gates the compliment of confirming all his standing orders. Greene was looking forward, not backward. He had been charged with an investigation of Gates' past conduct. He ignored it. The task ahead was formidable enough in all conscience, without spending time raking old coals.

Confronted with the true state of the army (and Gates did nothing to conceal the bitter truth) Greene was appalled. Much of the trouble lay in Gates' Quartermaster and Commissary Departments. The quartermaster was "an honest young man" of limited experience and narrow viewpoint. Greene promptly

7. John O'Bannon, ca. 1760-1810, was a son of William and Anne (Neville) O'Bannon who lived near Marshall. He is listed by Capt. William Triplett as a cornet in his company, who resigned 6 Aug. 1781. He married, 1784, Mary Ann Winn. He later moved to Ohio where he made many surveys for Virginians entitled to bounty land.

8. James Rogers, 1760-post 1840, had served as a guard under Lt. John Combs of Fauquier escorting Hessian prisoners taken at Trenton from Noland's Ferry to Albemarle Barracks. He volunteered as a horseman under William Triplett and was with him 20 Aug. 1781. About 1784 he moved to Franklin Co., then called "New Virginia".

9. William King went as a substitute for his father "under General Gates." He served under William Triplett in Mecklenburg County. He was not the William King previously mentioned. (see Note No. 23, Chap. VII)

10. Springfield, N. J., 7-23 June 1780. Greene repulsed an attack by General Knyphausen and between 5,000 and 6,000 men. Greene had about 1,000 regulars and another 1,000 militia under General William Maxwell harassing the enemy's advance.

replaced him with Lieutenant Colonel Carrington. In every respect Carrington lived up to Greene's expectations. So also did William Richardson Davie,[11] whom Greene chose to replace the superannuated Colonel Polk as Commissary General. Having been a brilliant field commander, Davie was less than enchanted with his new post. To his protest that he knew nothing of money and accounts, Greene replied calmly, "Don't concern yourself. There is no money, hence no accounts." Once resigned to his fate, Davie faced the overwhelming difficulties resolutely and with considerable success.

Realizing the need for removing the troops from the neighborhood of Charlotte where their addiction to plundering had made them "a terror to the inhabitants", Greene sent his brilliant young Polish engineer, Thaddeus Kosciuszko,[12] to find a suitable alternate campsite, so that he might establish a "camp of repose for the purpose of repairing our waggons, recruiting our horses and disciplining our troops." He approved Gates' reorganization plans without change. He confirmed Morgan in command of the light infantry brigade and, after carefully going over Morgan's plans in detail, made only minor suggestions.

While all this was taking place William Washington's horsemen were absent with some of Morgan's light infantry. Camp life bored them and, though instructed not to become embroiled in any major engagement, they were encouraged to seek a little adventure at the expense of the enemy. They had galloped over to Salisbury and down into Mecklenburg County to cooperate with the local

11. William Richardson Davie, 1756-1820, born in England, was taken by his father to the Waxhaw settlement in South Carolina in 1763. After graduating from Princeton in 1776 he became a brilliant partisan leader in South Carolina. He married, 1782, Sarah Jones, the wealthy daughter of Gen. Allen Jones. He was Governor of North Carolina in 1798 and Peace Commissioner to France the year following.

12. Thaddeus Kosciuszko, 1746-1817, was a son of an impoverished Lithuanian gentleman. He was graduated from the Ecole Royale in Warsaw and studied engineering at Mezieres, France. He borrowed money to come to America but was soon employed by the Pennsylvania Committee of Defense to plan the Delaware River Forts. His fortifications at Saratoga played a large part in the American victory. He became a close friend of Gates and came to the Southern Department, arriving after Gates' defeat at Camden. He remained to give valuable advice to Greene, until 1783. After returning to Poland, his later career was even more distinguished than his service in America.

militia, but nothing "of consequence" happened. Then Washington heard that Colonel Henry Rugeley,[13] an American Loyalist officer, had fortified the barn on his estate "Clermont", about 12 miles north of Camden, and was holed up there with more than a hundred Tories. Washington remembered the place (usually called Rugeley's Mill) well. It was there that the American troops had gathered before Camden and Gates had delivered his considered opinion that the Southern Theatre was "not good cavalry country." Washington decided that it would do no harm to investigate.

Colonel Rugeley occupied a log barn surrounded by a ditch and abatis. It was impregnable to bullets, so Washington's horsemen could do nothing with it. Washington had no artillery but he had considerable native guile. No one had tried the "Quaker gun" trick lately. That ploy was to cut a pine log in the shape of a gun and move it into position, propped up on three stubs of its limbs. From a distance it could be quite convincing. This contraption was pushed boldly into a comspicuous location by some of his dismounted cavalry. Washington suggested politely to Colonel Rugeley that he had better surrender before his fortress was blown to smithereens. The trick worked. Out tumbled Colonel Rugeley, a major, and 107 privates. The promising military career of Colonel Rugeley had met a sudden end. On the 5th of December, when Greene badly needed something to cheer him up, Washington and his men appeared on the scene at Morgan's camp at "New" Providence [14] with their prisoners. It helped enormously - well out of proportion to the importance of the incident.

The Fauquier men quickly promoted the engagement to fullfledged battle status, and few who took part failed to mention it in their claims for pensions. There were no casualties, only the quiet satisfaction of a successful prank. One participant was Thomas O'Bannon, [15] a foot soldier from Captain Winn's company, perhaps riding behind his brother, John O'Bannon, a cavalryman.

13. Henry Rugeley, according to Lorenzo Sabine in **The American Loyalists**, was a "Loyalist with a foot in each camp."

14. Providence, about a half mile southeast of Charlotte, was Morgan's headquarters. Martin calls it "New" Providence.

15. Thomas O'Bannon, ca. 1758-post 1816, was a brother of John O'Bannon (see Note No. 7 above). He married, 1783, Hannah Barker. He lived at "Flint Hill" near Marshall, where his home, in ruins, still stands.

Another was Samuel Sands,[16] one of Captain Tate's men. He remembered the day vividly when he and his mounted companion were old men content to sit by the fireside. George Rogers, not quite sixteen, and his brother, James, had an arrangements similar to the O'Bannons. James had brought his own horse down with Major Triplett with the intent of joining William Triplett's company; George was from Francis Triplett's own company of foot. Together they rode to Rugeley's Mill on James' horse and had a perfectly splendid time. Lord Cornwallis was, however, not amused. "Rugeley," he wrote grimly to Tarleton, "will not be made a brigadier."[17]

Washington's enterprise may have amused General Nathanael Greene but it did not divert his attention long from more important considerations. Kosciuszko had selected a site on the Pee Dee River near Cheraw Hill, just south of the North Carolina border as most suitable for his "camp of repose". Its only drawback was that it was farther from the enemy than Charlotte. His removal there might look like a retreat that would increase the enemy's confidence and dishearten the people of the country who looked to him for defense. At all cost this should be avoided without bringing on a general engagement, which he could not afford. He must carry on some encouraging operations, limited in nature, but threatening Cornwallis' flanks, interrupting his communications, cutting off his supplies and animating Marion, Sumpter and Pickens with their partisan bands to similar enterprises.

To meet the situation Greene made a daring decision, contrary to all the classic rules of warfare. He decided to divide his already insufficient army. Washington, Howe and Burgoyne had all made this potentially disastrous mistake at least once. Only at Barren Hill had the consequences been less than fatal, and Lafayette had escaped from Barren Hill only by the skin of his teeth. Yet there were excellent, even compelling, reasons for Greene to disregard the military canon; that to divide an inferior force in the face of a superior enemy was to invite the piecemeal destruction of its parts. Only a really great general would have known that the time had

---

16. Samuel Sands (or Sans) 1752-post 1818, was one of those sent from Augusta County late in 1780. It was his belief that Captain Tate, under whom he served, was under Major Triplett but the arrangement of the line at Cowpens indicates that Tate's immediate superior was Major Brookes of Maryland.

17. Tarleton's **Memoirs**.

come. He embarked on "the most audacious and ingenious piece of military strategy of the war."[18]

The first division was to be Morgan's light infantry, with Lieutenant Colonel Howard in command of the infantry and Lieutenant Colonel William Washington in command of the cavalry. Under Howard were 200 Maryland Continentals under Brookes, 140 Delaware Continentals under Kirkwood, Francis Triplett's battalion of Virginia sharpshooters, which included about 150 men under Captains Combs and Winn as well as about half the men from Amherst and Rockbridge Counties, 200 in all. Under Captain James Tate were the Virginia Continentals, remnants of Buford's 3rd Virginia Regiment, Tate's own rifle corps and the remainder of the Amherst and Rockbridge contingent, about 150 men. Washington had about 80 light dragoons. The nucleus of Morgan's command totalled about 770 men who were both trained and equipped, the flower of Greene's army.[19]

The second division was to be the remainder, about 1,100 Continentals and militia under the command of General Isaac Huger of South Carolina. Because they were less experienced and had a long and grueling march ahead of them, Greene remained with them. They were of course encumbered with the heavy baggage, what little artillery they possessed, and stores enough to carry them until additional supplies could be found.

The land in which Greene must perforce operate was crossed by three great rivers. An accurate knowledge of the fords and ferries available was indispensable to his safety and success. Accordingly he sent Colonel Edward Carrington to explore and map as far north as the Dan River in southern Virginia. To the Yadkin and Catawba Rivers to the west, he sent Generals Edward Stevens and Kosciuszko, for the same purpose. They were also to collect or build flatboats to be carried on wheels or in wagons from one river to another. Later these sensible precautions were to pay off in coin of purest gold.

On the 16th of December Greene ordered Morgan to cross the Catawba to the west and join the North Carolina militia under

---

18. Sydney G. Fisher, **The Struggle for American Independence**, Vol. II, p. 377.

19. The figures, generally are taken from Ward's **The War of the Revolution**, Vol. II, p. 755. However, Ward seems not to have heard of or taken into account the militia from Augusta and Rockbridge Counties and overlooked several other small units known to have taken part in the battle. His figure of 200 Virginia riflemen is short by at least 100, probably 150.

General William Davidson, to operate between the Broad and Pacolet Rivers, as they saw fit. Should Cornwallis threaten Greene at Cheraw Hill, Morgan would rejoin him or fall upon the enemy's flank or rear.

An excessive rainfall that flooded the lowlands delayed Greene's departure; but on the 20th he was on his way. The roads were deep with mud, the horses too weak from want of food to drag the heavy wagons and the men were not much better off. Somehow he managed to reach Cheraw Hill in six days. Kosciuszko had chosen well. He was now in a position to give active support to Marion's force which was carrying out successful raids against the British supply lines, to threaten Camden, and he was nearer to Charleston than Cornwallis was. It was not a bad situation, though he was 140 miles from Morgan across the Catawba.

New recruits began to come in to Greene's camp. He had not been entirely altruistic in giving Morgan all his cavalry. Washington had promised him Lee's Legion. They arrived at Cheraw Hill on the 13th of January; 100 horse and 180 foot, "the most thoroughly disciplined and best equipped scouts and raiders in the Revolution." Almost at the same time Colonel John Green of Culpeper appeared on the scene with 400 militia from all parts of Virginia.

After crossing the Catawba Morgan faced 58 miles of difficult travel across deep swamps and rugged terrain before camping on Christmas Day on the banks of the Pacolet River. He, too, received additional reinforcement: 120 North Carolina militia under Davidson and 190 North Carolina riflemen under Major Joseph McDowell. Not long after a fine detachment of mounted South Carolina and Georgia militia, mostly Scotch-Irish, arrived, led by the indefatigable Lieutenant Colonel James McCall.[20] In the clinches the Scotch-Irish are always with us, unruly, but ready for a good scrap! Morgan quickly found something for them to do. He sent them with William Washington and his dragoons against a party of 250 Loyalists who were said to be ravaging the countryside along Fairfort Creek in South Carolina. After a forty mile ride, they found their quarry near Ninety-Six, killed or wounded 150, captured 40 and returned to camp without a single casualty.

Cornwallis, resting at Winnsboro, had also been reinforced by 1,500 men, sent by Clinton from New York under Major General

---

20. McCall's gang was a boisterous outfit, constantly in trouble, but apparently worth their keep. Disdaining firearms, they were armed with sabres to fight from horseback. There were only 45 of them but it seemed like more.

Leslie.[21] He now had better than 4,000 men, well-trained, armed and equipped, against Greene's whole army of 3,000, of whom most were in rags. One would expect him to have been elated and confident. Instead he was mired deep in despondency. Greene's splitting of his army threw him off balance. Few could believe that Greene would have done so had he known of Leslie's addition to the British force, but Cornwallis was not so sure. He had seen what Greene had counted on; if he attacked Huger's force at Cheraw Hill, Morgan might take Ninety-Six or Augusta or both. If he went for Morgan the way was open for Greene to cut his supply line and, perhaps, recover Charleston. Much as he hated to do so, he could only follow the example of his antagonist and divide his own army. He sent Leslie to hold Camden and block Huger's advance. He directed Tarleton to find Morgan and crush him. With his main army he inched cautiously north to pick up any pieces that might tumble into his lap. For once Cornwallis was not thinking clearly. Caught in the trough betwixt Scylla and Charybdis he knew not which side to favor.

Tarleton's force totalled about 1,100 rank and file, with two light field pieces (3-pounders, called "grasshoppers"). Morgan's corps was about equal in numbers. It has been said that Tarleton's trained regulars outnumbered Morgan's three to one but the figure is misleading. It is true that Morgan's Continentals were few, only 400, but some of his militia like Triplett's and Tate's Virginians were top-notch troops, and McCall's Georgians were not to be trifled with. Still, Morgan was at a disadvantage in that he was the pursued and Tarleton the pursuer. Crossing the Pacolet only a hair's breadth ahead of Tarleton's advanced elements, Morgan beat his way precipitately to Thicketty Creek, a branch of Broad River near the North Carolina line. There, tired of running, he turned at bay.

The site Morgan had selected to make his stand had little to recommend it. Called "Hannah's Cowpens" because it had been used as a place for wintering cattle, it was shorn of every vestige of foliage. Three hillocks, the highest about 70 feet, rose from this barren plain, one behind the other. Between were grassy swales and beyond, for nearly five miles, the slope descended to the Broad River which swept in a wide arc, cutting off possible retreat on

---

21. Alexander Leslie was the same British officer who had slept soundly while the Americans marched around him at Princeton. That episode did not stop his promotion to Major General. He succeeded Cornwallis in command of Charleston which he held until 14 Dec. 1782.

three sides. Morgan's officers were appalled. Obviously a position astride this mole hill must have its flanks "in the air", vulnerable to any flanking movement and offering dangerous opportunities for encirclement. They could see only one advantage; the place was well-known. Their friends could easily find them when it was over and bury the dead. Morgan sent back word to Colonel Andrew Pickens [22] to meet him there with his South Carolina militia. The taciturn Pickens who "would first take the words out of his mouth and examine them in his hands before uttering them", emitted a reluctant "yup". He was there at sundown on the 16th of January, bringing other partisans with small detachments with him. Ward says he brought only 70 men but others credit him with many of the militia that had joined Morgan along the Pacolet.

In their improvised camp on the grassy swale on the night of 16-17 January 1781, fires were lit, rations distributed, food cooked, militia groups straggled in and mounted patrols moved in and out. Amid the confusion Morgan hobbled among the campfires, half-crippled with sciatica, to make sure each unit knew exactly what was expected of them on the morrow. His plan was unorthodox, in fact, unheard of, but he had no doubts about it. It had to work; there was no retreat. He intended that the forward line of 150 picked riflemen (Georgia and North Carolina militia) would be concealed in the tall grass. He knew that they could shoot - and run. They would do both. "Hold up your heads, boys, give me but three good fires and you are free. Then, when you get home, will your parents bless you and your girls cover you with kisses."[23] He wanted them to let the enemy get within 50 paces, to get two hits, then to run, but not too far. He would need them later.

The second line commanded by Pickens, would be along the first ridge 150 yards behind the first. Here the bulk of the militia, 300 North and South Carolinians, would wait for the first line and cover their retreat. They were to fire twice but in a special way. They were to get the officers and platoon sergeants. They must not shoot too high. When the enemy got within range for a bayonet

22. Andrew Pickens, 1739-1817, was born in Pennsylvania. He moved south with his parents and other Scotch-Irish families through the Shenandoah, where they lived for a while. He was a farmer and Justice of Peace before the war. As a prominent partisan leader, he had attained the rank of Colonel before Cowpens. He was wounded at Eutaw Springs, but contributed to the final operations in the south by his expedition against the Cherokees in 1782.

23. Thomas Young, "Memoir", quoted in **The Orion**, (Penfield, Ga., 1844) Vol. III, p. 88.

charge, they too, would run. There is a fancier military term, "deploying to the rear", but the meaning is the same. They would, to be exact, run around the American left flank to draw the enemy to their right. This was important because the third, or main, line was arranged in a particular way.

The third line was 150 yards uphill from the second line. Commanded by Lieutenant Colonel John Eager Howard, about 600 men would hold a front of about 400 yards. The Delaware and Maryland Continentals were to be in the center. The all-important left wing was Major Francis Triplett's Virginia battalion. Here the front line, kneeling, was instructed to lay down a field of musket fire. Over their heads the riflemen would fire, crouch to load, and fire again. Similarly on the right was Captain Tate with his mixture of regulars and Virginia militia, to which was added Captain Beale's small company of veteran Georgia militia. Their order of battle was the same as Triplett's.

In the rear Lieutenant Colonel William Washington's 80 Virginia dragoons and Lieutenant Colonel James McCall's 45 Georgia infantrymen, armed with sabres to fight from horseback, would survey the scene. They were not to expose their precious horses to the initial small-arms crossfire. When the time was right they were to make a long sweep around the left and hit the enemy on their right flank. After that they were on their own.

All night, like Henry V at Agincourt, Morgan talked to his men in small groups. He had heard a lot about the Carolinians as sharpshooters. Now was their time to prove it. The men were scared of Tarleton. His Virginians had been scared of Burgoyne at Saratoga, yet look what they had done! "His Virginians!" A burst of pride surged in every Virginia heart. One of Washington's men wrote,[24] "It was upon this occasion I was more perfectly convinced of General Morgans qualifications to command militia than I had ever before been. He went among the volunteers, helped them fix their swords, joked with them about their sweethearts, told them to keep in good spirits and the day would be ours. And long after I laid down he was going about among the soldiers ... I don't believe he slept a wink that night." He was right. Morgan kept patrols and scouts close to the enemy, brought in several small detachments of militia during the night. An hour before daylight his pickets were driven in. They brought word that Tarleton was within five miles, marching light and fast.

"Boys, get up! Benny is coming," he roared.

---

24. *Ibid.*

The morning was bitterly cold. As they formed the men slapped their hands together to keep warm, "an exertion not long necessary ..." Tarleton advanced cautiously but by 6 o'clock his advance cavalry patrol reported that they had made contact and that Morgan was preparing for battle. He lost no time getting ready to attack. By 6:45 o'clock, still before sunrise, he moved his troops out of the woods about 400 yards in front of the first American position. Then, with orders to drive in the skirmishers, - the standard opening move, - the dragoons under Captain Charles Ogilvie trotted out, spread into a thin red line, - and charged.

"It was the most beautiful line I ever saw," wrote young Thomas Young in rapture.

It was not so long. The unseen riflemen picked their targets, aligned their sights, held their breaths, and fired. Even Tarleton should have known when his dragoons returned with 15 empty saddles out of 50, that something strange was in the wind and that something stranger might lay beyond. He did not notice. He was too busy getting ready for the grand assault. Precisely at 7 o'clock he led the line forward, field music setting the step. Left in reserve were the cavalry and 200 kilted Highlanders, some of his best troops. The front line of American riflemen fell back slowly, firing as they did so. This unnerved some of Tarleton's infantry because, in proper warfare, such a thing was simply *not done*.[25] When the range had closed to 100 yards from Pickens' line, his officers bellowed "Fire!" The result was devastating. This phase of the action accounted for about half the British casualties, of whom about 40 percent were officers. Still the British kept coming, bayonets fixed. To their utter delight, Pickens' line broke and fled. It was exactly what they expected of a bunch of raw militia. It seemed to them rather odd that they all fled to the right, but that might be because of the terrain - or something. The planned stampede was not the smooth operation that some accounts make it. It was disorganized enough to fool anyone. Certainly the British never expected to see those militiamen again.

The false sense of security did not last long. The British dragoons charged toward the American left to hack up the fleeing militia. Suddenly they received a nasty jolt. They had run head-on into Francis Triplett's Virginians. They were greeted by a withering burst of musketry interspersed by accurate rifle fire. The American

---

25. The European soldiers considered the rifle an inferior weapon and were astonished and annoyed that the riflemen could load and fire while running. As they could not do it themselves, they regarded it as unsportsmanlike.

line stood solid, unwavering. The British faltered for an instant, but came on. Suddenly, without warning, they were hit in their right flank by Washington's and McCall's cavalry. The cavalry had been instructed not to alert them to the danger by shooting. They came in with sabres flashing in the morning sun. The line of British dragoons broke and fled for safety with heavy losses.

It was 7:15 before Tarleton could reform his infantry line to resume the attack on the American center. The flight of the second line of militia had been taken by the British infantry for the beginning of a retreat of Morgan's whole force. They had not grasped the significance of the flight of the dragoons on their right. They were cheering in triumph when the first volley hit them. The cheers died in their throats. Howard's Maryland and Delaware regulars fired volley after volley, kneeling, firing low, picking out the epaulettes. Over their heads came the rifle fire, accurate, unusually intense. They had no idea that the fleet-footed Georgians and South Carolinians were returning to the fray, filtering into the line from the rear.

About 7:30 Tarleton knew that the day was lost unless he could bring in his reserve Highlanders to turn the American right wing. As the pipes began to skirl and the 200 kilted veterans started forward, Howard sensed the threat. He ordered Tate to change the front of his right company to meet them. The company was to face about in line and wheel to the left so as to make a right angle with the main line and repel the flankers. It was a difficult and dangerous manoeuvre with any but the most experienced troops, but it was absolutely necessary.

The order was misunderstood. Believing that a general withdrawal was called, the whole line started to the rear in good order. Howard immediately realized what had happened, but was unable to stop it. He decided to complete the withdrawal to the new position. Morgan rode up in alarm. Quickly seeing that Howard's new position had certain tactical advantage, Morgan ordered Howard to face about and fire as soon as the new line was formed. The British rushed in for the kill. They were not 50 yards away when Tate's men turned, firing from the hip at point-blank range, and charged with their bayonets. From his position on the flank, Washington could see what was happening.[26]

"They're coming on like a mob. Give them one fire and I will charge them."

---

26. Washington had just returned to the field after pursuit of the dragoons on the American left.

Faced with blistering fire in front and with charging cavalry on their flank and rear, the British left collapsed. The British right, though badly mauled by Triplett's Virginians, were still struggling. Now they tried to escape to the rear but were cut off by the American cavalry. Only the Highlanders and a few dragoons on the extreme left refused to quit. Just as Howard's entire line was able to give them their undivided attention, Pickens appeared on their flank with some of his militia who had made a complete circle of the battlefield. Colonel James Jackson led his Georgians into the midst of the embattled Scots. Surrounded, locked in hand-to-hand combat, with nine of their sixteen officers dead, the Highlanders gave up. Their commanding officer handed his sword to Pickens. Pickens received it without comment. As has been previously observed, he had no talent for small talk.

It must be said of Tarleton that he was no quitter. He rode back to his 200 man cavalry reserve to lead them to a counterattack which he thought might still save the day. To a man, they rode off and left him! Tarleton's handful of British artillery were still firing the grasshoppers ineffectually into the American lines. Some 40 British dragoons and 14 officers rallied around Tarleton in a dash to save the guns. Before they could reach them Captain Robert Kirkwood and his Delaware men charged their position and took it. The hapless artillerists never surrendered. Almost without exception, they died by their guns.

The time had come for Tarleton to quit the scene of the disaster that had wiped out nine tenths of his army. His horse was near collapse but his regimental surgeon, Dr. Robert Jackson,[27] urged that he take his. When Tarleton demurred, Jackson said simply that his place was with his wounded comrades. He was going nowhere, and the rebels might find him useful.

Tarleton and his small force galloped off with Washington in hot pursuit. Noting that Washington was well in advance of the pack, Tarleton and two officers turned back to attack him. When Washington slashed at one officer he broke his sabre near the hilt. A 14 year old American bugler shattered his opponent's sword arm with a bullet in the shoulder. The other British officer was

---

27. Robert Jackson, 1750-1827, was the son of a small farmer on the Clyde, in Scotland. He financed his medical education by serving as a surgeon on whaling ships. He was an assistant to a doctor in Jamaica when he decided to join a militia unit in New York. He was accepted as a surgeon's mate and ensign in the 71st Highland Regiment. After the Revolution he launched a personal crusade to reform the medical service in the British army.

wounded by Washington's sergeant major. Reining his horse in a circle, Tarleton, fired his pistol, missing Washington but wounding his horse. The agonized animal reared in pain, but Washington kept his seat. Tarleton galloped off after his fleeing cavalry.

Morgan wasted no time gloating over his triumph. He knew that Cornwallis with a vastly superior force was near; how near he did not know. By noon he and his entire army had put the Broad River between themselves and the war-torn field of Cowpens. Pickens was left to take care of the wounded. The young British surgeon was a Godsend. After speeding Tarleton on his way, he whipped his hankerchief out of his pocket and, fastening it to his cane, he strolled casually toward the American positions. When challenged he said, "I am assistant surgeon to the 71st Regiment. Many wounded men are in your hands. I have come to offer my services to help care for them." The last thing that Morgan wanted was to be further encumbered with more than 200 enemy wounded. Dr. Jackson suggested that they be paroled in his care. Morgan agreed. Under British tents and with all the food and British medical supplies he could use, a flag of truce fluttering overhead, Jackson set about mending the broken bodies of his gallant comrades. When he offered his own parole to Pickens the latter merely bowed. From such men the Americans required no parole.

Oh, yes! it was a triumph for Morgan and his men. The hour's fighting had cost the British 100 killed, 229 wounded and 600 captured unhurt. *Sixty-six* officers were lost of whom 39 were dead as mackerels. Captured also were 60 Negro batmen, 100 dragoon horses, 800 muskets, 35 loaded wagons and the colors of the 7th Regiment. Further interesting booty included a travelling forge, the two useful "grasshoppers", and all the enemy's musical instruments. More important than the loot was the damage done to Tarleton's mystical reputation, the enormous increase in the self-confidence of the militia and the lift in American morale given by what was, even in London, called "the worst British defeat since the surrender of Burgoyne at Saratoga."[28]

However, the Americans did not get off unscathed. Morgan reported 12 dead and 60 wounded. Major Triplett and his men mourned the loss of the brave and much beloved Captain John Combs who had fallen in the first assault of the British infantry on the American left. Lieutenant Alexander Keith had stepped into

---

28. Boatner, **Encyclopedia of the American Revolution**, p. 299. However, the **London Chronicle**, 29 March said: "By all accounts Col. Tarleton was never more distinguished for spirit and gallantry than on this occasion."

his place but the vacancy in their hearts would remain. According to first sergeant Benjamin Martin more than 50 years later, "I was in the lead all the time of the action. I loved Captain Combs, he was killed. Captain Dobson and Lieutenant Ewen was on the left of the Maryland Troops near me." Not far away was the youthful Daniel Payne of "Locust Shade", near Orlean.[29] There was a look of surprise on his face as the bullet lodged in his young heart. There were probably one or two more from Fauquier, but their names are lost.

As the years rolled on the stories of Hannah's Cowpens took on the special virtue of Agincourt. Old soldiers remembered who stood next to them on that day, behind whose body they had crouched to reload their rifles, whose sudden warning had saved them from certain death. They teased each other about the parts they had played. Dempsey Jackson[30] swore that his greatest consolation in battle had been that John Fishback had stood in the front rank before him, as some shield against British bullets. Fishback stoutly denied any intention of saving Jackson's worthless life. As a musketeer he was only doing his duty. Presumably Jackson was a rifleman.

Thomas O'Bannon bewailed the fact that, just before the battle, Morgan had sent him to collect the sick in front of the British lines and bring them into Salisbury out of harm's way. It was a dangerous and difficult assignment, but what bothered him was that he had missed his share of the glory. His sometime friend, John Murphey, added to his frustration by feigning certainty that Thomas was not collecting the sick at all, but merely hiding.

---

29. Daniel Payne, d. 1781, son of William and Mary (Ball?) Payne, he moved from King George Co. to Fauquier at an early age with his older brother, Francis Payne of "Locust Shade." General Edward Stevens, writing to Jefferson, 24 Jan. 1781, reports 10 killed and 55 wounded, including 3 "subalterns" from the Virginia troops, one a Continental and two from the Militia. "One," he wrote, "would die." He had not, appararently, learned of Capt. Comb's death.

30. Dempsey Jackson was a neighbor of the Philip Fishback family and married, 1787, Mary Pickett, dau. of William S. Pickett. They moved to Mason Co., Ky. John Fishback married Mary (Pickett) Jackson's sister, Martha, in 1785.

Orderly sergeant Spencer Withers [31] had an even sadder story. He had been sick, and so missed the battle. This was especially galling because his cousin, Lewis Withers, had fought splendidly, received a slight but decorative wound, and was receiving applause from every quarter. Spencer could imagine the effect on the girls at home.

John Franklin, [32] who had been with Colonel George Baylor's Horse, said that he had ridden with Washington at Ninety-Six and Cowpens. It was not his fault that some of his excited descendants, assuming the wrong Washington, later promoted him to the position of aide-de-camp to his Excellency. He was just a cavalry private, doing his duty. There was John Forrester, who had been with Captain John Ashby in the 3rd Virginia Regiment at Brandywine, John Austin of Morgan's rifles at Saratoga, and the indestructible William Asberry. [33] Asberry's wife's prim parents, the Glascocks, thought that, because he had been a soldier, he must be a dissipated man, unfit to marry their daughter. In their view service in the patriot cause was no passport to Heaven. In later years, when pensions were sought, some of those who fought at Cowpens were cryptic, some expansive, but all were proud.

The Congress was delighted with Morgan's victory and in a burst of enthusiasm voted him a gold medal, and Washington and Howard each silver medals. To Pickens they gave a sword. Virginia gave Morgan a horse, "richly comparisoned", and a sword. Not to be outdone, South Carolina made Pickens a Brigadier. In dispatches dated the 19th of January, the day after the battle, Morgan credited Major Triplett and Captain Tate with distinguished service. The splendid performance of Captain Robert Kirkwood seems to have gone unnoticed. Perhaps the most notable

31. Spencer Withers, 1756-1843, was a son of William and Elizabeth (Hord) Withers. He enlisted as a substitute for Peter Crim. He married Esther Potts, 1759-1818. He moved to Mason Co. but after the death of his wife and the destruction of his home by fire, he returned to Culpeper Co. where he died. His pension record gives the year of birth as 1756. In the Withers genealogy (by Franz V. Recum) it is given as 1765, which seems most unlikely.

32. John Franklin, 1748-post 1820, enlisted in 1780 in South Carolina under Capt. Churchill Jones and served until 1783. He married Elizabeth ? It is not certain that he lived in Fauquier before the Revolution.

33. William Asberry, 1755-1814, m. 1784, Susannah Glascock, dau. of Thomas and Catherine (Rector) Glascock. She m. (2) Thomas Bateman.

accolade received by the Fauquier men is found in a letter from General Edward Stevens to Governor Thomas Jefferson. In part it reads, "tho it adds greatly to my satisfaction that the detachment of Virginia Militia under the immediate command of Triplett is spoke of with great applause for their behavior that day."[34]

The Fauquier men behaved like Continentals, fought like Continentals and, in several instances, died like Continentals, but in one important respect they were still militia. They had volunteered for six month's service. They were still farmers and, at the end of February, they expected to go home. The officers tried to persuade them to stay, but to no avail. One cannot blame them. The pay that they received in Continental currency was virtually worthless. Their only negotiable asset was the produce of their farms. They could not leave their families destitute.

Morgan had on his hands upward of 600 prisoners. In a letter to Greene, written at Sherrald's Ford on the 29th of January,[35] he said that he was sending the prisoners captured at Cowpens northward:

> Sir: I arrived here this morning. The prisoners crossed at the Island Ford seventeen miles higher up the river. I expect them to join me this evening. Shall send them on to Salisbury guarded by Major Triplett's Militia whose time expires this day. If they are to be sent any further, Major Triplett wishes, and thinks it right, that the Militia under Gen. Stevens should have the trouble of them, as they have not underwent so much fatigue as his men—

Peter Bashaw said that he accompanied them as far as Charlotte, North Carolina and was discharged there. Most of the others took them as far as Salisbury, some forty miles further north. At Salisbury on the last day of February, with reluctance but with gratitude for what they had done, Francis Triplett signed discharges for James Emmons,[36] John Fishback, Spencer Withers, George Rogers and Thomas O'Bannon. The last named was to

34. Letter, Edward Stevens to Thomas Jefferson, 24 Jan. 1781, from Camp at Hick's Creek, in: **Papers of Thomas Jefferson**, Vol. 4.

35. Letter, Morgan to Greene, 29 Jan. 1781 in: Graham, **Life of Morgan**, p. 328.

36. James Emmons, 1761-1839, m. 1784 in Fauquier, Sarah ? . He moved, about 1800, to Stokes Co., N.C. He died near Niles, Territory of Michigan where he had lived since 1835.

continue on and take the sick and wounded Americans to Richmond.

Benjamin Martin tells of receiving his discharge and of what happened to it, a circumstance that must have been often repeated. While marching with the prisoners to Salisbury, he was on a road near the North Carolina line when Major Triplett rode up with the discharge in his hand. Doubtless the Major wished him luck and perhaps sent with him a message to his friends. A few years later Martin moved to Kentucky. Before going, he wrote, "I destroyed all my useless papers and among them my discharge papers as I expected never to have any use for them again." Fifty years would pass before he needed them.

Only one pensioner from Fauquier, 32 year old John Kemper, [37] reported that he had been with the group that had escorted the prisoners all the way to "Albemarle Barracks". He was not of Major Triplett's battalion, having been drafted in Shenandoah County. He had spent the winter at Cheraw Hill under General Stevens. When news reached them of the Cowpens victory, he was sent on detachment to Charlotte and thence home by way of Albemarle, where he was discharged.

On the afternoon of the 31st of January, about 2 o'clock, with his army under Colonel Howard already on the march toward Salisbury, Morgan and Washington rode to Beattie's Ford on the Catawba to meet General Nathanael Greene. Although the news of Cowpens had been most gratifying, Greene had sensed that Morgan needed help. At enormous personal risk, he had galloped 125 miles through Tory-infested country with only an aide, a guide and a sergeant's guard of dragoons. Only his safe arrival could justify so rash a venture.

By that time Morgan was truly ill. His sciatica had increased to the point that the pain impaired his ability to function rationally. A severe case of hemorrhoids made riding perfect agony. Fearing that his condition would place a burden on his army, he had no choice but to ask Greene for a leave of absence. He suggested retreating beyond the mountains to the west in order to

---

37. John Kemper (Camper), 1749-1842-3, son of Harman and Catharine (Cuntze) Kemper, was born in Fauquier Co. but was living in Shenandoah Co. when he was drafted in 1780. He was a grandson of John Kemper of Germantown (see Note No. 11, Chap. IX).

save the army, but Greene had other plans.[38] Greene realized that a retreat to the west would lay the entire State of Virginia open to Cornwallis. He agreed that retreat was necessary but was determined to move northward to the Dan River. He would draw Cornwallis after him, pulling him farther from his base of supply, but Greene's army would always be between Cornwallis and his goal.

At Guilford, North Carolina, not far from the Dan, on the 10th of February, Greene reluctantly allowed Morgan to leave for home. No specific record has been found, but it seems highly probable that Major Francis Triplett accompanied him at least part of the way. Triplett now had no command in the south and there was much for him to do in Virginia. Someone had to attend the ailing general whose progress was limited to a few miles a day. Captain William Triplett must have started north about the same time. He intended to raise a cavalry company in Fauquier to join Washington and no time was to be lost.

At Guilford, Greene reunited his two armies. Cornwallis was hot on his trail with 2,500 regulars. He had burned all his baggage at Ramseur's Mill, destroying even stores and rum, in order to speed up the chase. Greene had, at most, 2,000 ill-equipped, threadbare troops to oppose him. He considered making a stand but a Council of War advised him against it and urged that he attempt to beat Cornwallis to the Dan. He had a close call but, when the army reached the banks of the Dan they found that Colonel Carrington had done his work well. The boats were in readiness.

Without Morgan the light infantry brigade was scattered and dismembered. To replace it Greene organized a 700 man light corps to serve as a rear guard and draw the enemy away from the line of retreat. William Washington commanded the mounted elements, 240 men, including his dragoons and the cavalry of Lee's Legion. John Eager Howard commanded the infantry, his 280 Maryland and Delaware Continentals, 120 foot soldiers from Lee's Legion and 60 Virginia riflemen remaining from Triplett's battalion. Before leaving Morgan was asked to command this unit, but it was obviously impossible. The "Old Waggoner" had reached the end of his rope.

38. Letter, Morgan to Jefferson, 1 Feb. 1781, from Sherrald's Ford, Morgan writes: "Great God! what is the reason I cant have more men?" He continues that an "old pain in the breast and Hip has aceazed me so that I shant be of much use in the field this winter—if ever I am."

The war in the Carolinas was far from over, but the participation of Fauquier men in its final stages was small and is largely undocumented. There was only one more major battle, which can be briefly described. Having crossed the Dan, Greene lost no time in reorganizing his main body with new recruits assembled in Virginia by General Steuben. The southern militia was beginning to turn out and equipment from the north was coming through as a result of the constant effort of Colonel Christian Febiger. "Old Denmark" was on his way to Virginia and, as we will soon see, no reverses, north or south, had dampened his spirits or diminished his enthusiasm for the patriot cause. On the 18th of February, Greene sent Lee's Legion and two companies of Maryland Continentals back across the Dan to cooperate with Pickens and his 700 newly-raised militia. Two days later Colonel Otho Williams crossed with the same light infantry that had formed the rear guard less than two weeks before. As soon as he was joined by General Edward Stevens and his 600 Virginia riflemen, Greene himself crossed the river. He did not want to give Cornwallis a chance either to resume the offensive or escape. By mid-March Greene was as ready for battle as he was ever likely to be, and Cornwallis was ready and waiting.

At Guilford Courthouse, on the 15th of March, Cornwallis attacked. Morgan, working his way painfully home through Virginia,[39] sent Greene sound advice, which Greene, in large measure, followed. His battle plan somewhat resembles that of Cowpens, but it was carried out without Morgan's flair. "If the militia fights," the old wagoner wrote, "you will beat Cornwallis; if not he will beat you and perhaps cut your regulars to pieces ... A number of old soldiers" are said to be among the militia. Select them and put them in the ranks with the regulars ... fight the riflemen on the flanks, put the militia in the center "with some picked troops in their rear with orders to shoot down the first man who runs. If anything will succeed, a deposition of this kind will."

Consequently Greene placed two North Carolina militia brigades in the forward line. It was "Lighthorse Harry" Lee who tried to calm their nerves. "Three rounds, my boys, and then you can fall back."[40] He said that he had "whipped the British three

---

39. Morgan was obliged to break his journey twice, first at Brigadier General Robert Lawson's plantation and secondly at Carter Harrison's plantation on the James, in order to recover strength to travel further. It was from the second stop that he wrote to Greene.

40. Henry Lee, **Memoirs of War in the Southern Department of the United States.**

times that morning and could do it again." It did not happen quite as he had planned. The North Carolinians fired once, and departed for home. Lee tried to rally them and even threatened to fall on them with his cavalry, to no avail. They had had enough.

The second line was composed of the two Virginia militia brigades commanded by Colonels Edward Stevens and Robert Lawson.[41] They were flanked on the east by Lee's Legion and on the west by Washington's cavalry. When the British hit the second line they met with stiff resistance, but the Virginians were finally beaten back. The British right wheeled against Lee and was able, temporarily, to put him out of action. Washington counterattacked to relieve the pressure, but the line was split. Stevens, who had seen the militia run at Camden and had therefore heeded Morgan's advice, had placed a line of sentinels to his rear "with orders to shoot every man who flinched."[42] His brigade held until he, himself, was wounded and had to be carried from the field.

Greene's third and main line was composed of the 5th Virginia Continental Regiment under Colonel Samuel Hawes,[43] right center, and the 1st Maryland Regiment under Colonel John Gunby,[44] left center. The right wing was the 4th Virginia Continental Regiment under Colonel John Green, and the left was the 5th Maryland Regiment under Colonel Benjamin Ford.[45] As Cornwallis massed his troops to attack the third line he directed his spearhead against the toughest part of Greene's line, the 1st Maryland Regiment. The British were thrown back with heavy loss. Returning to the attack they met similar resistance from Hawes' Virginians.

41. Robert Lawson, 1748-1805, served as a Major in the 4th Virginia Regiment, 13 Feb. 1776; Col., 19 Aug. 1777; resigned 17 Dec. 1777. Brigadier General, Virginia Militia.

42. Henry Lee, **Memoirs.**

43. Samuel Hawes, the Colonel commanding the 5th Virginia Regiment at Guilford Courthouse, was relatively unknown until he and his men distinguished themselves at Hobkirk's Hill, 25 Apr. 1781.

44. John Gunby, Colonel of the 1st Maryland Regiment, called "the finest battalion in the American Army," (Fortescue) was made the scapegoat for Greene's defeat at Hobkirk's Hill.

45. Benjamin Ford, Colonel of the unfortunate 5th Virginia Regiment, was in command at Hobkirk's Hill where his regiment did little better. Ford was wounded and carried from the field, after which his line broke and retired in disorder.

Having met a stalemate in the center, Cornwallis next turned his attention to the American left, the 5th Maryland Regiment. Here the American line wavered. It was a largely new regiment of recruits, now in their first battle. Furthermore they were without the flanking support they had expected from Lee's Legion. The sight of scarlet and steel was too much for their nerves. Without firing a shot, they turned and fled. Rushing into the gap William Washington's dragoons and Kirkwood's ever-splendid Delaware Continentals halted the enemy advance. The 1st Maryland Regiment, now commanded by Colonel Howard after Gunby had been unhorsed, finally succeeded in closing the gap, but it was still a greatly attenuated line.

There were several times when a strong counter-attack might have turned the tide of battle for General Nathanael Greene. Now some of the weakness of his battle plan began to show up. The conditions were not as at Cowpens and the battle did not follow the same course. To the immense chagrin of Colonel John Green, his Virginians were not engaged, although the Americans had no reserve. The separation of Lee's Legion early in the battle from the main line deprived them of support where it was most needed, on the right flank. Greene rejected the idea of a counter-movement as too risky and, about 3 o'clock in the afternoon, decided to retreat. He withdrew Colonel Green's 4th Virginia Regiment from the line to cover it. It was an important service but the old colonel from Culpeper did not see it that way. In answer to his grumbling, Greene assured him that he would have the first blow next time. "This delighted him and he always reckoned upon the promised boon with pleasure," wrote Lee.[46] The "promised boon" never came.

Of the few Fauquier men who were at Guilford Courthouse, John Franklin, formerly of Baylor's Horse, was with Washington. He remained with him until the battle at Eutaw Springs, 8 September, 1781, when both he and his commander were wounded and captured. They were taken to Charleston, where they remained prisoners until the end of the war. Franklin then returned to Fauquier County. Washington, having married "a young lady in whom are concentrated the united attractions of respectable

---

46. Lee, **Memoirs**, p. 282n.

descent, opulence, polish and beauty," (in that order!) [47] decided to remain in Charleston.

Captain Alexander Keith probably returned, at least for a time, to Colonel John Green's 4th Virginia Regiment. Green, himself, returned to Virginia, as his regiment was commanded by Lieutenant Colonel Richard Campbell at Hobkirk's Hill. Keith served until the end of the war, according to his military record.

Although he was from Shenandoah County and only by accident in a Fauquier unit, it is Godfrey Smith [48] who gives us the best idea of what may have happened to those of Major Francis Triplett's battalion who stayed behind. He was a veteran of many years' hard campaigning and, for him, the end was not in sight. He had first enlisted early in the war with Colonel Abraham Buford for eighteen months. Before his term expired he enlisted for the war with General Edward Stevens at Petersburg. However he continued with Buford's Regiment on the long, dismal road to Waxhaws, where he had seen most of his companions slain. Somehow he escaped and returned to Petersburg, where Captain Francis Triplett picked him up on the way to Cowpens. When the Fauquier men left in the spring of 1781, he was transferred to Captain Rudolph's company of "Lighthorse Harry" Lee's Corps of Light Infantry. With Lee he served at Guilford Courthouse, and at the battle of Camden or "Pine Tree the same place where Gates was before defeated." He meant, of course, Hobkirk's Hill, a mile and a half north of Camden near Pine Tree Creek. He was also in the battle of Eutaw Springs and "smaller affairs." However, when the time came for him to go home, he had the measles at Georgetown, South Carolina.

The measles was no laughing matter in those days and he was very ill. They ordered him to return to Virginia as soon as he could walk, and they would give him a discharge. He returned to Virginia but could never locate any of his old officers. By the time it really mattered to him they had died. He mentions also that he was under the command of Colonel Samuel Hawes of the 5th Virginia Regiment, but does not say when. Had we a roster of that regiment

---

47. *Ibid.*, p. 588. Lee continues: "The gallant soldier soon became enamoured of his amiable acquaintance, and afterwards married her." Much of Lee's prose is like that.

48. Godfrey Smith, 1760-1820, was living in Greenup Co., Ky., when he applied for a pension 27 Oct. 1817. Presumably he was in indigent circumstances, or he would not have been eligible under the pension act.

we might find on it the name of William Asberry. It is known that he remained to fight at Guilford Courthouse, according to the testimony of Burtis Ringo, who could not remember under whose command he had served.

After Cowpens there had been John Deering [49] to see that the Fauquier men got safely home. Now those who returned to Virginia had to find their way by themselves, dodging Tarleton and his raiders along the way.

Greene's losses at Guilford Courthouse were heavy, but not so heavy as those of Cornwallis. Ward puts the American losses at 78 killed and 183 wounded. Captain Tate, who commanded the right wing at Cowpens, had his thigh broken. Captain Andrew Wallace, who had commanded his right company whose fortuitous mistake had nearly won the battle, was killed. The men from Augusta and Rockbridge Counties fought on the road between Stevens and Lawson, the right flank of Stevens and the left of Lawson. Here casualties were especially heavy and, according to Lossing, many of them were left on the field. [50]

On the morning of the 16th of March, Lord Cornwallis looked out over the field at Guilford Courthouse that he had won at such heavy cost. The night had been rainy, dark and cold. The dead were unburied, the wounded unsheltered and the groans of the dying broke the gloomy silence. Of his force of 1,900 men, he had lost one quarter, of whom 93 had been killed in action and 50 more died of wounds on the field. Half of his elite Guards were lost. General James Webster, [51] one of his bravest officers, was dying.

49. John Deering (or Dearing), 1746-1822, is mentioned in several pension records as Captain, but he was recommended as an Ensign in the Fauquier Militia, 27 Aug. 1781. The pension records may reflect a later rank. He was probably a sergeant at Cowpens. He was later prominent in Fauquier and in 1797 was one of the original trustees of Salem (Marshall). He lived on Thumb Run in the Manor of Leeds where he had leased 200 acres and in July 1798 he petitioned the Court to condemn one acre belonging to Isaac Arnold opposite his own to erect thereon a water grist mill.

50. B. J. Lossing, **Pictorial Field-Book of the Revolution**, Vol. II, p. 608-09. Also Oren F. Morton, **History of Rockbridge County**.

51. James Webster, ca. 1743-1781, was a son of an Edinburgh clergyman. As a career officer he served with distinction at Monmouth. He came South with Clinton's Charleston expedition 26 Dec. 1779 and fought well at Camden, where he was slightly wounded. He particularly distinguished himself at Guilford Courthouse, but died of wounds a fortnight later.

General Charles O'Hara [52] was dangerously wounded. He had won the battle but he had lost the campaign. It was soon known in London that another such victory would mean the end of the army in the south.

Sadly Cornwallis decided to pull back his famished and exhausted army. Greene had sent back his American army surgeons under a flag of truce to help him take care of the wounded of both sides. Gratefully Cornwallis left his own wounded in their care and headed southeast along the Haw River. A retreat to Camden to join Lord Rawdon would have been too much of an admission that his entire campaign had been a failure. He decided to take his army toward Wilmington, North Carolina, where he could, at least, obtain food and supplies. He started withdrawing on the 18th of March with Greene in cautious pursuit. At Ramsay's Mill, where the Haw joins Deep River to form the Cape Fear River there was an opportunity for Greene to strike, but he felt that he lacked the strength to assure success. Cornwallis continued unmolested into Cross Creek (now Fayettesville) and reached Wilmington by the 7th of April. On the 24th he marched to Virginia.

It remains for Aquilla Blakely [53] to round out the story of the Fauquier men at Guilford Courthouse. Blakely was born in what is now Fauquier County on the 10th of October, 1740. After that nothing ordinary ever happened to Aquilla Blakely. He moved to Patrick County, on the banks of the Dan, where he enrolled in September of 1776 in a company of Captain Henry Lynes under Colonel William Christian. On the day that he left home the sun was eclipsed and it was so dark that the fowls went to roost. After this ominous portent, he marched against the Cherokee to Long Island on the Holston, from which vantage point they raided Indian town on the Tellico Plains. Three more brief tours of duty followed before Guilford Courthouse. On the last one he marched under Captain Abram Penn of Patrick County to the Shallow Ford

52. Charles O'Hara, 1740?-1802, was an illegitimate son of James O'Hara, 2nd Lord Trawley. He had served in Germany, Portugal and Senegal before coming to America in July 1778. He spearheaded Cornwallis' pursuit of Greene to the Dan River.

53. Aquilla Blakely, 1740-1838, said that he was born in Fauquier Co. As the county did not exist in 1740, it must be assumed that he lived there at least until 1759. His parents are unknown and he outlived all his family except Ruth (Blakely) Anderson, his "only known surviving child."

of the Yadkin where, he said, they captured eighty or ninety Tories marching to join Cornwallis.

His adventures lose nothing in the telling, but when he marched in the company of Captain George Hairston about the 1st of March, 1781, to Guilford Courthouse, they managed to arrive too late for the battle. They joined Greene's army the next day and marched in pursuit of Cornwallis as far as Deep River. Here, according to Aquilla, General Greene's army and Earl Cornwallis encamped within three miles of each other, both north of the Deep River but with the latter immediately on the bank. There they "killed 15 or 20 bullocks and in the night made a bridge by cutting saplings long enough to reach from one rock that projected above the water to another." That the starved British had overlooked 15 or 20 bullocks seems unlikely, but perhaps they did. However, the bridge was used only briefly because General Greene stopped pursuit. Blakely's tale is interspersed with many macabre details. At the Haw River one of his comrades was hanged on a walnut limb for attempted desertion. A white oak tree at Cornwallis' camping ground just across the Deep River provided a suitable gallows for another deserter. Apparently some of the militia that had run away early in the battle did not make it all the way home.

Blakely's unit was ordered to Cape Fear, where they were discharged after about four days. Blakely trudged back to Patrick County. War, he thought, could be dangerous. It was his last tour. He died in Blount County, Alabama, on the 7th of December, 1838, at the age of 98 years and 58 days. He still remembered that solar eclipse.

Interlude
The War Returns to Virginia

So, after nearly five years, the war returned to Virginia, almost to the same place where, in 1775, the Virginians had first met the enemy. During the intervening years Virginia had supplied men and treasure, perhaps more than any other of the states, but, aside from a few sporadic raids, her shores had remained inviolate. Clinton could no longer neglect to strike at the heart of the rebellion, if he had any hope of a successful conclusion of a war in which even the British were losing interest.

In May, 1779, a British raid on Norfolk and Portsmouth had resulted in substantial loss of shipping, naval supplies, ordnance and tobacco, but the raiders departed as quickly as they had come. The attack on the 30th of December, 1780, was, however, an entirely different matter. Cornwallis was convinced that the conquest of Virginia would be followed by control of all the colonies and tried to persuade Clinton to that view. He was unsuccessful but Clinton did consent to send a large detachment under Benedict Arnold to Virginia with somewhat limited objectives; destruction of military stores, preventing reinforcement of Greene and rallying of Tory sympathizers.

Having little confidence in Arnold, Clinton sent Lieutenant Colonels Thomas Dundas and John Graves Simcoe with him to tell him what to do. Both were experienced officers but Arnold was, in effect, more capable than either, Arnold had the 18th British Regiment, Simcoe's Queen's Rangers and detachments of Loyalist volunteers from New York and Bucks County, Pennsylvania, about 1,600 men in all. A violent gale off the Virginia capes reduced the number to 1,200 when a war vessel and three transports were forced to turn back.

Nevertheless, within one week he took Richmond, destroyed the iron foundry at Westham, about six miles up the James, a powder factory, machine shops and five or six tons of gunpowder. Returning to Portsmouth on the 6th of January, Arnold entrenched and encamped for the winter. All of this took place without the slightest effective opposition. In fact the raids came at a time when the military establishment in Virginia was in complete disarray. There were four military units in the state, at Elk Hill on the James about 40 miles above Richmond, Fredericksburg, Yorktown and Williamsburg.

At Elk Hill Baron Steuben had about 200 newly enlisted Virginia Continentals. Their training had only begun, but it was better than the small body of militia under Brigadier General George Weedon at Fredericksburg or Muhlenberg's and Nelson's scattered forces near Williamsburg. Thomas Marshall's artillery regiment at Yorktown was in shambles. Jefferson, almost at his wit's end, was calling frantically for help from any source, to little avail. Washington had often warned him to expect an invasion of the state but Jefferson had neither the military experience nor the resources to take adequate precautions. He sent General Thomas Nelson, Jr. of the militia down to the coastal region ("the lower country,") to call up the militia in that quarter, "but waited further intelligence before we would call for militia from the middle or upper country." The response was disappointing.

By the middle of February, with rumors flying around that Clinton was sending substantial reinforcement to Arnold, the Governor and Council could no longer pretend that the local militia could meet the increasingly dangerous situation. They called for militia from the "middle and upper country", post haste. Even then they dared not ask for all the militia and, so doubtful were they of their own effectiveness, they used Baron Steuben's name to spark the patriotic flame. The resolution, on the 16th of February, 1781, read:

> Baron Steuben having requested that an additional force of Militia be immediately called into service; the Governor is advised to order a fourth of the Militia from the Counties of Loudoun, Fairfax, Prince William and Fauquier to march without delay to Williamsburg under proper field Officers, Captains & Subalterns and with their arms.

The homegrown patriots, under the inept military leadership of Governor Jefferson obviously needed help from outside Virginia. Washington, though he did not feel too secure himself outside New York, decided to send Major General Lafayette with three regiments of light infantry - 1,200 rank and file drawn from New England and New Jersey Continental regiments - to march southward. He asked the French fleet to cooperate, but the French ran into their customary misadventure, bad weather, and were forced to limp back to Newport. Lafayette reached Head of Elk on the 3rd of March and five days later a French expeditionary force finally left Newport with the British under Admiral Arbuthnot in hot pursuit. The two fleets met at the mouth of the Chesapeake Bay. Although the French had the upper hand, they abandoned the expedition. Arbuthnot on the other hand, sought refuge in the Chesapeake and linked up with Arnold. With the sea routes now open, Clinton could send Major General William Phillips with 2,000 more troops to join Arnold and take over his command.

On the 1st of April, 1781, the fortunes of the patriots in Virginia had again touched bottom. The men returning from the victory at Cowpens found the enemy on their threshold, ready to strike.

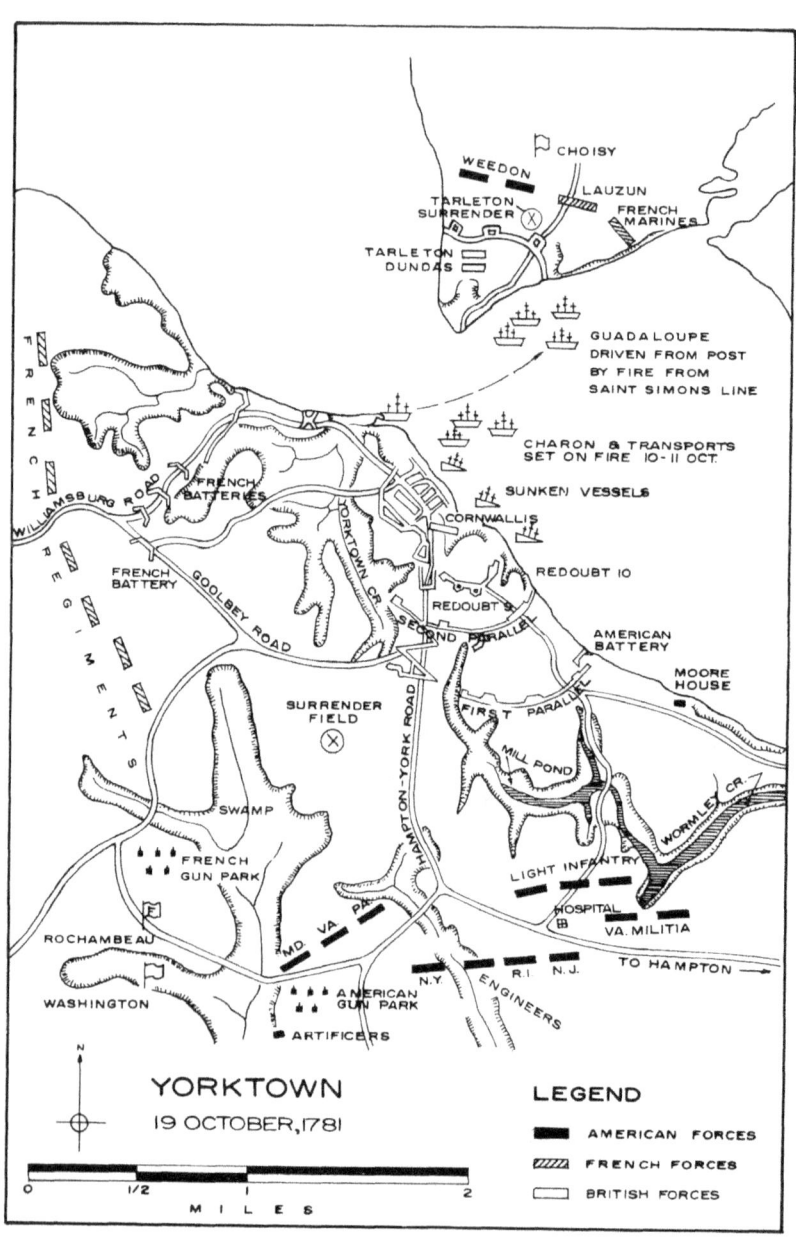

XII
Yorktown

In the winter of 1780-81 the county officials of Fauquier were deeply worried. They knew only too well that the enemy might soon be at their gates and there was little but empty land between them and the British invaders, should they appear. An attack on Virginia appeared almost inevitable and, from the enemy's point of view, it was eminently desirable to cut the colony in half. This would entail a thrust deep into the interior as far as the Blue Ridge. Their great problem was in awakening an apathetic populace to the urgency of the situation.

Not long after Francis Triplett and his men had departed to join Greene in the Carolinas, in October of 1780, Colonel Humphrey Brooke, the County Lieutenant, had been handed a quota calling for 69 men to be raised to serve as Continentals under Baron Steuben.[1] Because the Continental enlistments were "for the war", they did not appeal very strongly to farmers who could not think beyond the next spring's planting. In addition the Congress had no enviable record for probity in financial matters and pay was not something one could count on. In spite of Brooke's most earnest efforts, he could corral only 46, whom he delivered to the Continental recruiting officer. Disgusted and frustrated, Brooke considered resigning his commission, but hesitated to do so before being assured of his back pay.

At the Court held in Fauquier, 26 March 1781, Brooke was given 2,289 lbs. of tobacco, the balance of last year's levy, plus an additional 2,248 for the current year and numerous "sundries" he had furnished the militia.[2] In May he resigned, leaving the county without a County Lieutenant. No one wanted the job. Not until August was it possible to prevail upon a reluctant Colonel William Edmonds to resume his old office.

---

1. Tyler's Quarterly Magazine, Vol. IX, No. 4, p. 235-6.

2. Fauquier County Court Minute Book, 26 March 1781.

Arnold's raids in January provided an incentive that the militia had lacked. The term of enlistment was considerably shorter than that of the Continentals, six months at most, often as little as two. Weedon, writing to Jefferson from Fredericksburg on the 15th of January, told him that he had warned the Northern Neck Counties of their imminent danger. He had then between 600 and 700 men at Fredericksburg and daily expected 500 more from west of the Blue Ridge,[3] but it was not enough. Colonel Armistead Churchill of the 2nd Fauquier Battalion at last realized the necessity of leading his unit to join Weedon, if only to justify the rank he had held so long. He had, in fact, begun signing up men for a six months tour as early as November, 1780. His captains were John O'Bannon and Tilman Weaver. Though they worked feverishly, they were unable to muster enough men to meet Weedon's call in mid-January. When Thomas Kincheloe, for instance, was drafted for a second time early in January, he was told to go home and await a later call.

Kincheloe, who, we remember, had been a recruiting sergeant for Captain Peter Grant for the 11th Virginia Regiment from 1778 to 1780, had been discharged by Grant at Fauquier Courthouse when it became apparent that further effort was useless. He remembered well Colonel Churchill's call to rendezvous at Fauquier Courthouse on the 1st day of February, 1781. It was a cold, clear morning and the sense of urgency to get the matter settled was electric in the crisp air but, even then, nothing much happened. No positive command had been received from Governor Jefferson and, without orders, they could not march.

It was not until the 17th of February that Jefferson summoned enough courage to order out the militia of the inland counties. In a letter to the County Lieutenants of Loudoun, Fairfax, Prince William and Fauquier Counties, he asked for one fourth of their militia to march to Fredericksburg, then to Williamsburg. He asked also that they supply one baggage wagon for every 75 men, to remain as long as they did. In a letter to General Thomas Nelson, informing him of this, he estimated that this order would produce about 1,090 men.[4] He added almost apologetically "These counties are indeed distant, but they have some time held in readiness."

3. Letter, Weedon to Jefferson, 15 Jan. 1781, in **Jefferson Papers**, (Boyd, ed.) Vol. IV. p. 376.

4. Ibid, p. 636.

In January Colonel Churchill added another Captain to his ranks, John Thomas Chunn,[5] a capable officer who was to play a prominent part in the last months of the war. The fourth and last company Captain to appear on the scene was Thomas Bronaugh, who was not apparently able to get his company in readiness in time to march with the rest. Aylett Buckner was the Major in the Fauquier Battalion. The struggle to get the Fauquier men armed, equipped and ready to march continued all through February. On the 3rd of March General George Weedon addressed Governor Jefferson somewhat testily:[6]

> Sir: I had the honour of addressing your Excellency the 28th ulto. The tedious delay of the Fauquier & Loudoun Militia has kept me here ever since in a very disagreeable situation. I have from reports the information that they are now on the march so I have hopes to be on my route to Williamsburg in two or three days.

Churchill took his men by the old Marsh Road to Stafford County, and then by the Lower, or Falls, Road to Falmouth. Weedon did not detain them in Falmouth as he, himself, was busy preparing to take his brigade further south. They then marched through Spotsylvania and Caroline Counties on the "Great Waggon Road", stopping at Bowling Green where they joined another company of militia from the Northern Neck. They followed the Pamunkey the full length of King William County, crossing at West Point where the Pamunkey flows into the York River. They were then only a short distance from Springfield Camp near Williamsburg.

Churchill's men were not all new recruits by any means. Captain O'Bannon had with him William Payne, then 23, who had fought at Great Bridge and had been one of the few who, under the command of Hezekiah Turner, had fought at Germantown. Also

---

5. John Thomas Chunn, 1749-1804, was a man of considerable means who came from Maryland to Fauquier Co. about 1774 and bought two 1,000 acre tracts in 1776 and 1779 from grandsons of Captain James Ball. His home was "Mount Independence" near Delaplane. His mill on Goose Creek, later called Woolf's Mill, still stands.

6. Letter, Weedon to Jefferson, 3 Mar. 1781 in **Jefferson Papers** (Boyd, ed.) Vol. V, p. 54.

with O'Bannon was John O'Rear,[7] who had served for 9 months with George Rogers Clark at Kaskaskia and Vincennes. After his return from Kentucky he had spent his time guarding lookout points along the Potomac and James Rivers. There were many other seasoned veterans.

Not all were. Both Payne and O'Rear brought with them younger brothers of somewhat tender age. William O'Rear was 18, and his friend, William Jett,[8] who was also along, barely 16. Augustine Payne was 19. Somewhere along the line Payne was wounded in the foot but, with a certain Spartan fortitude, refused to turn back.

One of the men with Captain Weaver was Tilman Kemper, another veteran of George Rogers Clark's Kentucky Regiment. He had served at Vincennes under Captain Leonard Helm. He was drafted in Fauquier late in 1780 but it was apparently well into March before he joined Weaver's unit. He claimed that he had served only two months and eight days, from the 23rd of March to the 31st of May. About the end of February Churchill's fourth and last company appeared on the scene under Captain Thomas Bronaugh. With Bronaugh was Jessee Withers,[9] recently returned from service against the Indians on the Holston River and full of stories of Indian villages laid waste and captured evidence of British attempts to incite them to war against the Americans.

However, according to both John O'Rear and Kincheloe, Colonel Churchill had no real intention of remaining permanently in command at Williamsburg. Having delivered his men, he turned

---

7. John O'Rear, 1749-post 1832. On 11 Aug. 1711, John and Daniel O'Rear patented 400 acres on Dorrell's Run. Presumably John and Daniel (see note No. 43, Chap. 3) O'Rear were descended from these men, but according to the will of Thomas Harrison (d. 1773) John O'Rear was living on Goose Creek adjoining Benjamin Harrison's "Glanville". He and his brother William moved to Montgomery Co., Ky., where both were living in 1832.

8. William Jett, 1764-1851, may have been a son of Francis and Mary Jett of Leeds Manor. He died testate at "Orleans" in Leeds Manor (probably the reference is to the house and not to the village). The name of his wife is not given in his will.

9. Jessee Withers, 1760-1834, m. 6 Aug. 1789, Catherine Porter, daughter of Samuel Porter, d. 1809.

over his command; some say to Colonel James Innes,[10] others to Colonel William Brent. Colonel Churchill returned to Fauquier, ostensibly to raise more troops, and was seen no more in the field. All of his enlistments expired on the 24th of April and many of his men, having seen enough of adventure, wanted to go home.[11] A number, however, stayed on, among them Jessee Withers, who re-enlisted, and Tilman Kemper, who was promptly drafted again. Those who went home had not been idle during their tour of duty, as we will see, but they missed the last act of the drama.

Not all of the Fauquier men then on duty were with Colonel Churchill by any means. We must not forget those who had marched off so proudly to join Colonel Thomas Marshall's Virginia State Regiment of Artillery. At "Oak Hill", his home in Fauquier, on the 4th of February, Colonel Thomas Marshall, recently returned from Kentucky, took a long and troubled look at what had happened to his regiment in his absence. Having made out, to the best of his ability, a detailed roster, he felt that some note of explanation was in order. According to a document on file in the State Auditor's office in 1848 (but since apparently lost) he wrote:

> From my long absence & the present dispersed situation of my Regiment, it is impossible for me to give an exact return but in the above the officers stand as they rank in the line (except Capt. Allan who perhaps has no rank at all in the line). The dates of their commissions I have given so far as they fall within my knowledge. As to the non-commissioned officers and privates, according to the last accounts I am able to get of them, their numbers & situation stand as follows: To the Southard with Capt.

10. James Innes (Innis) 1754-1798. Son of Robert and Catherine (Richards) Innes of Caroline Co. He was a lawyer and orator, considered by many superior to Patrick Henry. As Lieut. Col. of the 15th Va. Regt., he served at Trenton, Princeton, Brandywine, Trenton and Monmouth. He resigned in September, 1778, but was asked by Washington to command a regiment of Virginia militia at Yorktown. He was a man of colossal stature and commanding presence. He married Elizabeth Cocke, daughter of James Cocke of Williamsburg. His daughter, Anne, married Peyton Randolph.

11. Letters, Jefferson to Muhlenberg (16 Apr.) Weedon (17 Apr.) in **Jefferson Papers,** (Boyd, ed.) Vol. V, pp. 475, 483. They wanted to go home before those who were to replace them had arrived. In his letter to Weedon, Jefferson instructs him to hold the old Fauquier militia at least until the 7th of May. On the 26th of April he wrote Steuben that he "still relied on them for 1 May."

(Roan), twenty-six for the war and between thirty and forty whose terms of enlistment are nearly expired. And in the State of Virginia, about thirteen for the War with Capt. Moody, one with me, one with Capt. Clay as I am informed & one with the adjutant; besides five or six others with Capt. Moody whose terms of enlistment are nearly expired.
T. Marshall, Col. U.S.A.

In short, more than two thirds of Marshall's command, upwards of 60 officers and men, were with Captain Christopher Roan in North Carolina under General Greene. At Yorktown Lieutenant Colonel Elias Edmonds and Major John Mazarett had only twenty men under Captain Edward Moody, a third of whom might leave at any moment. Captain Gideon Johnston, his able quartermaster, his son Captain Thomas Marshall, Jr., the regimental paymaster and Captain-Lieutenant Henry Vowles, the adjutant, had no commands, though Vowles did have a clerk. Captain John Allan "of ye Artificers" (gunsmiths) stood ready to maintain whatever field pieces they could commandeer, and 1st Lieutenant Walter Scott was in the "laboratory" (presumably making gunpowder).

Of the remaining officers Captain Samuel Blackwell, who had rashly taken some of his men to Charleston, was still a prisoner. His nephew, Humphrey Marshall and John Spencer were "invalid". The dismal fact remained that six additional Captains, eight Captain-Lieutenants and eight 1st Lieutenants, who were without commands and therefore supernumerary, had absolutely nothing to do. There was nothing wrong with the Virginia State Regiment of Artillery that could not be cured by the infusion of three or four hundred artillery recruits and a dozen or so guns. The outlook for obtaining even a fraction of that number of men or guns was, Marshall knew, bleak indeed.

The Gentlemen Justices of Fauquier County, with the best intentions in the world of sending clothing and provisions to Williamsburg in the wake of Colonel Churchill's battalion, were without means to do so. The treasury was bare. On the 5th of February they hastily called a special meeting of the County Court to consider ways and means of replenishing it. They especially needed some means of transporting supplies—specifically a wagon and team. They decided upon a special levy of 30 lbs. of tobacco for each tithable and appointed a Commission to see to its collection. They knew it was not enough, but they believed that it was all the traffic would bear. As a matter of fact, it was accepted more readily than they expected, encouraging them to order another levy in March.

On the 26th of February, at the regular court session, it was realized that no provision had been made for storing the levied tobacco. Martin Pickett offered the use of one of his warehouses near Fauquier Courthouse—for a price. He was allowed £875 rent, a figure that occasioned a wry smile. In Continental currency it was next to nothing. In March Robert Ashby was allowed £750 for his trouble and the rent of his "houses" (probably barns) near Delaplane for the same purpose. At the same court William Edmonds and John Blackwell were allowed £500 for trouble in procuring beef. William Pickett was ordered to deliver the wagon and team, purchased by the county from William Bryan for $2,400, to John Blackwell, deputy commissioner, presumably to deliver beef and grain to the army. The possible value of 2,400 of the new Continental dollars at the time defies imagining.

The enlistments of the few remaining rank and file in the Virginia Regiment of Artillery were fast expiring. At the March court Joshua and James Keneard[12] produced discharges signed by Major Mazarett and asked that they be recorded. Thomas White had one signed by Lieutenant Colonel Elias Edmonds. Edmonds was getting heartily sick of commanding a phantom unit. Before the 28th of May he had resigned and accepted a colonelcy in the militia. In May, John Ridley, quartermaster sergeant, and Enoch Smith and William Waddell, gunners, presented discharges signed by John Mazarett, still a Major, but now *Commandant* of the regiment.

In 1853, in Wilkes County, Georgia, a document was found that gives us an interesting glimpse of the Fauquier men in the Virginia Regiment of Artillery under Colonel Edmonds. William Benson left a brief autobiography in which he named all of the Fauquier men he remembered, 46 in all. After outlining the details of a rather poignant childhood, he says that he enlisted for three years when he was eighteen, on the 24th of August, 1777. He marched to "Little York" (Gloucester) with Colonel Thomas Marshall, but was taken sick in March and was sent to the "horspittle" in Williamsburg with three of his comrades, William Waddell, Mason Watts and Peter Hitt. They continued sick and finally, in May, had to be sent home on furlough to recover. They returned to Yorktown late in 1778 and remained there until the spring of 1780. Then they were ordered up to Williamsburg to

---

12. Joshua and James Keneard are not easily traced. James married, 26 Nov. 1804, Margaret (Peggy) Jeffries. Joshua witnessed the will of William Sinklair, d. 1798 and posted bond for the marriage of Frances Keneard to William Hall in 1789.

march to Charleston. Charleston was taken before they arrived, so he "went about" until his enlistment expired on the 24th of August 1780.

However, the only real home that William Benson had known after his father's death in 1765 was his regiment, and he was miserable outside it. On the 5th of September he was back, as shown by an order on the commissary department as follows:

> This is to certify that William Benson a Soldier in Colo. Marshall's Regiment of Artillery have due him from the State of Virginia one Coate, one Vest, one pr. Breeches, Two Shirts, Two pr. Stockings, Two pr. Shoes & one hatt.
> Richmond Sept. 5th, 1780
> Yancey Lipscomb, Capt-Lt. U.S.A.

The roster he gives us includes the names of all those who were discharged before the 28th of May, 1781, but William Benson, serving in some capacity under Colonel Elias Edmonds, whom he revered, stayed on. Years later, when Colonel Edmonds and many others were dead, he compiled his list with the help of his friend John Hammonds. We will meet him later at the "seage at York."

The March Court produced few other developments of interest. In spite of the parlous times land speculation on the "Monongalia River below the mouth of Elk" was evidently rife. The Sheriff, James Bell, was ordered to summon a grand jury for the May Court. In May it developed that the Sheriff, for some reason or another, had neglected to do so. He was fined 1,000 lbs. of tobacco and dismissed. John Moffett was appointed in his place.

During March, one by one, the Fauquier militiamen came back from Cowpens. They were exhausted by the fatigue they had "underwent" but, to their credit, most of them joined up later. Before the 23rd of March Morgan, ill, dejected and stony broke, reached "Saratoga", his home near Berryville. In addition to his other worries, he had received no pay whatever since returning to the army in September, 1780, he could get no reimbursement for the corn he had furnished the army, and even a mare he had brought with him to sell to defray his expenses (it was useless to bring currency) went unpaid for. Duncan Rose of Petersburg,[13] who had care of the animal, wrote Jefferson 3 March urging payment for the last as "General Morgan's family is distressed for money."

---

13. Letter, Rose to Jefferson, 3 Mar. 1781, **Jefferson Papers** (Boyd, ed.) Vol. V, p. 53.

On reaching "Saratoga" the "old Waggoner" roared his displeasure to Jefferson. He was "in great want" and so "bare of cloaths" that he was ashamed to be seen in public. What irked him particularly was that the State Auditor, as State Auditors do, took refuge behind a technicality—he could not ascertain the precise date of Morgan's commission, so he could not compute his pay, he said. Morgan continued to roar until the 15th of October, when he was paid in discounted notes.

Nevertheless Morgan was not giving up. He had a plan for raising a troop of cavalry in Frederick for Colonel William Washington's Horse and asked Jefferson's permission to do so.

In March Arnold had been biding his time at the great Byrd plantation, "Westover" on the James, awaiting reinforcements promised by Clinton. They arrived at Portsmouth on the 26th of March. The 2,600 new men were under the command of Major General William Phillips,[14] an especially unattractive character, who outranked Arnold and was expected to take over his command.

Against this greatly augmented British force were only 3,000 American troops, widely scattered. Most of them were raw militia. In and around Petersburg Brigadier General Peter Muhlenberg had about 1,000 men to guard the supplies of tobacco and military stores in its warehouses. In spite of its importance, the town was unfortified and its approaches were guarded only by small detachments of pickets. Between Fredericksburg and Williamsburg Brigadier General George Weedon had at least 1,000 men. "Joe Gourd's" expectations of January had proved somewhat sanguine with respect to reinforcement from beyond the Blue Ridge, but there had been other notable acquisitions. Among these were the Fauquier Militia under Colonel Churchill and several other militia companies from Fauquier and Culpeper, brought down by Captains William Grigsby, Gabriel Green[15] and Armistead White, to serve under General Edward Stevens. The difficulty with General Weedon's command was that, if the need arose to assemble in one

---

14. William Phillips, 1731?-1781, was a highly efficient officer who served with distinction at Ticonderoga and Saratoga as General of Artillery. Although something of a hero in the **Royal Artillery**, the Americans found him insolent and obnoxious in extreme.

15. Gabriel Green, was a son of James and Elizabeth (Jones) Green of Culpeper Co. Col. John Green was his uncle. He married, in Fauquier, 22 Sept. 1783, Sarah Ann Grant. After the war he moved to Green River, Kentucky.

place, it was so widely scattered that it is doubtful that even General Weedon could have remembered where they all were.

For instance, William King, who had been discharged at Valley Forge, and his younger brother Robert were brought in by Captain Grigsby and spent most of their three month tour at Camp Maubin at Malvern Hill near the James River about half way between Richmond and Williamsburg. They were discharged 2 April 1781, having seen no action. Grigsby returned to Fauquier County for more men and reappeared later.

Thomas Kincheloe was detached from Chunn's company and sent under Captain John Edens[16] with 24 men to Yorktown where they remained until driven out by a "body of British supposed to be about a thousand strong." They made their escape across the York River under heavy British fire. However this time the British left Yorktown and the Virginians returned three days later. Ten days later Captain Edens discharged them, apparently early in May.

Then there was Joseph Oder, who wandered around vaguely between Fredericksburg and "Little York", seldom sleeping two successive nights in the same place, with the British always just around the bend in the road. John Blackwell,[17] one of Captain Gabriel Green's men, did about the same thing, but with a more certain knowledge of where he had been—Richmond, Norfolk, Cabin Point on the James and up the river to Sandy Point, to Carter's Ferry across the James, back to Richmond and then to Malvern Hill—all with the enemy after them. It must have been interesting serving under General Weedon—interesting and somewhat disconcerting.

It was possibly just as well that Weedon's boys were out and about because Baron Steuben, stolidly guarding the supply depot at Point of Forks, on the James about 30 miles above Richmond,

16. John Edens. It has been claimed that he was John Eddens of Fauquier Co., but no proof that the latter held the rank of Captain has been found.

17. John Blackwell, 1758-post 1834, was a son of James Blackwell of Culpeper Co. Their relationship, if any, to the Blackwells of Fauquier is untraced. He first entered service in 1780 as a substitute for three months for his father. He served under Col. James Slaughter. In September he entered as a substitute for Henry Coons, who paid him $500 in Continental paper. This time he was under Col. John Green and was stationed at Richmond, Manchester and Norfolk. He was discharged in October, 1780, "Col. Green's regiment being too weak" to remain where it was. This was before Arnold's raid! After 1794 he moved to Shelby Co., Kentucky. There is no mention of a family.

was sulking in his tent. His regiment of Virginia Continentals had risen from 200 in January to 500, and was now well trained, but he was far from happy. Correctly surmising on the 29th of March that Cornwallis in Wilmington, North Carolina had little choice but to effect a union with Phillips in Virginia, Steuben proposed taking his Continentals, together with most of the Virginia militia, and marching to join Greene with the purpose of crushing Cornwallis before he could move north. The plan was not without merit, that is if Virginia would risk giving Phillips free rein to ravage the tidewater. The Governor and Council, understandably, declined with thanks.

Steuben, with a European's fundamental lack of understanding of state pride and politics, could see only the tactical situation. He found it hard to believe that a strategy having the support of Washington, Lafayette, Greene, the Virginia Brigadiers, Weedon and Muhlenberg, and even of Richard Henry Lee, could be frustrated by the elected representatives of a single state. Angered by the refusal to follow his recommendations, he threatened to march south anyway, to join Greene. As his troops were on Continental establishment he could, in fact, have done so, but Greene wisely refused to issue the order. Steuben pondered resignation.

Lafayette was still waiting at Head of Elk for some word that the French fleet would join him when he reached Virginia. In fact the fleet was on its way, but the young Marquis did not know it. Neither did Washington. Only Rochambeau had the information and he was telling no one, especially not Washington. At that particular time relations between the two men were somewhat strained.

Jean Baptiste Donation de Vimeur, Comte de Rochambeau[18] had been in Newport almost a year, following Vergennes' orders to give Washington the impression of French cooperation without, in fact, committing his 5,500 French troops to any scheme that might prove dangerous. The strategy was becoming increasingly

18. Jean Baptiste Donation de Vimeur, Comte de Rochambeau, 1725-1807. Born at Vendome of an old and distinguished family, he was first trained for the church. Having no vocation and a decided leaning toward a military career, he was commissioned at the outbreak of the War of the Austrian Succession (1740). His rise was rapid, surprisingly because of his ability rather than influence at court. He later became a Marshal of France. He was arrested during the Terror and narrowly escaped the guillotine because of the timely death of Robespierre.

apparent to Washington. The incident that triggered a near-confrontation took place early in April. Washington had written a letter, dated at New Windsor 28 March 1781, addressed to Lund Washington, his estate manager at Mount Vernon. It was not one of his nobler epistolary efforts. It was intercepted by the British and Clinton gleefully published it in an effort to stir up trouble between Washington and Rochambeau.[19]

The letter began somewhat testily with a comment concerning Washington's next-door neighbor and old hunting companion, William Triplett.[20] The subject is irrelevant but it was couched in Washington's typically top-lofty style which dispelled, for those who knew him, any suspicion of forgery. It continued with this amazing paragraph:

> We have heard nothing certain of the two Fleets since they left their respective ports. We wait with impatient anxiety for advices from Chesapeake and the Southern Army. God send they may be favourable to us; a detachment from New York has made two or three attempts to put to Sea (for the purpose, it is said, of reinforcing either Arnold or Cornwallis) and as often returned. My last accts. from New York mention another attempt on the 25th; but whether with truth or not, it is not in my power to say. It is unfortunate; but this I mention in confidence, that the French Fleet and detachment did not undertake the enterprize they are now upon when I first proposed it to them; the destruction of Arnold's Corps would then have been inevitable before the British Fleet could have been in condition to put to Sea. Instead of this, the small squadron which took the *Romulus* and other Vessels was sent and could not, as I foretold, do any thing without a Land force at Portsmouth.

---

19. The letter was published in Rivington's "Gazette", a New York paper sympathetic to the British, 4 April 1781.

20. William Triplett, 1730-1803, was a son of Thomas and Sarah (Harrison) Triplett of Fairfax Co. The victim of this unwelcome notoriety was usually on excellent terms with the Commander-in-Chief. His brother, Captain Thomas Triplett of Grayson's Regiment, escorted Mrs. Washington to and from Camp Middlebrook on occasion and was one of the officers who warned Washington of the Conway Cabal. Francis Triplett of Fauquier was his first cousin.

Rochambeau chose to slide over the incident but he was not mollified by Washington's rather flimsy excuses. He was certainly amply justified in questioning Washington's discretion as, of all people, Lund Washington was probably least entitled to know what those at Washington's headquarters thought of the French alliance. It was not until 26 May that Washington received from his Paris representative, John Laurens,[21] his first inkling that the French West Indian fleet had been ordered to send a major detachment to America.

Two weeks later Rochambeau finally divulged the news that de Grasse had reached Cape Haitien with 20 ships of the line, 3 frigates and 3,000 troops. Rochambeau was guilty of still another bit of dissembling. Washington, of course, expected and wanted the French fleet off New York to join in a proposed attack on that city. He still cherished the belief that conquest of that British stronghold was the only way to end the war. Washington has been accused of myopia in his concentration on New York, but the charge is unfair. New York, where Clinton had more than 14,000 men, *was* important and its successful investiture *would*, probably, have ended the war.

Rochambeau, who could not speak English and was not interested in learning, saw the matter as Steuben did, as a tactical problem. He correctly foresaw that the war could come to a swift military conclusion by a combined land and naval operation at the mouth of the Chesapeake Bay. Shamelessly, therefore, he conspired with de Grasse to turn up with his fleet in the wrong place at the right time. Nothing of the sort was even guessed at Washington's headquarters or in Virginia.

Early in April Jefferson began to worry in earnest about the early expiration of enlistments of the militia. He had sent Lafayette a list of the militia from 18 counties totalling 3,226 men, including 292 from Fauquier then in the field. On the 28th he warned him that those from Loudoun, Fauquier, Prince William, Fairfax, Spotsylvania, Caroline and Culpeper would soon expire and, though he was issuing a call for men to replace them, he could not

---

21. John Laurens, ca. 1754-1782, son of Henry Laurens of South Carolina, was educated in England and Geneva. He served with distinction at Brandywine, Germantown and Monmouth. He was at Charleston during the siege and was captured. On parole, he was sent to France in 1781 to help Franklin. He was active at Yorktown and, with the Viscomte de Noailles, negotiated the surrender. He was killed in a minor skirmish in South Carolina, 27 Aug. 1782.

be sure of its success.²² On the 11th of April he received a disquieting letter from Weedon who was alarmed that the British fleet might make an attempt to destroy Hunter's works and the gun factory operated by Fielding Lewis, Washington's brother-in-law, at Fredericksburg. He suggested that Steuben march some troops back to defend them. Steuben refused, saying that in "trying to guard everything, nothing would be defended." In passing Weedon mentioned that the militia of Loudoun, Fauquier, Prince William and Fairfax were talking of "their tour being out on the 24th of April."²³

The Fauquier militia was in the throes of another crisis. Major Aylett Buckner had come with them on the march to Williamsburg but had had to give up because of his health and had returned home. On the 12th of April the officers recommended to the Governor that he appoint Captain John O'Bannon in his place, pointing out that he was the oldest commissioned Captain in the Fauquier Battalion and was well qualified for the rank of Major. For once the officers were in accord. It was signed by Captain John Thomas Chunn and 10 other officers. However the promotion apparently was given to Captain Chunn.²⁴

As April rolled on and Phillips and Arnold were obviously preparing an excursion into the hinterland, the Governor and Council sent out another frantic call for militia. On the 14th of April letters were sent to Fauquier, Loudoun, Caroline, Albemarle, Fluvanna, Goochland and Henrico counties, demanding immediate response. Fauquier was to furnish 252 men and Loudoun no fewer than 407.²⁵ Both counties promptly protested, claiming with some justice that they had already in the field more men than they could afford and far more than some Virginia counties.²⁶

22. Letters, Jefferson to Lafayette (19 Mar, 28 Mar.) in **Jefferson Papers**, (Boyd, ed.) Vol. V, pp. 181, 271.

23. Ibid, p. 410.

24. Ibid, p. 423.

25. **Journal of the Council of the State of Virginia**, Vol. II, p. 335.

26. Letter, Jefferson to Samuel Cox, 14 Apr. 1781, in **Jefferson Papers**, Vol. V, p. 444. Cox appealed on behalf of Fauquier and Loudoun, citing previous service. On the 1st of April Jefferson had taken the trouble to investigate the claim and discovered that Fauquier men had indeed performed more individual tours of duty than any other county, the incredible sum of 9,078. The only close rival was Caroline Co. Nevertheless, he replied to Cox that the militia of both counties could not be spared and he would "require continuance until the others arrive."

Four days later, on the 18th, Arnold made the first move. Lafayette, on his way from Baltimore, was out of arm's reach. Arnold sailed up the James River toward Petersburg with 2,500 trained British regulars, destroying whatever they came upon. On the 24th they disembarked at City Point and marched to Petersburg. Muhlenberg put up a still resistance but he had no artillery and was forced to withdraw. Petersburg, with its quantities of military stores and 4,000 hogsheads of tobacco, was left open to the enemy.

The success of these marauding expeditions and the lack of any effective resistance encouraged Phillips to continue. At Chesterfield Courthouse a great range of barracks was burned and 300 barrels of flour taken. At Osborne's, on the James about 15 miles below Richmond, the Americans lost a considerable naval force assembled to cooperate with the French fleet, if it ever came. There the *Tempest, Renown* (26 guns), and the *Jefferson* (14 guns) were disabled. With the capture of 2 ships, 3 brigantines, 2 schooners and 5 sloops, went 2,000 hogsheads of tobacco and great quantities of flour and naval stores. Among those captured was naval Captain James Markham of Fauquier,[27] skipper of the *Tempest*.

The next stops were Manchester, across the river from Richmond, where they burned 1,200 hogsheads of tobacco, and Warwick, where they took 500 barrels of flour, destroyed the mills, warehouses and more tobacco. May 1st found them back at Manchester, eyeing speculatively the Virginia capital across the river. They were just a little late. On the 29th of April Lafayette had arrived in Richmond with his 1,200 Continentals.

On Tuesday, the 1st of May, 1781, the General Assembly of the Commonwealth of Virginia was, as usual, scheduled to meet in Richmond. The circumstances were hardly propitious for convening a deliberative body. The atmosphere was electric, the scene one of pure chaos. Obtaining a quorum was next to impossible. The members of the House of Delegates behaved as one might expect legislators to do when, momentarily, they expect cannon fire to explode in the council chamber.

---

27. James Markham, probably a cousin of Thomas Marshall, married 29 Nov. 1770, Catherine Kenner, daughter of Howson Kenner. He was first captain of the galley *Page* and later the *Dragon*. He was appointed to the command of the *Tempest* 1 Dec. 1780. He attempted to escape capture in a small boat. He and Lieut. William Steele were captured but Lieut. William Harwar Parker made his escape by swimming ashore under enemy fire.

The County of Fauquier had sent to represent them Major Francis Triplett and Captain William Pickett.

Just how or why these worthies were elected to replace Colonel Martin Pickett and Captain Charles Chilton who had served for the preceding three years remains a mystery. Neither had any legislative experience, other than serving on the county court, and neither was especially well-known or well-connected in Richmond. Both had more important things to do for which they were better qualified. If the county wanted to honor a hero, a medal would have been a more acceptable reward for Francis Triplett than an uneasy seat in the House of Delegates. He was there, though, as shown by the account book the following December, when he was paid £1,664 for attending the May session.[28] Both he and Pickett were appointed to committees which would have been important under calmer conditions. In May, 1781, the only really important committee was the one appointed to consider moving the capital to Charlottesville, Staunton or even Winchester, out of range of General Phillips' trigger-happy gunners. On Thursday, the 10th of May, the Assembly gave up and adjourned to meet in Charlottesville on the 24th of May.

Although the situation was now critical, Jefferson was still reluctant to abandon his principles of democracy and seize the power necessary to raise an army by conscription. When there was a clamor in the legislature that General Daniel Morgan be given anything necessary to induce him to take the field again, he was glad to oblige. There were stories of whole rifle battalions lurking in the hills who would serve, but only under Morgan.[29]

Morgan was not unwilling. He had written to Francis Triplett that his health was much improved. His old friend Colonel Christian Febiger was visiting him in Frederick County when there was an eruption of violence in Hampshire County caused by disaffected Loyalist sympathizers. Morgan was asked to lead a

---

28. National Archives, Record Group 93. Revolutionary Receipts, "No. 38985, 26 Dec. 1781: Received for Francis Triplett sixteen hundred & sixty four pounds 8/, his wages as a Delegate for the County of Fauquier to May session 1781, & for John Bryon five thousand three hundred and sixty two pounds 10/ for waggon hire attending the Fauquier Militia on duty to the relief of South Carolina."

29. This belief appears to have been mistaken although Colonel John Smith confirmed it in a letter to Horatio Gates, 18 June 1781. Gates Papers, New York Historical Society.

militia army against the insurgents.[30] The uprising was quickly put down and Morgan, leaving Febiger in command, hurried back home to prepare to join Greene in South Carolina. He felt so well that he was convinced that he was ready for strenuous service. In truth, Morgan had his good and bad days, depending on the weather. As spring brought warmer weather, the good days began to outnumber the bad. Letters from his friends in the Assembly and from Lafayette changed his plans. Lafayette wanted Morgan to raise a brigade of riflemen and cavalry, which he would personally command. "I ever had a great esteem for riflemen," he assured Morgan and nothing would give him greater pleasure than to have Morgan at his side.

On the 2nd of June the House of Delegates passed a resolution directing Jefferson to call on Brigadier General Daniel Morgan to take the field, allowing him the widest discretionary powers in organizing his brigade. Morgan's mind churned with plans for a brigade of light infantry composed of three regiments, each consisting of eight companies of riflemen and a troop of cavalry. He already had the cavalry. All that was required was enlisting the infantry, nearly 2,000 men. It was a tall order, but Morgan believed it could be done.

Letting no time go by, Jefferson wrote Morgan on the 2nd of June enclosing commissions for officers of three battalions and urging him to proceed with all deliberate speed.[32] It was one of the last acts of Jefferson's ill-starred two years as Governor of the Commonwealth. Conscious of his inadequacy as a military leader, he had suggested that General Thomas Nelson, Jr. take his place. The Assembly agreed.

As Steuben had predicted, Cornwallis marched from Wilmington, arriving in Petersburg, Virginia on the 20th of May. While on the way he learned to his dismay that General Phillips had died of typhoid fever in Portsmouth. Phillips' army with an additional 1,500 men sent by Clinton and his own force gave Cornwallis command of a united British army totalling 7,200 rank

30. The principal leader of the mob was John Claypool, a Scotsman and prominent farmer, who organized his neighbors to resist conscription and impressment of beef. As Morgan approached at the head of a body of militia the uprising collapsed.

31. Letter, Lafayette to Morgan, 17 May 1781. Quoted in Don Higginbotham, **Daniel Morgan, Revolutionary Rifleman,** p. 161.

32. **Jefferson Papers,** J. Boyd, ed., Vol. VI, pp. 70, 71n, 72n. **Journals of the House of Delegates** (1781) pp. 1-10.

and file. In the meantime, Lafayette had been joined by Muhlenberg's and Weedon's brigades, totalling 2,000 militia and a handful of dragoons. Against the British he had but 3,250 men of whom two-thirds were militia. "Were I to fight a battle," he wrote Washington laconically on the 24th of May, "I should be cut to pieces, the militia dispersed and the arms lost. Were I to decline fighting, the country would think itself given up. I am therefore determined to skirmish, but not engage too far ... Were I always equal to the enemy, I should be extremely happy in my present command, but I am not strong enough even to get beaten."[33]

In the face of Cornwallis' overwhelming superiority, Lafayette had no choice but to retreat. There were only two possibilities of reinforcement, Steuben's 500 Continentals at Point of Forks, or the Pennsylvania Line which had been ordered south under General Anthony Wayne before the 1st of March. Wayne, whose men were recovering from the effects of a traumatic mutiny, encountered serious organizational and supply problems that delayed his march from York, Pennsylvania, until 20 May. Though his force numbered only 800 men,[34] many fewer than expected, Lafayette led his army by forced marches to Ely's Ford on the Rapidan to meet him. Cornwallis pursued only as far as Cook's Ford on the North Anna, where, despairing of preventing a junction between Lafayette and Wayne, he turned his attention elsewhere.

Tarleton was sent to Charlottesville after the Virginia legislators, only to find that all but seven had fled. On the 4th of June, while his dragoons were beating at the gates of Monticello, Jefferson took to the hills. Simcoe was sent to Point of Forks to engage Steuben. Steuben evaded them, though, having been taken in by an obvious trick, he lost the supplies he had been so zealously guarding. Tarleton and Simcoe then rejoined Cornwallis who was encamped at Elk Hill on the James below Point of Forks.

33. **Memoirs, Correspondence and Manuscripts of General Lafayette,** Vol. I, p. 417, quoted by Ward, **The War of the Revolution,** Vol. II, p. 873.

34. There is a wide difference in the estimate of the numbers Wayne commanded. Ward, **op. cit.,** gives 800. Boatner, **Encyclopedia of the American Revolution,** p. 1154, has "about 1,000 good troops." Neither figure came up to Washington's and Lafayette's expectations.

Fauquier County played host to an army from outside her borders for only three days during the Revolution.[35] It rained steadily and they had a terrible time. "Mad" Anthony Wayne had ridden on ahead to meet Lafayette, but his men, and artillery, marching from York, reached Noland's Ferry across the Potomac in the midst of a violent storm. In crossing the river four soldiers were drowned when their boat capsized. On the 31st of May they camped by the Potomac. The officers spent the night in Colonel Joshua Clapham's Negro quarters because of the rain, the men in the mud outside. The next day, after making only five miles they camped until the 3rd of June. They then marched through Leesburg and camped for the night on Goose Creek 15 miles further on. The rain must have subsided because the next day they marched 18 miles and reached Red House (Haymarket). Another 12 miles on the old Shenandoah Hunting Path brought them into Fauquier County, southeast of present day Catlett.

The rain began again, but, on the 6th of June, they pushed on to Elk Run Church. They stayed there all of the 7th because of the rain. John Crump, who lived on Elk Run, complained that they damaged his plantation to the tune of £15 and had taken off with two of his horses. He had a certificate for £60 for them and would, he said, expect to be paid in specie.[36] George Fitzhugh also claimed that damage had been done to his plantation on Cedar Run. Many had lost horses and, of course, the Pennsylvania Line had to be fed. Brereton Jones[37] not only furnished beef and fodder but also pasturage for their horses. Thomas Withers and others furnished wagons and teams for the use of Wayne's brigade as well as for the local militia. The amounts of beef, corn, wheat and whiskey furnished by the people of Fauquier during that period was prodigious. It was, of course, exactly what was happening all over Virginia and they had no reason to complain. They expected when the war was over, to be paid, however, and were not bashful about saying so.

35. It is probable that militia from Frederick, Berkeley or Hampshire Cos. crossed Fauquier, but their passage is not recorded.

36. Fauquier County Court Minutes, 1784-86, p. 269. As these claims were not processed until 1784 when currency had stabilized, payment in specie was possible. However Crump's request indicates some doubt in Fauquier as to the value of paper.

37. Brereton Jones, 1716-1795, was a prosperous farmer who lived near Elk Run Church on land adjoining John Crump. He married, 1740, Elizabeth Warner, who survived him. (See G. H. S. King, **The Register of Overwharton Parish**, p. 61)

FAUQUIER COUNTY IN THE REVOLUTION

On the 8th of June, the rain having subsided, the Pennsylvania Line started early and crossed the Rappahannock at Norman's Ford at 10 o'clock. The march across Culpeper to Raccoon Ford on the Rapidan was short and they joined Lafayette's army about midday. Although they could hardly have been impressed with the beauty of Fauquier during their brief, soggy visit, the officers apparently admitted that they had fared well, enough so as to encourage visits from other of Lafayette's units. Captain James Markham and his wife, Catherine (Kenner) Markham, were promptly visited by gentlemen from Colonel Lee's [38] Corps and Colonel Armand's [39] Legion in search of flour, beef and fodder. Colonel Lee's men also visited Brereton Jones, as did four men from Major William Nelson's cavalry. When the latter ate dinner, pastured their horses and rode off leaving a certificate for only one bushel of oats, Jones decided that hospitality had gone far enough. He put in a claim for the food.

It was probably with some relief that Wayne assembled his men at Raccoon Ford, especially his artillery unit with six precious guns which, he feared, might be permanently stuck in Fauquier mud.

Although this reinforcement did not, by any means, give Lafayette the strength to engage Cornwallis in battle, he could move closer and stop the unopposed raids. The day Wayne arrived he started south from his camp at Raccoon Ford on the Rapidan and by the morning of the 12th of June held a strong position behind Mechunk Creek (a tributary of the upper James) to fend off any British move toward Charlottesville. The stores had been moved to Albemarle Old Courthouse and, to protect them he had to move west across the enemy's front without exposing his left to a flank attack. William Butler tells about it: [40]

38. Colonel Lee, who was with Lafayette, was not "Lighthorse Harry" who was rather busily engaged at Ninety-Six, S. C.

39. Armand-Charles Tuffin, Marquis de La Rouerie, 1750-1793, after distinguished service at Short Hills, Brandywine, and Monmouth was second in command under Pulaski. After Pulaski's death at Savannah, he joined de Kalb. He was given an improper mission by Gates at Camden and did badly. Early in 1781 he returned to France for clothing and equipment, but his men joined Lafayette. He was "urbane, polished, a gallant leader and greatly beloved."

40. William Butler, 1762-post 1834, moved to Bourbon Co., Kentucky about 1785 and, in 1825, to Lincoln Co., Missouri.

I served as a substitute in place of Joseph Butler in ... Colonel Blackwell's Regiment and in May, 1781 rendezvoused in Fauquier County where I had moved after receiving my former discharge (he had been with Colonel John Slaughter of Culpeper guarding the fords of the Dan). Mr. Butler, for whom I served resided there. We marched to join Lawson's brigade at Petersburg and then crossed the James River into Hanover County and joined Gen. Wayne's army at Raccoon Ford, where the British under Cornwallis succeeded in getting between our army and its public stores which had been removed from Richmond to Albemarle Courthouse. The army had to cut out an old, disused road for twelve miles so as to intersect the road between the British and the public stores, which they succeeded in doing two miles in advance of the enemy. They drew up in order of battle, expecting the enemy every minute, but they came not.

John Blackwell was at Raccoon Ford, also, though he approached it from a different direction. Immediately upon completing his recent tour, while still at Malvern Hill, he was "prevailed upon" to begin another by Captain Edmonds.[41] Under Edmonds, Blackwell marched from Camp Maubin to the Chickahominy Swamp west of Williamsburg, where there was an American supply depot. The British marched to "Pogue's Mill" and they were forced to retreat to Albemarle Courthouse. Just how they achieved this is left in doubt by failure to identify Pogue's Mill, but after a short period they joined General Wayne at Raccoon Ford.

William Allen, who had gone to Germantown with Captain Charles Chilton, must have been on the same march. He was still serving with Chilton, who had brought his company down to serve under the "Marquis De La Fayette at Richmond." With two others of his company he was sent on a scouting party under Colonel Call[42] and Major Boyes to "Mobbins" Hills where they remained until the army marched from Richmond. The next day the British

---

41. Elias Edmonds, b. ca. 1758, was probably a son of William and Anne (Cralle?) Edmonds of Northumberland Co.

42. Richard Call was a 1st Lieut, in the 1st Continental Dragoons, 4 June 1776, and Capt. six months later. He served later in Col. George Baylor's Horse and escaped the Tappan massacre. He came from Prince George Co.

light horse under Tarleton came upon them and compelled them to make a hasty retreat. They were pursued and "sorely pressed" until they joined the main army in Culpeper, Virginia.

Peter Bashaw, back from Cowpens, was substituting for Harmon Utterback under Colonel Edmonds during this rather tedious excursion into the interior. William Jett remembered that they were stationed at Williamsburg until they were driven from that place by British troops. They were "forced from the seaboard and compelled to march in the interior of the country." He was "quite young" and, in 1834, had forgotten just where they went. However Captain John Barbee[43] remembered his comings and goings. Barbee was in the commissary department and, somehow, had to see that they were fed. Rather amusingly Jett described Barbee, who was ten years older than he was, as "a sprightly, promising young man" whom he often saw at Williamsburg and elsewhere.

Fortunately Lafayette was picking up reinforcements as he marched. At Mechunk Creek on the 13th General William Campbell, who had led the successful attack on King's Mountain, brought in 600 experienced riflemen from the southwest corner of the state. On the 19th Baron Steuben arrived with 500 Continentals. Steuben was ailing and could not continue but, to Lafayette's vast relief, "Old Denmark" rode at the head of his column. Colonel Christian Febiger had hastily shed his responsibilities in Hampshire County and rushed to his friend's assistance. Lafayette even had a respectable artillery. In addition to the six guns Wayne had brought with him, units of the 2nd and 4th Continental Artillery had arrived with eight more.[44]

In the face of this growing threat, Cornwallis broke his camp at Elk Hill and hurried east to "shorten his supply line and secure more rapid communication between himself and General Clinton in New York;" or so he said.[45] Having promised Clinton that "the boy cannot escape me", he had to say something. Lafayette followed some twenty miles behind, not yet strong enough to open

---

43. John Barbee, 1753-1835, was a son of Andrew (d. 1790) and Jane Barbee. He married 27 June 1782, Mary Dyson, 1763-1845. He received a land warrant in June 1783 for service in the Revolution but died in Fauquier.

44. Col. John Lamb commanded the 2nd Continental Artillery (New York and Connecticut) and Col. Thomas Proctor the 4th until April 1781 when it was split between the 1st and 2nd.

45. Ward, **The War of the Revolution**, Vol. II, p. 874.

battle but well able to harass the rear and send out spies and "deserters" to give exaggerated reports of his strength. Cornwallis retreated through Richmond to Williamsburg. There, awaiting him, was a message from Sir Henry Clinton that almost left him speechless. Clinton wanted him to send 3,000 men to New York!

The letter written by Governor Jefferson to General Morgan on the 2nd of June reached him in record time. On the 7th he wrote his friend Colonel Tavener Beale outlining his plans. We do not know in what county Beale was living at the time. Early in the war he had been a 1st Lieutenant in Colonel Peter Muhlenberg's "German Regiment" from the Valley, but had resigned in March, 1777. He was probably a colonel of militia in an adjoining county, possibly Rockingham, the next south of Shenandoah, which had been set apart from Augusta in 1778. Morgan's letter reads:[46]

> Winchester, 7th of June.
> Dr. Sir: I am directed by the Legislature of Virginia to raise a Brigade of Volunteers for the term of three months for the immediate defence of this state which is threatened with immediate destruction except we can make head and stop the progress of the enemy. They have given me ample powers to appoint officers for that purpose and have sent me a number of commissions to fill up as I think proper. Colo. Triplett I have appointed to raise a Brigade below the Ridge in Fauquier & Loudoun, Colo. Darke in Berkeley and Hampshire, Colo. Smith in Frederick and Shendoe; will you undertake to raise what men you can in your County and join Colo. Smith?
> The matter is just this, - if we do not make head and oppose the enemy they will destroy us. My dear Sir, delay no time on this occasion, our all depends on our exertions. Please communicate success in this matter to Colo. Smith from time to time. All this must be performed in a few days. *I have now taken the field.*
> I am Sir, yr. Obdt. Servt. DAN MORGAN

We do not know whether or not Colonel Beale was able to act promptly in accordance with Morgan's urgent appeal, but it appears that he could not "communicate success" in time to do much good.

Colonel William Darke, who had also been in the "German

Regiment," was wounded and taken prisoner at Germantown. He had only recently been exchanged and was living at his home in Berkeley County. He did his best and led a unit of unknown size to join Morgan. Colonel John Smith was one of Morgan's old riflemen, having been in Captain Peter Bruin's Company in February, 1777. He was then colonel of the Frederick County Militia.

As for Colonel Francis Triplett, no explanation of Morgan's trust is necessary. It had been a long time since Morgan had written to him, explaining a period of unusual silence and failure to repay a small loan, "and I intend Down after harvest and try if I can settle it - I have often Inquired of you ... and always has had pleasure to hear you shine, - which gives infinite satisfaction."[47] Now, God willing, they would shine together or not at all.

If Francis Triplett's time had been occupied in the House of Delegates on the run, hotly pursued by Tarleton, at least his son had not been idle. The first order of business for Captain William Triplett on his return from Cowpens had been to raise a troop of cavalry to join Colonel William Washington in the Carolinas. He was assisted by his old companion of the Kentucky days, Parmanus Bullitt,[48] a much younger half-brother of Colonel Thomas Bullitt, as 1st Lieutenant. He had no 2nd Lieutenant but John O'Bannon, who had been with him at Cowpens, was a cornet. Recruiting, difficult as it was, was apparently not impossible. However, as months passed and the situation in Virginia became increasingly grave, there was no more thought of riding to the Carolinas. When Francis Triplett was commissioned Colonel of a light infantry regiment under Morgan, he had his cavalry troop already made.

They were about all he did have. Colonel Francis Triplett and his two colleagues in Frederick and Berkeley Counties were faced with almost incredible difficulty in recruiting. Morgan's friends warned him that it would take another act of the Assembly to raise troops at that time of year, since the critical condition of the spring crops and the approaching harvest season would discourage the farmers from volunteering. Morgan plunged ahead as best he could. At least he had a cavalry for which he secured the finest horses, mostly by impressment. Colonel Francis Triplett, possibly

---

47. Higginbotham, **Daniel Morgan, Revolutionary Rifleman**, p. 13.

48. Parmanus Bullitt, fifth son of Capt. Benjamin (d. 1766) Bullitt and his second wife, Sarah Burditt (?). He apparently returned to Kentucky after the war and does not appear in later Fauquier records.

reminded of the old days when he had conducted race meets in Charles County, Maryland, seemed to know where the best horses were. That, at least, was the way it seemed to such recognized connoisseurs of horseflesh as Catesby Woodford (General Woodford's brother), William Fitzhugh, James Hathaway, William Crosby and even his comrade in arms, Captain James Winn. Morgan boasted to Governor Nelson that his three troops of dragoons would ride the fastest mounts in western Virginia.[49]

However the delays he encountered provoked the speakers of the two houses of the Assembly to urge him to speed up his preparations. The jittery Assembly in Charlottesville still clung to the belief that there were numbers of riflemen in the back country who would come out of hiding to follow Morgan. Morgan assured Governor Nelson on the 26th of June that he had wasted no time, but he admitted his disappointment that he had only a fraction of the 2,000 men he needed for the infantry. The Governor, he wrote, could not "conceive how reluctantly the people leave their homes at this time of year."[50] A few days later, with as many trained riflemen and dragoons as he could muster, Morgan struck off at a rapid pace to overtake Lafayette.

The young Frenchman was hovering around Cornwallis' rear spoiling for an opening to bring off some spectacular coup. Quite obviously he was not yet strong enough to take on Cornwallis' entire army. If only, he thought, he could catch the British off guard at a time and under circumstances that would preclude their operation as a single combat unit. On the 5th of July such an opportunity seemed to arise.

Cornwallis believed that Sir Henry Clinton's message would almost certainly be rescinded once his superior was fully apprised of his situation in Virginia. Yet he could neither refuse to comply, nor could he afford to give Clinton the impression that he was dilatory in his reaction. He hoped that, while seemingly obeying orders, he could pull off a *coup de main* that would change Clinton's mind.

In response to Clinton's demands, Cornwallis wrote a guarded reply suggesting that a purely defensive post in Virginia was hardly worth while and that he might better return to South Carolina. Nevertheless, on the 4th of July, he struck off for Portsmouth as the best embarkation point for the troops he felt compelled to send to New York. While his army was moving along the narrow, shady

---

49. Morgan to Nelson, 26 June 1781, Charles Roberts Autograph Collection, Haverford College, Penna.

50. **Ibid.**

road to Jamestown where he planned to ferry them across the James, he sent out a false report by supposed deserters that they would cross on the 5th and 6th. Lafayette was taken in by the ruse and attempted to catch them crossing the river. He sent out Wayne and 500 Pennsylvanians to harass Cornwallis' rear which was covered by Tarleton's Legion.

Tarleton drew back under sharp fire and faded into a thin-set pine forest. Unknown to Wayne, Cornwallis' entire army was drawn up behind these woods, hoping that Lafayette would bring up his whole force. Instead the young Marquis sent several hundred more Pennsylvanians to Wayne, who moved forward to pounce upon what he thought was a large rear guard. Suddenly Cornwallis brought his whole army out of the woods. With great presence of mind Wayne ordered his forward units to advance with bayonets level, checking the enemy until his men could come off without confusion. Under the circumstances, it was a brilliant action, but one of his frightened men wrote home, "Madness! Mad Anthony, by God, I never knew such a piece of work ... 800 troops opposed to 5 or 6,000 upon their own ground."[51]

Lafayette, at the old Ludwell plantation, Greenspring, heard the news with dismay. Again, as at Barren Hill, he had risked his whole army. Again he was saved only by the British failure to press their advantage. Cornwallis continued to march to Portsmouth only to find that Clinton had changed his mind as he had expected, but not in a way that improved his position. In fact the new plan was, if anything, worse. He instructed Cornwallis to send troops, not to New York, but to Philadelphia, to divert Washington's attention there. Then he ordered them hurried to New York; then he told Cornwallis to make a stand at Yorktown; then he suggested Old Point Comfort for a naval base, supported by Yorktown. He again asked for reinforcements, but authorized Cornwallis not to send them if he did not want to do so. On the 20th of July Cornwallis received categorical orders from Clinton to take a post and hold it, but he did not say which one.[52]

Old Point Comfort seemed to be his preference, but, on examination, Cornwallis and his engineers decided that it was not

---

51. Letter, Robert Wharry to Reading Beatty, 27 July 1781, in **Penna. Mag. of Hist.**, Vol. LIV, p. 160.

52. It must be remembered that the time necessary for an interchange of ideas between the two commanders made strategic planning difficult. Furthermore Lord George Germaine was trying to direct the war from London and only succeeded in muddying the waters further.

suitable because the channel was too wide to be covered by shore batteries, and there was no adequate protection for shipping. Cornwallis, therefore, selected Yorktown for his main base and established a supporting position across the York River at Gloucester. Early in August he took his stand that he would only leave as a prisoner of war.

When Brigadier General Daniel Morgan rode up to Lafayette's headquarters on the 7th of July, the day after the battle, he found the young Marquis still trembling in the delayed realization that he had very nearly lost his army. "One hour more of daylight must have produced the most disastrous conclusion," wrote Henry Lee. Neither Lafayette nor Morgan had more ambitious plans than to retire to Malvern Hill and await developments. Cornwallis sent Tarleton to destroy stores in Bedford County. Morgan and Wayne galloped after him, but Tarleton had no stomach for another encounter with Morgan or Wayne. He evaded them and, after an exhausting circuit of 400 miles in fifteen days, during which he accomplished little, he rejoined Cornwallis, at Portsmouth.

On the long, slow ride from Goode's Bridge on the south side of the James, where he had gone to intercept Tarleton, Daniel Morgan finally faced the truth, and with it the ruin of all his plans. He had concealed the state of his health from Lafayette as long as there was a chance for a blow at Tarleton, but on the 24th of July he wrote Greene that he was "broke down" and could no longer continue. About the same time with the most profound anguish, he notified Governor Thomas Nelson that he saw no alternative to another leave of absence; sciatica had done its worst. Reaching Malvern Hill on the 31st of July, he broke the news to Lafayette. Still he hoped that he would not be away long. On the 15 of August Lafayette wrote, "You are the general and the friend I want, and both from inclination and esteem, I lose a great deal when you go from me and I will think it a great pleasure and a great reinforcement to see you again," but, he cautioned, "do not depart so soon as to expose your health." Morgan was too ill to reply.

Morgan's departure left his command in shambles. In fact no very clear picture emerges from the conflicting records of the various components. Certainly Colonel Francis Triplett remained in command of something, but of just what, is not easily determined.

---

53. Letter, Morgan to Butler, 17 Jan. 1782. Draper Papers, State Hist. Soc. of Wisconsin. Morgan wrote that between August and October he had twice "literally peeped into the other world."

His relationship with Colonel Elias Edmonds of the Fauquier Militia appears to vary. His commission was received from the State whereas Edmonds was recommended by the county, but what, if any, effect that may have had on their relative rank is uncertain. Sometimes they seem to act jointly, at others with complete independence. Even the men who served under them seem confused.

We have, for instance, the "Pay Roll of Captain William Triplett's Company of Mounted Cavalry from Fauquier County for two months commencing the 20th of June, under the command of Col^o. Francis Triplett."[54] In fact, the pay roll covers an additional 15 days served by the officers, Captain Triplett, Lieutenant Parmanus Bullitt and Cornet John O'Bannon, from June 5th to June 20th. June 5th was the date of Morgan's authority to raise his brigade. On the 6th of August, John O'Bannon resigned and Thomas Gibson was appointed to his place. The pay roll lists 29 troopers of whom four later applied for pensions. From them we learn much about the short, frustrating existence of Captain Triplett's company.

Elisha Barton[55] was the first to volunteer, for six months, early in April of 1781. Captain Triplett marched him and others to Fauquier Courthouse to serve in his company, "designed to defend those places where danger was apprehended from the enemy." However, for seven dull weeks they defended Fauquier Courthouse, waiting for enough to be recruited to form a respectable troop. Early in June they proceeded to Falmouth, where they waited another three weeks for the rest to catch up. About the 1st of July they were ordered to Bowling Green "on the Great Road leading from Richmond to Fredericksburg." After a few days they were sent, in company with others, to Yorktown where they remained until he was discharged. Barton does not make a distinction between Yorktown and Gloucester or "Little York",[56] north of the

---

54. Original MS in the Virginia State Library. In the heading the word "cavalry" was written twice. The first was partially erased and the word "mounted" written over it.

55. Elisha Barton, 1757-post 1834. His brief pension application gives no information other than that he moved to Bedford Co., Va. in 1784. Oddly the pay roll lists both an Elisha and an Elijah Barton.

56. The name "Little York" is used without any recognizable consistency. Some obviously applied it to Gloucester but many applied it to Yorktown and York, Pennsylvania, was also called "Little York" by some. It can only be identified if the context is unmistakable.

river, which was their destination. However he does say that "they never joined the main army", which is clear inference that they were with Weedon on the Gloucester side. He remembered a "Lieutenant Samuel" Gibson and an "ensign" (cornet in a cavalry troop) named John Barker, whose name does not appear on the pay roll. He was discharged about two weeks before the Battle of Yorktown.

Reuben Bramblet volunteered under Captain William Triplett early in June. After his brief tour at Brandywine he had been in South Carolina on "the Indian line" where he had been taken prisoner by Tories, but soon released. More recently he had been employed with his team, by the Commissioners of Fauquier County "drawing grain &c. to the Quartermaster in Fredericksburg", as certified by Colonel Elias Edmonds 28 September, 1780.[57] He rode with Triplett's company to Falmouth and ultimately to "Little York." His enlistment was for only three months and he returned home early in September. He "heard of the surrender a few weeks after his return."

Neither of these men was present at the surrender, but Sergeant William Jones[58] was, in a rather unusual way. He joined Captain William Triplett's company of Colonel Francis Triplett's regiment on the 20th of May at Fauquier Courthouse. He was taken prisoner in an engagement near Gloucester and confined to a prison ship in the York River for four months, he says. It may have seemed like four months, but it probably wasn't much more than three. However, he must have had a good view of the fireworks.

James Rogers volunteered again as a horseman under Captain William Triplett. He alone mentions that Francis Triplett was Colonel of the regiment only part of the time, and that his command was taken over by Colonel James Innes. His discharge was signed by Colonel Innes and Captain Triplett.

There were, of course, other companies from Fauquier County formed in the early summer of 1781. Prompt action was taken on

57. Bramblett was apparently hired for this service by the county on a continuing basis, as opposed to those who were pressed into service for a few days on an emergency basis. Elder Robert Sanders of the Broad Run Baptist Church had his wagon and team impressed in the Continental Army and it was captured by the British. He asked to be reimbursed £150 in April, 1782.

58. William Jones, 1759-1834, married 24 June 1784, Mary Fishback, 1760- liv. 1860. It appears unlikely that he was taken prisoner before 15 July or that he was detained long after the surrender, 19 October.

the recommendation of Thomas Helm[59] to be captain of militia, 23 April 1781. He took the oath at the next session of the Fauquier Court. He managed to get his company under way about the 1st of August. We have the pension records of five of his men of whom three had seen previous service at Cowpens. It would seem probable, therefore, that Helm intended joining Colonel Francis Triplett under Morgan. His men included the perennial Peter Bashaw, now a substitute for Josiah Holtzclaw, James Emmons, substituting for his brother William, and George Rogers, who thought he was drafted. After Cowpens Bashaw had served three months earlier in 1781 under Lafayette, and was now ready to march to "Little York" under "Capt. Helloms." Emmons had not served since his tour under Colonel Washington at Rugeley's Mill and Cowpens.

George Rogers woke up in the middle of August with the firm conviction that he had been drafted and that his company had gone off without him. Accordingly he raced after them and caught up with them between Fredericksburg and Bowling Green. They told him that he was mistaken about the draft, but it would be nice to have him along. He mentions that his Lieutenant was named Bradley, but he probably meant John Bradford,[60] who had taken the oath on the 23rd of July. Armstead and Berryman Shumate also apparently served with Captain Thomas Helm but their records are deficient in detail.

According to Jeremiah Brown, Helm's company marched to Deep Spring or Springfield Camp near Williamsburg. Brown had been one of those who had marched north, only to arrive after the Battle of Germantown was over. In 1781 he was drafted, along with his brother, Jesse Brown, about 16 years old. Jeremiah was taken sick at Springfield and hired a cousin, Joseph Brown, to take his place. Joseph and Jesse Brown served until after the surrender.

Captain John Ball, fully recovered from the wound he had received at Brandywine, marched a company of Fauquier militia to join the army under Colonel Elias Edmonds on the

---

59. Thomas Helm, b. ca. 1750, was a grandson of Thomas Helm who patented 283 acres on Dorrell's Run in 1727. He was probably a nephew of Capt. Lynaugh Helm of Clark's Ohio Regiment. He married 23 Jan. 1779 Elizabeth Gillison but, in 1800, they petitioned for divorce, the first in Fauquier. The petition was denied by the General Assembly.

60. John Bradford was a son of Daniel and Alsey (Morgan) Bradford of Marr's Run. He married, 14 Sept. 1787, Sarah Barbee, dau. of Andrew Barbee and sister of John Barbee, see **supra**, Note No. 34.

21st of July. We have their pay roll which shows that their enlistments were for only two months, though they were granted eight days additional pay for returning home. In addition to Captain Ball there was Lieutenant James Hathaway, formerly with Captain Scott at Quibbletown, and Ensign Joseph Nelson. Non-commissioned officers included sergeants William Metcalf, William McBride, John Kemper, and Francis Sudduth; corporals William Mulliken, James Ellis and Tilman Kemper. There were, in addition, 51 rank and file.

The pay roll does not tell us much about their activities except to indicate that something happened about the 12th of August of a most serious nature. Three men were summarily discharged on the 12th and 13th of August and, on the 19th, two more. On the latter date a young man named Richard Northcutt died. On the 29th another man was discharged and on September 9th Ensign Joseph Nelson. Officers are not normally discharged; they are either asked to resign or are declared supernumerary and their pay is suspended. Nelson must have been discharged for cause but, had the cause been grievous, he would have been court-martialled. The probable reason was negligence which caused the death of Northcutt.

William Metcalf was promoted to Ensign to replace Nelson and William Scoggin was made sergeant. Tilman Kemper, who had finished his tour with Captain Thomas Conway instead of Tilman Weaver, had been with Lafayette ("Gen[l]. Le Marquis, as we called him") on the march to Culpeper, was now a corporal. Charles Kemper, the brother of John and Tilman, was a private. None of them mentioned the incident of August 12th. So Captain Ball's company came and went, leaving others to taste the joy of victory.

Somewhat surprisingly the Gentlemen Justices of Fauquier County recommended, on the 23rd of July, a captain who was not one of their own. However, the credentials of William Bayliss of Frederick County could not be overlooked. We remember him from Brandywine and Monmouth, and as the brilliant young engineer at West Point. We last saw him in the wild scrimmage at Paulus Hook, where he was wounded. Before he recovered from his wound, his regiment had been ordered to Charleston and that city was so closely invested that he could not join it. Because he was without troops and "not wishing the country to pay without his being in a condition to render service", he resigned his commission in July or August, 1780.

John Marshall, a close friend, found him a command. His 1st Lieutenant was Lewis Jennings and enlistment was for six months, beginning the 23rd of June. According to William Ford,[61] the "Corps" was called the "Flying Camp", just why is obscure. Ford had been wounded in the hip at the battle of Jamestown (probably Greenspring) but the wound had healed. In July William Ford, his younger brother, Henry, George Ford (no known relation) and Charles Shaw were on the march. After reaching Yorktown, probably after the battle, Bayliss took over the command of Alexander Scott Bullitt,[62] according to Richard Rosser, one of his men. John Kemper and Thomas M. Maddux, who had messed with Rosser there, testified to the same effect.

On the 1st of August Captain James Winn took another company of Fauquier men to the vicinity of Yorktown. Linsfield Sharpe, recommended for a captaincy on the 23rd of July, was second in command and Thomas Conway was 1st Lieutenant. Sharpe soon took over as captain. Among the men were Nicholas Lawler and Samuel Shumate. Both were there when the last gun was fired.

While the Virginia troops were converging on Yorktown and Gloucester the most encouraging news reached them from the north. Rochambeau received from de Grasse a clear, concise and unequivocal promise that cleared the air, resolved all doubts and determined the course of the war.[63] De Grasse would sail on the 13th of August from Santo Domingo with three regiments (3,000 men), 100 dragoons, 100 artillerists, 10 field pieces and a number of siege cannon and mortars, in 25 or 29 ships of war. He would go directly to the Chesapeake where he would remain until 15 October, when he would return with his troops to the West Indies.

Rochambeau lost no time in communicating this intelligence to Washington on the 14th of August. Washington acted promptly. He knew that the defeat of Cornwallis was possible and was

61. William Ford was born in Charles Co., Md. in 1762 but was living in Fauquier at the time of his enlistment in 1777. That tour was spent under Capt. William Kincheloe guarding prisoners taken at Saratoga. He served again in 1779 in Capt. William Jenning's Co. In 1833 he was living in Monongalia Co., Va. Henry Ford, m. 16 Dec. 1790, Nancy Payne, dau. of Thomas and Sarah (Glendenning) Payne. Charles Shaw m. 19 Jan. 1790, Catherine Jett, dau. of William Jett of Leeds Manor.

62. Alexander Scott Bullitt, 1761-1816, was the son of Cuthbert and Helen (Scott) Bullitt. In 1784 he sold his Fauquier property to his uncle, the Reverend John Scott, and moved to Kentucky. There he was the first Lieutenant Governor, 1800-1804.

63. Sparks, **Writings of George Washington**, Vol. VIII, pp. 522-23.

compelled to accept the risk that Clinton, with 15,000 men in New York, might make a strong move to cut off New England. With great secrecy and careful planning, he and Rochambeau prepared to move south, leaving a token force of New England Continentals to convey the notion to Clinton that nothing unusual had happened. Hastily, on the 15th of August, Washington wrote to Lafayette to resist to the utmost any attempt by Cornwallis to break out of the narrow corner into which he had backed himself.

Washington could rely safely on Clinton's inertia. Although reinforced about that time by 2,500 Hessians, raising his force in New York to just under 17,000 men, he still failed to notice that General Heath opposing him, had been left with fewer than 2,500 men. He was not worried about Cornwallis who, he thought, could easily be reinforced or, if necessary, evacuated by the British fleet. Not until September 2nd could he say "By intelligence I have this day received, it would seem that Mr. Washington is moving an army to the southward, with an appearance of haste and gives out that he expects the co-operation of a considerable French armament."[64] By that time the allied armies had reached Philadelphia and concealment of their destination was no longer possible.

Washington did not have a strong force; mostly New York and New Jersey Continentals, detachments of light infantry from Connecticut and Rhode Island, an artillery regiment and a small corps of engineers, about 2,000 in all. As they passed through Philadelphia, hot and dusty in late August, the tattered Americans offered a marked contrast to the glittering array that followed; Rochambeau's four regiments "dressed in complete uniforms of white broadcloth, faced with green and ... furnished with a complete band of music."[65] There was no news of de Grasse, whose last letter was dated July 8th. In addition Admiral de Barras, who had sailed from Newport with eight ships of the line carrying most of the heavy siege guns, had not been heard from.

The British Admiral Graves with 19 ships of the line and seven frigates, left New York for the Chesapeake intending to intercept Barras and prevent his junction with de Grasse. He had no idea of the strength of the French fleet and found, to his horror, when he peeped into the Chesapeake Bay, that de Grasse had landed his 3,000 troops under the Marquis Saint-Simon and was all set to do battle. At the sight of the enemy, de Grasse slipped his cables and

64. Ward, **The War of the Revolution**, Vol. II, p. 883.

65. **Ibid.**, p. 884.

sailed out to meet them. The two forces were ill matched. De Grasse's 24 ships of the line included the magnificent *Ville de Paris,* 110 guns, probably the greatest warship afloat. Most of the rest had at least 74 guns. Furthermore, in the two hour engagement, de Grasse seems to have out-sailed the enemy fleet and left them reeling from the effect of his heavier armament.

At 6 o'clock in the evening of September 5th, the British fleet withdrew. While the fighting had been going on de Barras had quietly slipped into the roads. The British fleet manoeuvered off the coast for several days but the French force was now too powerful to offer hope of successful combat. Then they sailed back to New York, leaving Cornwallis to his doom.

At Chester, Pennsylvania, on the 4th of September, a dispatch from General Mordecai Gist brought Washington news of the arrival of the French fleet in the Chesapeake. Meanwhile Lafayette had disposed his forces to prevent any possibility of Cornwallis' escape to North Carolina. His main army he arranged in a wide arc south of Yorktown between Williamsburg and the road to Hampton. He posted Wayne's force at Cabin Point on the James and brought Weedon's 1,500 militia down to encircle Gloucester on the north. Cornwallis showed no disposition to stir. The addition of three French regiments to Lafayette's army on the 4th of September was soon known to him. Then he must have realized that he was lost.

The stately, tree-lined Duke of Gloucester Street was crowded during those scorchingly hot September days. Off-duty soldiers strolled under the Dutch elms; Americans and French idling away the time in good fellowship, playing billiards in the taverns, crabbing in twisting College Creek, "playing whist" and of an evening going "to a hop." Then, on the 14th, excitement swept the town and the outlying camps. Drums pulsed insistently announcing the arrival of Washington and Rochambeau, who had ridden ahead to announce the arrival of their approaching armies. Rising from a sickbed, and accompanied by Governor Nelson and General Saint-Simon, Lafayette rushed to meet them. His stewardship was over and, with pride, he consigned to their care the brave men who had marched with him during the past weary months, the Virginia militia of 1781, who, with his few Continentals and loyal Pennsylvanians, had brought Cornwallis to bay.

By the 26th of September all of the actors in the drama on which the curtain would soon rise were assembled in the wings. At daybreak on September 28th, a fine, clear day, the allied troops set out in light marching order on parallel course from Williamsburg.

It was an impressive parade of military strength. The right under the command of General Washington, including Continentals and militia, totalled 8,845 rank and file. The left, under Rochambeau, fewer in number truly, but incomparably better armed and disciplined than the 3,000 militia that made up a third of Washington's force, totalled 7,800. Within the besieged town Cornwallis sat with about 7,000 men. He detached another 700 men under Lieutenant Colonel Thomas Dundas to garrison Gloucester on the opposite side of the York River.

It would be pleasant to visualize the men of Fauquier as playing key roles on the immense stage that was Yorktown. A siege is quite unlike a battle of movement, in that it offers little opportunity for individual distinction. Center stage is occupied by the Generals, and on them the spotlight falls. The lowly spearbearer is lost in the scenery. It is not our purpose to describe the pageant as it unfolded; only, if possible, to find our spearbearers and see them safely home.

The Virginia troops at Yorktown were organized under the overall command of Governor Thomas Nelson. They consisted of George Weedon's Brigade (1,500 men), Robert Lawson's (750 men) and Edward Stevens' (750 men). There were also the Virginia State Regiment, 200 men under Charles Dabney, and a body of south Virginia riflemen under William Campbell. There were several men from Fauquier under General Stevens and Colonel Dabney, but the vast majority were with Weedon, most of them under the immediate command of Colonel Elias Edmonds. It was therefore with more than passing interest to them that they learned that the task assigned to Weedon's brigade was the siege of Gloucester. To reinforce them Rochambeau sent Lauzun's Legion and some marines from Barras' ships.

The first meeting between Brigadier General George Weedon and the Duc de Lauzun must have been interesting to watch. Their mutual dislike was instantaneous, loud and vituperative. Armand Louis de Gontaut, Comte de Biron and Duc de Lauzun[66] was a product of the French court where military preferment is earned by intrigue in the ante-chamber of the reigning favorite. His diminutive Lordship was "disgusted" by the Virginian's boorish manners. On the other hand "Joe Gourd" regarded the foppish little Frenchman with utter contempt. Hastily Rochambeau sent

---

66. Armand Louis de Gontaut, Duc de Lauzun, executed 1793, was a notorious libertine. His "Memoirs", although widely quoted by historians, are considered unreliable and self-serving.

General de Choisy[67] who outranked both, to resolve their differences and take command.

On the 2nd of October Cornwallis sent Tarleton and his Legion to reinforce Dundas at Gloucester and, on the next day the last battle in which Fauquier men are known to have engaged took place. That morning Choisy started to move his force nearer to the British fortification. Dundas had come out of the works on a grand foraging expedition in the Gloucester peninsula. The wagons, loaded with corn, were on their way back, covered by Tarleton's Legion, when Choisy's van came upon the rear guard. Lauzun's dragoons charged upon them and there was a sharp encounter during which Tarleton and Lauzun almost met in hand-to-hand combat.[68] Tarleton's horse was overthrown and he had to be rescued by the rest of the British cavalry. Remounted, he sounded a retreat and reformed his men behind a company of Dundas' infantry.

The French dragoons pushed on, closely followed by the Virginia militia under the command of Lieutenant Colonel John Mercer. When Tarleton attempted to drive the French back he struck the solid, unyielding line of Virginians who opened fire with telling effect. "They received the onslaught with a steadiness that surprised Choisy as much as it did the enemy," according to Freeman.[69] Tarleton was brought to a crashing halt, sounded a retreat and retired within the fortifications. Within a half hour Choisy's entire force was on the field and the siege of Gloucester had begun.

By the evening of October 6th the preparations for the siege of Yorktown were also complete, the heavy guns were at hand and trenches were being dug along the first parallel. Steuben, the only American officer with siege experience, was busy advising as to the best defense against sorties. By the 9th enough batteries were in place to begin the bombardment of the town. The French battery on the extreme left spoke first, soon followed by the American battery on the right. Until the 11th the artillery alone carried on the fight; but now the infantry was to take its part. Two British redoubts near the river east of the town prevented the completion

---

67. Claude Gabriel de Choisy, was a French Brigadier General of such slight importance that information about him is scarce.

68. Lauzun, **Memoirs**, quoted in the **Magazine of American History**, Vol. VI, p. 53. Lauzun gives a rather extensive account of this encounter in which he is the inevitable hero. (See above)

69. Douglas Southall Freeman, **George Washington**, Vol. V, p. 387.

of the earthworks in that sector. One was assigned to Colonel de Deux-Ponts[70] with 400 picked chasseurs and grenadiers; the other to Lieutenant Colonel Alexander Hamilton with 400 picked New England and New York Continentals. Both task forces met stiff resistance, but their success was never in doubt.

Completion of the trenches in the area of these redoubts, allowed the allies to move their guns within closer range of the enemy lines and also permitted batteries to enfilade them. The normal reaction to such a threat is for the defenders to sally forth and attempt to spike the guns. A brave but only partially effective sortie was made by the British under Lieutenant Colonel Robert Abercrombie[71] on the afternoon of October 16th. The Americans soon had the guns back in working order and the noose was further tightened.

Earl Cornwallis was now desperate. He wrote to Clinton:[72]

> My situation now becomes very critical; we dare not show a gun to their old batteries and I expect their new ones will open to-morrow morning ... The safety of the place is, therefore, so precarious that I cannot recommend that the fleet and army should run great risque in endeavoring to save us.

Only one last, slim chance remained—to retreat across the York River, overwhelm the Virginia militia and Lauzun's Legion, and escape to the north. If that could be done he could, by forced marches through Maryland, Pennsylvania and New Jersey, where there were no organized American forces to oppose him, reach Clinton in New York. As a last resort it offered scarcely a glimpse of hope, but a good general must try everything.

About midnight of the 16th of October Cornwallis embarked the greater part of his Guards, the light infantry and part of one regiment in small boats and landed them on the Gloucester side. Fate deprived the Virginia militia of their last chance to meet

---

70. Guillaume de Deux-Ponts, commanded a regiment called the Royal Deux-Ponts. He was painfully wounded in the face toward the end of the action.

71. Robert Abercrombie, 1740-1827, served in the French and Indian Wars. He was at Brandywine, Germantown and was wounded at Monmouth. He later distinguished himself in India. Among Britain's greater generals, he was noted for incorruptibility.

72. Ward, **The War of the Revolution**, Vol. II, p. 893.

Cornwallis in battle. A violent storm dispersed the boats, swept away most of the equipment and ended all chance of escape. On the following morning the allies opened on the doomed town with all their cannon. The British works were tumbling into ruin; not a gun could reply. Their ammunition was exhausted.

According to William Benson of Colonel Elias Edmonds' militia from Fauquier:

> The 29 day of September We began the seage at York and the 17 day of october they com to A Capatelation and the 19th day they Marched out and laid down there armes.

Elaborate descriptions of the pageant of the surrender at Yorktown were written, but not to our knowledge by men of Fauquier. Few occupied any point of vantage from which to do so. Most of the leaders under whom they had fought were no longer with them. Morgan was ill in Winchester. William Washington was wounded, a prisoner in Charleston. Colonel Thomas Marshall was in Kentucky, Nathanael Greene in South Carolina. Greene had, however, sent "Lighthorse Harry" Lee to be "in at the kill." Lee had something to do with the action at Gloucester on the 3rd of October and refers to it in his "Memoirs" but does not make clear the part he played.

But where was Weedon? And where, for that matter, were Colonels Elias Edmonds and Francis Triplett? We do not know.

The reason is probably to be found in a little known fact about the surrender at Yorktown. Not all of the British surrendered at the same time or in the same place. Lieutenant Colonel William Dundas, the commander at Gloucester, was one of two commissioners asked by Cornwallis to arrange terms of surrender. In his absence the command at Gloucester fell to Banastre Tarleton.[73] Suddenly this cold-hearted, vindictive, utterly ruthless man was paralyzed with fright. He told Choisy that he feared for his life if he were left to the tender mercies of the Virginia militia. Choisy was all sympathy.

At Gloucester where Tarleton surrendered, therefore, Choisy had only Lauzun's Legion and a picked group of Virginians under Lieutenant Colonel John Mercer drawn up to witness the ceremony.

---

73. As Gloucester was still intact (it had been watched but not besieged) the cavalry there was allowed to come out with swords drawn, to the sound of trumpets. This was a minor concession to Cornwallis' complaint that the British were denied the "usual honors." Flexner, **George Washington in the American Revolution**, p. 461.

The remainder of the Virginia militia were kept in camp.[74] While it seems likely that many Fauquier men were among the victims of this gratuitous insult, perhaps they did not care. Or, if they cared, disdained to say so. Only a few mentioned having been on parade during the surrender.

Nevertheless the British did surrender and the Fauquier men were certainly not left out of the jollification that followed.

Like the rest "the officers and soldiers could scarcely talk for laughing, and they could scarcely walk for jumping and dancing and singing as they went about."[75] They did not know, as we know today, that the last major battle of the war was over and that the Virginia militia had performed almost their last service in the cause of independence. They knew only that the threat to Virginia had been turned aside and, for a time at least, they could turn their thoughts from war.

The prisoners, of course, had to be dealt with. Cornwallis and his principal officers were paroled and allowed to go to New York. The rank and file, of whom there were 7,241, were divided, according to one account, into three "parcels" and sent to prison camps, one to Albemarle, one to Winchester and one "somewhere else" (Fort Frederick, Maryland). It seemed both sensible and appropriate that those intended for Winchester be escorted by the militiamen whose homes were in that area, so that they could be discharged nearby. Selected to take charge of this operation was Major Nathaniel Welch.

It seems especially fitting that Nathaniel Welch should have commanded these returning victors, for few had served longer or more faithfully the patriot cause in Virginia. He came from that part of Culpeper that would later (1792) become Madison County. He was with the Culpeper Minutemen at Great Bridge and then fought with Daniel Morgan. He was a Lieutenant under Morgan in 1777, and in 1779 was a Captain and brigade quartermaster in the 2nd Virginia State Regiment. He was a splendid drill officer and also known to many as an efficient adjutant in charge of the distribution of arms, ammunition and stores. In February of 1781 he was at Malvern Hill as a Major under Colonel Elias Edmonds. He commanded the battalion at the surrender to which the only Fauquier men who mention having "paraded" at the time were then attached.

74. Ward, **The War of the Revolution**, Vol. II, p. 894.

75. Scheer and Rankin, **Rebels and Redcoats**, p. 572.

While settling his accounts on the eve of their departure for Winchester, Nathaniel Welch was standing in a room in which there was a store of arms and ammunition. A servant accidentally set fire to the lot and there was a loud explosion. Welch was not badly hurt but regretted the loss of his sword and belt and, incidentally, the record of his military commission, which was to plague him later. The next morning, the 21st of October, they took off for home.

Marching through the autumnal sunshine with their "parcel" of prisoners (about 2,500), their hearts were gay and their steps were light. Two of the companies were almost wholly from Fauquier, those of Captains James Winn and Thomas Helm. The former marched under the orders of newly promoted Captain Linsfield Sharpe. John Barbee, long quartermaster sergeant and assistant commissary, was commissioned as lieutenant before they left. Many of our old friends were on that last, best march of all; Sergeant Reuben Murray, Nicholas Lawler, Samuel Shumate and William Jett of Winn's company; James Emmons, Peter Bashaw, William Butler, Armistead Shumate and Jeremiah Brown of Helm's. Young Jett had been sick during the siege but recovered immediately when there was talk of going home. Quite a few of the men were sick. Thomas Kincheloe, for instance, was so "ill and emaciated ... that two of his mess, Peter Rust and Edward (?) Shacklett, owing to his great debility were permitted to attend him and assist him home." Captain William Grigsby gave him a discharge after the surrender.

Several, like John Blackwell and Joseph Oder were discharged at Fauquier Courthouse before reaching Winchester. Oder's duties in the last days had been partly at Yorktown, but mostly "acting under orders guarding & waggoning, bringing in provisions &c to the American troops Engaged in the Siege." The prodigious quantity of food required to supply the combined armies is reflected in the claims against the Commonwealth presented to the Fauquier County Court in March and April of 1782.

When the troops reached Winchester they found Daniel Morgan, miraculously revived from what he had about decided would be his death-bed, by news of Cornwallis' surrender. The Winchester barracks were, of course, quite inadequate to house such a flood of prisoners and Morgan busied himself seeking ways and means to house and feed them. There were, as usual, no funds. Some he hired out to farmers, who usually found them more trouble than they were worth. Others he set about building new barracks, a task they considered beneath their dignity.[76] The militia companies were not asked to remain long to guard them. On the 15th of November General Peter Muhlenberg wrote from Winchester, "The troops are now removed from Cumberland Courthouse and are now in Winchester. I have taken charge of them and have dismissed the militia."[77]

Some served a little longer. Richard Rosser says that Captain William Baylis' company marched some prisoners to Albemarle Barracks, and then continued on with others destined for Winchester. William Ford, in the same company, was not discharged until the 23rd of December. Spencer Withers says that he was discharged at Ashby's Bent on Christmas Eve. Baylis, himself, ended his service at Winchester before 1 January 1782. Others, mostly officers and N. C. O.s with experience in the commissary and quartermaster departments were even less fortunate. Lieutenant John Barbee's specialized experience kept him in the service until the "Spring after Corn Wallace's defeat."

General Washington, expecting at least another year of fighting led his Continentals back to their posts on the Hudson where they resumed their vigil over New York. General St. Clair started south with 2,000 Pennsylvania, Maryland and Delaware regulars to reinforce Greene. With him went "Mad" Anthony Wayne and his rugged Pennsylvanians. Rochambeau's troops remained in Virginia until the following spring. On the 23rd of June, 1782, they, too, started back to Newport. It was necessary for some of the Virginians to remain to fill in trenches to prevent their use by a returning enemy, demolish fortifications and repair the roads. Jessee Rector,[78] who enlisted as a private under Captain Dudley, 1 September 1781, writes of marching to Portsmouth to assist in demolishing the breastworks there. When not so occupied they mounted an expedition to the seacoast against a pocket of

---

76. Captain Joseph Graham, senior officer among the prisoners had some difficulty explaining this to Daniel Morgan. Morgan replied amiably that a little work would not hurt them and, if they did not know how, now was a good time to learn.

77. The troops at Cumberland Courthouse were trained guards whereas the militia was unaccustomed to this duty. Most of the prisoners taken at Cowpens escaped from the hands of the militia.

78. Jessee Rector, 1759-1843. He first enlisted in 1780 but did not serve because of illness. No further record of him has been found in Fauquier Co., though his pension application states that he was born there.

Tories and captured a few. Having done so they were at a loss to know what to do with them.

In the first flush of victory the Fauquier Militia concluded that, along with the immediate danger to Virginia, the draft had also vanished. They soon learned differently. The only thing to be said in favor of the new draft was that it was unlikely to lead to fatal consequences, only boredom. It was extremely difficult to get men to face even that hazard. Burtis Ringo, once a dragoon with Colonel Charles Dabney's Virginia State Regiment, was "chosen" to carry messages for Governor Nelson. Richard Bailey, one of the few who escaped the slaughter at Waxhaws, was drafted to guard the prisoners at Winchester. Jeremiah Boggess was drafted *twice*, once for three months duty in Williamsburg in 1782, and again in March, 1783 for two months at Winchester.[79]

Generally speaking, however, the men resisted the draft and the officers resisted any exertion to make them comply. On the 9th of November, 1782, the County Lieutenant of Fauquier received a stern rebuke from the Virginia War Office in Richmond:[80]

> Sir: I am directed by his Excellency the Governor in council to call upon you for the names of those officers who have refused to attend to the execution of the act of the last Session of the Assembly for recruiting this States' quota of troops to serve in the Continental army. I must beg your immediate attention to this matter and to forward it without delay. I am, I confess, somewhat surprised that your County should be deficient on this occasion, when almost the whole state, without exception, are proceeding with the execution of the law.

Colonel William Edmonds had again allowed himself to be pressured into another term as County Lieutenant and had taken the oath in the September Court, 1782. He apparently made no reply because, on the 27th of February, 1783, he received a letter from the Governor, who was very angry indeed. Governor Benjamin

---

79. Jeremiah Boggess (or Boggus), 1753-1846. He was born in Prince William Co. and moved to Wilkes Co., Ga. He was a son of Thomas (d. 1771) and Hannah Boggess of Fauquier. A number of letters in his pension file indicate that he was senile in 1842 and the accuracy of his memory may be questioned. It is certain however, that he served under Captain William Grigsby in the regiment of Col. Elias Edmonds.

80. National Archives, RG 93, Photostat No. 038185.

Harrison wrote in part:[81] "I expect you will without delay forward to me the information required (in the above letter), that such steps may be taken with the delinquent officers as their misconduct calls so loudly for!" The outcome of that letter is not recorded.

If the rank and file sought release from military service eagerly, the officers were, perforce, more cautious. Most of them had accumulated vast arrearages of pay and many were accountable for huge debts contracted for the benefit of the military. One such was General Morgan. He not only had been paid in worthless notes but the State Auditor refused to honor obligations to Winchester artisans who had equipped his cavalry when all Virginia had implored him to take the field in the summer of 1781. Furthermore he was obligated to those who had furnished provisions and materials to feed and house the hundreds of prisoners who had been dumped on Frederick and neighboring counties.[82] Morgan dared not give up his commission for fear that these people might never be paid. Colonel Francis Triplett was in a somewhat similar position. On the 26th of December, 1781 he signed a receipt for £18,562.10s "for waggon hire performed to the Fauquier Militia during the last invasion."[83] It was but a fraction of the amount for which he had obligated himself and covered a period already six months in arrears. Early in 1782 he was "appointed to make purchases of horses for the Southern Army."[84] Make purchases, yes; pay for them, well, we will talk about that later. In the spring of 1782 he ranged the piedmont in search of horses. There are records in Louisa County in April, in Fauquier the same month, all concerning horses impressed "for the command of Colonel Francis Triplett." In this capacity he served until the end of the war. More than three months after the peace treaty was signed we find in the Auditor's Account Book a warrant "to Francis Triplett for his services as a Colonel of Militia in this State."[85] It would buy little more than the seed for next year's crop.

81. **Ibid.** Photostat No. 036021.

82. Morgan was forced to call on Fauquier and other counties for food for which he could give only promissory notes. A few prisoners also worked on farms near Paris.

83. National Archives, RG 93, Photostat No. 039016.

84. **Calendar of State Papers,** Vol. III, p. 15.

85. State Auditor's Account Book, XVIII, p. 164.

It is impossible to estimate how many officers were left nearly penniless and heavily obligated at the end of the War for Independence. Those who had served in the state militias were far better off than those in the Continental Line, for Congress was not only bankrupt but without any source of revenue. Only the steady hand and majestic presence of Washington saved the infant nation from disaster.

So perhaps the men from Fauquier were among the lucky ones. They had no money in their pockets and no immediate prospect of having any, but they had their youth, their imagination, their liberty and their beautiful land, undamaged, at the foot of the blue mountains.

Epilogue
The Forest Land Revisited

After the eight year struggle for independence the men of Fauquier returning from the far-flung battlefields could detect little change in their homeland. The rolling hills, the crystal streams, the fresh and fragrant air, were still the same. The new-turned earth smelled sweet in the springtime, the corn was tall and green in summer, the hillsides breathtaking in their autumn splendour. The mountains gleamed in the morning sunlight, loomed darkly against the setting sun. No, the land had not changed.

The change was in themselves.

They had travelled far and witnessed scenes beyond their descriptive powers, heard things that did not bear repeating. They had seen men die for their country, and others live to disgrace it. They had learned the awesome lesson that men everywhere were much the same, brave, generous, tolerant; or, cowardly, greedy, bigoted. No colony, no class, no nation had a monopoly on these virtues or vices. They had fought for their homeland but, by their side and with equal gallantry, had fought the brave de Fleury, the brilliant Kosciuszko and the unperturbable "Old Denmark." The Virginians had scorned the Connecticut men at Kip's Bay—but it was men of Connecticut who had stormed Redoubt Number Ten at Yorktown. They had boasted of their valor after Trenton, but from Camden the Virginians had run away. Some of these things they did not admit, even to themselves but, deep down, they knew. They would never again be as they were before the war.

Changed, also, was their sense of values. They had fought for freedom and, to many, that meant freedom from tithes, from taxes, from landlords and from the authority of church and state. Wiser men knew that it could not be so, but wise men did not always prevail. The Congress, weak, ineffectual and without any source of revenue, could not even pay its debts and was helpless in the face of wider obligations. The only tangible asset was land, and that belonged to the states.

Beyond the Blue Ridge lay the Alleghenies and beyond the Alleghenies lay Kentucky, vast, rich, almost untouched. After the recapture of Vincennes George Rogers Clark had retained complete control of the Illinois country, assuring the safety of the inhabitants of the western lands. The British still held Detroit, but they showed little interest in forays outside their outer defenses. The Indians were less tractable, especially the Shawnees who continued to mount sporadic raids with some success. However Clark's expedition which destroyed Chillicothe, the Shawnee "capital" in 1780, put an end to the threat by the Shawnee for a while.

The news of Yorktown did not end the war west of the mountains. Indeed, it was not until 5 June 1782, that the luckless Colonel William Crawford, Washington's friend and former commandant at Fort Pitt, at the head of 480 volunteers, met defeat near Upper Sandusky, Ohio. Crawford's horrible death at the hands of the Indians and further raids culminating in the defeat of 200 Kentucky riflemen at Lower Blue Licks on the 19th of August, provoked Clark to a devastating attack on the Shawnee Indian towns. On the 4th of November, 1782, Clark, at the head of 1,000 mounted riflemen with some artillery, attacked and burned Piqua (the new "Chillicothe"). Five other Shawnee towns were also burned and large quantities of corn and other provisions belonging to the Indians were destroyed. It was a blow that the Shawnees did not soon forget.

It was also one of the last acts of the war. Because Virginia had furnished almost all of the men and supplies to conduct the war west of the Alleghenies, there was no question of the ownership of Kentucky. It belonged to Virginia as did, according to the most extravagant claims, the land north of the Ohio extending to the Great Lakes. Some contested those claims, but they did not contest Kentucky and the immense Virginia military reserves in Ohio and Illinois. To those distant lands of unimaginable plenty, the eyes of many of the veteran soldiers turned. They were not the rich, who had no incentive to leave their profitable acres in Virginia, nor were they the poor, who lacked means even to break their chains. They were the young, the self-reliant and, by and large, the middle class.

Only a little over a month after Yorktown, hardly noticed at the time, an event took place that was unimportant in itself, but marked the end of an era. At Greenway Court, Thomas, Sixth Lord Fairfax, surrendered his soul to God and his vast suzerainty to his indifferent heirs. The ubiquitous Parson Weems dreamed up the unlikely tale that he died of a broken heart as a result of Cornwallis' surrender. The truth is that he was almost ninety and had long since ceased to know or care what was happening to the American claims of an arrogant king he had always disliked. In his lucid moments, however, he must have realized that the days of the Fairfax Proprietary, along with other such entities within the new democracy, were numbered.

Most of the Proprietary descended to his feckless brother Robert, but his sixth part, which he had inherited from his mother, he left to the Reverend Denny Martin, his oldest nephew, on condition that he change his name to Fairfax. Denny Martin Fairfax, who had read but left no known answer to the egalitarian effusion of his brother Thomas before the war, had no interest in coming to Virginia. However, to protect his inheritance, he did. For a long while, until 1793, he or Thomas Bryan Martin, acting as his agent, continued to grant leases in Leeds Manor to the sons of his tenants and others who had means to secure them. The men of Fauquier had a choice. They could either settle in Fauquier on a lease for lives, which would expire with the death of their youngest child, or move to Kentucky where land was free and inalienable—but remote and untamed. It was not an easy choice, but many took the latter road.

The steady drain of young, middle-class farmers on the population of Fauquier County opened the gulf between rich and poor ever wider. Other social changes were taking place; old barriers falling, new ones being built. In the May Court of 1781 the Justices of Fauquier granted licenses to perform marriages to "dissenting teachers", David Thomas, Robert Sanders and John Monroe. A fourth license, to John Pickett, followed shortly after. This action was in response to an act of the General Assembly the previous December. It was the beginning of the end of the established church. Tithes to support the church had already been abolished and it did not take too long for the beautiful church at Elk Run, Turkey Run Church and the chapels of Leeds Parish to fall into disuse and total ruin.

A cardinal tenet of the Baptist faith as preached by the Elders named above was the complete separation of church and state. No longer would tithes be used to support "riotous priests, unworthy of their cloth", as some said they were. It was forgotten that the clergy, even the "unworthy" ones, had accounted for only a tiny part of the monies raised in tithes. Tithes had also opened new roads, kept old ones in repair, built bridges, swept the courthouse and erected the new gaol. In their place came the "personal property tax", not one whit less onerous and far less leniently administered.

There were other aspects of the new democracy that came as a sudden shock to the good people of Fauquier. Denny Martin Fairfax soon returned to England leaving his affairs in the hands of the aging Gabriel Jones and the rising young attorney, John Marshall. In 1792 John Marshall formed a syndicate consisting of himself, his brother, James Markham Marshall, and his brother-in-law, Raleigh Colston, proposing to buy the Fairfax Proprietary from Robert, the 7th Lord. Before the deal could be consummated, Lord Fairfax died. His heir, Denny Martin Fairfax, soon deeded all of his Virginia holdings except Leeds Manor to James Markham Marshall. Denny Martin Fairfax, too, died soon after, leaving Leeds Manor to his younger brother, Major General Philip Martin. Philip Martin, who had visited Virginia in 1765 and had spent most of his adult life avoiding the necessity of doing so again, was ready to sell the 160,382 acre Leeds Manor at bargain rates.

Between 1783 and 1793 Thomas Bryan Martin as agent for his brother, had executed 225 additional leases in Leeds Manor to men not quite ready to move to Kentucky. Only when the Marshalls took over did the tenants of Leeds Manor remember with affection the years of benign neglect under his ancient Lordship. Now a syndicate of hard-eyed American businessmen was in charge, intent on making a profit on its investment. By dozens, even hundreds, the tenants of Leeds Manor and other similar tracts owned by the Carters, Lees and even Washingtons, abandoned their leases on the rocky hillsides and moved to Kentucky or Ohio. The census of 1810 shows a drop in the white population of ten per cent below the 1800 census. By 1820 the loss was even greater and in 1840 Fauquier had only eighty per cent of its 1800 white population. Not all of those who went to Kentucky remained there. The gold at the end of the rainbow often turned to baser metal in the hands of speculators, but few reversed their steps.

The administration of the land bounty program in Virginia readily lent itself to abuse by unscrupulous speculators ready to take advantage of the gullible. Warrants were issued upon application by veterans without surveys, and sometimes to those who hardly knew where Kentucky was. Many, desperate for ready cash, sold them for absurdly low prices or assigned them as collateral for loans at usurous interest rates. Not all of those who bought bounty land warrants were speculators. Officers and men of some means were besieged by their less fortunate comrades to take warrants at any price so that they could ward off starvation. Many reluctantly dipped into their own pockets for money they could ill afford to spare.

Many sold their bounty warrants in order to improve their Fauquier estates. Frances Edmonds, widow of Colonel Elias Edmonds, built the handsome house "Edmonium" (Loretto) from the proceeds of the sale of his Revolutionary bounty lands. Many used the money to buy farm lands adjacent to their own, or extend their holdings into more fertile areas. Some, of course, spent it foolishly, maintaining a life-style beyond their means.

Yet, as the years passed by, Fauquier County prospered. The War of 1812 came and was gone without altering the course of progress. More land was planted by slave labour, turnpikes were built, new mills ground corn. There was even talk of building a canal to open Hedgman's River, now the upper Rappahannock, to coastal shipping. The courthouse succumbed to decay and was replaced in 1818 by a new one with a stately Doric portico. Log cabins and early farm houses were replaced, or added to, with solid houses of brick or stone in the early Federal style. Such splendid examples as "Oakwood" (1805) of the Scotts, the Paynes' "Bellevue" (1810), Morgan's "Clover Hill" with its silver door knobs throughout the house, Chunn's "Mount Independence" (1804) and Edmonds' "Belle Grove" (1812), still stand.

In 1780 Colonel Thomas Marshall, before going to Kentucky, sold 1,000 acres of his "Oak Hill" property to Major Thomas Massey. In 1781 he was named County Surveyor of Fayette County. In 1782 he opened a surveying office one mile west of Lexington. Returning briefly to Fauquier in 1785, he deeded the balance of the "Oak Hill" property to his son, John Marshall. He died in Kentucky in 1802. At "Oak Hill" John Marshall built (1818) a fine brick house alongside the old one built in 1773.

The death of Colonel Marshall in Kentucky was only one of many as the Revolutionary leaders dropped off one by one. Daniel Morgan also died in 1802 in the great stone house, "Saratoga", he had built in 1782, some say by Hessian prisoners. Colonel William Edmonds died in 1816 at the age of 82. His house at "Oak Spring", built in 1789 was destroyed by fire in 1807. The new one, still standing, is a picturesque and interesting hodge podge of styles. His nephew, Colonel Elias Edmonds, had preceded him in death in 1800, mourned by an old soldier who had been with him in Marshall's Virginia Artillery and had re-enlisted to serve under him at Yorktown. William Benson wrote:

Elias Edmonds, cirnel. I live in hopes this world. Poor dear Col. Edmonds, the last time I Seed him was at Fauquier court house, and we drank som grog together for the last time that I ever seed him in this world or ever Shall again. He is gone to the other world.

Colonel Francis Triplett died in Fauquier in 1794 having never realized his most ardent wish, to move with his family to Kentucky. His will provided that they should do so after his death and settle on his enormous Kentucky holdings around Maysville and Lexington. He instructed them to sell the remainder of his Fauquier lease to finance the move. By contrast Captain (later Colonel) Joseph Blackwell of Elk Run remained in Fauquier. He lost his fortune because of "too much Virginianism", but remained politically active until his sudden death after a disputed election in 1823.

In 1825 Fauquier County had an honoured guest.

On a hot and sultry day, the 23rd of August, an immense concourse of people assembled on the north bank of the Rappahannock (near Fauquier Springs). The militia, splendid in uniform—their buttons glittering in the sunlight, lined the roadway. The finest carriages, drawn by the most magnificent horses in the county, were gathered. The old man who arrived from Culpeper County, escorted by a similar retinue, was tall and straight as an arrow. The quiet elegance of his dress contrasted with the gold braid and epaulettes around him. At sixty-five, he looked every inch a king, but he was not a king. He was, as far as he was concerned, not even a marquis. He was simply General Lafayette. The small, middle-aged man beside him was his son, George Washington Lafayette. On his other side was his recent host, James Monroe, until the previous March, President of the United States.

For more than a year General Lafayette had toured his adopted country as a guest of the nation. Now he was on his way home. It had been an exciting year, stimulating but, at the same time, exhausting. His hosts had been more than generous. Congress had mended his broken fortunes. He had been showered with gifts, some useful (a "superb" umbrella), some strange (a live rattlesnake), some rather cumbersome (a model of the Erie Canal seventy feet long). The price he had had to pay was rigorous. There had been too many triumphal arches to walk under, too many paths lined by maidens in white strewing rose petals, too much food (a dinner given in his honour in Boston had 24 entrees in the first course), too much to drink. Above all there had been those endless speeches. The old man's appetite for adulation was almost insatiable, but there were limits. The ivy clad walls of La Grange, his home in Auvergne, beckoned.

As his carriage neared Warrenton bells rang, cannon boomed and the people lining the roadway cheered and cheered. On the portico of the courthouse he was welcomed by Fauquier's professional orator, Thomas L. Moore, at whose voice "the courthouse windows rattled." His reply was gracious, but brief. Then they moved to a shady marquee on the lawn of the Warren Green (Mrs. Norris' Tavern) where he faced the inevitable stupifying banquet. Then came the real speeches. As orotund sentences piled one upon another, his face assumed a mask of benign endurance. One might almost think that he was asleep, were it not for the fact that, whenever the orator's praise fluttered around the name "Lafayette", he bowed slightly, as became the "hero of two worlds."

Then came the toasts. The reporter for the Washington *National Intelligencer* was asleep, for he missed the first three. He was fully awake to record the fifth:

> To the memory of our countrymen—officers and soldiers of the *third* Virginia Regiment, who gallantly fell in defence of the rights of man.

The old soldier came alive, his eyes lit by a sudden glow. They were on the field at Brandywine at a place called Marshall's Woods. It was the day the gallant Chilton fell. A musket ball had knocked him from his horse. He remembered John Ashby's worried face bending over him—

John Ashby, they told him, had been dead ten years.

The toasts went on and on as each speaker mounted his favorite political steed. Finally it was the old man's turn. Slowly he rose to his full height. The wine sparkled in the crystal goblet. He raised it high:

> To the *old Virginia Line*, the *Militia of 1781* and the present generation of Fauquier: May the Revolutionary services of the fathers find everlasting reward in the republican prosperity and happiness of their children.

The waves of applause swept over him but the old soldiers of the Militia of 1781 were silent, too moved for utterance.

They had not been the best of soldiers. They were not well-trained, but they had tried, Good God, how hard they had tried!

They had made mistakes, but they had remained by his side until it was over. Now they knew that the old man ("General le Markwis, as we liked to call him") remembered and understood.

What more could they ask of fame?

Williamsburg April 12th 1781

We the Subscribing Officers belonging to the Fauquier Militia now in Service, do hereby Certify that John O'Bannon Gentleman is the Oldest Commission'd Captain in the said County and as Major Aylett Buckner has resign'd and return'd home and on his resignation having given his Command up in favor of said Obannon do hereby recommend said Obannon as a Gentleman qualified in every respect to fill the place of a Major for said County.

Given under our Hands—

  John T. Chunn Capt.
  John Rust Capt.
  Turner Morehead Capt.
  Tilman Weaver Capt.
  Joshua Tulloss Lieut.
  Commandr. of Capt. Bronaugh's Company
  James Foley Lieut.
  Rodham Tullos Ensign
  Peter Kamper Ens.
  George Adams Lieut.
  Wharton Ransdell Ensign

(Request to Governor Thomas Jefferson, from the Officers of the Fauquier Militia, recommending Captain John O'Bannon's appointment to Major. Virginia State Library, Executive Papers, Apr. 1-15, 1781, Box 7)

Fauquier Countians in the Revolution

This list contains the names of men who rendered military service, who were either natives or who proved service while a resident of the county. The list does not assume to be complete - the sources are few and scattered but every effort has been made to locate each soldier and his service record. According to numbers published in the **Papers of Thomas Jefferson** (edited by Julian P. Boyd) the Fauquier Militia alone numbered in 1780 some 1222 soldiers. In comparison with the estimated population at the outbreak of the war, nearly every able-bodied man served in the militia. We would appreciate having additions and corrections for the county records to be maintained by the Fauquier County Public Library.

ABBREVIATIONS

Adj. — adjutant
comd. — commanded
comm. — commissioned
CL. — Continental Line
cpl. — corporal
Ens. — ensign
enl. — enlisted
MB. — Fauquier Co. Court Minute Book
Mil. — militia
OB. — Fauq. Co. Court Order Book
pens. — pension
POW. — prisoner of war
pvt. — private
resgd. — resigned
ret. — retired
sgt. — sergeant
vols. — volunteers

SOURCES

Eckenrode—	Eckenrode, H. J. comp. Index of the Revolutionary Records in the Virginia State Archives. (Richmond, 1912, 1914)
DAR-PI—	DAR Patriot Index. (Washington, 1966) and Supplements
Gwathmey—	Gwathmey, John H. Historical Register of Virginians in the Revolution. (Richmond, 1938)
Heitman—	Heitman, Francis B. Historical Register of Officers of the Continental Army. (Baltimore, 1914, 1967)
Stewart—	Stewart, Robert Armistead, The History of Virginia's Navy of the Revolution, (Richmond, 1933)

FAUQUIER COUNTIANS IN THE REVOLUTION 447

Military Rosters—

1775-76   "A pay Roll of William Pickett's Company of the first minute Battalion, from the 8th day of November, 1775, to the 2 day of April, 1776." Unidentified newspaper clipping filed 7 Dec. 1905. National Archives, RG 93, War Dept. Collection of Revolutionary War Records (M 246, Roll 114, Jacket 364) Marked "not official", but names checked with pension records are found accurate.

1777-78   "Muster Roll of Capt. John Chilton's Company in the 3rd Virginia Regiment, commanded by Colo. Thomas Marshall for the Month of June, 1777."

Same for the Month of September, 1777.

Same for the Month of October, 1777.

"Muster Roll of Capt. John Blackwell's Co. (No. 4) 3rd Virginia Regiment, as it stood April 1, 1778."

Revolutionary War Rolls 1775-1783 (Virginia Jackets Nos. 62-73) M246, Roll 97 (National Archives, Washington, D.C.).

1777   Roster of Captain Benjamin Harrison's Company, Fauquier Militia. Taken from: Gwathmey, John H., Historical Register of Virginians in the Revolution. (Richmond, 1938) Original roster not located.

1777   Roster of Capt. James Scott's Fauquier Independent Company, a volunteer company serving from January to April, 1777. Taken from Gwathmey, John H., Historical Register of Virginians in the Revolution. (Richmond, 1938). Original not located and Gwathmey did not give the source but, when checked against pension records, it is found to be correct in all instances of a pension or bounty claim.

1778-81   "This is a list of our Army, Colonel Edmonds' Artillery at Yorktown. William Benson, his hand. John Hammonds, his hand." A list of members of Captain Elias Edmonds' Company in the 1st Virginia State Regiment of Artillery, compiled by two old soldiers after 1800. They continued together until Yorktown when Elias Edmonds was Colonel in command of the regiment. The list may be incomplete but a high percentage can be checked with pension records.

1781   "Pay Roll for Captain John Ball's Company, Fauquier Militia under the command of Colo. Elias Edmonds. Joined the Army July 21st. Discharged Sept. 21. Egiht days for returning home." Endorsed 26 Oct. 1782, by William Pickett. Examined, Elias Edmonds, Colo. (Original in the Virginia State Library, Archives Division, Richmond, Va.)

1781   "'Pay Roll of Capt. William Triplett's Company of Mounted Cavalry from Fauquier County for two months, Commencing the 20 June under the Comd. of Colo. Francis Triplett." (Original in the Virginia State Library, Archives Division, Richmond, Va.

1781   "Roster, 4 Febr. 1781: A Return of the names & rank of the Officers of the Regiment of Artillery raised for the defense of the Commonwealth of Virginia. Thomas Marshall, Senr. Colo." Taken from a copy made 11 May, 1848, of an original in the Virginia State Auditor's Office, Richmond, Va., but since lost. (Copy in the Virginia State Library, Archives Division, Richmond, Va.).

—A—

ADAMS, George (W.8393) Pvt., James Scott's Fauq. Indep. Co. 1777; Lt., Fauq. Mil. 1781. Signed O'Bannon petit. Apr. 1781. Died in service in a "campaign to the south".

ADAMS, Littleton (W.5597) 1753-1834. Pvt., James Scott's Co., Culp. Min. Bn. 1775. Pvt., Valentine Peyton's Co., 3rd Va. Regt., CL. Sept. 1777. Dischgd. Valley Forge, Mar. 1778.

ADDAMS, Gavin. Pvt., John Chilton's Co., 3rd Va. Regt. CL. 1777.

ALLASON, David. Pvt., John Ball's Co., Fauq. Mil. 1781.

ALLEN, Archibald (R.102) Pvt., Charles Chilton's Co., Fauq. Mil.

ALLEN, Henry (W. 20579) 1764-18)1. Pvt., Armistead Minor's Co., 3rd Va. Regt. CL. At Brandywine, Germantown, Monmouth and Stony Point. Public Armory, Fredericksburg, 1782.

ALLEN, James. Pvt., Wm. Pickett's Co., Culp. Min. Bn. 1775.

ALLEN, John. Pvt., Wm. Blackwell's (No. 6) 11th Va. Regt.

ALLEN, Moses. (S.2487) 1754-1843. Sgt., John Chilton's Co., 3rd Va. Regt., CL. Re-enl. same co. under John Blackwell. At Brandywine, Germantown and Monmouth. POW Charleston, May 1780.

ALLEN, William (W.8318) 1758-1841. Pvt., John Chilton's Co. Culp. Min. Bn. 1775; Pvt., Charles Chilton's Co., Fauq. Mil., 1777; Drafted 1781, same co. With Lafayette at Richmond.

ANDERSON, Elijah. Pvt., John Ball's Co., Fauq. Mil. 1781.

ANDERSON, John. Sgt., Wm. Blackwell's Co. (No. 6), 11th Va. Regt. CL. June 1777. Morgan's Rifle Regt. 1778.

ANDERSON, John. Pvt., John Ball's Co., Fauq. Mil. 1781.

ANDERSON, Joseph (R. 193) 1756-1820. Pvt., Richard Stevens' Co. 11th Va. Regt. CL. Sept. 1779. Received a "hurt" from which he never recovered.

ANDERSON, Spencer (S.37672) Pvt., Wm. Pickett's Co., Culp. Min. Bn. 1775. Pvt., Philip R. F. Lee's Co., 3rd Va. Regt. 1777.

ARMSTRONG, George. Pvt. John Ball's Co., Fauq. Mil. 1781.

ARNOLD, Benjamin. Pvt., Wm. Pickett's Co., Culp. Min. Bn., 1775.

ARNOLD, Samuel. 1750-d.p. 1829. Pvt., Fauq. Mil.

ARRINGTON, Thomas. Pvt., Fauq. Mil. (suspended claims, Va. Sta. Lib.)

ARROWSMITH, James. Pvt., Fauq. Mil. (MB 1820-21, service not given)

ARROWSMITH, William. Drummer-fifer, 8th Va. Regt. CL.

ASBERRY, William. (W.2988) 1755-1814. Pvt. His widow believed that he served in "Capt. Blackwell's Co.".

ASH, Francis, (R.274) Pvt., Benj. Harrison's Co. Fauq. Mil. 1777 2nd Lt., Fauq. Mil., Recom. Mar. 1778; oath 1779.

ASH, Uriel. Pvt., Benj. Harrison's Co., Fauquier. Mil. 1777.

ASHBY, Enoch. 1744-d.p. 1790. Pvt., Benj. Harrison's Co., Fauq. Mil. 1777.

ASHBY, John. 1740-1815. Capt., 3rd Va. Regt., CL. appd. 18 Mar. 1776. Wdd. Germantown. resgd. 30 Oct. 1777. Maj., Fauq. Mil. 1780-81. (Heitman)

ASHBY, Lewis, 1746-1806. Pvt., Benj. Harrison's Co., Fauq. Mil. 1777; Ens., Fauq. Mil., recom. 1778.

ASHBY, Nathaniel. 1750-1812. Ens., 3rd Va. Regt., CL. appd. 18 Mar. 1776; 2nd Lt., 8 Oct. 1776; 1st Lt. 1777; resigned 14 Nov. 1777. (Heitman) (DAR-PI)

ATTWELL, Francis. 1750-1781. Capt., Fauq. Mil. Nov. 1777 in room of Capt. Charles Bell, resgd.
AUBER, John. Drummer. John Chilton's Co., 3rd Va. Regt. 1777.
AUSTIN, George. Pvt., Wm. Triplett's Cav. Co., Fauq. Mil. 1781.
AUSTIN, John. (R.318) Pvt., John Porterfield's Co., Morgan's Rifle Regt. 1776; Pvt., Gabriel Long's Co., 11th Va. Regt. 1778. Served at Quebec, Saratoga, Monmouth, Cowpens and Yorktown.
AYRES, John. Pvt., Elias Edmonds' Co., 1st Va. State Regt. of Artillery.

—B—

BAILEY, Carr. Pvt., Wm. Triplett's Cav. Co. 1781.
BAILEY, George. Pvt., James Scott's Fauq. Inde. Co. 1777.
BAILEY, James. Pvt., John Chilton's Co. 3rd Va. Regt. June 1777. Pvt., Francis Triplett's Co. Fauquier Mil. 1780.
BAILEY, J. D. Pvt., Francis Triplett's Regt. of Va. Militia at Cowpens.
BAILEY, John. Pvt., Thomas Helm's Co. Fauquier Mil. 1781.
BAILEY, Richard (R.387) 1762-post 1841, drafted 1781 in William Jenning's Co. Sgt. Elias. Edmond's Regt. Va. Mil. Discg. July 1781. Substitute for Benjamin O'Rear.
BAILEY, Stephen (R.393) Pvt., Martin Pickett's Regt. of Fauq. Mil. 1781. substitute for brother Simon Bailey. (DAR-PI).
BAILEY, William. Pvt., John Chilton's Co. 3rd Va. Regt. June 1777. Pvt., 9th Va. Regt.
BAILEY, Wright. Pvt., Wm. Triplett's Cav. 1781.
BAKER, John. 1st Lt., Wm. Kincheloe's Co., Fauq. Mil. 1779.
BAKER, Matthias: Pvt. James Scott's Fauq. Inde. Co. 1777.
BAKER, Samuel S. (S.10354) 1740-post 1835. Pvt. Wm. Blackwell's Co. Culp. Min. Bn. 1775.
BALCH, Nicholas. Pvt., 4th Va. Regt. of Light Dragoons. (MB 1781-84., 23 Sept. 1782.)
BALL, Benjamin. 1st Lt. Fauq. Mil. rec. 22 Mar. 1779. oath June 1779.
BALL, Charles. Capt. Fauq. Mil. resigned 24 Nov. 1777
BALL, David. (S.37730) Pvt. John Blackwell's Co. 3rd Va. Regt. Feb. 1778. (MB 1820-21. No service given.) (DAR-PI)
BALL, John. 1742-1806. Soldier. 6th Va. Regt. Wdd. at Brandywine 1778. Ens., Francis Attwell's Co. Fauq. Mil. oath July 1779; recom. Capt. Fauquier Mil. Oct. 1779, oath Feb. 1780. (DAR-PI)
BALL, Robert. Capt. 9th Va. Regt. (MB. 1781-84, p. 244).
BALL, William. Capt. Fauquier Mil. oath Aug. 1777, in room of John Webb, dec'd.
BALL, William. Ens., Fauq. Mil, 1779; 2nd Lt. 1780.
BALLANCE   , (listed by **Eckenrode**) Wife Patty drew subsistance from the county.
BALLARD, William. 1732-1799. Lt. Fauq. Mil.
BANKS, John. Ens., Fauq. Mil. oath 1778.
BARBEE, Benjamin. Pvt., John Ball's Co. Fauq. Mil. 1781.
BARBEE, John. (W. 24626) 1753-1835 QM. Sgt., William Payne's Co. 1st Va. Regt; Commissary Dept.
BARBER, William. Soldier 1st Va. Regt. CL. service cert. signed by Brig. Gen. Muhlenberg. 25 Oct. 1779.

BARKER, John. Pvt., James Scott's Fauq. Inde. Co. 1777; Ens. recom. March 1778; 1st Lt., William Kincheloe's Co. recom. Oct. 1779, oath Feb. 1780; 1st Lt. Wm. Triplett's Cav. Co. 1781.
BARKER, Peter. Cpl., Wm. Pickett's Co., Culp. Min. Bn. 1775.
BARNE, Henry, Pvt., John Ball's Co. Fauq. Mil. 1781.
BARNETT, Ambrose. Ens., Fauq. Mil., recom. 25 Oct. 1779. oath 27 Mar. 1780.
BARNETT, George Ens., Thomas Helm's Co. Fauq. Mil. 1781.
BARNWELL, James (S.37727) d: 1824. Capt., Booker's Co. Fauquier pensioner 1823.
BARR, Isaac. (S.41419) 1751-post 1821. Pvt. John Ashby's Co., 3rd Va. Regt. 1776-78. Trans. to Capt. Pike's Cav. Co. At Haarlem, Trenton, Princeton, Brandywine, Germantown and Monmouth, Discg. 1781.
BARTLETT, John. c. 1760-1816. Soldier, Fauq. Mil. (DAR-PI)
BARTON, Elijah, Pvt., Wm. Triplett's Cav. Co., Fauq. Mil. 1781.
BARTON, Elisha, (S.19198) 1758-1834. Pvt., Wm. Triplett's Cav. Co., Fauq. Mil. 1781.
BARTON, Kimber. 1746-1800. Pvt., James Scott's Fauq. Indep. Co., 1777.
BARTON, Stephen. Pvt., James Scott's Fauq. Indep. Co., 1777.
BASHAW, Peter (S.2962) 1763-d.p. 1864. Pvt., Francis Triplett's Co., Fauq. Mil. 1780, as a substitute for Joseph Jones; Pvt., Col. Elias Edmonds' Fauq. Mil. Regt., 1781, as a substitute for Harmon Utterback. Later served as a substitute for Josiah Holtzclaw in Thomas Helm's Co., Col. Edmonds' Regt.
BASQUE, Benjamin. Pvt., Fauq. Mil. (Eckenrode)
BASQUE, Jesse. Pvt., Fauq. Mil. (Eckenrode)
BASYE, Richard. (W.8755) c.1755-1822. Pvt., John Blackwell's Co., 3rd Va. Regt. CL., enl. 1777. At Brandywine and Germantown.
BATES, Thomas. Pvt., John Chilton's Co., 3rd Va. Regt., CL. June and Sept. 1777.
BAUCETT, William. Pvt., John Chilton's Co., 3rd Va. Regt. CL. June and Sept. 1777; Sgt., same company comd. by Capt. John Blackwell, Apr. 1778.
BAYLIS, Henry. Ens. and Capt., Fauq. Mil., 1781.
BAYLIS, William. (S.12953) 1759-1844. 1st Lt., 12th Va. Regt., CL., at Brandywine, Monmouth, West Point and Paulus Hook. Capt., Fauq. Mil., at Yorktown. 1781. (Heitman)
BAYLOR, William. Capt., Fauq. Mil., (MB. 1781-84, pg. 12)
BAZZILL, John. (S.37805) Pvt., Henry Bedinger's Co., Col. Thomas Gaskins' 3rd Va. Regt., CL. Apr. 1781, at Winchester.
BEALE, Richard E. (W.1128) Pvt., John Chilton's Co., 3rd Va. Regt. CL. After Germantown he was Sgt. Maj. 3rd Va. Regt. under Col. Heth, later adjutant. Dischg. Valley Forge, Mar. 1778.
BELL, Charles. Capt., Fauq. Mil. resigned 1777.
BELL, James. Pvt., James Scott's Fauq. Inde. Co. 1777.
BENSON, William. (W. 5218) 1759-1834, Pvt., Col. Thomas Marshall's 1st Va. Regt. of Artillery. Under Col. Elias Edmonds at Yorktown.
BERRY. William. Pvt. Fauq. Mil. (MB. 1832-33.)
BERRYMAN, Robert Sgt. John Ashby's Co., 3rd Va. Regt. CL. 1777.
BINGHAM, Benjamin. Pvt. Fauq. Mil. discg. at Williamsburg 1781 by Capt. Wm. Triplett and Col. Elias Edmonds.
BISHOP, David, Pvt., James Scott's Fauq. Indep. Co. 1777.
BISHOP, William, Pvt. John Ball's Co. Fauq. Mil. 1781.

FAUQUIER COUNTIANS IN THE REVOLUTION 451

BLACKERBY, Jeduthan. c. 1750-1829. Pvt. 6th Va. Regt. CL. (DAR-PI).
BLACKMORE, George. Pvt., Col. Alexander Spotswood's 2nd Va. Regt. Co. (No. 2,) 1 Mar. 1777. Ens., 2nd Va. Regt. July 1779. POW Charleston, May 1780. Lt. Feb. 1781. exchanged July, 1781. resigned Apr. 1782. **Heitman.**
BLACKMORE, Thomas. Pvt., Col. Alexander Spotswood's 2nd Va. Regt. Co. (No. 2) 1 Mar. 1777. Killed at Germantown.
BLACKWELL, David. (W.9358) 1753-1841, John Chilton's Co. Culp. Min. Bn. 1775. Fauq. Mil. 1777. Commisary Sept. 1780, John Brett's Co., Lee's Legion.
BLACKWELL, James. b: 1743. 1st Lt., Tilman Weaver's Co. Fauq. Mil. oath June 1779.
BLACKWELL, John 1755-1808. 1st Lt., John Chilton's Co. 3rd Va. Regt. Apr. 1776; wdd. Brandywine, 11 Sept. 1777; Capt. 15 Sept. 1777; POW Charleston May 1780; on parole to end of war. Brevet Maj. 1783. Gen. of Mil. 1790. **Heitman.**
BLACKWELL, John. 1735-post 1795. Lt. Col., 2nd Bn. Fauq. Mil. recom. 24 Nov. 1777; Lt. Col., 1st Bn. Fauq. Mil. oath Sept. 1778.
BLACKWELL, John. (S.30873) 1758-post 1834. Pvt. enl. Apr. 1780 as a substitute for his father, James Blackwell, in John Waugh's Co., Col. James Salughter's Regt. Culp. Mil.; enl. Sept. 1780, as a substitute for Henry Coons, in Brown's Co. under Col. John Green; drafted Mar. 1781, Gabriel Green's Co. under Gen. Edward Stevens; enl. June 1781 in Capt. Elias Edmonds' Co. Fauq. Mil.
BLACKWELL, Joseph. (S.37781), 1755-1823. Pvt. Capt. William Blackwell's Co. Culp. Min. Bn. 1775; cadet, John Ashby's Co. 3rd Va. Regt. 1776; 2nd Lt., Thomas Blackwell's Co. 10th Va. Regt., Feb. 1777; 1st Lt. Nov. 1777; POW Charleston, May 1780; exchanged June 1781: Capt. 1779; ret. Jan. 1783. **(Heitman).**
BLACKWELL, Joseph. (Wid. Ctf.1191) 1752-1826; 2nd Lt. in John Chilton's Co. 3rd Va. Regt. Apr. 1776. Eye injury forced ret. April, 1778. Later recruiting officer and in the CommissaryDept. Richmond, Va.
BLACKWELL, Samuel. 1745-1782-83. Maj., 1st. Bn. Fauq. Mil. recom. Nov. 1777; oath Sept. 1778; Lt. Col., Fauq. Mil. recom. Aug. 1781, oath 1782; Capt. Col. Thomas Marshall's 1st Va. Regt. of Artillery; POW Feb. 1781. **(Heitman).**
BLACKWELL, Thomas. 1752-1831. Capt. 10th Va. Regt. CL. Mar. 1777 res. (supernumerary) 14 Sept. 1778.
BLACKWELL, William. 1738-1782. Capt. Culp. Min. Bn. 1775; Capt. 11th Regt. July 1776-Jan. 1778; Capt. Co. (No. 6), Morgan's Rifle Regt. Jun. 1777; Wdd. Brandywine Sept. 1777; Capt. Fauq. Mil. oath July 1779. **(Heitman).**
BLAKELY, Aquilla. (S.31558) 1740-1838. Pvt., Capt. Henry Lyne's Co. under Col. Christian against Cherokees, Sept. 1776; Ord. Sgt. James Lyon's Co. Va. Vols. 1777; pvt. James Poteet's Co., N.C. Vols. 1780; enl. as substitute for Thomas Goff Mar. 1781, George Hairston's Co. Gen. Green's Div. At Guilford Courthouse.
BLENNINGHAM, Morris. Pvt., John Blackwell's Co. 3rd Va. Regt. CL., Apr. 1778.
BLISS, William. drummer. Wm. Pickett's Co. Culp. Min. Bn., 1775-6 Deserted.

BOARD, John. Fauquier pensioner 1832-33. (Suspended claims awaiting further proof).
BOGGESS (BOGGS), Jeremiah. (R.986) 1753-1845-6. Ens. recom. Sept. 1780. Wm. Grigsby's Co. Fauq. Mil. under Col. Wm. Edmonds; Ens. same company 1781 under Col. Elias Edmonds. Ens. Simmons Co. under Col. Homes, Mar. 1783.
BOLT, Abraham. b: Fauquier Co. 24 Aug. 1764. enl. So. Car. Was at Cowpens.
BONHAM, Peter. Sgt., William Blackwell's Co. (No.6), Morgan's Rifle Regt. Apr. 1778.
BOOTHE, James. Pvt., Elias Edmonds Co., 1st Va. State Regt. of Artillery.
BOWEN, James. 1750-1815. Pvt. Fauq. Mil. (DAR-PI).
BOWLING, Charles. (S.16041) b: Westmoreland Co. Served as a substitute for Samuel Thornbury, drafted Fauq. Mil. 1781.
BOYD, Archibald. Pvt. Benjamin Harrison's Co. Fauq. Mil. 1777.
BOYD, Daniel (S.41454) Pvt. enl. 1779 in Capt. Wales Co. Loudoun Co., Col. Abraham Buford's 3rd Va. Regt. Fauquier Co. Pension declaration Sept. 1821.
BOYD, Samuel. Pvt., John Chilton's Co., 3rd Va. Regt. C.L. 1776.
BRADFORD, Alexander. 1st Lt. Fauq. Mil. recom. Mar. 1779.
BRADFORD, Enoch. (R.1126) c.1760-1823. Pvt. Fauq. Mil. 1779-80; enl. 1781 as a substitute for Benjamin Settle, in Wm. Greene's Co. Culpep. Mil.
BRADFORD, Henry, 1757-1815. Sgt., John Chilton's Co. 3rd Va. Regt. CL. June 1777. Wdd at Brandywine 11 Sept. 1777.
BRADFORD, John. Ens. Fauq. Mil. oath July 1781.
BRADFORD, William. QM Sgt., Benjamin Harrison's Co. Fauq. Mil. 1777.
BRADFORD, William, (S.39240), 1760-1832. Pvt., enl. 1777. John Chilton's Co. 3rd Va. Regt. CL.; Pvt., same company under Capt. John Blackwell, Apr. 1778. Dischgd. Fauquier, 1780.
BRAGG, William. (W.3764) 1755-1834. Pvt., John Chilton's Co. 3rd Va. Regt. CL. Wdd. while working on entrenchments in New York. Dschgd. Phila. July 1777.
BRAMBLET (BRAMLETT), Hugh. Pvt., Benjamin Harrison's Co. Fauq. Mil. 1777.
BRAMBLET, Reuben. (S.30896). 1757-post 1832. Pvt., enl. 1777. Samuel Blackwell's Co. Fauq. Mil. under Col. Armistead Churchill; pvt. 1779 in Wm. Berry's Co. under Col. Williamson to So. Car.; Pvt. Wm. Berry's Co. under Col. Williamson to So. Car.; Pvt. Wm. Triplett's Cav. Co. Fauq. Mil. under Col. Francis Triplett. Dischg. 1781 before Yorktown. (Pens. appl. 5 Sept. 1832, Gallatin Co. Ill.)
BRAMBLET, Reuben. (R.1152) 1758-post 1832. Pvt., Elias Edmonds' Co. 1st Va. Regt. of Artillery under Col. Thomas Marshall. (Pens. appl. Oct. 1832, Laurens Dist. S.C.)
BRAY, Timothy, Jr., Soldier, Fauq. Mil. (**Eckenrode**) Listed as pensioner, d: 4 Mar. 1830, (MB. 1829-31, pg. 394)
BRISCOE, Reuben. Capt. Co. 6, Morgan's Rifle Regt. 1 Apr. 1778.
BRONAUGH, Samuel. Ens. Fauq. Mil. recom. 22 May 1780.
BRONAUGH, Thomas, 1741-1794. Capt. Fauq. Mil. in room of John Blackwell. Oath May, 1778. (DAR-PI)

BRONAUGH, William. Pvt. William Pickett's Co. Culp. Min. Bn., 1775-76.
BROOKE, Humphrey. 1728-1802. County Lt. and commander Fauq. Mil. resigned 28 May 1781. (**Heitman**). J. H. Brooke, Col. Fauquier Mil. (**Eckenrode**) is probably the same person.
BROOKS, Joseph, Soldier. Fauquier pension 1832. no other record.
BROOKS, Thomas, 1760-1800. Pvt. Fauq. Mil.
BROOKS, William, 1752-1841, born in Fauquier Co. Pvt., militia.
BROWN, Jeremiah. (S.6764) 1757-post 1833, Pvt. Wm. Blackwell's Co. Culp. Min. Bn. 1775-76. Drafted 1777. Samuel Blackwell's Co. Fauq. Mil., Col. Wm. Edmonds' Regt. Drafted 1781 in Thomas Helm's Co. Fauq. Mil. Hired Joseph Brown as a substitute when he became sick at Williamsburg.
BROWN, Jesse. Liv. Fauq. Co. 1832. Pvt., drafted with brother Jeremiah (see above) 1781 in Thomas Helm's Co. Fauq. Mil. Served at Yorktown.
BROWN, John. Pvt., John Chilton's Co. 3rd Va. Regt. CL. June 1777. Wdd at Brandywine 11 Sept. 1777. Pvt. John Ball's Co. Fauq. Mil. 1781.
BROWN, Jonathan. Pvt. Wm. Pickett's Co. Culp. Min. Bn. 1775-76.
BROWN, Marmaduke. Pvt., John Ball's Co. Fauq. Mil. 1781.
BROWN, Martin. Pvt. Wm. Triplett's Cav. Co. Fauq. Mil. 1781.
BROWN, Swanson. Sgt., Col. Francisco Byrd's Va. Reg. 27 Mar. 1780. (MB. 1773-80.) **Gwathmey**, p. 102.
BROWN, Thomas. 1760-1844. Pvt. Fauq. Mil. (DAR-PI)
BROWN, William. Pvt., Benjamin Harrison's Co. Fauq. Mil. 1777.
BRUCE, William. 1759-1842. Pvt., Fauq. Mil. (DAR-PI)
BRUIN, Peter Bryan. d: 1827. Lt., Morgan's Va. Rifle Co. July 1775. Wdd and POW at Quebec, Dec. 1775; exchanged July 1776; Capt. 11th Va. Regt. Dec. 1776; Maj. and Aide-de-Camp to Gen. Sullivan Nov. 1777. Served to end of war.
BRYANT, John. Pvt., Benjamin Harrison's Co. Fauq. Mil. 1777.
BRYAN, James. Pvt. James Scott's Fauq. Indep. Co. 1777. Pvt. 11th Va. Regt. CL. 1779.
BRYAN (BRYANT), Reuben. (S.41462) 1756-post 1826. Pvt., John Ashby's Co. 3rd Va. Regt. CL. 1776. Selected for Col. Daniel Morgan's Rifle Regt. Gabriel Long's Co., later comd. by William Knox. At Saratoga and Valley Forge. (**Eckenrode**).
BUCKNER, Aylett. 1745-1811. Maj. Fauq. Mil. oath May 1778. Commanded 2nd Fauquier Mil. Bn. to Williamsburg 1781 but was forced to resign because of ill health.
BULLITT, George. Pvt., Elias Edmonds' Co., 1st Va. State Regt. of Artillery.
BULLITT, Permanus. 1st Lt., Wm. Triplett's Cav. Co., 1781.
BULLITT, Thomas. 1730-1778. Col., Adjutant General of Virginia. resigned 1 May 1777.
BURDETT, James. Pvt., Benjamin Harrison's Co. Fauq. Mil. 1777.
BURDETT, Joseph. Pvt., John Ball's Co. Fauq. Mil. 1781. dischgd. 19th Aug. 1781.
BURGESS, Dawson. Pvt. James Scott's Fauq. Indep. Co. 1777.
BURK, Samuel. (W.2912) 1759-1841. enl. 1775 in Wm. McClanahan's Co. (see McClanahan); Pvt. Capt. Abraham Buford's Co. Culp. Minute. Bn.; Pvt., Rucker's Co. to Delaware River Forts 1777; Pvt., John Ball's Co. Fauq. Mil. 1781.

BURK, William. (W.5951) c.1750-1803. Pvt. Wallace's Co. King Geo. Co. 1778. Served to Oct. 1781. Lived in Fauquier 1783-1803.
BUTLER, Edward. Pvt., John Chilton's Co., 3rd Va. Regt. CL. 1777. enl. in a Penna. Regt. Aug. 1777.
BUTLER, William, (S.16671) 1762-post 1833. Pvt., Armistead White's Co. Col. John Slaughter's Regt. Jan. 1781. Marched to Dan River; enl. as substitute for Joseph Butler in Joseph James Co. of Fauq. Mil. May 1781. Joined Wayne's army at Raccoon Ford. Dischg. July 1781.

—C—

CAFFREY, Lewis Pvt., Wm. Triplett's Cav. Co., Fauq. Mil., 1781.
CANNADAY, Thomas, Pvt., James Scott's Fauq. Indep. Co. 1777.
CANTWELL, John (R.1668) 1744-post 1833. Pvt. Daniel Floweree's Co., Fauq. Mil. 1781.
CATLETT, William. Pvt. James Scott's Fauq. Indep. Co. 1777.
CAYNOR, Matthew. Soldier. Certf. by Lt. Col. John Webb, 5th Va. Regt. that he had served 3 years in the 6th Va. Regt. (Fau. MB.)
CHANCELLOR, Thomas. 1745-1823. Pvt. Fauq. Mil.
CHAPMAN, Joseph. Pvt. John Chilton's Co., 3rd Va. Regt. CL. Sept. 1777. Deserted.
CHILTON, Charles. 1741-1793. 1st Lt., James Bell's Co., Fauq. Mil., Mar. 1778; Capt. Fauq. Mil. oath Apr. 1779; served to end of war.
CHILTON, John. 1739-1777. Capt. Culp. Min. Bn. 1775; Capt. 29 Apr. 1776. 3rd Va. Regt. CL. Killed at Brandywine 11 Sept. 1777.
CHUMLEY, Daniel. (S.3152) 1759-post 1853. Pvt. William Triplett's Co. of Grayson's Additional Cont. Regt.; At Monmouth. Discgd. by Gen. Lincoln at Charleston, S.C.
CHUNN, John Thomas. Pvt. James Scott's Fauq. Indep. Co. 1777. Maj. Fauq. Mil., recom. Aug. 1781; oath May 1783.
CHURCHILL, Armistead, 1733-1795. Col., 2nd Bn. Fauq. Mil. recom. Nov. 1777; oath May 1778.
CLAGGETT, Samuel, M.D. Served as surgeon, CL, from Charles Co. Md. Widow, Amie Jane Ramey Claggett, granted pension, 1833, listed as "Annie" - lived with son, Ferdinand, in Fauq. Co. Dr. Claggett d. in Fauq. Co., 1820.
COLVIN, Henry. (S.12600). 1762-1839. Pvt., enl. Culp. Co. 1779 under Capts. Wallace and Anderson, in regt. of Col. John Campbell. (DAR-PI)
COFFEE, Robert, Pvt., John Chiltons Co., 3rd Va. Regt. CL. June 1777. Killed at Brandywine 11 Sept. 1777.
COMBS, John. d: 1781. Ens. Fauq. Mil., oath May 1778. Capt. Dec. 1780. Killed at Cowpens, 17 Jan. 1781.
COMBS, Robert. 1753-1842. enl. 1775. Simon Triplett's Co., Loudoun Co. Mil. Fauquier pens. 21 Aug. 1832.
CONNEHILL, Jacob. Soldier, Fauq. Mil. (**Eckenrode**)
CONNER, Stephen. Soldier. Col. Francis C. Byrd's Regt. Proof of service rec. (MB. 27 Mar., 1780).
CONWAY, George. Pvt., Wm. Triplett's Cav. Co., Fauq. Mil. July 1781.
CONWAY, Peter. Pvt., Wm. Blackwell's Co. Culp. Min. Bn. 1775.
CONWAY, Thomas, Ens., Benj. Harrison's Co. Fauq. Mil. 1777; Lt. in Wm. Pope's Co. Fauq. Mil., oath May 1778.

COOK, William. Soldier, Fauq. Mil. (**Eckenrode**)
COPPAGE, John. 1754-1823-25. Pvt., Valentine Peyton's Co., 3rd Va. Regt. CL.
CORDELL, John. Chaplain (Capt.) Fauq. Mil. (DAR-PI)
CORDER, Benjamin. Pvt. John Ball's Co. Fauq. Mil. 1781.
CORDER, John. 1761-1849. Pvt. Fauq. Mil.
CORDER, William. Soldier, Clark's Illinois Regt.
CORLEY, Manoah. Pvt. (DAR Magazine, Dec. 1974)
CORNHILL, Daniel. Pvt. Fauq. Mil.
CORNISH, Daniel. Pvt. Fauquier Mil.
CORNWELL, Daniel. Pvt. Elias Edmonds' Co. 1st Va. State Regt. of Artillery.
CORUM, Richard. Pvt. John Ball's Co., Fauq. Mil., 1781.
COURTNEY, Samuel (S.39346) 1755-post 1837. enl. Feb. 1776 in marines under Capt. Alexander Dick. Pvt. 1776 in John Gillison's Co., Col. John Green's 10th Va. Regt.; re-enl. 1779. At Germantown, Stony Point. Paulus Hook; POW Charleston, May 1780.; exchg 1781: served in Alexander Parker's Co. Va. Vols. to end of war.
COWLING, George. Pvt., John Blackwell's Co., 3rd Va. Regt. CL. 1778.
COWNE, Augustine. 1st Lt. Col. Elias Edmonds' Fauq. Mil. Regt. Commissioned 15 April, 1780.
COX, Samuel. Pvt., John Ashby's Co., 3rd Va. Regt. CL. 1777. Dischgd. after Brandywine.
CRAINE, John Ens., Fauq. Mil., recom. Nov. 1780.
CRAVEN, John. Ens., Fauq. Mil., recom. 27 Nov. 1780.
CROOKE, Jonathan. Pvt., Capt. Chilton's 3rd Va. Regt. CL. 1777. Attended wounded after Brandywine: Pvt., same Co. under Capt. John Blackwell, Apr. 1778.
CROOKE, Ozias. Pvt., John Ball's Co. Fauq. Mil. 1781 Dischgd. 13 Aug. 1781.
CROSBY, John. Sgt., Benjamin Harrison's Co. Fauq. Mil. 1777.
CROSBY, William. Pvt., Benjamin Harrison's Co. Fauq. Mil. 1777; Pvt. John Ball's Co. Fauquier Mil. July 1781.
CRUMP. Travis. Pvt., Wm. Pickett's Co. Culp. Min. Bn. 1775.
CUMMINS, Thomas. Pvt., Benjamin Harrison's Co. Fauq. Mil. 1777.
CURTS, Frederick. Pvt., James Scott's Fauq. Indep. Co. 1777.

—D—

DARNALL, Joseph. Pvt., John Ball's Co. Fauq. Mil. July 1781.
DARNALL, Rollay (Rawley) Pvt., Wm. Pickett's Co. Culp. Min. Bn. 1775-76
DAVIS, Richard. 1725-1809. Pvt., Fauq. Mil.
DAVIS, William, Pvt., John Chilton's Co., 3rd Va. Regt. CL. Sept. 1777. Pvt., same company under John Blackwell, Apr. 1778.
DAVISON, William, Pvt., John Chilton's Co., 3rd Va. Regt. CL. In June 1777 he enl. in a New Jersey Regt. but returned to the 3rd Va. Regt. and was sick in the hospital after Brandywine. Pvt., same company under John Blackwell, Apr. 1778.
DAY, William, Pvt. John Chilton's Co., 3rd Va. Regt. CL. June and Sept. 1777 with Gen. Washington's Guard.
DEANE, John. 1748-post 1818. Pvt., John Chilton's Co., 3rd Va. Reg. CL. At Haarlem Heights, Trenton, Princeton and Brandywine.

DEARING (DEERING), John. 2nd Lt., Wm. Ball's Co., Fauq. Mil. 24 Mar. 1778.; 1st Lt. under Maj. Francis Triplett at Cowpens. Brought Fauquier troops back after Cowpens, Jan. 1781.
DEARON, Peter. Pvt., John Blackwell's Co., 3rd Va. Regt. CL. 1778.
DENING, John. Lt. Fauq. Mil., comm. Aug. 1781.
DENNIS, William. Pvt., Wm. Blackwell's Co. (No. 6), Col. Daniel Morgan's 11th Va. Regt., 1 June 1777.
DICKERSON, John. Pvt., Fauq. Mil. Substitute for Samuel Baker.
DIGGES, Edward. Maj., 2nd Bn. Fauq. Mil. recom. Nov. 1777.
DIXON, George. Pvt., John Ball's Co. Fauq. Mil. 1781
DODD, John. 1759-1815, Pvt., Philip Love's Co. of Vols. in defense of frontier, 1774; enl. Capt. Alexander Dick's Co., captured on board the **Muskite**, Nov. 1778; exchgd. and re-enl. dischgd: Set. 1780.
DONALDSON, Stephen. Pvt. James Scott's Fauquier Indep. Co. 1777.
DONALDSON, William, Ens., Fauq. Mil. recom. Mar. 1778, oath June 1778.
DONAPHAN, Joseph. Q.M. Sgt., Wm. Triplett's Cav. Co., Fauq. Mil. 1781.
DOYLE, Robert. Pvt., John Blackwell's Co., 3rd Va. Regt. CL. 1778.
DRISKILL, Timothy, Soldier, 4th Va. Light Dragoons. (MB. 1781-84, p. 67, Sept. 1781).
DRONE, William. (W.3785) 1762-1824. Enl., Loudoun Co. John Randolph's Cav. Co. of Lee's Legion. (MB. 1820-21 30 Aug. 1820).
DRUMMON, Joshua. Pvt., Elias Edmonds' Co., 1st Va. Regt. of Artillery.
DRUMMON, William, 1750-1794. Sgt., Fauq. Mil. (DAR-PI)
DULIN, Daniel. Pvt., Wm. Johnston's Co. 11th Va. Regt. CL. Nov. 1778.
DULIN, John (S.394-68) 1743-post 1827. Pvt., Wm. Pickett's Co., Culp. Min. Bn. 1775; enl. Apr. 1776 in John Chilton's Co., 3rd Va. Regt. (according to pension rec.) His name does not appear on rosters of that company in June and Sept. 1777. Samuel Cox, Apr. 1828, said he enlisted in Capt. John Ashby's Co. at the same time and was discharged with him by Col. Thomas Marshall after Brandywine, Sept. 1777.
DUNCAN, Charles. (W.22973) 1761-1838. Enl. 12 Jan. 1777 in Wm. Blackwell's Co., 11th Va. Regt. CL. Dischgd. 12 Jan. 1780, Frederick, Md. by Maj. Williams.
DUNCAN, James. Pvt. Benj. Harrison's Co. Fauq. Mil. 1777.
DUNCAN, Joseph. Armorer. Clark's Illinois Regt.
DYSON, Aquilla. Pvt. Benj. Harrison's Co. Fauq. Mil. 1777; Lt. Fauq. Mil., recom. July 1782.

—E—

EDMONDS, Daniel. (S.8394) 1757-post 1833. Pvt., enl. 1777 in Williamsburg under Capt. John Triplett of Culpeper in Regt. commanded by Col. Wm. Brent. Transferred to Cont. Line. At Valley Forge, Monmouth, Stony Point and Yorktown.
EDMONDS, Elias. 1754-1800. Capt., Fauq. Mil., 1776-7 (**Eckenrode**). Lt. Col., 1st Va. State Regt. of Artillery (MB. 1781-84, p. 2) Col., Fauq. Mil. 1781-1783.
EDMONDS, William, 1734-1816, Col., 1st Bn. Fauq. Mil., recom. Mar. 24 Mar. 1778; County Lt., recom. Aug. 1781; resigned May 1783. (**Heitman**).

EDWARDS, Benjamin, Pvt., Benj. Harrison's Co. Fauq. Mil. 1777.
EDWARDS, John. Pvt., Fauq. Mil. (DAR Mag. June-July 1974).
EDWARDS, Joseph. Pvt. Fauq. Mil. (DAR Mag. Aug.-Sept. 1972).
EDWARDS, Liney. Pvt. Wm. Triplett's Cav. Co. 1781.
EDWARDS, Thomas. Ens., Fauq. Mil., oath Sept. 1778; 2nd Lt. in Francis Atwell's Co., July 1779; 2nd Lt. in Daniel Floweree's Co., recom. Sept. 1780.
EFAUGH, David. Soldier, Fauq. Mil. (**Eckenrode**).
ELLIOTT, John. Pvt. Wm. Triplett's Cav. Co. July, 1781.
ELLIOTT, Samuel. Pvt. Wm. Blackwell's Co. 11th Va. Regts. CL. Later 7th Va. Regt. CL.
ELLIS, James. Cpl., John Ball's Co. Fauq. Mil. July 1781.
ELLIS, Nathan. Pvt., John Ball's Co. Fauq. Mil. July 1781.
EMMONS, James. (W.7108) 1761-1839. Pvt., enl. Oct. 1780 in James Winn's Co. Va. Mil. Regt; under Major Francis Triplett at Cowpens. Enl. 1781 as substitute for brother, Wm. Emmons, in Thomas Helm's Co., Fauq. Mil.
ENGLISH, Robert. Pvt. JOHN Chilton's Co., 3rd Va. Regt. CL. Deserted at Brandywine.
ETHALL, Anthony. 1757-post 1832. Enl. Sept. 1775 in Simon Triplett's Co., Loudoun Mil. Drafted 1777 under Daniel Feagans to guard Hessian prisoners taken at Trenton, to Charlottesville. Drafted Thomas Connor's Co., Col. Meriwether's Regt. of Va. Mil. July 1781.
ETHERINGTON, John, Jr. Pvt., John F. Mercer's Co., 3rd Va. Reg. CL.
ETHERINGTON, John, Sr. Pvt., John F. Mercer's Co., 3rd Va. Regt. CL.
EUSTACE, William. Pvt., Benj. Harrison's Co. Fauq. Mil. 1777. 1st Lt. Fauq. Mil., recom. July, 1781.
EVANS, Thomas. Sgt., Benj. Harrison's Co., Fauq. Mil. 1777.

—F—

FEWELL, Henry. Pvt., Wm. Pickett's Co., Culp. Min. Bn. 1775-76.
FIELD, Reuben. Soldier., Fauq. Mil. Fauq. Pens. Military Record not given.
FIELDS, Stephen. Pvt., Wm. Triplett's Cav. Co. Fauqier Mil. July 1781.
FILBART, Fewel. Pvt., Wm. Pickett's Co., Culp. Min. Bn. 1775-76.
FISHBACK, Jacob. 1749-1821. Pvt., wagoner, Fauq. Mil. (DAR-PI)
FISHBACK, John. (R.3563) 1760-post 1839. Pvt., James Winn's Co. in Va. Mil. Regt. commanded by Maj. Francis Triplett at Cowpens.
FLETCHER, James. Pvt., John Ball's Co., Fauq. Mil. July 1781.
FLETCHER, John. 2nd Lt., Fauq. Mil. recom. Oct. 1779; Lt., Fauq. Mil. May 1780.
FLETCHER, Joshua. 1750-1811. Pvt. Turner Morehead's Co. Fauq. Mil. (DAR-PI)
FLORENCE, William, Lt., Fauq. Mil. (MB. 1781-83, p. 73)
FLOWERREE, Daniel. Capt., Fauq. Mil.
FLOYD, Henry. Soldier, Fauq. Mil. (DAR Mag. July 1976).
FOLEY, Enoch. Pvt. Elias Edmond's Co. 1st Va. State Regt. of Artillery.
FOLEY, James. Lt., in Wm. Ball's Co., Fauq. Mil. Mar. 1777.

FOLEY, James, Jr. Lt., Fauq. Mil., oath Aug. 1777; Capt. recom. Oct. 1779 and again Aug. 1781. Oath as Capt. 32 Sept. 1782. (MB. 1781-84, p. 68) Signed O'Bannon Petition, 12 Apr. 1781.

FOLEY, Martin. Capt. Fauq. Mil., oath (MB. 1781-83. p. 68.)

FOOTE, Richard. ca. 1753-1779. Lt., Va. Marines. Killed in Chesapeake. Fauq. Will, 24 Feb. 1779. Estate to brother Wm. Foote.

FORD, Henry. Pvt., Served with brother, William Ford, in Col. Elias Edmonds' Regt. Fauq. Mil. 1781. (see: William Ford.)

FORD, James. Pvt., Fauq. Mil. substitute for Samuel Baker. q.v.

FORD, William. (S.8506) 1762-post 1833. Pvt., Wm. Kincheloe's Co. 1777, guarding prisoners taken at Saratoga. Pvt. Wm. Jennings' Co. in the fall of 1779. Marched to Richmond with Capt. Francis Triplett's Co. Served in Wm. Frost's Co., Col. Elias Edmonds' Regt. Enl. 1781 Wm. Baylis' Co. Fauq. Mil. under Col. Elias Edmonds. ("the Corps was called the Flying Camp") Wdd. at Jamestown. Dischgd: Dec. 1781.

FORESTER, John. (S.35948) 1739-post 1820. Pvt., enl. 1776 John Ashby's Co., 3rd Va. Regt. CL. Enl. 1779 in Wm. Triplett's Co., Morgan's Rifle Regt.

FOWKE, Chandler. Sgt., 1st Bn. Fauq. Mil. under Col. Wm. Edmonds.

FOWKE, Gerard. Pvt., Benj. Harrison's Co., Fauq. Mil. 1777.

FOWKE, Robert. Pvt., Benj. Harrison's Co., Fauq. Mil. 1777.

FRANKLIN, John. (S.39541) Cpl., enl. 1780 in S.C. in Capt. Churchill Jones' Co. of Col. George Baylor's 3rd Regt. of Light Dragoons. At Camden, Ninety-six and Cowpens. Wdd. Eutaw Springs. Fauquier pension (MB. 1820-21, 27 Nov. 1820).

FRAZER, John. Pvt., Benj. Harrison's Co. Fauq. Mil. 1777. Died in the service.

FREEMAN, Edward. Pvt., Wm. Triplett's Cav. Co., July 1781.

FRENCH, John, Jr. C. 1760-post 1806. 2nd Lt., Fauq. Mil., (MB. 1773-80, pp. 311-12.)

FRENCH, Mason. c. 1757-1819. Pvt., Benj. Harrison's Co. Fauq. Mil. 1777. Ens., Peter Grant's Co., Grayson's Additional Cont. Regt. 2nd Lt., Dec. 1777. Resignd: 12 May 1778.

FULLER, Joshua. Lt., Fauq. Mil., Mil., oath Aug. 1777.

FULLER, Rodham. Ens., William Blackwell's Co., Fauq. Mil., oath Sept. 1778.

—G—

GAFNEY, James. Pvt., John Ball's Co., Fauq. Mil. 1781.

GAINES, Thomas Hollinger, Sr. Soldier. Fauq. Mil. (DAR Mag. Dec. 1971).

GARNER, Charles. Pvt., Wm. Blackwell's Co., Culp. Min. Bn. 1775-76. Enl. June 1777, Wm. Blackwell's Co. (No. 6) 11th Va. Regt. Served to Oct. 1778. d: in Ga. 1837.

GARNER, Jonas. Pvt., Wm. Pickett's Co., Culp. Min. Bn. 1775-76.

GARNER, Joseph. d: 1840. Sgt., Wm. Blackwell's Co. (No. 6), 11th Va. Regt. Wdd. at Brandywine.

GARRETT, Henry. Pvt., John Blackwell's Co., 3rd Va. Regt. CL. 1778.

GARINGTON, John. 2nd Lt., Fauq. Mil., recom. Mar. 1778 and again in Sept. 1780.

GARROTT, Robert. Pvt., Leonard Helm's Co., Clark's Illinois Regt. At Kaskaskia and Vincennes.

GEORGE, Aaron. Soldier. Mil. (**Eckenrode**)

FAUQUIER COUNTIANS IN THE REVOLUTION

GEORGE, Nicholas. Capt., Fauq. Mil. 1777. Resigned because of ill health, 1778. d: June, 1779. (DAR Mag. Dec. 1972).
GIBSON, Jacob. Pvt., Elias Edmonds' Co., 1st Va. State Regt. of Artillery.
GIBSON, John Pvt., John Ball's Co. Fauq. Mil. 1781.
GIBSON, Thomas. Cornet. Wm. Triplett's Cav. Co. Fauq. Mil. 1781. Capt. Fauq. Mil. (MB. 1793-95, p. 177.)
GLASCOCK, Spencer. Pvt. Fauq. Mil. (**Eckenrode**); Ens., Recom. 23 Sept. 1782. (MB. 1781-84, p. 67).
GLASCOCK, Thomas. Soldier. Fauq. Mil. (**Eckenrode**).
GLIVER, Thos. Pvt., John Blackwell's Co. 3rd Va. Regt. CL. 1778.
GODDARD, Joseph. (R.4078) 1761-1844. Pvt., enl. Jan. 1777 in Fauquier in Thomas Blackwell's Co. 10th Va. Reg. under Col. Edward Stevens. Served as pvt. and cpl. to Dec. 1778. Re-enl. for war in Blackwell's Co.
GRAHAM, ———, Capt., Fauq. Mil. (**Eckenrode**).
GRANT, Daniel. Pvt., Wm. Pickett's Co., Culp. Min. Bn., 1775-76. Pvt. Gabriel Long's Co. Morgan's Rifle Regt. Cert. from Brig. Gen. Wm. Woodford for service. (MB. 1773-80, p. 434).
GRANT, Isaac. Pvt., Simon Triplett's Co. Loudoun Mil. 1777.
GRANT, John. Pvt., Wm. Pickett's Co., Culp. Minute Bn. 1775-76. Pvt. Wm. Blackwell's Co. (No. 6), 11th Va. Regt. 1 June 1777. (**Saffell**).
GRANT, William. Pvt., Charles Gallahue's Co. (No. 2), 11th Va. Regt., May 1777.
GRASTY, George. Soldier, Fauq. Mil. (DAR Mag. Aug. - Sept. 1969).
GRAYHAM (GRAHAM), Walter. Pvt., Benj. Harrison's Co. Fauq. Mil. 1777. Capt., 1st. Va. State Regt. of Artillery under Col. Elias Edmonds. Com. Apr. 1780. (Same as above?).
GREEN, Andrew. Soldier, Fauq. Mil. No service given, (MB. 1820-21, 30 Aug. 1820.)
GREEN, Duff. 1759-1778, 2nd Lt., Col. John Green's 10th Va. Regt. Killed in a duel at Valley Forge.
GREEN, Jonathan. Pvt. Wm. Triplett's Cav. Co. Fauq. Mil. 1781.
GREEN, George. 1761-post 1841, Soldier. Fauquier pensioner, 1841.
GREEN, Moses. Pvt., James Quarles Co. 2nd Va. Regt. (Va. Liber II, f. 48).
GREEN, Thomas. d: 1777. Pvt. 6th Va. Regt., killed at Brandywine 11 Sept. 1777. (MB. 1781-83, p. 108).
GREEN, William. (W.8868) 1755-1835. Pvt., drafted 1777 in James Pendleton's Co. Culpeper Mil. Dischgd: Oct. 1777.
GRESPY, Martin. Pvt., Wm. Pickett's Co. Culp. Min. Bn., 1775-76.
GRIFFITH, Martin. Soldier, dischg. signed by Lt. Col. Richard Campbell and Capt. Hezekiah Morton. (MB. Oct. 1781.) Pension for wound continued, July 1783. (MB. 1781-84. pg. 151.)
GRIGSBY, Taliaferro. c. 1754-c. 1826, Pvt., Wm. Triplett's Cav. Co. 1781. (**Eckenrode**) (DAR-PI).
GRIGSBY, William. Capt. Fauq. Mil., recom. Mar. 1778, oath Apr. 1779.
GROVE, Phillip. 1755-post 1833. Soldier. Fauquier pensioner 1833.
GROVES, Thomas. (W.4211) d: 1822 Musician. Enl. in 1779 in a company from Fauquier "Posey's Detachment" of the 7th Va. Regt. under Lt. Col. Thomas Posey. Served to June 1783. Fauquier pension (MB. 1820-21, Aug. 1820).
GUNNELL, James. Soldier. Fauq. Mil. d: 1 Jan. 1819. Obituary in **National Intelligencer**, Washington, D.C.

—H—

HALEY (HAILEY), Anthony. (S.41624) Soldier. Nothing in pension file. (DAR-PI).
HADDOX, Nimrod. Pvt., John Ball's Co. Fauq. Mil. 1781.
HADELMAN, William. Pvt., James Scott's Fauq. Indep. Co. 1777.
HAILEY, John. Pvt., James Scott's Fauq. Indep. Co. 1777.
HALL, William. Pvt., Col. Byrd's Regt. (MB. 1773-1780, p. 456.)
HAMBRICK, Sephers. Soldier. Fauq. Mil. (Eckenrode).
HAMMRICK (HAMBRICK), Benjamin. Pvt., John Chilton's Co. 3rd Va. Regt. June and Sept. 1777. Pvt., same company under John Blackwell, Apr. 1778.
HAMRICK, David. Cpl. 4th Va. Light Dragoons, dischgd. 1781. (MB. 1780-81, p. 8).
HAMMONDS, John. Pvt., Elias Edmonds' Co. 1st Va. State Rgt. of Artillery. (MB. 1781-84, p. 108.) (DAR-PI).
HAMILTON, James. Pvt., John Chilton's Co., 3rd Va. Regt. CL. June and Sept. 1777.
HANEY, William. Pvt., Elias Edmonds' Co., 1st Va. State Regt. of Artillery.
HANSBOROUGH, John. Pvt., Fauq. Mil. (DAR-PI).
HARDIN, Benjamin. (S.3110) 1753-1839. Pvt., Stephen Ashby's Co., Col. Nevill's Regt. Va. CL. Served under Col. Laughlin McIntosh at Fort Pitt, June or July 1778. At Yorktown again with Capt. Stephen Ashby.
HARRIS, James (S.37996) Pvt., enl. in Fauquier Co. 1779 under Capt. Seldon, attached to 1st Va. Regt. CL., commanded by Col. Davis., dischgd. 1781.
HARRIS, John. Pvt., 4th Va. Light Dragoons. (MB. 1781-84, p. 67, Sept. 1782.)
HARRIS, Thomas. 2nd Lt. Fauq. Mil., oath May 1778.
HARRISON, Burr, Capt., Fauq. Mil., recom. July 1782. (MB. 1781-84, p. 59.); 1st Lt., in Wm Grigsby's Co., Fauq. Mil., recom. Mar. 1778; oath Apr. 1779.
HARRISON, Cuthbert. 1747-1778-9. Lt., Va. Dragoons, 1776; Capt. 1st Cont., Dragoons, Feb. 1777. Died in service.
HARRISON, William. Soldier, Fauq. Mil. (Eckenrode).
HATHAWAY, James. 2nd Lt., James Bell's Co. Fauq. Mil. recom. Nov. 1777. (MB. 1773-1780, p. 311-12.); 2nd Lt. James Scott's Fauq. Indep. Co. 1777; 1st Lt. John Ball's Co. Fauq. Mil. 1781; promoted Capt. 9 Aug. 1781. Dischgd. 1781.
HATHAWAY, John. 1733-1786. 1st Lt., James Scott's Fauq. Indep. Co. 1777.; Capt., Fauq. Mil., recom. Oct. 1779; oath Feb. 1780. Resgd. 1781. (MB. 1781-84, p. 108.)
HAWKINS, William. Soldier. Fauq. Mil. (DAR Mag. Aug-Sept. 1969)
HEALE, William. Ens., Wm Kincheloe's Co., oath Apr. 1779; 2nd Lt. Fauq. Mil., recom. 1779; oath Feb. 1780.
HEATON, Thomas, 1761-1858. Pvt. Fauq. Mil. (DAR-PI)
HELM, Lynaugh (Leonard) 1730-ante 1796 Capt., Clark's Illinois Regt. 1778. Captured at Vincennes.
HELM, Thomas. 1750-1816. 2nd Lt., 3rd Va. Regt. CL, Mar. 1776; 1st Lt. Nov. 1776; resigned Nov. 1777; Capt. Fauq. Mil. oath May. 1781. (OB. 1832-33, p. 267, 295.)
HELM, William. Capt. (OB. 1832-33, p. 64. 30 May 1832.)

FAUQUIER COUNTIANS IN THE REVOLUTION 461

HENSON, Robert. Soldier Fauq. Mil. (Suspended claims for further proof of service)
HERRINGTON, Robert. Pvt., John Eustace's Co., 2nd Va. Regt. CL. Service certified Fauquier (MB. 1773-80, p. 442.)
HEWES, Benjamin. Soldier, Fauquier pensioner. (Gwathmey) No record found.
HIGGINS, John. Pvt., Elias Edmonds' Co., 1st Va. State Regt. of Artillery.
HIGGINS, William. Pvt., Elias Edmonds' Co., 1st Va. State Regt. of Artillery.
HITT, John. Soldier Fauq. Mil. (DAR Mag. Aug-Sept. 1972)
HITT, Lazarus. Soldier Fauq. Mil. (DAR Mag. June-July 1971)
HITT, Peter. Pvt., Elias Edmonds' Co., 1st Va. State Regt. of Artillery. Fauq. Mil. (**Eckenrode**) (DAR Mag. Jan. 1974)
HOGAIN, John. 2nd Lt., Fauq. Mil., recom. Oct. 1780.
HOGAN, John. Pvt., James Scott's Fauq. Indep. Co. 1777.; Pvt. 5th Va. Regt. CL.
HOGAN, Rawley. Pvt., Benj. Harrison's Co. Fauq. Mil. 1777.
HOLLEY, Rawley. Soldier, Fauq. Mil. (**Eckenrode**)
HOLMES, James. Pvt., Benj. Harrison's Co. Fauq. Mil. 1777.
HOLTZCLAW, Jacob. Soldier. Fauq. Mil. (DAR-PI)
HOLTZCLAW, Nathan. Pvt., Elias Edmonds' Co., 1st Va. State Regt. of Artillery.
HOPPER, John. Pvt., John Chilton's Co., 3rd Va. Regt. CL. June and Sept. 1777; Pvt., 1st Va. State Regt. of Artillery. Cert. of service signed by Lt. Col. Edward Carrington. (MB. 1773-80., 27 Mar. 1780.)
HOPPER, Joseph. Soldier, Slaughter's Co., DAR Mag. Jan. 77.
HORD, Peter. c. 1749-1817. Pvt., Fauq. Mil. (DAR-PI)
HORRELL (HARRELL), John. Soldier. (MB. 1820-21, Mar-Apr 1821) Service not given.
HORTON, Henry. Pvt., John Ball's Co., Fauq. Mil. 1781.
HUBBARD, Epaphroditus. Pvt., 4th Va. Light Dragoons. (MB. 1781-84, p. 67, 23 Sept. 1782)
HUDLING, Richard. Soldier, Fauq. Mil. (**Eckenrode**)
HUDNALL, (HUDNELL), Joseph. Pvt., Benj. Harrison's Co. Fauq. Mil. 1777.
HUDNALL, Thomas. Pvt., Elias Edmonds' Co., 1st Va. State Regt. of Artillery. Fauq. Mil. (**Eckenrode**)
HUDSON, Rush. Soldier. Fauq. Mil. (MB. 1820-21, 30 Aug. 1820.) Service not given.
HUGHLETT (HULETT), William. Pvt., Benj. Harrison's Co. Fauq. Mil. 1777. (MB. 1820-21, 30 Aug. 1820.) Service not given.
HULL, Edwin. d: 1780. Capt. 15th Va. Regt. Nov. 1776. Resignd. Sept. 1778. Killed in service 15 Sept. 1780. (**Heitman**)
HUME, Charles, 1739-1821. Soldier. (DAR-PI)
HUME, Francis, 1730-1813. Capt. (DAR-PI)
HUME, Hubbard, Pvt., Benj. Harrison's Co. Fauq. Mil. 1777.
HUME, William. Soldier, Fauq. Mil. (**Eckenrode**)
HUMPHRIES, Samuel. Pvt., James Scott's Fauq. Indep. Co. 1777; Pvt. in Clark's Illinois Regt.
HUNT, William. 2nd Lt., Fauq. Mil., recom. Oct. 1780.
HUNTON, William, 1730-1809. Pvt. Fauq. Mil., Oct. 1780.

HYND, Michael, Drummer. John Chilton's Co. 3rd Va. Regt. CL. June 1777. Missing after Brandywine. (Gwathmey)

—I—

IRONMONGER, Robert. Fifer. Pvt. 2nd Va. Brigade, 10th Va. Regt. later 6th Va. Regt. CL. (Eckenrode)

—J—

JACKMAN, Richard. Pvt. Fauq. Mil. (DAR-PI)
JACKSON, Dempsey. Pvt., James Winn's Co. Fauq. Mil. under Maj. Francis Triplett at Cowpens. (See pens. appl. John Fishback R. 3563.)
JACOBS, John. Pvt., Samuel Blackwell's Co. Fauq. Mil. 1778. In pens. appl. Jeremiah Brown (S.6764) q.v.
JACOBS, William. Wagoner. Pension rejected, not considered military service.
JAMES, George. Soldier. No service record found.
JAMES, John. Pvt., Benj. Harrison's Co. Fauq. Mil. 1777. Ens., Fauq. Mil., July 1781.
JAMES, Joseph. Capt., Fauq. Mil. recom. Nov. 1777 in place of Samuel Blackwell. Oath Sept. 1778.
JAMES, Thomas. 2nd Lt. Fauq. Mil. May 1779.
JASPER ?, Benjamin. Pvt., Elias Edmonds' Co., 1st Va. Regt. of Artillery, 1777.
JEFFRIES, Alexander. 1764-1841. Fauquier pension list. 1832-33.
JEFFRIES, Henry. Soldier. Fauq. Mil. (DAR-PI)
JEFFRIES, Joseph. Soldier, Fauq. Mil. (Eckenrode)
JEFFRIES, Thomas. Pvt., Benj. Harrison's Co. Fauq. Mil. 1777.
JEFFRIES, William. Pvt., Benj. Harrison's Co. Fauq. Mil. 1777. Pvt. 11th Va. Regt.
JAMESON, David. 1754-post 1833. Pvt., John Brett's Co. Prince William Mil. 1780. Pension rec. David Blackwell (W. 9358) q.v.
JENKINS, Anthony. Soldier, Fauq. Mil. (Eckenrode)
JENKINS, Joshua. Sgt., John Chilton's Co., 3rd Va. Regt. killed at Brandywine, 11 Sept. 1777. Cert. by Col. Thomas Marshall, Fauquier Co. Court, 27 Mar. 1780.
JENKINS, Josiah. Pvt., died in service. Certificate of death August, 1779.
JENKINS, Thomas. Soldier, Fauq. Mil. (Eckenrode)
JENNINGS, Augustin. 2nd Lt., Fauq. Mil. (MB. 1773-1780, p. 341); 1st Lt., Fauq. Mil., 28 Feb. 1780.
JENNINGS, Baylor. Ens., Fauq. Mil., recom. Oct. 1779; oath May 1780.
JENNINGS, Berryman. Pvt., Wm Pickett's Co., Culp. Min. Bn. 1776; Ens., Thomas Bronaugh's Co., recom. Nov. 1777; oath May 1778.
JENNINGS, George, Ens., Fauq. Mil., (MB. 1784-86, p. 253.)
JENNINGS, Lewis. Ens., Wm. Jennings Co., Fauq. Mil. 1781.
JENNINGS, William. Capt., Fauq. Mil., (MB. 1773-80, p. 325.)
JESSOPS, Jacob. Pvt., Wm Pickett's Co., Culp. Min. Bn. 1775.
JETT, Anthony. Pvt., John Ball's Co., Fauq. Mil. 1781.

FAUQUIER COUNTIANS IN THE REVOLUTION 463

JETT, James. Pvt., 11th Va. Regt., died in service, 25 Mar. 1777 at Bound Brook, N.J.
JETT, Thomas. Pvt., Wm. Pickett's Co., Culp. Min. Bn. 1775; Pvt., Elias Edmonds' Co. 1st Va. Regt. of Artillery, 1777.
JETT, William. 1764-1851. Pvt., John O'Bannon's Co., Fauq. Mil., Col. Churchill's Regt.; Pvt., James Winn's Co., Col. Elias Edmonds' Regt. Fauq. Mil. 1781. At Yorktown.
JETT, William S. d: Fauquier Co. 1817. Enl. 3 Feb. 1776. Pvt., Goerge Slaughter's Co., 8th Va. Regt., comd. by Col. Abraham Bowman.
JOHNSON, David. Sgt. Fauquier Mil. (DAR-PI)
JOHNSON, George. Pvt., 4th Va. Light Dragoons. (MB. 1781-84, p. 67, 23 Sept. 1782.)
JOHNSON, Marshall. Pvt., John Ball's Co. Fauq. Mil. 1781.
JOHNSON, William. Pvt. Benj. Harrison's Co., Fauq. Mil. 1777; Pvt. 4th Va. Light Dragoons, (MB. 1781-84, p. 67, 23 Sept. 1782.)
JOHNSON, Yellis. Pvt., Wm. Pickett's Co. Culp. Min. Bn. 1775. (DAR Mag. Dec. 1771.)
JOHNSTON, Archibald. c. 1750-post 1834. Enl. Loudoun Co. Sept. 1777 as Lt. in Jacob Reed's Co., Col. Josias Clapham's Regt.; Enl. Apr. 1781 as Orderly Sgt. Robert Sandford's Co. Maj. Dennis Ramsay's Regt.
JOHNSTON, Gideon. (S.38089) 1749-1825. Enl. as pvt. 1776, R. K. Meade's Co., 2nd Va. Regt.; Lt., Arundell's Co. Va. Artillery; Capt. and Brigade QM, Col. Thomas Marshall's 1st Va. State Regt. of Artillery. (MB. 1820-21, 30 Aug. 1820).
JONES, Charles. Pvt., Wm Pickett's Co., Culp. Min. Bn. 1775.
JONES, James. Pvt., James Scott's Fauq. Indep. Co. 1777; Pvt., Elias Edmonds' Co., 1st Va. State Regt. of Artillery. Fauquier pensioner 1832-33.
JONES, John. Pvt., Wm. Pickett's Co., Culp. Min. Bn. 1775; Sgt., Corps of Guards, certified service Oct. 1779. (MB. 1773-80, p. 434.)
JONES, John Warner. Pvt., Wm. Triplett's Cav. Co., Fauq. Mil. 1781.
JONES, Moses. Pvt. 8th Va. Regt. CL. (**Eckenrode**)
JONES, Reuben. Pvt., Benjamin Pollard's Co., 2nd Va. State Regt. **Virginia Gazette**, Williamsburg, 1 Nov. 1777. "Lewis Seale of Culpeper and Reuben Jones of Fauquier, whose furloughs have expired some time, are ordered to repair to headquarters immediately or send certificates of their inability to do so, otherwise they will be deemed deserters and treated accordingly...Benj. Pollard, Capt." He furnished an acceptable excuse because in 1781 he was a pvt. in Wm. Triplett's Cav. Co., Fauq. Mil.
JONES, Thomas. Soldier, Fauq. Mil. (DAR Mag., Nov. 1969)
JONES, William. 1759-1834. Pvt., Wm. Pickett's Co. Culp. Min. Bn. 1775; enl. Fauquier CH, 20 Apr. 1776. Re-enl. Sgt., May 1781, Wm. Triplett's Cav. Co. of Col. Francis Triplett's Regt. POW at Yorktown 15 July-17 ct. 1781.
JORDON, Thomas. (R. 5759) Pvt., 3rd Va. Regt. CL Wdd. at Trenton. Fauquier pensioner, d: 1817.

—K—

KEIN, Thomas. Paid for recruiting in Fauquier, 14 Feb. 1776. (**Gwathmey**, p. 435)

KEIRNES, (KEARNS), William. Pvt., Wm. Blackwell's Co. (No. 6), Morgan's Rifle Regt.; Pvt. 7th Va. Regt. CL. proved service Fauquier Co. (MB. Nov. 1779.)
KEITH, Alexander, 1748-1822. Pvt. Co. No. 2, Col. Alexander Spotswood's 2nd Va. Regt. CL. Mar. 1777.; Lt. in Col. John Green's 6th Va. Regt. 1779. Promoted to Capt. vice Capt. John Combs at Cowpens, under Maj. Francis Triplett. Served to end of war. (Heitman)
KEITH, Isham, 1735-1787, Ens., Wm Pickett's Co. Culp. Min. Bn. 1775. 2nd Lt., 3rd Va. Regt. CL. Mar. 1776; 1st Lt. 3rd Va. Regt. CL. Jan. 1777. Resigned Apr. 1778 because of eye damage caused by smallpox. (Heitman)
KEITH, Thomas. d: 1802. 2nd Lt. Capt. Turner Morehead's Co. Fauquier Mil., recom. Mar. 1778. Later promoted to Capt.
KELLY, Thomas. Pvt., John Chilton's Co., 3rd Va. Regt., on command at Morristown, June 1777. In hospital after Brandywine, Sept. 1777.
KEMPER, Charles. (W. 20292) 1756-1841. Pvt., enl. 1777 in Hezekiah Turner's Co., Fauq. Mil.; Pvt. and gunner, Elias Edmonds' Co., 1st Va. State Regt. of Artillery. 1777. Orderly Sgt. in Wm Jennings Co., Col. Elias Edmonds' Regt. Fauq. Mil. Promoted to Ens. same company.
KEMPER, Henry. Soldier, Fauq. Mil. (DAR Mag. Dec. 1972)
KEMPER, James. 1st Sgt. James Winn's Co. Fauq. Mil. at Cowpens, Jan. 1781.
KEMPER, John. (S. 9142) 1749-post 1833. Drafted from Shenandoah Co. 1780 in Neville's Co., Col. Richard Campbell's Regt. Drafted in Jacob Wrinker's Co., Gen. Edward Steven's Regt. Wintered at Cheraw and guarded prisoners taken at Cowpens to Albemarle Barracks.
KEMPER, John. Cpl. Benj. Harrison's Co., Fauq. Mil. 1777. Sgt. John Ball's Co., Fauq. Mil. 1781.
KEMPER (KAMPER), Peter, Jr. Ens., Fauq. Mil., recom. Mar. 1778, oath Mar. 1780. Signed O'Bannon petition, Apr. 1781.
KEMPER, Tilman. (W.8573) 1759-1836. Pvt., enl. 1778 in Leonard Helm's Co., Clark's Illinois Regt. Drafted 1780 in Tilman Weaver's Co., Col. Armistead Churchill's Bn. Fauq. Mil. Cpl. in John Ball's Co. Fauq. Mil. 1781.
KENEARD, James. Pvt., Elias Edmonds' Co., 1st Va. State Regt. of Artillery. Proved service. (MB. Mar. 1781.)
KENEARD, Joshua. Pvt., Elias Edmonds' Co., 1st Va. State Regt. of Artillery. Proved service. (MB. Mar. 1781.)
KENTON, Benjamin. Pvt., Wm. Blackwell's Co. (No. 6) 11th Va. (Morgan's Rifle) Regt. CL.
KENTON, Mark. Cpl., Henry Lee's Co., of Col. Theodorick Bland's 1st Regt. of Light Dragoons, Dec. 1777. Sgt. Lee's Legion. 1780.
KENTON, Simon. 1755-1836. Capt., Lincoln Militia, Clark's Illinois Regt. Later Brig. Gen. of the Ohio Mil.
KENTON, John. 1757-1829. Sgt., Fauq. Mil. (DAR-PI)
KENTON, William. 2nd Lt., Fauq. Mil., recom. Mar. 1778., oath May 1778.
KERWIN, Andrew. Pvt., Wm. Pickett's Co., Culp. Min. Bn. 1775.
KEY, James. 1st Lt., Benj. Harrison's Co., Fauq. Mil. 1777.
KEY, (KEYS), Price. Pvt., Wm. Triplett's Cav. Co. Fauq. Mil. 1781. QM Sgt., Ord. Sgt. (DAR-PI)

KIBBLE, William. Pvt., Elias Edmonds' Co., 1st Va. State Regt. of Artillery.
KINCHELOE, Thomas. (W.1620) 1761-post 1832. Recruiting Sgt., Peter Grant's Co., 11th Va. Regt. CL. Drafted Feb. 1781 John Thomas Chunn's Co., Col. Armistead Churchill's Bn. Fauq. Mil. Released at Williamsburg Sept. 1781 by Gen. Robert Lawson because of illness.
KINCHELOE, William. 1736-1797. Lt. in James Scott's Fauq. Indep. Co. 1777. Capt. 1778. He removed to Kentucky where he built Ft. Kincheloe near Louisville 1779. The fort was burned by Indians Nov. 1781, but he and his family escaped.
KING, Joshua. Pvt., served 3 years in CL, then sent Charles Neale as a substitute, reserving right to bounty land. (MB. 1773-1780, p. 446, Mar. 1780.) (DAR-PI)
KING, Richard. Pvt., Wm. Grigsby's Co. Fauq. Mil. 1781. Pvt., John Ball's Co., Fauq. Mil. 1781.
KING, Robert. Pvt., Wm. Grigsby's Co. Fauq. Mil. 1781.
KING, William. (S.30524) 1760-63-post 1833. Pvt., enl. John Blackwell's Co., Fauq. Mil. 1777. Pvt., William Grigsby's Co. Fauq. Mil. 1781.
KIRK, John. Pvt., John Chilton's Co., 3rd Va. Regt. CL. June and Sept. 1777.
KIRK, Thomas. Soldier in Penna. with Jeremiah Brown, q.v.
KISTERSON, John. Soldier, Fauq. Mil. (**Eckenrode**)
KNEELON, John. Pvt., James Scott's Fauq. Indep. Co. 1777.

—L—

LAWLER, Nicholas. (S.32372) 1743-post 1831. Pvt., James Winn's Co., Col. Elias Edmonds' Regt. 1777.; Pvt., Leonard Sharp's Co., Col. Armistead Churchill's Regt. of Fauq. Mil. Pvt., James Winn's Co., Fauq. Mil. 1781.
LAWLER, Thomas. Pvt., Wm. Pickett's Co., Culp. Min. Bn. 1775.
LAWS, John. Pvt., Fauq. Mil. (MB. 1820-21, Aug. 1820.)
LAYTON, Robert. 1st Lt., Fauq. Mil., recom. Mar. 1778; oath May 1778.
LEACH, George, Jr. 1756-1838. Pvt., Elias Edmonds' Co., 1st Va. State Regt. of Artillery. Wdd. at Williamsburg. Sgt., service certified Fauquier (MB. 1781-84, p. 108.)
LEACH, George, Sr. Pvt., Elias Edmonds' Co., 1st Va. State Regt. of Artillery.
LEACH, Thomas. Pvt., Fauq. Mil. (**Eckenrode**)
LEACH, Valentine. 1755-1821. Sgt., Elias Edmonds' Co. 1st Va. State Regt. of Artillery. (DAR-PI)
LEE, James. Soldier, Fauq. Mil. (DAR Mag. Apr. 1972)
LEE, John. Soldier. Died in army, heir James Lee. (**Gwathmey**, p. 465)
LEE, William. Pvt., Wm. Pickett's Co., Culp. Min. Bn. 1775.
LEGG, John. Pvt., John Blackwell's Co., 3rd Va. Regt. CL. Apr. 1777.
LEONARD, Michael. Pvt., John Chilton's Co., 3rd Va. Regt. CL. June and Sept. 1777.
LEWIS, Francis. Soldier. Fauq. Mil. (**Eckenrode**)
LEWIS, James. 1752-1802. Pvt., Benj. Harrison's Co., Fauq. Mil., 1777.

LEWIS, William. 1750-1832. Pvt., Benj. Harrison's Co., Fauq. Mil., 1777. Pvt., Lee's Legion. (DAR-PI)
LINE, Cornelius. Pvt., James Scott's Fauq. Inde. Co. 1777.
LINOR, Philip. Pvt. Fauquier pensions.
LINTON, Michael. Pvt., Wm. Pickett's Co., Culp. Min. Bn. 1775.
LLOYD, George Embry, Sr. 1758-1853. Pvt., Fauq. Mil. (DAR-PI)
LUNSFORD, Rodham (S.13803) Pvt., Lawrence Butler's Co., 3rd Va. Regt., CL. Fall of 1779 marched to Charleston, S.C. POW, May 1780 to end of war.
LUTTRELL, Daniel. Pvt., Benj. Harrison's Co., Fauq. Mil., 1777.
LUTTRELL, John. Pvt., John Ball's Co., Fauq. Mil., 1781.
LUTTRELL, Joshua. Pvt., John Ball's Co., Fauq. Mil. Dischgd. 19 Aug. 1781.
LUTTRELL, Richard. Pvt., Benj. Harrison's Co., Fauq. Mil., 1777.
LUTTRELL, Robert. Pvt., John Ball's Co., Fauq. Mil., 1781.
LUTTRELL, Rodham. Pvt., Benj. Harrison's Co., Fauq. Mil., 1777.
LYNAUGH, Philip. Pvt., John Chilton's Co., 3rd Va. Regt., CL. June and Sept. 1777.
LYNN, William. Pvt., John Ball's Co., Fauq. Mil., 1781.
LYON, James. Pvt., Fauq. Mil. (MB. 1820-21, 30 Aug. 1820) Service not given.

—Mc—

McBRIDE, William. Pvt., James Scott's Fauq. Indep. Co. 1775. Sgt., John Ball's Co. Fauq. Mil. 1781.
McCALL, John. Pvt., Elias Edmonds' Co., 1st Va. State Regt. of Artillery.
McCANNON, Christopher. Pvt., 1st Va. Regt. CL. cert. signed by Col. Allison, (MB. Mar. 1780.) Sgt., 1st Va. Regt. CL. Dischgd. by Brig. Gen. Muhlenberg, (MB., Oct. 1781.)
McCLAIN, Thomas. Pvt., John Chilton's Co., 3rd Va. Regt. CL., Sept. 1777. In hospital after Brandywine; Pvt., same company under John Blackwell, Apr. 1778.
McCLANAHAN, David. Pvt., John Ball's Co. Fauq. Mil. 1781.
McCLANAHAN, James. Pvt., Elias Edmonds' Co., 1st Va. State Regt. of Artillery.
McCLANAHAN, Thomas. (W.1052) 1753-1845. Pvt., enl. 1775 under Capts. John Green and Richard Taylor, Col. Patrick Henry's Regt. Son of Wm. McClanahan, q.v. (DAR-PI)
McCLANAHAN, William. 1730-1802. Capt. A Baptist Elder authorized to raise a company among his parishioners in Culpeper and Fauquier Co. 1776.
McCLANAHAN, William. (S.5742) Pvt., enl. under Capts. Thomas Wailes, John White and Thomas Howard, 3rd Va. Regt. CL. under Col. Abraham Buford. Received 13 wounds at Waxhaws, May, 1780. Re-enl. Pvt. in Tilman Weaver's Co., Feb. 1781. Dischgd. 30 May, 1781.
McCOWN, John. Pvt., John Chilton's Co., 3rd Va. Regt. CL. June and Sept. 1777.
McCOY, Daniel (S.36083) 1761-1836. Pvt., enl. June 1779 in Fauquier Co. in Col. John Green's 2nd Va. Regt. Dischgd. 1781.
McGRAW, James. Pvt., 3rd Va. Regt. CL. Killed at Waxhaws, May, 1780. John McGraw, heir. (MB. 1798-99, p. 526.)

McGUIRE, Conner. Pvt., John Chilton's Co., 3rd Va. Regt. CL. Sept. 1777. Pvt. same company under John Blackwell, Apr. 1778.
McKNIGHT, Benjamin. Soldier. (MB. 1820-21, 30 Aug. 1820.) Service not given.
McLAIN, John. Sgt., John Ashby's Co., 3rd Va. Regt. CL. Died in Philadelphia, 7 Jan. 1777.
McMECKIN, Robert. Pvt., John Chilton's Co., 3rd Va. Regt. CL. Sept. 1777. Pvt., same company under John Blackwell, Apr. 1778.

—M—

MADDIN, Samuel. Pvt., John Chilton's Co., 3rd Va. Regt. CL. Sept. 1777. Pvt. same company under John Blackwell, Apr. 1778.
MADDOX, John. Pvt., Wm. Pickett's Co., Culp. Min. Bn., 1775.
MADDUX, Alexander. Pvt. 3rd Va. Regt. CL. Killed at Stony Point, June, 1779. Thomas Maddux, heir. (**Gwathmey**, p. 492)
MADDUX, Ezekiel. Pvt., Wm. Pickett's Co., Culp. Min. Bn. 1775.
MADISON, Ambrose (?). Soldier, Fauq. Mil. (**Eckenrode**)
MAHORNEY, Benjamin. (S.32393) Pvt., Benj. Harrison's Co. Fauq. Mil. 1777. Re-enl. Mar. 1779, Capts. William Wales and Thomas Hord's Co., 3rd Va. Regt. under Col. Abraham Buford. Trans. to Col. Epp's Co., Col. Wm. Washington's Light Dragoons. Dischgd. Oct. 1780.
MALONE, Thomas. Soldier. Enl. New Jersey Regt. comd. by Col. Peter Schuyler. Had lived in Va. more than 7 years in 1780. (MB 28 Feb. 1780.)
MARKHAM, James. 1752-1816 Capt. Va. Navy. Apptd. Apr. 1776. Capt. *Dragon,* 1777-80; Capt. *Tempest.* 1780. POW at Osborne's 27 Apr. 1781. Paroled 28 Apr. 1781.
MARKWILL, Joseph. Pvt., Elias Emonds' Co. 1st Va. State Regt. of Artillery.
MARR, John. Soldier. Died in the service. Daniel Marr, heir. (MB. 1773-80, p. 449, 27 Mar. 1780.)
MARSHALL, James Markham. 1764-1848. 2nd Lt., 1st Va. State Regt. of Artillery, 1778 (?), 1st Lt. 13 Apr. 1780. Lt. Col. Elias Edmonds acting comdr. Mentioned in 1781 as Capt. (**Heitman**).
MARSHALL, John. 1755-1832. Lt., Culp. Min. Bn., 1775; 1st Lt., 3rd Va. Regt. CL. July 1776; Capt-Lt., 15th Va. Regt. Cl. (Morgan's Rifle Regt.) Dec. 1776; Deputy Judge Advocate, 30 Nov. 1777; Capt. July, 1778; trans. to 7th Va. Regt. CL. Sept. 1778. Resigned 12 Feb. 1781. (**Heitman**).
MARSHALL, Thomas, 1730-1802. Major, Culp. Min. Bn., 1775; Maj., 3rd Va. Regt. CL. 13 Feb. 1776; Lt. Col., 13 Aug. 1776; Col. 21 Feb. 1777; Resigned 4 Dec. 1777. Col. 1st Va. State Regt. of Artillery, Nov. 1777. Served to end of war. (Note: The statement in **Heitman** and elsewhere that he was a POW in Charleston, May 1780, is incorrect.)
MARSHALL, Thomas Jr., 1761-1817. Pvt., Wm. Pickett's Co., Culp. Min. Bn. 1775; Capt. 1st Va. State Regt. of Artillery Apr. 1780,; Regimental Paymaster, Feb. 1781. Supernumerary 4 May, 1782.
MARSHALL, William. 1735-1809. He was an elder in the Baptist Church, said to have served in the Revolution, (DAR-PI), but his service is not confirmed.

MARTIN, Benjamin. (R. 6965) 1758-post 1833. Pvt., Wm. Pickett's Co., Culp. Min. Bn. 1775; Enl. James Winn's Co., Fauq. Mil. 1776; Cpl. Benj. Harrison's Co., Fauquier Mil. 1777; Served as a substitute for James Kemper in Francis Triplett's Co. 1780. Cpl., John Combs' Co. at Cowpens. Dischgd. Feb. 1781.
MARTIN, John. Pvt., Benj. Harrison's Co., Fauq. Mil. 1777; 2nd Lt. Tilman Weaver's Co. Fauq. Mil., oath July, 1779.
MASSIE, Thomas. c. 1745-1801. Capt. 6th Va. Regt. CL. 1776; Maj. 11th Va. Regt. CL. Feb. 1778; trans. to 2nd Va. Regt. CL. Sept. 1778. Resigned June 1779.
MATTHEW, Jonathan. Pvt., James Scott's Fauq. Indep. Co. 1777.
MATTHEW, Thomas. Pvt., James Scott's Fauq. Indep. Co. 1777.
MATTHEWS, Chichester. Sgt., John Chilton's Co., 3rd Va. Regt. CL. June and Sept. 1777.
MAUZY, John. 2nd Lt., Fauq. Mil., recom. May 1780.
MAY, James. Pvt., Elias Edmonds' Co., 1st Va. State Regt. of Artillery. (MB. 1781-84, p. 199.)
METCALF, John. Ens., Fauq. Mil., recom. Aug. 1781.
METCALF, William. Sgt., John Ball's Co. Fauq. Mil. 1781 promoted to Ens. 19 Sept. 1781.
MILLER, Henry, Pvt., Fauq. Mil. (**Eckenrode**).
MILLER, William. Pvt., Wm. Pickett's Co., Culp. Min. Bn., 1775.
MITCHELL, James. Pvt., John Blackwell's Co. 3rd Va. Regt. CL. 1778.
MIZENER, John. Pvt., James Scott's Fauq. Indept. Co. 1777.
MOFFETT, Henry. Pvt., Wm. Pickett's Co., Culp. Min. Bn. 1775. Sgt. 3rd Va. Regt. CL. John Ashby's Co. 1777.
MOFFETT, Jesse. (W. 3446) 1759-1836. Pvt., Benj. Harrison's Co. Fauq. Mil. 1777. Enl. July 1781 in Wm. Grigsby's Co., Col. Elias Edmonds' Regt.
MOFFETT, John. Maj. 2nd Bn. Fauq. Mil., recom. 24 Mar. 1778. Recommendation denied.
MOFFETT, William. Pvt., John Chilton's Co., 3rd Va. Regt. CL. Sept. 1777; Pvt., John Blackwell's Co., 3rd Va. Regt. CL. 1778.
MONDAY, George. Pvt., Wm. Pickett's Co., Culp. Min. Bn., 1775. Fauquier Mil. 1777.
MONROE, Alexander. Soldier. (DAR Mag. Mar. 1971).
MONROE, George. 1762-post 1832. Pvt., John T. Chunn's Co. Fauq. Mil. enl. Nov. 1780. Fauquier pension 1832-33
MONROE, James. Pvt., Wm. Pickett's Co., Culp. Min. Bn. 1775.
MOODY, Isaiah. Capt. Fauq. Mil. (Fauquier petitions, Va. State Library)
MOORE, Hendley, Pvt., Elias Edmonds' Co., 1st Va. State Regt. of Artillery.
MOORE, Peter. Pvt., John Chilton's Co., 3rd Va. Regt. CL. June and Sept. 1777. Wdd. at Brandywine. Pvt., Elias Edmonds' Co., 1st Va. State Regt. of Artillery.
MOORE, William. 1753-1818. Sgt., John Chilton's Co. 3rd Va. Regt. CL. June 1777. Ens. Sept. 1777. Capt. Fauquier Mil. recom. July 1782. (DAR-PI)
MOREHEAD, Charles, Jr. 1762-1828. Sgt., Lee's Legion.
MOREHEAD, Turner. Sgt., James Scott's Fauq. Indep. Co. 1777. Capt., Fauq. Mil., oath May 1778. Signed O'Bannon petition Apr. 1781.

MORGAN, Benjamin. 1762-1814. Pvt., Fauq. Mil. (DAR-PI)
MORGAN, Charles. Pvt., Wm. Blackwell's Co. (No. 6) 11th Va. (Morgan's Rifle) Regt., June 1777.
MORGAN, John. Sgt., Wm. Blackwell's Co. (No. 6), Morgan's Rifle Regt., June 1777. Died in service. Charles Morgan, heir. (MB. 1781-84, p. 108.)
MORGAN, Simon. (W. 8475) 1755-1810. Capt., wdd. at Eutaw Springs, for which he received a pension. (DAR-PI)
MORRISON, Edward. Soldier. Fauquier pension 1832-33.
MORTON, Hezekiah. Capt. Fauq. Mil. (MB. 1781-84, p. 22.)
MOSS, Thomas. Armorer. Claim for tools retained by Col. Finnie, Q.M.G., cert. July, 1783. (MB. 1781-84, p. 152.) (Fauquier petitions, Va. State Lib.).
MULLIKIN, William. Cpl., John Ball's Co., Fauq. Mil. 1781.
MURPHEY, John. Pvt., John Chilton's Co., 3rd Va. Regt. CL. June and Sept. 1777. Wdd. at Brandywine. Pvt. 4th Regt. Light Dragoons. Served under Col. William Washington at Cowpens. (Dischgd. by Lt. Col. Benjamin Temple. (MB. May 1781.) Pvt., Wm. Triplett's Cav. Co. 1781. Fauquier pensioner, 1832-33.
MURPHY, William. Pvt. Fauq. Mil. (Eckenrode).
MURPHY, James. Pvt., Fauq. Mil. (Eckenrode).
MURRAY, Reuben. 1762-post 1832. Pvt., enl. in James Winn's Co. Fauq. Mil., later comd. by Linsfield Sharp. Sgt., Turner Morehead's Co., Fauq. Mil. 1781. Dischgd. Winchester, 1781.
MURRAY, Shadrack. Pvt., James Scott's Fauq. Indep. Co. 1777.

—N—

NALLS, William. Pvt., James Scott's Fauq. Indep. Co. 1777.
NASH, Elijah. c. 1760-1777. Pvt., John Ashby's Co., 3rd Va. Regt., CL. Died in service. Will, Fauquier Co. 26 May 1777. (W.B. 1, p. 313).
NASH, Travis. Pvt., Benj. Harrison's Co. Fauq. Mil. 1777.
NASH, William. 2nd Lt., Fauq. Mil., Wm. Grigsby's Co., recom. 24 Mar. 1778.
NEAL, Richard. Pvt., Fauq. Mil. (Eckenrode).
NEALE, Charles. Pvt., Fauq. Muq., served as a substitute for Joshua King, Mar. 1780.
NEALE, Matthew. Ens., Francis Triplett's Co., Fauq. Mil., recom. Mar. 1779; oath Sept. 1779.
NEAVILL, Thomas (?). Pvt., James Scott's Fauq. Indep. Co. 1777.
NELSON, John. 1747-d.p. 1829. Pvt., Benj. Harrison's Co., Fauq. Mil. 1777. Lt. Fauq. Mil. (DAR-PI).
NELSON, Joseph. 1750-1837. Ens., John Ball's Co. Fauq. Mil., recom. Oct. 1779; oath May 1780. (DAR-PI).
NELSON, Thomas. Ens. Fauq. Mil., recom. Oct. 1779; oath Mar. 1780.
NELSON, William. Lt., Wm. Blackwell's Co., Culp. Min. Bn., 1st Lt., John Ashby's Co., 3rd Va. Regt. CL. 1776. Died in Philadelphia, Dec. 1776.
NEWMAN, Abner, 1755-d.p. 1824. Pvt., Fauq. Mil. (DAR-PI).
NICHOLSON, John. Soldier. Col. Francis Otway Byrd's 3rd Dragoons. (MB. March 1780.).
NICHOLS, Samuel. Pvt., Wm. Pickett's Co., Culp. Min. Bn. 1775.

NORMAN, Hugh. Pvt., Wm. Pickett's Co., Culp. Min. Bn. 1775.
NORRIS, James. Pvt., John Ball's Co. Fauq. Mil. 1781.
NORRIS, John. (W. 19930) 1760-1836. Pvt., James Scott's Fauq. Indep. Co. 1777. Drafted Turner Morehead's Co., Fauq. Mil. Mar. 1781. Drafted, Thomas Helm's Co. Fauq. Mil. Sept. 1781.
NORRIS, William. 1st Lt., Francis Attwell's Co., Fauq. Mil., recom. Nov. 1777, and again Mar. 1778.
NORTHCUTT, Richard. Pvt., John Ball's Co. Fauq. Mil. July 1781. Died or accidentally killed, 19 Aug. 1781.

—O—

O'BANNON, Aaron. Pvt., Co. No. 2, Col. Alexander Spottswood's 2nd Va. Regt., Mar. 1777.
O'BANNON, Andrew. (R.168211) Wagonmaster. Pvt., Wm. Pickett's Co., Culp. Min. Bn. 1775. Enl., John Chilton's Co., 3rd Va. Regt. CL. 1777., as regimental wagonmaster. Served at Brandywine, Germantown and Monmouth.
O'BANNON, Benjamin. (S.4629) 1759-d.p. 1832. Enl., in John Blackwell's Co., 3rd Va. Regt. 1777. He raised a company in Fauquier Co. and joined the Cont. army at Valley Forge. Comm. Capt. Col. Wm. Heth's 3rd Va. Regt. Served with Col. Daniel Morgan. Wdd. at Monmouth.
O'BANNON, Benjamin. (S.31886) 1750-d.p. 1832. Born in Fauquier Co. Enl. 1780, Salisbury, N.C.
O'BANNON, George. 1757-1776. Pvt. John Ashby's Co., 3rd Va. Regt. CL. Killed in action at Haarlem Heights, 16 Oct. 1776. Fauquier Co. WB. 1, p. 311.
O'BANNON, John. Cornet. Wm. Triplett's Cav. Co. under Col. Francis Triplett, 1781. Resigned 6 Aug. 1781.
O'BANNON, John. 1735-1797. Capt. comm. ante 1776. Recom. Maj. by 11 officers of the Fauquier Mil., Apr. 1781, as the Captain who had served longest. Petition apparently denied. (DAR-PI).
O'BANNON, Samuel. 2nd Lt. Fauq. Mil., recom. Sept. 1780; Lt. Fauquier Mil., recom. July 1782.
O'BANNON, Thomas, 1756-1832. Pvt., enl. Abel Westfall's Co. 8th Va. Regt., comd. by Col. Abraham Bowman. 1777. Pvt., Abraham Kirkpatrick's Co., 4th Va. Regt., comd. by Col. John Neville.
O'BANNON, Thomas (S.5851), 1757-1834. Drafted Sept. 1780 in James Winn's Co. Fauq. Mil., comd. by Gen. Wm. Smallwood. At Hillsborough, N.C. trans. to Maj. Francis Triplett's Regt. of Va. Mil. under Brig. Gen. Daniel Morgan. Dischgd. as QM Sgt. Feb. 1781. by Maj. Triplett.
O'BANNON, William. 1730 (?)-1807, Pvt. Fauq. Mil. (DAR-PI).
OCDEN (sic), Joseph. Pvt., James Scott's Fauq. Indep. Co. 1777.
ODER, Joseph. 1751-1833-4, Pvt., enl. 1777 in Samuel Blackwell's Co., Fauq. Mil., comd. by Col. Wm. Edmonds., later by Lt. Col. Martin Pickett. (DAR-PI).
OGLE, Thomas. DAR Mag. Jan. 1977.
O'REAR, Daniel. (S.7376) Pvt., Leonard Helm's Co., Clark's Illinois Regt.

O'REAR, Daniel. (S.31892) 1759-d.p. 1834. Pvt., enl. Wm. Blackwell's Co., Culp. Min. Bn. 1775. Enl. in John Ashby's Co., 3rd Va. Regt. CL; Enl. Sept. 1779, Richard Allen's Co., Col. Wade Hampton's Regt. S. C. Mil; Ord. Sgt. John G. Lowman's Co., Col. Williams' Regt.; POW Charleston May, 1780.
O'REAR, John. (S.31285) Ord. Sgt., Leonard Helm's Co., Clark's Illinois Regt., 1778. Ord. Sgt., John O'Bannon's Co. Fauq. Mil. Regt. comd. by Col. Armistread Churchill.
O'REAR, William. Pvt., John O'Bannon's Co., Fauq. Mil. Regt. comd. by Col. Armistead Churchill.
ORDAM (OLDHAM), George. Pvt., Wm. Triplett's Cav. Co., Col. Francis Triplett's Regt. under Gen. Daniel Morgan, 1781.
OWENS, Charles. Sgt. 3rd Va. Regt., comd. by Col. Abraham Buford.

—P—

PARKER, Benjamin (S.46062) 1759-d.p. 1832. Pvt., Benj. Harrison's Co. Fauq. Mil. 1777. Pvt., Wm. Jenning's Co., Fauq. Mil. Apr. 1781.
PARKER, Joseph (S.38285) 1756-1821. Pvt., Wm. Blackwell's Co. (No. 2) 11th Va. Regt. CL 1777. Promoted cpl. 1778.
PARKER, Martin. Pvt., John Ball's Co. Fauq. Mil. 1781 (DAR-PI)
PATTESON, Tilman. Capt., Fauq. Mil. (Eckenrode).
PATTIE, William. 1763-d.p. 1841. Fauq. pensioner.
PATTON, Alexander. 1745-d.p. 1820. Pvt., John Ashby's Co., 3rd Va. Regt. CL 1776. Re-enl., Valentine Peyton's Co., 3rd Va. Regt. CL 1778. Fauq. pensioner.
PAYNE, Augustine. 1762-d.p. 1832. Pvt., John O'Bannon's Co., Fauq. Mil., Nov. 1780. Wdd. in service.
PAYNE, Francis, 1743-1816. Ens., Fauq. Mil., oath Feb. 1779 (DAR-PI).
PAYNE, George. Pvt., enl. about 1 Sept. 1780.
PAYNE, William, 1759-d.p. 1834. Pvt., Wm. Pickett's Co., Culp. Min. Bn. Sgt., Hezekiah Turner's Co. Fauq. Mil., Sept. 1778. Sgt. John O'Bannon's Co. Fauq. Mil. 1780-81.
PAYNE, Winter, 1755-1837. Capt. Died in Fauq. Co. (DAR-PI).
PEAKE, George. Pvt., Wm. Triplett's Cav. Co., Fauq. Mil. 1781.
PEAKE, John. 1756-1841. Pvt. Henry Lee's Co. of Virginia Light Dragoons, 1776; Pvt., Benj. Harrison's Co., Fauq. Mil., Sept. 1777.
PEAKE, Joseph. Pvt., Scott's Fauq. Indep. Co., 1777.
PEARLE, Samuel. Ens. Fauq. Mil., recom. June 1780; 2nd Lt., Fauq. Mil., recom. Nov. 1780.
PEARL, William. Sgt. Fauq. Mil. (DAR Mag. Dec. 1969).
PENNINGTON, Daniel. Pvt., John Chilton's Co., 3rd Va. Regt. CL. June and Sept. 1777; Pvt., same company under John Blackwell, Apr. 1778.
PEPPER, Samuel. 1756-1824. Pvt., Benj. Harrison's Co., Fauq. Mil. 1777. (DAR-PI).
PETERS, James. Seaman. Galley *Henry.* Naval Board Min. Nov. 1777.
PETERS, John. (W.8511) 1762-1833. Pvt., Tilman Weaver's Co., Fauq. Mil.; 2nd Lt., Wm. Pope's Co., Fauq. Mil., recom. Sept. 1778.
PETTIT, Nathaniel. Pvt. (DAR-PI).
PEYTON, Henry. 1st Lt., Fauq. Mil., recom. Oct. 1779.
PEYTON, Robert. Ens. 3rd Va. Regt., Nov. 1776; 2nd Lt. Jan. 1777; Killed at Brandywine, 11 Sept. 1777.

PEYTON, Valentine. 1st Lt. 3rd Va. Regt. 1777. Capt. 3rd Va. Regt. after resgn. Capt. John Ashby. Comm. dated 11 Sept. 1777.

PHILIPS, Samuel. Sgt., Wm. Blackwell's Co. (No. 6), Morgan's Rifle Regt. June 1777.

PHILLIPS, Elijah. Pvt. Charged in Fauq. Ct. with dessertion but released. (MB. 1781-84, p. 4).

PICKETT, Martin. 1740-1809. Lt. Col., 1st Bn. Fauq. Mil., Nov. 1777; Col., 2nd Bn., Fauq. Mil., recom. Aug. 1781.

PICKETT, William, 1742-1814. Capt., Culp. Min. Bn., 1775-76. Lt. Col. 2nd Bn. Fauq. Mil., Recom. Mar. 1778. Not apptd. Served as Maj., Fauq. Mil., 1778-9.

PICKETT, William Sanford. 1735-1798. Capt. Fauq. Mil. (DAR-PI).

PIPER, Benjamin. Pvt., Elias Edmonds' Co. 1st Va. State Regt. of Artillery.

POPE, Benjamin. 1740-1816. Ens. Fauq. Mil. (DAR-PI).

POPE, William. Capt., Fauq. Mil., oath May 1778.

PORTER, John. Pvt., Elias Edmonds' Co., 1st Va. State Regt. of Artillery. (MB. 1781-84, p. 115).

POWELL, John. Pvt., Fauq. pensioner.

PRIEST, Peter. Pvt., Fauq. Mil. 1777. Wdd. near Brandywine.

PRINCE, Hubbard. 2nd Lt., Fauq. Mil., recom. Mar. 1778.

PROCTOR, John. Pvt., Fauq. Mil. (DAR Mag. Dec. 1974).

PROVO, William. Pvt. Eustace's Co., 2nd Va. Regt. CL. (MB 27 Mar. 1780).

PURCELL, George. 1751-d.p. 1841. Pvt., Fauq. pensioner.

—Q—

QUAIL, John. Pvt., John Chilton's Co., 3rd Va. Regt. CL. June and Sept. 1777.

—R—

RAMEY, John, (W.11104) 1753-1834. Pvt., (pension folder empty) (DAR-PI).

RANKIN, Moses. NCO in "last war". Certf. signed by Gen. Geo. Washington. (MB 1773-80, p. 451., Apr. 1780).

RANSDELL, Edward. Pvt., Wm. Blackwell's Co. (No. 6). Morgan's Rifle Regt., June 1777.

RANSDELL, Presley. Sgt., Scott's Fauq. Indep. Co. 1777.

RANSDELL, Thomas. Pvt., Wm. Triplett's Cav. Co., Fauq. Mil., 1781.

RANSDELL, Thomas. 3rd Lt., Wm. Blackwell's Co. (No. 6) Morgan's Rifle Regt., June 1777.; 1st Lt., John Cropper's Co., Col. Daniel Morgan's 11th Va. Regt., CL. Nov. 1778.

RANSDELL, Wharton, Sr. Pvt., Scott's Fauq. Indep. Co., 1777.

RANSDELL, Wharton, Jr. Pvt., Scott's Fauq. Indep. Co., 1777; Ens., Fauq. Mil., oath Sept. 1778. Signed O'Bannon petit. Apr. 1781.

RAWDEN, John. B: England, res. Fauq. 1780. Enl. Fauq. Mil., after 1 Sept. 1780 (Chesterfield Supplement, Va. Sta. Lib.).

RECTOR, James, (R.8635) b: 1754. Pvt., enl. in Henry Dudley's Co., Col. Charles Dabney's Va. State Regt., 1778. Dischgd. Nov. 1781.

RECTOR, Henry. Solder. (DAR Mag., Aug-Sept 1972).

RECTOR, Jesse. (R.8639) 1759-1843 Pvt., enl. 1780 but did not serve because of illness. Pvt., Henry Dudley's Co., Col. Charles Dabney's Va. State Regt., 1781.

REDMAN, Richard. Soldier. (Chesterfield Supplement, Va. Sta. Lib.).
REEVE, William (S.31924) 1766-d.p. 1833. Pvt., James Scott's Fauq. Indep. Co., 1777.
RICE, Bailey. Soldier, enl. after 1 Sept. 1780 (Chesterfield Supplement, Va. State Lib.).
RICE, James B. Soldier. Suspended claims; did not serve 6 mos.
RICE, William, Pvt., Elias Edmonds' Co., 1st Va. State Regt of Artillery, 1778.
RIDDLE, William. 1757-d.p. 1833. Soldier, Fauq. pensioner.
RIDLEY, John. QM Sgt., Elias Edmonds' Co., 1st Va. State Regt. of Artillery. (MB. 1781-84, p. 7).
RIELY, Edward Soldier, Fauq. Mil. (Eckenrode).
RILEY, George. Pvt., John Ball's Co., Fauq. Mil. 1781.
RILEY, John. Pvt., James Scott's. Fauq. Indep. Co. 1777; Pvt. John Blackwell's Co., 3rd Va. Regt. CL. Apr. 1778. (Eckenrode).
RINGO, Burtis (S.31329) b: N.J. 1763-1855. Pvt. Wm. Armstead's Co. of Dragoons, Charles Dabney's Va. Regt. 1779. Sgt. 1782 express rider for Gov. Nelson.
RIXEY, Richard. 1st Lt., Fauq. Mil., oath May 1778; Capt. Fauq. Mil., recom. May 1780; oath June 1780.
ROACH, John. Cpl., John Green's Co., Col. Charles Harrison's 1st Cont. Artillery, CL. (MB 1781-84).
ROACH, William. Cpl. John Chilton's Co., 3rd Va. Regt. CL. June and Sept. 1777. Assigned to Gen. Washington's Guard.
ROBERTS, Joseph. Soldier, Fauq. Mil. (Eckenrode).
ROBINSON, Dixson (Dickson) Pvt., John Chilton's Co., 3rd Va. Regt. CL. June and Sept. 1777. Assigned to Gen. Washington's Guard.
ROBINSON, Mach. Pvt., Wm. Blackwell's Co. (No. 6), Morgan's Rifle Regt., June 1777.
ROBINSON, William, 1758-1833. Fauq. pensioner. 1833.
ROGERS, Edward. 1763-1813. Pvt., Fauq. Mil. (DAR-PI).
ROGERS, George. (W.10240) 1764-1858. Pvt., Francis Triplett's Co. Fauq. Mil., 1780; Pvt. John Combs' Co., Fauq. Mil., at Cowpens, Jan. 1781.; Pvt., Thomas Helm's Co., Col. Wm. Darke's 4th Va. Regt., Aug. 1781. Discgd. May 1782.
ROGERS, George. Ens., James Bell's Co., Fauq. Mil., recom. Nov. 1777; 2nd Lt., oath June 1779.
ROGERS, James. Pvt., Wm. Triplett's Cav. Co., Fauq. Mil., 1781.
ROGERS, Reuben. Pvt., Wm. Triplett's Cav. Co., Fauq. Mil., 1781.
ROLLINS, Vincent. Pvt., John Eustace's Co., 2nd Va. Regt. CL. (MB. 1773-80, pg. 442. 27 Mar. 1780).
ROSSER, John. Pvt., Benj. Harrison's Co. Fauq. Mil. 1777.
ROSSER, Richard. (S.31344) 1757-d.p. 1832. Pvt., Benj. Harrison's Co., Fauq. Mil. 1777.
ROUTT, Richard. d: 1806. Ens., 12th Va. Regt. CL. Dec. 1776; 2nd Lt., Apr. 1777; retired 14 Sept. 1778. (OB. 1834-35, p. 70).
ROWLES, William. 1759-d.p. 1832. Pvt., Capt. Norrard's Co., Col. Josias Carvil Hall's 4th Md. Regt., Cl. Res. of Fauq. 1832.
RUSSELL, George. Pvt., John Chilton's Co., 3rd Va. Regt. June and Sept. 1777; Pvt., same company under John Blackwell, Apr. 1778.
RUSSELL, Joseph Pvt., Wm. Triplett's Cav. Co., Fauq. Mil. 1781.
RUSSELL, William. Col., 5th Va. Regt., 1778. POW Charleston, May 1780. Excg. Nov. 1780. (MB. 1773-80, p. 444).

RUST, Benjamin. Pvt., James Scott's Fauq. Indep. Co. 1777.
RUST, John Lt., Turner Morehead's Co., Fauq. Mil. 1781. Signed O'Bannon petit. Apr. 1781.
RUST, Vincent. Ord. Sgt., John Ashby's Co., 3rd Va. Regt., CL. 1777.

—S—

SCANLAND, John Fielding. Pvt., John Ball's Co., Fauq. Mil. 1781. (DAR-PI).
SCOGGIN, William. Pvt., John Ball's Co., Fauq. Mil., 1781. Promoted to Sgt., 24 Aug. 1781.
SCOTT, Alexander. Lt., Thomas Helm's Co., Fauq. Mil., Sept. 1781.
SCOTT, James. 1742-1779. Capt., Fauq. Mil. 1775-76. Capt., Culp. Min. Bn., 1775. Capt. Fauq. Independent Co. 1777.
SCRIBBING, William. Pvt., Fauq. Mil. Fauq. pension (**Gwathmey**).
SEATON, George. Pvt., Benj. Harrison's Co., Fauq. Mil. 1777.
SEATON, William Ens., Francis Triplett's Co., Fauq. Mil., Mar. 1778.
SETTLE, Edward. (S.4907) 1764-1839. Pvt., Wm. Triplett's Cav. Co. Fauq. Mil. 1781.
SETTLE, Francis. b: Fauq. Co. Enl. Culp., Mil. after 1 Sept. 1781. (Chesterfield Supplement, Va. Sta. Lib.).
SETTLE, Strother. Pvt., Col. Stephen Moylan's 4th Regt. of Light Dragoons (MB. 1781-84, p. 67. 23 Sept. 1782).
SETTLE, William. Capt., Fauq. Mil. Resigned Mar. 1777.
SHACKLEFORD, George. Pvt., Wm. Johnston's Co., 11th Va. Regt. CL.
SHACKLEFORD, James. 1763-1825. Pvt., John Ball's Co., Fauq. Mil. 1781.
SHACKLETT, Edward. (W.6037) 1758-1826. Pvt., Nathaniel Burwell's Co., Col. Charles Harrison's 1st Cont. Artillery Regt. 1777-79. Sgt. 1st Va. State Regt. of Artillery. Cert. of service July 1780 signed by Lt. Col. Edward Carrington. (MB. July 1780).
SHARP, James. Pvt., John Ball's Co., Fauq. Mil. 1781.
SHARPE, Linsfield. 2nd Lt., Benj. Harrison's Co., Fauq. Mil. 1777; Capt., Fauq. Mil., recom. July 1781. (MB. 1773-80, pg. 311-12).
SHAVER, George. Virginia Battalion (?) (**Eckenrode**).
SHAVER, John. 8th Va. Regt. CL., 9th Va. Regt. Cl. (Va. Bn. ?) (**Eckenrode**).
SHERRINGTON, Robert. Pvt., John Eustace's Co., 2nd Va. Regt. Cl. Proved service Fauq. Co. 27 Mar. 1780. (MB. 27 Mar. 1780).
SHUMATE, Armstead. (R.9551) 1761-d.p. 1846. Pvt., Thomas Helm's Co., Fauq. Mil. 1781. Pvt., Wm. Blackwell's Co., Fauq. Mil. in place of uncle, James Shumate.
SHUMATE, Berryman (R.9552) d: 1802. Pvt., Thomas Helm's Co., Fauq. Mil. 1779. Substitute for uncle, John Shumate.
SHUMATE, Daniel. 1749-1826. Ens., Nicholas George's Co., Fauq. Mil. apptd. Mar. 1777; 2nd Lt., Fauq. Mil., oath Nov. 1778.
SHUMATE, Samuel (S.15646) Pvt., Samuel Blackwell's Co., Fauq. Mil. 1777; Pvt., James Winn's Co., Fauq. Mil. 1779.
SHUMATE, William. Pvt., Wm. Blackwell's Co. (No. 6) Morgan's Rifle Regt. (11th Va. Regt. CL) June, 1777.
SIDEBOTTOM, John. Pvt., Morgan's Rifle Regt. 1777.

FAUQUIER COUNTIANS IN THE REVOLUTION 475

SIDWELL, Stephen. b: Penna. Fauq. Pensioner. (Chesterfield Supplement, Va. Sta. Lib.).
SINCLAIR, John. Pvt., Wm. Pickett's Co., Culp. Min. Bn. 1775.
SINGLETON, Joshua. Ens., Turner Morehead's Co. Fauq. Mil. 1781.
SINGER, George. Pvt., Benj. Harrison's Co., Fauq. Mil. 1777; Pvt., John Ball's Co., Fauq. Mil., 1781.
SLAGLE, Abram. Pvt., James Scott's Fauq. Indep. Co., 1777.
SMALLWOOD, Hebron. 1755-d.p. 1833. Pvt., enl. 1777 in Williamsburg in John Triplett's Co., Col. Wm. Brent's Regt. Transferred to Cont. Line.
SMITH, Andrew. Pvt., Elias Edmonds' Co., 1st Va. State Regt. of Artillery.
SMITH, Augustine. Cpl., Benj. Harrison's Co., Fauq. Mil. 1777; Ens., Tilman Weaver's Co., Fauq. Mil., oath 26 July 1779.
SMITH, Enoch. Gunner. Elias Edmonds' Co., 1st Va. State Regt. of Artillery. (MB. 1781-84, p. 8). Sgt., Wm. Triplett's Cav. Co. Fauq. Mil., 1781.
SMITH, Gerrard. Pvt., Wm. Pickett's Co., Culp. Min. Bn. 1775.
SMITH, Isaac. Pvt., John Chilton's Co. 3rd Va. Regt. CL. June and Sept. 1777.
SMITH, James A. Pvt., Fauq. Mil. Fauq. pensioner.
SMITH, John. Soldier. (MB. 1820-21, 30 Aug. 1820. No service given.)
SMITH, Joseph. Lt. Fauq. Mil., recom. Aug. 1781.
SMITH, Robert. Pvt., 1st Va. Regt., CL.
SMITH, Rolly (Rowley). 1st Lt., Fauq. Mil., oath Mar. 1781.
SMITH, Spencer. Pvt., Wm. Pickett's Co., Culp. Min. Bn. 1775.
SMITH, Thomas. 1747-1796. 2nd Lt., Fauq. Mil., oath June 1778.
SMITH, William. 1755-1823. Ens., Fauq. Mil., Mar. 1779.
SMITH, William. Pvt., Benj. Harrison's Co. Fauq. Mil., 1777; Pvt., 1st Va. State Regt., Cert. of service from Gen. Edward Stevens presented to Mar. Court, 1780.
SOUTHARD, William. Pvt., Wm. Pickett's Co., Culp. Min. Bn. 1775.
SOUTHERN, George. Soldier, Fauq. Mil. (Eckenrode).
SPICER, William. Pvt., Benj. Harrison's Co., Fauq. Mil. 1777.
SPILLER, Philip. Pvt., John Ball's Co., Fauq. Mil., 1781.
STALLARD, Randolph (S.6165) 1757-d.p. 1832. Lt. (DAR-PI).
STAMPS, John. Pvt., Wm. Triplett's Cav. Co., Fauq. Mil., 1781.
STANTON, William. Soldier. Lived in Fauq. Co. (DAR-PI).
STEWART, William. Pvt., John Ball's Co., Fauq. Mil., 1781. Continued in service.
STONE, Nimrod. 1764-1841. Pvt., Wm. Triplett's Cav. Co., Fauq. Mil., 1781. (DAR-PI).
STRAUGHN, John. Pvt., Wm. Blackwell's Co. (No. 6), Morgan's Rifle Regt. June 1777.
STRONG. John. Pvt., John Chilton's Co., 3rd Va. Regt. CL. June and Sept. 1777.
STROTHER, Benjamin. Pvt., Lee's Legion.
STROTHER, William. Sgt., Lee's Legion.
SUDDOTH, Francis. Sgt., John Ball's Co., Fauq. Mil., 1781.
SUDDOTH, John. Pvt., John Ball's Co., Fauq. Mil., 1781.
SUDDOTH, William. Pvt., Charles Gallahue's Co. (No. 2), Morgan's Rifle Regt., May 1777; Cpl., Wm. Blackwell's Co. (No. 6) same Regt., June 1777.

SYDNOR, Philip. Soldier (MB. 1820-21, 30 Aug. 1820) Service not given.

—T—

TALBOT, Cornelius. Pvt., James Scott's Fauq. Indep. Co., 1777.
TAYLOR, Benjamin. Pvt., Benj. Harrison's Co., Fauq. Mil. 1777. Fauquier Petitions (Virginia State Lib.).
TAYLOR, Joseph. 2nd Lt., Fauq. Mil., Francis Attwell's Co., Nov. 1777; 1st Lt., Fauq. Mil., oath July, 1779.
TAYLOR, Nimrod. Pvt., John Ball's Co., Fauq. Mil., 1781. Dischgd. 13 Aug. 1781.
TAYLOR, Thornton. Ens., Wm. Blackwell's Co. (No. 6), Morgan's Rifle Regt. 1 Apr. 1778.
TAYLOR, Zachariah. Pvt., Elias Edmonds' Co., 1st Va. State Regt. of Artillery.
TEMPLE, Benjamin. Capt., Va. Dragoons, June 1776; Lt. Col. 1st Cont. Dragoons, Mar. 1777. trans. 4th Dragoons, Dec. 1779; (Heitman).
THAYER, William. Sgt. 5th Va. Regt. CL. (MB. 1820-21, 27 Feb. 1821). Service not given.
THOMAS, David. Pvt., James Scott's Fauq. Indep. Co. 1777.
THOMAS, Elisha. (W.2974) 1760-1834. Pvt., Robert Bell's Co., Col. George Gibson's 1st Va. Regt., CL. Jan. 1777. Proved service 9th Va. Regt. (MB. 1773-80, p. 244).
THOMAS, John. Pvt., John Chilton's Co., 3rd Va. Regt. CL. Sept. 1777; Pvt., same company under John Blackwell, Apr. 1778.
THOMAS, Joseph. Pvt., 9th Va. Regt. Cl. (MB. 1773-80, p. 244).
THORNBERRY, Samuel. Pvt., James Scott's Fauq. Indep. Co. 1777.
THORNTON, John. Pvt., Elias Edmonds' Co., 1st Va. State Regt. of Artillery.
THORNTON, Reuben. Pvt., Elias Edmonds' Co., 1st Va. State Regt. of Artillery.
TIMBERLAKE, Epaphroditus. 2nd Lt., Fauq. Mil., in room of Thomas Edwards, 26 Sept. 1780.
TOMLIN, John. Pvt., Charles Porterfield's Co., Morgan's Rifle Regt. (11th Va. Regt. CL) 1778.
TOMLIN, Stephen. Pvt., John Chilton's Co., 3rd Va. Regt. CL. Sept. 1777.; Pvt., same company under John Blackwell, Apr. 1778.
TOMLIN, William, Sr. (S.6261) 1758-d.p. 1832. Cpl., John Chilton's Co., 3rd Va. Regt. CL. June and Sept. 1777; Sgt., 4th Va. Light Dragoons. (MB. 1780-84, p. 67, 23 Sept. 1782).
TRIPLETT, Francis. 1728-1794. Adj. Fauq. Mil., 1777; Capt. Fauq. Mil., in room of Capt. Wm. Ball, Mar. 1778; oath Sept. 1778; Maj. Fauq. Mil., Dec. 1780, at Cowpens; Col. in Morgan's Va. State Regt., apptd. June 1781. Served to 1783.
TRIPLETT, Hedgman. 1762-1826. Sgt., Fauq. Mil., 1780.
TRIPLETT, Peter (S.6032) 1750-1851. Marine, on sloop **Liberty**, 1776; Pvt., John Lee's Co., Col. George Gibson's 1st Va. State Regt., 1777; sapper, Gen. Anthony Wayne's Brig. in attack at Stony Point; Wdd. at Stony Point, 16 July, 1779; Pvt., George Slaughter's Co., Clark's Illinois Regt., 1781. Served to 1783.

TRIPLETT, William. 1759-1812. Ens., Grayson's Add. Cont. Regt., 1777; 1st Lt. same Regt., 1778; Capt., Col. Wm. Washington's 3rd Cont. Dragoons, 1779; Capt. of Cav., Col. Francis Triplett's Regt., Morgan's Va. State Regt., apptd. June 1781. (Note: His military record in Heitman is confused with that of his cousin Wm. Triplett of Fairfax Co., also an officer in Grayson's Regt.).
TRIPLETT, William, c. 1735-1822. Pvt., Benj. Harrison's Co., Fauq. Mil. 1777.
TUFFNELL, James. Pvt., John Chilton's Co., 3rd Va. Regt. CL. Sept. 1777; Pvt., same company under John Blackwell, Apr. 1778.
TULLOSS, Benjamin. Ens., Fauq. Mil., (MB. 1773-80, p. 311).
TULLOSS, Joshua. Lt., Nicholas George's Co., Fauq. Mil., 1777; Capt., Fauq. Mil., acting comd. Capt. Thomas Bronaugh's Co., Apr. 1781. Signed O'Bannon petition 12 Apr. 1781.
TULLOSS, Rodham. Ens., Fauq. Mil. (MB. 1773-80, p. 341) Signed O'Bannon petition 12 Apr. 1781.
TUNNEL, George. Pvt., Fauq. Mil. (Eckenrode).
TURNER, Hezekiah. Capt., paymaster, 3rd Va. Regt. CL. June 1777 to May 1778. (Heitman).
TURVY, William, Pvt., John Chilton's Co., 3rd Va. Regt. CL. Sept. 1777; Pvt., same company under John Blackwell, Apr. 1778.
TYLER, John. Pvt., James Scott's Fauq. Inde. Co. 1777.

—U—

URTON, James (S.15690) 1752-d.p. 1834. Pvt., Simon Handcock's Co. Loudoun Mil. under Maj. George West, 1777; Cpl. July 1781, served as press master for the impressment of cattle in Loudoun Co.
URTON, Peter (S.16561) 1765-d.p. 1833. Drafted Fairfax Mil. 1780. Pvt., John O'Bannon's Co., Fauq. Mil. 1781; Served as a substitute for Henry Rector of Fauquier Co.
UTTERBACK, Benjamin. 1754-1842. Ord. Sgt., Samuel Blackwell's Co. 1st Va. State Regt. of Artillery.
UTTERBACK, Harman, 1746-1826. Soldier. (DAR-PI).
UTTERBACK, Harmon. 1755-1854. Pvt., Wm. McClanahan's Co. of Baptist Vols. 1776.
UTTERBACK, Jacob. 1743-1842. Soldier. (DAR-PI).
UTTERBACK, Joel. Soldier, Fauq. Mil. No further information.
UTTERBACK, Joseph. Soldier. (DAR-PI).

—V—

VOWLE, John. Pvt., Benj. Harrison's Co., Fauq. Mil., 1777.

—W—

WADDELL, William. 1758-1831. Pvt., Elias Edmonds' Co., 1st Va. State Regt. of Artillery. (MB. 1781-84, p. 8) (DAR-PI)
WALKER, John. Pvt., John Chilton's Co., 3rd Va. Regt. CL. Sept. 1777; Pvt., same company under John Blackwell, Apr. 1778.
WALLACE, Thomas. Pvt., Benj. Harrison's Co., Fauq. Mil., 1777.
WALTON, John. Pvt., John Chilton's Co., 3rd Va. Regt. CL. June and Sept. 1777; Pvt., same company under John Blackwell, Apr. 1778.

WARREN, William. Ens., Fauq. Mil., recom. 28 Sept. 1778.
WATTS, Bennett. Pvt., Elias Edmonds' Co., 1st Va. State Regt. of Artillery.
WATTS, Mason. Pvt., Elias Edmonds' Co., 1st Va. State Regt. of Artillery.
WATTS, Thomas, Jr., 1747-1797. Lt. (DAR-PI).
WEALEY, Daniel. Pvt., Wm. Pickett's Co., Culp. Min. Bn. 1775.
WEAVER, Philip (S.14785) Pvt., Fauq. Mil., Kentucky pensioner.
WEAVER, Tilman. Capt., Fauq. Mil., recom. Mar. 1778. Signed O'Bannon petition 12 Apr. 1781.
WEBB, John. Capt., Fauq. Mil., recom. Mar. 1777. Died soon after comm.
WEBB, John. Capt., 7th Va. Regt. CL. 1776; Maj. 1778; Lt. Col. 5th Va. Regt. CL. July 1779. Ret. Feb. 1781. (MB. 1773-80, pg. 458).
WEEDON, Joseph. Pvt., Elias Edmonds' Co., 1st Va. State Regt. of Artillery.
WELCH, Patrick. Ord. Sgt. 3rd Va. Regt. Died leaving brother Alexander Welch as only heir. (MB. 1834-35, p. 71, 28 May 1834).
WELCH, Sylvester, Sr. 1762-d.p. 1832. Pvt., Samuel Denny's Co., 1st Va. State Regt. of Artillery. Fauq. Co. pension 1832.
WHALLEN (WHALON), Patrick. 1738-1826. Pvt. Fauq. Mil. (DAR-PI).
WHEATLEY, Joseph. Capt., Fauq. Mil., recom. Oct. 1779; oath 22 May 1780.
WHITE, John. Pvt., John Chilton's Co., 3rd Va. Regt. CL., June and Sept. 1777.
WHITE, Joseph. Soldier. Fauquier pension.
WHITE, Thomas. Pvt., Elias Edmonds' Co., 1st Va. State Regt. of Artillery. Proved service (MB. 1781-84, p. 2).
WHITECOTTON, Axton. Pvt., Wm. Pickett's Co., Culp. Min. Bn. 1775.
WHITTEN, John. "On hearing the complaint of John Whitten who is unwillingly detained as a Soldier by John Rust, the Court are of opinion the said John Whitten has not been legally enlisted and therefore ought to be discharged." (MB. 28 Sept. 1778).
WICKLIFFE, Benjamin. Pvt., Gallahue's Co., 11th Va. Regt. CL. May 1777; Cpl. Co. No. 9, Morgan's Rifle Regt. 1778.
WICKLIFFE, Charles. Pvt., Wm. Triplett's Cav. Co., Fauq. Mil. 1781.
WICKLIFFE, David. (S.6409) 1755-1836. Pvt., 3rd Va. Regt. CL.
WICKLIFFE, William. Sgt., Benj. Harrison's Co. Fauq. Mil. 1777. Ens., Wm. Pope's Co., Fauq. Mil., recom. Sept. 1778.
WILDER, Reuben. Pvt., John Chilton's Co., 3rd Va. Regt. CL. June and Sept. 1777.
WILKINSON, John. Pvt., John Blackwell's Co., 3rd Va. Regt. CL. 1778.
WILLIAMS, Charles. Capt., Fauq. Mil., oath 25 Aug. 1777.
WILLIAMS, George, Sr. 1732-1800. Pvt., Fauq. Mil. (DAR-PI).
WILLIAMS, Simon. Pvt., Benj. Harrison's Co. Fauq. Mil. 1777.
WILLIS, Bailey. Soldier. Fauquier pensioner 1832-33.
WILSON, Joseph. Soldier. Fauq. Mil. (**Eckenrode**).
WILSON, Richard, Pvt., 1st Va. Regt. CL. Proved service. Fauq. Co. (MB. 28 Feb. 1780).

WINE, Benjamin. Pvt., Fauq. Mil. (**Eckenrode**).
WINN, James. Capt., Fauq. Mil. 1776; Capt., Col. Wm. Crawford's Va. Regt. at Fort Pitt. 1779; Capt., Fauq. Mil. under Maj. Francis Triplett's Va. Mil. Regt. at Cowpens.
WINN, Minor. 1st Lt., Fauq. Mil., recom. Oct. 1779; oath Feb. 1780.
WINKFIELD, William. Pvt., Wm. Pickett's Co., Culp. Min. Bn. 1775.
WISE, Samuel. Pvt., 6th Va. Regt. CL. Proved service Fauq. Co. Court (MB. 22 May 1780).
WITHERS, Benjamin. c. 1760-1823. Pvt., Fauq. Mil. (DAR-PI).
WITHERS, Enoch Keene, 1760-1813. Sgt., Grayson's Add. Cont. Regt., 1777; Ens., 1 Nov. 1777; res. 13 Mar. 1778; Adj., Col. Richard Campbell's 4th Va. Regt. CL. Feb. 1781. (**Heitman**).
WITHERS, James (son of James) 1743-1808. 1st Lt. Thomas Bronaugh's Co., Fauq. Mil., recom. Nov. 1777; Capt., Fauq. Mil., recom. Aug. 1781.
WITHERS, James (son of Thomas) 1745-1791. 2nd Lt., Thomas Bronaugh's Co., Fauq. Mil., recom. Mar. 1778.
WITHERS, James, (W.4399) 1757-1834. Sgt., Wm. Pickett's Co., Culp. Min. Bn.; Ens., John Lee's Co., Col. George Gibson's 1st Va. State Regt. 1777-78; Lt., Winsor Brown's Co., Gibson's Regt. 1779. Pvt., (sic) Armstead White's Co., Culp. Mil., 1781. (**Heitman**).
WITHERS, Jesse. (S.11819) 1760-1834. Pvt., John Craig's Co., Fauq. Mil., June 1779; Ord. Sgt., Thomas Bronaugh's Co., Fauq. Mil., May, 1781; Pvt., Abraham Kirkpatrick's Co., Col. Christian Febiger's Regt., Sept. 1781.
WITHERS, John. Pvt., John Ball's Co., Fauq. Mil., 1781.
WITHERS, Joseph. 1761-2-1825. Wdd. at Eutaw Springs, S.C., 8 Sept. 1781. Crippled for life.
WITHERS, Lewis. c. 1758-1821. Pvt., James Winn's Co., Fauq. Mil. 1781. Wdd. at Cowpens, brought back to Va., June, 1781.
WITHERS, Matthew Keene, Pvt., James Scott's Fauq. Inde. Co., 1777.
WITHERS, Spencer. (S.6400) d: 1843. Pvt., substitute for Peter Crimm, Fauq. Mil., 1780; Ord. Sgt., Francis Triplett's Co., Fauq. Mil., Aug. 1780; served at Cowpens; Ord. Sgt., Col. Elias Edmonds' Va. State Regt., June 1781.
WITHERS, William (son of Thomas). 1754-1809 Pvt., Wm. Pickett's Co., Culp. Min. Bn., 1775; Pvt., John Ball's Co., Fauq. Mil., 1781.
WITHERS, William (son of John) Sgt., Wm. Pickett's Co., Culp. Min. Bn., 1775; 2nd Lt., Thomas Bronaugh's Co., Fauq. Mil., recom. Nov. 1777.
WITHERS, William, (son of Keene) Pvt., Wm. Pickett's Co., Culp. Min. Bn., 1775.
WITHERS, William Ramblin (W.18351) b: 1758. Pvt., Wm. Pickett's Co., Culp. Min. Bn. 1775; Sgt. Peter Grant's Co., Grayson's Add. Cont. Regt., 1776; Lt., James Winn's Co., Col. Wm. Crawford's Regt. at Fort Pitt., 1779; Lt. Felix Worley's Co., Col. Charles C. Pinckney's South Car. Regt., 1781.
WITLEY, Shadrack. Soldier. born and raised in Fauq. Co. (Chesterfield Supplement, Va. State Lib.).
WOOD, John. Pvt., Charles Porterfield's Co. (No. 4), 11th Va. Regt. CL. June 1777; Morgan's Rifle Regt., 1778.
WOOD, James. Pvt., Benj. Harrison's Co., Fauq. Mil. 1777.

WOOD, Robert. Pvt., John Blackwell's Co., 3rd Va. Regt., CL. Apr. 1778.

WOODHAM, George. Soldier, Fauq. Mil. (**Eckenrode**).

WRIGHT, James. 2nd Lt., 11th Va. Regt. CL. 1776; 1st Lt., Mar. 1777; Capt., 7th Va. Reg. CL. July 1779; POW. Charleston, S.C., May 1780; Maj. (MB. 1784-86, p. 179) (**Heitman**).

WRIGHT, William. Pvt., John Eustace's Co., 2nd Va. Regt., CL. Proved service Fauq. Co. (MB. 27 Mar. 1780).

—Y—

YOUNG, William. Ens., Fauq. Mil. (MB. 1781-84, p. 73).

Index

-A-

Abercrombie, Robert, 429
Aberdeen Univ., Scotland, 46, 61
Adams, John, 172
Adams, Richard, 239
Agincourt, 371, 376
Albany, N. Y., 188
Albemarle Barracks, 363n, 379, 433
Albemarle Co., 59, 252, 297, 431
Albemarle Militia, 406
Albemarle Old Courthouse, 412
Aldie, Va., 115, 199
Alexander, James, 121n
Alexander, John, 301n
Alexander, Lucy (Thornton), 301n
Alexander, Morgan, 266
Alexandria, Va., 69n, 174, 176-177, 262, 333, 349
Allan, John, 397-398
Allason, David, 254
Allason, William, 7, 8, 249
Allegheny Mts., 438
Allen, Catherine (McConchie), 303n
Allen, Frances (Pepper), 88n
Allen, Henry, 281, 303, 304
Allen, Moses, 99, 143, 186, 206, 266, 281, 331
Allen, Richard, 331
Allen, William, 88, 227, 304, 413
Allentown, 277, 278
Amboy, N.J., 277, 441n
Amherst Co., 367
Amherst, Gen'l., 294n
Ancaster, Duke of, 327n
Anderson, John, 186
Anderson, Richard, 141, 184
Anderson, Ruth (Blakely), 386n
Andrews, Matthew Page, 103n
Anna (ship), 322
Annapolis, Md., 163, 360
Aquackanock, N.J., 281
Arbuthnot, Marriott, 321, 328, 390
Arell, David, 199
Armand, 344
Armand's Legion, 412
Arminianism, 18
Armistead, William, 75
Armistead's Store, 99n

Arnold, Benedict, 91-92, 171, 298n, 388-390, 394, 401, 402n, 404, 406-407
Arnold, Benjamin, 84
Arnold, Isaac, 385n
Asberry, Susannah (Glascock), 377n
Asberry, William, 377, 385
Asbury, George, 166
Ashby, Benjamin, 220
Ashby, Jack, 29, 69, 98, 99
Ashby, Jane (Combs), 99n, 258n
Ashby, John, 11, 29, 79, 81n, 88, 98, 99, 100, 109, 110, 113, 115, 121, 128, 137, 144, 146, 153, 154, 155, 156, 166, 168, 177, 186, 195, 196n, 198, 205, 214, 219, 240, 246, 247, 258n, 267, 331, 377, 443
Ashby, Leannah (Darnall), 258n
Ashby, Lewis, 258
Ashby, Margaret (Mauzy), 99n, 246
Ashby, Mary (Hardin), 267n
Ashby, Mary (Turner), 81n, 98
Ashby, Nathaniel, 99, 137, 152-153, 181, 186, 214,, 246, 258n
Ashby, Robert, 9, 29, 43, 98, 399
Ashby, Stephen, 196, 267n
Ashby, Thomas, 29n
Ashby's Bent (Gap), 8, 29n, 32, 171, 352, 433
Ashley River, S.C., 331
Ashville (Bolling) Run, 11
Assumpink Bridge, 142, 145
Assumpink Creek, 148
Atlantic Ocean, 197, 321-322
Attopin Creek (W'land Co.), 61
Attwell, 290
Attwell, Francis, 239, 241, 256
Attwell, Mary McDonald, 241n
Attwell, Thomas, 241n
Auburn, 10, 40, 171
Augusta Co., 29n, 52, 362, 367n, 369, 385
Augusta (ship), 349
Austin, Elizabeth (Lindsey), 69
Austin, John, 69, 93, 181, 280, 377

Aylett, 11
Aylett, Wm., 12n

-B-
Bailey, James, 275, 351
Bailey, Richard, 333-334, 336, 434
Bailey, Stephen, 38
Bailey, William, 186, 266
Baker, Leonard, 55n, 66n
Baker, Moses, 80n
Baker, Samuel, 80
Baker, Sgt., 303
Balaklava, 85
Balch, Hezekiah, 21, 22
Balch, Thomas, 160
Baldwin's Ridge, 41, 62n, 89, 138
Ball, Benjamin, 290
Ball, Burgess, 39, 308
Ball, Edward, 239
Ball, Elias, 334
Ball, Elizabeth (Burgess), 308n
Ball, Frances (Washington), 308n
Ball, James, 258n, 395
Ball, Jeduthan, 308n
Ball, John, 290, 313, 422-423
Ball, Mary (Chichester), 308n
Ball, William, 177, 224, 227, 256-257, 290, 338
Ballance, Patty, 339
Ballard, Robert, 269, 297
Baltimore, Md., 163, 172, 360, 407
"Baptist Company", 351n
Baptists, 17, 21, 65
Barbee, Andrew, 414n, 422n
Barbee, Elizabeth, 113n, 114
Barbee, Jane, 414n
Barbee, John, 314, 414, 422n, 432-433
Barbee, Mary (Dyson), 414n
Barbee, Thomas, 113n
Barber, William, 314
Barker, John, 172, 258, 314, 421
Barker's Branch, 17
Barnes, John, 266
Barnett, Ambrose, 240, 314
Barr, Isaac, 144, 281
Barras, de, 425-426
Barren Co., Ky., 100n, 348n
Barren Hill, Pa., 273-274, 299, 304, 366n, 418
Barrett, Ann, 178
Barron, James, 104n

Barron, Richard, 104n
Bartenstein, Thomas E., v.
Bartlett, Thomas, 215n
Barton, Elijah, 420n
Barton, Elisha, 420
Barton, James, 166
Bashaw, Frances (Taylor), 350n
Bashaw, James, 350n
Bashaw, Peter, 350, 378, 414, 422, 432
Basking Ridge, N.J., 188n
Bateman, Thomas, 377n
Battut, John, 85, 86
Bawcut, William, 266
Baylis, John, 30, 223
Baylis, William, 30, 286, 308-309, 423-424, 433
Baylor, George, 377, 413n
Baylor's Horse, 327, 383
Baynham, Joseph, 190
Bayse, Nancy (Taylor), 266
Bayse, Richard, 266
Beale, Capt., 371
Beale, G. W., 18n
Beale, Mary Elizabeth Smallwood Grayson, 117n
Beale, Richard (Dickey), 117, 143, 179, 247
Beale, Richard, 214
Beale, Tavener, 415
Beale, Winifred Eustace, 179
Beall, Gen'l., 127n
Beattie's Ford, 379
Beatty, Reading, 418n
Beaufort, S.C., 329n
Beaver Dam Brook, N. J., 189
Beaver, Sgt., 116n
"Bedford" (Fitzhugh home), 268
Bedford County, Va., 419
Bee's Plantation (S.C.), 327
Bell, Charles, 224, 241
Bell, Frances (Edmonds), 39
Bell, James, 165, 178, 227, 238, 242, 254, 256, 259, 290, 311, 400
Bell, John, 33, 37, 39
"Belle Air" (Grayson home), 174n
"Belle Grove" (Edmonds estate), 441
"Bellevue" (Payne estate), 441
"Belmont" (Ashby home), 195n, 246, 258n
"Belvoir" (Fairfax estate on Potomac), 9

INDEX

Benson, William, 399-400, 430, 441
Bergen, N.J., 184-185, 306-307
"Berkeley" (Harrison home), 172
Berkeley County, 68, 104, 222, 415-416
Berkeley Mil., 411n
Berkeley Springs, 115n
Berry, William, 254
Bethel, 16
Bethlehem, Pa., 69, 212
Beverley, Robert, 1
Birmingham Meeting House (Brandywine), 203, 206
Birmingham, N.J. (now West Trenton), 141
Biron, see Lauzun, Duc de
Bishop Madison Map, 5
Black Watch Regt. (British), 185
Blackmore, 206n
Blackmore, Elizabeth (Payne), 247n
Blackmore, George, 267
Blackmore, Thomas, 267
Blackwell, Agatha Ann (Eustace), 101n, 330
Blackwell, Ann, 120n, 169n, 224, 258n
Blackwell, Ann (Eustace), 101n
Blackwell, Ann Grayson (Gibson), 79n
Blackwell, Ann (Lewis), 88n
Blackwell, Celia (Helm), 76n, 254n
Blackwell, David, 81, 88, 105
Blackwell, Elizabeth, 25
Blackwell, Elizabeth (Crump), 62n, 76n, 79, 121, 169n, 223, 224, 258n
Blackwell, Elizabeth (Steptoe), 63n, 88n, 102n, 169, 258n
Blackwell family, 31, 56, 79, 101n
Blackwell, George, 169n
Blackwell, James, 258, 402n
Blackwell, John, 41, 62, 74, 101, 110, 117, 127, 143, 154, 165-166, 168-169, 178-179, 182, 186, 206, 214, 219, 220n, 223-224, 226-227, 230, 232, 238, 240-242, 247-248, 250-251, 254, 256, 259, 266, 290, 311, 330, 399, 402-413, 432
Blackwell, Joseph, 5-7, 10, 16, 25, 33-34, 41, 62n, 63n, 79, 87, 89, 99, 101, 102n, 110, 112n, 113n, 117, 121, 127, 143n, 146, 153-155, 160-161, 169, 179, 183, 186, 201, 213-214, 220, 224, 231-232, 247, 249, 263, 269-270, 272n, 297, 331, 442
Blackwell, Judith, 25
Blackwell, Judith (Grant), 99n, 169n
Blackwell, Laetitia, 25
Blackwell, Lucy (Steptoe), 62n, 224
Blackwell, Margaret (Gillison), 224n
Blackwell, Margery (Downing), 34
Blackwell, Samuel, 25, 34, 41, 88n, 101, 169, 224-228, 230, 240-241, 256, 258n, 276, 398
Blackwell, Sarah (Beale), 224n
Blackwell, Susannah, 263
Blackwell, Thomas, 25, 99, 169, 213, 231, 235-237, 263, 267, 272n, 292, 297
Blackwell, William, 3, 33-34, 62n, 66, 74, 76-81, 87-88, 121, 169-171, 180-181, 186-187, 191, 200, 213, 220, 224, 231, 248-249, 254n, 256, 258n, 267-269, 289
Blackwell, William, Jr., 43n
Blakely, Aquilla, 386-387
Bland, Martha, 120n
Bland, Mary, 248n
Bland, Richard, 59
Bland, Theodorick, 260, 327
Bloomingdale Road, (N.Y.), 113
Blount Co., Ala., 387
Blower, John, 250n
Blower's Run, 238, 250
Blue Ridge Mts., 29, 29n, 31-32, 60, 108n, 170, 242, 245, 353-354, 393, 401, 415, 438
Board of War, 166, 172, 319, 323, 325, 359, 361
Boatner, Mark M. 70n, 121n, 212n, 261n, 305n, 375n, 410n
Boggess, Hannah, 434
Boggess, Jeremiah, 338, 434
Boggess, Thomas, 434n
Booger, Wm. Fletcher, 97n
Booker, Richard, 276
Boone, Daniel, 68n
Bordentown, N.J., 135, 140-141
Bordentown Road, 145
Boru, Brian, 114
Boston, Mass., 68n, 77, 90, 94, 104, 108, 139, 442
Boston Port Bill, 49

Boston Tea Party, 48
Botetourt Co., 52
Botetourt, Lord, 46
Boudinot, Elias, 265
Boudinot, Hannah (Stockton), 265n
Bound Brook, N.J., 184n
Bourbon Co., Ky., 412n
Bowling Green, Va., 395, 420, 422
Bowman, Abraham, 167
Bowman, Capt., 294
Bowman, Joseph, 252-253, 293
Boyd, Julian, 409n
Boyd, Mary (Brooke), 201
Boyd, Samuel, 110, 201, 240
Boyes, Major, 413
Bracken Co., Ky., 226n, 351n
Braddock, Edward, 29, 32, 343n, 349
Braddock's Expedition, 30, 61, 83n, 98, 135n, 136n, 186n
Bradford, Alexander, 290
Bradford, Alsey (Morgan), 422n
Bradford, Ann, 206n, 247n
Bradford, Daniel, 422n
Bradford, Elizabeth (Payne), 206n, 247n
Bradford, Henry, 186, 198, 214, 247, 259, 266
Bradford, John, 21, 290n, 422
Bradford, Mary (Marr), 290n
Bradford, Mary (Morgan), 206n, 247n
Bradford, Molly (Steel), 206n
Bradford, Sarah (Barbee), 422n
Bradford, William, 206n, 214, 247n, 259n, 281
"Bradley" (Peake home), 312n
Bradley, 422
Brady, Capt. 181n
Bragg, William, 143, 186, 223
Braintree, Mass., 111n
Bramblet, Reuben, 225, 421
Brandywine, Battle of, 88, 165, 186, 194, 165-206, 208, 211-212, 214-215, 220-221, 229, 239, 247, 250, 255, 260, 266, 286, 301n, 304, 306, 350, 353, 377, 405n, 421, 423, 429n, 443
Brandywine Creek, 194, 196
Braxton, Carter, 26n, 33
Braxton, Mary (Carter), 26n
Breckinridge Co., Ky., 250n
Brent, Col. 225
Brent, Elizabeth (Carroll), 106n
Brent, George, 268

Brent, Giles, 3
Brent Town, 2, 267
Brent, William, 3, 45, 106, 397
Bristow, Robert, 268
British Grenadiers, 85
British War Office, 299
Broad River, 355, 368-369, 375
Broad Run, 10, 17, 44, 240n, 338n
Broad Run Baptist Church, 18, 21, 421
Broadway (N.Y.C.), 116, 119
Broglie, Comte de, 340n
Bronaugh, Catherine, 241n
Bronaugh, Elizabeth (Newton), 241n
Bronaugh, Samuel, 241n
Bronaugh, Thomas, 241, 248-249, 255-256, 259, 395-396
Bronaunt, Martha, 76n
Bronaunt, Sarah, 76n
Bronx, (N. Y.), 122
Bronx River, 123
Brooke, Elizabeth (Braxton), 26n, 33
Brooke family, 33
Brooke, Francis, 33
Brooke, Humphrey, v, 16, 26, 33, 50, 179, 201n, 235, 248n, 255, 393
Brooke, Robert, 26n
Brooke, Walter Darrell, 304
Brookes, Benjamin, 352, 366n, 367
Brooklyn Heights, 94
Broughton, Sgt. Major, 204
Brown, Ann (Kelly), 79n
Brown, Dixon, 313
Brown, Jeremiah, 79, 106, 225, 422, 432
Brown, Jesse, 79n, 225, 422
Brown, John, 206, 247, 304, 312
Brown, Joseph, 422
Brown, Stuart E., 32n
Brown, Swanson, 337
Browne, Montfort, 120
Brown's Run, 313
Brownsville, Pa., 253
Bruin, Elizabeth (Edmonds), 171n
Bruin, Peter Bryan, 171, 352, 416
Brunskill, John, Jr., The Rev., 16-17, 34
Brunswick, N.J., 151, 182
Brunswick Parish, 241n
Bryan, James, 258
Bryan, Reuben, 180, 181
Bryan, William, 399
Bryon, John, 408n

INDEX

Buck Run, 36
Buckner, Aylett, 239, 248-250, 255, 259, 289, 395, 406
Buckner, Mordecai, 102n, 129, 158-160
Bucks Co., Pa., 388
Buffalo Ford, 340
Buford, Abraham, 77, 219n, 297, 325, 333-336, 352, 367, 384
Bull Run, 16
Bull Run Mts., 2, 4-5, 31, 111, 323, 351n
Bullitt, Alexander Scott, 228n, 424
Bullitt, Benjamin, 48n, 259n, 416n
Bullitt, Cuthbert, 48n, 76, 254, 259, 311n, 424n
Bullitt, Elizabeth (Harrison), 48n, 254n
Buttlitt, Helen (Scott), 424n
Bullitt, Joseph, 249
Bullitt, Parmanus, 416, 420
Bullitt, Sarah (Burditt), 416n
Bullitt, Thomas, 48, 76, 176, 249, 270, 416
Bunker Hill, Battle of, 68, 77, 91, 115n, 343n
Burgess, Charles, 12n
Burgess patent, 257n
Burgoyne, John, 162, 188, 198, 232-235, 366, 371, 375
Burk, Samuel, 237
Burlington, N. J., 149
Burwell, Lewis, 253
Burwell's Ferry, 64
"Bushy Park," Middlesex Co., 25n
Butler, Frances, 254
Butler, Joseph, 413
Butler, Richard, 298, 302-303
Butler, William 412, 432
Byrd, Col., 337
Byrne, Richard, 30

-C-

Cabin Point, 402, 426
Cadwalader's, John, 134-135, 139n, 141, 145, 150
Caesar, 198
Cahokia, 293-294
Calhoon, 299
Call, Richard, 413
Calmes Gap, 9
Cambridge, Mass., 70, 90
Camden, S. C., 319, 326, 335, 340, 342-344, 346, 353n, 354, 360n, 364n, 365, 368, 382, 384-385, 412n, 437
Camp Crossroads, Pa., 192n, 198
Camp Maubin, 402, 413
Camp Middlebrook, 404n
Campbell, Archibald, 291
Campbell, John, 31
Campbell, Richard, 384
Camp Springfield (Va.), 157
Campbell, William, 355, 414, 427
Canada, 41n, 162, 216n, 294n
Cannon, Matthew, 102
Cantwell, John, 254
Cape Fear, 292
Cape Fear River, N.C., 84n, 354, 386-387
Cape Hatteras, 327
Cape May, N.J., 108
Carleton, 112n
Carolandville, 248n
"Carolina Gamecock", 343n
Carolina Road, 9, 111, 323
Caroline County, 72, 308n, 395
Caroline Militia, 405
Carpenter's Hall, 153
Carrington, Edward, 279, 337, 361, 364, 367, 380
Carroll, Daniel, 106n
Carroll, Eleanor (Darrell), 106n
Carter, Charles, 1n, 248n, 260n
Carter, Col., 250
Carter, Dale, 275
Carter, George, 43
Carter, Landon, 4, 248
Carter, Robert "King", 3-4, 25, 26n, 31, 38n
Carter, Robert (of "Nomini Hall"), 5, 25
Carter's Ferry, 402
Carter's Run, 10, 113n
Carter's Run Baptist Church, 19-20
Cartwright, Dorinda, iv
Caswell, Richard, 335, 346
Catawba River, 335, 354-355, 367
Catholics, 15
Catlett, John, 251
Catlett, Lawrence, 308n
Catlett, Thomas, 308
Catlett, Va., 411
"Cedar Grove" (Foote home), 268
"Cedar Grove" (Kemper home), 290n
Cedar Run, 10-11, 165, 171, 250n, 251, 268-269, 311n, 411

Centre Point, 216
Chadd's Ford, Pa., 202, 204, 216
"Chantilly" (Lee home, Westmoreland Co.), 37
Chapman, Jonathan, 10
Chappawamsic, 22, 98n
Chappelear, Nancy, 246n
Charles Co., Md., 98, 224n, 417, 424n
Charleston Harbour, 331
Charleston, S.C., 77n, 138, 162, 195n, 292, 295, 297, 308n, 315-318, 322-353, 359, 369, 383-384, 385n, 398, 400, 405n, 423, 430
Charlotte, N.C., 341, 345, 351, 354-355, 361, 364, 366, 378-379
Charlottesville, 252n, 343n, 408, 412, 417
Chatham, N.J., 159, 181, 183-184
Cheesequake, N.J., 189n
Cheraw Hill, S.C., 366, 368-369, 379
Cherokee Indians, 108n, 362, 370n, 386
Chesapeake Bay, 77, 104, 162, 202, 390, 405, 424-426
Chester, N.J., 190, 197
Chester, Pa., 129, 204, 426
Chesterfield Co., 407
Chesterfield Courthouse, 336
Chew, Benjamin, 218, 353n
Chew house (Cliveden), 218, 221, 349
Chickahominy Swamp, 413
Chillicothe, 438
Chilton, Betsy, 138
Chilton, Betsy (Blackwell), 200
Chilton, Betty, 183
Chilton, Charles, 25n, 41, 62, 88, 100, 110, 116, 126n, 127n, 138, 153, 159n, 160, 182-183, 187, 198, 201, 206n, 211, 224, 227, 232, 240, 242, 248-249, 259, 268n, 290, 408, 413
Chilton, Elizabeth (Blackwell), 62n, 100
Chilton family, 31, 56, 297
Chilton, George, 201
Chilton, Jeminna (Cooke), 62n
Chilton, John, 16, 25, 41, 62, 66, 74, 76, 81, 88, 89, 99-101, 110-113, 116-117, 120, 126-127, 137, 143-144, 146, 149, 151, 153, 154, 155, 156, 158, 159, 161, 166, 170, 179, 180, 181, 182, 183, 184, 186, 187, 188, 191n, 196, 197, 198, 199, 200, 202, 205, 206, 211, 213, 214, 219, 224, 227, 239, 247, 248, 249, 268, 443
Chilton, Joseph, 201
Chilton, Laetitia (Blackwell), 25, 62n, 89
Chilton, Lucy, 201
Chilton, Nancy, 201
Chilton, Stephen, 100
Chilton, Thomas, 41, 62n, 110, 201
Chilton, William, 41, 100
Chinn, Charles, 10, 16, 240
Chinn, Rawleigh, 240n
Choisy, Claude Gabriel de, 428, 430
Chotank, 26n, 268
Christian, William, 95, 104, 105, 108, 362, 386
Christina, Del., 194, 195
Chrybdis, 369
Chumley, Daniel, 176, 281, 332
Chunn, John Thomas, 258, 395, 402, 406
Churchill, Armistead, 19, 25, 38, 127n, 176, 224-227, 229-231, 235, 238-240, 255, 259, 289, 394-398, 401
Churchill, Elizabeth, 25
Churchill, Elizabeth (Blackwell), 224
Churchill family, 31
Churchill, Hannah (Harrison), 25n
Churchill, Henry, 38
Churchill, John, 11, 25, 33, 38
Churchill, Priscilla, 25
Churchill, William, 25
Cincinnatus, 237
Citadel, 330
City Point, 407
Claiborne, Dandridge, 253
Clapham, Joshua, 411
Clarke, George Rogers, 252, 253, 258, 293-294, 304, 396, 422n, 438
Clark, Joseph, 205
Clarke Co., Va., 353n
Clarke, Jonathan, 307, 310
Clay, Capt., 398
Clay, Elijah, 251
Clay, Thomas, 276
Claypool, John, 409n
Clayton, Philip, 73
Clements, Mace, 286, 287
"Clermont" (Rugeley estate, S.C.), 365

INDEX

"Clermont" (Scott estate), 46, 102
Clermont, S.C., 343
Clinch River, 354
Clinton, Henry, 187, 273-275, 277-278, 280, 282, 285, 298-300, 306, 321, 327-330, 331, 343n, 356, 368, 385n, 388-390, 401, 404, 409, 414-415, 417-418, 425, 429
Clontarf, Ireland, 114n
"Clovelly" (Cedar Grove), 290n
"Clover Hill" (Morgan estate), 441
Clyde, Scotland, 374n
Cobham, 83
Cocke, James, 397n
Coffee, Mary, 206n, 255
Coffee, Robert, 206
Colchester, Va., 177, 261n, 312n
Cole, Howson W., iv
Coleman, Lt., 315
Coleman, Mary, 254
College of R. I., 21
College of William and Mary, 21, 34, 76, 339
Collier, George, 291
Collins, Sara, iv
Colston, Raleigh, 440
Columbia University (King's College), 150n
Colvin, John, 177n
Combs, Ennis, 258n
Combs, John, 258, 349, 362, 367, 375-376
Committee of Safety, 84, 93, 98n, 103
Concord, Battle of, 64, 66, 298n
Concord Meeting House, 206
Confederacy, ii, 337n
Connecticut, 112, 115n, 117, 121n, 437
Connecticut Regt., 302
Connor, Stephen, 337
Conshohocken, 273n
Continental cavalry, 327
Continental Congress, 53, 58, 68, 71, 163, 168, 172, 174, 177, 185, 202, 208, 230, 236, 244, 252, 261-263, 271, 283, 285, 295, 298n, 301n, 305, 317-319, 340, 346-347, 359, 377, 393, 436-437
Continental Line, 87, 88n, 91n, 93, 95, 101, 103, 111n, 170-171, 177, 179n, 180, 202, 208, 212n, 219, 222, 224, 249, 254, 257, 260, 264-266, 277, 290-292, 295, 302, 327n,
329, 331, 333, 339, 341, 346, 350
Conway Cabal, 230n, 235, 404n
Conway, Gen., 192
Conway, Lydia (George), 338n
Conway, Peter, 78
Conway, Thomas, 257-258, 338, 423-424
Cook, John, 106, 206n, 247n
Cooke, Elizabeth, 25n
Cooke, John Esten, 70n
Cooke, Mordecai, 25n, 268n
Cook's Ford, Va., 410
Coone, Robert, 276
Coons, Henry, 402n
Cooper, Apollos, 205
Cooper River, 326
Coote, Mrs. Patrick, 57
Cople Parish (Westmoreland Co.), 41, 62n
Coppage, Moses, 30
Corn, Island, 253n, 293
Cornwallis, Lord, 126, 134, 145, 148-150, 215-216, 219, 278-279, 321, 332, 335, 342-345, 347, 354-355, 366, 368-369, 375, 380-383, 385-388, 403-404, 409-410, 412-413, 415, 417-419, 424-432, 439
Cornwell, John, 30, 311
Coryell's Ferry, 135, 277
Courtney, Samuel, 308, 332
Courtney, Sarah (Courtney), 308n
Covington's Ordinary, 228n
Cowpens, S.C., i, 121n, 359-387, 390, 400, 414, 416, 422, 433n
Cox, Samuel, 249, 406n
Coxe's Mill, 341
Craig, Rev. James, 7, 16
Craine, John, 338
Cranberry, N. J., 278
Crawford, William, 167, 186, 195, 212, 222, 349-350, 438
Crim, Peter, 377n
Croesus, 313
Cross, Nathaniel, 350n
Cromwell's Run, 10
Crook, Johnathan, 266
Crooke, Jonathan, 214
Crooked Run, 10, 258n, 311n
Cropper, John, 212, 266, 280, 283, 286, 287n, 297
Crosby, George, 177
Cross Creek (now Fayettesville, N. C.), 386
Croton River, 124

"Crow's Next" (Daniel estate), 332n
Crump, Elizabeth (Triplett), 270
Crump, George, 304
Crump, John, 256n, 411
Crump, Richard, 276
Culpeper Co., 3, 20, 35, 38, 42. 49, 50, 51, 58, 65, 73, 74, 99n. 104, 113n, 121, 168-169, 181, 190n, 222, 237, 261n, 263, 304, 341, 351n, 368, 377n, 383, 402n, 412-414, 423, 431, 442
Culpeper Courthouse, 73
Culpeper Military District, 58
Culpeper Militia, 30, 237n, 337, 401, 405
Culpeper Minute Men (Culp. Min. Bn.), 65, 73, 74, 75n, 77, 80, 82, 84, 85, 89n, 90n 93, 99, 103, 121, 431
Cumberland Co. 251, 433
Cunninghame, Alexander, 7
Curry, Daniel, 68n
Custis, Geo. Wash. Parke, 150n

-D-

Dabney, Charles, 427, 434
Dade, Baldwin, 81n
Dade, Sarah (Alexander), 81n
Daingerfield, William, 105
Dan River, 367, 380-381, 386
Danbury, Conn., 283
Daniel, Frances (Moncure), 332n
Darke, William, 415
Darnall, Jeremiah, 3, 165-166, 258n, 310-311
Darnall, Katherine (Holtzclaw), 165
Darnall, Waugh, 165, 250n
Dartmouth, Lord, 53, 58, 90
Davidson Co., Tenn., 350n
Davidson, William, 266, 368
Davie, Sarah (Jones), 364n
Davie, William Richardson, 364
Davies, Samuel, 17
Davies, William, 316
Davis, John, 240n
Davis, Lt., 196
Davis, Mildred (Higgins), 240n
Davis, Scytha (Seth), 240n
Davis, William, 271
Day, Major, 204
Day, William, 186
Declaration of Independence, 94, 172, 354
Deep River, 340-341, 386-387

Deep Run, 10, 80, 228n
Deep Spring, 422
Deering, John, 177, 257, 385
de Fermoy, Roche, 139-140, 143, 148
Defiance (ship), 276
Delany, Sharp, 300-301
Delaplane, Va., 43, 81n, 98, 258n, 395, 399
Delaware, 302, 433
Delaware Cont. Line. 340, 352, 367, 371, 380, 383
Delaware Militia, 129
Delaware Regiment, 123
Delaware Regulars, 143
Delaware River, 112, 137, 147-149, 191, 193, 197, 209, 213, 215, 225, 232, 234, 236-238, 277, 349, 364n
Denmark, 91n
Dennis, William, 180
Denny, Edmund, 275
Derby, Conn., 298n
Detroit, 69, 252, 293, 294n, 438
Dettingen Parish, 5, 44-46
Deux-Ponts, Guillaume de, 429
deWilde, Dorothea, iv
Dickerson, John, 80
Dickinson, Josiah Look, 32, 45n
Dickinson, Philemon, 278
Digges, Edward, 224, 228, 240, 248-250, 254-257, 259
Digges, Edward, Jr., 224n
Digges, Thomas, 248, 254, 290
Dinwiddie, Gov. Robert, 16, 29n, 31
Dixon and Hunter, 8
Dobbs Ferry, N. Y., 112
Dobson, Capt., 376
Doeller, William D., v
Doniphan, 81n
Donizetti, 144
Dorchester Co., Md., 46
Dorchester Heights, 94
Dorman, John Frederick, 79n
Dorrell's Run, 22, 33, 251, 396n, 422
Dover, Del., 167
Downman, Margaret (Ball), 240n
Dragon (ship), 407n
Dryden, 35
Dublin, Ireland, 114n
Dudley, Capt., 433
Dudley, John W., iv
Duelling, 264
Dulin, John, 247

INDEX

Dumfries, Va., 30, 49, 69n, 97, 98n, 101, 109, 11, 167, 174, 177, 190n, 260n, 319
Dumfries-Rappahannock Rd., 6
Dumfries Road, 9, 323
Dundas, Thomas, 388, 427-428
Dundas, William, 430
Dunmore Co., 44, 49
Dunmore's War, 52, 69, 95, 98, 252
Duncan, Joseph, 181n
Duncan, William, 8
Dunlop, Sgt. 303
Dunmore, Lord, 27, 44, 46, 48-49, 52-54, 58, 63, 67-68, 74-75, 77, 80-83, 85-87, 90, 94, 102, 104-105, 107, 119, 121
Dunmore (ship), 90, 105
Dunmore's War, 186n
Duportail, Gen'l., 326
Durham boats, 140

-E-

Eckenrode, H. J., 361n
Ecole Royale, 364n
Eden, Robert, 46
East River, N. Y., 94, 113
Eden, Sir Robert, 102
Edens, John, 402
Edinburgh, Scotland, 385n
Edmonds, Anne (Cralle?), 413n
Edmonds, Elias, 33, 37, 74, 171n, 223, 229, 246, 251, 348, 360, 398-400, 413-414, 420, 422, 427, 430-431, 434, 441
Edmonds, Elias, Jr., 62
Edmonds, Elizabeth (Blackwell), 25, 62n
Edmonds, Elizabeth (Miller), 62n, 171n, 246n
Edmonds, Frances, 246n, 441
Edmonds, Hester (Foote), 331n
Edmonds, John, 246n
Edmonds, Judith (Sydnor), 62
Edmonds, William, 16, 19, 25, 38-39, 62-63, 121, 165, 171n, 176, 212, 223, 225, 230-232, 235, 238-240, 246, 250, 255-256, 259, 393, 399, 413n, 434, 441
Edmonds, William, Jr., 331
"Edmonium" (Loretto) (Edmonds estate), 269n, 441
Edrington, Christopher, 268n
Education, Fauquier Co. 1775, 13
Edwards, Andrew, 7
Edwards, Morgan, 20n
Edwards, Thomas, 241, 290, 338

Elizabeth River, 82, 296
Elizabethton, Tenn., 355
Elizabethtown, N. J., 112n
Elk, Head of, Md., see Head of Elk, Md.
Elk Hill, Va., 389, 410, 414
Elk Marsh, 2, 10, 37, 169
Elk Run, 5, 16, 169, 224, 256n, 259n, 263, 267, 304, 331
Elk Run Church, 9, 411, 439
Elliott, Hannah, 255
Elliott, Winny, 249
Ellis, James, 423
Ely's Ford, Va., 410
Embrey, Alvin T., 286n
Emmons, James, 378, 422, 432
Emmons, Sarah, 378n
Emmons, William, 422
England, 94, 102
English, Robert, 214
Englishtown, N. J., 278
Ennis, Col., 226
Eppes, Francis, 84, 108
Erie Canal, 442
Estaing, Comte d', 282, 283, 284, 414
Ethiopian Regiment, 105
Eustace, Capt., 337
Eustace, Hancock, 41
Eustace, Isaac, 101n, 330
Eustace, John, 220
Eustace, William, 33, 44, 220n
Eutaw Springs, 370, 383
Eversham Parish, Md., 46n, 102
Ewell, Bertram, 33n
Ewen, Lt., 376
Ewing, James, 135, 139, 140, 145, 148

-F-

Fairfax, Bryan, 48
Fairfax County, 43, 61, 71, 250n, 261n, 312n, 313, 394, 404n
Fairfax, Denny Martin, 440
Fairfax Militia, 30, 57, 389, 405-406
Fairfax Proprietary, 28, 56, 439
Fairfax, Robert, 7th Lord, 14, 40n, 439-440
Fairfax, Thomas, 6th Lord, 4, 5, 8, 13, 14, 28, 29n, 30-33, 35, 39, 45-47, 52, 254, 438
Fairfax, William, 35
Fairfort Creek, S. C., 368
"Fairview" (Harrison home), 173n

Falmouth, 1n, 7-9, 323, 395, 420
Farrow, Micajah, 214
Faucette, Rachel, 150n
Fauquier Co. Jail, 255
Fauquier Co. Resolves, 49, 52, 102
Fauquier Courthouse, 6, 7, 8, 165
Fauquier, Francis, 43
Fauquier Hist. Soc., 16n, 25n, 49n
Fauquier Independent Co., 182, 215, 242, 312
Fauquier Militia, 38, 171n, 176-177, 212, 223-224, 226-229, 231, 233n, 234-235, 240, 242-243, 247-249, 254-260, 276, 290n, 313n, 347, 349, 351n, 362n, 385n, 389, 393-395, 397n, 400-401, 405-406, 408n, 420, 422, 434-435
Fauquier White Sulphur Springs, 40n, 304, 442
Fayette Co., Ky., 441
Fayetteville, N. C., 332
Febiger, Christian, 91, 92, 168, 181, 186, 196, 204, 212-213, 217, 220-221, 266, 271, 280, 283, 288, 297-298, 301-305, 314-315, 318, 381, 408-409, 414
Ferguson, Patrick, 328, 354-356
Filson, John, 253
Fincastle Co., 52
First Continental Dragoons, 413n
First Continental Artillery Regt., 245, 275, 361
First Virginia Regt. of Artillery, 281, 337, 340, 345, 360
First Virginia Regt. of Light Dragoons, 230
Fishback, 3
Fishback, John, 30, 351, 376, 378
Fishback, John Philip, 351n
Fishback, Martha (Pickett), 351n, 376n
Fishback, Philip, 351, 376n
Fishback's Ridge, 351n
Fisher, Sydney, 367n
Fishing Creek, N.C., 346
Fitzhugh, George, 248n, 411
Fitzhugh, Henry, 268
Fitzhugh, John Thornton, 268n
Fitzhugh, Lucinda (Edrington), 268n
Fitzhugh, Susannah (Cooke), 268n
Fitzhugh, Thomas, 268n
Fitzhugh, William, 417
Fitzgerald, John, 120, 121, 150n

Fitzpatrick, John C., 111n, 236n
Fleming Co., Ky., 292n
Fleming, 168
Fleming, John, 151
Fleming, Thomas, 167
Fletcher, John, 314
Fleury, Francois Louis de, 301-302, 437
Flexner, James Thomas, 116n, 120n, 145n
"Flint Hill" (O'Bannon estate), 365n
Florida, 291
Flowerree, Daniel, 75, 76, 338
Fluvanna Mil., 406
Flying Camp, 108, 111, 129, 353n, 424
Foley, Elizabeth (Oglevie), 313n
Foley, James, 177
Foley, James, Jr., 313
Foley, Sarah (O'Bannon), 313n
Foote, Celia (Helm), 3, 268, 331n
Foote, Elizabeth, 268
Foote family, 268-269
Foote, George, 268-269, 331n
Foote, Henry, 76n
Foote, Hester, 26n
Foote, George, 3
Foote, Hester (Hayward), 3, 268
Foote, Jane (Stuart), 269n
Foote, Katherine (Fossaker), 268n
Foote, Margaret (Helm), 268
Foote, Richard, 3, 26n, 33, 268-269
Foote, Richard Helm, 269
Ford, Benjamin, 382
Ford, George, 424
Ford, Henry, 424
Ford, Nancy (Payne), 424n
Ford, W. C., 98n
Ford, William, 257, 424, 433
Fordyce, Charles, 74n, 85, 86n, 88, 348
Forman, David, 208, 217
Forrester, John, 100, 377
Fort Ashby, 69
Fort Duquesne, 61, 186n
Fort Frederick, 48n, 319, 431
Fort Lafayette, 299
Fort Lee, 122, 126
Fort Montgomery, Pa., 197, 300, 314
Fort Mifflin, 209, 213, 234n, 236
Fort Montgomery, Pa., 300, 314
Fort Moultrie, 329

INDEX 491

Fort Pitt, 61, 252, 298n, 336, 350, 438
Fort Washington, 119n, 122, 124, 126, 130, 135n, 140, 341n
Fortescue, 336, 382n
4th Cont. Artillery, 414
4th Cont. Dragoons, 327n
Fowey (ship), 64, 67
Fowke, Chandler, 240n
Fowke, Mary (Fossaker), 240n
France, 270, 271, 364n
Frankfort, Ky., 276n
Franklin, Benjamin, 134n, 264, 405n
Franklin Co., Tenn., 363n
Franklin, Hugh F. 92n
Franklin, John, 377n, 383
Frederick County, 26n, 29, 32, 38-39, 42, 49, 52, 68, 104, 252-253, 262n, 267n, 286, 295, 337, 341, 346, 401, 408, 423
Frederick Mil., 411n, 416
Frederick, Md., 70, 103, 111, 173, 177, 211n, 225, 319, 341n
Frederick the Great, 142n, 264
Fredericksburg, Va., 49, 60-62, 64-65, 72, 95, 262, 275, 296, 303n, 319, 323-324, 332n, 333, 351, 389, 401, 406, 420-422
Freeman, D. S., 207, 428
Freeman's Farm, 208
French and Indian War, 69, 115n, 123n, 159, 338, 429n
French Revolution, 301n
Fristoe, William, 20, 65
Frogg, Maj. John, 30, 33
Fry and Jefferson Map, 5

-G-

Gadsden, Christopher, 73n, 328-329
Gadsden Flag, 73n
Gage, Gen'l., 53, 82, 83n
Gallatin Co., Ill., 226n
Garner, Charles, 187
Garner, Joseph, 186, 213
Garrard Co., Ky., 239n
Garrington, John, 338
Garrish, 91
Gates, Horatio, 91, 130, 136, 156, 208, 234-236, 283, 288, 340-346, 349, 352-353, 359, 361, 363-365, 408, 412n
George, Margaret, 338n
George, Nicholas, 177, 224, 256, 312, 338n

Georgetown, Md., 262
Georgetown, S. C., 384
Georgia, 291-292, 336, 341n, 342, 350n
Georgia militia, 291, 370-371
Germain, Lord, 321, 418n
German Regiment (Pa. & Md.), 134, 148
Germantown, Battle of, 256, 258n, 266, 267n, 281, 283
Germantown, Pa., 197, 204, 207, 209, 211-242, 298n, 304, 348, 353n, 360n, 395, 413, 416, 422, 429n
Germantown, Va., 3, 6, 9, 10 12, 16, 177n, 193, 348, 351n, 379n
Germany, 386n
Gerry, Elbridge, 139n
Gibault, Father, 293
Gibbons, James, 302, 304
Gibbs, Caleb, 314
Gibson, 338n
Gibson, George, 208, 222, 303n, 304
Gibson, John, 79, 271
Gibson, Mary (Brent), 79
Gibson, Samuel, 421
Gibson, Thomas, 420
Gillison, John, 272n, 297, 308
Gilmore, James, 362
Girty, Simon, 257n
Gist, 345
Gist, Christopher, 175n, 360n
Gist, Mordecai, 360, 426
Gist, Nathaniel, 175, 297, 309-310, 319, 324, 360n
Gist's Additional Regiment, 297
Gist's Maryland Brigade, 345
"Glanville' (Harrison home), 22n, 177, 396n
Glascock, Catherine (Rector), 377n
Glascock family, 377
Glascock, John, 17
Glascock, Thomas, 341n, 377n
"Glenwillis" (Marshall home), 276
Gloucester Co., 25n, 319, 419, 421, 424, 426-428, 430
Gloucester Neck, 105
Glover, John, 139-140, 147
Goddard, Frances (Rector), 292n
Goddard, Joseph, 292, 303-304
Gontaut, see Lauzun, Duc de
Goochland Militia, 406
Goode's Bridge, 419

Goodwin, Mary R. M., 109n
Goose Creek, 9, 10, 16, 26n, 258n, 395n, 411
Goose Creek Baptist Church, 20
Gordon, John, 61n
Gordon, Margaret (Tennant)
Gordon, Thomas, 102
"Gordon's Dale" (Scott home), 103, 240n, 312
Gosport, 296
Gott, John K. 246n
Graham, George, 76n, 268n
Graham, John, 26n
Graham, Joseph, 433n
Grand Door (Indian chief), 293-294
Grant, 151
Grant, Daniel, 180, 314
Grant, General, 273
Grant, James, 142, 148, 218n
Grant, John, 26n, 50n, 180
Grant, Peter, 26n, 41, 50, 65n, 248-250
Grant, Margaret (Watts), 50n
Grant, Peter, 394
Grant, William, 20, 25, 26n, 33, 65, 165, 238-239, 254, 313
Grant's Tomb, 115
Grasse, Comte de, 405, 424-425-426
Graves, 425
Grayson, Ann, 22n
Grayson, Benjamin, 174n
Grayson, Susanna (Monroe), 174n
Grayson, William, 117, 174-175, 177, 278
Grayson's Additional Cont. Reft., 97n, 175, 176, 236, 249, 278-281, 297, 332, 362, 404n
Great Awakening, 17
Great Bridge, Va., 60, 73n, 80, 82-83, 87-89, 98n, 99, 168-169, 180, 201, 225, 227, 239, 247, 256, 274, 347-348, 395, 431
Great Kanawa River, 52, 338
Great Lakes, 438
Great Run, 290n
Great Wagon Road, 69
Green, Duff, 33, 37, 121n, 263-264, 290
Green, Eleanor (Dunn), 121
Green, Elizabeth (Jones), 401n
Green family, 277
Green, Gabriel, 401-402
Green, James, 401n

Green, John, 121, 123, 263, 267, 271, 276, 280, 283, 290, 292, 297, 308, 331, 337, 368, 382-384, 401n
Green, Lucy (Blackwell), 248n
Green, Moses, 248n
Green, Richard, 311
Green, Robert, 121
Green, Sarah Ann (Grant), 401n
Green, Susannah (Blackwell), 121
Green, T.M., 77n
Green, William, 42, 276
Green Meadows, Pa., 29
"Green Meadows" (Withers' home), 313n
Green River, Ky., 401n
Greene, Nathanael, 119, 125-126, 133n, 139-141, 169, 194, 204-205, 209, 213, 216-217, 219, 222, 263, 277, 279-280, 282, 315, 346n, 352n, 353n, 359-361, 363-369, 378-381, 383, 385-388, 393, 398, 403, 409, 419, 430, 433
"Greenland" (Ashby home), 81n, 98, 195n
"Green Meadows" (Withers' home), 81n
"Greenspring" (Ludwell estate), 418, 424
Greenup Co., Ky., 384n
Greenville, S.C., 335
Greenway Court (Fairfax estate), 9, 13, 14, 29, 32, 35, 40, 52, 67, 438
Grey, General, 274
Griffith, David, 134, 157, 173, 205
Griffith, Hannah, 205n
Grigsby, Elizabeth (Bullitt), 259n
Grigsby, John, 259n
Grigsby, Samuel, 16
Grigsby, William, 259, 401-402, 432, 434n
Groome, H.C. 28n, 31, 47n
Guilford, N.C., 380-381, 383-385, 387
Gulf Stream, 322
Gunby, John, 382-383
Gwathmey, John H. 257
Gwinnett, Button, 350n
Gwynn's Island, 105, 109

-H-
Haarlem Heights, N. Y., 113, 120, 123, 239, 250
Hackensack, N. J., 112, 124, 126

INDEX

493

Hackensack River, N. J., 185, 189, 307-308
Hackittstown, N. J., 191, 197
Hackley, Woodford G. 20n
Haddrel's Point, S.C., 330, 332-333
Hairston, George, 387
Halifax Co., Va., 176
Halifax, N. C., 332
Hall, Frances (Keneard), 399n
Hall, John, 159
Hall, William, 337, 399n
Hamilton, Alexander, 150, 275, 277, 429
Hamilton, Henry, 293-294
Hamilton, James, 150n
Hamilton Parish, 3, 15, 16, 34, 45, 65n, 165-170n, 257, 311
Hammonds, John, 400
Hampshire Co., 38, 42, 196n, 408, 414-415
Hampshire Co. Militia, 30, 411n
Hampton, 77-80, 87, 93, 106, 121, 225, 426
Hampton Roads, 105, 162
Hampton, Wade, 331
Hamrick, Benjamin, 266
Hancock, John, 111
Hancock, Thomas, 111n
Hand, Edward, 122n, 148, 150, 350
Handcock's Bridge, N. J., 149n
Hanging Rock, S. C. 343, 346
"Hannah's Cowpens" (Cowpens, S. C.), 369, 376
Hanover Co., 54, 55, 413
Hanover, N. J., 188
Hanover, Pa., 111, 184
Hardin, Mark, 5
Hardin, Martin, 257n
Hardin's Ordinary, 257n
Hardy, Stella Pickett, 25n, 34n, 101n
Harlem River, 112
Harper's Ferry, 69
Harris, 292, 304
Harrison, 345
Harrison, Ann (Barnes), 98n
Harrison, Ann (Grayson), 224
Harrison, Benjamin, 22n, 59, 172, 177, 182, 224, 226-228, 230, 248, 249, 257, 348, 396, 435
Harrison, Burr, 22, 23n, 98n, 224n, 259
Harrison, Carter, 381n
Harrison, Charles, 245, 263, 267, 275, 279, 325, 340-341, 361
Harrison, Cuthbert, 45, 46n, 173

Harrison, Fairfax, 3, 45n
Harrison family, 42, 65
Harrison family (James River), 172n
Harrison, family (Northern Neck), 172n
Harrison, Frances Osborne (Barnes), 45, 173n
Harrison, Jane, 23n
Harrison, Lucy, 23n, 225n
Harrison, Thomas, 10, 20, 22, 33, 38, 42, 46n, 224
Harrison, Robert Hanson, 316n
Harrison, Sarah (Hawley), 312n
Harrison, Thomas, 396n
Harrison, William, 22, 23n, 312n
Harrod, William, 253, 293
Haslet, John, 123
Hathaway, James, 171, 226, 240, 242, 417, 423
Hathaway, Joanna (Neavil), 171
Hathaway, John, 171, 215, 226, 242, 305
Hathaway, Sarah Lawson (Timberlake), 171
"Hatherage" (Hathaway home), 171
Hausseger, Nicholas, 134, 148
Haverstraw, 315
Haverstraw Mt. (N. J.), 190
Haw River, 386-387
Hawes, Samuel, 382-384
Hay, Samuel, 303
Hayden, H. E., 288n
Haymarket, 111
Hayward, Hester, 3
Hayward, Nicholas, 3, 268
Head of Elk (Elkton) Md., 129, 202, 209, 216, 317, 390, 403
Heale, William, 248, 314
Heard, Gen'l., 127n
Heath, 130, 425
Hedgman, Peter, 39, 304
Hedgman River Baptist Church, 20n
Hedgman's River, 2, 5, 32, 304, 441
Heitman, 176n
Hell Gate (N. Y.), 112, 122
Helm, Achillis, 251n
Helm, Elizabeth (Gillison), 422
Helm family, 268-269
Helm, Hester (Edrington), 76n, 268
Helm, Leonard, 251, 256, 258, 270, 293-294, 396

Helm, Lynaugh, 76n, 251-252, 268, 422
Helm, Thomas, 248n, 251, 422, 432
Henderson, William, 329
Hening, W. W., 72n
Henrico Militia, 406
Henry V, 371
Henry, Patrick, 41, 54, 55, 56, 58, 72, 74, 82, 84, 89, 95, 108, 176, 179, 208, 231, 248, 252, 253, 259, 285, 324, 397n
"Hereford" (Chilton home), 62n, 138
Hesse-Cassel, 142
Hessians, 135, 137, 141, 142, 143, 144, 146, 150, 160,. 182, 217, 226, 280, 306, 308, 322, 363n, 425, 441
Heth, Eliza (Briggs), 92n
Heth, William, 69, 92, 168, 181, 185, 195, 197, 199-200, 203n, 204n, 207-208, 214, 225, 246, 280, 283, 297, 314n, 315, 317n
Higginbotham, Don, 409n
Hillsborough, N. C., 334, 336, 340, 346-347, 349, 361, 363
Hitchcock, 150
Hite, Col., 39
Hitt, Peter, 399
Hobcaw Ferry, 326
Hobkirk's Hill, 382n, 384
Hog Island, 234n
Hogains, John, 338
Hogan, John, 258
Hollinsworth, Col., 182, 194
"The Hollow" (home of Thomas Marshall), 11, 12, 17, 43
Holston River, 354, 386, 396
Holston Valley, 108n
Holtzclaw, 3
Holtzclaw, Jacob, 351n
Holtzclaw, John, 351n
Holtzclaw, Josiah, 351, 422
Hopewell Gap, 52
Hopewell, N. J., 17, 21, 277
Hopper, John, 337
Hornsby, Joseph, 75
Horry, Hugh, 327
Hough, Franklin B., 329n
Houses, Fauquier Co., 11
Howard, John Eager, 351, 353, 362, 367, 371, 373-374, 377, 379-380, 383
Howard, Margaret Oswald (Chew), 353n
Howe, Admiral Lord, 94, 162

Howe, Robert, 84, 89, 93, 291-292, 328n, 359
Howe, William, 74, 94, 112n, 113, 122, 124, 134, 135, 162-163, 179, 185, 187-188, 202, 205, 208-209, 215-217, 231, 237-238, 244, 246, 270, 273-274, 366
Howell's Ferry, 197
Hudnall, John, 38
Hudnall, Joseph, 19
Hudson Highlands, 217n
Hudson River, 70, 112, 113, 119, 122, 125, 127, 140, 146, 188, 197, 283, 285, 298, 300, 306, 314, 433
Huger, Daniel, 326n
Huger, Isaac, 326-328, 367, 369
Huger, Mary (Cordes), 326n
Huguenots, 3, 268
Hull, William, 298
Hume, 17
Hull, Edwin, 101n
Hull, William, 302
Humphrey, John, 92
Humphries, Samuel, 258
Humston, Edward, 23n
Humston, Jane, 23n
Hunter, 406
Hynd, Michael, 186, 206

-I-

Illinois, 251n, 294
Illinois Regiment, 251n, 258
Illinois, 438
Indiana, 301
Inner Hebrides, Scotland, 217n
Innes, Catherine (Richards), 397n
Innes, Elizabeth (Cocke), 397n
Innes, James, 397, 421
Innes, Robert, 397n
Inverness, Scotland, 350n
Ireland, 114, 123n, 148n
Ireland, James, 20
Irvine, James, 237
"Ivy Hill" (Edmonds home), 223, 246n

-J-

Jackson, Dempsey, 376
Jackson, James, 374
Jackson, Mary (Pickett), 376n
Jackson, Robert, 374-375
Jackson, T. J. ("Stonewall"), 313n
Jacobs, John, 225

INDEX 495

Jamaica, 374n
Jamaica Assembly, 54
James City Co., 49
James I, 46
James, George, 341n
James, John, 106
James, Joseph, 241, 259-260, 290
James, Mary (Wheeler), 241n
James, Thomas, 290
James River, i, 54, 77, 80-83, 89, 296, 319, 381n, 388, 396, 401-401, 407, 410, 412-413, 418-419, 426
Jameson, David, 73n
Jamestown, 83, 105, 418, 424
Jay, John, 286n
Jefferson Co., Tenn., 333n
Jefferson (ship), 407
Jefferson, Thomas, 36, 56, 59, 252n, 324, 347, 352, 360, 362, 376n, 378, 380n, 389, 394-395, 397n, 400-401, 405, 406n, 409-410, 415, 424n
Jeffersonton Baptist Church, 20n
Jeffries, William, 257
Jeffries Ford, Pa., 202
Jenkins, Joshua, 186, 206
Jennings, Augustine, 313
Jennings, Baylor, 314
Jennings, Berryman, 241
Jennings, John Melville, iv
Jennings, Lewis, 423
Jennings, William, 276
Jett, Francis, 390n
Jett, Mary, 396n
Jett, William, 396, 414, 424n, 432
"Joe Gourd" (George Weedon), 109, 126
Johnson, Henry, 303
Johnson, Herbert A., 213n, 340n
Johnson, Moses, 239
Johnson, William, 342, 353n
Johnston, Francis, 267n
Johnston, George, 74, 107n
Johnston, Gideon, 275-276, 281, 340, 398
Johnston, Margaret, 267n
Jones, Allen, 364
Jones, Brereton, 411, 412
Jones, Churchill, 377n
Jones, Elizabeth (Warner), 411n
Jones, Gabriel, 440
Jones, James, 173
Jones, John, 314
Jones, Joseph, 262n, 347, 350
Jones, Mary (Fishback), 421
Jones, William, 421

-K-

Kalb, Johann de, 340-341, 345, 360n, 412
Kaskaskia, i, 252, 293-294, 396
Kecocton Hills (Loudoun Co.), 15
Keirnes, Ann, 290
Keirnes, William, 314
Keith, Alexander, 267, 375, 384
Keith, Alexander D., 25n
Keith, Isham, 25n, 66, 79, 81, 99, 110, 127, 137, 146, 153, 154, 186, 240, 266
Keith, John A. C., iv
Keith, Rev. James, 15, 16, 25n, 36, 63n, 81n, 267n
Keith, John, 81
Keith, Judith (Blackwell), 25, 183, 247
Keith, Mary Ann (Callihue), 267n
Keith, Mary Isham Randolph, 25n, 36, 63n, 81n, 267n
Keith, Thomas, 25, 63, 110, 116, 224, 240, 248-249, 254-255, 258
Kelly John, 20, 65
Kelly, Thomas, 247
Kemp, Peter, 276, 290
Kemper, Catherine (Cuntze), 379n
Kemper, Charles, 246, 423
Kemper, Harman, 379n
Kemper, Henry, 30
Kemper, James, 349-350
Kemper, John, 290n, 294n, 379, 423-424
Kemper, Peter, 294n, 349n
Kemper, Tilman, 304-305, 396-397, 423
Keneard, James, 399
Keneard, Joshua, 399
Keneard, Margaret (Jeffries), 399n
Kenner, Howson, 407n
Kennett Square, Pa., 196n, 202
Kenton, Simon, 52n
Kenton, William, 258
Kentucky, 21, 37, 48, 176, 252-253, 257n, 270, 295, 304, 311, 360, 396-397, 416, 424n, 430, 438-440, 442
Kettle Run, 97
Key, James, 257, 348
Kincheloe, Elizabeth (Canterbury), 257n
Kincheloe, Fort, (Ky.), 257n
Kincheloe, John, 257n
Kincheloe, Nancy, 250n

Kincheloe, Thomas, 250, 257n, 394, 402, 432
Kincheloe, William, 171, 215, 257, 424
King, George H. S., 411n
King George Co., 31, 44, 268, 376n
King, Robert, 226n, 402
King, William, 226, 242, 363, 402
King William Co., 26n, 253, 395
King's Bridge, N. Y., 112, 118, 122, 298
King's College, Aberdeen, 102n
King's Ferry, N. Y., 298
Kings Mountain, 354-356, 414
Kip's Bay, 113, 118, 140, 159, 437
Kirbride's Ferry, 135
Kirk, Thomas, 225
Kirkwood, Robert, 352, 367, 374
Knowlton, Thomas, 115
Knox, George, 302
Knox, Henry, 126n, 139-140, 218, 245, 279
Knox, John, 40, 303-304
Knyphausen, General von, 363n
Kosciuszko, Thaddeus, 364, 366-368, 437

-L-

Lackley and Company, 75
Lafayette, George Washington, 442
Lafayette, Marquis de, 205, 244, 264, 272-274, 277-280, 282, 284, 286, 301n, 340n, 366, 389-390, 403, 405, 407, 409-414, 417-419, 422-423, 425-426, 442-443
"La Grange" (Lafayette estate), 443
Lake Budd (N. J.), 191
Lake Champlain, 156, 163
Lamb, John, 414n
Lamkin, George, 10, 33
Lancaster County, 31, 62, 171, 246n
Lancaster, Pa., 69, 112, 163, 225, 237, 319, 323, 348-349
Lauderdale Co., Ala., 333n
"Laurel Hill" (Lindsay home), 261n
Laurens, Henry, 405n
Laurens, John, 405
Lauzun, Duc de, 427-428
Lauzun's Legion, 429-430
Lawler, Nicholas, 424, 432
Lawrence Co., Ala., 333n
Lawrence Co., Tenn., 333n

Lawson, Robert, 129, 381n, 382, 385, 427
Lawson's Brigade, 413
Layton, Robert, 258
Lear, Hannah (Bailey), 228
Lee, Ann Hill (Carter), 260n
Lee, Casenove G., Jr., 56n
Lee, Charles, 71, 95, 105n, 124, 129, 130, 136, 167, 265, 277-279, 281, 316
Lee, Col., 412
Lee, Elizabeth (Steptoe), 260n
Lee, Francis Lightfoot, 166
Lee, G., 188
Lee, Hancock, 40, 179, 304
Lee, Hannah Harrison (Ludwell), 37n
Lee, Henry (Lighthorse Harry), 175n, 260-261, 299, 302, 306-310, 315, 346n, 352n, 353n, 381-382, 384, 419, 430
Lee, John, 304
Lee, John, Jr., 41
Lee, Lucy (Grymes), 260n
Lee, Matilda, 260n
Lee, Philip Francis, 198, 205
Lee, Philip, Ludwell, 41, 260n
Lee, Richard Henry, 6, 12, 37, 40, 41n, 56, 153n, 230, 403
Lee, Robert Edward, 260n
Lee, Thomas, 37n, 56, 153n
Lee, Thomas Ludwell, 12n
Leeds, Duke of, 136n
Leeds Manor, 13, 32, 385n, 396n, 424n, 439-440
Leeds Parish, 5, 10, 16, 51, 65n, 157, 311, 439
Leedstown Resolutions, 41, 56
Leesburg, Va., 111, 167, 173, 175, 206n, 214, 225, 319, 323, 411
Lee's Legion, 261, 368, 380-383
"Leesylvania" (Lee home), 260n
Lefevre, Mrs. (Phila.), 153
Leitch, Andrew, 108, 109, 115, 117, 120
Leslie, Alexander, 149, 150, 151, 152, 369
Leslie, Samuel, 83n, 85, 86
Leslie, William, 85n
Levin, Earl of, 85n
Lewis, Andrew, 39, 52, 95, 105, 107, 129, 167n
Lewis, Charles, 105
Lewis, Fielding, 6, 42, 303n, 406
Lewis, Mary (Brent), 88n
Lewis, Zacharias, 88n, 249-249

INDEX

Lexington, Battle of, 64, 66, 298n
Lexington, Ky., 48, 441
Liberty Bell, 320
Liberty Pole, 307n
Liberty (ship), 104n
Licking Run, 3, 10, 81n, 258n
Light Infantry Brigade, Cont. Line., 297-298
Lime Kiln Road, 219
"Limerick" (Huger home), 326n
Limestone (now Maysville) Ky., 48, 270
Lincoln, Benjamin, 197, 204, 291-292, 295-296, 315-317, 324, 328-329, 332, 359
Lincoln Co., Mo., 412n
Lindsay, Ann (Calvert), 261n
Lindsay, Robert, 261n
Lindsay, Susannah (Austin), 261n
Lindsay, William, 261
Linud's Ferry (Lenud), 334, 342, 362
Lipscomb, Daniel, 276
Lipscomb, Yancey, 276, 400
Little Falls 241n
Little River, 17
Little York (Gloucester), 399, 402, 420, 422
Little York, Pa., 225
Liverpool, England, 327n
Livingston, Henry, 279
Livingston, Robert, 91n
"Locust Shade" (Payne estate), 376
Loman, John, 331
London, England, 43, 282, 300, 321, 386
London Military Academy, 328n
Long, Gabriel, 181, 314
Long Island, N. Y., 111, 136n, 140, 168, 186n, 218, 274, 360n
Long Island Sound, 121, 1221, 123
Loretta (Edmondium), 269n
Loring, Elizabeth (Lloyd), 135n
Loring, Joshua, 135n
Lossing, B. J. 85, 385
Loudoun County, 32, 38, 42, 97, 104, 115, 157, 173, 190n, 198-199, 222, 236, 251n, 394
Loudoun County Resolves, 98n
Loudoun Militia, 389, 395, 405-406
Louisa County, 435
Louisville, Ky., 253
Lovell, Sarah (Marshall), 36
Lovell, William, 36

Lower Blue Licks, Ky., 438
Lucken's Mill, 216
"Ludwell Park" (Carter home), 248n
Luttrell, Richard, 338
Lynes, Henry, 386

-Mc-

McAllister, J. T. 65
McBride, William, 423
McCall, James, 368-369, 371
McClanahan, Thomas, 33
McClanahan, William, 351n
McCollestown, Pa., 173
McCormick, Margaret, 39
McCormick, Stephen, 39
McDonald, Angus, 68
McDonald, Daniel, 241n
McDonald, Ellen (Barret), 241n
McDonnell, John C. (Mrs.), iv
McDougall, Alexander, 208, 217, 283
McDowell, Joseph, 368
McDowell, Samuel, 362
McGraw, Jemima, 254, 339
McIntosh, Lachlan, 350
McKonkey's Ferry, N. J., 135, 137, 140-141
McLain, John, 109, 110, 152-153, 177
McLane, Allan, 274, 299, 300, 302, 307
McSherrystown, Pa., 173

-M-

Maddox, Alexander, 305
Maddux, Thomas, 7, 126n, 239
Maddux, Thomas M. 424
Madison County, 35n, 58n, 431
Magaw, Robert, 122n
Magdalen (ship), 64
Maidstone, Kent, England, 47
Maidstone (Rectortown), 5
Maine, 91
Mallory, Philip, 23n
Mallory, William, 23n
Malvern Hill, 402, 419, 431
Mamaroneck, 123
Manassas Gap Railroad, 5
Manchester, Va., 407
Manhattan, N. Y., 94, 111n, 122
Manning, James, 21, 22
Marblehead, Mass., 140, 147
Marcus Hook, Pa., 193
Marion, Francis, 342, 366, 368

Marion's Brigade (S.C.), 327n
Markham, Catherine (Kenner), 407n, 412
Markham, James, 403, 407, 412
Markham (village), 11, 43, 269
Marlborough Point, 199n
Marr, Daniel, 337
Marr, John, 337
Marr, John Quincy, 337n
Marr's Run, 206n, 247n, 259n, 337, 422n
Marsh Road, 395
Marsh Run, 289-290, 304
Marshall, Abraham, 36
Marshall, Elizabeth (Markham), 34
Marshall, Humphrey, 276, 398
Marshall, James Markham, 440
Marshall, John, 12-14, 34, 36, 55n, 63, 66-67, 73n, 87-88, 92n, 99, 170, 213, 220, 247, 266, 286, 310, 339, 340n, 348, 423, 440-441
Marshall, John ("of the Forest"), 36
Marshall, Markham, 36
Marshall, Mary Ann, 276n
Marshall, Mary (Quesenbury), 36, 276n
Marshall, Mary Randolph Keith, 36, 37
Marshall (Salem), 16-17, 44, 103, 171, 177, 363n, 365n, 385n
Marshall, Thomas, 11-12, 14-17, 19, 25-26, 30, 33-37, 42-44, 51, 54-55, 57, 59-60, 62-65, 67, 72, 83, 86, 88, 89n, 95, 102, 109, 119, 139, 146, 156, 180-181, 185, 191, 197, 200, 203-205, 212-213, 217-218, 220-221, 225, 228, 231, 233, 245-247, 251, 269, 275-276, 285, 340, 348-349, 353, 361n, 389, 397-400, 407n, 430, 441
Marshall, Thomas, Jr., 276, 398
Marshall, William, 19
Marshall's Wood, 206, 443
Martin, Benjamin, 348, 350-352, 362n, 365n, 379
Martin, Bryan, 52, 53, 254
Martin, Denny, 47, 439
Martin, Frances (Fairfax), 47n
Martin, Henry, 348
Martin, John Joseph, 348
Martin, Nancy (Kemper), 348n
Martin, Philip, 40, 440
Martin, Thomas Bryan, 14, 29, 32, 33, 36, 40, 47, 439-440

Martinique, 139n, 282
Maryland, 32, 46, 68, 102, 167, 174-175, 208, 270, 277, 302, 307, 335n, 354, 366n, 429, 433
Maryland Board of War, 360
Maryland Brigade, 345
Maryland Continental Line, 302n, 336, 340, 346, 351-352, 367, 371, 376, 380-381
Maryland Convention, 102, 103
Maryland Militia, 129, 208
Maryland Regiments
  First: 382
  Second: 353n
  Third: 360n
  Fifth: 382-383
Mason and Dixon Line, 260
Mason Co., Ky., 276n, 376n, 377n
Mason, David, 186
Mason, George, 252n
Massachusetts, 64, 68, 91n, 139, 273, 277, 292n, 298
Massachusetts Continentals, 122n
Massachusetts Regt.
  Third: 298n
Massey, Rev. Lee, 312n
Mathews, George, 219
Matson's Ford, Pa., 273-274
Matthew, General, 324
Matthews, Chichester, 186, 214
Matthews, Edward, 296
Matthews, George, 168
Matthews, Sampson, 301n
Mattox Creek, 34
Mattox, Martha, 249
Matuchin, N. J., 184
Mauzy, Hester (Foote), 99n
Mauzy, John, 99n
Mawhood, Charles, 149, 150
Maxwell, Gen., 195n, 277
Maxwell, Helen, 86
Maxwell, James, 86n
Maxwell, William, 203-204, 207, 218, 363n
Mayo River, 30
Maysville, Ky., 270, 442
Mazarett, John, 399-400
Meade, Bishop William, 5, 13, 51n
Meade, Capt., 85
Meade, Richard, 275
Meade, Richard Kidder, 322
Mechunk Creek, 412, 414
Mecklenburg Co., N. C., 253, 333n, 363n, 364
Meigs, Return J., 298, 302

INDEX 499

Mercer, Catherine (Mason), 199n
Mercer, Fort, 237
Mercer, Hugh, 61-62, 72, 95-97, 105, 108, 111, 125n, 135, 139-140, 143, 149-152, 185, 199n, 353n
Mercer, James, 199n
Mercer, John, 199n, 428, 430
Mercer, John Francis, 190, 199
Mercersburg, Pa., 61
Metcalf, William, 423
Metuchen, N. J., 187
Mezieres, France, 364n
Middlebrook (Bound Brook), N.J., 181, 184, 187, 283, 292, 295, 297, 308n, 331-332
Middlebrook, Camp, 291
Middlesex County, 103
Midland, 37
Miffin, Thomas, 147, 148, 359n
Mill Point, 104
Mill Run, 250
Miller, John Frederick, 64
Mills: Saw, grist, 9, 10
Millstone, N.J., 151
Minor, Armistead, 304
Mississippi River, 252
Mitchell, Capt., 332
Moffett, Elizabeth (Bailey), 228n
Moffett, Jesse, 228, 259
Moffett, John, 16, 65, 165, 239, 249, 254, 256, 259, 311, 400
Moffett, Lee, 10, 65n
Moffett, William, 214
Moffett, Willie, 266
Monck's Corner, 326-327, 334, 342, 362
Monckton, Lt. Col., 279, 280
Monmouth, Battle of, 245-281, 285-286, 298n, 304, 315, 332, 353n, 362, 385n, 423, 429n
Monongahela River, 253, 400
Monongalia County, 424n
Monroe, James, 144, 442
Monroe, John, 439
Montague, Captain, 82
Montclair, N. J., 112
"Monterey" (Harrison home), 224n
Montgomery Co., Ky., 397n
Montogomery, Janet (Livingston), 91n
Montgomery, John 253-293
Montgomery, Richard, 91, 92
"Monticello" (Jefferson estate), 410
Moody, Edward, 398

Moore, Peter, 206
Moore, Thomas L., 443
Moore, William, 214
Morayshire, Scotland, 44
More, William, 186
Morehead, Ann (Ransdell), 258n
Morehead, Charles, 240, 258n, 261, 338n
Morehead, John, 176n, 261n, 338n
Morehead, Margaret (Slaughter), 261n
Morehead, Mary (Turner), 258n
Morehead, Turner, 258-259, 261
Morgan, Abigail (Curry), 68n
Morgan, Charles, 76
Morgan, Daniel, 68-70, 91-93, 95, 100, 112, 155, 168, 170-171, 180-181, 186, 197-198, 200n, 204n, 208, 212-213, 221, 235, 238, 249, 251, 256, 266, 278, 280, 283, 288-289, 295, 297-298, 316, 346-347, 349, 352-353, 362, 364-365, 367-368-369-370-371-372-373, 375-376-377-378-379-380-381, 400, 408-409, 415-416-417, 419, 422, 430-431-432, 435, 441
Morgan, John, 153, 180, 186
Morgan's Rangers, 314
Morgan's Riflemen, 69n, 298n
Morningside Heights, N. Y., 113
Morris Heights, N. Y., 120, 122
Morris, Robert, 167
Morrison, Elizabeth, 239
Morrison, Lydia, 239
Morristown, N. J., 152, 156, 162, 167, 169, 171, 180-181, 185, 187-188, 199, 315, 322
Morrisville, 30n, 37, 228
Morton, Oren F., 385n
Motley, Archie, iv
Moultrie, John, 329n
Moultrie, William, 329-330
"The Mount" (Lindsay home), 261n
Mt. Holly, N. J., 135, 189, 277
"Mt. Independence" (Chunn estate), 258n, 291n, 441
Mountjoy, Alvin, 160, 184, 192, 201
Mt. Pleasant, S. C., 330
"Mt. Vernon" (Washington estate), 368n, 301, 404
Moylan, Stephen, 327
Muccaboy, Thomas, 338
Mud Island, 213, 234n
Muhlenberg, Peter, 167, 169, 185, 209, 221-222, 243, 262-263, 271,

272n, 273, 277, 280, 283, 288, 291, 297, 306, 310, 314, 316, 331, 389, 397n, 401, 403, 407, 410, 415, 433
Mulliken, William, 423
Murderers Creek, (N.J.), 189
Murfree, Hardy, 298, 302-303
Murphey, John, 206, 247, 259, 376
Murray Hill, N. J., 113
Murray, Reuben, 432
Murray, Virginia, 53
Musconaconk Brook, (N. J.), 192
Musgrave, Thomas, 218

-N-

Napier, Lt., 85n
Nash, 204
Nash, Elijah, 109, 110
Nash, Mary (Morgan), 259n
Nash, William, 206n, 239, 247n, 259
Nashville, Tenn., 206, 350n
Nassau, Germany, 351n
Nassau Hall (Princeton), 150
Neabsco Creek, 312n
Neale, Matthew, 290
Neavil, George, 171
Neill, Edward D., 31
Neilson, Charles, 103
Nelson, 137, 338n
Nelson Co., Ky. 257n
Nelson, Hugh, 248, 249
Nelson, Jane Byrd-Page, 248n
Nelson, John, 99n, 177, 253
Nelson, Joseph, 311, 314, 423
Nelson, Nathaniel, 248n
Nelson, Thomas, 72, 314, 332, 389, 394
Nelson, Thomas, Jr., 56, 282, 409, 417, 419, 426-427, 434
Nelson, William, 80n, 99, 153n, 177, 186, 257, 412
Nevill, Robert, 30
Neville, George, 9, 10
Neville, John, 283, 316, 323, 326
Neville, Joseph, 9
Neville, Presley, 286, 308
New Bern, N.C., 84n
New Brunswick, N. J., 124, 126, 129, 133, 149, 187, 281
New England Continentals, 429
New Hampshire, 123n, 279
New Hope, Pa., 192n
New Jersey, 70, 113, 127, 138, 165-166, 176, 179, 186, 208, 250, 265n, 266, 277, 291, 352, 439

New Jersey Continental Line, 389
New Jersey Militia, 278n
New Market, 39
New Rochelle, N. Y., 123
New Windsor, 300
New York, 94, 107, 109, 113, 118, 135, 187, 198, 217n, 277, 280, 282, 294, 299-300, 315, 333, 368, 374, 388, 414, 417-418, 425, 431
New York Continental Line, 122n, 425, 429
New York Harbour, 319, 321
New York Militia, 139
Newark Bay, 185
Newark, Del., 196n
Newark, N.J., 126, 184, 308, 316
Newcastle, Del., 193, 352
Newport, R. I., 282, 390, 403, 425
Newton, Elizabeth (Kenyon), 241n
Newton, William, 241n
Newtown, Pa., 136
Nicholas, George, 168
Nicholas, Robert Carter, 57
Nicholson, John, 337
Nightingale, Forence, 153
Niles, Michigan, 378n
Ninety-Six, S.C., 368, 377
Nisbett, James, 81n
Noailles, Viscomte de, 405n
Noel-Hume, Ivor, 57, 90n
Noland's Ferry, 111, 112, 173, 212, 225, 262, 275, 323, 363n, 411
Norfolk, Va., 64, 77, 82, 85-89, 93, 119, 162, 348, 388, 402
Norfolk Intelligencer, 8
Norman's Ford, 248n, 323, 412
Norris, Mrs. 443
Norris, William, 38, 241
Norristown, N.J., 112
North Anna River, 410
North Carolina, 84, 108, 277, 298, 302, 317, 341, 353-354
North Carolina Militia, 328, 335, 345-346, 368, 370, 381
North Carolina Regts., 5th, 299
North Castle, N. Y., 124
North, Lord, 285
North River, N. Y., 186
North, William, 265n
Northcutt, Richard, 423
Northen, W. J. 341n
Northern Neck, 33, 211n, 254, 394
Northumberland County, 25, 31, 34, 41, 88n, 169, 258n, 275, 413n

INDEX

-O-

"Oak Hill" (Marshall home), 11, 66, 246, 397, 441
"Oak Spring" (Edmonds estate), 62n, 223, 441
"Oakwood" (Scott estate), 441
Oath of Allegiance, 272
O'Bannon, Aaron, 267
O'Bannon, Andrew, 228n, 239, 280
O'Bannon, Anne (Neville), 363n
O'Bannon, Benjamin, 115, 117, 250, 259n, 280
O'Bannon, Briant, 114
O'Bannon, Bryant, 267n
O'Bannon, Eleanor (Ash), 117n
O'Bannon, George, 100, 110, 113, 114, 117, 119, 239, 250, 259n
O'Bannon, Hannah (Barker), 364n
O'Bannon, John, 16, 113n, 114, 117n, 239, 313n, 338n, 363, 365, 372, 396, 406, 416, 420
O'Bannon, Joseph, 259n
O'Bannon, Mary Ann (Winn), 363n
O'Bannon, Mary Pepper (Smith), 239n
O'Bannon, Samuel, 338
O'Bannon, Sarah (Barbee), 113n, 114, 117, 239n, 313n, 338n
O'Bannon, Thomas, 351, 365, 376, 378
O'Bannon, William, 363n
Occoquan River, 219
Oder, Joseph, 227-229, 402, 432
Ogilvie, Charles, 372
O'Hara, Charles, 386
O'Hara, James, 386n
Ohio, 350, 352n, 363n
Ohio River, i, 52, 252-253, 270
Ohio Valley, 48, 52
Okinawa, 109
Old Fort, N.C., 354
Old Point Comfort, 418
Oneida Indians, 274
Orange County, 58, 65, 73, 74, 323
Ordinary Fees, 339
O'Rear, Benjamin, 336
O'Rear, Daniel, 78, 79, 331, 396n
O'Rear, John, 78n, 396
O'Rear, William 396
Orlean, 10, 17, 376
"Orlean" (Jett estate), 396n
Osborne's, 407
Oswald, Eleazer, 279
Otter (ship), 77, 83, 85, 86, 105

Oven Top Mt., 36
Overhill Cherokees, 108
Overwharton Par, 15, 44
Oxford, N.J., 190
Oxford (ship), 104

-P-

Pacolet River, 368-370
Page, John, 118, 121, 124, 145, 152, 159, 160n, 202, 205, 221, 222n, 237n, 260, 262, 296, 347
Page, Mann, 25, 38, 64
Page, Mann, Jr., 160
Page (ship), 407n
"Pageland" (Churchill estate), 38
Paine, Thomas, 24
Pamunkey River, 395
Paoli, Pa., 216, 348
Paramus, N.J., 281
Paris, France, 264
Paris, Va., 43
Parker, Alexander, 332
Parker, Catherine (Martin?), 181n
Parker, Elizabeth (Duncan), 181n
Parker, Hyde, 291
Parker, Joseph, 181
Parker, Josiah, 158, 159
Parker, Martin, 181n
Parker, Richard, 283, 297, 317, 328-329, 332
Parker, Thomas, 181n
Parker, William Harwar, 407n
Parson's Plantation (N.C.), 340
Patrick County, 386-387
Patriot, (ship), 104n
Patterson Creek, 69
Patton, Alexander, 281
Paulus Hook, N.J., 175, 306-307, 319, 332, 423
Payne, (Flowerree), 87n
Payne, Augustine, 87, 396
Payne, Brooke, 66n
Payne, Daniel, 376
Payne, Francis, 376n
Payne, John, 87n
Payne, Josias, 206n, 247n
Payne, Mary (Ball?), 376n
Payne, Sarah (Glendenning) 424n
Payne, Thomas, 424n
Payne, William, 66, 74, 76, 81, 87, 215, 227, 376n, 395-396

Peachy, William, 96
Peake, John, 312
Peake, Mary (Harrison) 312n
Peake, William, 30, 312n
Pearle, Samuel, 339
Pearson, Harvey H., v
Pearson, Lt., 335
Pee Dee River, 342, 366
Peekskill, N. Y., 124, 208
Pierce, Joseph, 41
Peirce, Peter, 30
Pendleton, Edmund, 59, 86
Pendleton, James, 237n
Penn, Abram, 386
Pennington, Daniel, 266
Pennington, N. J., 135
Pennsburg, Pa., 139
Pennsylvania, 15, 17, 63, 68, 111, 165, 167, 176-177, 186, 218, 225, 270, 277, 298, 303, 327n, 354, 370n, 429, 433
Pennsylvania Associators, 134, 135
Pennsylvania Committee of Defense, 364n
Pennsylvania Continental Line, 410-412
Pennsylvania "German Troops", 182
Pennsylvania Militia, 129, 139, 151, 217
Pennsylvania Regiments
  Third: 122n
  Fourth: 122n
  First Rifle: 122n
  Sixth: 302n
  Ninth: 298n, 302n
Pennsylvania Rifle Regiment, 143
Pennsylvania troops, 196
Pennypacker's Mill, 216, 219, 225-226, 231
Pension Act, 1832, 87
Pequannock River, N. J., 189
Perth Amboy, N. J., 1108, 109, 158, 187, 188
Peters, B. J., 29n
Peters, John, 177n
Peters, Richard, 319
Petersburg, Va., 316, 319, 324, 333, 336, 351, 384, 407, 409
Pettits, N. J., 191
Peyton, Ann (Thornton), 261n
Peyton, Eleanor, 240n
Peyton family, 31
Peyton, Henry, 16, 239-240, 261, 308, 313-314
Peyton, John, 160n, 195n, 198, 240n
Peyton, Robert, 160, 190, 205
Peyton, Seth (Harrison), 160n, 195n
Peyton, Susanna (Fowke), 240n
Peyton, Valentine, 186, 195, 214, 220, 246, 250, 266
Peyton, Yelverton, 33
Philadelphia, Pa., 49, 53, 58, 61, 69, 94-95, 111, 129, 133, 138, 167, 169, 171, 173, 175, 186, 188, 193, 196, 198, 202, 207, 213, 216, 219, 225-227, 234-235, 237-238, 242, 269, 271, 273-275, 285, 289, 291, 304, 318-320, 323, 418, 425
Philadelphia Associators, 150
Philadelphia Baptist Church, 17
Phillips, Samuel, 354
Phillips, William, 79, 106, 390, 401, 403, 406-408
Piankatank River, 105
Pickens, Andrew, 366, 370, 372, 374-375, 377, 381
Pickering, Timothy, 359
Pickett, Ann, 183
Pickett, Ann (Blackwell), 7
Pickett, Elizabeth (Cooke), 102n, 241n
Pickett, Elizabeth (Crump), 248n
Pickett, Elizabeth (Metclaf), 351n
Pickett family, 10
Pickett, John, 19, 439
Pickett, Lucy (Blackwell) 224
Pickett, Martin, 7, 16, 19, 25-26, 38, 62, 102, 110, 116, 158n, 165, 179, 187, 223-236, 239-241n, 248-249, 254, 256, 259, 399, 408
Pickett, Mary, 376n
Pickett, William, 16, 19, 25n, 62, 66, 74, 76, 81, 84, 87, 99, 102n, 180, 187, 224n, 239, 241n, 248-250, 253-256, 259, 289, 348, 399, 408
Pickett, William Sanford, 369n, 351n, 376
Pignut Mt., 4, 44, 113n, 114, 165, 240n, 250n, 351n
Pike, Capt., 144n
Pinkney, John, 8
Piper's Church, 10, 17, 20
Piper's Mill, 10
Piqua, 438
Piscataway, N. J., 185

INDEX 503

Pittstown, N. J., 130, 192
Plainfield, N. J., 112
Pluckimin, N. J., 151
Poque's Mill, 413
Point Levi, 91
Point of Forks, 402
Point Pleasant, 52, 95
Polk, Col., 364
Pomfret, John E., 21
Pompey, 303
Pompton, 315
Pontiac's War, 69, 123n, 298n
Poor, Enoch, 273
Pope, 35
Pope, William, 257-259
Port Island, 234n
Port Tobacco, Md., 113n
Porter, Samuel, 396n
Porterfield, Charles, 69, 92, 171, 181, 221, 280, 341-342, 346
Porterfield, Robert, 266
Portsmouth, 104, 162, 292, 296, 388, 401, 417-419, 433
Portugal, 386n
Posey, John, 301n
Posey, Martha (Price), 301n
Posey, Mary (Alexander), 301n
Posey, Thomas, 301, 303
Potomac Creek, 332n
Potomac River, 9, 26n, 39, 69, 79, 97, 106, 111, 173, 212, 225, 260n, 275, 323, 396, 411
Powell, Eleanor (Peyton), 96n, 190n
Powell, Leven, 97, 98n, 107n, 157, 173, 175, 177, 236
Powell, Robert, 198
Powell, Robert C., 107n, 157n, 173n
Powell, Sarah (Harrison), 98n
Powell, William, 98n, 190
Presbyterians, 15
Prescott, Richard, 265
Price, Thomas, 341n
Priest, Peter, 233
Prince George Co., 49, 413n
Prince, Hubbard, 258
Prince William Co., 5, 15, 16, 28, 33, 34, 42, 46, 49, 61, 65n, 71, 81n, 97, 100, 108, 111, 171, 174n, 190n, 222, 257n, 261n, 267-268, 312n, 394, 434n
Prince William Co., Independent Co., 174n
Prince William Militia, 30, 69, 106, 389, 405-406

Princeton, Battle of, 133-161, 298n
Princeton College, 205
Princeton, N. J., 21, 85n, 123n, 128, 134, 140, 184, 186, 274, 364n, 369n
Proctor, Thomas, 414n
Prove, William, 337
Providence, N. C., 365
Providence, R. I., 21
Pulaski, Casimir, 327, 341n, 412n
Pulaski's Legion, 341, 344
Pumpton, N. J., 192
Pumpton Plains, N. J., 188, 287
Purdie, Alexander, 74n, 78n, 108, 119
Putnam, Israel, 120, 122, 123, 283-284

-Q-

Quaker Meeting House (Trenton), 150
Quakers, 15, 30
Quantico, 106n
Quarles, John, 22n, 276
Quebec, i, 31, 70n, 91-92, 100, 112, 168, 171, 181, 197, 294n, 346
Queen's American Rangers, 123, 388
Queen's Loyal Virginia Regiment, 83
Queen's Loyalist Regiment, 85
Queensbury, Marquis of, 8
Quibbletown, N. J., 158, 173, 182-183, 423

-R-

Raccoon Ford, 412-413
Radnor, Pa., 300
Raleigh Tavern, 49
Rall, Johann Gottlieb, 142, 143, 144
Ramapo River, N. J., 185
Ramey, Emily G., iv
Ramsay's Mill, 386
Ramseur's Mills, 380
Randolph, Anne (Innes), 397n
Randolph family 36
Randolph, Peyton, 59, 64, 397n
Rankin, Hugh F., 299n
Ransdell, Edward, 41
Ransdell family, 31, 56
Ransdell, Mary (Chilton), 49
Ransdell, Thomas, 154, 170
Ransdell, Wharton, 11, 33, 37, 41, 49, 258

Ransdell, William, 38, 49, 223, 258
Rapidan River, 410
Rappahannock Co., 35n, 58n
Rappahannock County (Ridemond), 33
Rappahannock River, 10, 20n, 44, 60, 97, 105, 323, 412, 441-442
Raritan River, 128, 134
Rawdon, Lord, 343, 386
Reade, Isaac, 108, 109, 133, 150
Rector, Henry, 292n
Rector, Jessee, 444
Rector family, 3
Rector, John, 6
Reading, Pa., 237
Rectortown, 6, 10
Red Bank, N. J., 237
Red House (Haymarket), 111, 411
Red Store, 7
Red Store (Haymarket), 319
Redstone, Pa., 253, 294
Reed, Joseph, 156
Reeve, William, 182, 183
Religion (Fauq. Co., - 1775), 15
Renown (ship), 322, 407
Rhinebeck, N. Y., 91n
Rhode Island, 21, 119n, 425
Rice, George, 171
Richardson, Holt, 282
"Richland" (Brent house), 106, 107
Richmond, Va., 60, 64, 65, 73, 239, 247, 324, 347, 351-352, 360, 379, 388, 402, 407-408, 415, 420
Richmond Co., 31, 49, 61, 71
Richmond Co. Courthouse, 97, 133
Ridley, John, 399
Riley, Christian, 59, 76, 173, 312n
Riley, John, 59, 76
Rind, Clementina, 8
Ringo, Burtis, 292n, 385, 434
Ringo, Hannah (Rector), 292n
Rio Santa Maria, 292
Rising Sun Tavern, 60, 95
Riverside Drive (N.Y.C.), i, 116
Rives Co., Mo. 286n
Rixey, Elizabeth (Morehead), 338n
Rixey, Richard, 338
Roach, John, 275
Roach, William, 186
Roan, Christopher, 361, 398
Roanoke River, 332

Robards, Maj., 237n
Roberts, Kenneth L., 92n
Roberts, Samuel, 160
Robertson, J. Dallas, 262n
Robespierre, 403n
Robinson, Dickson, 186
Robinson, McKinney, 180
Robust (ship), 322
Rochambeau, Comte de, 403-404-405, 424-425-426-427, 433
Rocheblave, Chevalier de, 294
Rochefort, George, 330
"Rock Spring" (Chilton estate), 62n, 89, 100, 110
Rockaway, 315
Rockbridge Co., 362, 367, 385
Rockingham County, 415
Rockaway River, N.J., 188
Rocky Mountains, S. C., 343
Rogers, Elizabeth (Lankford), 352n
Rogers, Elizabeth (Randall), 352n
Rogers, George, 240, 242, 352, 366, 378, 422
Rogers, Henry, 352n
Rogers, James, 363, 366, 421
Rogers, Robert, 123
Rogers, Robert, Sr., 80
Rollins, Vincent, 337
Romulus (ship), 404
Rose, Duncan, 400
Ross, David, 175
Rosser, Richard, 228, 231, 424, 433
Rousseau, 24
Routt, James, 6
Rucker, Capt., 237
Rudolph, Michael, 307, 384
Rugeley, Henry, 365
Rugeley's Mill, S. C., 335, 343-344, 365-366, 422
Rush, Dr. Benjamin, 71n
Russell, George, 266
Russell (ship), 321
Russell, William, 97n, 283, 323, 338
Rust, Elizabeth, 215n
Rust, Ellsworth Marshall, 311n
Rust, John, 215n, 311
Rust, Peter, 432
Rust, Sarah (Mason), 311n
Rust, Sarah (Singleton), 311n
Rutherford, Thomas, 42
Rutledge, Edward, 172, 327
Rye, N. Y., 123

INDEX   505

-S-
Sabine, Lorenzo, 365n
Sackville, Fort, 293
St. Augustine, Fla., 74n, 107, 323
St. Clair, Arthur, 139, 140, 144, 156, 187, 433
St. Croix, B.W.I., 150n
St. John's Church, 54, 56
St. Lawrence River, 91, 112n
St. Louis, 293
Saint Mary's Church (Turkey Run), 16
St. Paul's Parish, 268
Saint-Simon, Marquis, 425-426
Salem, Mass., 139n
Salisbury, N. C., 341, 364, 376, 378-379
Samara, 109
Sanders, Elizabeth (Nash), 110
Sanders, James, 110
Sanders, Robert, 421n, 439
Sands, Samuel, 366
Sandy Hook, 112n, 277-278, 282, 291, 314, 321
Sandy Point, 83, 402
Santee River, S.C., 334
Santo Domingo, 424
Saratoga, N.Y., 91n, 208, 212-213, 234-235, 257, 262n, 295, 298n, 347, 364n, 371, 375, 377, 401n, 424n
"Saratoga" (Morgan estate), 316n, 353n, 400-401, 441
Sargent, John, 139-140
Saunders Creek, S.C., 344-345
Savannah, Ga., i, 291, 314, 322, 329n, 341n, 359
Savannah River, 332
Sayer and Bennett, 9
Scheer, George F., 92n, 299n
Schoepf, Johann, 269
Schuyler, Gen'l., 91n, 116
Schuylkill River, 193, 198, 204, 207, 215-216, 226, 238, 271, 273
Scoggin, William, 423
Scotch Highlanders, 267
Scotch-Irish, 15, 368, 370n
"Scotchtown" (Henry estate), 324
Scotland, 46, 102, 113n, 332n
Scott, Alexander, 250n, 254n
Scott, Alexander II, 45
Scott, Rev. Alexander, 44, 45
Scott, Catherine (Stone), 254n
Scott, Charles, 83, 86, 89, 108, 129, 146, 149, 160, 185, 188, 196, 204, 209, 218, 221, 237, 243-244, 262, 273, 277, 279-281, 288, 295-297, 310, 316-317, 325-326, 328, 332, 338, 348
Scott, Elizabeth (Harrison), 45, 312-313
Scott family, 44
Scott, James, 14, 16, 44, 46, 49, 54, 56, 57, 59, 60, 62, 65, 66, 67, 72, 74, 75, 81, 87, 94, 101, 102, 103, 165, 171, 172, 173, 182, 183, 201, 215, 228n, 248, 250, 254, 255, 257, 258, 312-313, 339, 423
Scott, Rev. James, 44, 45, 102, 254n
Scott, Rev. John, 312, 424
Scott, Rev. Mr., 338n
Scott, Robert, 254
Scott, Sarah (Brown), 254n
Scott, Sarah Gibbons Brent, 45
Scott, Walter, 398
Scylla, 369
Seaton, James, 30
Seaton, William, 290
Seaton, William, Jr., 257
2nd British Grenadier Battalion, 279
Second Continental Artillery, 279, 414
Selden, Rev., 59
Sellers, John Robert, 70n, 148n
Semple, Robert B., 18, 19
Senegal, 386n
Separate Baptists, 19
Settle, Isaac, 30
Settle, William, 224
Seven Year's War, 142n, 340n
71st Highland Regiment, 374n
Shackleford, George, 227n
Shacklett, Edward, 275, 337, 432
Shakespeare, 138
Shallow Ford, 386
Sharpe, Linsfield, 257, 424, 432
Shaw, Catherine (Jett), 424n
Shaw, Charles, 424
Shawnee Indians, 48, 108n, 438
Shee, John, 122n
Sheeler, Harva, iv
Shelburne Parish, Va., 157
Shelby Co., Ky. 402n
Shelton, Clough, 297
Shenandoah County, 49, 379, 384, 415
Shenandoah Hunting Path, 2, 411
Shenandoah River, 26n
Shenandoah Valley, 28, 39, 63, 174

Shepherd, Capt. 181n
Sherman, Roger, 172
Sherrald's Ford, 378n, 380n
Sherrington, Robert, 337
Shippen, Alice (Lee), 153n
Shippen, Edward, 153n
Shippen, William, 153
"Shirley" (Carter home), 260n
Shirley, Gov. (Mass.), 121n
Shumate, Armistead, 422, 432
Shumate, Berryman, 422
Shumate, Daniel, 177, 262
Shumate, John, 256n
Shumate, Samuel, 424, 432
Simcoe, John Graves, 388, 410
Simpson's Creek (Ky.), 257n
Sinclair (Sincler), William, 110, 139n, 177n
Sineputent Inlet, Md., 198
Sinklair, William, 399n
Skinner, Cortlandt, 121n
Skippack Creek, 232
Skippack Road, 216-217
Slaughter, Philip, 73, 75
Slaughter, Cadwallader, 261n
Slaughter, James, 402n
Slaughter, John, 413
Slaughter, Margaret (Ransdell), 261n
Smallpox, 177n
Smallwood, William, 208, 217
Smith, Abner, 239
Smith, Ann (Marshall), 36
Smith, Augustine, 36
Smith, Capt. 336
Smith Co., Tenn., 333n
Smith, Enoch, 399
Smith, Godfrey, 384
Smith, John, 253, 262-263, 408n, 415-416
Smith, Joseph, 239, 314
Smith, Joseph Thomas, 239n
Smith, Mary (Pepper), 239
Smith, Robert, 337
Smith, Rolly, 338
Smith, Ruth, 239
Smsith, Wilhelmina, 239
Smith, William, 218, 239, 257, 290, 337
Smith, William B., 252, 253
Smith's Cove, N. J., 189, 299
Smyth, J. F. D., 60n
Somerset County, Md., 46n, 103
Somerset Courthouse, N. J., 151
Somerville, Va., 352n
South Carolina, 73, 199, 354, 405n, 409, 417, 421
South Carolina Militia, 328, 370
South Carolina Partisans, 343
Southall, Capt., 89n
Southampton, Pa., 192n
Sowego, 20, 22
Spencer, John, 398
Spencer, Joseph, 122
Spencer, Sgt., 303
Spotswood, Alexander, 2, 3, 119, 129, 167, 351n
Spotsylvania Co., 61, 64, 71, 323, 395
Spotsylvania Militia, 405
Springfield Camp, 348, 395, 422
Springfield, N. J., 363n
Springsteel, David, 300-301
Squire, Matthew, 77-78
Stafford County, 26n, 31, 106, 113n, 115, 123, 171, 190n, 220, 240n, 241n, 268, 304, 330, 395
Stafford Courthouse, 44
Stafford Militia, 79, 106
Stamp Act, 40, 41, 56
Staten Island, 94, 343n
Staunton, 343n, 408
Steel, Samuel, 206n
Steele, William, 407n
Steel's Gap, N. J., 187
Stephen, Adam, 29n, 38, 81n, 129, 133-135, 139-141, 158, 166, 169, 184-185, 194, 196-197, 199, 203, 205, 207, 209, 217, 219, 221, 244, 306
Stephen, G., 196
Stephenson, Hugh, 68, 341n
Steuben, Baron, 264,270,274,277, 279, 305, 352n, 361, 381, 389, 393, 397n, 402-403, 405-406, 409-410, 414, 428
Stevens, Edward, 65, 81, 84, 85, 87, 90, 93, 99, 155, 168-169, 213, 263, 337, 341, 343-346, 360-361, 367, 376n, 378-379, 381-382, 384-385, 401, 427
Stewart, Catesby Willis, 108n
Steward, John, 302, 305
Steward, Robert Armistead, 104n
Stille, Charles J., 300n, 305n
Stirling, Lord (William Alexander), 54, 106n, 121, 123-125, 134, 135, 139, 140, 142, 146, 158, 182, 183, 188, 197, 203, 205, 215, 217, 218, 250, 277, 279, 299, 308, 309, 310, 316
Stokes Co., N. C. 378

INDEX

Stokes, John, 315
Stony Brook (N.J.), 149-150
"Stony Hill" (Peyton home) 240n
Stony Point, 197, 285-320, 332, 352
Story, Joseph, 34n
Strange, William, 311
"Stratford" (Lee home), 37n
Straughn, John, 180
Strawberry, S. C., 334
Stricker, Col. 182
Strother, Mary (Fishback), 352
Strother, William, 26n
Stryker, William S., 142n
Stuart, Rev. William, 269n
Sudduth, Francis, 423
Sudduth, William, 180
Suffolk, 83
Suffolk County, 82, 296, 348
Sullivan, John, 136, 139-140, 142, 144-145, 196-197, 204n, 205, 207, 217-219, 222, 282
Sullivan's Island, 329
Sumner Co., Tenn., 206n, 247n
Sumpter, 366
Sumpter, Thomas, 343, 345-346
Susquehanna River, 225
Sutherland, William, 306
Swede's Ford (Norristown), 216
Sycamore Shoals, Tenn., 355
Sydnor, Charles S., 44n

-T-

Taliaferro, Elizabeth (Hay), 81n
Taliaferro, Francis, 81n
Taliaferro, Lawrence, 65, 74, 76, 81
Taliaferro, Mary (Jackson), 81n
Taliaferro, Sarah (Dade), 81n
Taliaferro, William, 109
Tappan Massacre, 327n, 413n
Tarleton, Banastre, 327-328, 334-336, 342-343, 345, 363, 366, 369, 371-375, 385, 410, 414, 416, 418-419, 428, 430
Tarleton, Susan Pricilla, 327n
"Tarleton's Quarter", 355-356
Tarpley, Col., 250n
Tate, James, 352, 366-367, 369, 371, 373, 377, 385
Taylor, Joseph, 241
Taylor, Richard, 30
Taylor's Church, 16
Tebbs, Foushee, 30, 190n
Tebbs, Lt., 190
"Tebbsdale" (Tebbs home), 30
Tellico Plains, 386

Tempest (ship), 407
Tennant Meetinghouse, 278
Tennessee, 354
Terrick, Bishop, 157
The Plains, 17
Thicketty Creek, 369
Thomas, David, 17-21, 439
Thomson, Humphrey, 276
Thomson, Rev. James, 12, 17, 51, 157, 228n
Thornton, Capt., 116
Thornton, Charles, 267n
Thronton, Frances (Gregory), 115n
Thornton, Francis, 115n
Thornton, Jane (Washington), 115n
Thornton, John, 72n, 115, 123, 199
Thornton, Mildred (Gregory), 72n
Thoroughfare Gap, 5
Three Mile Run, 274
Throg's Point (N. Y.), 122
Thruston, Charles Mynn, 68, 174-175, 337
Thumb Run, 10, 17, 78, 289, 385n
Thumb Run Baptist Church, 20
Ticonderoga, 130, 136, 187, 401n
Tilton, James, 177
Timberlake, Eppahroditus, 338
Tin Pot Run, 248n
Tomlin, Mrs., 182
Tomlin, Stephen, 214, 266
Tomlin, William (Billy), 182, 183, 186, 214-215, 266
Tories (Loyalists), 63, 89, 90, 103, 104, 123, 127, 135, 149n, 158, 184-185, 234, 327, 329n, 331, 342, 354-356, 365, 368, 379, 387-388, 408, 421, 434
Toulon, France, 282
Town Run, 2, 338n
Townsend, Doris, iv
Travis, Edward, 85
Trawley, Lord, 386n
Treaty of Albany, 2
Treaty of the Long House, 29n
Trenton, Battle of, 133-161
Trenton Ferry, 135, 140
Trenton, N. J., i, 128, 129, 133, 135, 137, 139-140, 142, 167, 173, 174n, 184, 186n, 274, 298n, 319, 353, 363n, 437
Trevelyan, George Otto, 281n
Trinity Church, (N. Y. C.), 119, 333

Trinity College (Dublin), 91n
Triplett, Benedicta (Sennett), 176
Triplett, Catherine, 303n
Triplett, Elizabeth (Hedgman), 69
Triplett, Elizabeth (Morehead), 176n
Triplett, Francis, 69, 74, 76, 226, 228-231, 248-249, 254, 257, 270, 289-290, 304, 349-351, 353, 362, 366-367, 369, 371-372, 374-375, 377-380, 384, 393, 404, 408, 415-416, 419-420, 422, 430, 435, 442
Triplett, George, 303n
Triplett, Hannah (Crump), 304
Triplett, Peter Hedgman, 303-304
Triplett, Sarah (Birkhead), 303n
Triplett, Sarah (Harrison), 404n
Triplett, Simon, 251n
Triplett, Thomas, 304, 404n
Triplett, William, 69n, 176, 261n, 270, 281, 332, 362, 380, 404, 416, 429-421
Trois Rivieres, 216
Troy, 352n
Trumbull, Joseph, 136n
"Truro" (Foote home), 268n
Truro Parish, 312n
Tullos, Joshua, 177
Tullos, Rodham, 257
Turkey Run, 16, 25, 38n
Turkey Run Church (St. Mary's), 7, 439
"Turk's March", 330
Turnbull, Stephen, 276
Turner, Mrs. Charles G., v
Turner, Hezekiah, 97, 198, 227-228, 231, 248-249, 254-255, 313, 395

-U-

Union Co., Ky., 286n
University of Pennsylvania, 147n, 153n
University of Va. Library, 92n
Upper Sandusky, Ohio, 438
Upperville, 20, 43
Utterback, Elizabeth (Crump), 351n
Utterback, Harmon, 351, 414
Utterback, Margaret (Strumatt), 351n

-V-

Valcour Island, 91
Valentine, Edward, 276
Valhalla, 85
Vallentine, Josiah, 361n
Valley Forge: 121n, 226, 238, 242-245, 247, 251, 254, 257, 260-261, 263-264, 267, 270, 273-276, 304, 350, 402
Vass, William, 286
Venn, H., 13
Vera Cruz, 91n
Vergennes, Comte de, 282
Verplanck's Ford, 298
Verplanck's Point, 299
Ville de Paris (ship), 426
Vincennes, i, 252, 293, 294, 396, 438
Virginia Baptist Historical Society, 20n
Virginia Brigades, CL
  First (Stirling), 133, 134, 135, 141, 143, 158
  Second (Stephen), 133, 134, 141, 142, 144
Virginia Convention, 72, 82, 86, 90, 94-95, 101, 106n, 107, 170
Virginia Continental Line, 101, 211, 217, 219, 238, 250, 265, 273, 283, 286, 288, 295, 317-318, 320, 323, 326, 330, 332-333, 335-336, 348, 352-353, 365, 367, 389, 403
Virginia Council of State, 176, 406
Virginia dragoons, 327
Virginia Gazette, 8, 64, 74n, 78, 106, 108, 275, 291, 307n, 309n, 325
Virginia General Assembly, 208, 248, 251, 253-254, 296, 324, 407, 417, 422, 439
Virginia House of Burgesses, 42-44, 46, 49-50, 52-53, 67, 72, 172
Virginia House of Delegates, 90n, 168, 170n, 179, 360, 361n, 407-409, 416
Virginia Militia, 222, 343, 345, 371, 378
Virginia Regiments
  First: 72, 80, 84, 89n, 95, 104, 105, 107, 108, 109, 111, 118, 120, 121, 123, 133, 135, 150, 151n, 151, 208, 222, 267, 279, 283, 297, 303n, 304, 308, 314, 317, 326, 329
  Second: 72, 74, 80, 82, 89n, 105, 107, 108, 129, 167, 190n, 220, 254, 256, 262, 266, 271, 275, 283, 289, 297, 315, 319, 326, 329, 337, 431

INDEX

Third: 22, 72, 77, 79, 88, 94-98, 100, 102, 105, 108-109, 111, 118, 120, 123, 133-135, 144, 146, 148-150, 151-153, 156-157, 159-160, 166, 168-169, 180, 185, 188, 197-198, 205, 208, 212-215, 218-220, 223, 225-226, 228, 231-232, 239, 245-247, 258-259, 265, 280-283, 286, 297, 304, 317n, 330-331, 333-334, 337, 349, 352, 267, 377, 443
Fourth: 108, 129, 135, 188, 283, 297, 316n, 329, 333, 382-384
Fifth: 97, 129, 135, 141, 146, 148, 184, 258, 283, 297, 329, 382, 384
Sixth: 102n, 129, 135, 169, 178, 283, 297, 308, 329, 331-332, 337
Seventh: 105, 167, 185, 186, 212, 225, 282, 283, 297, 314, 329, 339
Eighth: 167, 188, 283, 297, 309, 329
Ninth: 167, 219, 283, 336
Tenth: 99, 155, 168, 169, 196, 213, 220, 231, 237, 263, 267, 270, 271, 272n, 280, 283, 292, 297, 329, 341
Eleventh: 77n, 95, 168, 169, 170, 180, 181, 185, 186, 196, 208, 212, 213, 220, 221, 224, 225, 249, 250, 256-258, 266, 280, 282, 283, 297, 329, 394
Twelfth: 188, 196, 282, 283, 286
Fourteenth: 1659, 271, 283
Fifteenth: 185, 186, 212, 218, 225, 266, 282, 283, 397n
Sixteenth: 97n, 309
Virginia State Regiment of Artillery, 245, 251, 275, 276, 397-398
Vowles, Henry, 398

-W-

Wabash River, 293-294
Waddell, William, 399
Waddy, Samuel, 153
Wake (now Raleigh), N. C., 335n
Wales, 341n
Wales, George, 333
Walker, Benjamin, 265
Walker, James W., iv
Wallace, A. D., 113n, 118n
Wallace, Andrew, 385
Wallace, Gustavus Brown, 113, 117, 118n, 190n, 198, 286-287, 297, 317, 332

Wallace, James Westwood, 190, 288
Wallace, Lt., 82
Wallace, Michael, 113n, 190n, 288n, 317n
Wallace, Tom, 332
"Walnut Lodge" (Blackwell home), 25, 169, 258n
Walton, John, 266
"Wambaw" (Ball home) S.C., 334
War of the Austrian Succession, 340n, 403n
Ward, Christopher, 144n, 145n, 367n, 370, 410n
Warren Academy, 21, 22
Warren Green, 443
Warren, Joseph, 22
Warren, R. I., 21
Warrenton, 6, 16, 22, 250n, 290n
Warsaw, Poland, 364n
Warsaw, Va., 96
Washington, Ann (Aylett), 115n
Washington, Anne (Fairfax), 35
Washington, Augustine, 61n, 115n
Washington, Bailey, 199n
Washington, Charles, 60, 115n, 308n
Washington, Elizabeth (Storke), 199n
Washington family, 56
Washington, George, 6, 11, 14, 29, 34-36, 42-43, 56-58, 60-62, 68-71, 74, 83, 90-92, 94, 100, 108-109, 111-113, 115-124, 129-136, 139-142, 144-152, 156, 159, 161-163, 168-170, 172, 174, 176-177, 179-180, 183-188, 197-198, 201-203, 205, 207-211, 215-219, 221, 225, 227, 229-230, 232, 234-238, 243, 245, 251, 254, 260-265, 269-270, 272-273, 275, 277-285, 289, 291-292, 295, 297-301, 303n, 305-306, 308, 310, 314, 316-318, 323n, 324, 326, 347-350, 359, 366, 389, 397n, 403-406, 410, 418, 424-427, 433, 436, 438
Washington, Jane Riley (Elliot), 199n
Washington, Lawrence, 35, 36
Washington, Lund, 268n, 404-405
Washington, Martha, 265, 404n
Washington, Mildred (Thornton), 115n, 308n
Washington, William, 144, 199, 327-328, 334, 342, 361-362, 364-

365, 367-368, 371, 373-375, 377, 379-380, 382-383, 401, 416, 422, 430
Washington, D. C., ii
Washington, Ky., 276n
Washington Parish, (Westmoreland Co.), 14, 36
Washington's Horse, 327, 338n
Washington's Life Guard, 181, 314
Watauga Valley, 108n
Watchung Mt., (N. J.), 158, 182, 187
Wateree Ferry, 346
Watery Mountain, 170n
Watlington, John, 361
Watson, John W. J., 342n
Watts, Margaret, 26n
Watts, Mason, 399
Watts, Thomas
Watts' Ordinary, 9
Wawayanda, Lake (N. J.), 190
Waxhaws, S. C., 297, 335, 338, 346, 364n, 384, 434
Wayne, Anthony, 204, 216-219, 221, 277-280, 297-306, 315, 348, 352, 410-411, 413-414, 418-419, 426, 433
Weaver, Ann Elizabeth
Weaver, John, 177n
Weaver, Tilman, 3, 177n, 258, 394, 396
Webb, John, 177, 224
Webb, Samuel, 136
Webster, James, 385
Weedon, Catherine (Gordon), 61n
Weedon, George, d 60-61, 95, 109, 111-112, 115-116, 118, 120-121, 123-126, 133, 135, 137, 145-146, 148, 152, 154-156, 169, 175, 185, 187, 202, 204-205, 209, 213, 220-221, 231, 233, 237-238, 243-244, 260-262, 264, 271-272, 275, 277, 280, 296, 347, 389, 394-395, 397n, 401-403, 406, 410, 421, 426-427, 430
Weedon, Sarah (Gray), 61n
Weehawken, 308
Weeks, Thomas, 276
Weems, Mason L., 438
Welch, Nathaniel, 431-432
Welch, Sylvester, 275, 281
West, Capt., 181n
West, Charles, 115-117, 198-199, 225

West Indies, 291, 314
West Point, N. Y., 283, 285, 298, 299, 314, 359, 423
West Point, Va., 395
West, William, 9, 115n
Westfall, Ens., 196
Westham, Va., 388
Westmoreland Co., 10, 12n, 25n, 31, 34, 36, 37, 40, 41, 49, 61, 241n, 257, 268
"Westover" (Byrd estate), 401
Westphalia, 3
West's Ordinary, 111, 323
Wharry, Robert, 418n
Wheatley, Joseph, 313
Whippany, N. J., 161, 184
White, Anthony, 334, 342
White, Armistead, 401
White Clay Creek (Pa.), 225
White Horse Tavern, 212, 215
White, Lt., 195
White, Nelle Rhea, 290n
White Marsh Church, Pa., 175, 236
White Marsh, Pa., 228, 235
White Plains, N. Y. 122-124, 127, 129, 274, 281-283, 285, 286, 353n
White Plains, 5, 298n
White, Thomas, 399
White, William, 205
Whitefield, George, 17
Whitehall Slip (N. Y.), 119
White's Creek, Tenn., 350n
Whiting, Mr., 235
Wickliffe, Lydia Ann Elizabeth (Hardin), 257n
Wickliffe, Elizabeth (Arrington), 257n
Wickliffe, Robert, 257n
Wickliff, William, 257
Wilkes Co., Ga., 399, 434n
Wilkesboro, N. C., 331
Wilkinson, James, 141n
Williams, 331
Williams, Charles, 224, 227, 256-257
Williams, James, 292
Williams, John, 276
Williams, Otho, 341, 344n, 345, 381
Williamsburg, 28, 32, 44, 48, 52-53, 63-64, 66, 71, 74-75, 77-79, 81-82, 90, 94, 98, 109, 121, 127-128, 157, 170, 248-249, 251n, 259, 262, 269, 282, 285, 291, 294, 296, 324-325, 333, 348, 389, 395, 401-402, 413-414, 434

INDEX

Willis, Lewis, 168-169, 196
Wilmington, Del., 129, 133, 193-194, 196, 237
Wilmington, N. C. 354, 386, 403, 409
Wilson, James, 172
Wilson, Richard, 337
Winchester, Va., 69, 167, 408, 431-435
Winn, Elizabeth (Withers), 313n
Winn, Hannah (Withers), 313n, 351
Winn, James, 313n, 348-353, 362, 365, 367, 417, 424, 432
Winn, Minor, 50n, 215n, 313, 349
Winn, Susannah, 50n
Winnsboro, 368
Wirt, William, 55, 56n
Wise, Catherine, 178
Wise, Samuel, 178, 337
Withers, Catherine (Barbee), 241
Withers, Catherine (Porter), 396n
Withers, Elizabeth (Hord), 377
Withers, Elizabeth (Nisbett), 81n
Withers, Elizabeth (Williams), 81n, 313n
Withers, Elizabeth (Withers), 241
Withers, Esther (Potts), 377n
Withers, James, 81n, 241
Withers, Jessee, 396-397
Withers, Lewis, 377
Withers, Martha Ann (Ashby), 81n
Withers, Sarah (Pickett), 241n
Withers, Spencer, 350, 377-378, 433
Withers, Thomas, 81n, 241, 313n, 411
Withers, William, 377n
Withers, William Rawlin, 81n, 349-350
Wolfe, James, 294n
Wood, 297
Wood, James, 282, 286, 309

Woodbridge, N.J., 187
Woodford, Anne (Cocke), 72n
Woodford, Catesby, 417
Woodford, Mary (Thornton), 72n
Woodford, Mr. 235
Woodford, William, 72, 77-78, 82-84, 86-89, 105, 107-108, 119, 129, 180, 185, 203-204, 212, 214, 217-219, 223, 225, 231, 233, 237, 243-244, 246, 261-263, 266, 271-273, 277, 279-280, 283-284, 287-289, 295, 298, 306-307, 309-310, 314, 316-319, 322-325, 328, 329n, 333, 417
"Woodstock" (Brent home), 268
Woolf's Mill, 258n, 395n
Wright family, 31
Wright, James, 170
Wright, John, 33, 177n
Wright, Joseph, 170n
Wright, Mary (Duncan), 170n
Wright, William, 337
Wyatt, Cary, 361
Wythe, George, 252n, 339

-Y-

Yadkin River, 367, 387
Yale, 298n
Yardleyville, 135
Yates, Bartholomew, 151, 152
"Yew Hill" (Ashby estate), 9, 11, 29, 43, 98
Yonkers, N.Y., 112
York, Pa., 69, 111, 163, 173, 208, 319, 410-411
York River, 296, 395, 402, 419, 421
York, Va., 251n
Yorktown, iii, 228n, 251, 263, 275, 330, 339, 360, 389, 393, 437
Young, Original, 20, 65, 177, 246, 258n
Young, Thomas, 370n

-Z-

Zane, Isaac, 68

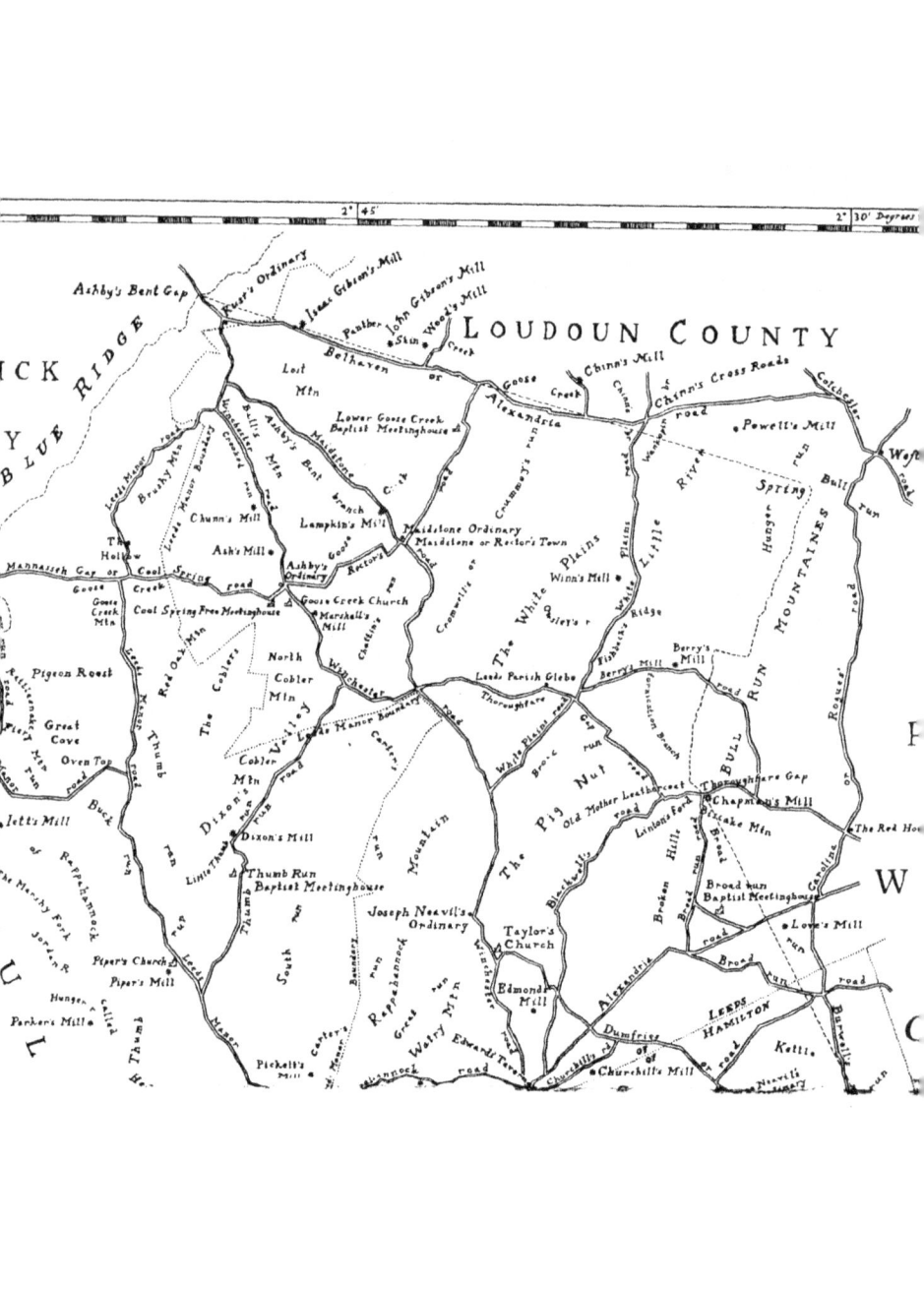

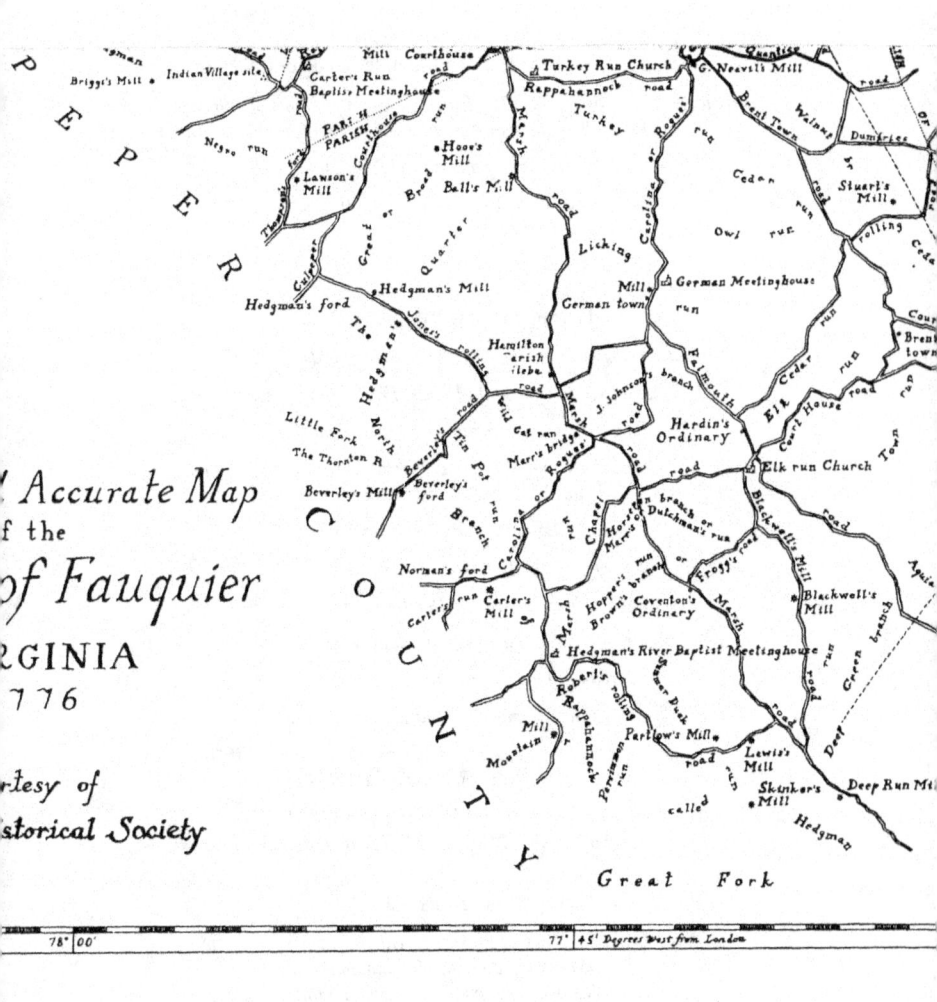

Heritage Books by T. Triplett Russell and John K. Gott

*An Historical Vignette of Oak Hill, Fauquier County: Home of John Marshall,
Chief Justice of the United States and Native Son of Fauquier County*

Fauquier County in the Revolution

The Dixon Valley, Its First 250 Years

Heritage Books by John K. Gott

CD: Fauquier County, Virginia Court Records, 1776–1782

CD: Fauquier County, Virginia Deeds, 1759–1785, Volumes 1 and 2

CD: Fauquier County, Virginia Guardian Bonds, 1759–1871

*CD: Fauquier County, Virginia Marriage Bonds, 1759–1854
and Marriage Returns, 1785–1848*

CD: Fauquier County, Virginia

Fauquier County, Virginia Court Records, 1776–1782

Fauquier County, Virginia Deed Abstracts, 1779–1785

Fauquier County, Virginia Guardian Bonds, 1759–1871

Fauquier County, Virginia Deeds, 1759–1778

Fauquier County, Virginia Deeds, 1778–1785

*Fauquier County, Virginia: Marriage Bonds (1759–1854),
and Marriage Returns (1785–1848)*

*One Hundred Years of Cochran Lodge, 1899–1999:
Cochran Lodge No. 271, A.F. & A.M., The Plains, Virginia*

The Years of Anguish: Fauquier County, Virginia, 1861–1865
Emily G. Ramey and John K. Gott

*Valiant Virginian: Story of Presley Neville O'Bannon, 1776–1850,
to Which is Added the O'Bannon Family*
Trudy J. Sundberg and John K. Gott

www.ingramcontent.com/pod-product-compliance
Lightning Source LLC
Chambersburg PA
CBHW071431300426
44114CB00013B/1389